Radical Perspectives on Social Problems

Radical Perspectives

READINGS IN CRITICAL SOCIOLOGY

EDITED BY **Frank Lindenfeld**

on Social Problems

Second Edition

The Macmillan Company, New York

Collier-Macmillan Publishers, London

The Macmillan Company
866 Third Avenue, New York, New York 10022

Collier-Macmillan Canada, Ltd., Toronto, Ontario

Library of Congress catalog card number: 75-190669

Printing: 2 3 4 5 6 7 8   Year: 3 4 5 6 7 8 9

Preface to the Second Edition

In preparing the second edition of this anthology, I have replaced some of the selections from the first edition with others that make a point more clearly or forcefully. I have added a section on *University and Society,* completely changed the contents of the section on *Politics and Social Change: The New Left,* and revised the introductions as well as my article "Work, Automation, and Alienation." I want to thank Peter Reinhard and most especially Paul Thaxter for their comments, suggestions, and help.

F. L.

PREFACE

My main purpose in compiling this anthology is to make available a set of texts that reflect a critical, engaged viewpoint in sociology. The readings are designed for generalists, not specialists, in the hope that these will be useful to students and citizens in their attempts to understand, cope with, and change the world around them. The anthology is an outgrowth of a course, "Man and Society," that I taught at Cal State for students who did *not* intend to specialize in the study of sociology. It may also be useful in college courses dealing with social problems.

Much of the work of sociologists has tended to be "ideological" in the sense that *its underlying assumptions* have reflected support of existing social institutions.* This anthology is intended to be a utopian antidote, an interpretation of the social world dedicated to the possibility and the desirability of radical change. My aim is to help cultivate the utopian sensibility: the ability to look at social patterns and to see them not only as they are and as they have been, but also as they might be, if. . . .

Man's self-consciousness makes possible the deliberate transformation of social institutions. It is not necessary that we put up with the social world as we find it. If history is not predetermined and inevitable, then one of our tasks should be to help change it in the direction that we want.

The utopian outlook leads to the general question of what varieties of social arrangements would maximize the possibilities for human fulfillment and the ability of men to control the conditions that affect their lives. As Mills put it: "Under what conditions do men come to *want* to be free and

---

* See Robert A. Nisbet, *The Sociological Tradition* (New York: Basic Books, 1966). Nisbet writes: "The paradox of sociology . . . lies in the fact that although it falls, in its objectives and in the political and scientific values of its principal figures, in the mainstream of modernism, its essential concepts and its implicit perspectives place it much closer, generally speaking, to philosophical conservatism" (p. 17).

capable of acting freely? . . . And on the negative side: can men be made to want to become *cheerful* robots?"*

Regarding work: How can we maximize men's control over their work, and pride in it? How can we reap the advantages of industrialization and automation without becoming victims of its disadvantages? What would be the social consequences of abandoning the principle of economic efficiency? What are the alternatives to bureaucratic organization of economic enterprises? Is social inequality inevitable?

What kinds of kinship and educational arrangements may be most successful in establishing the conditions under which individuals can attain freedom and fulfillment?

Regarding politics: Under what social conditions might warfare be eliminated? What would be necessary in order to move America closer to a "society of publics"? Is a minimum degree of coercion necessary for the maintenance of any social order? What social arrangements will help to preserve the integrity of "open" institutions from encroachment by individuals who set out to take advantage of others, or by groups that may be organized to oppress, exploit, torture, and kill others?

I do not pretend to have the answers, nor is there necessarily any one best answer to such questions. Some of the questions raised will be touched on by the selections in this book. Others remain to be dealt with. But this anthology should at least help sensitize readers to the possibilities of social invention and to some of the obstacles in the way.

I did not intend this to be a "balanced" book. Because the book was designed largely to help American students deal with their environment, many of the articles refer to the United States. The social prescriptions represented in the selections run along the spectrum from piecemeal reform to wholesale radical changes and revolution. In making choices I purposely selected writings which I felt constituted radical critiques of the established social order. I included a large number of articles dealing with education and with politics because I felt these were two of the most crucial problem areas. I tried to place a limit of no more than two articles by any one author, but I could not resist including several articles by C. Wright Mills.

Because of limited space, it has been necessary to abridge a number of articles. Omissions from the original text are indicated by asterisks (one or more paragraphs omitted) or three periods (minor omissions).

Comments on proposed selections for this anthology were given by Paul Booth, Jim Jacobs, Bill Harrell, Bernard Rosenberg, John R. Seeley, Maurice Stein, and Heather Tobis. Their help is gratefully acknowledged. Responsibility for the final choice of selections, however, is mine. Thanks are also due to Paul Thaxter, whose help in getting together material for this book and editing the introductions was indispensable.

F. L.

* C. Wright Mills, *The Sociological Imagination* (New York: Oxford University Press, 1961), p. 175.

CONTENTS

ix

Part Three IDEOLOGIES AND
AGENCIES OF CHANGE

PART ONE

Introduction

SOCIAL SCIENCE
AND HUMAN VALUES

PSYCHOLOGISM and the myth of value neutrality are two major obstacles to understanding social problems. Psychologism is the explanation of social phenomena in terms of the attitudes and behavior of individuals rather than the structure of society. It is the attribution of structural characteristics to a mere sum of individual attitudes or milieux.[1] The myth of value neutrality is simply that social scientists can be objective, when in fact they cannot. Although these are two separate obstacles, believers in value neutrality tend to prefer psychologistic to structural theories of social problems.

Sociology is necessarily value-directed.[2] Seeley points out that our very choice of problems and our phrasing of them are determined by what we take for granted. If we take for granted the existing social structure,

[1] See C. Wright Mills, *The Sociological Imagination* (New York: Oxford University Press, 1961), p. 67.

[2] History, psychiatry, indeed all the social sciences, are value-directed. For a discussion of psychiatry as partisan, see Thomas S. Szasz, *Ideology and Insanity* (New York: Doubleday, 1970). On biases in history, see Howard Zinn, "History as Private Enterprise," in Kurt H. Wolff and Barrington Moore, Jr., eds., *The Critical Spirit* (Boston: Beacon Press, 1967).

we will focus on reforms of the system or on the failure of individuals to adjust to it, but we will not search for structural alternatives. Take poverty, for example. Supporters of the prevailing system might ask such questions as "What social reforms might reduce the extent of poverty?" or "How can we re-educate the poor so that they can better participate in the economy?" Critics, however, might begin by asking whether the cause of poverty is not to be found in the system of private property itself.

Not even mere description is neutral. Seeley calls it a form of social intervention, because it necessarily has an effect on the phenomenon described. For example, accounts of racial segregation, police brutality, or poverty call these things to public attention and may trigger attempts at social change.

Sociologists try to be neutral, but their theories are necessarily based on certain assumptions. All theories are normative, according to Horton. They are based either on the assumption that the existing social order ought to be maintained or that it ought to be changed. The former he calls order theories, the latter conflict theories. Order theories define social problems in terms of individual failure to adjust to prevailing mores. Conflict theories define problems as struggles between competing groups. They are based on dissatisfaction with the prevailing system.

Horton shows how order and conflict theorists conceptualize the relationship of blacks to whites. Order theorists assume consensus among Negroes and whites on the American creed; they see the problem as one of incomplete assimilation and unequal opportunity of sharing in the rewards of the great society. Conflict theorists define the problem as one of conflict, or as a struggle for black liberation.

Mills distinguishes between personal troubles and public issues. Troubles affect individuals and their immediate social milieux; their statement and resolution lie within the scope of the individual and his relations with family and friends. Issues transcend the local troubles felt by individuals; they are experienced by many persons at the same time, and often reflect a "crisis in institutional arrangements."

The distinction between troubles and issues shows why psychologism is inadequate to explain social problems. Psychologism views contradictions within political or economic institutions as though they were merely a sum of individual problems, and directs us to solve them by helping individuals. A social problem can be coped with on a personal basis by the few who are smart, aggressive, or rich, but they cannot be solved for everybody except by changing the social structure.

Applying Mills' conception we see racism as a system of institutionalized segregation and discrimination, instead of merely the prejudiced attitudes of individuals. The cure for racism is not the education of whites to see blacks as equal, but the provision of jobs or income for unemployed blacks and greater power for them as a social group. Similarly, we see the causes of unemployment in capitalism and the use of automation rather than in individual laziness or lack of skills. No matter how qualified a man may be, he will not find a job in a capitalist system where his work can be done more cheaply by machines. For the causes of war, we look to the existence of sovereign states with their arms races and military conscription, rather than to the aggressiveness of individual soldiers or statesmen. Belligerent political leaders may precipitate wars, but they cannot do so without armies and organized military production.

To say that psychologism does not adequately explain social phenomena is not to criticize psychology or psychiatry per se. These disciplines can be a source of personal growth and liberation. But they become potential instruments of repression when they hold that poverty or alienation, which are the faults of an exploitative system, can be ameliorated through personal effort or psychotherapy. Often such remedies only help individuals to adjust to a sick social order, when instead they should join with other people to change it.

Answers to social inquiry are largely determined by the nature of our questions. Social phenomena can best be understood by asking questions about the social structure rather than about individuals within it. Furthermore, because objectivity is impossible in the study of human affairs, the only practical alternative is to recognize and explicate our assumptions and values.[3]

[3] See Alvin W. Gouldner, "Anti-Minotaur: The Myth of a Value-Free Sociology," *Social Problems* (Winter 1962), pp. 199–213. See also Gouldner, *The Coming Crisis of Western Sociology* (New York: Avon Equinox, 1972).

The Promise

C. Wright Mills

Nowadays men often feel that their private lives are a series of traps. They sense that within their everyday worlds, they cannot overcome their troubles, and in this feeling, they are often quite correct: What ordinary men are directly aware of and what they try to do are bounded by the private orbits in which they live; their visions and their powers are limited to the close-up scenes of job, family, neighborhood; in other milieux, they move vicariously and remain spectators. And the more aware they become, however vaguely, of ambitions and of threats which transcend their immediate locales, the more trapped they seem to feel.

Underlying this sense of being trapped are seemingly impersonal changes in the very structure of continent-wide societies. The facts of contemporary history are also facts about the success and the failure of individual men and women. When a society is industrialized, a peasant becomes a worker; a feudal lord is liquidated or becomes a businessman. When classes rise or fall, a man is employed or unemployed; when the rate of investment goes up or down, a man takes new heart or goes broke. When wars happen, an insurance salesman becomes a rocket launcher; a store clerk, a radar man; a wife lives alone; a child grows up without a father. Neither the life of an individual nor the history of a society can be understood without understanding both.

Yet men do not usually define the troubles they endure in terms of historical change and institutional contradiction. The well-being they enjoy they do not usually impute to the big ups and downs of the societies in which they live. Seldom aware of the intricate connection between the patterns of their lives and the course of world history, ordinary men do not usually know what this connection means for the kinds of men they are becoming and for the kinds of history-making in which they might take part. They do not possess the quality of mind essential to grasp the interplay of man and society, of biography and history, of self and world. They cannot cope with their personal troubles in such ways as to control the structural transformations that usually lie behind them.

Surely it is no wonder. In what period have so many men been so totally exposed at so fast a pace to such earthquakes of change? That Americans have not known such catastrophic changes as have the men and women of other societies is due to historical facts that are now quickly becoming "merely history." The history that now affects every man is world history. Within this scene and this period, in the course of a single generation, one sixth of mankind is transformed from all that is feudal and backward into all that is modern, advanced, and fearful. Political colonies are freed; new and less visible forms of imperialism installed. Revolutions occur; men feel the intimate grip of new kinds of authority. Totalitarian societies rise, and are smashed to bits—or succeed fabulously. After two centuries of ascendancy, capitalism is shown up as only one way to make society into an industrial apparatus. After two centuries of hope, even formal democracy is restricted to a quite small portion of mankind. Everywhere in the underdeveloped world, ancient ways of life are broken up and vague expectations become urgent demands. Everywhere in the overdeveloped world, the means of authority and of violence become total in scope and bureaucratic in form. Humanity itself now lies before us, the super-nation at either pole concentrating its most co-ordinated and massive efforts upon the preparation of World War Three.

The very shaping of history now outpaces the ability of men to orient themselves in accordance with cherished values. And which values? Even when they do not panic, men often sense that older ways of feeling and thinking have collapsed and that newer beginnings are ambiguous to the point of moral stasis. Is it any wonder that ordinary men feel they cannot cope with the larger worlds with which they are so suddenly confronted? That they cannot understand the meaning of their epoch for their own lives? That—in defense of selfhood—they become morally insensible, trying to remain altogether private men? Is it any wonder that they come to be possessed by a sense of the trap?

It is not only information that they need—in this Age of Fact, information often dominates their attention and overwhelms their capacities to assimilate it. It is not only the skills of reason that they need—although their struggles to acquire these often exhaust their limited moral energy.

What they need, and what they feel they need, is a quality of mind that will help them to use information and to develop reason in order to achieve lucid summations of what is going on in the world and of what may be happening within themselves. It is this quality, I am going to contend, that journalists and scholars, artists and publics, scientists and editors are coming to expect of what may be called the sociological imagination.

1

The sociological imagination enables its possessor to understand the larger historical scene in terms of its meaning for the inner life and the external career of a variety of individuals. It enables him to take into account how individuals, in the welter of their daily experience, often become falsely conscious of their social positions. Within that welter, the framework of modern society is sought, and within that framework the psychologies of a variety of men and women are formulated. By such means the personal uneasiness of individuals is focused upon explicit troubles and the indifference of publics is transformed into involvement with public issues.

The first fruit of this imagination—and the first lesson of the social science that embodies it—is the idea that the individual can understand his own experience and gauge his own fate only by locating himself within his period, that he can know his own chances in life only by becoming aware of those of all individuals in his circumstances. In many ways it is a terrible lesson; in many ways a magnificent one. We do not know the limits of man's capacities for supreme effort or willing degradation, for agony or glee, for pleasurable brutality or the sweetness of reason. But in our time we have come to know that the limits of "human nature" are frighteningly broad. We have come to know that every individual lives, from one generation to the next, in some society; that he lives out a biography, and that he lives it out within some historical sequence. By the fact of his living he contributes, however minutely, to the shaping of this society and to the course of its history, even as he is made by society and by its historical push and shove.

The sociological imagination enables us to grasp history and biography and the relations between the two within society. That is its task and its promise. To recognize this task and this promise is the mark of the classic social analyst. It is characteristic of Herbert Spencer—turgid, polysyllabic, comprehensive; of E. A. Ross—graceful, muckraking, upright; of Auguste Comte and Emile Durkheim; of the intricate and subtle Karl Mannheim. It is the quality of all that is intellectually excellent in Karl Marx; it is the clue to Thorstein Veblen's brilliant and ironic insight, to Joseph Schumpeter's many-sided constructions of reality; it is the basis of the psychological sweep of W. E. H. Lecky no less than of the profundity and clarity of Max Weber. And it is the signal of what is best in contemporary studies of man and society.

No social study that does not come back to the problems of biography, of history, and of their intersections within a society has completed its intellectual journey. Whatever the specific problems of the classic social analysts, however limited or however broad the features of social reality they have examined, those who have been imaginatively aware of the promise of their work have consistently asked three sorts of questions:

1. What is the structure of this particular society as a whole? What are its essential components, and how are they related to one another? How does it differ from other varieties of social order? Within it, what is the meaning of any particular feature for its continuance and for its change?

2. Where does this society stand in human history? What are the mechanics by which it is changing? What is its place within and its meaning for the development of humanity as a whole? How does any particular feature we are examining affect, and how is it affected by, the historical period in which it moves? And this period—what are its essential features? How does it differ from other periods? What are its characteristic ways of history-making?

3. What varieties of men and women now prevail in this society and in this period? And what varieties are coming to prevail? In what ways are they selected and formed, liberated and repressed, made sensitive and blunted? What kinds of "human nature" are revealed in the conduct and character we observe in this society in this period? And what is the meaning for "human nature" of each and every feature of the society we are examining?

Whether the point of interest is a great power state or a minor literary mood, a family, a prison, a creed—these are the kinds of questions the best social analysts have asked. They are the intellectual pivots of classic studies of man in society—and they are the questions inevitably raised by any mind possessing the sociological imagination. For that imagination is the capacity to shift from one perspective to another—from the political to the psychological; from examination of a single family to comparative assessment of the national budgets of the world; from the theological school to the military establishment; from considerations of an oil industry to studies of contemporary poetry. It is the capacity to range from the most impersonal and remote transformations to the most intimate features of the human self—and to see the relations between the two. Back of its use there is always the urge to know the social and historical meaning of the individual in the society and in the period in which he has his quality and his being.

That, in brief, is why it is by means of the sociological imagination that men now hope to grasp what is going on in the world, and to understand what is happening in themselves as minute points of the intersections of biography and history within society. In large part, contemporary man's self-conscious view of himself as at least an outsider, if not a permanent stranger, rests upon an absorbed realization of social relativity and of the transformative power of history. The sociological imagination is the most fruitful form of this self-consciousness. By its use men whose mentalities have swept only a series of limited orbits often come to feel as if suddenly awakened in a house with which they had only supposed themselves to be familiar. Correctly or incorrectly, they often come to feel that they can now provide themselves with adequate summations, cohesive assessments, comprehensive orientations. Older decisions that once appeared sound now seem to them products of a mind unaccountably dense. Their capacity for astonishment is made lively again. They acquire a new way of thinking, they experience a transvaluation of values; in a word, by their reflection and by their sensibility, they realize the cultural meaning of the social sciences.

2

Perhaps the most fruitful distinction with which the sociological imagination works is between "the personal troubles of milieu" and "the public issues of social structure." This distinction is an essential tool of the sociological imagination and a feature of all classic work in social science.

Troubles occur within the character of the individual and within the range of his immediate relations with others; they have to do with his self and with those limited areas of social life of which he is directly and personally aware. Accordingly, the statement and the resolution of troubles properly lie within the individual as a biographical entity and within the scope of his immediate milieu—the social setting that is directly open to his personal experience and to some extent his willful activity. A trouble is a private matter: values cherished by an individual are felt by him to be threatened.

Issues have to do with matters that transcend these local environments of the individual and the range of his inner life. They have to do with the organization of many such milieux into the institutions of an historical society as a whole, with the ways in which various milieux overlap and interpenetrate to form the larger structure of social and historical life. An issue is a public matter: some value cherished by publics is felt to be threatened. Often there is a debate about what that value really is and about what it is that really threatens it. This debate is often without focus if only because it is the very nature of an issue, unlike even widespread trouble, that it cannot very well be defined in terms of the immediate and everyday environments of ordinary men. An issue, in fact, often involves a crisis in institutional arrangements, and often too it involves what Marxists call "contradictions" or "antagonisms."

In these terms, consider unemployment. When, in a city of 100,000, only one man is unemployed, that is his personal trouble, and for its relief we properly look to the character of the man, his skills, and his immediate opportunities. But when in a nation of 50 million employees, 15 million men are unemployed, that is an issue, and we may not hope to find its solution within the range of opportunities open to any one individual. The very structure of opportunities has collapsed. Both the correct statement of the problem and the range of possible solutions require us to consider the economic and political institutions of the society, and not merely the personal situation and character of a scatter of individuals.

Consider war. The personal problem of war, when it occurs, may be how to survive it or how to die in it with honor; how to make money out of it; how to climb into the higher safety of the military apparatus; or how to contribute to the war's termination. In short, according to one's values, to find a set of milieux and within it to survive the war or make one's death in it meaningful. But the structural issues of war have to do with its causes; with what types of men it throws up into command; with its effects upon economic and political, family and religious institutions, with the unorganized irresponsibility of a world of nation-states.

Consider marriage. Inside a marriage a man and a woman may experience personal troubles, but when the divorce rate during the first four years of marriage is 250 out of every 1,000 attempts, this is an indication of a structure issue having to do with the institutions of marriage and the family and other institutions that bear upon them.

Or consider the metropolis—the horrible, beautiful, ugly, magnificent sprawl of the great city. For many upper-class people, the personal solution to "the problem of the city" is to have an apartment with private garage under it in the heart of the city, and forty miles out, a house by Henry Hill, garden by Garrett Eckbo, on a hundred acres of private land. In these two controlled environments—with a small staff at each end and a private helicopter connection—most people could solve many of the problems of personal milieux caused by the facts of the city. But all this, however splendid, does not solve the public issues that the structural fact of the city poses. What should be done with this wonderful monstrosity? Break it all up into scattered units, combining residence and work? Refurbish it as it stands? Or, after evacuation, dynamite it and build new cities according to new plans in new places? What should those plans be? And who is to decide and to accomplish whatever choice is made? These are structural issues; to confront them and to solve them requires us to consider political and economic issues that affect innumerable milieux.

In so far as an economy is so arranged that slumps occur, the problem of unemployment becomes incapable of personal solution. In so far as war is inherent in the nation-state system and in the uneven industrialization of the world, the ordinary individual in his restricted milieu will be powerless—with or without psychiatric aid—to solve the troubles this system or lack of system imposes upon him. In so far as the family as an institution turns women into darling little slaves and men into their chief providers and unweaned dependents, the problem of a satisfactory marriage remains incapable of purely private solution. In so far as the overdeveloped megalopolis and the overdeveloped automobile are built-in features of the overdeveloped society, the issues of urban living will not be solved by personal ingenuity and private wealth.

What we experience in various and specific milieux, I have noted, is often caused by structural changes. Accordingly, to understand the changes of many personal milieux we are required to look beyond them. And the number and variety of such structural changes increase as the institutions within which we live become more embracing and more intricately connected with one another. To be aware of the idea of social structure and to use it with sensibility is to be capable of tracing such linkages among a great variety of milieux. To be able to do that is to possess the sociological imagination.

3

What are the major issues for publics and the key troubles of private individuals in our time? To formulate issues and troubles, we must ask what values are cherished yet threatened, and what values are cherished and supported, by the characterizing trends of our period. In the case both of threat and of support we must ask what salient contradictions of structure may be involved.

When people cherish some set of values and do not feel any threat to them, they experience *well-being*. When they cherish values but *do* feel them to be threatened, they experience a crisis—either as a personal trouble or as a public issue. And if all their values seem involved, they feel the total threat of panic.

But suppose people are neither aware of any cherished values nor experience any threat? That is the experience of *indifference*, which, if it seems to involve all their values, becomes apathy. Suppose, finally, they are unaware of any cherished values, but still are very much aware of a threat? That is the experience of *uneasiness*, of anxiety, which, if it is total enough, becomes a deadly unspecified malaise.

Ours is a time of uneasiness and indifference—not yet formulated in such ways as to permit the work of reason and the play of sensibility. Instead of troubles—defined in terms of values and threats—there is often the misery of vague uneasiness; instead of explicit issues there is often merely the beat feeling that all is somehow not right. Neither the values threatened nor whatever threatens them has been stated; in short, they have not been carried to the point of decision. Much less have they been formulated as problems of social science.

In the 'thirties there was little doubt—except among certain deluded business circles—that there was an economic issue which was also a pack of personal troubles. In these arguments about "the crisis of capitalism," the formulations of Marx and the many unacknowledged re-formulations of his work probably set the leading terms of the issue, and some men came to understand their personal troubles in these terms. The values threatened were plain to see and cherished by all; the structural contra- dictions that threatened them also seemed plain. Both were widely and deeply experienced. It was a political age.

But the values threatened in the era after World War Two are often neither widely acknowledged as values nor widely felt to be threatened. Much private uneasiness goes unformulated; much public malaise and many decisions of enormous structural relevance never become public is- sues. For those who accept such inherited values as reason and freedom, it is the uneasiness itself that is the trouble; it is the indifference itself that is the issue. And it is this condition, of uneasiness and indifference, that is the signal feature of our period.

All this is so striking that it is often interpreted by observers as a shift in the very kinds of problems that need now to be formulated. We are frequently told that the problems of our decade, or even the crises of our period, have shifted from the external realm of economics and now have to do with the quality of individual life—in fact with the question of whether there is soon going to be anything that can properly be called individual life. Not child labor but comic books, not poverty but mass leisure, are at the center of concern. Many great public issues as well as many private troubles are described in terms of "the psychiatric"—often, it seems, in a pathetic attempt to avoid the large issues and problems of modern society. Often this statement seems to rest upon a provincial nar- rowing of interest to the Western societies, or even to the United States —thus ignoring two-thirds of mankind; often, too, it arbitrarily divorces the individual life from the larger institutions within which that life is enacted, and which on occasion bear upon it more grievously than do the intimate environments of childhood.

Problems of leisure, for example, cannot even be stated without considering problems of work. Family troubles over comic books cannot be formulated as problems without considering the plight of the contemporary family in its new relations with the newer institutions of the social structure. Neither leisure nor its debilitating uses can be understood as problems without recognition of the extent to which malaise and indifference now form the social and personal climate of contemporary American society. In this climate, no problems of "the private life" can be stated and solved without recognition of the crisis of ambition that is part of the very career of men at work in the incorporated economy.

It is true, as psychoanalysts continually point out, that people do often have "the increasing sense of being moved by obscure forces within themselves which they are unable to define." But it is *not* true, as Ernest Jones asserted, that "man's chief enemy and danger is his own unruly nature and the dark forces pent up within him." On the contrary: "Man's chief danger" today lies in the unruly forces of contemporary society itself, with its alienating methods of production, its enveloping techniques of political domination, its international anarchy—in a word, its pervasive transformations of the very "nature" of man and the conditions and aims of his life.

It is now the social scientist's foremost political and intellectual task—for here the two coincide—to make clear the elements of contemporary uneasiness and indifference. It is the central demand made upon him by other cultural workmen—by physical scientists and artists, by the intellectual community in general. It is because of this task and these demands, I believe, that the social sciences are becoming the common denominator of our cultural period, and the sociological imagination our most needed quality of mind.

Social Science? Some Probative Problems

John R. Seeley

It seems to me that sociologists—and psychologists and other social scientists, analogically—broadly do three things. They state or *define* or recognize *problems*. They write what I shall call, analogically with elementary geography, *sociography*. They do *sociology*. By sociography I mean an enterprise of description, perhaps an idiographic enterprise; by soci-

FROM John R. Seeley, "Social Science? Some Probative Problems" in *Sociology on Trial*, Maurice Stein and Arthur Vidich, Eds., © 1963, pp. 57–65. Reprinted by permission of John R. Seeley and Prentice-Hall, Inc., Englewood Cliffs, New Jersey.

ology I mean an attempt at a causal analysis, a nomothetic enterprise. In all cases, however, the social scientist makes, to my mind, a decisive intervention, one attended by very difficult intellectual problems of self-location, and ethical problems of warrantability.

I shall deal lightly with the first case, though it is no light matter. The very "recognition" of something as a scientific problem, instead of some other kind of problem, marks a shift, an implicit act of legislation so profound as to deserve the title revolutionary. Nothing, I should think, except the commonness in our day of these acts of scientific territory-seizing, could obscure the radical change involved, a change that by itself threatens to shake the foundations of the present society and to erect a new one of unforeseeable characteristics—perhaps an iatrocratic one—in its place.

Numerous illustrations will readily come to mind. A recent one is alcoholism: the minute alcoholism is *defined* as a problem for science, even before any causal connections are established, let alone controls or remedies found, *in virtue of the definition* what alcoholism is held to be, and therewith attitudes to, practices upon and even custody of, care and responsibility for the alcoholic are immediately implicitly, and later explicitly, altered. *The social relation is altered by the definition per se*; society is reconstituted out of the simple fiat (if effective) that alcoholism is a problem for science. With "mental disease" and "neurosis" as forerunners, with "sexual deviation" trembling on the border of redefinition, with delinquency half in, half out, but coming in, with no bar in principle to the admission under the rubric of any desired or undesired condition—"authoritarianism," for instance—is it not visible, almost patent, that more and more is being defined out of the old and nonscientific society and into the new one taking gigantic shape in its womb? I see no bars in principle. If the causes of authoritarianism can be scientifically determined, why cannot the causes of democratism?—and why cannot the one be countered while the other is nurtured?—except, of course, that an induced or caused democratism is not what we really wanted to begin with. (The last point has to do with what someone recently called the problem of the "morality pill.") All I want to establish for now is the *science-as-legislation theorem*: that "recognition" of a problem as scientific at all, as clearly legislates a revolutionary difference into human affairs as any nineteenth-century Act of Annexation did in affairs political.

I now want to deal with what looks like the most innocent, innocuous, or least interventive aspect of our trade: mere sociography or psychography: description of what is—map-making, if you will, or data assembling and ordering.

Description of a vital human activity in and of and by itself constitutes, in my opinion, an attack upon that activity, both from the viewpoint of the participants and from the viewpoint of the disinterested (neither participant, nor social scientist) observer. To the degree that it is a successful description, ethically neutral, deadpan, it tears apart for the participants the veil of unreality that is the foundation of the activity. A scientific description—of a social gathering, for instance—might well yield the participants something, even something of considerable worth, but could not leave something that was also valuable to them unaffected for the worse. Everyone purports to value light, but too much light is pitiless glare, and what goes on in and after the glare is impossibly what went on in the welcome and familiar twilight. How could a love relationship survive, for instance, an extended equitable enumeration of the characteristics of the beloved? How does other-directed behavior survive its categorization (stigmatization) as such? What becomes of the organization man, once he is identified by self and others as such? I am almost tempted to analogize: the light of social science is ultra-violet; the bacteria cannot survive the light; life cannot live without bacteria; social science sterilizes; the sterility kills.

We have long confronted this problem as the problem of "unmasking." I think nearly every description, again in and of itself, of any vital social or psychological matter, involves or risks such unmasking. In both sciences we have comforted ourselves (I think, falsely) by protecting the identity of the unit we are describing (the patient, person, community, or factory). I suggest it is false comfort, if only because it is insufficient: it avoids the inequity of fining a particular speeding motorist, as it were, by fining them as a group. When, finally, our initial operation results in a new "descriptive" image of parents, doctors, academics, teachers, professional men generally, businessmen, executives, unwed mothers, suburbs, churches, parishes, community chests, neurotics, alcoholics, pedophiles, hoboes, slums, gold coasts, Americans, Japanese, Indians, Protestants, Catholics, Jews, fundamentalists, or mystics, the living conditions for definable classes of people are altered—generally, I think, in the direction of a more complex, strenuous set of demands on them accompanied by a diminished armamentarium of available defenses.

It may or may not be significant that a long-standing point of friction between Americans and Russians in Geneva has been the issue of *inspection*. As Kenneth Boulding has repeatedly pointed out, we have little or nothing of a sociology or psychology of inspection. Social and psychological descriptions are not merely inspection but *reported inspection*, and in the long run, continuous inspection. It is not even clear which way, ethically and psychologically, the categorical, nonpersonal form of the reporting works; for the true professional, perhaps a description, a potential exposure, of the *enterprise* with which he is associated—the Church, the teaching profession, his type of community—is infinitely worse than an exposure of *himself*, as a mere actual repository of an ideal embodied in the naïve social definition.

Again, we cannot, I think, console ourselves in any easy way. We cannot, as indicated above, get off the hook by shifting the focus from individuals to groups or categories. Nor, which may be less obvious, by shifting from persons or institutions to types of behavior—say, antagonistic cooperation, or sibling rivalry, or gamesmanship—without again encountering the probability that we merely make life harder for everyone; or, more commonly, harder for some who share preferentially in the behavior and easier for those who do not. Nor may we comfort ourselves, I think, by believing that in time we will get around to everyone in all respects, so that at least we will hold the balance of disadvantage even. There is an infinity of possible categorizations to be viewed in an infinity of possible perspectives; and there will not be an infinity of infinities of monographs written or read. So we exert a *judicial* function in deciding what to describe. Description is like taxation; the right to describe absolutely is the right to destroy absolutely.

What we do, in practice is, I think, to intervene (by description) against some "bad guys" in favor of some "good guys"—but by unacknowledged canons and on no ordered, let alone explicit and shared, principle.

If sociography and psychography are implicit intervention, what is to be said of the bulk of psychology and sociology, if by these we mean the sciences that trace supposed cause and effect relations in their fields?

A *fortiori*, these represent, as I have said elsewhere, not mere findings, but findings *for* and *against*, judgments as well as verdict and, in their redefinitional effects, acts of legislation as well.

Let me assert first that there is a fatal peculiarity about the normal notion of cause when an attempt is made to apply it in the social sciences. I take it for granted that, in society as in nature, everything is related to everything else and hence in some ultimate, metaphysical sense everything is the cause of any one thing. But by "*the* cause" or "a cause" we mean in science, as in practical everyday life, that particular thing which it would be most "convenient," economical, or efficient to change in order to secure a desired change in what we are pleased to call an effect. Thus mosquitoes, if we do not mind exterminating them, are "the cause" of malaria in men; though apart from this canon of convenience we might equally have said that blood was the cause of malaria if we could do without it, or men, if we were prepared to exterminate them.

The differences on this score between the natural and social sciences is that, in the former but not in the latter, there exist two plain, open and public canons of causal selection: there is, first, a basic judgment for man *against* the rest of the animate, and, *a fortiori*, the inanimate universe; and second, in general, in reference to things there is an economics mediated by a single fungible medium, money, that permits or appears to permit comparative measures of convenience and inconvenience in terms of relative costs. (A whole set of social conventions does underlie this procedure, but the natural scientist is not bound to examine them.)

But the minute we try to apply this mode of reasoning in the social sciences we are faced with two problems: one perhaps only technically difficult (interconvertibility of costs or disutilities), and the other, I think, insuperable. For when we say "convenient" in the social sciences, we must ask further *"Convenient to whom?"* And unless we can either identify a general interest—which we have so far failed to do—or a supervenient criterion (such as pleasingness to God) we cannot fail, in effect, in attributing causality at all, simply to award costs to X out of the social, psychological, or material pocket of Y. For by the very act of picking out of the infinity of actual causal connections some one or ones as designated and hence recognized causes, we are altering definitions, redistributing tasks and responsibilities, increasing and decreasing prestige or repute, changing balances of psychic and social incomes, assets and liabilities.

Take the problem of accounting for "delinquency" as an instance. Admittedly, this is selected from the field of "social problems," where the procedure is most evident, but an attempt to account for apathy or anxiety, or administration or bureaucracy would serve nearly as well. As I have said elsewhere, the cause of delinquency, "other things being equal," is any one or more of the following: poor street lighting, alleys, immigration, paternal infidelity, differential association, neurotic acting out, broken homes, the American income distribution, lack of alternate meaningful activities, advertising and display, failure to nail down prized objects, the slum, the ecological organization of the American city, materialism, its opposite; preoccupation with one's worth as a person, the law itself, the absurdity of society or the human condition; the want of religion, the nuclear family, the political system which needs crime which needs as a training ground prisons and reformatories; schools that engage few or no loyalties, the perversity of the individual delinquent, or his parents, or theirs; psychological ignorance, the unconscious wishes of those who deplore the activity or condemn the actors. "Choose your pick," as they say. There can hardly be a question that all are involved, and an infinity—literally—of other candidates for causal ascription besides. And each of these "causal factors" is also connected for the purposes of science with an infinity of other causes. The selection for reporting and hence attention of any one cause—say, the ghettoization of Negroes in the Black Belt, leading to rent extortion, leading to overcrowding, leading to heightened necessities for certain types of experiences and escapes—is as clear an act of judgment (in the legal sense) as if when a bridge collapsed a judge were to select a particular passenger over it as the cause of its downfall from the combined excessive weight of all of them on it at the time.

The selection of any one of these for study *is* a political act, an expression of a political position—a power-redistributing value-function that the social scientist knowingly or unknowingly holds. Let me leave this here for now as the *cause-tax or etiology-fine theorem.*

I would like to turn next to the problem involved in the *ceteris paribus,* or context-taken-for-granted problem. Let me suppose a sociologist or psychologist interested in the rehabilitation of the imprisoned delinquent. He might be asked and he might assent to the study of any of the following, roughly ordered, problems. How, after we have thoroughly strapped a defiant child, can we mitigate his feelings, so that he is not led by the feelings into a vicious cycle of further defiance and increased punishment (surely a humane desire, within its context)? Or, how can we find a substitute punishment for strapping that would have the same effect—the breaking of resistance—without the too patent sadomasochistic risks (surely also humane enough in its context)? Or, how can administration be smooth and overwhelming without resort to patent punishment, defined as such? (I think this is the commonest type of problem our clients bring us.) Or, given morally meaningless confinement, how can we minimize coercion? Or, given the need for order and the absurd rules of the society, what alternatives can we find for confinement (e.g., free marijuana)? Or, what alternatives are there to the absurd rules, given the present sociopolitical structure? Or, what alternatives are there to that structure, given the need for national stability in the face of the cold war? Or, what alternatives to cold war, given no radical reconstruction in the minds and hearts of men?

With every shift in context, it is obvious that the whole scientific problem shifts. With every success at an early level in the list, the likelihood that a subsequent item might be successfully examined is reduced. If a really successful outcome for strapping could be assured with the aid of science (as perhaps it could), the view that we might need to re-examine larger problems would be most unlikely to find research funds—or listeners. So the decision as to where to cut into a social problem, what other things to take as being equal or to be taken for granted, is in effect an act of intervention tending to ensure that they remain not only equal but unchanged. One way to reduce theft from department stores, for instance, would be to institute a pay-what-you-like system (including no payment), with losses turned into profits by tax subsidies. Why not? But the problem is not usually posed so. Which means that the problem, as set, is within a complex net of assumptions and goals, the *ceteris paribus*, that in effect constitutes an invitation to join the conservative party. Hence, the way to deal with alcoholism is likelier to be found by science to be the setting up of more clinics where the socially hurt can be reconciled to their fate and persuaded to find substitute comforts, than it is to be the elimination of the sources of anxiety, aggression, self-denial, and self-castration that appear to underlie all or most self-defeating self-indulgence. Even when we shift away from the study of *problems*, defined as such, to the study of persons or small groups—again "all other things being equal" being the very precondition for the study—we flee, I believe, in motive as well as effect, from the larger questions, just as we divert resources, and, worse, attention from these much more far-reaching matters. American sociology and psychology go that way, I believe, not on the mere ground of scientific safety, or ease of management of the problem, but from covert alliances with the going order, in its major aspects, already in the heart of the scientist.

I am sure it does not need emphasis that, just as the best is sometimes the enemy of the better, so most often the better is the enemy of the best. A sure-fire psychotherapy might well put off for three thousand years any attempt to cope with the institutional ways that ensure the breakdowns that the therapy deals with. I will leave this as the *accepted context equals alliance theorem.* The Communists used to use the phrase "blunting the edge of revolution" for the effect of minor (or perhaps particularly major) reforms; and while we may not wish to espouse the politics, the perplexity remains; whether we are electing to deal with a narrow-context social problem or a sociological problem: one is more likely to stand in the way of more radical action, the other in the way of more significant knowledge.

Let me drive home the point of the context once more, but in a different way: a social scientist studying, say, the psychology of resignation in the context of Belsen is doing something far different from someone studying the same problem in the context of midtown Manhattan, or for that matter, Lhasa, Tibet. No less, I believe, with the development of learning theories that explore the analogies of human learning with the behavior of machines, pigeons, or students of Zen.

Nor can we comfort ourselves, I think, with the consolation that we all act freely on manifold interests, and that these individual impulses can be ordered by the market, intellectual or commercial. Our "interests" are themselves potential matters of scientific investigation, and would, I doubt not, turn out to be closely connected with a personal politics that gains no advantage from being inexplicit, if not denied. The actual and practical upshot seems to me even short of Louis Wirth's attribution to the whole, to sociology as such, of the term "an omnium gatherum"; it fails the completeness of the first term and the orderliness of the second. Indeed, its first-order social consequence—and it may not be unintended, it may be the very condition under which we are socially allowed to practice—looks very like the scattering and frittering away of most of the best minds of any given generation over the whole field of the variously trivial. Perhaps not; perhaps there is more order or sense than I see; but my first impression is that the result would well justify the opening stanzas of Allen Ginsberg's *Howl.*

Another insufficiently explored set of problems in the social sciences flows, I believe, out of the interpenetrations of knowledge and commitment. I have sufficiently, I hope, indicated my view as to how such knowledge in general flows only out of commitments (or implies them) whether one is more or less witting as to the nature of, or basis for, the commitments in question. It goes without saying that the commitment may well be and quite generally is made over in the light of the knowledge gained on the basis of it.

I want to drive the point home somewhat further by beginning with psychoanalysis—of any school, as far as I know—as a model, and I want to ask: What kind of social scientific knowledge is not analogical *in the proc-*

ess necessary to reach it? I do not wish to enter here into any discussion of any particular psychoanalytic tenet. But the formal status of the knowledge gained in analysis is, *ex hypothesi,* that it cannot be embraced (or tested) until certain kinds of experiences have been had which alter, probably irrevocably, the intelligence that proposes to assess them. It is open to those who have not made the commitment and had the experience to say either that the deliverances are false or not demonstrable. But this will no more —and properly so—shake the devotees, than the like arguments against the existence of God shake the religious. Indeed, the arguments are formally similar in that a first act of faith brings into vision—and to the participant it appears a vision that is at least as uncontestable as everyday or "scientific" vision—an object or class of objects, that justifies a further venture of faith, that brings into sight more objects or more of the same object . . . and so indefinitely.

Now I do not believe that this form of discovery, if you are willing to admit the word, is limited to psychoanalysis. Nothing short of a mature mind is capable, I believe, of defining (or even recognizing more than perfunctorily) what a mature mind might be. But such a definition in effect moves ahead of, rather than behind, the maturing mind: the insight contributes to the maturity, and thereby brings new visions, and the necessity of redefinition into sight.

We attempt commonly, in sociology at least to pay tribute to something of what is involved by speaking of the process of "participant-observation." Sometimes we speak as though we could occupy a position anywhere on a scale from total observation without participation to total participation without observation. And for limited purposes such talk may serve us well enough. But it seems to me there is a major class of matters in which nothing but total, unreserved participation will bring the object to be observed into sight in anything except a fatally distorting light. The model might be the mystical experience: I doubt if it can be had on the basis of a trial or a limited or divided commitment; neither perhaps can a love experience, although obviously celibate sociologists could write some things learnedly about love and marriage. But the central social facts—love, hate, friendship, enmity—are constituted by faith, and entered upon, for any purpose except the most trivial comprehension, only in ways that set up the process of building of knowledge on faith and faith on knowledge in a succession of steps that simultaneously opens one to some observations while blinding one to others. The most obvious statement might be that we can understand nothing until our modes of perception have been ineradicably set in many ways by some culture; but once this process is well begun, we can understand some things and not others. The knowledge has thus essentially in its very structure the nature of an historic or ontological process, in which successive steps in the activity produce irreversible changes in the actor, so that the convention that approximates reality in the natural sciences—the contrary of Heraclitus' assertion that you cannot step into the same river twice—has no counterpart in the social sciences, or finds only a minor echo there. Insofar as this view is adopted in any large part, I should think it ought to give a quite different perspective upon a career in social science, and the training appropriate for it, and the meaning of contrasting deliverances by different social scientists. Commonly, these are viewed as erroneous judgment on one part by the other, or explained away in terms of a sociology of knowledge. But the possibility that they may be equi-valid as consequences of different commitment-knowledge sequences, while invoked as a criticism in terms of ideology, is rarely allowed as legitimate and desirable as well as, perhaps, unavoidable.

There are a number of other intriguing problems connected with the practice of our trade which I have touched on at other times and places, and which are closely connected with some of the foregoing.

There is a problem concerning even manner and place of publication, for insofar as knowledge is useful or even comforting, the manner of publication involves the problem of redistributing power (or gratification) in certainly unplanned and perhaps undesired ways. The present laissez-faire effect is, I believe, at best to secure and maintain a Pareto-curve for the distribution of vital knowledge of self and others; at worst, the effect of present publication practices is to heighten inequalities in access to important inside dope, and hence further to favor the managerial society.

There is a problem connected with the activity itself in its bearing on social stability: social change is already quite directly tied to technological change, in turn directly tied to quasi-autonomous natural science research. We are just entering the period where the society will be ever more rapidly changed (and I believe, shaken) by the much more far-reaching products of social scientific research. But again, this problem is not the natural scientists' concern, whereas it must be ours. In Lenin's words, "What is to be done?" Are we to take no "scientific" or ethical interest in the results of our own social intervention? Whose "field of study" is this, if not ours?

There is a problem connected with the ambiguities of the notion of "mastery" in relation to social affairs. With the aid of social science, what is to be mastered by whom, for whom, and with what conceivable results? There is also the opposite problem; the impotency-perception problem, as thinking in terms of causes and effects—the essential vocabulary of science —gradually replaces thinking in terms of agency, the essential vocabulary of action and drama, the former gradually leading man to view and feel himself as product rather than producer of himself and his "world."

There are so many such fundamental questions, so far-reaching in terms of the consequences that different answers to them would imply, that I am often left with the feeling that the house of social science is still largely founded on sand. Whether that is so or not, it seems evident that men do increasingly turn to social science, directly or indirectly, to structure perception and guide conduct, individual and collective, in more and more of their affairs. Before we have to take the strain that must ensue as our style of perception and explanation becomes the dominant style, as they shortly may, I should like to know more surely that we know, at least in large outline, what we are about.

Order and Conflict Theories of Social Problems

John Horton

A recent best seller, *The One Hundred Dollar Misunderstanding*,[1] should be required reading for every student of social problems and deviant behavior. The novel makes clear what is often dimly understood and rarely applied in sociology—the fundamentally social and symbolic character of existing theories of behavior. In the novel a square, white college boy and a Lolitaesque Negro prostitute recount their shared weekend experience. But what they have shared in action, they do not share in words. Each tells a different story. Their clashing tales express different vocabularies and different experiences. Gover stereotypically dramatizes a now hackneyed theme in the modern theater and novel—the misunderstandings generated by a conflict of viewpoints, a conflict between subjective representations of "objective" reality.

Paradoxically, this familiar literary insight has escaped many social scientists. The escape is most baffling and least legitimate for the sociologists of deviant behavior and social problems. Social values define their phenomena; their social values color their interpretations. Whatever the possibilities of developing empirical theory in the social sciences, only normative theory is appropriate in the sociology of social problems. I would accept Don Martindale's definitions of empirical and normative theory:

> The ultimate materials of empirical theory are facts; the ultimate materials of normative theory are value-imperatives . . . empirical theory is formed out of a system of law. Normative theory converts facts and laws into requisite means and conditions and is unique in being addressed to a system of objectives desired by the formulator or by those in whose service he stands.[2]

The problem for the sociologist is not that normative theories contain values, but that these values may go unnoticed so that normative theories

FROM *American Journal of Sociology*, May 1966, pp. 701–713, reprinted with permission of The University of Chicago Press.

[1] Robert Gover, *The One Hundred Dollar Misunderstanding* (New York: Ballantine Books, 1961).

[2] Don Martindale, "Social Disorganization: The Conflict of Normative and Empirical Approaches," in Howard Becker and Alvin Boskoff (eds.), *Modern Sociological Theory* (New York: Dryden Press, 1959), p. 341.

pass for empirical theories. When his own values are unnoticed, the sociologist who studies the situation of the American Negro, for example, is a little like the middle-class white boy in Gover's novel, except that only one story is told, and it is represented as *the* story. The result could be a rather costly misunderstanding: the Negro may not recognize himself in the sociological story; worse, he may not even learn to accept it.

One of the tasks of the sociologist is to recognize his own perspective and to locate this and competing perspectives in time and social structure. In this he can use Weber, Mills, and the sociology of knowledge as guides. Following Weber's work, he might argue that in so far as we are able to theorize about the social world, we must use the vocabularies of explanation actually current in social life.[3] This insight has been expanded by C. W. Mills and applied to theorizing in general and to the character of American theorizing in particular. The key words in Mills's approach to theorizing are "situated actions" and "vocabularies of motive." His position is that theories of social behavior can be understood sociologically as typical symbolic explanations associated with historically situated actions.[4] Thus, Mills argues that the Freudian terminology of motives is that of an upper-bourgeois patriarchal group with a strong sexual and individualistic orientation. Likewise explanations current in American sociology reflect the social experiences and social motives of the American sociologist. Mills contends that for a period before 1940, a single vocabulary of explanation was current in the American sociologist's analysis of social problems and that these motives expressed a small-town (and essentially rural) bias.[5] He interpreted the contemporary sociological vocabulary as a symbolic expression of a bureaucratic and administrative experience in life and work.[6]

Continuing in the tradition of Weber and Mills, I attempt to do the following: (1) propose a method of classifying current normative theories of deviant behavior and social problems; (2) discuss liberal and sociological approaches to the race question as an example of one of these theories; and (3) point out the implications of the normative character of theory for sociology. My general discussion of competing theories will be an elaboration of several assumptions:

1. All definitions and theories of deviation and social problems are normative. They define and explain behavior from socially situated value positions.

[3] For Weber's discussion of explanation in the social sciences see *Max Weber: The Theory of Social and Economic Organizations*, trans. A. M. Henderson and Talcott Parsons (Glencoe, Ill.: Free Press, 1947), pp. 87–114.
[4] C. Wright Mills, "Situated Actions and Vocabularies of Motive," *American Sociological Review*, V (December, 1940), 904–913.
[5] C. Wright Mills, "The Professional Ideology of the Social Pathologists," *American Journal of Sociology*, XLIX (September, 1942), 165–80.
[6] C. Wright Mills, *The Sociological Imagination* (New York: Oxford University Press, 1959).

2. Existing normative theories can be classified into a limited number of typical vocabularies of explanation. Contemporary sociological theories of deviation are adaptations of two fundamental models of analysis rooted in nineteenth-century history and social thought. These are *order* and *conflict* models of society. Order models imply an *anomy* theory of societal discontent and an *adjustment* definition of social deviation. Conflict models imply an *alienation* theory of discontent and a *growth* definition of deviation.

3. In general, a liberalized version of order theory pervades the American sociological approach to racial conflict, juvenile delinquency, and other social problems. I use the term "liberal" because the sociological and the politically liberal vocabularies are essentially the same. Both employ an order model of society; both are conservative in their commitment to the existing social order.

4. Alternatives to the liberal order approach exist both within the context of sociological theory and in the contemporary social and political fabric of American society. More radical versions of order models have been used by European sociologists such as Emile Durkheim; radical versions of order models are presently being used in American society by political rightists. The conflict vocabulary has been most clearly identified with Karl Marx and continues today in the social analysis of socialists and communists, while an anarchistic version of conflict theory pervades the politics of the so-called new left.

5. Current vocabularies for the explanation of social problems can be located within the social organization of sociology and the broader society. As a generalization, groups or individuals committed to the maintenance of the social status quo employ order models of society and equate deviation with non-conformity to institutionalized norms. Dissident groups, striving to institutionalize new claims, favor a conflict analysis of society and an alienation theory of their own discontents. For example, this social basis of preference for one model is clear in even the most superficial analysis of stands taken on civil rights demonstrations by civil rights activists and members of the Southern establishment. For Governor Wallace of Alabama, the 1965 Selma-Montgomery march was a negative expression of anomy; for Martin Luther King it was a positive and legitimate response to alienation. King argues that the Southern system is maladaptive to certain human demands; Wallace that the demands of the demonstrators are dysfunctional to the South. However, if one considers their perspectives in relationship to the more powerful Northern establishment, King and not Wallace is the order theorist.

In sociology, order analysis of society is most often expressed by the professional establishment and its organs of publication. Alienation analysis is associated with the "humanitarian" and "political" mavericks outside of, opposed to, or in some way marginal to the established profession of sociology.

Order and Conflict Theories: Anomy and Alienation Analysis of Social Problems As Ideal Types

The terms "alienation" and "anomy" current in the analysis of social problems derive historically from two opposing models of society—order and conflict models.[7] A comparison of the works of Marx and Mills (classical and contemporary conflict models) and Durkheim and Merton or Parsons (classical and contemporary order models) highlights the differences between the two social vocabularies. These competing vocabularies can be abstracted into ideal types of explanation, that is, exaggerated and ideologically consistent models which are only approximated in social reality.

The Order Vocabulary

Order theories have in common an image of society as a system of action unified at the most general level by shared culture, by agreement on values (or at least on modes) of communication and political organization. System analysis is synonymous with structural-functional analysis. System analysis consists of *statics*—the classification of structural regularities in social relations (dominant role and status clusters, institutions, etc.)—and *dynamics*—the study of the intrasystem processes: strategies of goal definition, socialization, and other functions which maintain system balance. A key concept in the analysis of system problems (social problems, deviation, conflict) is anomy. Social problems both result from and promote anomy. Anomy means system imbalance or social disorganization—a lack of or breakdown in social organization reflected in weakened social control, inadequate institutionalization of goals, inadequate means to achieve system goals, inadequate socialization, etc. At a social-psychological level of analysis, anomy results in the failure of individuals to meet the maintenance needs of the social system.

Order theories imply consensual and adjustment definitions of social health and pathology, of conformity and deviation. The standards for defining health are the legitimate values of the social system and its requisites

---

[7] In contemporary sociology, the concepts of alienation and anomy are often used synonymously. In practice, this usually means that alienation, a key term in conflict analysis, has been translated into a more conservative-order vocabulary; for a discussion of differences between past and present uses of these concepts see John Horton, "The Dehumanization of Anomie and Alienation," *British Journal of Sociology*, XV (December, 1964), 283–300.

for goal attainment and maintenance. Deviation is the opposite of social conformity and means the failure of individuals to perform their legitimate social roles; deviants are out of adjustment.

A contemporary example of an order approach to society and an adjustment interpretation of health and pathology has been clearly stated in Talcott Parsons' definition of mental health and pathology:

Health may be defined as the state of optimum *capacity* of an individual for the effective performance of the roles and tasks for which he has been socialized. It is thus defined with reference to the individual's participation in the social system. It is also defined as *relative* to his "status" in the society, i.e., to differentiated type of role and corresponding task structure, e.g., by sex or age, and by level of education which he has attained and the like.[8]

The Conflict Vocabulary

Conflict theorists are alike in their rejection of the order model of contemporary society. They interpret order analysis as the strategy of a ruling group, a reification of their values and motivations, a rationalization for more effective social control. Society is a natural system for the order analyst; for the conflict theorist it is a continually contested political struggle between groups with opposing goals and world views. As an anarchist, the conflict theorist may oppose any notion of stable order and authority. As a committed Marxist, he may project the notion of order into the future. Order is won, not through the extension of social control, but through the radical reorganization of social life; order follows from the condition of social organization and not from the state of cultural integration.

Conflict analysis is synonymous with historical analysis: the interpretation of intersystem processes bringing about the transformation of social relations. A key concept in the analysis of historical and social change (as new behavior rather than deviant behavior) is alienation—separation, not from the social system as defined by dominant groups, but separation from man's universal nature or a desired state of affairs. Change is the progressive response to alienation; concepts of disorganization and deviation have no real meaning within the conflict vocabulary; they are properly part of the vocabulary of order theory where they have negative connotations as the opposites of the supreme values of order and stability. Within the conflict framework, the question of normality and health is ultimately a practical one resolved in the struggle to overcome alienation.

Conflict theory, nevertheless, implies a particular definition of health, but the values underlying this definition refer to what is required to grow and change, rather than to adjust to existing practices and hypothesized

---

[8] Talcott Parsons, "Definitions of Health and Illness in the Light of American Values and Social Structure," in E. Gartley Jaco (ed.), *Patients, Physicians and Illness* (Glencoe, Ill.: Free Press, 1963), p. 176.

requirements for the maintenance of the social system. Health and pathology are defined in terms of postulated requirements for individual or social growth and adaptation. Social problems and social change arise from the exploitive and alienating practices of dominant groups; they are responses to the discrepancy between what is and what is in the process of becoming. Social problems, therefore, reflect, not the administrative problems of the social system, nor the failure of individuals to perform their system roles as in the order explanation, but the adaptive failure of society to meet changing individual needs.

A growth definition of health based on a conflict interpretation of society is implicit in Paul Goodman's appraisal of the causes of delinquency in American society. Unlike Parsons, he does not define pathology as that which does not conform to system values; he argues that delinquency is not the reaction to exclusion from these values, nor is it a problem of faulty socialization. Existing values and practices are absurd standards because they do not provide youth with what they need to grow and mature.

As was predictable, most of the authorities and all of the public spokesmen explain it (delinquency) by saying there has been a failure of socialization. They say that background conditions have interrupted socialization and must be improved. And, not enough effort has been made to guarantee belonging, there must be better bait or punishment.

But perhaps there has *not* been a failure of communication. Perhaps the social message has been communicated clearly to the young men and is unacceptable.

In this book I shall, therefore, take the opposite tack and ask, "Socialization to what? to what dominant society and available culture?" And if this question is asked, we must at once ask the other question, "Is the harmonious organization to which the young are inadequately socialized, perhaps against human nature, or not worthy of human nature, and *therefore* there is difficulty in growing up?"[9]

The conflict theorist invariably questions the legitimacy of existing practices and values; the order theorist accepts them as the standard of health.

Paradigm for the Analysis of Conflict and Approaches to Social Problems

In order more sharply to compare order and conflict models in terms of their implications for explanations of deviation and social problems, essential differences can be summarized along a number of parallel dimensions. These dimensions are dichotomized into order and conflict categories. The resulting paradigm can be used as a preliminary guide for the content analysis of contemporary as well as classical studies of social problems.

[9] Paul Goodman, *Growing Up Absurd* (New York: Random House, 1960), p. 11.

ORDER PERSPECTIVE	CONFLICT PERSPECTIVE

1. UNDERLYING SOCIAL PERSPECTIVE AND VALUE POSITIONS (IDEAL)

a. Image of man and society Society as a natural boundary-maintaining system of action Transcendent nature of society, an entity *sui generis,* greater than and different from the sum of its parts; lack of transcendence as lack of social control means anomy	Society as a contested struggle between groups with opposed aims and perspectives Immanent conception of society and the social relationship; men are society; society is the extension of man, the indwelling of man; the transcendence of society is tantamount to the alienation of man from his own social nature
Positive attitude toward the maintenance of social institutions	Positive attitude toward change
b. Human nature *Homo duplex,* man half egoistic (self-nature), half altruistic (socialized nature), ever in need of restraints for the collective good <div align="center">or</div>*Tabula rasa,* man equated with the socialization process <div align="center">or</div>*Homo damnatus,* the division into morally superior and morally inferior men	*Homo laborans,* existential man, the active creater of himself and society through practical and autonomous social action
c. Values The social good: balance, stability, authority, order, quantitative growth ("moving equilibrium")	Freedom as autonomy, change, action, qualitative growth

2. MODES OF "SCIENTIFIC" ANALYSIS

Natural science model: quest for general and universal laws and repeated patterns gleaned through empirical research Structural-functional analysis	Historical model: quest for understanding (*Verstehen*) through historical analysis of unique and changing events; possible use of ideal type of generalization based on historically specific patterns
Multiple causality; theory characterized by high level of abstraction, but empirical studies marked by low level of generalization (separation of theory from application)	Unicausality; high or low level of theoretical generalization; union of theory and practice in social research and social action
Conditions of objectivity: accurate correspondence of concepts to facts; rigid separation of observer and facts observed—passive, receptive theory of knowledge	Utility in terms of observer's interests; objectivity discussed in the context of subjectivity—activistic theory of knowledge

ORDER PERSPECTIVE	CONFLICT PERSPECTIVE
Analysis begins with culture as major determinant of order and structure and proceeds to personality and social organization	Analysis begins with organization of social activities or with growth and maintenance needs of man and proceeds to culture
Dominant concepts: ahistorical; high level of generality; holistic; supra-individual concepts; ultimate referent for concepts— system needs considered universally (i.e., the functional prerequisites of any social system) or relativistically (i.e., present maintenance requirements of a particular social system)	Historical, dynamic; low level of generality and high level of historical specificity; ultimate referent for concepts—human needs considered universally (i.e., man's species nature) or relativistically (demands of particular contenders for power); referent often the future or an unrealized state of affairs.

3. ORDER AND CONFLICT THEORIES OF SOCIAL PROBLEMS AND DEVIATION

a. Standards for the definition of health and pathology

Health equated with existing values of a postulated society (or a dominant group in the society), ideological definition	Health equated with unrealized standards (the aspirations of subordinate but rising groups), utopian definition

b. Evaluation of deviant behavior

Pathological to the functioning of the social system	Possibly progressive to the necessary transformation of existing relationships

c. Explanation of deviation or a social problem

A problem of anomy, inadequate control over competing groups in the social system; disequilibrium in the existing society	A problem of self-alienation, being thwarted in the realization of individual and group goals; a problem of illegitimate social control and exploitation

d. Implied ameliorative action

Extension of social control (further and more efficient institutionalization of social system values); adjustment of individuals to system needs; working within the system; the administrative solution	Rupture of social control; radical transformation of existing patterns of interaction; revolutionary change of the social system

4. ORDER AND CONFLICT THEORIES AS SOCIALLY SITUATED VOCABULARIES

Dominant groups: the establishment and administrators of the establishment	Subordinate groups aspiring for greater power
Contemporary representatives: Parsonian and Mertonian approach to social problems as a liberal variant of order models; politically conservative approaches	C. W. Mills, new left (SNCC, SDS, etc.) approaches and old left (socialistic and communistic)

The order and conflict models as outlined represent polar ideal types which are not consistently found in the inconsistent ideologies of actual social research and political practice. If the models have any utility to social scientists, it will be in making more explicit and systematic the usually implicit value assumptions which underlie their categories of thinking. In this paper as an exercise in the use of conflict-order models, I examine some of the normative assumptions which can be found in the approach of the sociologist and the political liberal to the Negro question. My thinking is intentionally speculative. I am not trying to summarize the vast literature on race relations, but merely showing the existence of an order pattern.

Liberals and Sociologists on the American Negro: A Contemporary Adaptation of Order Theory

Contemporary liberalism has been popularly associated with a conflict model of society; actually it is a variant of conservative order theory. Within the model, conflict is translated to mean institutionalized (reconciled) conflict or competition for similar goals within the same system. Conflict as confrontation of opposed groups and values, conflict as a movement toward basic change of goals and social structures is anathema.

The liberal tendency of American sociology and the essentially conservative character of contemporary liberalism are particularly marked in the sociological analysis of the Negro question. In the field of race relations, an order model can be detected in (1) consensual assumptions about man and society: the "over-socialized" man and the plural society; (2) a selective pattern of interpretation which follows from these assumptions: (a) the explanation of the problem as a moral dilemma and its solution as one requiring adjustment through socialization and social control; (b) the explanation of the minority group as a reaction-formation to exclusion from middle-class life; (c) an emphasis on concepts useful in the explanation of order (shared values as opposed to economic and political differences); an emphasis on concepts useful in the explanation of disorder or anomy within an accepted order (status competition rather than class conflict, problems of inadequate means rather than conflicting goals).

The Liberal View of Man: Egalitarian Within an Elitist, Consensual Framework; All Men Are Socializable to the American Creed

No one can see an ideological assumption as clearly as a political opponent. Rightist and leftist alike have attacked the liberal concept of man implicit in the analysis of the Negro question: conservatives because it is egalitarian, radicals because it is elitist and equated with a dominant ideology. The rightist believes in natural inequality; the leftist in positive, historical differences between men; the liberal believes in the power of socialization and conversion.

A certain egalitarianism is indeed implied in at least two liberal assertations: (1) Negroes along with other men share a common human nature socializable to the conditions of society; (2) their low position and general inability to compete reflect unequal opportunity and inadequate socialization to whatever is required to succeed within the American system. These assertations are, in a sense, basically opposed to the elitist-conservative argument that the Negro has failed to compete because he is naturally different or has voluntarily failed to take full advantage of existing opportunities.[10]

The conservative, however, exaggerates liberal egalitarianism; it is tempered with elitism. Equality is won by conformity to a dominant set of values and behavior. Equality means equal opportunity to achieve the same American values; in other words, equality is gained by losing one identity and conforming at some level to another demanded by a dominant group. As a leftist, J. P. Sartre has summarized this liberal view of man, both egalitarian and elitist. What he has termed the "democratic" attitude toward the Jew applies well to the American "liberal" view of the Negro:

> The Democrat, like the scientist, fails to see the particular case; to him the individual is only an ensemble of universal traits. It follows that his defense of the Jew saves the latter as a man and annihilates him as a Jew . . . he fears that the Jew will acquire a consciousness of Jewish collectivity. . . . "There are no Jews," he says, "there is no Jewish question." This means that he wants to separate the Jew from his religion, from his family, from his ethnic community, in order to plunge him into the democratic crucible whence he will emerge naked and alone, an individual and solitary particle like all other particles.[11]

The conservative would preserve a Negro identity by pronouncing the Negro different (inferior), the radical by proclaiming him part of the superior vanguard of the future society; but the liberal would transform him altogether by turning him into another American, another individual competing in an orderly fashion for cars, television sets, and identification with the American Creed. In their attack on the liberal definition of man, the conservative and leftist agree on one thing: the liberal seems to deny basic differences between groups. At least differences are reconcilable within a consensual society.

---

[10] For a conservative argument, see, among many others, Carleton Putman, *Race and Reason* (Washington, D.C.: Public Affairs Press, 1961).

[11] Jean-Paul Sartre, *Anti-Semite and Jew*, trans. George J. Becker (New York: Grove Press, 1962), pp. 56–57.

The Liberal Society: Structural Pluralism
Within a Consensual Framework

Thus, the liberal fate of minorities, including Negroes, is basically containment through socialization to dominant values. Supposedly this occurs in a plural society where some differences are maintained. But liberal pluralism like liberal egalitarianism allows differences only within a consensual framework. This applies both to the liberal ideal and the sociological description: the plural-democratic society *is* the present society.

This consensual pluralism should be carefully distinguished from the conflict variety. J. S. Furnivall has called the once colonially dominated societies of tropical Asia plural in the latter sense:

In Burma, as in Java, probably the first thing that strikes the visitor is the medley of peoples—European, Chinese, Indian, native. It is in the strictest sense a medley, for they mix but do not combine. Each group holds to its own religion, its own culture and language, its own ideas and ways. As individuals they meet, but only in the market-place, in buying and selling. There is a plural society, with different sections of the community living side by side, but separately, within the same political unit. Even in the economic sphere there is a division along racial lines.[12]

For Furnivall, a plural society has no common will, no common culture. Order rests on political force and economic expediency. For liberals and sociologists, American society has a common social will (the American Creed). Order rests on legitimate authority and consensus. The whole analysis of the Negro question has generally been predicated on this belief that American society, however plural, is united by consensus on certain values. Gunnar Myrdal's influential interpretation of the Negro question has epitomized the social will thesis:

Americans of all national origins, classes, regions, creeds, and colors, have something in common: a social ethos, a political creed. . . . When the American Creed is once detected the cacophony becomes a melody . . . as principles which ought to rule, the Creed has been made conscious to everyone in American society. . . . America is continuously struggling for its soul. The cultural unity of the nation is sharing of both the consciousness of sin and the devotion to high ideals.[13]

In what sense can a consensual society be plural? It cannot tolerate the existence of separate cultural segments. Robin M. Williams in a recent book on race relations writes: "The United States is a plural society which cannot settle for a mosaic of separate cultural segments, nor for a caste

[12] J. S. Furnivall, *Colonial Policy and Practice* (London: Cambridge University Press, 1948), p. 304.
[13] Gunnar Myrdal, *An American Dilemma* (New York: Harper & Bros., 1944), pp. 3–4.

system."[14] Norman Podhoretz, a political liberal who has written often on the Negro question, has stated the issue more bluntly. In his review of Ralph Ellison's *Shadow and the Act*, a series of essays which poses a threat of conflict pluralism by asserting the positive and different "cultural" characteristics of Negroes, Podhoretz states his consensual realism:

> The vision of a world in which many different groups live together on a footing of legal and social equality, each partaking of a broad general culture and yet maintaining its own distinctive identity: this is one of the noble dreams of the liberal tradition. Yet the hard truth is that very little evidence exists to suggest that such a pluralistic order is possible. Most societies throughout history have simply been unable to suffer the presence of distinctive minority groups among them; and the fate of minorities has generally been to disappear, either through being assimiliated into the majority, or through being expelled, or through being murdered.[15]

The liberal and the sociologist operating with an order ideology positively fear the conflict type of pluralism. As Sartre rightly observed, the liberal who is himself identified with the establishment, although avowedly the friend of the minority, suspects any sign of militant minority consciousness. He wants the minority to share in American human nature and compete like an individual along with other individuals for the same values.

As Podhoretz has observed, pluralism never really meant co-existence of quite different groups:

> For the traditional liberal mentality conceives of society as being made up not of competing economic classes and ethnic groups, but rather of competing *individuals* who confront a neutral body of law and a neutral institutional complex.[16]

How then can ethnic groups be discussed within the plural but consensual framework? They must be seen as separate but assimilated (contained) social structures. Among sociologists, Milton Gordon has been most precise about this pluralism as a description of ethnic groups in American society.

> Behavioral assimilation or acculturation has taken place in America to a considerable degree. . . . Structural assimilation, then, has turned out to be the rock on which the ships of Anglo-conformity and the melting pot have foundered. To understand that behavioral assimilation (or acculturation) without massive structural intermingling in primary relationships has been the dominant motif in the American experience of creating and developing a nation out of diverse peoples is to comprehend the most essential sociological fact of that experience. It is against the background of "structural pluralism" that strategies of strengthening intergroup harmony, reducing ethnic discrimination and preju-

[14] Robin M. Williams, Jr., *Strangers Next Door* (Englewood Cliffs, N.J.: Prentice-Hall, Inc., 1964), p. 386.

[15] Norman Podhoretz, "The Melting-Pot Blues," *Washington Post*, October 5, 1964.

[16] Norman Podhoretz, as quoted in "Liberalism and the American Negro—a Round-Table Discussion" with James Baldwin, Nathan Glazer, Sidney Hook, Gunnar Myrdal, and Norman Podhoretz (moderator), *Commentary*, XXXVII (March, 1964), 25–26.

dice, and maintaining the rights of both those who stay within and those who venture beyond their ethnic boundaries must be thoughtfully devised.[17]

Clearly then the liberal vocabulary of race relations is predicated on consensual assumptions about the nature of man and society. The order explanation of the Negro problem and its solution may be summarized as follows:

1. *An order or consensual model of society.*—American society is interpreted as a social system unified at its most general level by acceptance of certain central political, social, and economic values. Thus, the Negro population is said to have been acculturated to a somewhat vaguely defined American tradition; at the most, Negro society is a variant or a reaction to that primary tradition.
2. *Social problems as moral problems of anomy or social disorganization within the American system.*—Social problems and deviant behavior arise from an imbalance between goals and means. The problems of the Negro are created by unethical exclusion from equal competition for American goals.
3. *The response to anomy: social amelioration as adjustment and extension of social control.*—Liberal solutions imply further institutionalization of the American Creed in the opportunity structure of society and, therefore, the adjustment of the deviant to legitimate social roles.

The Race Question As a Moral Dilemma

A familiar expression of liberal-consensualism is Gunnar Myrdal's interpretation of the American race question as a moral dilemma. According to this thesis, racial discrimination and its varied effects on the Negro—the development of plural social structures, high rates of social deviation, etc.— reflect a kind of anomy in the relationship between the American Creed and social structure. Anomy means a moral crisis arising from an incongruity between legitimate and ethical social goals (for example, success and equality of opportunity) and socially available opportunities to achieve these goals. American society is good and ethical, but anomic because the American Creed of equality has not been fully institutionalized; the ethic is widely accepted in theory but not in practice.

Sidney Hook as a political liberal has likewise insisted that American society is essentially ethical and that the Negro problem should be discussed in these ethical terms:

Of course, no society has historically been organized on the basis of ethical principles, but I don't think we can understand how any society functions without observing the operation of the ethical principles within it. And if we ex-

[17] Milton Gordon, "Assimilation in America: Theory and Reality," *Daedalus*, XC (Spring, 1961), 280, 283.

amine the development of American society, we certainly can say that we have made *some* progress, to be sure, but progress nevertheless—by virtue of the extension of our ethical principles to institutional life. If we want to explain the progress that has been made in the last twenty years by minority groups in this country—not only the Negroes, but other groups as well—I believe we have to take into account the effect of our commitment to democracy, imperfect though it may be.[18]

The Solution: Working Within the System

The liberal solution to the racial question follows from the American-dilemma thesis: the belief in the ethical nature and basic legitimacy of American institutions. Amelioration, therefore, becomes exclusively a question of adjustment within the system; it calls for administrative action: how to attack anomy as the imbalance of goals and means. The administrator accepts the goals of his organization and treats all problems as errors in administration, errors which can be rectified without changing the basic framework of the organization. Karl Mannheim has aptly characterized the bureaucratic and administrative approach to social problems. What he says about the perspective of the Prussian bureaucrat applies only too well to his counterpart in American society:

The attempt to hide all problems of politics under the cover of administration may be explained by the fact that the sphere of activity of the official exists only within the limits of laws already formulated. Hence the genesis or the development of law falls outside the scope of his activity. As a result of his socially limited horizon, the functionary fails to see that behind every law that has been made there lie the socially fashioned interests and the *Weltanschauungen* of a specific social group. He takes it for granted that the specific order prescribed by the concrete law is equivalent to order in general. He does not understand that every rationalized order is only one of many forms in which socially conflicting irrational forces are reconciled.[19]

The liberal administrator's solution to the Negro question entails the expansion of opportunities for mobility within the society and socialization of the deviant (the Negro and the anti-Negro) to expanding opportunities. Hence the importance of education and job training; they are prime means to success and higher status. Given the assumption that the American Creed is formally embodied in the political structure, the liberal also looks to legislation as an important and perhaps sole means of reenforcing the Creed by legitimizing changes in the American opportunity structure.

---

[18] Sidney Hook, "Liberalism and the American Negro—a Round-Table Discussion," *Commentary*, XXXVII (March, 1964), p. 31.
[19] Karl Mannheim, *Ideology and Utopia* (New York: Harcourt, Brace & World, 1936), p. 118.

Negro Life As a Reaction Formation

Another important deduction has followed from the assumption of the political and cultural assimilation of the American Negro: whatever is different or distinct in his life style represents a kind of negative reaction to exclusion from the white society. The Negro is the creation of the white. Like the criminal he is a pathology, a reaction-formation to the problem of inadequate opportunities to achieve and to compete in the American system.

Myrdal states:

The Negro's entire life, and consequently, also his opinions on the Negro problem are, in the main, to be considered as secondary reactions to more primary pressures from the side of the dominant white majority.[20]

More recently Leonard Broom has echoed the same opinion:

Negro life was dominated by the need to adjust to white men and to take them into account at every turn. . . Taken as a whole, the two cultures have more common than distinctive elements. Over the long run, their convergence would seem inevitable. . . . Because Negro life is so much affected by poverty and subservience, it is hard to find distinctive characteristics that can be positively evaluated. In the stereotype, whatever is admirable in Negro life is assumed to have been adopted from the white man, while whatever is reprehensible is assumed to be inherently Negro.[21]

Conflict Theorist Looks at Order Theorist Looking at the Negro

A liberal order model—consensual pluralism, with its corollary approach to the race question as moral dilemma and reaction-formation—colors the sociological analysis of the race question. It is interesting that the fundamental assumption about consensus on the American Creed has rarely been subjected to adequate empirical test.[22] Lacking any convincing evidence for the order thesis, I can only wonder who the sociologist is speaking for. He may be speaking for himself in that his paradigm answers the question of how to solve the Negro problem without changing basic economic and political institutions. He probably speaks least of all for the Negro. The liberal sociologists will have some difficulty describing the world from the viewpoint of Negro "rioters" in Los Angeles and other

[20] Gunnar Myrdal as quoted by Ralph Ellison, "An American Dilemma: A Review," in *Shadow and the Act* (New York: Random House, 1964), p. 315.

[21] Leonard Broom, *The Transformation of the American Negro* (New York: Harper & Row, 1965), pp. 22–23.

[22] For a recent attempt to test the American dilemma thesis see Frank R. Westie, "The American Dilemma: An Empirical Test," *American Sociological Review*, XXX (August, 1965), 527–38.

cities. In any case, he will not agree with anyone who believes (in fact or in ideology) that the Negro may have a separate and self-determining identity. Such a view suggests conflict and would throw doubt on the fixations of consensus, anomy, and reaction-formation.

Conflict interpretations are minority interpretations by definition. They are rarely expressed either by sociologists or by ethnic minorities. However, a few such interpretations can be mentioned to imply that the end of ideology and, therefore, the agreement on total ideology has not yet arrived.

Ralph Ellison, speaking from a conflict and nationalistic perspective, has made several salient criticisms of the liberal American dilemma thesis. He has argued that Myrdal's long discussion of American values and conclusion of multiple casuality have conveniently avoided the inconvenient question of power and control in American society.

All this, of course, avoids the question of power *and* the question of who manipulates that power. Which to us seems more of a stylistic maneuver than a scientific judgment. . . . Myrdal's stylistic method is admirable. In presenting his findings he uses the American ethos brilliantly to disarm all American social groupings, by appealing to their stake in the American Creed, and to locate the psychological barriers between them. But he also uses it to deny the existence of an American class struggle, and with facile economy it allows him to avoid admitting that actually there exist two American moralities, kept in balance by social science.[23]

Doubting the thesis of consensus, Ellison is also in a position to attack Myrdal's interpretation of the American Negro as a reaction-formation, and assimilation to the superior white society as his only solution.

But can a people (its faith in an idealized American Creed notwithstanding) live and develop for over three hundred years simply by reacting? Are American Negroes simply the creation of white men, or have they at least helped to create themselves out of what they found around them? Men have made a way of life in caves and upon cliffs, why cannot Negroes have made a life upon the horns of the white men's dilemma?

Myrdal sees Negro culture and personality simply as the product of a "social pathology." Thus he assumes that "it is to the advantage of American Negroes as individuals and as a group to become assimilated into American culture, to acquire the traits held in esteem by the dominant white American." This, he admits, contains the value premise that *"here in America*, American culture is 'highest' in the pragmatic sense. . . ." Which aside from implying that Negro culture is not also American, assumes that Negroes should desire nothing better than what whites consider highest. But in the "pragmatic" sense lynching and Hollywood, fadism and radio advertising are products of "higher" culture, and the Negro might ask, "Why, if my culture is pathological, must I exchange it for these?" . . . What is needed in our country is not an exchange of pathologies, but a change of the basis of society.[24]

[23] Ralph Ellison, *Shadow and the Act, op. cit.*, p. 315.
[24] *Ibid.*, pp. 316–17.

Conclusion

The hostile action of Negro masses destroying white property is perhaps a more convincing demonstration of conflict theory than the hopes of Negro intellectuals. But as a sociologist I am not really interested in raising the question of whether a conflict definition of the race question is more correct than the more familiar order model. Each view is correct in a normative and practical sense in so far as it conforms to a viable political and social experience. What indeed is a correct interpretation of the Negro problem or any social problem? The answer has as must to do with consensus as with correspondence to the facts. Normative theories are not necessarily affected by empirical evidence because they seek to change or to maintain the world, not describe it.

Whenever there is genuine conflict between groups and interpretations, correctness clearly becomes a practical matter of power and political persuasion. This seems to be the situation today, and one can expect more heated debate. If conflict continues to increase between whites and Negroes in the United States, the liberal sociologist studying the "Negro problem" had better arm himself with more than his questionnaire. A militant Negro respondent may take him for the social problem, the sociologist as an agent of white society and the scientific purveyor of order theory and containment policy.

This clash of perspectives would be an illustration of my general argument: explanations of the Negro question or any other social problem invariably involve normative theory, values, ideologies, or whatever one may care to call the subjective categories of our thinking about society. Concepts of deviation and social problems can be discussed only in the context of some social (and therefore contestable) standard of health, conformity, and the good society. Terms like "moral dilemma," "pluralism," "assimilation," "integration" describe motives for desirable action: they are definitions placed on human action, not the action itself independent of social values.

The error of the sociologist is not that he thinks politically and liberally about his society, but that he is not aware of it. Awareness may help him avoid some of the gross errors of myopia: (1) mistaking his own normative categories for "objective" fact; thus, the liberal sociologist may mistake his belief in the consensual society for actual consensus; (2) projecting a normative theory appropriate to the experience of one group onto another group; this is what Ellison means when he says that the liberal sociologist is not necessarily speaking for the Negro. Indeed, the errors of myopia are perhaps greatest whenever the middle-class sociologist presumes to describe the world and motivation of persons in lower status. Seeing the lower-class Negro within a white liberal vocabulary may be very realistic politics, but it is not very accurate sociology.

Once the sociologist is involved in the study of anything that matters, he has the unavoidable obligation of at least distinguishing his vocabulary from that of the groups he is supposedly observing rather than converting. As a scientist, he must find out what perspectives are being employed, where they are operating in the society, and with what effect. Perhaps this awareness of competing perspective occurs only in the actual process of conflict and debate. Unfortunately, this is not always the situation within an increasingly professionalized sociology. The more professionalized the field, the more standardized the thinking of sociologists and the greater the danger of internal myopia passing for objectivity. But outside sociology debate is far from closed; conflict and order perspectives are simultaneously active on every controversial social issue. The liberal order model may not long enjoy uncontested supremacy.

PART TWO

Some Problems of Advanced Industrial Societies

SECTION 2

EDUCATION FOR WHAT?

THE IMPLICIT VALUES of educational institutions have far greater impact on youngsters than any explicit curriculum may have. Henry shows that the real subject matter is not spelling or arithmetic but the ways of the culture. Children are not merely taught but "invaded" and "possessed" by the spirit of competition, the horror of failure, the authority of the teacher. As both Friedenberg and Marin point out, students learn from the very existence of compulsory attendance that they are powerless. Friedenberg shows how the school functions to control students with a diffuse authority that has nothing to do with formal instruction. What the students learn is that they have no rights. Illich points to a "hidden curriculum," which is the assumption that children can be prepared for adulthood in society only by going to schools and consuming knowledge as a commodity under the authority of a certified teacher, that learning about the world is better than learning from the world, that "what is not taught in school is of little value."

The purpose of education, says Henry, has never been to free the mind and spirits of human beings, but to bind them. The school's implicit message is that children should mistrust their own judgment and perception in favor of the "right" way of the teacher. In English composition, art, or music, the teacher's conceptions of what is proper push into the background the children's originality.

The very origin of the term curriculum—from the Latin, meaning race track—indicates what schooling is really about. Students are taught to compete. They learn that one can succeed only at the cost of another. The school is a cultural instrument for instilling the fear of failure, which then functions to perpetuate the culture. The nightmarish fear of failure comes to haunt those socialized in our schools, even at the heights of any later success.

Conformity, obedience, and acquiescence are the major subjects learned in high school, according to both Marin and Friedenberg. Compulsory attendance deprives adolescents of the opportunity to act on their own volition. Students have no voice in selecting curriculum, hiring teachers, or determining what the school is about. Some schools practice a sham democracy where students decide between alternatives predetermined by the school authorities.[1]

The frustration of adolescent energy in schools leads to its own reaction. High school and even junior high school students are beginning to revolt on a gut level against the whole system. They organize strikes and demonstrations, they use drugs to deaden themselves against the system or escape it, they drop out of school altogether.

I agree that attempts to reform the schools do not make sense, because it is not only the methods but the goals that must be changed. As Marin puts it, "Revision of curriculum, teaching machines, smaller classes, encounter groups, redistributions of power—all of these are stopgap measures, desperate attempts to keep the young in schools that are hopelessly outdated."

One alternative to traditional schooling is the free school, where there are no grades or compulsory classes, and where children and adults treat each other as equals. At their best, free schools are communities where young children acquire their learning naturally, in a protected environment that allows them to grow at their own pace.[2] Even free schools, Illich warns, incorporate much of what they profess to reject. Teachers who have grown up in an unfree society find it difficult to break away from its hidden assumptions, and often unconsciously perpetuate the old system in a new guise.

Whether they are free or traditional, schools seem less useful for adolescents than for younger children. My own view is that the free high school works best as a place where young people can live together and as a

[1] This prepares students to participate in politics with the proper spirit, because the citizen is only free to decide between alternatives predetermined by those who run the major political parties.

[2] See the selection by A. S. Neill in Section 13 of this book. See also Paul Goodman, "The Present Moment in Education," New York Review of Books, April 10, 1969; George Dennison, The Lives of Children (New York: Random House, Inc., 1969); and Jonathan Kozol, Free Schools (Boston: Houghton Mifflin Company, 1972).

home base they can return to. The chief "subject" in such a school is usually the interaction of the young people with each other in a community they themselves are helping to build. Adolescents learn most readily by experiencing the world as apprentices, workers, or travelers. The school Marin speaks of allowed teenagers to come and go at will; the assumption was that all freely chosen activities contribute to learning.

Illich envisages a decentralized, post-industrial society where knowledge is communicated from adults to children and between each other in everyday activities instead of in schools. He says we must deprofessionalize education and rid ourselves of the superstition that only those with the proper credentials can teach. Further, we must extend the same principle to other fields, so that all men and women learn a variety of trades and skills formerly the exclusive possession of specialists and technicians. We must build simple tools and machines so that ordinary persons can repair them. We must share medical knowledge so we can keep our bodies healthy without having to rely on doctors. Illich does not, however, discuss the problem of how to bring about such a society. This topic is dealt with in later sections of the present anthology.

American Schoolrooms: Learning the Nightmare

Jules Henry

School is an institution for drilling children in cultural orientations. Educators have attempted to free the school from drill, but have failed because they have always chosen the most obvious "enemy" to attack. Furthermore, with every enemy destroyed, new ones are installed among the old fortifications that are the enduring contradictory maze of the culture. Educators think that when they have made arithmetic or spelling into a game; made it unnecessary for children to "sit up straight"; defined the relation between teacher and children as democratic; and introduced plants, fish, and hamsters into schoolrooms, they have settled the problem of drill. They are mistaken.

The paradox of the human condition is expressed more in education than elsewhere in human culture, because learning to learn has been and

FROM *Columbia University Forum* (Spring 1963), pp. 24–30. © Copyright 1963 by Jules Henry. An expanded version of this article appears in *Culture Against Man*, by Jules Henry. Reprinted by permission of Random House, Inc.

continues to be *Homo sapiens'* most formidable evolutionary task. Although it is true that mammals, as compared to birds and fishes, have to learn so much that it is difficult to say by the time we get to chimpanzees which behavior is inborn and which is learned, the learning task has become so enormous for man that today, education, along with survival, constitutes a major preoccupation. In all the fighting over education we are simply saying that after a million years of struggling to become human, we are not yet satisfied that we have mastered the fundamental human task, learning.

Another learning problem inherent in the human condition is this: We must conserve culture while changing it, we must always be *more* sure of surviving than of adapting. Whenever a new idea appears, our first concern as *animals* must be that it does not kill us; then, and only then, can we look at it from other points of view. In general, primitive people solved this problem simply by walling their children off from new possibilities by educational methods that, largely through fear, so narrowed the perceptual sphere that nontraditional ways of viewing the world became unthinkable.

The function of education has never been to free the mind and the spirit of man, but to bind them. To the end that the mind and the spirits of his children should never escape, *Homo sapiens* has wanted acquiescence, not originality, from his offspring. It is natural that this should be so, for where every man is unique there is no society, and where there is no society there can be no man. Contemporary American educators think they want creative children, yet it is an open question as to what they expect these children to create. If all through school the young were provoked to question the Ten Commandments, the sanctity of revealed religion, the foundations of patriotism, the profit motive, the two-party system, monogamy, the laws of incest, and so on, we would have more creativity than we could handle. In teaching our children to accept fundamentals of social relationships and religious beliefs without question we follow the ancient highways of the human race.

American classrooms, like educational institutions anywhere, express the values, preoccupations, and fears found in the culture as a whole. School has no choice; it must train the children to fit the culture as it is. School can give training in skills; it cannot teach creativity. Since the creativity that *is* encouraged—as in science and mathematics, for example—will always be that which satisfies the cultural drives at the time, all the American school can do is nurture that creativity when it appears.

Creative intellect is mysterious, devious, and irritating. An intellectually creative child may fail in social studies, for example, simply because he cannot understand the stupidities he is taught to believe as "fact." He may even end up agreeing with his teachers that he is "stupid" in social studies. He will not be encouraged to play among new social systems, values, and relationships, if for no other reason than that the social studies teachers will perceive such a child as a poor student. Furthermore, such a child will simply be unable to fathom the absurdities that seem transparent *truth* to the teacher. What idiot believes in the "law of supply and demand," for example? But the children who do, tend to *become* idiots; and learning to be an idiot is part of growing up! Or, as Camus put it, learning to be *absurd.* Thus the intellectually creative child who finds it impossible to learn to think the absurd the truth, who finds it difficult to accept absurdity as a way of life, usually comes to think himself stupid.

Schools have therefore never been places for the stimulation of young minds; they are the central conserving force of the culture, and if we observe them closely they will tell us much about the cultural pattern that binds us.

Much of what I am now going to say pivots on the inordinate capacity of a human being to learn more than one thing at a time. A child writing the word "August" on the board, for example, is not only learning the word "August," but also how to hold the chalk without making it squeak, how to write clearly, how to keep going even though the class is tittering at his slowness, how to appraise the glances of the children in order to know whether he is doing it right or wrong. If a classroom can be compared to a communications system—a flow of messages between teacher (transmitter) and pupils (receivers)—it is instructive to recall another characteristic of communications systems applicable to classrooms: their inherent tendency to generate *noise. Noise,* in communications theory, applies to all those random fluctuations of the system that cannot be controlled, the sounds that are not part of the message. The striking thing about the child is that along with his "messages about spelling" he learns all the noise in the system also. But—and mark this well—it is *not* primarily the message (the spelling) that constitutes the most important subject matter to be learned, but the noise! The most significant cultural learnings—primarily the cultural drives—are communicated as *noise.* Let us see the system operate in some of the contemporary suburban classrooms my students and I studied over a period of six years.

It is March 17 and the children are singing songs from Ireland and her neighbors. The teacher plays on the piano, while the children sing. While some children sing, a number of them hunt in the index, find a song belonging to one of Ireland's neighbors, and raise their hands in order that they may be called on to name the next song. The singing is that of pitchless quality always heard in elementary school classrooms. The teacher sometimes sings through a song first, in her off-key, weakishly husky voice.

The usual reason for this kind of song period is that the children are "broadened" while they learn something about music and singing. But what the children in fact learn about singing is to sing like everybody else. (This phenomenon—the standard, elementary school pitchlessness of the English-speaking world—was impressive enough for D. H. Lawrence to mention it in *Lady Chatterley's Lover.* The difficulty in achieving true pitch is so pervasive among us that missionaries carry it with them to distant jungles, teaching the natives to sing hymns off key. Hence on Sundays we would hear our Pilagá Indian friends, all of them excellent musicians in the Pilagá scale, carefully copy the missionaries by singing Anglican hymns, translated into Pilagá, off key exactly as sharp or as flat as the missionaries sang.) Thus one of the first things a child with a good ear learns in elementary school is to be musically stupid; he learns to doubt or to scorn his innate musical capacities.

But possibly more important than this is the use to which teachers and pupils put the lesson in ways not related at all to singing or to Ireland and her neighbors. To the teacher this was an opportunity to let the children somehow share the social aspects of the lesson with her. The consequence was distraction from singing as the children hunted in the index, and the net result was to activate the children's drives toward competition, achievement, and dominance. In this way the song period was scarcely a lesson in singing, but rather one in extorting the maximal benefit for the Self from *any* situation.

The first lesson a child has to learn when he comes to school is that lessons are not what they seem. He must then forget this and act as if they were. This is the first step toward "school mental health"; it is also the first step in becoming absurd. The second lesson is to put the teachers' and students' criteria in place of his own. The child must learn that the proper way to sing is tunelessly and not the way he hears the music; that the proper way to paint is the way the teacher says, not the way he sees it; that the proper attitude is not pleasure, but competitive horror at the success of his classmates, and so on. And these lessons must be so internalized that he will fight his parents if they object. The early schooling process is not successful unless it has produced in the child an acquiescence in its criteria, unless the child *wants* to think the way school has taught him to think. What we see in kindergarten and the early years of school is the pathetic surrender of babies. How could it be otherwise?

Now nothing so saps self-confidence as alienation from the Self. It would follow that school, the chief agent in the process, must try to provide the children with "ego support," for culture tries to remedy the ills it creates. Hence the effort to give children recognition in our schools. Hence the conversion of the songfest into an exercise in Self-realization. That anything essential was nurtured in this way is an open question, for the kind of individuality that was recognized as the children picked titles out of the index was mechanical, without a creative dimension, and under the strict control of the teacher. In short, the school metamorphoses the child, giving it the kind of Self the school can manage, and then proceeds to minister to the Self it has made.

We can see this at work in another example:

The observer is just entering her fifth-grade classroom for the observation period. The teacher says, "Which one of you nice, polite boys would like to take [the observer's] coat and hang it up?" From the waving hands, it would seem that all would like to claim the honor. The teacher chooses one child, who takes the observer's coat. . . . The teacher conducted the arithmetic lessons mostly by asking, "Who would like to tell the answer to the next problem?" This question was followed by the usual large and agitated forest of hands, with apparently much competition to answer.

What strikes us here are the precision with which the teacher was able to mobilize the potentialities in the boys for the proper social behavior, and the speed with which they responded. The large number of waving hands proves that most of the boys have already become absurd; but they have no choice. Suppose they sat there frozen?

A skilled teacher sets up many situations in such a way that *a negative attitude can be construed only as treason*. The function of questions like, "Which one of you nice, polite boys would like to take [the observer's] coat and hang it up?" is to bind the children into absurdity—to compel them to acknowledge that absurdity is existence, to acknowledge that it is better to exist absurd than not to exist at all. The reader will have observed that the question is not put, "Who *has* the answer to the next problem?" but, "Who *would like to tell* it?" What at one time in our culture was phrased as a challenge to skill in arithmetic, becomes here an invitation to group participation. The essential issue is that *nothing is but what it is made to be by the alchemy of the system*.

In a society where competition for the basic cultural goods is a pivot of action, people cannot be taught to love one another. It thus becomes necessary for the school to teach children how to hate, and without appearing to do so, for our culture cannot tolerate the idea that babes should hate each other. How does the school accomplish this ambiguity? Obviously through fostering competition itself, as we can see in an incident from a fifth-grade arithmetic lesson.

Boris had trouble reducing 12/16 to the lowest terms, and could only get as far as 6/8. The teacher asked him quietly if that was as far as he could reduce it. She suggested he "think." Much heaving up and down and waving of hands by the other children, all frantic to correct him. Boris pretty unhappy, probably mentally paralyzed. The teacher, quiet, patient, ignores the others and concentrates with look and voice on Boris. After a minute or two, she turns to the class and says, "Well, who can tell Boris what the number is?" A forest of hands appears, and the teacher calls Peggy. Peggy says that four may be divided into the numerator and the denominator.

Boris's failure has made it possible for Peggy to succeed; his misery is the occasion for her rejoicing. This is the standard condition of the contemporary American elementary school. To a Zuñi, Hopi, or Dakota Indian, Peggy's performance would seem cruel beyond belief, for competition, the wringing of success from somebody's failure, is a form of torture foreign to those noncompetitive cultures. Yet Peggy's action seems natural to us; and so it is. How else would you run our world?

Looked at from Boris's point of view, the nightmare at the blackboard was, perhaps, a lesson in controlling himself so that he would not fly shriek-

ing from the room under enormous public pressure. Such experiences force
every man reared in our culture, over and over again, night in, night out,
even at the pinnacle of success, to dream not of success, but of failure. In
school the external nightmare is internalized for life. Boris was not learning arithmetic only; he was learning the *essential nightmare also. To be
successful in our culture one must learn to dream of failure.*

When we say that "culture teaches drives and values" we do not state
the case quite precisely. We should say, rather, that culture (and especially
the school) provides the occasions in which drives and values are *experienced in events* that strike us with *overwhelming and constant force.* To
say that culture "teaches" puts the matter too mildly. Actually culture
invades and infests the mind as an obsession. If it does not, it will be
powerless to withstand the impact of critical differences, to fly in the face
of contradiction, to so engulf the mind that the world is seen only as the
culture decrees it shall be seen, to compel a person to be absurd. The
central emotion in obsession is fear, and the central obsession in education
is fear of failure. In school, one becomes absurd through being afraid; but
paradoxically, *only by remaining absurd can one feel free from fear.*

Let us see how absurdity is reinforced: consider this spelling lesson in
a fourth-grade class.

The children are to play "spelling baseball," and they have lined up to be
chosen for the two teams. There is much noise, but the teacher quiets it. She
has selected a boy and a girl and sent them to the front of the room as team
captains to choose their teams. As the boy and girl pick the children to form
their teams, each child takes a seat in orderly succession around the room. Apparently they know the game well. Now Tom, who has not yet been chosen,
tries to call attention to himself in order to be chosen. Dick shifts his position
to be more in the direct line of vision of the choosers, so that he may not be
overlooked. He seems quite anxious. Jane, Tom, Dick, and one girl whose name
the observer does not know are the last to be chosen. The teacher even has to
remind the choosers that Dick and Jane have not been chosen. . . .
The teacher now gives out words for the children to spell, and they write them
on the board. [Each word is a pitched ball, and each correctly spelled word is a
base hit. The children move around the room from base to base as their team-
mates spell the words correctly.] The outs seem to increase in frequency as each
side gets near the children chosen last. The children have great difficulty spelling
"August." As they make mistakes, those in the seats say, "No!" The teacher
says, "Man on third." As a child at the board stops and thinks, the teacher says,
"There's a time limit; you can't take too long, honey." At last, after many
children fail on "August" one child gets it right and returns, grinning with
pleasure, to her seat. . . . The motivation level in this game seems terrific. All the
children seem to watch the board, to know what's right and wrong, and seem
quite keyed up. There is no lagging in moving from base to base. The child who
is now writing "Thursday" stops to think after the first letter, and the children
snicker. He stops after another letter. More snickers. He gets the word wrong.
There are frequent signs of joy from the children when their side is right.

"Spelling baseball" is an effort to take the "weariness, the fever, and the
fret" out of spelling by absurdly transforming it into a competitive game.

Children are usually good competitors, though they may never become good spellers; and although they may never learn to *spell* success, they know what it *is*, how to go after it, and how it feels not to have it. A competitive game is indicated when children are failing, because the drive to succeed in the *game* may carry them to victory over the subject matter. But once a spelling lesson is cast in the form of a game of baseball a great variety of *noise* enters the system; because the sounds of *baseball* (the baseball "messages") cannot but be *noise* in a system intended to communicate *spelling.* If we reflect that one could not settle a baseball game by converting it into a spelling lesson, we see that baseball is bizarrely irrelevant to spelling. If we reflect further that a child who is a poor speller might yet be a magnificent ballplayer, we are even further impressed that learning spelling through baseball is learning by absurd association.

In making spelling into a baseball game one drags into the classroom whatever associations a child may have to the impersonal sorting process of kid baseball, but there are differences between the baseball world and the "spelling baseball" world also. One's failure is paraded before the class minute upon minute, until, when the worst spellers are the only ones left, the conspicuousness of the failures has been enormously increased. Thus the *noise* from baseball is amplified by a *noise* factor specific to the classroom.

It should not be imagined that I "object" to all of this, for in the first place I am aware of the indispensable social functions of the spelling game, and in the second place, I can see that the rendering of failure conspicuous cannot but intensify the quality of the essential nightmare, and thus render an important service to the culture. Without nightmares human culture has never been possible. Without hatred competition cannot take place except in games.

The unremitting effort by the system to bring the cultural drives to a fierce pitch must ultimately turn the children against one another; and though they cannot punch one another in the nose or pull one another's hair in class, they can vent some of their hostility in carping criticism of one another's work. Carping criticism, painfully evident in almost any American classroom, is viciously destructive of the early tillage of those creative impulses we say we cherish.

Listen to a fifth-grade class: The children are taking turns reading stories they have made up. Charlie's is called *The Unknown Guest.*

"One dark, dreary night, on a hill a house stood. This house was forbidden territory for Bill and Joe, but they were going in anyway. The door creaked, squealed, slammed. A voice warned them to go home. They went upstairs. A stair cracked. They entered a room. A voice said they might as well stay and find out now; and their father came out. He laughed and they laughed, but they never forgot their adventure together."

Teacher: Are there any words that give you the mood of the story?
Lucy: He could have made the sentences a little better. . . .
Teacher: Let's come back to Lucy's comment. What about his sentences?

Gert: They were too short. [Charlie and Jeanne have a discussion about the position of the word "stood" in the first sentence.]

Teacher: Wait a minute; some people are forgetting their manners. . . .

Jeff: About the room: the boys went up the stairs and one "cracked," then they were in the room. Did they fall through the stairs, or what?

The teacher suggests Charlie make that a little clearer. . . .

Teacher: We still haven't decided about the short sentences. Perhaps they make the story more spooky and mysterious.

Gwynne: I wish he had read with more expression instead of all at one time.

Rachel: Not enough expression.

Teacher: Charlie, they want a little more expression from you. I guess we've given you enough suggestions for one time. [Charlie does not raise his head, which is bent over his desk as if studying a paper.] Charlie! I guess we've given you enough suggestions for one time, Charlie, haven't we?

If American children fail while one of their number succeeds, they carp. And why not? We must not let our own "inner Borises" befog our thinking. A competitive culture endures by tearing people down. Why blame the children for doing it?

The contemporary school is not all horrors; it has its gentler aspects as well. Nearing a conclusion, let us examine impulse release and affection as they appear in many suburban classrooms.

Impulse is the root of life, and its release in the right amount, time, and place is a primary concern of culture. Nowadays the problem of impulse release takes on a special character because of the epoch's commitment to "letting down the bars." This being the case, teachers have a task unique in the history of education: the fostering of impulse release rather than the installation of controls. Everywhere controls are breaking down, and firmness with impulse is no part of contemporary pedagogy of "the normal child." Rather, impulse release, phrased as "spontaneity," "life adjustment," "democracy," "permissiveness," and "mothering," has become a central doctrine of education. It persists despite tough-minded critics from the Eastern Seaboard who concentrate on curriculum. The teachers know better; the real, the persisting, subject matter is *noise*.

How can the teacher release children's emotions without unchaining chaos? How can she permit so much *noise* and not lose the message? Were they alive, the teachers I had in P.S. 10 and P.S. 186 in New York City, who insisted on absolute silence, would say that chaos does prevail in many modern classrooms and that the message *is* lost. But lest old-fashioned readers argue that the social structure has fallen apart, I will point out what does *not* happen: The children do not fight or wrestle, run around the room, throw things, sing loudly, or whistle. The boys do not attack the girls or vice versa. Children do not run in and out of the room. They do not make the teacher's life miserable. All this occurs when the social structure *is* torn down, but in the average suburban classrooms we studied, it never quite happens. Why not? Here are some excerpts from an interview with a second-grade teacher I'll call Mrs. Olan.

In the one-room schoolhouse in which I first taught, the children came from calm homes. There was no worry about war, and there was no TV or radio. Children of today know more about what is going on; they are better informed. So you can't hold a strict rein on them.

Children need to enjoy school and like it. They also need their work to be done; it's not all play. You must get them to accept responsibility and to do work on their own.

To the question, "What would you say is your own particular way of keeping order in the classroom?" Mrs. Olan says:

Well, I would say I try to get that at the beginning of the year by getting this bond of affection and relationship between the children and me. And we do that with stories; and I play games *with* them—don't just teach them how to play. It's what you get from living together comfortably. We have "share" times. . . . These are the things that contribute toward discipline. Another thing in discipline—it took me a long time to learn it, too: I thought I was the boss, but I learned that even with a child, if you speak to him as you would to a neighbor or a friend you get a better response than if you say, "Johnny, do this or that."

Mrs. Olan has a creed: Love is the path to discipline through permissiveness; and school is a continuation of family life, in which the values of sharing and democracy lead to comfortable living and ultimately to discipline. She continues:

With primary children the teacher is a mother during the day; they have to be able to bring their problems to you. They get love and affection at home, and I see no reason not to give it in school.

To Mrs. Olan, mother of a 21-year-old son, second-grade children are pussy-cats. When asked, "Do you think the children tend to be quieter if the teacher is affectionate?" she says:

If a teacher has a well-modulated voice and a pleasing disposition, her children are more relaxed and quiet. Children are like kittens; If kittens have a full stomach and lie in the sun, they purr. If the atmosphere is such that the children are more comfortable, they are quiet. It is comfortable living that makes the quiet child. When you are shouting at them and they're shouting back at you, it isn't comfortable living.

It is clear to the observer that Mrs. Olan is no "boss," but lodges responsibility in the children. She clarifies the matter further:

It means a great deal to them to give them their own direction. When problems do come up in the room we talk them over and discuss what is the right thing to do when this or that happens. Usually you get pretty good answers. They are a lot harder on themselves than I would be; so if any punishment comes along like not going to an assembly you have group pressure.

As the interviewer was leaving, Mrs. Olan remarked, "My children don't rate as high [on achievement tests] as other children. I don't push, and that's because I believe in comfortable living." *Noise* has indeed become subject matter.

In such classrooms the contemporary training for impulse release and fun is clear. There the children are not in uniform, but in the jerkins and gossamer of *The Midsummer Night's Dream;* it is a sweet drilling without pain. Since impulse and release and fun are a major requirement of the classroom, and since they must be contained within the four walls, the instrument of containment can only be affection. The teacher must therefore become a parent, for it is a parent above all who deals with the impulses of the child.

It is hard for us to see, since we consider most people inherently replaceable, that there is anything remarkable in a parent-figure like a teacher showering the symbols of affection on a child for a year and then letting him walk out of her life. However, this is almost unheard of outside the stream of Western civilization; and even in the West it is not common. As a matter of fact, the existence of *children* willing to accept such demonstrations is in itself an interesting phenomenon, based probably on the obsolescence of the two-parent family. (Today our children *do not have enough parents,* because parents are unable to do all that has to be done *by* parents nowadays.) The fact that a teacher can be demonstrative without inflicting deep wounds on *herself* implies a character structure having strong brakes on involvement. Her expressions of tenderness, then, must imply "so far and no farther"; and over the years, children must come to recognize this. If this were not so, children would have to be dragged shrieking from grade to grade and teachers would flee teaching, for the mutual attachment would be so deep that its annual severing would be too much for either to bear. And so this noise, too, teaches two lessons important to today's culture. From regular replacement-in-affection children learn that the affection-giving figure, the teacher, is replaceable also, and so they are drilled in uninvolvement. Meanwhile, they learn that the symbols of affectivity can be used ambiguously, and that they are not binding—that they can be scattered upon the world without commitment.

Again, the reader should not imagine that I am "against" affectionate classrooms. They are a necessary adjunct to contemporary childhood and to the socialization of parenthood (the "three-parent family") at this stage of our culture. Meanwhile, the dialectic of culture suggests that there is some probability that when love like this enters by the door, learning leaves by the transom.

What, then, is the central issue? The central issue is *love of knowledge* for its own sake, not as the creature of drive, exploited largely for survival and for prestige. Creative cultures have loved the "beautiful person"—meditative, intellectual, and exalted. As for the individual, the history of great civilizations reveals little except that creativity has had an obstinate way of emerging only in a few, and that it has never appeared in the mass of the people. Loving the beautiful person more, we may alter this.

The contemporary school is a place where children are drilled in very general cultural orientations, and where subject matter becomes to a very considerable extent the instrument for instilling them. Because school deals with masses of children, it can manage only by reducing children all to a common definition. Naturally that definition is determined by the cultural preoccupations and so school creates the *essential nightmare* that drives people away from something (in our case, failure) and toward something (success). Today our children, instead of loving knowledge, become embroiled in the nightmare.

Coming of Age in America

Edgar Z. Friedenberg

The Cradle of Liberty

In my judgment, the kind of tutelage and status that the high school assigns students affects their lives and subsequent development far more crucially than the content and quality of formal instruction. What is learned most thoroughly by attendance at Milgrim or Hartsburgh is certain core assumptions that govern the conditions of life of most adolescents in this country and train them to operate as adult, if not as mature, Americans. The first of these is the assumption that the state has the right to compel adolescents to spend six or seven hours a day, five days a week, thirty-six or so weeks a year, in a specific place, under the charge of a particular group of persons in whose selection they have no voice, performing tasks about which they have no choice, without remuneration and subject to specialized regulations and sanctions that are applicable to no one else in the community nor to them except in this place. So accustomed are we to assuming that education is a *service* to the young that this statement must seem flagrantly biased. But it is a simple statement of what the law provides. Whether this provision is a service or a burden to the young —and, indeed, it is both, in varying degrees—is another issue altogether. Compulsory school attendance functions as a bill of attainder against a particular age group, so the first thing the young learn in school is that there are certain sanctions and restrictions that apply only to them, that they do not participate fully in the freedoms guaranteed by the state, and that, *therefore, these freedoms do not really partake of the character of inalienable rights.*

When services are to be provided to an individual whom the law respects as it does the agency providing the services the normal legal instrument is, of course, a contract, which defines the rights and obligations of both parties and provides each with legal remedies against the contract's breach.

Compulsory school attendance, however, is provided by a law which recognizes no obligation of the school that the students can enforce. He cannot petition to withdraw if the school is inferior, does not maintain standards, or treats him brutally. There are other laws, certainly, that set standards for school construction and maintenance, the licensing of teachers, technics of discipline, and so forth; and proceedings under these may be invoked if the school does not abide by them. But they do not abate the student's obligation to attend the school and accept its services. His position is purely that of a conscript who is protected by certain regulations but in no case permitted to use their breach as a cause for terminating his obligation.

Of course not. The school, as schools continually stress, acts *in loco parentis*; and children may not leave home because their parents are unsatisfactory. What I have pointed out is no more than a special consequence of the fact that students are minors, and minors do not, indeed, share all the rights and privileges—and responsibilities—of citizenship. Very well. However one puts it, we are still discussing the same issue. The high school, then, is where you really learn what it means to be a minor.

For a high school is not a parent. Parents may love their children, hate them, or like most parents, do both in a complex mixture. But they must, nevertheless, permit a certain intimacy and respond to their children as persons. Homes are not run by regulations, though the parents may think they are, but by a process of continuous and almost entirely unconscious emotional homeostasis, in which each member affects and accommodates to the needs, feelings, fantasy life, and character structure of the others. This may be, and often is, a terribly destructive process; I intend no defense of the family as a social institution. Salmon, actually, are much nicer than people: more dedicated, more energetic, less easily daunted by the long upstream struggle and less prudish and reticent about their reproductive functions, though inclined to be rather cold-blooded. But children grow up in homes or the remnants of homes, are in physical fact dependent on parents, and are too intimately related to them to permit their area of freedom to be precisely defined. This is not because they have no rights or are entitled to less respect than adults, but because intimacy conditions freedom and growth in ways too subtle and continuous to be defined as overt acts.

Free societies depend on their members to learn early and thoroughly that public authority is *not* like that of the family; that it cannot be expected—or trusted—to respond with sensitivity and intimate perception to the needs of individuals but must rely basically, though as humanely as possible, on the imperial application of general formulae. This means that it must be kept functional, specialized, and limited to matters of public policy; the meshes of the law are too coarse to be worn close to the skin. Especially in an open society, where people of very different backgrounds and value systems must function together, it would seem obvious that each must understand that he may not push others further than their common undertaking demands or impose upon them a manner of life that they feel to be alien.

After the family, the school is the first social institution an individual must deal with—the place in which he learns to handle himself with strangers. The school establishes the pattern of his subsequent assumptions as to which relations between the individual and society are appropriate and which constitute invasions of privacy and constraints on his spirit— what the British, with exquisite precision, call "taking a liberty." But the American public school evolved as a melting pot, under the assumption that it had not merely the right but the duty to impose a common standard of genteel decency on a polyglot body of immigrants' children and thus insure their assimilation into the better life of the American dream. It accepted, also, the tacit assumption that genteel decency was as far as it could go. If America has generally been governed by the practical man's impatience with other individuals' rights, it has also accepted the practical man's respect for property and determination to protect it from the assaults of public servants. With its contempt for personal privacy and individual autonomy, the school combines a considerable measure of Galbraith's "public squalor." The plant may be expensive—for this is capital goods; but nothing is provided graciously, liberally, simply as an amenity, either to teachers or students, though administrative offices have begun to assume an executive look. In the schools I know, the teachers' lounges are invariably filled with shabby furniture and vending machines. Teachers do not have offices with assigned clerical assistance and business equipment that would be considered satisfactory for, say, a small-town, small-time insurance agency. They have desks in staffrooms, without telephones.

To justify this shabbiness as essential economy and established custom begs the question; the level of support and working conditions customarily provided simply defines the status of the occupation and the value the community in fact places on it. An important consequence, I believe, is to help keep teachers timid and passive by reminding them, against the contrasting patterns of commercial affluence, of their relative ineffectiveness; and to divert against students their hostilities and their demands for status. Both teachers and students, each at their respective levels, learn to regard the ordinary amenities and freedoms of middle-class life as privileges. But the teacher has a few more of them. He hasn't a telephone, but he may make calls from a phone in the general office, while, in some schools, the public pay phone in the hallway has a lock on it and the student must get a key from the office before he can dial his call. Where a hotel or motel, for example, provides in its budget for normal wear and tear and a reasonable level of theft of linens and equipment and quietly covers itself with liability insurance, the school—though it may actually do the same thing —pompously indoctrinates its students with "respect for public property," "good health habits," and so forth before it lets them near the swimming pool. In a large city, the pool may have been struck out of the architect's plans before construction began, on the grounds that it would be unfair to provide students in a newer school with a costly facility that students in older schools do not have.

If the first thing the student learns, then, is that he, as a minor, is subject to peculiar restraints, the second is that these restraints are general, and are not limited to the manifest and specific functions of education. High school administrators are not professional educators in the sense that a physician, an attorney, or a tax accountant are professionals. They are not practitioners of a specialized *instructional* craft, who derive their authority from its requirements. They are specialists in keeping an essentially political enterprise from being strangled by conflicting community attitudes and pressures. They are problem-oriented, and the feelings and needs for growth of their captive and disfranchised clientele are the least of their problems; for the status of the "teen-ager" in the community is so low that even if he rebels the school is not blamed for the conditions against which he is rebelling. He is simply a truant or juvenile delinquent; at worst the school has "failed to reach him." What high school personnel become specialists in, ultimately, is the *control* of large groups of students even at catastrophic expense to their opportunity to learn. These controls are not exercised primarily to facilitate instruction, and, particularly, they are in no way limited to matters bearing on instruction. At several schools in our sample boys had, for example, been ordered by the assistant principal —sometimes on the complaint of teachers—to shave off beards. One of these boys, who had played football for the school all season, was told that, while the school had no legal authority to require this, he would be barred from the banquet honoring the team unless he complied. Dress regulations are another case in point.

Of course these are petty restrictions, enforced by petty penalties. American high schools are not concentration camps; and I am not complaining about their severity but about what they teach their students concerning the proper relationship of the individual to society. The fact that the restrictions and penalties are petty and unimportant in themselves in one way makes matters worse. Gross invasions are more easily recognized for what they are; petty restrictions are only resisted by "troublemakers." What matters in the end, however, is that the school does not take its own business of education seriously enough to mind it.

The effects on the students of the school's diffuse willingness to mind everybody's business but its own are manifold. The concepts of dignity and privacy, notably deficient in American adult folkways, are not permitted to develop here. The high school, certainly, is not the material cause of this deficiency, which is deeply rooted in our social institutions and values. But the high school does more than transmit these values—it exploits them to keep students in line and develop them into the kinds of people who fit the community that supports it.

A corollary of the school's assumption of custodial control of students is that power and authority become indistinguishable. If the school's authority is not limited to matters pertaining to education, it cannot be derived from educational responsibilities. It is a naked, empirical fact, to be accepted or controverted according to the possibilities of the moment. In this world power counts more than legitimacy; if you don't have power it is naïve to think you have rights that must be respected; wise up. High school students experience regulation only as control, not as protection; they know, for example, that the principal will generally uphold the teacher in any conflict with a student, regardless of the merits of the case. Translated into the high school idiom, *suaviter in modo, fortiter in re* becomes "If you get caught, it's just your ass."

Students, I find, do not resent this; that is the tragedy. All weakness tends to corrupt, and impotence corrupts absolutely. Identifying, as the weak must, with the more powerful and frustrating of the forces that impinge upon them, they accept the school as the way life is and close their minds against the anxiety of perceiving alternatives. Many students like high school; others loathe and fear it. But even these do not object to it on principle; the school effectively obstructs their learning of the principles on which objection might be based; though these are among the principles that, we boast, distinguish us from totalitarian societies.

Yet, finally, the consequence of submitting throughout adolescence to diffuse authority that is not derived from the task at hand—as a doctor's orders, or the training regulations of an athletic coach, for example, usually are—is more serious than political incompetence or weakness of character. There is a general arrest of development. An essential part of growing up is learning that, though differences of power among men lead to brutal consequences, all men are peers; none is omnipotent, none derives his potency from magic but only from his specific competence and function. The policeman represents the majesty of the State, but this does not mean that he can put you in jail; it means, precisely, that he cannot—at least not for long. Any person or agency responsible for handling throngs of young people—especially if it does not like them or is afraid of them—is tempted to claim diffuse authority and snare the youngster in the trailing remnants of childhood emotion, which always remain to trip him. Schools are permitted to infantilize adolescence and control pupils by reinvoking the sensations of childhood punishment, effective because it was designed, with great unconscious guile, to dramatize the child's weakness in the face of authority. In fact, they are strongly encouraged to do so by the hostility to "teen-agers" and the anxiety about their conduct that abound in our society.

In the process, the school affects society in two complementary ways. It alters individuals: their values, their sense of personal worth, their patterns of anxiety and sense of mastery and ease in the world on which so much of what we think of as our fate depends. But it also performs a Darwinian function. The school endorses and supports the values and patterns of behavior of certain segments of the population, providing their members with the credentials and shibboleths needed for the next stages of their journey, while instilling in others a sense of inferiority and warning the rest of society against them as troublesome and untrustworthy. In this way, the school contributes simultaneously to social mobility and social stratification. It helps to see to it that the kinds of people who get ahead are those who will support the social system it represents; while those who might, through intent or merely by their being, subvert it are left behind as a salutary moral lesson.

The Alternative to Schooling

Ivan Illich

For generations we have tried to make the world a better place by providing more and more schooling, but so far the endeavor has failed. What we have learned instead is that forcing all children to climb an open-ended education ladder cannot enhance equality but must favor the individual who starts out earlier, healthier, or better prepared; that enforced instruction deadens for most people the will for independent learning; and that knowledge treated as a commodity, delivered in packages, and accepted as private property once it is acquired, must always be scarce.

In response, critics of the educational system are now proposing strong and unorthodox remedies that range from the voucher plan, which would enable each person to buy the education of his choice on an open market, to shifting the responsibility for education from the school to the media and to apprenticeship on the job. Some individuals foresee that the school will have to be disestablished just as the church was disestablished all over the world during the last two centuries. Other reformers propose to replace the universal school with various new systems that would, they claim,

FROM Saturday Review (June 19, 1971), © 1971 Saturday Review, Inc. Reprinted by permission.

better prepare everybody for life in modern society. These proposals for new educational institutions fall into three broad categories: the reformation of the classroom within the school system; the dispersal of free schools throughout society; and the transformation of all society into one huge classroom. But these three approaches—the reformed classroom, the free school, and the worldwide classroom—represent three stages in a proposed escalation of education in which each step threatens more subtle and more pervasive social control than the one it replaces.

I believe that the disestablishment of the school has become inevitable and that this end of an illusion should fill us with hope. But I also believe that the end of the "age of schooling" could usher in the epoch of the global schoolhouse that would be distinguishable only in name from a global madhouse or global prison in which education, correction, and adjustment become synonymous. I therefore believe that the breakdown of the school forces us to look beyond its imminent demise and to face fundamental alternatives in education. Either we can work for fearsome and potent new educational devices that teach about a world which progressively becomes more opaque and forbidding for man, or we can set the conditions for a new era in which technology would be used to make society more simple and transparent, so that all men can once again know the facts and use the tools that shape their lives. In short, we can disestablish schools or we can deschool culture.

In order to see clearly the alternatives we face, we must first distinguish education from schooling, which means separating the humanistic intent of the teacher from the impact of the invariant structure of the school. This hidden structure constitutes a course of instruction that stays forever beyond the control of the teacher or of his school board. It conveys indelibly the message that only through schooling can an individual prepare himself for adulthood in society, that what is not taught in school is of little value, and that what is learned outside of school is not worth knowing. I call it the hidden curriculum of schooling, because it constitutes the unalterable framework of the system, within which all changes in the curriculum are made.

The hidden curriculum is always the same regardless of school or place. It requires all children of a certain age to assemble in groups of about thirty, under the authority of a certified teacher, for some 500 to 1,000 or more hours each year. It doesn't matter whether the curriculum is designed to teach the principles of fascism, liberalism, Catholicism, or socialism; or whether the purpose of the school is to produce Soviet or United States citizens, mechanics, or doctors. It makes no difference whether the teacher is authoritarian or permissive, whether he imposes his own creed or teaches students to think for themselves. What is important is that students learn that education is valuable when it is acquired in the school through a graded process of consumption; that the degree of success the individual will enjoy in society depends on the amount of learning he consumes; and that learning *about* the world is more valuable than learning *from* the world.

It must be clearly understood that the hidden curriculum translates learning from an activity into a commodity—for which the school monopolizes the market. In all countries knowledge is regarded as the first necessity for survival, but also as a form of currency more liquid than rubles or dollars. We have become accustomed, through Karl Marx's writings, to speak about the alienation of the worker from his work in a class society. We must now recognize the estrangement of man from his learning when it becomes the product of a service profession and he becomes the consumer.

The more learning an individual consumes, the more "knowledge stock" he acquires. The hidden curriculum therefore defines a new class structure for society within which the large consumers of knowledge—those who have acquired large quantities of knowledge stock—enjoy special privileges, high income, and access to the more powerful tools of production. This kind of knowledge-capitalism has been accepted in all industrialized societies and establishes a rationale for the distribution of jobs and income. (This point is especially important in the light of the lack of correspondence between schooling and occupational competence established in studies such as Ivar Berg's *Education and Jobs: The Great Training Robbery.*)

The endeavor to put all men through successive stages of enlightenment is rooted deeply in alchemy, the Great Art of the waning Middle Ages. John Amos Comenius, a Moravian bishop, self-styled Pansophist, and pedagogue, is rightly considered one of the founders of the modern schools. He was among the first to propose seven or twelve grades of compulsory learning. In his *Magna Didactica*, he described schools as devices to "teach everybody everything" and outlined a blueprint for the assembly-line production of knowledge, which according to his method would make education cheaper and better and make growth into full humanity possible for all. But Comenius was not only an early efficiency expert, he was an alchemist who adopted the technical language of his craft to describe the art of rearing children. The alchemist sought to refine base elements by leading their distilled spirits through twelve stages of successive enlightenment, so that for their own and all the world's benefit they might be transmuted into gold. Of course, alchemists failed no matter how often they tried, but each time their "science" yielded new reasons for their failure, and they tried again.

Pedagogy opened a new chapter in the history of Ars Magna. Education became the search for an alchemic process that would bring forth a new type of man, who would fit into an environment created by scientific magic. But, no matter how much each generation spent on its schools, it always turned out that the majority of people were unfit for enlightenment by this process and had to be discarded as unprepared for life in a man-made world.

Educational reformers who accept the idea that schools have failed fall into three groups. The most respectable are certainly the great masters of alchemy who promise better schools. The most seductive are popular magicians, who promise to make every kitchen into an alchemic lab. The most sinister are the new Masons of the Universe, who want to transform the entire world into one huge temple of learning. Notable among today's masters of alchemy are certain research directors employed or sponsored by the large foundations who believe that schools, if they could somehow be improved, could also become economically more feasible than those that are now in trouble, and simultaneously could sell a larger package of services. Those who are concerned primarily with the curriculum claim that it is outdated or irrelevant. So the curriculum is filled with new packaged courses on African Culture, North American Imperialism, Women's Lib, Pollution, or the Consumer Society. Passive learning is wrong—it is indeed—so we graciously allow students to decide what and how they want to be taught. Schools are prison houses. Therefore, principals are authorized to approve teach-outs, moving the school desks to a roped-off Harlem street. Sensitivity training becomes fashionable. So, we import group therapy into the classroom. School, which was supposed to teach everybody everything, now becomes all things to all children.

Other critics emphasize that schools make inefficient use of modern science. Some would administer drugs to make it easier for the instructor to change the child's behavior. Others would transform school into a stadium for educational gaming. Still others would electrify the classroom. If they are simplistic disciples of McLuhan, they replace blackboards and textbooks with multimedia happenings; if they follow Skinner, they claim to be able to modify behavior more efficiently than old-fashioned classroom practitioners can.

Most of these changes have, of course, some good effects. The experimental schools have fewer truants. Parents do have a greater feeling of participation in a decentralized district. Pupils, assigned by their teacher to an apprenticeship, do often turn out more competent than those who stay in the classroom. Some children do improve their knowledge of Spanish in the language lab because they prefer playing with the knobs of a tape recorder to conversations with their Puerto Rican peers. Yet all these improvements operate within predictably narrow limits, since they leave the hidden curriculum of school intact.

Some reformers would like to shake loose from the hidden curriculum, but they rarely succeed. Free schools that lead to further free schools produce a mirage of freedom, even though the chain of attendance is frequently interrupted by long stretches of loafing. Attendance through seduction inculcates the need for educational treatment more persuasively than the reluctant attendance enforced by a truant officer. Permissive teachers in a padded classroom can easily render their pupils impotent to survive once they leave.

Learning in these schools often remains nothing more than the acquisitions of socially valued skills defined, in this instance, by the consensus of a commune rather than by the decree of a school board. New presbyter is but old priest writ large.

Free schools, to be truly free, must meet two conditions: First, they must be run in a way to prevent the reintroduction of the hidden curriculum of graded attendance and certified students studying at the feet of certified teachers. And, more importantly, they must provide a framework in which all participants—staff and pupils—can free themselves from the hidden foundations of a schooled society. The first condition is frequently incorporated in the stated aims of a free school. The second condition is only rarely recognized, and is difficult to state as the goal of a free school.

It is useful to distinguish between the hidden curriculum, which I have described, and the occult foundations of schooling. The hidden curriculum is a ritual that can be considered the official initiation into modern society, institutionally established through the school. It is the purpose of this ritual to hide from its participants the contradictions between the myth of an egalitarian society and the class-conscious reality it certifies. Once they are recognized as such, rituals lose their power, and this is what is now beginning to happen to schooling. But there are certain fundamental assumptions about growing up—the occult foundations—which now find their expression in the ceremonial of schooling, and which could easily be reinforced by what free schools do.

Among these assumptions is what Peter Schrag calls the "immigration syndrome," which impels us to treat all people as if they were newcomers who must go through a naturalization process. Only certified consumers of knowledge are admitted to citizenship. Men are not born equal, but are made equal through gestation by Alma Mater.

The rhetoric of all schools states that they form a man for the future, but they do not release him for his task before he has developed a high level of tolerance to the ways of his elders: education *for* life rather than *in* everyday life. Few free schools can avoid doing precisely this. Nevertheless they are among the most important centers from which a new life-style radiates, not because of the effect their graduates will have but, rather, because elders who choose to bring up their children without the benefit of properly ordained teachers frequently belong to a radical minority and because their preoccupation with the rearing of their children sustains them in their new style.

The most dangerous category of educational reformer is one who argues that knowledge can be produced and sold much more effectively on an open market than on one controlled by school. These people argue that most skills can be easily acquired from skill-models if the learner is truly interested in their acquisition; that individual entitlements can provide a more equal purchasing power for education. They demand a careful separation of the process by which knowledge is acquired from the process by which it is measured and certified. These seem to me obvious statements. But it would be a fallacy to believe that the establishment of a free market for knowledge would constitute a radical alternative in education.

The establishment of a free market would indeed abolish what I have previously called the hidden curriculum of present schooling—its age-specific attendance at a graded curriculum. Equally, a free market would at first give the appearance of counteracting what I have called the occult foundations of a schooled society: the "immigration syndrome," the institutional monopoly of teaching, and the ritual of linear initiation. But at the same time a free market in education would provide the alchemist with innumerable hidden hands to fit each man into the multiple, tight little niches a more complex technocracy can provide.

Many decades of reliance on schooling have turned knowledge into a commodity, a marketable staple of a special kind. Knowledge is now regarded simultaneously as a first necessity and also as society's most precious currency. (The transformation of knowledge into a commodity is reflected in a corresponding transformation of language. Words that formerly functioned as verbs are becoming nouns that designate possessions. Until recently dwelling and learning and even healing designated activities. They are now usually conceived as commodities or services to be delivered. We talk about the manufacture of housing or the delivery of medical care. Men are no longer regarded fit to house or heal themselves. In such a society people come to believe that professional services are more valuable than personal care. Instead of learning how to nurse grandmother, the teen-ager learns to picket the hospital that does not admit her.) This attitude could easily survive the disestablishment of school, just as affiliation with a church remained a condition for office long after the adoption of the First Amendment. It is even more evident that test batteries measuring complex knowledge-packages could easily survive the disestablishment of school—and with this would go the compulsion to obligate everybody to acquire a minimum package in the knowledge stock. The scientific measurement of each man's worth and the alchemic dream of each man's "educability to his full humanity" would finally coincide. Under the appearance of a "free" market, the global village would turn into an environmental womb where pedagogic therapists control the complex navel by which each man is nourished.

At present schools limit the teacher's competence to the classroom. They prevent him from claiming man's whole life as his domain. The demise of school will remove this restriction and give a semblance of legitimacy to the life-long pedagogical invasion of everybody's privacy. It will open the way for a scramble for "knowledge" on a free market, which would lead us toward the paradox of a vulgar, albeit seemingly egalitarian, meritocracy. Unless the concept of knowledge is transformed, the disestablishment of school will lead to a wedding between a growing meritocratic system that separates learning from certification and a society committed to provide therapy for each man until he is ripe for the gilded age.

For those who subscribe to the technocratic ethos, whatever is technically possible must be made available at least to a few whether they want it or not. Neither the privation nor the frustration of the majority counts. If cobalt treatment is possible, then the city of Tegucigalpa needs one apparatus in each of its two major hospitals, at a cost that would free an important part of the population of Honduras from parasites. If supersonic speeds are possible, then it must speed the travel of some. If the flight to Mars can be conceived, then a rationale must be found to make it appear a necessity. In the technocratic ethos poverty is modernized: Not only are old alternatives closed off by new monopolies, but the lack of necessities is also compounded by a growing spread between those services that are technologically feasible and those that are in fact available to the majority.

A teacher turns "educator" when he adopts this technocratic ethos. He then acts as if education were a technological enterprise designed to make man fit into whatever environment the "progress" of science creates. He seems blind to the evidence that constant obsolescence of all commodities comes at a high price: the mounting cost of training people to know about them. He seems to forget that the rising cost of tools is purchased at a high price in education: They decrease the labor intensity of the economy, make learning on the job impossible or, at best, a privilege for a few. All over the world the cost of educating men for society rises faster than the productivity of the entire economy, and fewer people have a sense of intelligent participation in the commonweal.

A revolution against those forms of privilege and power which are based on claims to professional knowledge must start with a transformation of consciousness about the nature of learning. This means, above all, a shift of responsibility for teaching and learning. Knowledge can be defined as a commodity only as long as it is viewed as the result of institutional enterprise or as the fulfillment of institutional objectives. Only when a man recovers the sense of personal responsibility for what he learns and teaches can this spell be broken and the alienation of learning from living be overcome.

The recovery of the power to learn or to teach means that the teacher who takes the risk of interfering in somebody else's private affairs also assumes responsibility for the results. Similarly, the student who exposes himself to the influence of a teacher must take responsibility for his own education. For such purposes educational institutions—if they are at all needed—ideally take the form of facility centers where one can get a roof of the right size over his head, access to a piano or a kiln, and to records, books, or slides. Schools, TV stations, theaters, and the like are designed primarily for use by professionals. Deschooling society means above all the denial of professional status for the second-oldest profession, namely teaching. The certification of teachers now constitutes an undue restriction of the right to free speech: the corporate structure and professional pretensions of journalism an undue restriction on the right to a free press. Compulsory attendance rules interfere with free assembly. The deschooling of society is nothing less than a cultural mutation by which a people re covers the effective use of its constitutional freedoms: learning and teaching by men who know that they are born free rather than treated to freedom. Most people learn most of the time when they do whatever they enjoy; most people are curious and want to give meaning to whatever they come in contact with; and most people are capable of personal intimate intercourse with others unless they are stupefied by inhuman work or turned off by schooling.

The fact that people in rich countries do not learn much on their own constitutes no proof to the contrary. Rather it is a consequence of life in an environment from which, paradoxically, they cannot learn much, precisely because it is so highly programed. They are constantly frustrated by the structure of contemporary society in which the facts on which decisions can be made have become elusive. They live in an environment in which tools that can be used for creative purposes have become luxuries, an environment in which channels of communication serve a few to talk to many.

A modern myth would make us believe that the sense of impotence with which most men live today is a consequence of technology that cannot but create huge systems. But it is not technology that makes systems huge, tools immensely powerful, channels of communication one-directional. Quite the contrary: Properly controlled, technology could provide each man with the ability to understand his environment better, to shape it powerfully with his own hands, and to permit him full intercommunication to a degree never before possible. Such an alternative use of technology constitutes the central alternative in education.

If a person is to grow up he needs, first of all, access to things, to places and to processes, to events and to records. He needs to see, to touch, to tinker with, to grasp whatever there is in a meaningful setting. This access is now largely denied. When knowledge became a commodity, it acquired the protections of private property, and thus a principle designed to guard personal intimacy became a rationale for declaring facts off limits for people without the proper credentials. In schools teachers keep knowledge to themselves unless it fits into the day's program. The media inform, but exclude those things they regard as unfit to print. Information is locked into special languages, and specialized teachers live off its retranslation. Patents are protected by corporations, secrets are guarded by bureaucracies, and the power to keep others out of private preserves—be they cockpits, law offices, junkyards, or clinics—is jealously guarded by professions, institutions, and nations. Neither the political nor the professional structure of our societies, East and West, could withstand the elimination of the power to keep entire classes of people from facts that could serve them. The access to facts that I advocate goes far beyond truth in labeling. Access must be built into reality, while all we ask from advertising is a guarantee that it does not mislead. Access to reality constitutes a fundamental alternative in education to a system that only purports to teach *about* it.

Abolishing the right to corporate secrecy—even when professional opinion holds that this secrecy serves the common good—is, as shall presently appear, a much more radical political goal than the traditional demand for public ownership or control of the tools of production. The socialization of tools without the effective socialization of know-how in their use tends to put the knowledge-capitalist into the position formerly held by the financier. The technocrat's only claim to power is the stock he holds in some class of scarce and secret knowledge, and the best means to protect its value is a large and capital-intensive organization that renders access to know-how formidable and forbidding.

It does not take much time for the interested learner to acquire almost any skill that he wants to use. We tend to forget this in a society where professional teachers monopolize entrance into all fields, and thereby stamp teaching by uncertified individuals as quackery. There are few mechanical skills used in industry or research that are as demanding, complex, and dangerous as driving cars, a skill that most people quickly acquire from a peer. Not all people are suited for advanced logic, yet those who are make rapid progress if they are challenged to play mathematical games at an early age. One out of twenty kids in Cuernavaca can beat me at Wiff 'n' Proof after a couple of weeks' training. In four months all but a small percentage of motivated adults at our CIDOC center learn Spanish well enough to conduct academic business in the new language.

A first step toward opening up access to skills would be to provide various incentives for skilled individuals to share their knowledge. Inevitably, this would run counter to the interest of guilds and professions and unions. Yet, multiple apprenticeship is attractive. It provides everybody with an opportunity to learn something about almost anything. There is no reason why a person should not combine the ability to drive a car, repair telephones and toilets, act as a midwife, and function as an architectural draftsman. Special-interest groups and their disciplined consumers would, of course, claim that the public needs the protection of a professional guarantee. But this argument is now steadily being challenged by consumer protection associations. We have to take much more seriously the objection that economists raise to the radical socialization of skills: that "progress" will be impeded if knowledge—patents, skills, and all the rest—

is democratized. Their argument can be faced only if we demonstrate to them the growth rate of futile diseconomies generated by any existing educational system.

Access to people willing to share their skills is no guarantee of learning. Such access is restricted not only by the monopoly of educational programs over learning and of unions over licensing but also by a technology of scarcity. The skills that count today are know-how in the use of highly specialized tools that were designed to be scarce. These tools produce goods or render services that everybody wants but only a few can enjoy, and which only a limited number of people know how to use. Only a few privileged individuals out of the total number of people who have a given disease ever benefit from the results of sophisticated medical technology, and even fewer doctors develop the skill to use it.

The same results of medical research have, however, also been employed to create a basic medical tool kit that permits Army and Navy medics, with only a few months of training, to obtain results, under battlefield conditions, that would have been beyond the expectations of full-fledged doctors during World War II. On an even simpler level any peasant girl could learn how to diagnose and treat most infections if medical scientists prepared dosages and instructions specifically for a given geographic area.

All these examples illustrate the fact that educational considerations alone suffice to demand a radical reduction of the professional structure that now impedes the mutual relationship between the scientist and the majority of people who want access to science. If this demand were heeded, all men could learn to use yesterday's tools, rendered more effective and durable by modern science, to create tomorrow's world.

Unfortunately, precisely the contrary trend prevails at present. I know a coastal area in South America where most people support themselves by fishing from small boats. The outboard motor is certainly the tool that has changed most dramatically the lives of these coastal fishermen. But in the area I have surveyed, half of all outboard motors that were purchased between 1945 and 1950 are still kept running by constant tinkering, while half the motors purchased in 1965 no longer run because they were not built to be repaired. Technological progress provides the majority of people with gadgets they cannot afford and deprives them of the simpler tools they need.

Metals, plastics, and ferro cement used in building have greatly improved since the 1940s and ought to provide more people the opportunity to create their own homes. But while in the United States, in 1948, more than 30 per cent of all one-family homes were owner-built, by the end of the 1960s the percentage of those who acted as their own contractors had dropped to less than 20 per cent.

The lowering of the skill level through so-called economic development becomes even more visible in Latin America. Here most people still build their own homes from floor to roof. Often they use mud, in the form of adobe, and thatchwork of unsurpassed utility in the moist, hot, and windy climate. In other places they make their dwellings out of cardboard, oildrums, and other industrial refuse. Instead of providing people with simple tools and highly standardized, durable, and easily repaired components, all governments have gone in for the mass production of low-cost buildings. It is clear that not one single country can afford to provide satisfactory modern dwelling units for the majority of its people. Yet, everywhere this policy makes it progressively more difficult for the majority to acquire the knowledge and skills they need to build better houses for themselves.

Educational considerations permit us to formulate a second fundamental characteristic that any post-industrial society must possess: a basic tool kit that by its very nature counteracts technocratic control. For educational reasons we must work toward a society in which scientific knowledge is incorporated in tools and components that can be used meaningfully in units small enough to be within the reach of all. Only such tools can socialize access to skills. Only such tools favor temporary associations among those who want to use them for a specific occasion. Only such tools allow specific goals to emerge in the process of their use, as any tinkerer knows. Only the combination of guaranteed access to facts and of limited power in most tools renders it possible to envisage a subsistence economy capable of incorporating the fruits of modern science.

The development of such a scientific subsistence economy is unquestionably to the advantage of the overwhelming majority of all people in poor countries. It is also the only alternative to progressive pollution, exploitation, and opaqueness in rich countries. But, as we have seen, the dethroning of the GNP cannot be achieved without simultaneously subverting GNE (Gross National Education—usually conceived of as manpower capitalization). An egalitarian economy cannot exist in a society in which the right to produce is conferred by schools.

The feasibility of a modern subsistence economy does not depend on new scientific inventions. It depends primarily on the ability of a society to agree on fundamental, self-chosen anti-bureaucratic and anti-technocratic restraints.

These restraints can take many forms, but they will not work unless they touch the basic dimensions of life. (The decision of Congress against development of the supersonic transport plane is one of the most encouraging steps in the right direction.) The substance of these voluntary social restraints would be very simple matters that can be fully understood and judged by any prudent man. The issues at stake in the SST controversy provide a good example. All such restraints would be chosen to promote stable and equal enjoyment of scientific know-how. The French say that it takes a thousand years to educate a peasant to deal with a cow. It would not take two generations to help all people in Latin America or Africa to use and repair outboard motors, simple cars, pumps, medicine kits, and ferro cement machines if their design does not change every few years. And since a joyful life is one of constant meaningful intercourse with others in a meaningful environment, equal enjoyment does translate into equal education.

At present a consensus on austerity is difficult to imagine. The reason usually given for the impotence of the majority is stated in terms of political or economic class. What is not usually understood is that the new class structure of a schooled society is even more powerfully controlled by vested interests. No doubt an imperialist and capitalist organization of society provides the social structure within which a minority can have disproportionate influence over the effective opinion of the majority. But in a technocratic society the power of a minority of knowledge capitalists can prevent the formation of true public opinion through control of scientific know-how and the media of communication. Constitutional guarantees of free speech, free press, and free assembly were meant to ensure government by the people. Modern electronics, photo-offset presses, time-sharing computers, and telephones have in principle provided the hardware that could give an entirely new meaning to these freedoms. Unfortunately, these things are used in modern media to increase the power of knowledge-bankers to funnel their program-packages through international chains to more people, instead of being used to increase true networks that provide equal opportunity for encounter among the members of the majority.

Deschooling the culture and social structure requires the use of technology to make participatory politics possible. Only on the basis of a majority coalition can limits to secrecy and growing power be determined without dictatorship. We need a new environment in which growing up can be classless, or we will get a brave new world in which Big Brother educates us all.

The Open Truth and Fiery Vehemence of Youth

Peter Marin

It is midnight and I am sitting here with my notes, enough of them to make two books and a half and a volume of posthumous fragments, trying to make some smaller sense of them than the grand maniacal design I have in my mind. I don't know where to begin. Once, traveling in summer

FROM *The Center Magazine*, Vol. II, no. 1 (January 1969), pp. 61–74. Reprinted by permission of the author.

across the country with a friend from Hollywood and my young son in a battered green Porsche, I stopped for lunch somewhere in Kansas on a Sunday morning. As we walked into the restaurant, bearded, wearing dark glasses and strange hats, and followed by my long-haired boy, one Kansas matron bent toward another and whispered: "I bet those two men have kidnapped that little girl." I took a deep breath and started to speak, but I did not know where to begin or how to explain just how many ways she was mistaken. Now, trying to write clearly about education and adolescence, I feel the same way.

For that reason I have chosen an eccentric method of composition, one that may seem fragmentary, jumpy, and broken. This article will be more like a letter, and the letter itself is an accumulation of impressions and ideas, a sampling of thoughts at once disconnected but related. There is a method to it that may disappear in its mild madness, but I do not know at this juncture how else to proceed. Shuffling through my notes I feel like an archeologist with a mass of uncatalogued shards. There is a pattern to all this, a coherence of thought, but all I can do here is assemble the bits and pieces and lay them out for you and hope that you can sense how I get from one place to another.

An entire system is hiding behind this, just beginning to take form, and these notes are like a drawing, a preliminary sketch. I feel comfortable with that notion, more comfortable than with the idea of forcing them together, cutting and pasting, to make a more conventional essay. I can perceive in myself at this moment what I also see in the young: I am reluctant to deal in sequence with my ideas and experience, I am impatient with transition, the habitual ways of getting "from here to there." I think restlessly; my mind, like the minds of my students, works in flashes, in sudden perceptions and brief extended clusters of intuition and abstraction —and I have stuck stubbornly to that method of composition. There is still in me the ghost of an apocalyptic adolescent, and I am trying to move it a few steps toward the future.

One theme, as you will see, runs through what I have written or thought: we must rethink our ideas of childhood and schooling. We must dismantle them and start again from scratch. Nothing else will do. Our visions of adolescence and education confine us to habit, rule perception out. We make do at the moment with a set of ideas inherited from the nineteenth century, from an industrial, relatively puritanical, repressive, and "localized" culture; we try to gum them like labels to new kinds of experience. But that won't do. Everything has changed. The notions with which I began my job as a high-school director have been discarded one by one. They make no sense. What emerges through these children as the psyche of this culture is post-industrial, relatively unrepressed, less literate and local: a new combination of elements, almost a new strain. Adolescents are, each one of them, an arena in which the culture transforms itself or is torn between contrary impulses; they are the victims of a culture raging within itself like man and wife, a schizoid culture—and these children are the unfinished and grotesque products of that schism.

They are grotesque because we give them no help. They are forced to make among themselves adjustments to a tension that must be unbearable. They do the best they can, trying, in increasingly eccentric fashions, to make sense of things. But we adults seem to have withdrawn in defeat from that same struggle, to have given up. We are enamored, fascinated, and deluded by adolescence precisely because it is the last life left to us; only the young rebel with any real passion against media, machines, the press of circumstance itself. Their elders seem to have no options, no sense of alternative or growth. Adult existence is bled of life and we turn in that vacuum toward children with the mixed repulsion and desire of wanton Puritans toward life itself.

As for me, an adult, I think of myself as I write as an observer at a tribal war—an anthropoloigst, a combination of Gulliver and a correspondent sending home news by mule and boat. By the time you hear of it, things will have changed. And that isn't enough, not enough at all. Somebody must step past the children, must move into his own psyche or two steps past his own limits into the absolute landscape of fear and potential these children inhabit. That is where I am headed. So these ideas, in effect, are something like a last message tacked to a tree in a thicket or tucked under a stone. I mean: we cannot *follow* the children any longer, we have to step ahead of them. Somebody has to mark a trail.

Adolescence: a few preliminary fragments . . .

(FROM MY STUDENT, V): *yr whole body moves in a trained way & you know that youve moved this way before & it contains all youve been taught its all rusty & slow something is pushing under that rusted mesh but STILL YOU CANNOT MOVE you are caught between 2 doors & the old one is much closer & you can grab it all the time but the other door it disappears that door you cant even scratch & kick (like the early settlers were stung by the new land) but this new land doesnt even touch you & you wonder if youre doing the right thing to get in*

(FROM FRANZ KAFKA): *He feels imprisoned on this earth, he feels constricted; the melancholy, the impotence, the sicknesses, the feverish fancies of the captive afflict him; no comfort can comfort him, since it is merely comfort, gentle headsplitting comfort glazing the brutal fact of imprisonment. But if he is asked what he wants he cannot reply. . . . He has no conception of freedom.*

(FROM TAPES RECORDED IN PACIFIC PALISADES, 1966, SEVERAL BOYS AND GIRLS AGED 12–14):—*Things are getting younger and younger. Girls twelve will do it now. One guy said I fuck a girl every Friday night. What sexual*

*pleasure do you get out of this (he's very immature you know) and he
would say, I don't know I'm just going to fuck.*

                                    or

—How old are you? —*Twelve.* —Will you tell us your first experience
with drugs, how you got into it?— *Well, the people I hung around with
were big acid-heads. So one day my friend asked me if I wanted to get
stoned and I said yes. That was about five months ago and I've been getting on it ever since. Started taking LSD about one month ago. Took it
eleven times in one month. I consider it a good thing. For getting high,
smoking grass is better, or hashish—it's about six times stronger than
marijuana.*

(FROM PAUL RADIN: Primitive Man As Philosopher): *It is conceivably
demanding too much of a man to whom the pleasures of life are largely
bound up with the life of contemplation and to whom analysis and introspection are the self-understood prerequisites for a proper understanding of
the world, that he appreciate . . . expressions which are largely non-
intellectual—where life seems, predominatingly, a discharge of physical
vitality, a simple and naive release of emotions or an enjoyment of sensations for their own sake. Yet . . . it is just such an absorption in a life of
sensations that is the outward characteristic of primitive peoples.*

Can you see where my thoughts lead? It is precisely at this point,
adolescence, when the rush of energies, that sea-sex, gravitation, the thrust
of the ego up through layers of childhood, makes itself felt, that the person
is once more like an infant, is swept once more by energies that are tidal,
unfamiliar, and unyielding. He is in a sense born again, a fresh identity
beset inside and out by the rush of new experience. It is at this point, too
—when we seem compelled by a persistent lunacy to isolate him—that
what is growing within the adolescent demands expression, requires it, and
must, in addition, be received by the world and given form—or it will
wither or turn to rage. Adolescence is a second infancy. It is then that a
man desires solitude and at the same time contact with the vivid world;
must test within social reality the new power within himself; needs above
all to discover himself for the first time as a bridge between inner and
outer, a maker of value, a vehicle through which culture perceives and
transforms itself. It is now, ideally, that he begins to understand the complex and delicate nature of the ego itself as a thin skin between living
worlds, a synaptic jump, the self-conscious point at which nature and culture combine.

In this condition, with these needs, the adolescent is like a primitive
man, an apocalyptic primitive; he exists for the moment in that stage of
single vision in which myth is still the raw stuff of being, he knows at first
hand through his own energies the possibilities of life—but he knows these
in muddled, sporadic, contradictory ways. The rush of his pubescent and

raw energy seems at odds with public behavior, the *order* of things, the tenor of life around him, especially in a culture just emerging—as is ours—from a tradition of evasion, repression, and fear.

The contradictions within the culture itself intensify his individual confusion. We are at the moment torn between future and past: in the midst of a process of transformation we barely understand. The development of adolescent energy and ego—difficult at any time—is complicated in our own by the increase in early sexuality, the complicated messages of the media, and the effects of strong and unfamiliar drugs. These three elements are, in themselves, the salient features of a culture that is growing more permissive, less repressive. They are profound, complex, and strong: heavy doses of experience demanding changes in attitude, changes in behavior. The direction and depth of feeling responds accordingly; the adolescent tries—even as a form of self-defense against the pressure of his own energies—to move more freely, to change his styles of life, to "grow." But it is then that he finds he is locked into culture, trapped in a web of ideas, laws, and rituals that keep him a child, deprive him of a chance to test and assimilate his newer self. It is now that the culture turns suddenly repressive. His gestures are evaded or denied; at best he is "tolerated," but even then his gestures, lacking the social support of acknowledgment and reward, must seem to him lacking in authenticity—more like forms of neurosis or selfishness than the natural stages in growth.

He is thrust back upon himself. The insistent natural press within him toward becoming whole is met perpetually by unbudging resistance. Schools, rooted as they are in a Victorian century and seemingly suspicious of life itself, are his natural enemies. They don't help, as they might, to make that bridge between his private and the social worlds; they insist, instead, upon their separation. Indeed, family, community, and school all combine—especially in the suburbs—to isolate and "protect" him from the adventure, risk, and participation he needs; the same energies that relate him at this crucial point to nature result in a kind of exile from the social environment.

Thus the young, in that vivid confrontation with the thrust of nature unfolding in themselves, are denied adult assistance. I once wrote that education through its limits denied the gods, and that they would return in the young in one form or another to haunt us. That is happening now. You can sense it as the students gather, with their simplistic moral certainty, at the gates of the universities. It is almost as if the young were once more possessed by Bacchanalian gods, were once again inhabited by divinities whose honor we have neglected. Those marvelous and threatening energies! What disturbs me most about them is that we lack rituals for their use and balance, and the young—and perhaps we ourselves—now seem at their mercy. The young have moved, bag and baggage, into areas where adults cannot help them, and it is a scary landscape they face, it is crowded with strange forms and faces, and if they return from it raddled, without balance and pitched toward excess, who can pretend to be surprised—or blameless?

At times they seem almost shell-shocked, survivors of a holocaust in which the past has been destroyed and all the bridges to it bombed. I cannot describe with any certainty what occurs in their minds, but I do know that most adults must seem to the young like shrill critics speaking to them in an alien language about a Greek tragedy in which they may lose their lives. The words we use, our dress, our tones of voice, the styles of adult lives—all of these are so foreign to that dramatic crisis that as we approach them we seem to increase the distance we are trying to cross. Even our attention drives them further away, as if adolescents perceived that adults, coming closer, diminish in sense and size.

The inner events in an adolescent demand from what surrounds him life on a large scale, in a grand style. This is the impulse to apocalypse in the young, as if they were in exile from a nation that does not exist—and yet they can sense it, they know it is there—if only because their belief itself demands its presence. Their demand is absolute and unanswerable, but it exists and we seem unable at this point in time to suppress or evade it. For one reason or another, massive shifts in cultural balances, the lessening of repression for whatever reasons—economic, technological, evolutionary—these energies, like gods, have appeared among us again. But what can we make of them? The simple problem is that our institutions are geared to another century, another set of social necessities, and cannot change quickly enough to contain, receive, or direct them—and as we suppress or refuse them they turn to rage.

Primitive cultures dealt with this problem, I think, through their initiation rites, the rites of passage; they legitimized and accepted these energies and turned them toward collective aims; they were merged with the life of the tribe and in this way acknowledged, honored, and domesticated—but not destroyed. In most initiation rites the participant is led through the mythical or sacred world (or a symbolic version) and is then returned, transformed, to the secular one as a new person, with a new role. He is introduced through the rites to a dramatic reality coexistent with the visible or social one and at its root; he is put in direct touch with the sources of energy, the divinities of the tribe. In many cultures the symbolic figures in the rites are unmasked at the end, as if to reveal to the initiate the interpenetration of the secular and sacred worlds. Occasionally the initiate is asked at some point to don the ritual mask himself—joining, as he does, one world with another and assuming the responsibility for their connection. This shift in status, in *relation*, is the heart of the rite; a liturgized merging of the individual with shared sources of power.

Do you see what I am driving at? The rites are in a sense a social contract, a binding up; one occurring specifically, profoundly, on a deep psychic level. The individual is redefined in the culture by his new relation to its mysteries, its gods, to one form or another of nature. His experience of that hidden and omnipotent mythical world is the basis for his relation to the culture and his fellows, each of whom has a similar bond—deep, personal, and unique, but somehow shared, invisibly but deeply. These ritualized relationships of each man to the shared gods bind the group together; they form the substance of culture: an invisible landscape that is real and felt, commonly held, a landscape which resides in each man and in which, in turn, each man resides.

I hope that makes sense. That is the structure of the kaleidoscopic turning of culture that Blake makes in "The Crystal Cabinet," and it makes sense too, in America, in relation to adolescents. What fascinates me is that our public schools, designed for adolescents—who seem, as apocalyptic men, to demand this kind of drama, release, and support—educate and "socialize" their students by depriving them of everything the rites bestow. They manipulate them through the repression of energies; they isolate them and close off most parts of the community; they categorically refuse to make use of the individual's private experience. The direction of all these tendencies is toward a cultural schizophrenia in which the student is forced to choose between his own relation to reality or the one demanded by the institution. The schools are organized to weaken the student so that he is forced, in the absence of his own energies, to accept the values and demands of the institution. To this end we deprive the student of mobility and experience; through law and custom we make the only legal place for him the school, and then, to make sure he remains dependent, manipulable, we empty the school of all vivid life.

We appear to have forgotten in our schools what every primitive tribe with its functional psychology knows: allegiance to the tribe can be forged only at the deepest levels of the psyche and in extreme circumstance demanding endurance, daring, and awe; that the participant must be given *direct* access to the sources of cultural continuity—by and in himself; and that only a place in a coherent community can be exchanged for a man's allegiance.

I believe that it is precisely this world that drugs replace; adolescents provide for themselves what we deny them: a confrontation with some kind of power within an unfamiliar landscape involving sensation and risk. It is there, I suppose, that they hope to find, by some hurried magic, a new way of seeing, a new relation to things, to discard one identity and assume another. They mean to find through their adventures the *ground* of reality, the resonance of life we deny them, as if they might come upon their golden city and return still inside it: at home. You can see the real veterans sometimes on the street in strange costumes they have stolen from dreams: American versions of the Tupi of Brazil, who traveled thousands of miles each year in search of the land where death and evil do not exist. Theirs is a world totally alien to the one we discuss in schools; it is dramatic, it enchants them; its existence forms a strange brotherhood among them and they cling to it—as though they alone had been to a fierce land and back. It is that which draws them together and makes of them a loose tribe. It is, after all, some sort of shared experience, some kind of foray into the risky dark; it is the best that they can do.

When you begin to think about adolescence in this way, what sense can you make of our schools? None of the proposed changes makes sense to me: revision of curriculum, teaching machines, smaller classes, encounter groups, redistributions of power—all of these are stopgap measures, desperate attempts to keep the young in schools that are hopelessly outdated. The changes suggested and debated don't go deeply enough; they don't question or change enough. For what needs changing are not the methods of the school system but its aims, and what is troubling the young and forcing upon their teachers an intolerable burden is the *idea* of childhood itself; the ways we think about adolescents, their place in the culture itself. More and more one comes to see that changes in the schools won't be enough; the crisis of the young cuts across the culture in all its areas and includes the family and the community. The young are displaced; there seems no other word for it. They are trapped in a prolonged childhood almost unique.

In few other cultures have persons of fifteen or eighteen been so uselessly isolated from participation in the community, or been deemed so unnecessary (in their elders' eyes), or so limited by laws. Our ideas of responsibility, our parental feelings of anxiety, blame, and guilt, all of these follow from our curious vision of the young; in turn, they concretize it, legitimize it so that we are no longer even conscious of the ways we see childhood or the strain that our vision puts upon us. That is what needs changing: the definitions we make socially and legally of the role of the young. They are trapped in the ways we see them, and the school is simply one function, one aspect, of the whole problem. What makes real change so difficult in the schools is only in part their natural unwieldiness; it is more often the difficulty we have in escaping our preconceptions about things.

In general the school system we have inherited seems to me based upon three particular things:

• What Paul Goodman calls the idea of "natural depravity": our puritanical vision of human nature in which children are perceived as sinners or "savages" and in which human impulse or desire is not to be trusted and must therefore be constrained or "trained."

• The necessity during the mid-nineteenth century of "Americanizing" great masses of immigrant children from diverse backgrounds and creating, through the schools, a common experience and character.

• The need in an industrialized state for energy and labor to run the machines: the state, needing workers, educates persons to be technically capable but relatively dependent and responsive to authority so that their energies will be available when needed.

These elements combine with others—the labor laws that make childhood a "legal" state, and a population explosion that makes it necessary now to keep adolescents off both the labor market and the idle street—to "freeze" into a school system that resists change even as the culture itself and its needs shift radically. But teachers can't usually see that, for they themselves have been educated in this system and are committed to ideas that they have never clearly understood. Time and again, speaking to them, one hears the same questions and anguish:

"But what will happen to the students if they don't go to school?" "How will they learn?" "What will they do without adults?"

What never comes clear, of course, is that such questions are, at bottom, statement. Even while asking them teachers reveal their unconscious and contaminating attitudes. They can no longer imagine what children will do "outside" schools. They regard them as young monsters who will, if released from adult authority or help, disrupt the order of things. What is more, adults no longer are capable of imagining learning or child-adult relationship outside the schools. But mass schooling is a recent innovation. Most learning—especially the process of socialization or acculturation—has gone on outside schools, more naturally, in the fabric of the culture. In most cultures the passage from childhood to maturity occurs because of social necessity, the need for responsible adults, and is marked by clear changes in role. Children in the past seem to have learned the ways of the community or tribe through constant contact and interchange with adults, and it was taken for granted that the young learned continually through their place close to the heart of the community.

We seem to have lost all sense of that. The school is expected to do what the community cannot do and that is impossible. In the end, we will have to change far more than the schools if we expect to create a new coherence between the experiences of the child and the needs of the community. We will have to rethink the meaning of childhood; we will begin to grant greater freedom *and* responsibility to the young; we will drop the compulsory-schooling age to fourteen, perhaps less; we will take for granted the "independence" of adolescents and provide them with the chance to live alone, away from parents and with peers; we will discover jobs they can do or want to do in the community—anything from mail delivery to the teaching of smaller children and the counseling of other adolescents. At some point, perhaps, we will even find that the community itself—in return for a minimum of work or continued schooling—will provide a minimal income to young people that will allow them to assume the responsibility for their own lives at an earlier age, and learn the ways of the community outside the school; finally, having lowered the level of compulsory schooling, we will find it necessary to provide different *kinds* of schools, a wider choice, so that students will be willing voluntarily to continue the schooling that suits their needs and aims.

All these changes, of course, are aimed at two things: the restoration of the child's "natural" place in the community and lowering the age at which a person is considered an independent member of the community. Some of them, to be sure, can be made in the schools, but my sense of things, after having talked to teachers and visited the schools, is that trying to make the changes in schools *alone* will be impossible.

One problem, put simply, is that in every school I have visited, public or private, traditional or "innovational," the students have only these two choices: to drop out (either physically or mentally) or to make themselves smaller and smaller until they can act in ways their elders expect. One of my students picked up a phrase I once used, "the larger and smaller worlds." The schools we visit together, he says, are always the smaller world: smaller at least than his imagination, smaller than the potential of the young. The students are asked to put aside the best things about themselves—their own desires, impulses, and ideas—in order to "adjust" to an environment constructed for children who existed one hundred years ago, if at all. I wonder sometimes if this condition is simply the result of poor schooling; I am more inclined to believe that it is the inevitable result of mass compulsory schooling and the fabrication of artificial environments by adults for children. Is it possible at all for adults to understand what children need and to change their institutions fast enough to keep up with changes in culture and experience? Is it possible for children to grow to their full size, to feel their full strength, if they are deprived of individual volition all along the line and forced to school? I don't know. I know only that during the Middle Ages they sometimes "created" jesters by putting young children in boxes and force-feeding them so that, as they grew, their bones would warp in unusual shapes. That is often how the schools seem to me. Students are trapped in the boxes of pedagogic ideas, and I am tempted to say to teachers again and again: more, much more, you must go further, create more space in the schools, you must go deeper in thought, create more resonance, a different feeling, a different and more human, more daring style.

Even the best teachers, with the best intentions, seem to diminish their students as they work through the public-school system. For that system is, at bottom, designed to produce what we sometimes call good citizens but what more often than not turn out to be good soldiers; it is through the schools of the state, after all, that we produce our armies. I remember how struck I was while teaching at a state college by the number of boys who wanted to oppose the draft but lacked the courage or strength to simply say no. They were trapped; they had always been taught, had always tried, to be "good." Now that they wanted to refuse to go, they could not, for they weren't sure they could bear the consequences they had been taught would follow such refusal: jail, social disgrace, loss of jobs, parental despair.

They could not believe in institutions, but they could not trust themselves and their impulse and they were caught in their own impotence: depressed and resentful, filled with self-hatred and a sense of shame.

That is a condition bred in the schools. In one way or another our methods produce in the young a condition of pain that seems very close to a mass neurosis: a lack of faith in oneself, a vacuum of spirit into which authority or institutions can move, a dependency they feed on. Students are encouraged to relinquish their own wills, their freedom of volition; they are taught that value and culture reside outside oneself and must be acquired from the institution, and almost everything in their education is designed to discourage them from activity, from the wedding of idea and act. It is almost as if we hoped to discourage them from thought itself by making ideas so lifeless, so hopeless, that their despair would be enough to make them manipulable and obedient.

The system breeds obedience, frustration, dependence, and fear: a kind of gentle violence that is usually turned against oneself, one that is sorrowful and full of guilt, but a violence nonetheless, and one realizes that what is done in the schools to persons is deeply connected to what we did to the blacks or are doing now in Vietnam. That is: we don't teach hate in the schools, or murder, but we do isolate the individual; we empty him of life by ignoring or suppressing his impulse toward life; we breed in him a lack of respect for it, a loss of love—and thus we produce gently "good" but threatened men, men who will kill without passion, out of duty and obedience, men who have in themselves little sense of the vivid life being lost nor the moral strength to refuse.

From first to twelfth grade we acclimatize students to a fundamental deadness and teach them to restrain themselves for the sake of "order." The net result is a kind of pervasive cultural inversion in which they are asked to separate at the most profound levels their own experience from institutional reality, self from society, objective from subjective, energy from order—though these various polarities are precisely those which must be made coherent during adolescence.

I remember a talk I had with a college student.

"You know what I love to do," he said. "I love to go into the woods and run among the trees."

"Very nice," I said.

"But it worries me. We shouldn't do it."

"Why not?" I asked.

"Because we get excited. It isn't *orderly*."

"Not orderly?"

"Not orderly."

"Do you run into the trees?" I asked.

"Of course not."

"Then it's orderly," I said.

In a small way this exchange indicates the kind of thinking we encourage in the schools: the mistaking of rigidity and stillness for order, of order as the absence of life. We try to create and preserve an order which depends upon the destruction of life both inside and out and which all life, when expressed, must necessarily threaten or weaken.

The natural process of learning seems to move naturally from experience through perception to abstraction in a fluid continuous process that cannot be clearly divided into stages. It is in that process that energy is somehow articulated in coherent and meaningful form as an act or thought or a made object. The end of learning is wisdom and wisdom to me, falling back as I do on a Jewish tradition, is, in its simplest sense, "intelligent activity" or, more completely, the suffusion of activity with knowledge, a wedding of the two. For the Hassidic Jews every gesture was potentially holy, a form of prayer, when it was made with a reverence for God. In the same way a gesture is always a form of wisdom—an act is wisdom—when it is suffused with knowledge, made with a reverence for the truth.

Does that sound rhetorical? I suppose it does. But I mean it. The end of education is intelligent activity, *wisdom*, and that demands a merging of opposites, a sense of process. Instead we produce the opposite: immobility, insecurity, an inability to act without institutional blessing or direction, or, at the opposite pole, a headlong rush toward motion without balance or thought. We cut into the natural movement of learning and try to force upon the students the end product, abstraction, while eliminating experience and ignoring their perception. The beginning of thought is in the experience through one's self of a particular environment—school, community, culture. When this is ignored, as it is in schools, the natural relation of self and knowledge is broken, the parts of the process become polar opposites, antitheses, and the young are forced to choose between them: objectivity, order, and obedience as against subjectivity, chaos, and energy. It doesn't really matter which they choose; as long as the two sets seem irreconcilable their learning remains incomplete. Caught between the two, they suffer our intellectual schizophrenia until it occupies them, too. They wait. They sit. They listen. They learn to "behave" at the expense of themselves. Or else—and you can see it happening now—they turn against it with a vengeance and may shout, as they did at Columbia, "Kill all adults," for they have allied themselves with raw energy against reason and balance—our delicate, hard-won virtues—and we should not be surprised. We set up the choices ourselves, and it is simply that they have chosen what we hold to be the Devil's side.

If this is the case, what are the alternatives? I thought at one time that changes in schooling could be made, that the school itself could become at least a microcosm of the community outside, a kind of halfway house, a preparatory arena in which students, in semi-protective surroundings, would develop not only the skill but the character that would be needed in the world. But more and more, as I have said, it seems to me impossible to do that job in a setting as isolated and restrictive as our schools. Students don't need the artificiality of schools; they respond more fully and more intelligently when they make direct contact with the community and are allowed to choose roles that have some utility for the community and themselves. What is at stake here, I suppose, is the freedom of volition, for this is the basic condition with which people must learn to deal, and the sooner they achieve within that condition wit, daring, and responsibility the stronger they will be. It seems absurd to postpone the assumption of that condition as long as we do. In most other cultures, and even in our own past, young people have taken upon themselves the responsibility of adults and have dealt with it as successfully as most adults do now. The students I have seen can do that, too, when given the chance. What a strain it must be to have that capacity, to sense in one's self a talent for adventure or growth or meaning, and have that sense continually stifled or undercut by the role one is supposed to play.

Thus, it seems inescapably clear that our first obligation to the young is to create a place in the community for them to act with volition and freedom. They are ready for it, certainly, even if we aren't. Adolescents seem to need at least some sense of risk and gain "out there" in the world: an existential sense of themselves that is vivid to the extent that the dangers faced are "real." The students I have worked with seem strongest and most alive when they are in the mountains of Mexico or the Oakland ghetto or out in the desert or simply hitchhiking or riding freights to see what's happening. They thrive on distance and motion—and the right to solitude when they want it. Many of them want jobs; they themselves arrange to be teachers in day-care centers, political canvassers, tutors, poolroom attendants, actors, governesses, gardeners. They returned from these experiences immeasurably brightened and more sure of themselves, more willing, in that new assurance, to learn many of the abstract ideas we had been straining to teach them. It was not simply the experience in itself that brought this about. It was also the feeling of freedom they had, the sense that they could come and go at will and make any choice they wanted— no matter how absurd—if they were willing to suffer what real consequences followed. Many wanted to work and travel and others did not; they wanted to sit and think or read or live alone or swim or, as one student scrawled on my office wall, "ball and goof." What they finally came to understand, of course, was that the school made no pretense at either limiting or judging their activities; we considered them free agents and limited our own activities to advice, to what "teaching" they requested, and to support when they needed it in facing community, parents, or law.

What we were after was a *feeling* to the place: a sense of intensity and space. We discarded the idea of the microcosm and replaced it with an increased openness and access to the larger community. The campus itself became a place to come back to for rest or discussion or thought; but we turned things inside out to the extent that we came to accept that learning took place more naturally elsewhere, in any of the activities that our students chose, and that the school was in actuality wherever they were, whatever they did. What students learned at the school was simply the feel of things; the sense of themselves as makers of value; the realization that the environment is at best an extension of men and that it can be transformed by them into what they vitally need.

What we tried to create was a flexible environment, what a designer I know has called permissive space. It was meant to be in a sense a model for the condition in which men find themselves, in which the responsibility of a man was to make connections, value, and sense. We eliminated from the school all preconceptions about what was proper, best, or useful; we gave up rules and penalties; we refused at all levels to resort to coercive force and students were free to come and go at will, to do anything. What we were after was a "guilt-free" environment, one in which the students might become or discover what they were without having to worry about preconceived ideas of what they had to be.

What we found was that our students seemed to need, most of all, relief from their own "childhood"—what was expected of them. Some of them needed merely to rest, to withdraw from the strange grid of adult expectation and demand for lengthy periods of introspection in which they appeared to grow mysteriously, almost like plants. But an even greater number seemed to need independent commerce with the world outside the school: new sorts of social existence. Nothing could replace that. The simple fact seemed to be that our students grew when they were allowed to move freely into and around the adult community; when they were not, they languished.

We came to see that learning is natural, yes, but it results naturally from most things adolescents do. By associating learning with one particular form of intellection and insisting upon that in school we make a grave error. When students shy away from that kind of intellection it doesn't mean they are turning away forever from learning or abstractions; it means simply that they are seeking another kind of learning momentarily more natural to themselves. That may be anything from physical adventure or experimental community work to withdrawn introspection and an exploration of their fantasies and dreams.

Indeed, it is hard for them to do anything without some kind of learning, but that may be what we secretly fear—that those other forms of learning will make them less manageable or less like ourselves. That, after all, may be one reason we use all those books. Levi-Strauss insists on the relation of increased literacy and the power of the state over the individual. It may well be that dependence on print and abstraction is one of the devices we use to make students manipulable, as if we meant to teach them that ideas exist in talk or on the page but rarely in activity. We tried to avoid that. When we permitted students the freedom of choice and gave them easy access to the community, we found that ideas acquired weight and value to the extent that students were allowed to try them out in action. It was in practical and social situations that their own strength increased, and the merging of the two—strengthened self and tested knowledge—moved them more quickly toward manhood than anything else I have seen.

One might make a formula of it: to the extent that students had freedom of volition and access to experience knowledge became important. But volition and access were of absolute value; they took precedence over books or parental anxiety; without them, nothing worked. So we had to trust the students to make their own choices, no matter what we thought of them. We learned to take their risks with them—and to survive. In that sense we became equals, and that equality may in the end be more educational for students than anything else. That, in fact, may be the most important thing we learned. New ways in seeing them were more effective than changes in curriculum, and without them nothing made much difference. But we must understand too that the old way of seeing things—the traditional idea of childhood—is in some way baked into the whole public-school system at almost every level and also hidden in most pedagogy.

In some ways it is compulsory schooling itself which is the problem, for without real choice students will remain locked in childhood and schools, away from whatever is vivid in life. But real choice, as we know, includes dominion over one's own time and energies, and the right to come and go on the basis of what has actual importance. And I wonder if we will ever get round, given all our fears, to granting that privilege to students.

One thing alone of all I have read has made recent sense to me concerning adolescents. That is the implicit suggestion in Erik Erikson's *Young Man Luther* that every sensitive man experiences in himself the conflicts and contradictions of his age. The great man, he suggests, is the man who articulates and resolves these conflicts in a way that has meaning for his time; that is, he is himself, as was Luther, a victim of his time and its vehicle and, finally, a kind of resolution. But all men, not only the great, have in some measure the capacity to experience in themselves what is happening in the culture around them. I am talking here about what is really shared among the members of a particular culture as a condition, a kind of internal "landscape," the psychic shape that a particular time and place assumes within a man as the extent and limit of his perceptions, dreams, and pleasure and pain.

If there is such a shared condition it seems to me a crucial point, for it means that there is never any real distance between a man and his culture, no real isolation or alienation from society. It means that adolescents are not in their untutored state cut off from culture nor outside it. It means instead that each adolescent is an arena in which the contradictions and currents sweeping through the culture must somehow be resolved, must be resolved by the person himself, and that those individual resolutions are, ideally, the means by which the culture advances itself.

Do you see where this leads? I am straining here to get past the idea of the adolescent as an isolate and deviant creature who must be joined—as if glued and clamped—to the culture. For we ordinarily think of schools, though not quite consciously, as the "culture" itself, little models of society. We try to fit the student into the model, believing that if he will adjust to it he will in some way have been "civilized." That approach is connected to the needs of the early century, when the schools were the means by which the children of immigrant parents were acculturated and moved from the European values of their parents toward more prevalent American ones. But all of that has changed now. The children in our schools, all of them, are little fragments of *this* culture; they no longer need to be "socialized" in the same ways. The specific experiences of every adolescent —his fears, his family crises, his dreams and hallucinations, his habits, his sexuality—all these are points at which the general culture reveals itself in some way. There is no longer any real question of getting the adolescent to "adjust" to things.

The problem is a different one: What kind of setting will enable him to discover and accept what is already within him; to articulate it and perceive the extent to which it is shared with others; and, finally, to learn to change it within and outside himself? For that is what I mean when I call the adolescent a "maker of value." He is a trustee, a trustee of a world that already exists in some form within himself—and we must both learn, the adolescent and his teachers, to respect it.

In a sense, then, I am calling for a reversal of most educational thought. The individual is central; the individual, in the deepest sense, *is* the culture, not the institution. His culture resides in him, in experience and memory, and what is needed is an education that has at its base the sanctity of the individual's experience and leaves it intact.

What keeps running through my mind is a line I read twelve years ago in a friend's first published story: *The Idea in that idea is: there is no one over you.* I like that line: *There is no one over you.* Perhaps that signifies the gap between these children and their parents. For the children it is true, they sense it: there is no one over them; believable authority has disappeared; it has been replaced by experience. As Thomas Altizer says, God is dead; he is experienced now not as someone above or omnipotent or omniscient or "outside," but inwardly, as conscience or vision or even the unconscious or Tillich's "ground of being." This is all too familiar to bother with here, but this particular generation is a collective dividing point. The parents of these children, the fathers, still believe in "someone" over them, insist upon it; in fact, demand it for and from their children. The children themselves cannot believe it; the idea means nothing to them. It is almost as if they are the first real Americans—suddenly free of Europe and somehow fatherless, confused, forced back on their own experience, their own sense of things, even though, at the same time, they are forced to defy their families and schools in order to keep it.

This is, then, a kind of Reformation. Arnold was wrong when he said that art would replace religion; education replaced it. Church became School, the principal vehicle for value, for "culture," and just as men once rebelled against the established Church as the mediator between God and man, students now rebel against the *public* school (and its version of things) as the intermediary between themselves and experience, between themselves and experience and the making of value. Students are expected to reach "reality" (whether of knowledge or society) through their teachers and school. No one, it is said, can participate in the culture effectively without having at one time passed through their hands, proven his allegiance to them, and been blessed. This is the authority exercised by priests or the Church. Just as men once moved to shorten the approach to God, they are moved now to do the same thing in relation to learning and to the community. For just as God was argued to appear within a man—unique, private, and yet shared—so culture is, in some way, grounded in the individual; it inhabits him. The schools, like the Church, must be the expression of that habitation, not its exclusive medium. This is the same reformative shift that occurred in religion, a shift from the institution (the external) to the individual (the internal), and it demands, when it occurs, an agony, an apocalyptic frenzy, a destruction of the past itself. I believe it is happening now. One sees and feels it everywhere: a violent fissure, a kind of quake.

I remember one moment in the streets of Oakland during the draft demonstrations. The students had sealed off the street with overturned cars and there were no police; the gutters were empty and the students moved into them from the sidewalks, first walking, then running, and finally almost dancing in the street. You could almost see the idea coalesce on their faces: The street is ours! It was as if a weight had been lifted from them, a fog; there was not at that moment any fury in them, any vengefulness, or even politics; rather, a lightness, delight, an exhilaration at the sudden inexplicable sense of being free. George Orwell describes something similar in *Homage to Catalonia:* that brief period in Barcelona when the anarchists had apparently succeeded and men shared what power there was. I don't know how to describe it except to say that one's inexplicable sense of invisible authority had vanished: the oppressive father, who is not really there, was gone.

That sudden feeling is familiar to us all. We have all had it from time to time in our own lives, that sense of "being at home," that ease, that feeling of a Paradise which is neither behind us nor deferred but is around us, a natural household. It is the hint and beginning of Manhood: a promise, a clue. One's attention turns to the immediate landscape and to one's fellows: toward what is there, toward what can be felt as a part of oneself. I have seen the same thing as I watched Stokely Carmichael speaking to a black audience and telling them that they must stop begging the white man, like children, for their rights. They were, he said, neither children nor slaves, no, they were—and here they chanted, almost cried, in unison—a beautiful people: *yes our noses are broad and our lips are thick and our hair is kinky . . . but we are beautiful, we are beautiful, we are black and beautiful.* Watching, you could sense in that released joy an emergence, a surfacing of pride, a refusal to accept shame or the white man's dominance—and a turning to one another, to their own inherent value.

But there is a kind of pain in being white and watching that, for there is no one to say the same things to white children; no "fathers" or brothers to give them that sense of manhood or pride. The adolescents I have seen— white, middle-class—are a long way from those words *we are beautiful, we are beautiful.* I cannot imagine how they will reach them, deprived as they are of all individual strength. For the schools exist to deprive one of strength. That is why one's own worth must be proven again and again by the same satisfaction of external requirements with no inherent value or importance; it is why one must satisfy a set of inexplicable demands; it is why there is a continual separation of self and worth and the intrusion of a kind of institutional guilt: failure not of God but of *the system*, the nameless "others," the authority that one can never quite see; and it explains the oppressive sense of some nameless transgression, almost a shame at Being itself.

It is this feeling that pervades both high schools and colleges, this Kafkaesque sense of faceless authority that drives one to rebellion or withdrawal, and we are all, for that reason, enchanted by the idea of the Trial, that ancient Socratic dream of confrontation and vindication or martyrdom. It is then, of course, that Authority shows its face. In the mid-fifties I once watched Jack Kerouac on a television show and when the interviewer asked him what he wanted he said: to see the face of God. How arrogant and childish and direct! And yet, I suppose, it is what we all want as children: to have the masks of authority, all its disguises, removed and to see it plain. That is what lies in large part behind the riots in the schools. Their specific grievances are incidental; their real purpose is to make God show his face, to have whatever pervasive and oppressive force makes us perpetual children reveal itself, declare itself, commit itself at last. It is Biblical; it is Freudian; it reminds me in some way of the initiation rites: the need to unmask the gods and assume their power, to become an equal—and to find in that the manhood one has been denied.

The schools seem to enforce the idea that there *is* someone over you; and the methods by which they do it are ritualized, pervasive. The intrusion of guilt, shame, alienation from oneself, dependence, insecurity—all these feelings are not the accidental results of schools; they are intentional, and they are used in an attempt to make children manipulable, obedient, "good citizens" we call it, and useful to the state. The schools are the means by which we deprive the young of manhood—that is what I mean to say—and we must not be surprised when they seek that manhood in ways that must of necessity be childish and violent.

But I must admit this troubles me, for there is little choice between mindless violence and mindless authority, and I am just enough of an academic, an intellectual, to want to preserve much of what will be lost in the kind of rebellion or apocalypse that is approaching. And yet, and yet . . . the rapidity of events leaves me with no clear idea, no solution, no sense of what will be an adequate change. It may be that all of this chaos is a way of breaking with the old world and that from it some kind of native American will emerge. There is no way of knowing, there no longer seems any way of estimating what is necessary or what will work. I know only that the problem now seems to be that our response to crisis is to move away or back rather than forward, and that we will surely, for the sake of some imagined order, increase in number and pressure the very approaches that have brought us to this confusion. I don't know. I believe that the young must have values, of course, be responsible, care, but I know too that most of the violence I have seen done to the young has been done in the name of value, and that the well-meaning people who have been so dead set on making things right have had a hand in bringing us to where we are now. The paradox is a deep and troubling one for me. I no longer know if change can be accomplished—for the young, for any of us, without the apocalyptic fury that seems almost upon us. The crisis of youth and education is symptomatic of some larger, deeper fault in our cities and minds, and perhaps nothing can be done consciously in those areas until the air itself is violently cleared one way or another.

So I have no easy conclusions, no startling synthesis with which to close. I have only a change in mood, a softening, a kind of sadness. It may be, given that, that the best thing is simply to close with an unfinished fragment in which I catch for myself the hint of an alternative:

. . . I am trying to surround you, I see that, I am trying to make with these words a kind of city so natural, so familiar, that the other world, the one that appears to be, will look by comparison absurd and flat, limited, unnecessary. What I am after is liberation, not my own, which comes often enough these days in solitude or sex, but yours, and that is arrogant, isn't it, that is presumptuous, and yet that is the function of art: to set you free. It is that too which is the end of education: a liberation from childhood and what holds us there, a kind of midwifery, as if the nation itself were in labor and one wanted to save both the future and the past—for we are both, we are, we are the thin bridge swaying between them, and to tear one from the other means a tearing of ourselves, a partial death.

And yet it may be that death is inevitable, useful. It may be. Perhaps, as in the myth, Aphrodite can rise only where Cronos' testicles have fallen into the sea. It may be that way with us. The death of the Father who is in us, the death of the old authority which is part of us, the death of the *past which is also our death; it may all be necessary: a rending and purgation. And yet one still seeks another way, something less (or is it more) apocalyptic, a way in which the past becomes the future in ourselves, in which we become the bridges between: makers of culture.*

Unless from us the future takes place, we are Death only, *said Lawrence, meaning what the Chassids do: that the world and time reside within, not outside, men! that there is no distance, no "alienation," only a perpetual wedding to the world. It is that—the presence in oneself of Time—that makes things interesting, is more gravid and interesting than guilt. I don't want to lose it, don't want to relinquish that sense in the body of another dimension, a distance, the depth of the body as it extends backward into the past and forward, as it contains and extends and transforms.*

What I am after is an alternative to separation and rage, some kind of connection to things to replace the system of dependence and submission—the loss of the self—that now holds sway, slanted toward violence. I am trying to articulate a way of seeing, of feeling, that will restore to the young a sense of manhood and potency without at the same time destroying the past. That same theme runs through whatever I write: the necessity for each man to experience himself as an extension and maker of culture, and to feel the whole force of the world within himself, not as an enemy—but as himself:

. . . *An act of learning is a meeting, and every meeting is simply the discovery in the world of a part of oneself that had previously been unacknowledged by the self. It is the recovery of the extent of one's being. It is the embrace of an eternal but elusive companion, the shadowy "other" in which one truly resides and which blazes, when embraced, like the sun.*

SECTION 3

UNIVERSITY AND SOCIETY

INSTITUTIONS of higher education produce two major commodities: research on products and policies for government and business, and trained personnel certified for higher or lower slots in the meritocracy. The colleges and universities are giant factories that transform millions of young people into "degree holders" and assign them to places in the stratified system. But education does not automatically lead to the higher positions it once did. Most of those who hold bachelors and even masters degrees will become technicians, functionaries, and middle-level employees whose position in the social structure is analogous to that of skilled workers a hundred years ago. Only a very small percentage, certain graduates of the elite colleges and universities, will become the upper-echelon managers and the top professionals of tomorrow.

Higher education is beset by internal contradictions. One is the split between research and teaching. Weiss reminds us that professors neglect teaching because their main rewards are based not on instruction but on the production of research papers. Driven by the obligation to produce research, professors cut down their teaching time with television courses, large classes, and multiple choice exams. And the teaching itself serves more to recruit students to the professor's own specialty than to help students understand themselves and the world.

A second contradiction, as the Cohn-Bendits point out, is that the university is supposed to be the guardian of culture and the repository of humanistic and spiritual values at the same time that it must produce technically trained personnel to run the system. The problem is that personnel processing can be accomplished most efficiently by ignoring humanistic values; only the fragmentation of knowledge will supply all the technicians and managers needed for the government and corporate bureaucracies.

Most students are enrolled primarily because large corporations and government agencies require college degrees for many jobs. Passing the course has become more important than learning the subject. For the sake of acquiring tickets to future jobs, students anxiously compete for grades, memorize answers for examinations, and write term papers they would rather not write. These exams and papers are often read by graduate assistants instead of the professors, who are too busy producing research and too overwhelmed by the sheer size of their classes to relate to their students on any personal basis.

Feeling that their education is irrelevant to their deepest concerns, that their professors don't care about teaching, and that the administration exists only to harass them with petty restrictions, students revolt. At first, the student rebels are concerned with liberalizing the bureaucratic rules. In the course of their struggles against university administrations, the student rebellions often become broadened. The purpose of their revolt becomes changing the university from a research-degree factory into a place where students learn about themselves and the world and how to change those aspects of the system they don't like. What students want, according to Weissman (one of the leaders of the Berkeley Free Speech Movement[1]), is more than the ability to choose among alternatives predetermined by others. What they want is the power to determine curriculum and institutional policy. To achieve these goals, Weissman suggests that the students organize around issues and form syndicates for collective bargaining. In addition to direct action demonstrations, he suggests that students create counter-curricula and anti-universities.

The educational system is interconnected with the economic and political systems. The modern university provides the research and the trained

---

[1] The Free Speech Movement was a student protest movement that erupted at the University of California at Berkeley in fall, 1964. University officials tried to enforce a rule against advocacy of direct political action. Students defiantly continued to set up tables, pass out literature, solicit members and collect money for partisan political groups. The arrest of a nonstudent for engaging in such activity was met by a sit-in around the police car that was to take him away. After a semester of agitation that culminated in further sit-ins, a mass arrest of eight hundred students, and a student strike, the students won the right of political advocacy.

personnel that industry and government need for their operation; government and industry finance the universities and provide members for their governing boards. Because of this interdependence it is not possible to radically alter one system without changing the others. There seems to be no way of changing the functions of the university short of social revolution.

The university contains within itself all the contradictions of the larger society. For this reason, according to the Cohn-Bendits, the students' revolt against the oppression of the university has a potential for spreading beyond its confines. Students who learn to question the operation and purposes of the university end up questioning the presuppositions of the entire social order. The university revolt then becomes the spearhead of a movement to change the whole society.

Campus radicals face a dilemma: whether to continue to work within the university, hoping to influence new generations in the struggle against corporate liberalism, or whether to go outside and form parallel "free" universities or work as community organizers.

It is difficult to stay in the university without being pressured to conform: radical graduate students become liberal professors. I agree with Weiss that most academicians who ought to provide a critical view of the social order have largely abdicated their responsibility. Enmeshed in the system, they strive for promotions, recommendations, and government research grants. They find it difficult to be critical, for they themselves hold privileged positions in an affluent society.

Some professors take seriously the vocation of the radical intellectual and remain college teachers. They have formed such organizations as the New University Conference.[2] They hope to "turn the universities into a major arena of struggle against imperialism, against militarism, against capitalist culture and ideology, and for the creation of an alternative culture and ideology."[3]

Others doubt the possibility of remaining in the university without becoming corrupted by its competitive ethos. Furthermore, the so-called radical academic sends his students out to face problems which he himself has not confronted.[4]

[2] There is a sociologists' group affiliated with the New University Conference. It publishes The Insurgent Sociologist.

[3] Richard Flacks, "Radicals in the Universities," New University Conference Newsletter, May 24, 1968.

[4] See Staughton Lynd, "The Responsibility of Radical Intellectuals," ibid.

The University As Corporation

John Weiss

The basic historical fact about higher education in the United States is this: in the late nineteenth century, a transformation began which ended by changing the theology-ridden, narrow, and classical College of the eighteenth century into a vast and truly social institution, broad in scope, secular and pragmatic in nature, and above all prepared to be of great use to a rising industrial society. The college became, and deliberately became, a necessary and major social institution far outstripping in aim and reality anything comparable in the American or European past. From this transformation have come both the major achievements and the tenacious defects of the beast.

The most basic change in the nineteenth century was the very conception of what and who should be taught. Led largely by administrative heads, often Presidents, (and resisted often by faculty), the vast areas of knowledge which had been developing since the early eighteenth century, both in the natural and social sciences, were admitted into the college, where they assumed equal rank with the traditional Latin, Greek, and allied classical studies. The college, and later the university, became for the first time the place where new knowledge in academic disciplines was not only admitted and passed on, but, with time, actively cultivated. Moreover, the disciplines themselves were being professionalized along with the college. National associations of scholars and disciplines were organized, with their meetings, journals, standards, and pedantic guildism. Slowly the college came to be regarded as the natural place for those who hoped to follow a life of scholarship. The advantages for the advance of knowledge and its teaching in all this are evident. What was not so evident then, however, was the way in which a unique and often destructive dialectic was set up between the claims of specialized research and the demand for mass education.

Hand in hand with scholarly or professional specialization went what one might call the democratization—or perhaps socialization—of the college curriculum and student body. Higher education was not really particularly useful or necessary in America before the last quarter of the nineteenth century. Previously the college had simply passed on, rather mechanically, the classical tradition plus a little advanced moral philosophy or deism. Its students were mainly future clergy and thin slice of the upper crust. Normally, one would not find future lawyers, physicians, engineers,

FROM *New University Thought* (Summer 1965), pp. 31–45. Reprinted by permission.

journalists, teachers, and business managers in attendance. They acquired their training outside the college, as apprentices. Had things remained this way, higher education in America would hardly play such a prominent social role today, nor could it possibly have the vast influence it has attained as the teacher of each new segment of the rising meritocracy.

In the late nineteenth century, dynamic administrators, usually Presidents, transformed the college by professionalizing its education offerings and bureaucracy, and by opening it to the managerial and professional elites. Increasingly, the professions required theoretical, hence teachable, knowledge. In a swiftly changing mass industrial society, theory becomes crucial in all occupations—even farming, as any faculty member at one of our agricultural colleges can testify. At first, independent schools, uncontrolled by the college, met the new need as scientific, technical, and business institutes. A steady decline in college enrollments, however, made obvious the irrelevance of a solely classical or liberal education in an industrial society. Furthermore, the new Presidents of the most advanced institutions of higher education were the first to sense that the traditional college would play an increasingly minor role in a market-oriented society, dedicated to democracy and utility. Under men like White of Cornell, Eliot of Harvard, Tappen of Michigan, and Wayland of Brown, the college began to pre-empt professional training and to assure itself of a really massive role in modern America. Francis Wayland, the President of Brown, put it all in compelling and business-like fashion in 1850, when reporting to the Trustees of Brown University:

Our colleges are not filled, because we do not furnish the education desired by the people . . . We have produced an article for which the demand is diminishing. We sell it at less than cost, and the deficiency is made up by charity. We give it away, and the demand still diminishes.

I take it that over-sensitivity to market terms is out of place here. The college and the university could not have become major social institutions without the insistence that higher education become a market commodity. And the American college President has, since the great transformation, known how to emphasize the commodity value of education as an article of trade. The rewards have been obvious: higher education in America has found ample room at the public trough. Typically, the important Morrill Land-Grant Act of 1862 set the market conditions which were the price for the unique ability of the American college to gain wealth from the public domain. The Act insisted that for this wealth each favored state or territory must set up at least one college:

. . . where the leading object shall be . . . to teach such branches of learning as are related to agriculture and the mechanic arts . . . in order to promote the liberal and practical education of the industrial classes in the several pursuits and professions of life.

From the eighties on, then, the great transformation began. The college, to paraphrase Ezra Cornell, was to become a place where any man could study anything. Courses in the useful arts—agriculture and engineering—applied science courses, even military studies and that favorite abomination of liberal arts professors, domestic economy, shouldered their way in alongside the classics and the natural and social sciences. Some of the first public relations activities of the college were expanded, and at first in vain, to convince local farmers that education and science could improve farming. Wives were to be better for having formal training in cooking (ennobled as domestic economy) and engineers and future business managers were to find college courses and degrees in the theoretical aspects of their vocations offered. One Regent of Illinois University—limitless in his ambitions and also normal in other respects—held that his institution ought to teach "every form of human learning which it has fallen to the fortune of mankind to devise or acquire."

Thus, higher education in the United States began its modern career as a social institution, capable of shaping the intellectual habits of a nation. Vast changes, still going on, were required to adjust the college to its role as a social utility subject to market conditions in a democratic business and mass culture. Entrance requirements, grading and credit systems, financial structure, administrative bureaucracies, course offerings, student life, and a general departmentalization and bureaucratization of all aspects of the college had to be undertaken. Essentially, the failure of many of the critics of higher education has been a failure to comprehend the necessities and limitations of such changes, as well as the opportunities they afford to those who develop a strategy for working within a given system for serious and radical reforms.

The social role of the American college helps to explain the brutal fact that ultimate authority is vested in men who are quite ignorant of education. The Boards and Trustees who hold final power have been, since the end of clerical influence in the nineteenth century, overwhelmingly composed of wealthy and prestigious businessmen and (secondarily) the professional elite of the community. Such men may have met a payroll but they have rarely taught a class. They are there because they are able to attract wealth and prestige as leaders of the business community, and to emphasize the social value of higher education. Critics have not been lacking to demonstrate that their control means that American higher education is a conservative bulwark of American society. It is not so much that university administrations do not believe in free speech, nor is it really a major defect that Communists are only reluctantly, if at all, allowed to speak on campus. What is really crucial is that as a social institution supported by those most satisfied with American society and unwilling to take seriously major criticisms of it, the university has simply refused to use its virtual monopoly of brains to stand apart from society and view it critically.

The universities' knowledge and expertise are used only to train people for the given tasks of society—among them the task of scholarship. It is not so much that the university is not leftish or radical. The basic trouble is that in its market-place wisdom of maximizing demand, the university has ignored its duty to press for change and reform in all directions.

Perhaps even more crucial, however, has been the increasing power of the administrative officers over their Boards and Trustees. Lack of time and lack of interest coupled with the increasing complexity of running a major social institution (in education as elsewhere) has given increased power to managers rather than owners. The administration, of course, acts within the limits set by the business and professional groups. At the same time they act as neutralizers and buffers as well as administrative specialists. The result seems to be that though the university and the college are part of the ruling establishment and work entirely in its uncritical spirit, few see the extent of such indirect control. And this is so because the subtle management techniques of bureaucratic administrators are designed to avoid the crude thrust of manly dictatorship, even while forcing all to yield to market pressures and dominant values. The stuffy, patronizing, and even parental air of the average Dean confronting his employees (called faculty) is one of the results. Furthermore, bureaucratic administrators in any vast social corporation consider it their primary duty to work according to policy as they find it. They simply refuse to lead the university in radical new paths unless outside pressures or a united and singleminded internal constituency group force them to it. How amusing and disheartening to discover that the editor of *Oxford Magazine*, a semi-official organ of Oxford University (England), senses the same compulsion at work as England moves to the socialization of her narrow-based education system. I quote:

> The University cannot in a democracy give the lead to public opinion . . . because it is more and more a public institution under public pressures. . . . Enlightened patronage of advanced principles is a privilege more easily exercised by a private rather than a public corporation.

Beyond these implications of the socialization of American higher education come the long-term consequences of having to justify the entire curriculum as useful to society but at the same time not critical and reformist. Within the college, natural selection works to give increases and funds to those programs which seem of obvious social utility, defined often enough as training upcoming members of the business and professional classes in their trade. This pragmatic community pressure was felt most strongly in the large state and land-grant institutions of the West, and still is. Their lack of a liberal arts tradition and more or less primitive cultural surroundings, their extreme need of public funds, and the financial power of the competing established private institutions have combined to make these institutions the most vulnerable and responsive to establishment attitudes.

As befits a corporate institution in a democratic economy, the college has had to introduce a vast array of new courses (commodities) and create a more or less free market for the exercise of consumer choice (the free elective system). Fortunately, a central concern with the liberal arts has managed to survive. Students of other things are still required to take courses in liberal arts. But is it too much to say that the contemporary trade school atmosphere of most liberal arts colleges has stifled that original sense of communicating an independent and critical lay culture to professional and business people?

Along with professional specialization there has been as well a fragmentation of the intellectual life of undergraduates. Whatever its defects, the eighteenth century college provided a unified and related intellectual life. We have multiplied our course offerings again and again with the excuse that knowledge has been similarly fragmented. But why has the college taken its task to be the representation of all disciplines fairly, rather than the purposeful communication of a unified intellectual culture? Basically, this is because the college has assumed the task of research as well as teaching and has insisted that its people do both—but especially research. The consequences for student life are apparent. Departmentalization shatters the student body and replaces it with student bodies. After the freshman year, students have no intellectual life in common. As for political activism, it cannot function where there is no true community. Students soon see that in spite of all the pseudo-democratic rhetoric indulged in by Deans of Students, no shreds of power will come to them. As elsewhere, we train our young in college to refuse responsibility for the society as a whole and retreat to their private concerns. As for the few student-lefties, shrewd administrative techniques can frustrate them and make them look foolish. If all else fails, one can always distribute a few tame faculty here and there in student government.

The student is pushed toward a mindless apathy to all but his career by virtue of the structure of the college itself. After some feeble exposure to highly simplified snippets of "surveyed" professional knowledge in several disciplines, the student gets on to his real business of preparing for a trade or profession. The parts are all there, but, except where general studies have been worked out, no one helps the student perceive the relationship between the various fields and, more importantly, between the knowledge he acquired and the culture he inhabits. Consequently, the student is aware above all of the vast irrelevance of most of the stuff he reads and hears—and on top of all that he must patiently listen to our accusations of apathy and conformity! Little wonder that he retreats to the at least real attractions of Mad magazine and the various gatefold girls! Those students who still cannot deny their intellectual curiosity most sensibly pick up bits and pieces of existentialist and revolutionary attitudes, and decide that their superiors are fools, that all must be redone, and that the only true education is self-education.

Correspondingly, the faculty and lower administration have been divided into all sorts of distinct interest and professional groups which have little or no intellectual or social unity. This is, of course, a result of the great diversity in curriculum of the modern college. We don't really have colleges, we have many departments in search of a college. Colleges, divisions, departments; each require administrative heads, and the whole follows the same political pattern prevalent in America at large—that is, the clash of small power units for power and affluence under the managerial supervision of higher establishment or upper administration. Only the upper administration is regarded, even by the faculty, as speaking for the college, and this because only they have a sense of the total and are concerned with the whole. But unfortunately the upper administration can only be concerned with the bureaucratic and financial management of the whole, and not with its intellectual life. Educational reforms, for example, in our vast state institutions are almost always confined to departments. General college-wide and serious educational reforms usually take place only in our small and private liberal arts colleges. Meanwhile the vast bulk of American students remain undirected and unreformed. Typically, the college teacher is ignorant of the total educational experience he and his colleagues are imparting to the students. The best of them can hardly find out what other courses their students take. Hence, even the faculty reformer is primarily concerned with improving his own course—not the complete intellectual life of his student.

The average faculty member, however, is like the average student, concerned with his private career and his department's private fate in the college power struggle. The departmental interest struggle to improve its competitive position *vis-a-vis* other departments is the reality underlying most of the important changes in college offerings and requirements. No department or division has responsibility for the total intellectual life of the student. And no department will surrender its claim to student time and budget allotment by bowing before an educational reform that lessens their credit hour requirement. The free election and major system, meanwhile, gives power (in liberal arts at least) to those departments and teachers who can command or attract the largest number of students. Such departments become the great powers on campus, and gain larger budgets, more faculty, and more influence over college decisions. The temptation is usually too strong for any to resist. Success is not defined as successful guidance of the general intellectual life of the student—it comes to mean recruiting the largest possible number of apprentices for one's guild.

Perhaps the most serious defects in undergraduate teaching stem ultimately from the refusal of the national guilds of scholars to consider teaching their major professional responsibility. Historians, sociologists, economists, anthropologists, and others, united in their professional association, distribute their awards of prestige and, indirectly, faculty rank and pay, according to their single-minded devotion to research and scholarship.

Such groups rarely take any responsibility for teaching methods, holding that such concern is nonsense emanating from the (unjustly) despised professors of education, and that, in any event, any research scholar can teach adequately. It is not too much to say that your average scholar confuses good teaching with smooth-flowing lecture rhetoric, mildly tough grading, and being liked by his students. Within such organizations, those who are devoted to the improvement of undergraduate education must form associations designed to remind the scholars of their neglect of duty. Someone must represent the teaching interest.

Any vital and sizeable institution designed to process large numbers of clients requires a business-like administrative bureaucracy. The rise of the college to such status has meant the increase and prospering of the bureaucratic type and his dominance over higher education. The skill of such men has nothing to do with teaching or scholarship—though that is often their background. An administrator is one who knows how not to offend the powerful, and how to tread carefully the tightrope drawn tight by contending forces. He is a "moderate" in the sense in which we use that much abused word, i.e., one who attempts no changes which will force him to move against the social pressures which surround him in any clearly defined way. The best administrator, as normally defined, is one who knows how to take advantage of prevailing conditions and gain students, status, and wealth for his administration. He will know how to stress the immediate utility of his medical and engineering schools; he will know how to represent, at one remove, the market demand for his various products. For the administrator must naturally look upon the college as producing a product (education) more or less efficiently (cost per credit hour per student and competing for customers (students) and private and public funds with other and similar corporations.

The teaching staff often assume an air of superiority to their administrative superiors, though it is hard to see any justification for this. For most of them treat students more or less as apprentice specialists—whether they are to be future literary scholars, electrical engineers, social scientists, dentists, undertakers, or chemists. Captured by the ideal of feeding his profession with ever more skilled apprentices, the college teacher pays little heed to the general intellectual life of the undergraduate. He can hardly be persuaded to give serious attention to those undergraduates—the vast majority—who attend his course but do not intend to become majors in his discipline. Before the student stands not a trained intellectual and generalist to help him reach an understanding of the world he inhabits, but a scholarly specialist, prepared only to communicate the lore and skills of his special field. The general student often becomes apathetic simply because he senses that his teachers have no real interest in improving his awareness as an educated layman. His instructor's work and prestige relates only to his fellow specialists and any in class who might become such.

The matter of prestige and status within one's specialty has been crucial for this trade-school orientation of modern liberal arts institutions. A college in America generally becomes famous and prestigious to the extent that it is able to purchase scholars of note who have achieved fame (among their few colleagues) through publication and paper-reading. This is the academic version of the "star" system. We hear it said again and again that there is no conflict between research and teaching. This would be true were it not for the simple fact that undergraduate teaching requires wide-ranging but not superficial generalists; whereas the only way to scholarly fame and higher wages is through steady and constant focus on a narrow area. One makes oneself a marketable commodity by developing intellectual skills that have little to do with general knowledge. Hence that extraordinary combination one so often finds among academic intellectuals: highly refined specialist knowledge but superficial irrelevance in all that pertains to general education. Increasingly, the academic intellectual does not regard himself as an intellectual and comes to scorn the very term, even as he condemns, perhaps, so-called American anti-intellectualism! In short, American higher education, by becoming socially useful and professionally competent, has drawn talent and energy away from a serious concern with stimulating an informed, general and critical awareness of our society and culture among those who need it most.

The evidence for all this is increasingly available. The administration, bent on decreasing costs, works for the introduction of the large lecture system, objective examinations, and flexible standards. Departmental chairmen, confronted with fixed budgets, are anxious to cram more students in the lecture halls so that the money thus saved may be used for hiring prestigious scholars, giving scholarships to their graduate students, and thereby obtaining budget increases, more staff, and campus power. The better and more ambitious faculty members, aware that promotion, scholarly fame, and the best posts go to the publisher rather than the teacher, will head for the nearest research grants, the most graduate seminars, and the fewest undergraduate courses.

The mass lecture system solves everybody's problem, even if at the expense of the undergraduate. Two hundred are taught, or shall we say "processed," where only twenty were before, and the professor can content himself with delivering two or three lectures a week. Exam grading and discussion sections can be left to graduate fellows who thus pay for their own fellowships. Teaching quality suffers because all real contact between teacher and student is lost, and ideas and facts cannot be related to the individual student's capacities and interests. All is tailored to fit the minimal needs of what one might call the mythical lecture room's most common denominator. The lecturer does not personally check the examinations, and he has little notion of what is happening to his students. The student is bereft of all opportunity to communicate his own grasp of the subject through extensive essay examination. This is not simply a matter of ignoring the rare creativity of a genius, it is a quite practical concern having to do with the daily work of all students. Examinations are merely graded in a mass system because there is no time to go over them carefully and demonstrate to the student *in writing* his own strengths and weaknesses of knowledge and understanding. If the individual student's mind and understanding are not revealed, discussed, and guided or enhanced at the junior college level, then teaching has not occurred. The whole system is simply and endlessly pumping out useless energy. The student level of performance is checked but not raised. Improvement, when it occurs, will be a chance by-product of irrelevance. In any sensible educational system, such utter failure would be recognized as a teaching failure. It is not so recognized because the administrator is concerned with efficiency and the teacher with scholarship. In the midst of a mass educational system we all become cynics and anti-democrats, because we have only the students left to blame.

Correspondingly, the all pervading objective examination, though often shown up for the absurdity it almost always is, increasingly dominates the college. And the reasons are clear. Few are really interested in giving the student a fair or so-called "objective" grade, and that is not in any event an important goal of college education. But efficiency and free time for research welcome an exam which can be graded swiftly and surely by any-one who can read and write. Objective exams have not been introduced because they measure the students' performance more accurately than the essay, they have been introduced because they save time and money. Only those who misunderstand the meaning of the word "objective" could con-tinue to apply it to our proliferating multiple-choice examinations. *Just as with an essay exam, a multiple-choice exam requires some person (i.e., sub-ject, not object) to select the questions and approve the answers.* Barring the simple parroting of brute names, dates, and semi-narratives (never any-body's educational ideal) all testing, *including* true-false and multiple choice, is subjective *and must be.* The nature of mind and knowledge is such that all testing of one mind by another must be subjective, tentative, and open to doubt—and one does not change matters by hiding one's inevitable subjectivity behind a graph, curve, percentage point, or numer-ical value. As for the usual textbook, it oversimplifies and describes where it should debate and analyze, and, contrary to the way of the real world, avoids all strong opinions and thematic treatment. It remains one of the most depressing obstacles to the communication of the ability to judge, generalize, and weigh evidence. But the textbook, like the mass lecture and objective exam, is there because it saves the teacher the trouble of building the course anew each time it is taught, and fitting his perceptions to the individual abilities of the students. Most importantly, the avoidance of strong opinion and complex interpretation makes the average liberal arts textbook a perfect product for a mass market of captive readers. Such texts are intended for the professors' convenience, not the student's needs. The end result is the overvaluing of passive memory over intelligent comprehension. One is asked to react, not think, and one aims at the selection of correct responses, rather than the careful composition of thematic statement by the perception of relevant facts and ideas, skillfully presented in a written essay. Meanwhile, we grade students as we grade beef, with no concern for improving the quality as we stamp the product.

As one contemplates the general run of undergraduate courses in our vast state institutions one wonders if much of what goes under the name of a liberal education doesn't simply dull the intellect. It doesn't really help matters to mitigate the lecture system by introducing graduate section men to conduct weekly discussion sections, as is often done. Only the lecturer can guide a worthwhile discussion in a course which is otherwise his; and in any event, the graduate student soon learns that he is primarily expected to keep his own research and course work up. Short of annoying female students, he will not be judged by what goes on in his classroom. Why are graduate assistants used? Simply because, once again, they lower costs and increase their department's power and quantity of teaching on the graduate level. By teaching, the graduate student pays for his fellowship and is available for the graduate seminars. All this increases the graduate program of the department. A further step, already taken in many institutions, is to simply hand over the hapless undergraduates to the graduate assistants— untrained, inexperienced, and overburdened. And these graduate students soon become faculty somewhere themselves, and have learned before they even started, that only fools, incompetents, or hopeless idealists take undergraduate teaching for anything more than the farce it so often is. As for the progressive administrator and department chairman, they are privy to the most saddening fact: the old system wasn't any better except here and there and just potentially. Over the loss of a here and there and a mere potential, no administrator can be expected to linger, but it is this loss of potential which is the most serious loss.

As Paul Goodman has rightly pointed out, this vast corporate educational system monopolizes the available brains, talent, and wealth. The potential reformers disappear into the machinery, quietly muttering witty remarks at their own expense and coming even to despise those students who, with crude naivete, take their own education and their teachers seriously—for a while. Aside from perhaps attempting to attract many students to his courses, the teacher wastes little time on his undergraduates. He will concentrate on research, majors, and graduate students. Most teachers in academia, unlike many of their high school counterparts, don't even know the difference between good and bad teaching. The wise chairman, meanwhile, will manipulate his teaching system so as to increase that portion of the budget he may spend to attract academic stars and graduate students. A man becomes an academic star or world class competitor in the market place by his ability to publish in accepted academic journals, read papers before his national association, and publish books that are well-received by his well-known colleagues. (Here there is, in the inexact studies, an amount of chicanery involved. For example, your publisher will ask you to name those who will be likely to give your book a favorable review and will act accordingly.) But however adequately set up, the standards of professional associations are not directly relevant to teaching; and increasingly these guilds set the standards for college and university appointment and promotion. For beyond this the terrible fact is that the system has no standards of its own.

The result is plain to see. In most large junior college classes, the majority of the students are not interested in the subject, and the instructors are not really interested in teaching them. At the same time, the department wants as many students in its classes as possible, and so for that matter does the teacher, unless he is concerned with teaching standards. To gain power with legislators, the corporation needs a vast number of customers. The situation is only made more absurd by the fact that the department genuinely feels its subject should be taught and for the best of reasons. As always, college politics are made all the more intense because ideals are at stake, and felt to be so. The students, for the most part, rarely know why, say, a future dentist or electrical engineer should be required to study sociology or history. And because courses are mainly taught by scholars on the lookout for potential scholars in the same discipline, the average student is right to assume that no rationale relevant to his needs lies behind his required presence. To suggest that the real purpose of liberal arts education for non-specialists is to teach them to help make their society and culture express the best that is in man would be to risk being labeled Victorian, naive, radical, or simply absurd. He will certainly find that a serious attempt to suggest that knowledge exists to be used will cause doubt to be cast on his credentials as an "objective" scholar. Meanwhile in the classroom, the tension and alertness which should follow the sensible teaching of a subject that undergraduates are brought to sense they want and need is rarely to be found. Instead one finds boredom, apathy, or worse, ignorant submissiveness, and the drone of endless lectures—the whole permeated by a strong sense of sham and fundamental questions never asked. There are exceptions, even glorious exceptions, but they are exceptions. They arise, perhaps, because of the extraordinary difficulty of destroying the natural curiosity of the young and true intellectual commitment even by the most well-contrived system.

The instructor who begins his career anxious to teach, too often ends as the professor bored at the very thought. Presented with a self-defeating task, he finds that the truth is complex, rarely spectacular and cannot be imparted without the direct meeting of mind and mind: all this the system avoids. Some few become campus characters—known as great teachers —who win student favor by purging their material of all but its dramatic and spectacular elements, and shouting these out with much effect. Most, however, unwilling or unable to "stimulate" (why not simply hook the chairs up to the nearest electric outlet?) yet plagued by the notion that they are boring their students, end by developing the appropriate cynical attitudes and concentrating on research and graduate students. The student may be entertained, he may be bored, or he may be trained. He is hardly ever taught anything of general significance beyond his trade that makes a difference to him, his society, or his culture.

The administration will and can do little to correct unaided what is more or less the responsibility of the faculty. Usually, administrations cooperate with curriculum reforms that do not increase costs, but few such proposals are forthcoming from the faculty. As with all bureaucracies, the administration is primarily interested in extending the power, prestige, and wealth of their institution. Left unopposed, they will always press for graduate school status, and they will encourage all means available for decreasing expenditures on undergraduates to that end. Hence the prevailing mood in the most progressive state universities is to dilute undergraduate education by doubling up the students. Given the system, individual departments dare not resist and must themselves press for Ph.D. granting programs whether they feel they have the resources or not—because that is how one gets resources. The more graduate students and academic "stars" one can boast, the more one can gain greater resources from the administration. As a result, there is a vast waste of resources in many states as major public universities set up competing graduate programs.

Ever since the great change of the late nineteenth century, the university has used public relations techniques to impress the businessmen of the community with its utility. Often, reading the press releases of the fraudulent professionals involved, one gets the impression that the faculty, with rocklike unity and earthy practicality, is working down to the last instructor for "better things for better living." There is, of course, nothing wrong with campus research for business and industry, especially when it is well paid. Why we must continue to train business executives without pay in our Colleges of Business Administration is not clear until one understands how convenient it is to have the business classes pass through the college and develop appropriate loyalties. Who ever bothered to establish a College of Labor Union Administration? Funds for research prospects increasingly hinge on the good will of business foundations and the approval of Pentagon defense research dispensers. If you don't think this determines where the bulk of research talent will direct itself, try applying to the Ford Foundation for a grant to study tax dodging in the modern corporation, or to the Pentagon for a grant to study ways of drastically reducing our arms budget. But I am unfair. A considerable sum of money is available for conferences in the fine arts, and festivals for the celebration of pure culture abound, peopled with somewhat surprised poets and novelists. More money for research and culture is not to be despised, and one does not expect, say, the Rockefeller Foundation to finance a symposium on the defects of modern capitalism. Still, this is another powerful temptation for the university and college to neglect their primary role as neutral critic and intellectual leader for progress and reform. To those who complain that this would mean a loss of scholarly objectivity, one can only say that scholarly objectivity is not to be equated with neutralism or letting others direct one's research. The university now deducts administrative expenses from all grants. Could it not find means of establishing a fund from its grants for the kind of research which society needs but which no wealthy group in the community can be expected to support? We should not allow the university to become merely an affluent research branch of government and business, with a few deviant groups of scholars pushing forward the frontiers of knowledge for their respective national guilds.

Freedom and the University

Stephan Weissman

. . . Student activists have staged numerous protests against specific arbitrary uses of the *in loco parentis* power (a power generally defended for its usefulness in protecting student inebriates from over-zealous sheriffs). More recently, the on-campus emphasis has been shifted from protests of particular infringements of political rights to a wholesale condemnation of the power of the college dean to act in the place of parents. This condemnation has been especially strong in the area of First Amendment liberties, but there have also been demands for the abolishment of *in loco parentis* power over "beer, sex, and cheating." The most wholesale challenge to the parietal power of administrators has been Berkeley's Free Student Union, an offspring of the Free Speech Movement (FSM), which openly demands that any rules concerning a student's nonacademic life be made and enforced by the students themselves.

In loco parentis is not, however, the major stumbling block to student freedom. At Berkeley and others of the big-name schools, for example, *in loco parentis* control of personal life is far less pervasive than at smaller universities and colleges. Compulsory chapel, strict regimentation of women's dormitories, class attendance requirements, and puritanical dress regulation, though still too frequently encountered, are slowly being overcome. In their place one finds free "cuts," careful nonenforcement of dorm and dress rules, and dorm keys for senior women. More important, fewer and fewer speakers are now denied access to campus facilities. But students

FROM a pamphlet published by Students for a Democratic Society. Reprinted by permission of the author.

should not exult in their new-found "freedom." The real challenge is the subtle "liberal" manipulation which passes for a democratic student personnel program.

Many analysts of the Berkeley conflict, including now-pessimistic student radicals, maintain that the velvet-glove application of just such "freedom" could have stifled the FSM. Serious errors were no doubt made by the administration. But one is hard pressed to imagine velvet soft enough to hide from experienced civil rights activists the iron fist inherent in any attempt to deny them use of the campus for organizing and advocating off-campus action. The administration could certainly have reversed the intent of their policy, they could have permitted the courts to determine the legality of on-campus advocacy. That is, the administration could have done voluntarily what they were later forced to do. Short of that, they had only one alternative to a massive confrontation: they could have ignored the premeditated guerrilla campaign of FSM to violate clamorously and massively *all* university restrictions on political activity.

With or without guerrilla warfare, educational authorities around the country have responded to the jangling echoes of Berkeley with just such nostrums as "shared responsibility," more personnel (sic) attention, and liberalized sex and political regulations. *In loco parentis* is thus giving way to a (scientific) bureaucratic paternalism like that which awaits the college grad in the world of industry. Perhaps this transition will hinder the ability of students to organize themselves for a real transformation of American education. But equally dangerous is the possibility that students and administrators alike will accept paternalism and private liberties as a definition of freedom.

Student activists have learned that "freedom" in America, on- or off-campus, too often means a choice between predetermined alternatives rather than participation in forming those alternatives, acting within a context fixed or manipulated by others rather than having a hand in shaping that context. Thus Mississippi Negroes are given the vote, but are hindered in developing a political party (the Mississippi Freedom Democratic Party) to make that vote meaningful, and by the same liberal Democrats who helped secure the vote. Similarly, suburban Americans can buy the cars of their choice, but they have no say in the production of those cars—will they be safe? etc. On campus the situation is the same. Does a student committee on curfews have freedom when limits are implicit in the probability of an administration veto? Does student government have freedom to disburse student funds when student leaders know that the administration will permit donations to the Red Cross, but not to SNCC? The on-campus struggle against such administered democracy, and the Dick and Jane student governments that sustain it, can only be viewed as part of the larger struggle to create in this country a meaningful definition of democracy.

A restricted sense of freedom is found not only in the Dean of Women's office, but in the classroom as well. For many, *this* restriction or absence of freedom is normal, even commendable. To quote a comment on Berkeley's Free Student Union in a Baton Rouge newspaper.

Education is impossible without authority and the recognition of authority. Management has to manage. That this affects one's place in life—and throughout life—is elementary. If a university can't teach that to its students it'll never be able to teach them anything.

Every institution—families, schools, enterprises, government, our armed forces, everything—falls apart on any other basis. And the future of American youth falls apart with it.

I would suspect that an equation of education with discipline and a resistance to classroom freedom marks the thought of people with far less authoritarian sentiments. There is even resistance to classroom freedom among those unafraid of the very unradical proposition that, as in most European universities, the nonacademic life of the student be no concern of the administration.

The classroom is the holy of holies, an AAUP (American Association of University Professors)-protected inner sanctum where professors are free (usually) to pass on the wisdom of the ages according to their own lights. But what of the student? "At Berkeley," report Professors Sheldon Wolin and John Schaar, "the educational environment of the undergraduate is bleak. He is confronted throughout his entire first two years with indifferent advising, endless bureaucratic routines, gigantic lecture courses, and a deadening succession of textbook assignments and bluebook examinations testing his grasp of bits and pieces of knowledge."*

In this "mass producing of men into machines," freedom is the loser. Although he is usually free to choose between various course offerings, the student has little freedom to determine what will be offered. Once enrolled in a class, the student must yield to the professor much of the decision-making power over the course and over the nature of that process through which learning is scheduled to take place. The student's recognition and acceptance of his subordinate status stem not from respect for his professor's intellect, but, simply stated, from an *acquiescence to authority*. This same pattern, plus the "necessities" of grading exams and papers, provides for the development of "production schedules" long before even initial personal contact between student and professor.

God forbid that the student challenge the schedule by getting "hung-up" on Dostoevsky the week in which the syllabus requires that he produce an exam on Tolstoy. Any personal involvement in the learning process, any unleashing of curiosity, might well result in intellectual *coitus interruptus*.

Fortunately for the university, the curiosity of childhood is usually disconnected in the public schools. In college the motivation to learn is not supposed to be found in personal satisfactions arising from the work itself.

---

* Sheldon S. Wolin and John H. Schaar, "The Abuses of the Multiversity," *The New York Review of Books*, March 11, 1965.—Ed.

The intellectual assembly line is not designed to produce such satisfactions, except as a by-product. Learning is a means to grades, to careers; the important questions are those which will appear on the next test. Even the persistent find that oversized classes, ritualized papers, and too-frequent examinations make one's own questions an extracurricular activity.

Of course students do learn something. Unfortunately, much of what they learn, from the point of view of developing men and women who are willing to determine the course of their own lives, is negative: blind acceptance of hierarchical authority, intellectual indifference, a willingness to do meaningless work, to produce according to schedule, to do without internal gratification in their work. Or to quote from a study by Christopher Jencks and David Riesman, "It is difficult to say to what extent colleges, along with the rest of the educational system, train students to respond with a disciplined attitude toward work not of their own devising (and therefore provide employers with a good yardstick for determining who will do well in a highly organized and authoritarian setting) and to what extent colleges help inculcate a distaste for work precisely because of its frequently imposed and alienated quality."*

"Alienation," "alienated learning," "alienated work"—unfortunately journalistic popularization and uncritical repetition have depleted these once-rich concepts of their meaning. Alienation can refer to the estrangement of the intellectual from his society, but few students are in truth intellectuals. Alienation can also refer to the work process, and it is in that sense that we must understand the malaise mirrored in the faces of a generation of student rebels. According to a noted nineteenth-century sociologist, alienation is that condition in which the individual worker has lost any sway over the condition of his work: ". . . the work is external to the worker, consequently he does not fulfill himself in his work, but denies himself . . . has a feeling of misery, not of well-being."† This description, as we have seen, exactly fits the work process on the assembly line of learning. And it explains why the worker on that assembly line—the middle-class student who has been deprived of little except the right to control his own life and work—could join with a Mississippi sharecropper in seeking a new definition of freedom.

When at Berkeley we sought to use *our* campus for the exercise of *our* constitutionally guaranteed rights, we learned that *our* campus was the "property of the Regents of the University of California." And *our* rights had to be yielded at the gates of *their* campus before they would allow us to become educated for jobs in *their* society. In point of fact, the State of California is to a large extent a society belonging to the Regents. Among their number are the states' major owners of banking, communications,

---

* David Riesman and Christopher Jencks, "The Viability of the American College" in Nevitt Sanford, ed., *The American College* (New York: John Wiley & Sons, Inc., 1962).—Ed.

† Karl Marx, *Economic and Philosophical Manuscripts.*—Ed.

transportation, mining, philanthropy, agriculture, and industry, plus its chief political figures. Their credentials for educating California's youth are, of course, their worldly success and their appointment to the Board by a governor dependent on their success for his.

But even if the Board were elected, as in Michigan, even if its membership included Martin Luther King and Allen Ginsberg, the problem of student alienation would remain. More important than *our* campus or *our* rights is the ownership and control of *our* lives, *our* personalities, *our* values. And it is in the work of learning that a student's life personality and values are unfolded and defined. Alienation from that work, and thus from ourselves and from others, will remain until that work becomes ours, until we can shape the process in which we learn. The general university environment will remain hostile to us as long as the administration and manipulation of that environment is geared by others to preparing us for the administered world of alienated work off the campus. Students will become "valued members of a genuine intellectual and moral community" (Wolin and Schaar) only when we gain control over that environment.

But, what of the faculty? As the university becomes a "knowledge factory," as it begins "to merge its activities with industry as never before," the now entrepreneurial professor takes on the styles, attitudes, ideals, and ideas of the industrial and governmental bureaucracies for whom and with whom he works. There seems to be "a point of no return," Clark Kerr continues, "after which research, consulting, and graduate instruction become so absorbing that faculty efforts can no longer be concentrated on undergraduate instruction as they once were." Or, to put the matter less generously, the professor comes to consider his product—knowledge—to be more important than the students to whom he is transmitting that knowledge.

And even that knowledge itself changes. For the nature of the product is determined not by the student consumers, but by the federal agencies, foundations, and industries who are the true purchasers of knowledge in our society. As William Appleman Williams explains, the professor "has become a full member of the system in direct proportion as he has become an expert or advisor concerned to rationalize and to sustain the system." Even when he does teach students, he is usually happy to be "a servant of established power." And the criticism remains applicable whether the establishment is represented by the giants on the California Board of Regents or by the merchants who run Braderton State Teachers' College. Certainly most professors deplore the grosser prejudices of this middle-class society. But how many make basic criticisms or suggest alternatives outside the "realities" of the conventional wisdom? How many go beyond "refining established revelation?"

Too often university intellectuals become "yes men" for society even when they say no—evidence, the academic debate over American action in Vietnam. For the majority of teachers present American policy stands condemned as an inept, even amateurial way to stop communism or block Chinese aggression. Few are the academics who have challenged, root and branch, America's underlying assumptions about present-day communism, Chinese countries, and our own role in the world.

Faced with such irrelevant and shallow teachers, students might well question their rhetoric about student-faculty government of the universities. For the faculty members are responsible, both in how they teach and what they teach, for the most alienating features of the university. Responsible? Are the professors to blame if society does not supply sufficient reward for teaching students rather than subjects? Are they responsible if there are not sufficient resources allocated to provide the small classes necessary for the kind of teaching which is its own reward?

At Berkeley, professors *were* held responsible by their students until, through student pressure, they fought against the curtailment of student political activity. In the Vietnam protest, professors are being urged to go beyond protesting this particularly brutal and inept war and to fight for overall alternatives to American foreign policy. In standing up on unpopular issues, some faculty members are unlearning the lessons taught by McCarthy. But they have far more to learn from their students. For, they have yet to fight in any numbers against the educational alternatives offered by society. They have yet to learn that it is never enough to make the best of one's conditions—that one must always struggle for the freedom to fashion new conditions.

A New Academic Freedom

Not unexpectedly, this impersonal, unfree assembly-line learning is producing its own opposition. Kerr himself points to "an incipient revolt against the faculty." At Berkeley the revolt was specifically against the administration, but great strength was drawn from general grievances against the Multiversity and against the society which it so faithfully mirrors. In that revolt the students took their desire for personal authenticity in learning and in life to the point of on-campus action only when the advocacy of off-campus civil rights action was denied them. But Kerr is correct: the revolt was there in the alienated condition of student life. Today's students demand a personal relevance to knowledge which is the direct opposite of the Multiversity's alienated process of learning. They demand a relationship between learning and their own moral concerns. Such a demand seems singularly appropriate to the existential attitudes of this post-nuclear generation, a generation which has the audacity to feel personally guilty for the condition of *their* world. To demand that the learning process be focused on personal involvement, however, is to demand freedom in the classroom, to demand "a situation in which there would be questioning, release from rigid squelching of initiative and expression."

Though not in reference to their own learning, this very definition of academic freedom has already impressed itself upon the present generation. It comes from a prospectus for the Mississippi Freedom Schools, in which so many northern volunteers served during the summer of 1964. The Freedom School idea has now spread, and there is continuous experimentation in the development of student-centered, question-oriented, loosely structured educational environments. Such an environment is vital if underprivileged children are to gain a sense of their worth.

But underprivileged children are not the only ones to ask, "Why are we not taken seriously?" Nor are they the only ones who would benefit from determining the course of their own learning. Would children of the middle class become less free or less educated if their teachers refrained from the exercise of dictatorial authority or from the more subtle, indirect manipulation inherent in the grading process? Could not students learn more (and remember more of that "learning" beyond exams) if their courses answered questions which they themselves asked? Should we not prefer the self-discipline which comes with problem-solving to the blind acceptance of external authority? Or, on another level, can an automated, leisure-time society endure without citizens who study because they are curious, who work because their work brings them pleasure?

Of course, the Freedom School cannot totally replace the Multiversity. It can, however, demonstrate the validity of a new kind of academic freedom. In the humanities and social sciences the need for intuitive involvement is already preached, although present-day university education makes the practice extracurricular. But even in math and the sciences, there is increased recognition of the need for free inquiry and the development of curiosity. Free Universities, like Freedom Schools, must provide personal confrontation with the concepts of science as well as of history, and encourage personal responsibility for the application of those concepts.

It is not, however, any inappropriateness of freedom to learning which blocks the growth of the Free University. Rather it is the very definition of the Multiversity, a definition which leaves as little room for freely given and freely accepted education as Senator Eastland's plantation leaves for Negro freedom.

A Free University

A Free University, like the free society upon which its long-term success depends, is at present only a distant vision. But that vision—based upon the belief that even students have a right to shape the environment in which they live and work—is our most powerful weapon for the subversion of the Multiversity. For most students accept the vision of the Multiversity. Though alienated, they do not comprehend the source of their alienation. They accept the authoritarian and conformist patterns of the

Multiversity as natural, inevitable. What right have they to do more than gripe over even the most demeaning and asburd regulation? Are they not being *given* an education? If they don't like it where they are, are they not *free* to be *given* that education at the Multiversity of their choice? Democracy? Most students would be honored to serve on some sandbox administration committee; they wouldn't even realize that their decision-making power was complete only if they made the "right" decisions.

On campus as off, the belief in human dignity, freedom, democracy, and participation in decision-making is in a sorry state. Our first tasks are thus educational:

1. *The Campus Freedom Party.* Throughout the country, and especially in the South, activists are organizing political parties to run candidates for student government offices. In most cases, however, they are not running to win, or even with the assumption that putting a good man in a crummy office would change the way in which their university does business. Rather they are running educational campaigns, calling the sandbox by its name, and building constituencies for the abolition of the most obnoxious *in loco parentis* rules: for elimination of compulsory ROTC; to protest the university keeping books for the draft board; for unlimited free speech and political activity; for an end to discriminatory admissions, housing, and hiring; to protest university purchases from and investments in discriminatory corporations; for co-op bookstores; and for the idea of eventual student-faculty government. With these platforms student activists raise the vision of student democracy ("rather than student government"), pressure those who do get elected to accept minimal programs leading to that vision, and develop a nucleus to lead action when a direct provocation occurs. After the elections, the parties (or SDS groups which sponsor them) attempt to engage their voters in a year-round multi-issue program of radical self-education, work in civil rights or with the poor, antiwar activity, educational reform, and participation in planning the next campaign.

2. *Free Student Unions.* One step beyond the political party is the student union. The union focuses not on twice-a-year elections, but on year-round collective bargaining with the administration. It also institutionalizes conflict, the sanction of a student strike, and the notion that students should govern themselves through a mass participation organization. Berkeley's FSU has so far had only limited success, partially because of the let down after FSM, partially because of the Vietnam protest. Perhaps FSU would now be strong and more "legitimate" if it had been started during—not after—the free speech controversy. Also, FSU faces a continuing need to expand on the idea of time locals. Union members are organized on smaller units on the basis of their willingness to meet at a certain time; for example there is an 11 A.M. Thursday local. But more union members are not active in time locals,

and there is an increasing desire to organize at least some of the time locals on the basis of common political and educational interests and ideologies.

3. *On-campus direct action and demonstrations.* Student activists should make quite clear that they do not expect any great changes to come about through voting: the Regents and the administration, even more of the faculty, think it their right to direct the lives of students. If we are serious about controlling our lives and education, then we must constantly affirm the right to revolt when we are affected by rules and practices over which we have no say. Compliance with rules should always be received as an unpleasant necessity, never as an obligation. When direct provocations arise, student activists are then prepared to organize massive noncompliance with the regulations in question (like the setting up of the prohibited political tables at Berkeley or sleep-outs against dorm curfews) or against the administration itself. Or, when possible, they can initiate guerrilla campaigns of demonstrations, pickets, and sit-ins to call attention to and build opposition against particular injustices.

4. *Organizing around ideas.* Radical activities must continually counterpose their vision of the university, and of human society to the liberal ideology which underlies most sources in history, political science, economics, sociology, philosophy, and literature. Professors might have all the answers, but to what questions? Moreover, the conventional academic view of human nature and possibilities of change is probably more pessimistic than that of the activist. One of our most important organizing jobs is to clarify, in papers, in classes, and in public forums the bias behind the conventional wisdom and to make explicit our own values. Equally important is the need, especially for graduate students, to define areas of radical research, to go beyond refining established revelation, to pose alternatives to the presently accepted reality. The Vietnam protest offers many such opportunities, as do discussions of the war on poverty, automation, urban problems, and the social responsibility of scientists.

Full-scale counter curricula have, unfortunately, shown little success in competition with the grade hunger which drives even "free" students back into their regular courses. But efforts should continue with a greater emphasis on demonstrating the validity of a freedom school methodology. The teach-in also offers possibilities for radical innovation, both with context and with method. And the eagerness to learn evident in past teach-ins should suggest a general policy of integrating radical self-education more closely into protest activities. Fixed counter courses share with standard university education a certain unreality.

Certainly other programs suggest themselves, but the important thing is to keep our eye on the prize—a new vision for a free university in a free society. Hopefully, there will be a greater sharing of experience, and even regional conferences and campaigns to move us closer to our goal. But for most of us, the movement itself will provide the education, the engagement, and the opportunity for self-realization which the Multiversity cannot offer.

The Student Revolt

Gabriel and Daniel Cohn-Bendit

. . . A modern university has two contradictory roles. To begin with, a university must churn out the trained personnel that is so essential for bureaucratic capitalism. The system needs an ever increasing number of engineers, technicians, scientists, teachers, administrators and sociologists to organize production, to "rationalize" industrial methods, to run the gigantic state machine, "to adjust the psychology of individuals and groups" and to preserve their sanity, even to "organize" leisure activities. Now, since the bourgeoisie itself cannot provide enough student material from among its own ranks, increasing numbers of bright lads are recruited from the lower middle classes and even the proletariat and the peasantry. The "right-thinking" Left concentrates its fire on the class structure of French higher education by stressing that only 6 per cent of the students are the sons of workers, when, in fact, they should be attacking the social function of the university: the production of a managerial élite. If some self-destructive fit should seize the bourgeoisie overnight and persuade it to recruit students exclusively from among the sons of manual workers, the university would become more democratic only in its composition. To the extent that the development of new manufacturing techniques is increasingly eliminating the need for unskilled labour, it is inevitable that psuedò-democratization by the recruitment of working class children to the universities will increase. In the past, the economic depression of the working and lower middle classes meant that sending one child, let alone several children, to the university, imposed an intolerable financial burden on the family, but higher wages and government grants now make it more and more possible. And what all the reformists—be they Communists, Social Democrats or left-wing Gaullists—really mean when they cry for the "democratization" of the universities, is that this process be speeded up.

FROM *Obsolete Communism: The Left-Wing Alternative,* by Gabriel and Daniel Cohn-Bendit. Copyright © 1968. English translation by André Deutsch Ltd. Used with permission of McGraw-Hill Book Company and André Deutsch Ltd.

But in any case it is obvious that, as capitalism increases its demands for graduates, not only the prize pigs, but more and more horses, sheep, even chickens, will all be pressed into the sausage machine. Now this is precisely where the contradiction in the system lies. The production of the maximum number of graduate workers in the minimum time calls for increasingly closer contacts between the universities and industry, for the ever greater adaptation of education to specific industrial needs. But at the same time, the university is supposed to be the supreme guardian of "culture," human reason and disinterested research, of unalloyed truth and objectivity. In brief, the university is supposed to be the temple and eternal repository of the spiritual values of society. Now if, for "spiritual values" we read the "ideology and values of the ruling class," we are left with the role the university has played from the Middle Ages down to the First World War. We might say that during this period the "social" and "cultural" role of the universities more or less overlapped. Society needed a relatively small number of lawyers, doctors, philosophers and professors, and chose them almost exclusively from among the sons of the ruling class. These enjoyed a humanistic and liberal education and were prepared to condone the most glaring social contradictions, while comforting themselves with the thought that the bourgeoisie was a champion of liberalization, democracy, universal education, etcetera. Later, a measure of petty bourgeois radicalism began to filter into the university, but was contained at a purely theoretical level: the crisis of society had not yet really occupied the academies.

Today, it is the economic rather than the theoretical role of the university which is predominant. This explains why the universities have been split up into a set of technical high schools, so many appendages to the major industries. But the system is internally inconsistent—it can only function by trying to suppress its own logic. The "cultural" function of the university is constantly assailed and has constantly to be reaffirmed. After all, even an alienated society cannot allow itself to become alienated to the point of psychosis. Even a totalitarian society, with its determination to subjugate every part of life to the will of the ruling class, group or party, cannot in the long run afford to suppress scientific *objectivity*, and without it, would quickly perish. For the strictest utilitarian reasons, modern societies need fundamental and "disinterested" research—because advances in applied technology depend on them. This the American bourgeoisie has come to realize more and more clearly.

Hence the basic problem of higher education is, then, that, while it cannot completely ignore the old humanistic values, since, after all, scientists and research workers must be produced, only the fragmentation of knowledge can supply all the faceless managers and technicians that are needed.

We have seen that the students are a socially heterogeneous group. They are also a transitory one, and their variety of social expectations increases their heterogeneity. Depending on his subject and the importance of his family connexions, a student may end up with a job worth 30,000 francs a month, and quite a few students want nothing better than that.

Their studies take from three to seven years. Hence while the younger students are still irresponsible adolescents, their older colleagues are men with a profession. Nor do these extremes always understand one another.

And yet it was these very students, the most heterogeneous of all social groups, who succeeded in banding together for collective political action, as witness their resistance to war in Algeria and the events of May 1968. The student movement was, in fact, the only "hard" reaction against the war in Algeria, what with violent demonstrations, and constant propaganda campaigns during the later years. It was always given out that "only a minority" participated in these student protests, but this minority represented at least 25 per cent of the French student population. As for the rest of the country, their protests remained largely verbal. The absence of organized protest outside of the universities can be laid squarely at the door of the Communist Party—it was both unwilling and unable to organize effective opposition to the war and support for the Algerian revolutionaries. Only towards the very end did the Communist Party see fit to hold a few demonstrations, including the one at Charonne Métro Station (Paris) where eight people were killed by the police.

The remarkable phenomenon of student opposition was due to several factors, chief among them what so many people call sneeringly "the revolt of modern youth." Now this revolt, which involves ever larger numbers of young people throughout the world, must not be confused with the old "conflict between the generations." The latter, as we know it, particularly in earlier forms of bourgeois society, reflected the impatience of the young to step into the shoes of the old. This impatience often took the form of an attack on the fossilized thinking of the older generation and sometimes crystallized into a liberal, radical or a reformist attitude. In the current revolt of youth, however, very much more is being questioned— the distaste is for the system itself. Modern youth is not so much envious of, as disgusted with, the dead, empty lives of their parents. This feeling began among bourgeois children but has now spread through all levels of society. Daniel Mothé (*Socialisme ou Barbarie* No. 33) has shown clearly how opposed young workers are to both the "values" that capitalist society has to offer them and also to working class values and traditional forms of organization (political parties and trade unions). Factory work, trade union "militancy," verbose party programmes, and the sad, colourless life of their elders are subjects only for their sarcasm and contempt.

The same sort of disdain is the reason why so many students have taken a radical stand, and have made common cause with young workers in the struggle against a repressive society.

Another factor in the student revolt was their own position in the system and the special problems it brings to light.

A minority of students accept the culture which is being dispensed to them, and the knowledge which is being ladled out, with the trust of small children. They have been completely taken in by what we have called the mythical secondary function of the modern university as the temple of values. They dutifully attend all their lectures, and try above all to pass off as their own their professor's ideas; their ambitions stop short at the coveted degree, or perhaps to become, if they are worthy of it, professors themselves. However, this fraction of student opinion is fast dwindling away—for reasons we shall examine below. Another fraction can see through the system, but keep their eyes firmly on the main chance: they are the opportunists, only concerned with their professional future. They realize that much of what they are taught is false, or at least inadequate, they have no illusions about the purely utilitarian function of their education, know that they will be fitted to hold down a "good" job, and are willing to accept the official bribes of privilege, a car, holidays abroad, money, a house in the country.

This section can always be mobilized in defence of the system. More often, however, they simply sit back and watch their more militant colleagues fight battles from which all students will benefit: for less overcrowding, better facilities, etcetera.

But for a third and constantly growing group, university life itself raises a series of fundamental questions. And once they start to analyse their own problems, the logic of their conclusions drives them on ultimately to reject the whole of contemporary society. This is because, as an essential part of the social system, the university necessarily contains all the contradictions, conflicts and paradoxes that characterize society itself.

We have said a university is supposed to be a seat of learning and rational inquiry. Now what young economist, for instance, can seriously believe in the rational character of the contemporary economic scene, whether planned or not? And only a few diehards among their teachers still pretend that the system is even capable of rationalization. How can an economist talk seriously about the rational distribution of goods in view of the glaring contradiction between the affluence of the highly industrialized countries and the misery of the Third World? How can a young industrial psychologist help being led to self-questioning when he sees that the object of his discipline is to "fit the man to the job" and that the job itself is deadly and quite futile? How can a young physicist ignore the theoretical crisis that is shaking the very foundations of contemporary physics and with it all its claims to be an exact science; how can he tell himself that his research is of benefit to humanity, in an age which has produced the H-bomb? Can he really avoid wondering about his personal responsibility when the greatest atomic scientists themselves are beginning to question the function of science and its role in society?

And how can students of social psychology possibly shut their eyes to their professional role: to help in the sacred interest of profit, to break in more workers to the conveyor belt, or to launch yet another useless product on the market?

· If these doubts about the value of one's studies are examined, inevitably the system which organizes it is brought into question as well. Subjects for courses are picked out of the hat; there is no logic in the curriculum, other than keeping research subservient to the demands of industry or, perhaps, the professor's next book.

These lectures reduce the student to the role of a listener; he is there to record, to remember, to reproduce in his exam the lecturer's threadbare arguments, opinions and style. The more opportunist a student is, the more he will try to ape his teacher's every word, in the certain knowledge that his final marks will be high. However, many students are becoming increasingly disgusted and sickened not only by this system but by the very culture that produces and fosters it.

*   *   *

. . . Most students will end up as managers and administrators, toiling away amid millions of other workers at their narrow little tasks, without any chance of deciding their place in society, their work, in short, the pattern of their lives. The so-called "liberal" professions will become less and less liberal as the values on which they are ostensibly based are increasingly perverted by the State.

For all that, we are not so much protesting that our education is out of touch with the needs of the future, nor complaining about the shortage of jobs, we totally reject the entire system. Our protest only turns into violent action because the structure of society cannot be smashed by talk or ballot papers. To dream of turning the university into an "island unto itself," where every man will be able to work in independence and peace, is in any case an empty dream because the future "intellectual worker" will not be able to accept the fragmented and alienated life which this dream entails.

As a result, the student movement has become revolutionary and not simply a university protest. It does not rule out reforms (its actions, in fact, provoke them) but it tries beyond its immediate aims to elaborate a strategy that will radically change the whole of society. This strategy will carry the student movement through success and failure, through periods of open conflict and apparent inaction, but as every year passes, and the educational system shows ever more clearly its ideological loyalties and its repressive nature, the student will find himself as alienated from the society in which he lives as the lowest wage earner.

SEX AND THE FAMILY

STUDIES BY ANTHROPOLOGISTS show that the family patterns and sexual attitudes and behavior that are familiar to us are only a few among many cultural possibilities. All family systems regulate sexual relationships, socialize children, and perpetuate the prevailing system of social stratification, but they do these things in different ways.[1]

Mead indicates that jealousy is neither natural nor inevitable, but culturally determined. The Eskimo encourage wife lending without evidence of the bad feelings this might occasion among more "civilized" peoples. She mentions such causes of jealousy as outraged personal dignity and threatened self-esteem. These, it seems to me, are related to the view of spouse as property. The jealous one is offended when another appropriates his property without permission. Mead says women appear to be more jealous than men because the social system usually makes them dependent on men for their status and security.

Goldfield, Munaker, and Weisstein remind us that the family fits into the economy and perpetuates the class system. The family functions as a consumer unit, and accumulates wealth to be transmitted to the children, who are socialized to accumulate property, marry, and continue

[1] See George P. Murdock, *Social Structure* (New York: The Macmillan Company, 1949).

the cycle. The economic functions of the family are most apparent among the middle and upper classes, who transmit not only property, but institutional positions, and the "right" attitude toward education.

Women are especially thwarted by the contemporary family structure, according to Goldfield et al. A woman must bend her efforts toward catching and keeping a man. When she is single she is expected to make herself attractive as a sexual commodity. Once she is married, a woman is expected to live for her husband, comfort him, raise his children, and give him sexual satisfaction. She is expected, in fact, to gain her identity through her husband.

Families often hinder the growth of children into healthy human beings because many parents have neither the patience nor the skill to care for their children's emotional needs. In punishing children for transgression of family or cultural taboos, parents often say, "I am only doing this because I love you," or, "This hurts me more than it hurts you." The so-called love found in many families is destructive to the personality of the child. As the English psychiatrist Laing says in his discussion of the socialization of the child in Western society:

> From the moment of birth, when the stone-age baby confronts the twentieth-century mother, the baby is subjected to these forces of violence called love, as its mother and father have been, and their parents and their parents before them. These forces are mainly concerned with destroying most of its potentialities. This enterprise is on the whole successful. By the time the new human being is fifteen or so, we are left with a being like ourselves. A half-crazed creature, more or less adjusted to a mad world. This is normality in our present age.[2]

One alternative to the family is group foster care, which reduces the dependence of children on their parents. This is usually a semibureaucratic environment where professional parents or nurses care for children in boarding houses.[3] In the Israeli Kibbutz, children are moved soon after birth to a communal nursery, where many of their needs are taken care of by the nurse. As the children grow older, the original nurse is replaced by others. The peer group takes the place of the parents as the center of the children's lives. However, unlike the typical boarding situation, children in the kibbutz visit their parents for a couple of hours a day.[4]

While I agree that the boarding home is feasible, and at its best is less damaging to children than the typical family, the commune seems a much better alternative for both parents and children. A commune, Cooper says, is a small group of persons who live either in the same

---

[2] Ronald Laing, *The Politics of Experience and the Bird of Paradise* (London: Penguin Books, 1967), p. 50.

[3] See Barrington Moore, Jr., "Thoughts on the Future of the Family," *Political Power and Social Theory* (Cambridge: Harvard University Press, 1958). See also Bruno Bettelheim, *Children of the Dream* (New York: The Macmillan Company, 1969).

[4] See Melford Spiro, "Children of the Kibbutz," in Section 13 of this anthology.

place or in close proximity and often work together. Ideally, there is room for individuals to be alone when they want to. Like the kibbutz, the commune is an enlarged family grouping that provides economic security for its members through sharing resources.

An important feature of the commune (as well as of the kibbutz) is that children have free access to adults other than their biological parents. This is liberating for both parents and children, because it allows for relationships to develop out of mutual sympathy and interest, rather than the accident of birth or the feeling that one is obligated to love someone. A second element of the commune, as Cooper describes it, is that central two-person sexual relationships continue but are supplemented by others. This works if members understand that giving love to one person does not mean there is less to give to others, and if each member has the unqualified right to say no.

Cooper says that making love is good and that the more it happens between as many as possible the better. He qualifies this by speaking about the need for relationships based on trust and tenderness; sex without love is not enough. Cooper's viewpoint is antithetical to the Playboy view of men and women as sexual commodities rather than total human beings who relate to one another out of mutual respect.[5]

[5] In the advanced industrial societies, so-called sexual freedom—the controlled release of sexual instincts—is permissible because it serves the ends of social cohesion. See Herbert Marcuse's discussion of repressive desublimation in his *Eros and Civilization* (Boston: Beacon Press, 1954) and *One-Dimensional Man* (Boston: Beacon Press, 1964).

Jealousy: Primitive and Civilized

Margaret Mead

> *Il y a dans la jalousie plus d'amour-propre que d'amour.*
> LA ROCHEFOUCAULD/MAXIMES

Some thinkers have included under the term jealousy all those defensive attitudes of fear, anger, and humiliation which centre about the loss of some object, be that object lands or flocks, spouse or title, position or reputation. Some theorists, like Müller-Lyer, have, erroneously, I think, insisted that primitive man does not know sexual jealousy because he often submits

FROM *Woman's Coming of Age*, edited by Samuel Schmalhausen and V. F. Calverton (New York: Liveright Publishing Corp., 1931), pp. 35–48. Reprinted by permission of the author.

with the best grace in the world to situations that would injure the ego of a present-day German citizen. Ernest Jones, claiming that the key to the meaning of sexual jealousy hangs side by side with all the other keys on the key ring of psychoanalysis, attributes sexual jealousy to a suppressed homo-sexuality which projects upon the suspected mate impulses of which the suspicious one is really guilty. The romantics have claimed that jealousy is the inevitable shadow cast by the perfect contours of real love. Here are contrasts enough: theories which would make jealousy any reaction to threatened self-esteem, set it down as special pathology, or justify it and even endear it to the world by tacking it on like a tail to the kite of romantic love. In this paper I shall adhere to the more catholic and less special view foreshadowed by Shand:

"If it is difficult to define jealousy by its feeling, which sometimes in-clines more to fear, sorrow and shame, at others to anger, suspicion and humiliation,—we can still define it by its end or function. It is that egoistic side of the system of love which has as its special end the exclusive posses-sion of the loved object, whether this object be a woman, or other person, or power, reputation, or property." I would only amend his definition to expunge the word "exclusive," for many people are jealous of a privilege which they share with others but which they maintain against outsiders.

Perhaps nothing illustrates more vividly the essentially egoistic and selfish nature of sexual jealousy than a comparison of the different cultural conditions under which one man may have first access to another man's wife. There is no evidence for claiming that an intensely proprietary atti-tude towards one's wife is characteristic of simpler or more complex cul-tures, for the most uncompromising exclusiveness has been found in all levels of society. Let us then investigate the contrasting attitudes of the French peasantry before the Revolution and the present-day Banaro of the Sepik River region in New Guinea.[1] The French peasant resented fiercely the exercise of the *jus primæ noctis* by his seigneur. The proponent of jealousy as the inalienable ornament of the lover's spirit would say that it was outraged love which resented this intrusion of another male—that any man subjected to such a trial would be filled with the keenest and most righteous jealousy. But is it not equally plausible that it was outraged dignity which tortured the peasant? He was no party to the scheme; his set of ideas did not include any soothing philosophy that he thought his bride was dignified by the lord's embrace. The exercise of the noble's power simply underscored in the most vigorous way possible the peasant's social impotence.

For legal arrangements under which another man has first access to a man's bride do not necessarily give rise to feelings of jealousy. Where the custom is merely that the chief's daughter should be deflowered by another, the eloping young chief will not approach his bride during the elopement,

---

[1] Thurnwald, R., "Banaro Society." *Memoirs of the American Anthropological Association.*

but, if he intends to marry her, bring her still a virgin to his father's house, where he knows she will submit to the cruel public defloration ceremony. He is more concerned with his reputation for having married a virgin than for the intimate ordeal to which he is subjecting the girl. And among the Banaro it is not only the defloration but a year's enjoyment of his bride, which the young bridegroom must yield to another man. Banaro society is divided into two exogamic moieties. Each of these moieties is subdivided into two divisions, making four divisions in all. In the other division of his own moiety, each man has a ceremonial friend, and it is the duty of this friend to initiate his friend's son's future wife into sex. This is done most formally in the "Goblin House" in front of the hidden sacred pipes upon which no woman may look, and the girl is then returned to her father-in-law's care. The ceremonial friend has access to her, always ritually, until a child is born, which is known as the "goblin child." Only then may the young man take his wife. Meanwhile he himself has been initiated by the wife of his father's ceremonial friend, whom he has been sent to seek out in the forest, carrying a charmed liana as invitation. Later on, on ceremonial occasions, the young bridegroom and *his* ceremonial friend of the other division will exchange wives, and their wives may even bear children to their husbands' friends, instead of to their husbands. So, in a lifetime, every individual has three goblin spouses in addition to a regular spouse.

Analysis will show that this social situation is simply packed with occasions which among us would give rise to jealousy: an old man's jealousy because his wife takes a young lover, an older woman's jealousy of her husband's interest in a fresh young girl, a young man's thwarted desire for his young wife—for he has to accept the embraces of a woman of his mother's age while another enjoys his pledged bride's virginity. Yet we have peculiar testimony of the peaceful and satisfactory way in which this apparent set for jealousy really operates. All over New Guinea and the adjoining islands, wherever the white man has gone, recruiting offers an escape to those who are permanently or temporarily at odds with their society. Working for the white man provides a refuge, unknown in the old days, to the disinherited son, the betrayed husband, the discredited magician, the deposed leader. The eagerness with which men come forward to meet the recruiter's tempting offers is a measure of the peace and content within their respective cultures. And among the Banaro the recruiter has little luck; every one is too contentedly involved in the fantastic intricacies of Banaro social life.

Or let us consider another familiar situation which may give rise to the most intense jealousy or to which jealousy may be entirely irrelevant. If a guest seduces his host's wife among us, or indeed in any society where the crowd are ready to cry "cuckold," the husband betrays the most furious resentment and jealousy. But let us go instead to a society where wife lending is the rule, as among the Eskimo, a society which cries, not "cuckold" but "stingy," "inhospitable," "mean," to a husband who does not give his wife to his guest. Here the husband will upbraid the wife who is slow to respond to his guest rather than resent the guest's demands. The most casual survey of primitive literature betrays the numerous ways in which exclusive sexual possession of the spouse is modified and contravened, and demonstrates how the self-interest of husband and wife is identified, not with the exclusive possession of each other, but with the appropriate carrying out, whether it be through wife lending, wife exchange, ceremonial license, or religious ceremony, of these very contraventions.

A conspicuous example of this is the attitude of women towards secondary wives in a culture where polygamy is the rule for the rich and influential. There is a case on record of a woman who actually haled her husband into court on the charge that she had been married to him three years and borne him two children, and he had not yet taken another wife. The native court allowed the husband six months in which to take unto himself without fail a second wife. Women urge their husbands to take other wives, which will add to their own prestige by conferring upon them the rank of first wife and also for the practical point of providing labourers and child bearers in the household. The self-esteem of the chief wife is enhanced by their entrance into the ménage and there is no occasion for jealousy—*unless* one of them tends to become the favourite and flexible custom permits usurpation of the first wife's dignities. In a society where there is emphasis upon virginity, a father will be jealous of his daughter's honour. In dissimilar case is the Maori father who has offered his daughter to an honoured guest, only to have her churlishly refuse the guest her favours. The guest is then entitled by custom to fasten a log by a long vine, and, naming the log after the ungracious girl, to drag it about his host's village, heaping the most definite and vigorous abuse upon this dummy. Such a father, although his daughter's virginity may be preserved, will bow his head in shame.

However varied the social setting, it will be seen to be the threatened self-esteem, the threatened ego which reacts jealously. Situations involving this self-esteem will, however, take widely different forms. One's reputation may be concerned with acquisition of wealth, display of wealth, distribution of wealth, or merely with having exchanged much wealth for value received. A man's personal reputation may be based upon the number of women he has purchased or the number of women he has captured, or, as among the Manus, upon the number of temptations which he has resisted —or again in certain parts of Micronesia, he may boast of the honourable scars which he has received from the shark tooth knives of belligerent and unwilling women. A woman's reputation may be tied up with absolute chastity, or with the type of pre-marital prodigality of favours which was so much admired among the ancient Natchez Indians that they pictured a spirit world entered by means of a bridge which was treacherously slippery beneath the feet of the over-virtuous maiden. There is hardly any limit of performance or apparent deprivation to which the individual may not be pushed by his society's standards. Whatever the social set, however, it will inspire him to zeal for his socially defined position. And if he feels his self-esteem is threatened, if his reputation as a gracious wife lender or as a successful ruler of a harem is in danger, jealousy will be the result.

The line between zeal and jealousy is a fine one; a line which the apologists for jealousy usually neglect to draw. An attentive interest in the attainment or the preservation of social or personal status is zeal, a positive attitude; a frightened, angry defence of such status, is jealousy, a negative attitude, always unpleasant in feeling tone. This can be seen clearly in a polygamous society. A zealous man anxious to enhance his own prestige will buy many wives. But the South African king, who, impotent himself, tries to draw a fast line of police about his two hundred wives, instead of winking at their amours as was the custom of over-married monarchs, is no longer merely zealous in carrying out the dictates of social usage, he is simply jealous.

The same distinction can be observed between the behaviour of the zealous suitor and the jealous one. He who is zealous studies his mistress's face to learn her pleasure, seeks out special gifts to please her, tries to arouse her interest and fulfil her slightest wish; all of his behaviour is positive, constructive, directed towards a goal. But the jealous suitor looks into her face only to read there his own dismissal or signs of his rival's triumph; he is far too busy worrying about his fate to be an acceptable tennis partner or dinner companion. Turned in upon himself, his whole duty is not to please the lady but to pity himself and to blame her or his rival for the humiliation which he is suffering. Although his goal is avowedly the same as his rival's, his whole behaviour serves to prevent his attaining it.

Compare also the behaviour of the woman, secure in herself, but anxious to please her lover, with the behaviour of her who fears to lose husband or lover. Aldous Huxley has drawn a vivid picture of the tears and tantrums of poor Margery, every one of which served to precipitate her impatient lover into the arms of her rival. The jealous man or woman seldom comes bearing flowers, and if one does so, it is with such a look in the eye as warns the recipient that conquest of the rival and rehabilitation of the injured self-esteem was the prime motive when the bouquet was selected.

So often, conduct which is zeal in one age or in one society, because it is motivated by an eager and lively appreciation of the social pattern or the customary values in personal relationships, is motivated in another society by feelings of insecurity which lead to fear, doubt, and suspicion. The mediæval crusader who cared so little for his chatelaine that he neglected to lock the metal girdle about her loins, would have been lacking in zeal and his wife might have felt just grounds for resentment, but the fifteenth century husband who kept up this practice would have been branded as a jealous monster.

The confusion between the two attitudes is increased by the inclusion in the romantic love pattern of certain conventional manifestations of jealousy. A failure to display a suitable amount of flattering anxiety, to greet a broken engagement with alarm, or a smile to another with glowering hostilities, if a man, with tearful pouts, if a woman, is written down as lack of zeal. But a closer scrutiny will always reveal the point at which the lover no longer acts to reassure his beloved but to reassure himself, from fear of loss or hurt to his self-esteem. Hence the ridiculous comment which is so often heard, "She likes him to be jealous of her." No one, not in some way pathological, likes to see another in an acute state of misery and humiliation. What such a commentator really means is: "She likes him to act in a way to which others are only impelled by self-love because she knows he is moved to it by love of her." The husband who dances close attendance from jealousy, the wife who goes meticulously over the events of an absence, from jealousy, is not appreciated.

In similar confusion was a woman who remarked to me recently: "Most men expect you to be jealous, and if you're wise you will be." What she meant was simply that most men were flattered by an amount of flutter which simulated jealousy.

If, then, jealousy be not a matter of a normal man defending his natural rights, but of a frightened man defending himself against the infringement of rights not natural but merely guaranteed to him by his society, we can admit frankly that it is an unfortunate phenomenon with nothing to be said in its favour. Jealousy is not a barometer by which depth of love can be read, it merely records the degree of the lover's insecurity. And jealousy is notably an attitude which arouses no sympathy in others. Yet if its display is really so strongly associated with true love, why should the world, having taken the lover to its bosom, evict the jealous lover? Is it not because jealousy, like all other forms of extreme egoism, is repellent, is necessarily of a sort with which others cannot identify themselves? Moreover jealousy defeats its own ends, renders many a lover *hors de combat* from the start. It is a negative, miserable state of feeling, having its origin in a sense of insecurity and inferiority.

In turning to a consideration of the causes of jealousy, as an occasional or chronic state of mind of large numbers of the human race, it is necessary to consider two types of causation, one social, one personal. Any society which places groups of individuals at a disadvantage because of racial, religious, or class distinctions, will be laying the groundwork for many jealous citizens. Furthermore, any society which arranges social or family life so as to provide inevitable clashes of interest of the sort which cannot be avoided will be opening the way to jealousy. Examples of this type of clash are those which arise from primogeniture, emphasis on the blood kin at the expense of the marriage tie, or such social rules as that which decrees that the eldest daughter must marry first. In this sense jealousy is directly dependent upon social causes; and in proof of it, some primitive peoples are far more jealous than others. Although every homogeneous culture inures those born within its confining walls to an unquestioning acceptance of its most difficult dictates, still some cultures force situations which produce less pleasant emotions than others.

An example of a culture in which jealousy is a conspicuous characteristic of the normal individual, is the Dobuan culture of the D'Entrecasteaux Islands,[2] east of New Guinea. Here the stage is set for jealousy and its expression in continual broils and dissension. The people are sorcery ridden and each maternal kin group of some half dozen families live to themselves in little villages where all others—even those married into the group—are regarded as strangers, and probable witches and sorcerers. There is complete pre-marital freedom, a freedom the exercise of which the old people insist upon by turning all the boys over twelve or thirteen out of the family huts at night. The boy is then forced to wander about among the various villages of his locality—for the girls of his own village are his "sisters"— until he finds some girl who will reply affirmatively to his plaintive jews-harp which he sounds hopefully from house to house. Several years' amorous vagabondage assures a youth's having slept with practically every girl in the locality except those of his own village.[3]

Into this habit of amorous and undiscriminating vagabondage, betrothal intrudes rudely, and not always by mutual consent. It is a fast rule that the boys must be up and away to their own villages by dawn. If a boy oversleeps and the mother of his partner of a night's intrigue, who sleeps in the same hut, considers him a suitable husband for her daughter, she can rise before him and sit in the house door. The villagers, early astir, knowing the significance of a woman's being so seated in her doorway, cluster about to gape rudely at the unfortunate youth who must finally emerge. He is now engaged. He and his fiancée must rigorously avoid each other during the day and meet only clandestinely, as before, at night. But meanwhile the engagement sets up a round of economic exchanges for which the boy and his relatives must work hard. He is away for days, fishing and hunting. And no longer may he even speak to the girls who last week were his careless partners in love. The most strict fidelity is enjoined upon the engaged couple, as upon the married couple, in Dobu. And each partner is tortured by the suspicion that the other is returning to the so recently abandoned amorous adventures.

After marriage a new impetus is given to jealousy. In keeping with the general spirit of jealousy, the young couple are not permitted to settle down either in his village or in hers but are required by custom to live alternate seasons in each of the two villages. Here the one who does not belong to the village is treated as a stranger, must walk humbly, avoiding the names of all the "owners of the village." Meanwhile the vigilance of each spouse has been unflagging. A Dobuan husband follows his wife about

---

[2] Based upon R. F. Fortune's *Sorcerers of Dobu.*
[3] With the additional provision that those with ringworm mate only with others similarly infected.

everywhere, sits idly by while she does woman's work in the garden, counts her footsteps if she leaves the verandah for the bush. She is never allowed to go to another village alone. Such jealous surveillance, coupled with the strain of a marriage where one spouse is always among alien and suspicious kin, combined with the pre-marital habits of licence, all combine to produce rather than to prevent infidelity. And here, the man or woman depending upon which one is resident in their own village, turns to village incest for intrigue—a type of intrigue not tasted before marriage. But where there is such close espionage, inter-village intrigues are hard to manage. Furthermore, a man who has been discovered as the seducer of another man's wife is liable to have a spear thrust in his back. But against his wife's intrigue with one of her village "brothers" a man has no such redress. If he protests, his wife's relatives simply throw him out of the village. Should he slay a member of his wife's village, it would become a "place of blood" to him and he might never enter it again. In desperate case indeed is the man whose wife has betrayed him with a village "brother" and in such case also is the wife of the latter who also is only an in-law and a stranger in the village. In such cases the betrayed spouse has only one resource, a sort of pseudo-suicide in which fish poison, which may or may not be fatal, is taken. The kin of the unfaithful spouse, alarmed lest death will follow which will involve them in a blood feud, may then exercise pressure and reunite the pair. But marriages maintained by attempted suicides against odds such as these, do not make for security and happiness, but rather for suspicion and jealousy.

It is worth noting that this jealous attitude which the Dobuan displays, bred from intolerable social arrangements, also characterises his attitudes towards property and trade. He stays up half the night uttering incantations to protect his own yams and to seduce the yams of his neighbour's gardens into his own. If he attains a sudden supply of tobacco as a workboy returning from work for the white man, he will distribute it all, fearful of the jealousy and envy of others should he keep any for himself. He spends his life pitting his magic against the inimical magic of his neighbours, in a state of morbid anxiety and insecurity. Into this house divided against itself, the recruiter steps, perhaps acquiring in one trip a divorced husband who is leaving in furious chagrin and the brother of the former wife who wants to escape the extra work of helping with his divorced sister's garden.

Samoa is keyed to a very different note. Here instead of the tiny hostile kin groups of Dobu, are large villages the members of which are united in formal ceremonial and allegiance to a chief. Instead of the limited and unfruitful garden lands of Dobu, where no amount of spells and hard work will produce a really fine crop, there is fertile land, and enough for all. Although there is freedom before marriage, marriage itself is not viewed primarily as sexual, but as a social contract between individuals who are old enough to turn their attention to more serious matters. Residence is within that household where the young couple fit most perfectly, in terms of temperament or carefully laid plans. Rank is so arranged that there are titles for all of those capable of holding them. And jealousy, as a widespread social phenomenon, is very rare in Samoa. Where it does occur it centers about those points in the system of rank which result in clashes of interest. So, occasionally, a Samoan wife is violently jealous of another woman who wishes to marry her husband, because as a divorced woman her rank is reduced and she has to sit among the young girls and the wives of untitled men. And in Samoa divorce is far less frequent than in Dobu, where intolerable circumstances breed jealousy, which breeds infidelity and divorce.

When my husband was leaving the Dobuans, the attitude they displayed was characteristic. All other emotions on the part of the men who had been his sailing and living companions for months were obscured by their jealous rage that he should actually choose to leave them. Sullenness, wounded self-esteem, was written on every face. But in Manus, of the Admiralties, where we had both lived for months, the people gathered in the thatched pile house which we were deserting and stood there silent, huddled together, possessing no customary phrase for so drastic a leave taking. But as our canoe was poled, solemnly, by the elders of the village, outside the last row of houses, the people we had left behind beat out upon the great slit drum first the call which we had used to call our house boys and, second, the death beat. The dignified gesture was not marred by any injured self-esteem. And this perhaps is one of the chief reasons why sophisticated people should wish to ban jealousy from their lives, because it tends to blur the important issues, to obscure the fundamentals of personal relations, to muffle hurt in sullenness, and to deck separations in rags of bitterness and abuse.

But aside from the social causes of jealousy, the sets which decree that a whole people, or a whole class will be ridden by a morbid doubt of keeping their winnings or winning their chosen prizes, there are the special reasons which predispose a given individual to react jealously to one situation after another. Some of these are purely culturally determined also. On the east coast of Africa, where marriageable girls are kept for months in the "Fatting House" and given a daily massage with butter to improve their physical attractiveness, the girl who refuses to put any weight upon her bones is at a social disadvantage which may well give her a haunting fear of failure and desertion. Among the Bush Negroes of Dutch Guiana the man who does not know how to carve, who has unfortunately no gift for handiwork, will be scorned by the maidens who are in a position to scorn, and be accepted grudgingly by the others. Whatever the mode of beauty or bravery, the style of accepted loverly address or premium upon ability, there will be some individuals who deviate strongly from the desirable type. And these, with rare exceptions, jealousy has marked down for her own.

Consider the historic cases of jealous obsession, and one finds the two causes for insecurity, cultural discrimination against groups and narrow cultural standards of beauty and achievement, as the motivating elements. Othello is perhaps the best example in literature of insecurity born of belonging to a racial group judged inferior by the group from whom he won his wife. Keats is as outstanding an example of the other type of jealousy, as he remarks in the revealing phrase in a letter in which he discusses the local maidens: "But much they care for Mr. John Keats, five feet and a quarter." I do not claim that matters of race or social status on the one hand, of physique or natural aptitudes on the other, are the only causes of the insecurity which has its expression in morbid jealousy, but they are perhaps the strongest contributory causes to its chronic existence. It does not dignify Othello's jealous emotion to have read it in terms of racial inferiority rather than the fair letters of true love, and the admirers of Keats could suffer more wholeheartedly with him under Fanny's cruelty were it not for the suspicion that he would have suffered with equal violence over others, because his jealousy was not relevant to Fanny but to himself and his self-doubts.

The only type of jealousy which can be regarded as strictly relevant to the personality of the lover and which cannot, in final analysis, be reduced to any sort of cultural causes, is the result of bad luck. The individual who has loved unhappily once, then twice, or perhaps oftener, develops a haunting fear of loss which is a comment neither upon an accident of birth nor upon his use of his own endowment, but rather upon forces which are completely out of human control. This same observation applies also to the artist, the scientist, or the business man, who, starting without any fundamental attitude of insecurity, is beaten into it by ill fortune. With pathetic violence, the unlucky cling to any good fortune which must of necessity appear to them as one lonely and unreliable spar salvaged from shipwreck. It is to be presumed that there will always be those who through a grain of unfortunate circumstances become chronically unsure and pitifully anxious to hold that which they have. In deprecating jealousy, one must include them, for jealousy adds to rather than mitigates their misery, but the revision of social or personal attitudes which give rise to jealousy can do nothing for these unfortunates for whose sake it is necessary to indict, not culture, but the nature of the universe.

It is also revealing to re-examine the terms upon which women have been indicted as "the jealous sex." Throughout history, with a few rare exceptions, women have been the *insecure* sex. Their status, their freedom of action, their very economic existence, their right over their own children, has been dependent upon the preservation of their personal relations with men. Into the field of personal relations have been thrust all these other considerations not germane to it. The wife threatened with the loss of her husband's affection, fidelity, interest, or loyalty, whichever point her society has defined as the pivot of wifely tenure, sees the very roots of her social existence being cut from beneath her. She has been in the position in which a man would be if he had to read in his wife's averted shoulder the depreciation of all his stocks, a loss of his business reputation, eviction from whatever position he holds, both social and political, as well as the loss of his home and possibly of all control over his children. If women's superior morbid anxiety concerning their relations with the all-necessary male purveyors of economic and social goods be read in these terms, it becomes a truism that women probably always have been "the jealous sex." It is also possible that the inescapable fact that women age earlier than men, and are more handicapped by child bearing and child care, will always render them relatively more insecure than men, and therefore relatively more anxious to keep their lovers and husbands. But the disassociation of social, economic, and legal security from the field of personal relations should go a long way towards giving women a security which is as great as that which their culture permits to the men born within it.

Granting that jealousy is undesirable, a festering spot in every personality so afflicted, an ineffective negativistic attitude which is more likely to lose than gain any goal, what are the possibilities if not of eliminating it, at least of excluding it more and more from human life? Samoa has taken one road, by eliminating strong emotion, high stakes, emphasis upon personality, interest in competition. Such a cultural attitude eliminates many of the attitudes which have afflicted mankind, and perhaps jealousy most importantly of all, but it also pays too high a forfeit for its pleasant serenity. High passion, intensity which produces great mystics and great artists, clash from which is born leadership and enterprise, all these are lacking also. And only the congenitally timid and the chronically disillusioned would want to pay so high a price for peace.

There is, however, another possibility latent in the very trends which different modern societies are pursuing at the present time. Russia perhaps exemplifies the strongest effort to create social conditions in which no inevitable sting will lie in any accident of race or economic status. Russia's prophecy of eventual racial and social tolerance, however, holds no promise of relief from the less explicit and more insidious results which flow from the standards of a homogeneous culture. There is always the possibility of strong selective mating, for instance, upon the basis of physical type or, perhaps, upon the basis of standard temperament. So, for example, Communism does not carry within its inclusive social programme any promise of personal security to a short man where height is considered the standard of manly beauty, or to the dreaming, introspective man, where activity and social participation happen to be the standards of temperamental fitness. By offering a coherent, exacting social programme which, if it succeeds, will tend to produce a strong homogeneity of attitude, Communism may increase rather than decrease the factors which doom the individual, not by virtue of class or race affiliations, but because of physical or temperamental factors, to a life of morbid anxiety and jealousy.

The other trend which offers a guarantee of more immunity from accidents which predispose to jealousy the individual who is short or fat, tongue-tied or undersexed, or deficient in mechanical ability, as the case may be, is the trend towards heterogeneity of culture, such as is found in great cities. The voluptuous prima donna type of beauty has a chance to compete favourably with the boyish form, the slight, small-featured youth with he of prize-fighting build. And as in matters of physical beauty, so in other matters of personal endowment. A variety of reputable professions and acceptable points of view makes it possible for many discrepant types to grow up, live and die, without the cankering sense of insecurity which is at the base of jealousy. Furthermore, because of the variety of national and sectional points of view represented, and because of the possibility of escape into one of these many different groups with sharply contrasting standards, an individual is less handicapped than he or she would be in any smaller or more homogeneous group. Matters like height, or relative blondness, or excitability or instability of temperament, can be adjusted by crossing from one group, which draws on Northern European stock, to another of Jewish or Southern European, or vice versa. The girl who revolts against the warm and exacting intimacy of some types of Jewish home need no longer shrink into herself under a stigma of being cold and unresponsive; she can instead carry her fierce reticences among those who make a virtue of meagreness of response. A cosmopolitan city even offers those peculiar groups who welcome any aberrations as original, and so offer soothing refuges to the most bizarre personality types. Even such characteristic sets for jealousy as being undersexed or old may be salved by association with groups who eschew or despise the emphasis upon sexual adjustment and emphasise instead pure intellect or religious ecstasy. In short, the least stratified society, the one which has the fewest social, racial, or religious classes, which has the strongest tendency to stress only humanity, *sui generis*, offers the greatest refuge for those whose jealousy is like that of Othello. But the type of muddling, heterogeneous, multiple standard, many-goaled society of a modern cosmopolitan city, like Paris or New York, offers the best hope of eliminating those types of jealousy which result from individual differences.

A Woman Is a Sometime Thing

Evelyn Goldfield, Sue Munaker, and Naomi Weisstein[1]

> *The Search for Fulfillment—*
> *Make Up – Make Out – Make It*

"Do you need anybody,
I just need someone to love,
Could it be anybody,
I want somebody to love."[2]

The media not only teach us to how to look but also how to think. We learn to see things in terms of their profit value; everything and everybody must be marketable. We, like business, seek the "saleable package." Men seek a particular commodity when shopping for a mate. Their image of what is ideal is in large part shaped by the kinds of images projected by the media. Since a woman's value lies in her body, her face, her legs, in sum her sex, in order to make herself into a saleable package—she must be "physically attractive." As long as a woman is pleasant to look at, she remains on the sexual market place. As she grows older she becomes less saleable. Every wrinkle, every grey hair is a mark of her decay . . . her depreciation. If she is useless as a beauty symbol, her true value is lost.

The female learns that she had better catch a man while she is able, if she wants any kind of love, companionship, respect or even economic security after her youth and beauty have faded. We must learn—and learn well—a whole lot of complicated lessons which we can forget only after we have that gold band securely on our left-hand, ring finger. We learn to compete with other women for the most eligible men: to project auras which hint at deep, secret, feminine mysteries, to flirt and charm, to play hard to get, to submit gracefully, to be cute and argumentative at one

FROM *The New Left*, Priscilla Long, ed., Boston, Mass.: Porter Sargent, Extending Horizons Books, 1969. Reprinted by permission. Only a portion of the original article is reprinted here.

1 We apologize to our sisters throughout the country for being so presumptuous as to speak for them, and regret that time did not permit circulation of the paper to allow for full discussion. We take total responsibility for all of the ideas stated here. But our thinking could not have progressed without the Chicago Writing Group, which besides ourselves includes Heather Booth, Amy Kessleman, and Fran Rominsky, nor without discussions with our sisters from across the country.

2 "With a Little Help From My Friends," © 1967 Northern Songs Limited. Words and Music by John Lennon & Paul McCartney. Reprinted by permission.

moment, passive and filled-with-worship at another moment. In short, we learn a whole lot of bull-shit which has nothing to do with who we really are.

And what do we seek: the all man, man. A man who is strong, aggressive, cool, ambitious, successful. A man who is certainly brighter, better, and stronger than we. Yet, because he fell for our tricks and wiles, we can't help suspecting, from time to time, that he and all other men like him, are really fools. A fool who doesn't want to love another human being but instead wants a phony, hollow stereotype who torments him and feeds his ego.

A recent newspaper cartoon depicts two old women speaking of a bride. One says to the other, "She can throw her diary away; she won't need it now." In other words, her life is over. Her beauty, her charm, her activity have fulfilled their goals: she has caught a man. From now on she can live through her husband, his successes and failures will be hers. His ambitions will be hers. Secure in her domesticity, he will be her contact with the outside world; from him she will get her ideas about important matters like politics and social change. His work will determine where they live, what kind of friends they have, their status and social class. Her role will be to back him up, support him, comfort him. After all, a wife is an important asset to a career; they say: behind every successful man is a woman.

Hard is the fortune of all womankind
She's always controlled, she's always confined
Controlled by her parents, until she's a wife
A slave to her husband, the rest of her life.[3]

Back in the old days when a certain amount of honesty prevailed in society, marriage was seen for what it was: a property relationship, a relationship of master to his slave, an exploitative relationship. A man married to have someone to serve him, bear and rear his children, manage his household, perpetuate his name and his property. A woman was married because she was forced to, because economic security demanded it, because it was the only upright, honorable thing to do. Conjugal love was a very secondary matter, so secondary that marriages were often arranged by parents, without husband and wife even knowing each other until the wedding day. Romantic love, sexual love, these had nothing to do with marriage.

Nowadays, women are taught that the ultimate love, romantic and sexual, is found only in marriage. Yet, marriage is still the same old property relationship. A woman is still her husband's servant. She cooks his meals, cleans his house, raises his kids in his name, and gains her identity through him. She usually has little or no contact with the outside world; her life is circumscribed. In addition marriage can be physically coercive—one of the defining qualities of a "good" husband is that he doesn't beat his wife.

Even if she has her own career or interest, the home is considered her

---

[3] American folk ballad.

"proper primary sphere." Her husband may encourage her outside interests and even "help" her around the house. The essential relationship hasn't changed; he is merely a benevolent master. When his career is at stake, she is expected to drop all of her interests in deference to his future. Most important, she has been trained to feel guilty or that she is being selfish if she resents any part of married life. Love is the name given to her isolation, sacrifice, dependence, boredom, loneliness and emptiness.

People do not really expect romantic love to last through marriage. It is part of our folk wisdom that the joys of new love cannot last. We look at the enraptured, excited engaged couple and say, wisely, "Just wait 'til they're married." Yet, people are disturbed that so many marriages, perhaps even their own, are moderately or desperately unhappy, that one out of four end up in divorce. Social commentators blame it on the fast-changing times, bad up-bringing, neurotic ever-present mothers, "frigid" women who don't give their men enough sex, or passive, absent fathers. No one calls into question the institution of marriage. Most often, those marrieds who are "trying hard" to make it are merely trying to make the best of a difficult situation. The fear of having to search and play the flesh game again is too threatening to most couples.

Yet, is it surprising that a master-servant relationship gives rise to resentment and bitterness rather than feelings of warmth and tenderness? Is it any wonder that when people begin to live together and see each other for the first time not playing the flesh game, that they may not like what they see? Why should a man who works outside of the home all day and a woman who keeps house and communicates with four-year-olds have anything in common? How can love, which implies warmth, mutuality, understanding, respect, excitement, flourish in an atmosphere infused with dullness, routine, with every element of domination and submission? When all of the romantic nonsense is swept away, marriage is still justified in terms of function and duty; it is the duty of human beings to perpetuate the race; it is the duty of women to bear and raise children.

Having Children

Females are told, "having a child is the most creative thing you can do." Of course, if simply bearing offspring were really creative, then rats, cats, rabbits—not to mention frogs—would be among the most creative things going, since they bear whole litters. Or is raising children into "warm, beautiful, human beings" the creative part? Much of child-raising is not creative at all; the bulk of the job is either custodial or janitorial. Nor is it clear that a child learns best about the world when she or he is totally dependent for warmth, affection and guidance upon one human being— particularly a human being who is permitted to experience life only through the activities of other people, usually children. Why should a child have only two adults as models in the most formative years? Why shouldn't childhood be spent in the company of many other children and a diverse grouping of adults? Why should the task of raising children be the burden of only the female sex?

Private Property Is a Total Concept[4]

If we strip marriage of the property function, what is left—an intimate relationship between two people? Most marriages, we are told, last only because there are children. Why should people be forced to decide at age *twenty* whom they will love at forty-five? Why should we be allowed only one intimate relationship? Why always a man and a woman? Why can't there be an intimate relationship between more than two people? Why must there be a legal contract? Why must it last a lifetime? Why does the world have to be divided up into couples who relate to everyone else as couples or else as "unfortunate" singles? Why should each couple live by itself, isolated from other friendships, other intimacies? Marriage is the cultural manifestation of a society based on private property. Married people possess one another and their children—they are each other's private property. The family is a basic consumption unit. It spends money and accumulates property which it passes down to its children, whom it has raised to love property. It teaches the children to need to possess and accumulate property and to marry to continue the cycle.

In the abstract, it is easy to imagine capitalism surviving the breakdown of the family. Single or communal units of consumption could prove even more profitable. Public institutions could inculcate the "proper" selfish values even better than the family does. Yet, a movement to abolish the family in favor of more communal, less property-oriented forms of living threatens the privatistic, anti-social, competitive values that the capitalist system is based upon.

"I will never marry, I will be no man's wife, I intend to live single, all the days of my life"[5]

Every game has its losers. Every game has those who refuse to play. In short, some females never marry. For such a woman, there is the threat of a life of sheer hell. She faces ridicule and humiliation. If she is a virgin, she is called a dried-up old prune. If she has affairs, she is a slut. Affairs are for young girls, not for women over thirty. If she lives with a man she constantly faces the fact that he can leave her anytime he wants, anytime she doesn't please him. It will not be so easy for her to get another man.

---

[4] According to *May Day*, No. 10, a weekly periodical, this was the postage meter slogan of a private school, founded by a John Bircher, which is dedicated to teaching "the libertarian philosophy of individualism."

[5] American folk ballad.

Women over thirty have low market value. Everyone, every day, subtly or bluntly, points out to her that her life is a failure, that she is unfulfilled, that she has lost out. When is she going to get a man, be respectable, settle down?

She faces loneliness and social ostracism. Her friends have all married and no longer have anything in common with her. She is an embarrassment to her family. People who have arranged their lives in couples only invite her to dinner if they can dig up a "date" for her or if some "eligible man" is in town. Out of loneliness, out of desperation, she may marry for convenience—to get people off her back—or she may let men walk all over her, hoping to get one before it is too late.

There are few places where single women can find male companionship merely for fun as well as for marriage prospects. With so much pressure to marry, single women seek out men in the most destructive ways. Young women in their mid-twenties who have skilled jobs such as secretaries, teachers, beauticians, case workers, nurses often spend many hours waiting for men in the humiliating atmosphere of a singles' bar. Some, less honest, will find men friends and go in crowds to similar bars, each hoping that by some magical happening, she will meet the man of her dreams: puff—all of her worries will end.

While the folk wisdom assures us that there is no such thing as the flashing knight in shining armour, there is hardly a girl who does not dream that there is someone special who will be hers, someone who is just a bit of a superman. With movies and TV so dominant in our lives, it is difficult to accept the known, ugly truth instead of the beautiful, romantic myth.

A single woman will often sleep with men who obviously don't respect her to prove that she is "hip," hoping that something of the "real" her will get to him in bed and he will want *her* forever. Why shouldn't she hope that in this way she may have her chance to capture the junior executive?

"I get by with a little help from my friends,
 With a little help from my friends
 Yes, with a little help from my friends."[6]

Since our society is so harsh on those who never marry, most single women are lonely and desperate. But, the single woman who digs being independent, for whom the prospect of marriage is not only not a panacea, but a horror, there is isolation as well. While she may believe and hope that single women together might provide each other warmth, companionship, community, most of her friends are preoccupied with finding a mate.

If the single woman is fortunate enough to have a good career, she is looked upon as a castrating bitch, too wrapped up in her own life to be able to love. Most single women aren't so lucky. Working-class single women, divorced women with children, women living on welfare, widows on small pensions or social security, these women face severe and horrible economic

---

[6] *Op. cit.*, Lennon & McCartney.

deprivation as well as social humiliation. If a single female wishes to raise children she faces total martyrdom since society frowns most extremely on "illegitimate" children and seldom allows her to adopt children. If she does have a child out of wedlock or if her husband deserts her, she is constantly faced with the threat that unless she leads a "model" existence, she will be considered an immoral and unfit mother and that her children will be taken away from her. Unwed mothers have a difficult time finding employment. More subtle and often more important ostracism, such as being the subject of morning coffee clatches in other homes in her town, will often prove deterrent enough. In every way imaginable, the single woman is constantly punished for not having found a husband, or for having found one and lost him.

Denied love, denied self-respect, denied companionship, denied economic security, a single woman often begins to believe that there is something wrong with her, that she is a freak. Few females can look at singleness as a positive state; for most, it is the worst of all possible worlds. The threat of being "single" once again deters many women from leaving husbands who mistreat them or husbands they can't stand. No matter what is wrong with marriage—she thinks—it is infinitely preferable to the single state.

Females have always been isolated from one another. Marriage isolates married women from each other and from single women. Single women who may be very close know that their friendship is predicated on both of them remaining single. Thus, single women are isolated by the nature of a search for a man. Perhaps that is why females have suffered for so many centuries without engaging in collective action to change their situation. If we want to create a revolutionary female movement, we are going to have to find ways of overcoming that isolation.

Sexual Liberation: For Whom and for What?

Today, we are told, women have been sexually liberated. Not very long ago, women were taught not to ever enjoy sex, not even in marriage. Now, in the age of the sex-manual, women are allowed to enjoy sex, encouraged to dig sex even without marriage. So how come so many females still don't like sex? Why do so many young females, hip females, groovy females, consider themselves frigid?

There are many reasons. One of them is that with all the sex talk, sex education, frank discussions and the rest, women are still not taught anything about their own sexuality by other females. Most women don't understand their own bodies, have hardly any idea of what their own genitals are like, even what they look like, and don't have the faintest notion of how to get sexual pleasure. Real honest discussions about such matters are not only taboo, they are unheard of. A woman isn't supposed to be so "crude" as to tell a man how to "turn her on." If she is forward enough to do so, she'll probably turn him off.

Sexual pleasure has been defined by men in accord with what gives the male pleasure. "Sex education" for women is learning how to satisfy a man. She knows what a male orgasm is. But, a whole lot of mystery and mystification surrounds the female orgasm. Freud, and his followers, spun theories about "two kinds of orgasm," the "wrong" kind received by direct clitoral stimulation, and the "right" kind, achieved with the penis inside the woman. If she can't get the "right" kind, the kind that gives direct pleasure to the man, then, baby, she is screwed up. But, large numbers of women just can't get the right kind; these women are called frigid. Since they don't like to screw the way the master likes it, they just don't deserve to get any pleasure.

Until recently, no one even bothered to take the trouble to find out what such an important thing as the female orgasm really was. Masters and Johnson[7] studied 7,500 orgasms, achieved by many different techniques, and found that all the orgasms were physiologically the same. Interesting, but even if there were two kinds, why should one be right, the other wrong? Why not do whatever will provide warmth, affection, sensual stimulation and erotic gratification for both partners? Why are we all so hung up?

Because that is not what sex is about in this society. Sex is also using people, conning people, messing over people, conquering people, exploiting people. Many of us who rebel under exploitative relationships, still have fantasies of mutilation, masochistic nightmares which excite us sexually. What we can't stomach in reality, we perpetuate in our dreams. Why? Because we women are taught that sexuality and love are to be dug in a context of cruelty and submission. That men are supposed to fuck us over. That sex means being fucked over.

It is a joke to talk about love in such a dehumanized context. This degraded form of man-woman relationship, master and slave, which is held ideal by our society, deprives all of us of our right to human love and human community. Cruelty, humiliation, domination and abject submission pervade the one area of our society where it is considered "proper" to show dependence, need for others, and intimacy.

These conditions disgust us. We are working to create a society where people don't have to get married in order to have love, respect or security. We want to eliminate marriage as we know it today. We want to have the freedom to love, to choose whom to love and how to love. We want the freedom to love more than one person; to love members of our own sex as well as men. We want people to be free to love in dyads, triads, tribes, packs or swarms, sexually or asexually. We want to liberate society from

---

[7] W. H. Masters & V. E. Johnson, *Human Sexual Response*, Little, Brown & Co., Boston, 1960, p. 15.

taboos about homosexuality, celibacy, promiscuity, perhaps even eradicate the concepts. We want to liberate love from economic necessity, from coercive, compulsive, exploitative sexuality, from all patterns of dominance and submission.

The Death of the Family

David Cooper

Before talking about new types of living arrangements between people that may avoid the restrictions and subtle violence of the family, one point has to be made clear. In the case of the capitalist countries of the first world one can only talk about communes as prototype situations that can never freely extend and flourish in a pre-revolutionary context. The psychology of appropriation, of treating other people to a greater or lesser extent as commodities that one may possess or exchange, is so objectively prevalent that instances of the transcendence of it must be rare and isolated. Even in those rare cases the transcendence is usually more apparent than real in so far as there seems to be an inevitable resort to suppression (trying not to think), repression and denial (the unconscious or prereflective manoeuvres) and various strategies of withdrawal. By these various means we can evade the spectacle of our possessing and using other people—usually of course in the form of a collusion, since people are so conditioned to be used and exploited in relationships.

What we have to do in this first-world context is to accumulate experience in the pre-revolutionary situation that can only achieve full social expression after revolution—which I believe has to be strategically reconsidered in the first world, and reconsidered precisely on the ground of micro-political experience, that is, the experience gained in groups that range from the two-person meeting to any meeting between people that is not so large that people cannot achieve a full internalization of each other that leads to a clear sense of recognition and of being recognized whatever confusion about the "exact" identity of each other remains in people's minds.

In this chapter I shall refer to certain forms of commune arrangement that have been attempted in the first world but I shall not consider types of anti-family arrangement that have been worked out particularly in Cuba and China. The parallels between first-world countries and revolutionary third-world countries are very few indeed until we define further the meaning of a hidden third world in the heart of the first world. Let me define, however, before proceeding, *commune* as a potential alternative form of micro-social organization in the first world: A commune is a micro-social structure that achieves a viable dialectic between solitude and being-with-others; it implies either a common residence for the members or at least a common work and experience area around which residential situations may spread out peripherally; it means that love relationships become diffused between members of the commune network far more than is the case with the family system, and this means of course that sexual relationships are not restricted to some socially approved two-person man-woman arrangement; above all, because this strikes most centrally at repression, it means that children should have totally free access to adults beyond their biological parental couple. These definitional elements point to an ideological *prise de position* that one may state thus: MAKING LOVE IS GOOD IN ITSELF AND THE MORE IT HAPPENS IN ANY WAY POSSIBLE OR CONCEIVABLE BETWEEN AS MANY PEOPLE AS POSSIBLE MORE AND MORE OF THE TIME, SO MUCH THE BETTER.

But let me retrench for a while from this position to register certain provisos. I think that the minimum condition for a relationship between people to be a love relationship is the experience . . . of tenderness which is the positive residue of feeling after all negativity, resentment, hostility, envy and jealousy have been dissolved away frequently enough and deeply enough. If one tightens one's definition of love considerably this feeling amounts to trust. This means an end to secrets, no relationship-act carried out behind anyone's back, although privacy, antithetic to family-modelled secrecy, always remains a possibility. But let us not fall into some sort of euphoric myth about openness at this point. Openness in the sense I am suggesting here means a lot of hard work. What I am suggesting means inevitably a considerable amount of suffering from the consequences of emotional mistakes one makes in one's relationships, and a disciplined, even ruthless clarification of blocks and compulsions that operate within one's mind. Openness means pain, and, despite attentive kindness and help and clarification that one may get from other people, the pain ultimately has to be suffered alone; and it is from this position of solitude that the ultimate clarification must come. Make no mistake about it, other people will always sense, even without realizing what they sense, when someone in the group has been through this sort of self-confrontation. It would be fatuous to speak of communes without the presence in the group of, in the first instance, at least one person who has rigorously enough dealt with his life in these terms.

*   *   *

When marriages "break up," I still feel a vestigial sense of amazement about the way that a state of not knowing about some affair that the other partner once had and now "confesses" is contorted into an issue of jealousy and anger. In fact, if one traces back the history of the relationship, the point of the partner having the affair that the other did not "know about" was often a point of liberation in sexual and relationship terms for the other (the "betrayed" one). But the divorce carries on of course because there is false resentment instead of real gratitude.—*But then the only evil of divorce is the prior evil of marriage.*

At this point I think one has to make a distinction between generations and their possibilities. I think that if we now, always in a first-world context, take the generation of people in early middle-age and also that of people now in their mid-teens to mid-twenties (the generation gap between these two groups now seems to be little more than twelve years) we find a common problem, albeit a problem that some of us might be grateful to have: the problem is the need for a strong, central two-person relationship that is inevitably felt by others to be somewhat excluding. Whether this need will apply in the future to the generation still in primary school is another matter, since the rate of breakdown of the institutional fabric of bourgeois society may be rapid enough in the next decade to introduce for them the possibility of a less centric system of relationships. There may be a shifting system of dyads leading to a polycentric relationship-structure even though there will probably be a degree of hierarchization in the emotional significance of the various two-person relationships that each person has.

But for the present let us try to be clearer about the "strong, central two-person relationship." As I see it this relationship in no sense entails the formation of a closed family system, i.e., an exclusion by relationship of other signficant relationships for each of the two people and the closely related claustration of the children within the small system of "primary" relationships. The clear possibility now actualized by many people is that more or less peripheral relationships with others may feed into the central two-person relationship in a way that enriches its quality on every level and reinforces its intensities. This realization, however, can again lead into euphoric idealism unless one recognizes certain qualifications. At certain stages of a two-person relationship either or both partners may need to make certain promises. In the exploration of the relationship one may need the other person to agree not to enter into another relationship until there is full concurrence about the "right time." No one of course is compelled to make or keep such a promise, *the right to say "no" is fundamental.* On the other hand, given the predatory nature of our society and the fact that we all internalize its predatoriness and reproduce it in our acts, despite our best intentions, in all our relationships, it seems reasonable for two people to arrive at a temporary contractual restriction on the extent of other relationships. This contract is antithetic to the marriage contract on the most essential point, the point of *relationship time.*

The marriage contract involves submission of personal need to an externally imposed time-scheme and through this submission one's social time and space is displaced into a region of otherness, leaving an emptiness in us that "given time" (which finally takes our time away) we no longer notice any more. If we do notice it we may want our time back but we then find that to get our time back involves a devastating shattering of our laboriously erected security structures and the full unleashing of the archaically implanted guilt about what we are doing to the security of others. We may well give up in despair but if we are alert enough to the issues we find ourselves impaled on the other horn of the guilt dilemma because there is then the progressive dissemination of our despair into all the others we relate to closely.

The way out of the situation seems to me to be the dawning realization that perhaps the most liberating thing one can do for other people is to do the thing that is most liberating for oneself. The "most liberating thing" is always the most joyful, but we must understand joy here as clearly distinct from happiness (which always devolves on to security in some form, that is to say a deceptively comfortable restriction of one's possibilities). Joy comprehends despair running through an end-point of pain into joy again. Whereas happiness is a unitary feeling-tone issuing from security, joy is the full, simultaneous expression of a spectrum—joy at one end, despair in the middle and then again joy at the other end. It is rare enough in my experience in this culture for people to weep freely enough in despair. It is far rarer for a noncontradictory joy to be present through such weeping. The fact that liberation is immediately pain and always means hard work on oneself from the decisive moment onwards is no enigmatic irony but an issue of our internalization of an objective contradiction in bourgeois society.

In a two-person relationship that chooses its own self-evolving definition rather than the choice of a static externally imposed definition, there is at least the chance of a respect for the natural history of a fully lived-out relationship. For instance in any two-person relationship there is a natural fluctuation in the intensity of sexual involvement. There may be fairly long periods of mutual or one-sided sexual withdrawal which cannot be reduced to resolvable "neurotic conflict"—try as one may, and however dutifully and obediently one tries to produce sexuality. Sexual involvement with people outside the dyad can clearly break down the intra-dyadic withdrawal if one most central illusion can be destroyed—*the illusion of the quantifiability of love.*

Love, of course, like every experience we may achieve, can be reduced to a state of being that may be reduced in turn to the status of a commodity and then fetishized like any other commodity. It becomes a sort of parcel with socially prescribed dimensions which cannot in the circumstances of any specific relationship be exceeded. One has, one is led to believe and then further leads oneself to believe, only so much love to offer. If one gives almost all one's love to one other person one has proportionately very little to parcel out to others. If one operates with this naïve algebra a corollary must be that any act of loving is experienced as loss of a certain inner quantity of love.

*   *   *

. . . For me it is a revolutionary act if in the course of months or years a person transcends the major bits of his micro- and macro-social conditioning in the direction of the spontaneous self-assertion of full personal autonomy which *in itself* is a decisive act of counterviolence against the system. It means that the person is *ready* in a way that few are. Beyond the one-person scale, but always coming in a sense from "one person," there is the explosive potential of a group or network who in the course of a long travail demonstrate the possibility of firstly viable and then good developing relationships that are antithetic along the most essential parameters to bourgeois relationships which are imposed, unchosen, uncreative and uncreating and which are always on the model of the nuclear family in either its original or its replicated forms.

In an earlier essay[1] I wrote of the need to develop Revolutionary Centres of Consciousness. These would take the form of anti-institutional spontaneous groupings of people who operate outside the formal bureaucratic structures of their factory, school, university, hospital, broadcasting corporation, art-institution (in the sense of either art school or gallery politics) and so on. In this form of grouping there would be no suppression of the personal reality of any member in the mode of serialization (i.e., forming bus-queues of people working in the institutional structure waiting for a bus that never arrives). Also there would be a paradigmatic influence mushrooming out to other potential groups.

The revolutionary nature of these groups (which, without a programme, are already emerging anyhow) lies in the exploding of the contradiction between the desperately controlling operations of bourgeois society that would anonymize, order and categorize people, and the impulse actually in people, despite this, to shout out their names in the world and to announce their work to the world; in fact to show themselves to the world because they can begin to look at their selves themselves.

But things cannot rest at this level of rapidly spreading subversion from the micro-political base of personal liberation. The fulfilment of liberation comes only with effective macro-political action. So the Centres of Revolutionary Consciousness have also to become Red Bases. Macro-political action here must be essentially negative and take the form of rendering bourgeois power-structures impotent by any and every means. This means might be a *revolutionary mimesis* of the tactics of the bourgeois power structure. The structure is greedy, it devours people and consumes their work, shitting out the indigestible residue as pay, as obscene holiday camps,

[1] Cooper, D. G., "Beyond Words," in *The Dialectics of Liberation*, Penguin Press, 1968.

and so on. So why not mimic the greed of the system by following its example as closely as possible. After all, one could hardly be more moral than that. In other words, if bosses or university authorities make concessions, one demands and exacts more and more "concessions" until *they* realize that they had nothing to give in the first place. Then, having abolished that false family structure, all one has to do is to make sure it is not set up again. Revolution becomes not a historical act but history itself— Continuous Revolution. Or, again, one may show that bourgeois power structures are powerless, apart from the power that we obediently invest them with, by arranging their disorganization. A few very simple but carefully concerted actions might do this.

Beyond this there are the more conventional tactics of strike and sit-in, but work on the micro-political level can rid these tactics of their economism, that is to say that in a first-world context it can never be simply a matter of more bread but more bread and much more reality.

What we want, in short, is not to chew our loaf but to consume the system so that at last we might get a taste of ourselves.

SECTION 5

MAN AND ENVIRONMENT

URBAN DEVELOPMENT in America during the nineteenth and the early part of the twentieth century was a movement of displaced farmers from rural areas to the cities in search of work and a better life. There is still movement into the cities by the poor from the countryside and from foreign lands, but nowadays the most rapidly growing areas are the suburbs. With the aid of the automobile and the freeway, the white middle class has moved to suburbia. Those who are left in the cities are mostly the poor, the foreign-speaking and ethnic minorities. If present trends continue, we may expect most large American cities to become ethnic enclaves with majorities of poor and black residents, surrounded by well-to-do white suburbs.

America, Riesman says, has a dual economy. It has a low-wage non-expense-account economy (in small business, domestic services, agricultural labor, sweatshops) and a high-wage managerial economy (in the large corporations and civil service). The slums in the countryside and central cities are the consumer side of the low-wage economy. The suburbs are the consumer side of the managerial economy. The suburbs are one vast supermarket where homes, automobiles, and appliances are bought on credit. The continual purchase of consumer goods by the well-to-do residents of suburbia is one of the main things that keep the whole system going.

Formerly men were judged (and judged themselves) largely by the work they did. But since industrialization and specialization have robbed many jobs of their meaning, says Riesman, what people do for a living has become less important than their style of life. This is especially true in the suburbs, where life is centered upon consumership. If life tends to be aimless and meaningless, it is because work is no longer the central focus. Meaningful life depends on meaningful work.

The topsy-turvy growth of cities and suburbs has polluted the environment and destroyed our natural resources. This destruction of the environment reflects a Western assumption that man can and should have dominion over nature. An alternative assumption, the ecological one, is that man should come to terms with the environment, that he should live with nature instead of against it.[1] According to Bookchin nothing short of adopting this view will prevent us from destroying the environment and eventually the human species itself.

Ecology provides a holistic perspective of relationships between man and nature, focusing on the interconnections between phenomena that are usually treated separately by specialists. Instead of taking it for granted that a new freeway must be built to accommodate greater auto traffic, for example, ecologists ask why so many persons have to travel so far, they examine decentralization of urban facilities as an alternative to road building, and ask whether alternatives such as rapid transit might not reduce deaths and casualties from car accidents. Where freeways are to be built nevertheless, ecologists calculate not only their monetary costs, but the social cost of greater urban congestion and the displacement of people to make room for the road, as well as the consequences of the additional pollution from motor vehicle exhausts.

The concentration of factories and people in huge metropolitan areas leads to complex logistic problems and requires inordinate amounts of electrical power. Ecological principles suggest decentraization into balanced communities that use local materials and energy, says Bookchin. Smaller regional economies can use a combination of sun, wind, water, and geothermal power in place of fossil fuels and atomic reactors. When communities are smaller, there is less need for cars, trucks, and freeways, because people can live closer to their work, and raw materials don't have to be carried so far. Even a small degree of decentralization would help alleviate some of the more pressing problems, because the difference between tolerable and intolerable crowding of schools, hospitals, and so on is often a matter of only a few percentage points.[2]

---

[1] See Ian McHarg, "Man and Environment," in Leonard J. Duhl, ed., *The Urban Condition* (New York: Basic Books, 1963).

[2] See Paul Goodman, "Ungovernable Cities," *WIN Magazine*, V, August 1969, p. 16.

The "ecology" campaigns that have become popular in the early 1970s have neutralized the critical and reconstructive aspects of ecology by dramatizing chiefly the less important issues. It is good that we have begun to recycle paper, metal and glass that used to be wastefully thrown away, and to install antismog devices in automobiles. But these things only make business more profitable by lowering costs of raw materials and providing markets for new products. They do not confront more basic problems such as automania, overconcentration of people and industries in metropolitan areas, and environmental pollution caused by big business in obtaining raw materials and in getting rid of wastes. Emphasizing the peripheral aspects of ecology makes us feel we have "done something," and thus blinds us to the need to radically reconstruct the society and create a truly liveable environment.

The Suburban Dislocation

David Riesman

Planned Utopia

The other day I went back to read that remarkable and neglected book, *Communitas: Means of Livelihood and Ways of Life*, by Percival and Paul Goodman.[1] This book includes a commentary on utopian community planning in the past and some suggestions as to potential utopias within the American scene of our day. It makes strange and disturbing reading now on at least two grounds. In the first place, it is easy to forget how much enthusiasm there was, during and immediately after World War II, for creative planning and reorganization of communal life, both here and in Europe. Ten years later, the air is sodden—as if a fall-out over intellectual life had already occurred—the cold war absorbs much of our political energy; and we struggle, not to plan, but even to register what is happening to our fantastically expanding economy, population, and metropolitan

FROM *The Annals of the American Academy of Political and Social Sciences* (November, 1957), pp. 125–46. Reprinted by permission of the author and the American Academy of Political and Social Sciences.

[1] [New York: Random House, Inc., 1960, revised edition. The book was originally published in 1947. See the selections from *Communitas* in Section 7 of this anthology—editor's note.] *Cf.* my discussion in "Some Observations on Community Plans and Utopia," *Yale Law Journal*, 1957. Reprinted in *Individualism Reconsidered* (Glencoe, Ill.: The Free Press, 1954).

malaise.[2] In the second place, it is curious how many of the Goodmans' then-utopian suggestions have been incorporated into our lives, ten years later, without planning and with fundamental change coming about interstitially only. We have come much closer to approximating their first ironical plan for a city of efficient consumption, although our shopping centers are suburban rather than urban. Certainly, our advertising is more "efficient" now than in prewar times, and our waste more exuberant.[3] Their second plan, for the decentralization of work and life, has come about in some measure: Through turning the home into a do-it-yourself workshop, through some degree of suburbanization of industry, and through greater labor mobility; but the quality of this plan, aimed at minimizing central political and economic control and at making work and leisure more meaningful, seems further away than ever. Their third plan, which aimed at a subsistence economy for security on top of which a luxury economy would be reared, has come about in an utterly paradoxical form. We have now a dual economy; one part is luxurious, pays high wages, lives in handsome plants, and generally engages in "conspicuous production"; the other part lives as if on another continent, paying low wages, not practicing Harvard Business School techniques, and seldom financing itself out of retained profits and quick depreciation accounts. The Goodman's third plan was intended to minimize government regulation and private price-administered regulation. Our dual economy, however, depends on continued war preparation, suitable tax and credit policies, and agreement between labor and management in the high-wage economy to let the consumer, and sometimes the stockholder, pay the costs of private socialism and creeping inflation.[4] Yet the consumer also benefits from the dual economy if he works for the high-wage, managerial side of it, or if, while working for the underprivileged economy, he can somehow use the former as leverage or "host" for raising his own income without the corresponding in-plant efficiencies and extra-plant responsibilities of the managerial side. Moreover, as Whyte makes clear in *The Organization Man*, the new neatly assembled suburbs, with their handsome school plants and their neighborly fraternalism, are

[2] The countries of Western Europe do not appear to be greatly in advance of America in these respects, but instead to be trying to enjoy with prosperity our new problems as well as their traditional ones—a far cry from, for example, the radically reconstitutive hopes expressed in the French Resistance press during the German Occupation. *Cf.*, e.g., the interesting book by Karl Bednarik. *The Young Worker of To-day: A New Type*, Renee Tupholme, Translator (Glencoe, Ill.: The Free Press, 1956); and see also recent articles in *Encounter* on "This New England" and "The Younger Generation" of the Welfare State.

[3] We buy more services than the Goodmans allowed for, which lowers our efficiency in production and distribution—and absorbs what would otherwise be a labor surplus.

[4] I am indebted to Eric Larrabee for stimulating discussions of the "dual economy." The concept is analogous to that of the dual state described by Ernest Frankel for Nazi Germany and resembles the contrast of controlled, *i.e.*, abundant, and free, *i.e.*, pinched, sectors in a totalitarian economy.

the consumption side of the managerial economy, valuing a similar "social ethic" and suffering from a similar lack of ultimate goals. Likewise, the residual but still immense slums to be found in both country and city are the domestic or consumer side of the low-wage, non-expense-account economy.[5]

This latter economy lacks the subsistence security at which the Goodmans aimed—rather, it remains the principal arena in which one is allowed to fail or to make a very fast buck. And the luxury economy exercises a ceaseless pull, both in its style of production and in the spread of these, via the expense account, into so-called private life.[6] Thus, private life gets further and further from even the possibilities of a subsistence minimum. At least it does so apart from the possibility, conceivable but unlikely, of a Savonarola-type revolt against high standards of living and dying and the economic and social structure that accompanies these.

Utopia and Reality

Perhaps the most significant difference between the Goodmans' book and the present state of the American experience and imagination is that the latter are encased in an additive or extrapolative mode of perception. When we have a problem, we have a standard remedy: More. We add a road, a wing to a school, a new department or government agency. Seldom do we rearrange the givens so that they become takens into a new configuration—as was done, for notable examples, in the Tennessee Valley Authority and the Marshall Plan. This is not merely the old American formula of "bigger and better" or the old American optimism, now in any case considerably attenuated. Rather, it is something which goes deeper into the way Americans structure their very image of physical and social reality. In his perceptive essay, "What is American about America?", John Kouwenhoven gives many illustrations of the additive principle: From the land-grant section to the reiterative beat of jazz, the roll of film, the highway grid of our cities, the added stories of the skyscraper or high-rise apartment, our soap-opera serials, our assembly lines.[7] Dorothy Lee, on the basis of

---

[5] To be sure, there live in the slums Negroes and other migrant groups who have jobs in the high-wage economy but have not yet had a chance to adopt, at least in residential pattern and usually also in family style of life, the suburban concomitants. And the slums also contain many elderly people, only rarely at work in the high-wage economy, whose skills and tastes antedate the spread of the dual economy both on the production and the consumption side.

[6] The low-wage economy has its expense accounts, too, and being mostly small business and small government, these have often more gravy if less finesse than those in the luxury economy; but they are confined to the boss and his nephews and friends: They are not institutionalized.

[7] *Colorado Quarterly* (Spring 1954) reprinted in *Harper's Magazine*, Vol. 213 (July 1956), pp. 25–33.

linguistic studies, has shown the lilt and drive of analogous tendencies in the changing patterns of American English.[8]

* * *

. . . For millions of suburbanites, their post-World War II experience has been prosperous and open far beyond their depression-born expectations. For them, the suburbs have been one vast supermarket, abundantly and conveniently stocked with approved yet often variegated choices. The children are less of a worry there than on city streets; the neighbors often more friendly than those city folk who "keep themselves to themselves"; life in general is more relaxed. The confidence such people often have that things will continue to go well for them is revealed in the story told one journalist in a Southern California suburb where employment depends on nearby defense plants. When he asked people what would happen to them in case of a depression or cancellation of defense contracts, they answered: "Why then the government will stockpile cars." Life on credit has worked out well for many such home owners, allowing them to have their children young and in circumstances far better than those in which they themselves grew up. Whatever the outsider might say about the risks blithely taken, with no allowance made for personal or social setbacks, or about the anemic quality of the relaxed life or its complacency, he would have to admit that such first-generation suburbanites have found the taste of abundance pleasant and, for the younger ones with wages rising faster than prices, not notably problematic.

Revolt Against Industrialism

This subjective attitude does not, however, alter the fact that, among such suburban dwellers and in general in our society, we are witnessing a tremendous but tacit revolt against industrialism. It is a very different sort of revolt from either that of the machine smashers of the early nineteenth century or that of the various anti-industrial sects—socialist, anarchist, agrarian, etc.—of an earlier day. Large manufacturing industry is increasingly moving to the luxury side of the "dual economy," and back-breaking toil and harsh physical conditions are vanishing (except in industrialized farming and the service trades) with the coming of electricity, full employment, unions, and personnel men. But the luxury, which is often used to make the work more gregarious and less of an effort, is seldom used to make it less monotonous.[9] Naturally, men treat their work as delinquents

[8] "Freedom, Spontaneity and Limit in American Linguistic Usage," *Explorations*, Vol. 6 (1956), pp. 6–14.

[9] *Cf.* Peter Drucker's discussion of job enlargement and related measures in *Concept of the Corporation* (New York: Harper & Brothers, 1946). Union leaders who once

treat school though schools are less likely than plants to pioneer the partial truancy of the four-day week, escaping and sabotaging when they can. Managers and foremen try in vain to restore the "old school spirit" to their employees and, failing, seek through automation and quality control to make up for the deliquescence of the "instinct of workmanship" once so painfully built into the labor force. Observers of factory life have repeatedly pointed out that status within the plant is no longer gained by hard work and craftsmanship, but rather by one's consumer skills outside. Men dream, not of rising in the factory, but of starting a small business such as a motel, gas station, or TV repair shop in the shabby and open-shop underside of our dual economy.[10] For youngsters from subsistence farms, for hillbillies, and Southern Negroes, a Detroit or Gary factory is still glamorous or at least a liberation from drastic poverty and insecurity; but for second- and third-generation factory workers, it no longer holds much meaning other than as a (hopefully temporary) source of funds and fringe benefits.

*   *   *

Life and Work Values

... When, a few years ago, I studied interviews done with several hundred college seniors at twenty representative universities, asking them what they would like or expect to be doing in fifteen years, I was struck by the fact that the great majority planned to live in the suburbs. They expected to be married, and in describing their prospective spouses they hoped for what we might call station-wagon types: educated, companionable, civic-minded, and profoundly domestic. There were few who recognized some incompatibility between focus on suburban life and focus on big-city ambitions (for instance, a senior who wanted to go into advertising, yet not live in or near New York). They were—with some exceptions especially among the Southerners—willing to sacrifice the heights of achievement, though not the plateaus of the luxury economy, in favor of their goals of suburban domesticity and peace. Those who hailed originally from the suburbs suffered from no disenchantment and wanted to return to them—often to the same one—while both city-bred and small-town boys also preferred the suburbs. I assume that some of the latter in an earlier day would have

---

were in the forefront of the drive to make work less exhausting—often an extrapolative matter of lowering hours, slowing the assembly line, lessening dirt and noise—have seldom moved into the more difficult area of making it less uncreative. (According to Nelson Foote, they have eliminated the former grim silence that suited a Puritanical management.)

[10] *Cf.*, e.g., Ely Chinoy, *Automobile Workers and the American Dream* (Garden City, N.Y.: Doubleday & Company, 1955), and, on older patterns of work morality, Eugene A. Friedmann and Robert J. Havighurst, *The Meaning of Work and Retirement* (Chicago: University of Chicago Press, 1954).

wanted to leave Main Street behind and make their mark in the big city, whatever lingering agrarian fears and suspicions of it they still harbored.[11] The city today, for many, spells crime, dirt, and race tensions, more than it does culture and opportunity. While some people still escape from the small town to the city, even more people are escaping from the city to the suburbs.

*   *   *

A recent fragmentary survey presents evidence that managers are less satisfied with their work even than unskilled workers, and it is conceivable that the middle-class occupations in general will soon be regarded as sources of funds and of periodic contacts and activity, much as the working-class occupations are now largely regarded.[12] If work loses its centrality, then the place where it is done also comes to matter less, and the access to variety in work that the central city provides may also come to matter less. Indeed, so much is this the case already that advertising for engineers in *Scientific American* and in trade journals looks more and more like the vacation advertising in *Holiday*. Minneapolis-Honeywell offers seasons and skiing as a counter-lure to the aircraft and electronic suburbs of the Far West.[13] In this regimen, white-collar and blue-collar move towards one another, as each group now emphasizes the consumption aspects of life.

Suburban Way of Life

This life, as just indicated, is increasingly focused on the suburbs which, since World War II, have grown so in quantity as to change their quality. For, although upper-class and upper-middle-class people have lived in the suburbs of our great cities since the 1880's or earlier, the cities before World War II still retained their hegemony: They engrossed commercial, industrial, and cultural power. The city represented the division and specialization not only of labor but of attitude and opinion: By discovering like-minded people in the city, one developed a new style, a new little magazine, a new architecture. The city, that is, provided a "critical mass" which made possible new combinations—criminal and fantastic ones as well as stimulating and productive ones. Today, however, with the continual loss to the suburbs of the elite and the enterprising, the cities remain big enough for

11 *Cf.* "The Found Generation," *The American Scholar*, Vol. 25 (1956), pp. 421–36; see also Eric Larrabee and David Riesman, "Company Town Pastoral: The Role of Business in 'Executive Suite,' " reprinted in Bernard Rosenberg and David Manning White, *Mass Culture* (Glencoe, Ill.: The Free Press, 1956), pp. 325–37.

12 See Nancy C. Morse and Robert S. Weiss, "The Function and Meaning of Work and the Job," *American Sociological Review*, Vol. 20 (1955), pp. 191–98. It should be noted that many men in the professions (the study included only men) and many in sales express great satisfaction with their work.

13 An occasional ad is more work-minded and will feature opportunities for responsibility and creativity along with the suburban fringe benefits.

juveniles to form delinquent subcultures, but barely differentiated enough to support cultural and educational activities at a level appropriate to our abundant economy. The elite, moreover, tend to associate with like-income neighbors rather than with like-minded civic leaders, thus dispersing their potential for leadership beyond township boundaries. Ironically, these people sometimes choose to live in communities which might be almost too manageable if millions of others did not simultaneously make the same choice.[14]

Indeed, the suburbs are no longer simply bedroom communities but increasingly absorb the energies of the men as well as the women and children. The men, that is, are not simply being good providers while still attached to the values of the industrial system: They are seekers after the good life in the suburbs on their own account. Early marriage and the rise in the birth rate are so many rivulets of individual, only barely self-conscious protest against the values inherited from industrialism and the low-birth-rate middle-class metropolis—so many decisions to prefer companionship in the present to some distant goal, and so many mortgages of the future in the benevolent shadow of the luxury economy and its escalator of slow inflation, promotion, and protection. Whereas men once identified themselves with commerce and industry—with its power, its abstractions, its achievements—and forced women to remain identified with domesticity— save for those women who broke through the barrier and became man-imitating career girls—now, as many observers have pointed out, a growing homogenization of roles is occurring. Women take jobs to support the suburban menage periodically while men take part in its work (do-it-yourself), its civic activities (Parent-Teachers Association, and so on), and its spirit. Rather than delegating religion to their womenfolk, men go to church in increasing numbers, occasionally as in an earlier day to be respectable or to climb socially, and occasionally out of a genuine religious call, but more typically because the church, like the high school and the country club, has become a center for the family as a social and civic unit.

*   *   *

Loss of Human Differentiation

There seems to me to be a tendency, though not a pronounced one, in the suburbs to lose the human differentiations which have made great cities in the past the centers of rapid intellectual and cultural advance. The sub-

---

[14] This is somewhat analogous to fad behavior, for individuals no longer live in suburbs as, so to speak, statistical isolates, but live there with recognition of the suburban style as theirs and their country's. *Cf.* Rolf Meyersohn and Elihu Katz, "Notes on a Natural History of a Fad," *American Journal of Sociology*, Vol. 62, No. 6 (1957), pp. 594–601.

urb is like a fraternity house at a small college—or the "close propinquity" to which Tocqueville referred—in which like-mindedness reverberates upon itself as the potentially various selves within each of us do not get evoked or recognized. For people who move to the suburb to live when adult, of course, matters are different than among those who never knew another milieu. And, to be sure, creative human contact need not be face to face but can often be vicarious, through print or other mediated channels. Certainly, highly differentiated human beings have grown up in locales which gave them minimal support. Moreover, though the nonneighborly seldom seek the suburbs,[15] a few doubtless manage to survive there. Ease of movement, in any case, permits periodic access to others, although as these others themselves scatter to the suburbs, this process becomes more difficult.

*　　*　　*

Uneven Distribution of Leisure

Let me stress again that the themes I am discussing are peculiar neither to the United States nor to the twentieth century. Just as cities are older than industry so are suburbs, their splendors, and miseries. It is the democratization and extension of the phenomena I am describing, and the resultant constriction of alternatives, which give them a new and cumulative quality. The modern suburb is the product of the car, the five-day week, and the "bankers' hours" of the masses. As hours drop further, we can anticipate that still fewer families with children will willingly live in the city. Exceptions would be cities like Minneapolis where the inhabitants can focus their leisure around their cottages on nearby lakes. But the same developments which have reduced hours for those white-collar and factory workers who do not go in for "moonlighting" or extra jobs have in turn put additional pressure on the still limited leisure of certain professional groups. These latter, in one way or another, cater to those whose enhanced income and leisure time allows them greatly to increase their consumption of services. People, that is, can now afford both the time and money for better medical care, more professional advice (therapeutic and otherwise), additional schooling, and so on. And the professions and service trades that supply these wants do not benefit from automation. Thus, the very developments that have increased the leisure of the masses have greatly reduced that of certain of the classes: Doctors, civil servants, teachers, school and college administrators, and some groups of managers and intellectuals work almost as long hours as steel-workers did in the nineteenth century. While

---

[15] Cf. Sylvia Fleis Fava, "Contrasts in Neighboring: New York City and a Suburban County," in William Dobriner, ed., Reader on the Suburbs (New York: G. P. Putnam's Sons).

some of these cadres, notably the doctors, have enough of a monopoly position to earn high incomes in partial revenge for being overworked, others, notably the civil servants and teachers, are poorly paid both in money and time. It is these groups who are becoming the principal victims of the anti-industrial or leisure revolution.[16]

*   *   *

The Aimless Quality of Suburban Life

In the days of Lincoln Steffens and later, people emphasized the "shame of the cities," and in the 1920's major novelists emphasized the constraints of small-town and occasionally of small-suburban life. Today, the comparable worry, in the books dealing with the suburbs, is conformity —*Point of No Return*, with its concern for place and competition, strikes a somewhat older note; writers point to the uniformity of the ranch style, the ever-present television antennae, the lamp, if not the crack, in the picture window—which usually provides a view of the nearly treeless street, the cars, and someone else's picture window. Actually, uniformity and conformity are quite different matters as Georg Simmel has observed in his essay on "Fashion."[17] The former may dictate to men only in inessentials, whereas the latter involves some psychological mechanism. And the conformity of the new suburbs is, in some important ways, far less stringent than that of the old; if it is not quite the case that "anything goes," lots of things do go which once would, if known, have brought ostracism. If one does not seek to force the new subordinate back across the ethnic tracks he has just crossed, he is quite tolerant, even bland. If he is political at all— rather than parochially civic-minded, tending to a "garden" which includes the local schools and waterworks—he is apt to be an Eisenhower Republican, seldom informed, rarely angry, and only spasmodically partisan.

No, what is missing in suburbia, even where the quality of life has not overtly deteriorated, is not the result of claustrophobic conformity to others' sanctions. Rather, there would seem to be an aimlessness, a pervasive low-keyed unpleasure. This cannot be described in terms of traditional sorrows but is one on which many observers of the American scene and the American visage have commented, notably Erich Fromm in *The Sane Society* and the Goodmans in *Communitas*. For millions of people, work no longer provides a central focus for life; and the bread-winner is

[16] *Cf.* the thoughtful comments on an "administrative depression" among white-collar workers in Harvey Wheeler, "Danger Signal in the Political System," *Dissent*, Vol. 4 (1957), pp. 298–310.
[17] The essay, which originally appeared in *International Quarterly*, Vol. 10 (1904), pp. 130–55, is reprinted in *American Journal of Sociology*, Vol. 62, No. 6 (1957), pp. 541–58.

no longer the chief protagonist in the family saga—just as Saturday night no longer provides a central focus for festivity. In fact, the decentralization of leisure in the suburbs is not only spatial but temporal, as evenings from Thursday through Sunday are oriented to play rather than work and are not individually accented or collectively celebrated.[18]

At the same time, leisure has not picked up the slack—as, in earlier writings, I was too sanguine that it might. Whatever balances of work and play might have been possible for preindustrial man, postindustrial man is keyed, as I remarked earlier, to greater expectations. He has learned more "needs" and cannot in any case reconstitute the institutions industrialism destroyed. It is almost inconceivable, for example, to imagine a reconstitution of the folk arts which everywhere—in Nigeria as in New Orleans, in Damascus as in Tennessee—prove fragile in the face of mass-produced music and imagery. In *Communitas*, the Goodmans devoted much ingenuity to suggesting how, in their New Commune, work could be made more varied and interesting: By job rotation on a grand scale, by alternating supervision and apprenticeship, by scrutiny of all work in terms of means as well as ends. But automation as presently interpreted moves us yet further away from such a re-examination of work routines, even though, were our values different, it could provide an opportunity for eliminating monotonous work and bringing far more variety and spark into it.

The Future of Leisure

I recently had the opportunity to talk about the future of leisure with some thoughtful union leaders and adult educators. They were looking forward, in dismay as much as in hope, to a far shorter working week and a less demanding working day. They were asking specialists on leisure how these vacua of time and energy could be filled with more creativity and less boredom. They were saddling leisure with the burden which indeed it did carry for a small minority of the leisure class in some aristocratic eras—the burden of supporting life's total commitment and significance. Suggestions were made for better adult education courses, even for sabbaticals for everybody or short periods of residence in an Aspen-like setting. And one leader spoke of efforts to link workers possessing underused craft skills with groups such as nursery schools possessing substandard facilities—groups which could greatly benefit from the energies and capabilities of people who would in their free time build jungle gyms, chairs, or other needed equipment. But it was clear from the tone of the meeting that these notions, valuable as they were, could not even claim the status of palliatives.

---

[18] I sometimes consider the drive-in movie the archetypical symbol of decentralization where people go to the theater not in stalls which permit circulation of elites but in cars which keep the family or the dating couple together with no sense of the audience or any shared experience outside the sedan.

It was not that they could not (given workers as they now are) compete with commercial recreation or polishing the car, but also that they did not provide the "moral equivalent of work." We can see in the bored teen-agers who don't like school, and are already sated with sex unmitigated by love, what leisure is like for most people when life lacks the accent and structure given it by work—not simply stand-by "work" but some effortful and periodically challenging activity.

In the studies of unemployed men made during the great depression, the observation of the demoralizing nature of being without work was often made, but it was sometimes assumed that this was mostly a matter of status and of poverty which forced the unemployed man to hang uselessly about the house. And in the studies of men who have retired, the same theme recurs. They are demoralized because the job gave status and income, and also because they grew up in a work-minded era and were not prepared for the age of leisure. I myself had thought that when a whole generation had been reared which was not driven to work by the agreed-upon motives of hunger and gain—often unconsciously driven because work-mindedness was instilled, so to speak, with mother's bottle feeding on schedule—such people could retire more comfortably than the elderly now do because they would have been preparing for it all life long. Presently, however, I am inclined to believe that work is still necessary because our inventiveness has not found ways of relating masses of men to creative activity or to each other outside of work. Though the artist, of whatever sort and for whom there is no real division between work and play, indicates what may someday be possible, even the artist, whatever his ideology of *l'art pour l'art*, needs usually to feel he is being of some use—if only in acting out a counterpoint to Philistine utilitarianism.

* * *

Conclusion

Writing ten years ago about the Goodmans' book, I was up against the perennial planners' problem: How to get from here to there, when "here" is the omnipresent educator, the agent of socialization. Yet, as makers of goods and ideas know, Americans are almost too ready to abandon one thing for another, provided they are persuaded by the media or friends that the other is somehow "better" or, preferably, "the best," along a dimension which is already given. To be sure, the range of such persuasion is not terribly wide, and it is wider of course in inessentials or externals, though the last ten years have seen radical changes in food habits, men's clothes, child rearing, and other (one might suppose) tenacious things. More problematic is the persuasion itself. When mobilized for the planners' good ends it is frequently self-defeating because it almost inevitably uses the given means such as appeals to snobbery or to a fake efficiency. Yet the fear of this problem, with its practical and ethical dilemmas, seems to me at present to have intimidated thinking about what the good ends are. Thus, even if people could be persuaded, there is nothing to persuade them of. Plans, as history occasionally shows, have their own persuasive power, particularly in unexpected historical junctures. Many Americans will soon discover the loss of urban and suburban texture and might then be ready to do something, were a model available. The social processes I have touched upon in this paper are moving people into the service trades and professions and out of industry and farming. We need to find meaningful work for the displaced ones rather than locating still more of them in selling, public relations, and looking after each other. The country can "use" poets, painters, planners, and prophets in virtually unlimited amounts. With poets in recent years the country has not done too badly; with painters—despite all I have said about visual blight and the country of the blind—not too badly, either. But planners and prophets?

Ecology and Revolutionary Thought

Murray Bookchin

There is one science . . . that may yet restore and even transcend the liberatory estate of the traditional sciences and philosophies. It passes rather loosely under the name "ecology"—a term coined by Haeckel a century ago to denote "the investigation of the total relations of the animal both to its inorganic and to its organic environment."[1] At first glance, Haeckel's definition is innocuous enough; and ecology narrowly conceived of as one of the biological sciences, is often reduced to a variety of biometrics in which field workers focus on food chains and statistical studies of animal populations. There is an ecology of health that would hardly offend the sensibilities of the American Medical Association and a concept of social ecology that would conform to the most well-engineered notions of the New York City Planning Commission.

Broadly conceived of, however, ecology deals with the balance of nature. Inasmuch as nature includes man, the science basically deals with the harmonization of nature and man. The explosive implications of an

FROM *Post-Scarcity Anarchism* by Murray Bookchin. Ramparts Books, 1971; Berkeley, Calif.
[1] Quoted in Angus M. Woodbury, *Principles of General Ecology* (Blackiston: New York, 1954), p. 4.

ecological approach arise not only because ecology is intrinsically a critical science—critical on a scale that the most radical systems of political economy have failed to attain—but also because it is an integrative and reconstructive science. This integrative, reconstructive aspect of ecology, carried through to all its implications, leads directly into anarchic areas of social thought. For, in the final analysis, it is impossible to achieve a harmonization of man and nature without creating a human community that lives in a lasting balance with its natural environment.

The Critical Nature of Ecology

The critical edge of ecology, a unique feature of the science in a period of general scientific docility, derives from its subject matter—from its very domain. The issues with which ecology deals are imperishable in the sense that they cannot be ignored without bringing into question the survival of man and the survival of the planet itself. The critical edge of ecology is due not so much to the power of human reason—a power which science hallowed during its most revolutionary periods—but to a still higher power, the sovereignty of nature. It may be that man is manipulable, as the owners of the mass media argue, or that elements of nature are manipulable, as the engineers demonstrate, but ecology clearly shows that the *totality* of the natural world—nature viewed in all its aspects, cycles and interrelationships—cancels out all human pretensions to mastery over the planet. The great wastelands of the Mediterranean basin, once areas of a thriving agriculture or a rich natural flora, are historic evidence of nature's revenge against human parasitism.

No historic examples compare in weight and scope with the effects of man's despoliation—and nature's revenge—since the days of the Industrial Revolution, and especially since the end of the Second World War. Ancient examples of human parasitism were essentially local in scope; they were precisely *examples* of man's potential for destruction, and nothing more. Often, they were compensated by remarkable improvements in the natural ecology of a region, such as the European peasantry's superb reworking of the soil during centuries of cultivation and the achievements of Inca agriculturists in terracing the Andes Mountains during the pre-Columbian times.

Modern man's despoliation of the environment is global in scope, like his imperialisms. It is even extraterrestrial, as witness the disturbances of the Van Allen Belt a few years ago. Today human parasitism disrupts more than the atmosphere, climate, water resources, soil, flora and fauna of a region: it upsets virtually all the basic cycles of nature and threatens to undermine the stability of the environment on a worldwide scale.

As an example of the scope of modern man's disruptive role, it has been estimated that the burning of fossil fuels (coal and oil) adds 600 million tons of carbon dioxide to the air annually, about .03 percent of the total atmospheric mass—this, I may add, aside from an incalculable quantity of toxicants. Since the Industrial Revolution, the overall atmospheric mass of carbon dioxide has increased by 25 percent over earlier, more stable, levels. It can be argued on very sound theoretical grounds that this growing blanket of carbon dioxide, by intercepting heat radiated from the earth, will lead to more destructive storm patterns and eventually to melting of the polar ice caps, rising sea levels, and the inundation of vast land areas. Far removed as such a deluge may be, the changing proportion of carbon dioxide to other atmospheric gases is a warning about the impact man is having on the balance of nature.

A more immediate ecological issue is man's extensive pollution of the earth's waterways. What counts here is not the fact that man befouls a given stream, river or lake—a thing he has done for ages—but rather the magnitude water pollution has reached in the past two generations. Nearly all the surface waters of the United States are now polluted. Many American waterways are open cesspools that properly qualify as extensions of urban sewage systems. It is a euphemism to describe them as rivers or lakes. More significantly, large amounts of ground water are sufficiently polluted to be undrinkable, and a number of local hepatitis epidemics have been traced to polluted wells in suburban areas. In contrast to surface-water pollution, the pollution of ground or subsurface water is immensely difficult to eliminate and tends to linger on for decades after the sources of pollution have been removed.

An article in a mass-circulation magazine appropriately describes the polluted waterways of the United States as "Our Dying Waters." This despairing, apocalyptic description of the water pollution problem in the United States really applies to the world at large. The waters of the earth are literally dying. Massive pollution is destroying the rivers and lakes of Africa, Asia and Latin America, as well as the long-abused waterways of highly industrialized continents, as media of life. (I speak here not only of radioactive pollutants from nuclear bomb tests and power reactors, which apparently reach all the flora and fauna of the sea; the oil spills and the discharge of diesel oil have also become massive pollution problems, claiming marine life in enormous quantities every year.)

Accounts of this kind can be repeated for virtually every part of the biosphere. Pages could be written on the immense losses of productive soil that occur annually in almost every continent of the earth; on lethal air pollution episodes in major urban areas; on the worldwide distribution of toxic agents, such as radioactive isotopes and lead; on the chemicalization of man's immediate environment—one might say his very dinner table— with pesticide residues and food additives. Pieced together like bits of a jigsaw puzzle, these affronts to the environment form a pattern of destruction that has no precedent in man's long history on earth.

Obviously, man could be described as a highly destructive parasite who threatens to destroy his host—the natural world—and eventually himself. In ecology, however, the word "parasite" is not an answer to a question, but raises a question itself. Ecologists know that a destructive parasitism of this kind usually reflects the disruption of an ecological situation; indeed, many species that seem highly destructive under one set of conditions are eminently useful under another set of conditions. What imparts a profoundly critical function to ecology is the question raised by man's destructive abilities: What is the disruption that has turned man into a destructive parasite? What produces a form of parasitism that results not only in vast natural imbalances but also threatens the existence of humanity itself?

Man has produced imbalances not only in nature, but, more fundamentally, in his relations with his fellow man and in the very structure of his society. The imbalances man has produced in the natural world are caused by the imbalances he has produced in the social world. A century ago it would have been possible to regard air pollution and water contamination as the result of the self-seeking activities of industrial barons and bureaucrats. Today, this moral explanation would be a gross oversimplification. It is doubtless true that most bourgeois enterprises are still guided by a public-be-damned attitude, as witness the reactions of power utilities, automobile concerns and steel corporations to pollution problems. But a more serious problem than the attitude of the owners is the size of the firms themselves—their enormous proportions, their location in a particular region, their density with respect to a community or waterway, their requirements for raw materials and water, and their role in the national division of labor.

What we are seeing today is a crisis in social ecology. Modern society, especially as we know it in the United States and Europe, is being organized around immense urban belts, a highly industrialized agriculture and, capping both, a swollen, bureaucratized, anonymous state apparatus. If we put all moral considerations aside for the moment and examine the physical structure of this society, what must necessarily impress us is the incredible logistical problems it is obliged to solve—problems of transportation, of density, of supply (of raw materials, manufactured commodities and foodstuffs), of economic and political organization, of industrial location, and so forth. The burden this type of urbanized and centralized society places on any continental area is enormous.

Diversity and Simplicity

The problem runs even deeper. The notion that man must dominate nature emerges directly from the domination of man by man. The patriarchal family planted the seed of domination in the nuclear relations of humanity; the classical split in the ancient world between spirit and reality —indeed, between mind and labor—nourished it; the antinaturalist bias of

Christianity tended to its growth. But it was not until organic community relations, feudal or peasant in form, dissolved into market relationships that the planet itself was reduced to a resource for exploitation. This centuries-long tendency finds its most exacerbating development in modern capitalism. Owing to its inherently competitive nature, bourgeois society not only pits humans against each other, it also pits the mass of humanity against the natural world. Just as men are converted into commodities, so every aspect of nature is converted into a commodity, a resource to be manufactured and merchandised wantonly. The liberal euphemisms for the processes involved are "growth," "industrial society" and "urban blight." By whatever language they are described, the phenomena have their roots in the domination of man by man.

The phrase "consumer society" complements the description of the present social order as an "industrial society." Needs are tailored by the mass media to create a public demand for utterly useless commodities, each carefully engineered to deteriorate after a predetermined period of time. The plundering of the human spirit by the marketplace is paralleled by the plundering of the earth by capital. (The liberal identification is a metaphor that neutralizes the social thrust of the ecological crisis.)

Despite the current clamor about population growth, the strategic ratios in the ecological crisis are not the population growth rates of India but the production rates of the United States, a country that produces more than half of the world's goods. Here, too, liberal euphemisms like "affluence" conceal the critical thrust of a blunt word like "waste." With a ninth of its industrial capacity committed to war production, the U.S. is literally trampling upon the earth and shredding ecological links that are vital to human survival. If current industrial projections prove to be accurate, the remaining thirty years of the century will witness a fivefold increase in electric power production, based mostly on nuclear fuels and coal. The colossal burden in radioactive wastes and other effluents that this increase will place on the natural ecology of the earth hardly needs description.

In shorter perspective, the problem is no less disquieting. Within the next five years, lumber production may increase an overall twenty percent; the output of paper, five percent annually; folding boxes, three percent annually; plastics (which currently form one to two percent of municipal wastes), seven percent annually. Collectively, these industries account for the most serious pollutants in the environment. The utterly senseless nature of modern industrial activity is perhaps best illustrated by the decline in returnable (and reusable) beer bottles from 54 billion bottles in 1960 to 26 billion today. Their place has been taken over by "one-way" bottles (a rise from 8 to 21 billion in the same period) and cans (an increase from 38 to 53 billion). The "one-way" bottles and the cans, of course, pose tremendous problems in solid waste disposal.

The planet, conceived of as a lump of minerals, can support these mindless increases in the output of trash. The earth, conceived of as a complex web of life, certainly cannot. The only question is whether the earth can survive its looting long enough for man to replace the current destructive social system with a humanistic, ecologically oriented society.

Ecologists are often asked, rather tauntingly, to locate with scientific exactness the ecological breaking point of nature—the point at which the natural world will cave in on man. This is equivalent to asking a psychiatrist for the precise moment when a neurotic will become a nonfunctional psychotic. No such answer is ever likely to be available. But the ecologist can supply a strategic insight into the directions man seems to be following as a result of his split with the natural world.

From the standpoint of ecology, man is dangerously oversimplifying his environment. The modern city represents a regressive encroachment of the synthetic on the natural, of the inorganic (concrete, metals, and glass) on the organic, of crude, elemental stimuli on variegated, wide-ranging ones. The vast urban belts now developing in industrialized areas of the world are not only grossly offensive to the eye and the ear, they are chronically smog-ridden, noisy, and virtually immobilized by congestion.

The process of simplifying man's environment and rendering it increasingly elemental and crude has a cultural as well as a physical dimension. The need to manipulate immense urban populations—to transport, feed, employ, educate and somehow entertain millions of densely concentrated people—leads to a crucial decline in civic and social standards. A mass concept of human relations—totalitarian, centralistic and regimented in orientation—tends to dominate the more individuated concepts of the past. Bureaucratic techniques of social management tend to replace humanistic approaches. All that is spontaneous, creative and individuated is circumscribed by the standardized, the regulated and the massified. The space of the individual is steadily narrowed by restrictions imposed upon him by a faceless, impersonal social apparatus. Any recognition of unique personal qualities is increasingly surrendered to the manipulation of the lowest common denominator of the mass. A quantitative, statistical approach, a beehive manner of dealing with man, tends to triumph over the precious individualized and qualitative approach which places the strongest emphasis on personal uniqueness, free expression and cultural complexity.

The same regressive simplification of the environment occurs in modern agriculture.[2] The manipulated people in modern cities must be fed, and to feed them involves an extension of industrial farming. Food plants must be cultivated in a manner that allows for a high degree of mechanization—not to reduce human toil but to increase productivity and efficiency, to

---

[2] For insight into this problem the reader may consult *The Ecology of Invasions* by Charles S. Elton (Wiley: New York, 1958), *Soil and Civilisation* by Edward Hyams (Thames and Hudson: London, 1952), *Our Synthetic Environment* by Murray Bookchin [pseud. Lewis Herber] (Knopf: New York, 1962), and *Silent Spring* by Rachel Carson (Houghton Mifflin: Boston, 1962). The last should be read not as a diatribe against pesticides but as a plea for ecological diversification.

maximize investments, and to exploit the biosphere. Accordingly, the terrain must be reduced to a flat plain—to a factory floor, if you will—and natural variations in topography must be diminished as much as possible. Plant growth must be closely regulated to meet the tight schedules of food-processing factories. Plowing, soil fertilization, sowing and harvesting must be handled on a mass scale, often in total disregard of the natural ecology of an area. Large areas of the land must be used to cultivate a single crop— a form of plantation agriculture that not only lends itself to mechanization but also to pest infestation. A single crop is the ideal environment for the proliferation of pest species. Finally, chemical agents must be used lavishly to deal with the problems created by insects, weeds, and plant diseases, to regulate crop production, and to maximize soil exploitation. The real symbol of modern agriculture is not the sickle (or, for that matter, the tractor), but the airplane. The modern food cultivator is represented not by the peasant, the yeoman, or even the agronomist—men who could be expected to have an intimate relationship with the unique qualities of the land on which they grow crops—but the pilot or chemist, for whom soil is a mere resource, an inorganic raw material.

The simplification process is carried still further by an exaggerated regional (indeed, national) division of labor. Immense areas of the planet are increasingly reserved for specific industrial tasks or reduced to depots for raw materials. Others are turned into centers of urban population, largely occupied with commerce and trade. Cities and regions (in fact, countries and continents) are specifically identified with special products —Pittsburgh, Cleveland and Youngstown with steel, New York with finance, Bolivia with tin, Arabia with oil, Europe and the U.S. with industrial goods, and the rest of the world with raw materials of one kind or another. The complex ecosystems which make up the regions of a continent are submerged by an organization of entire nations into economically rationalized entities, each a way station in a vast industrial belt-system, global in its dimensions. It is only a matter of time before the most attractive areas of the countryside succumb to the concrete mixer, just as most of the Eastern seaboard areas of the United States have already succumbed to subdivisions and bungalows. What will remain in the way of natural beauty will be debased by trailer lots, canvas slums, "scenic" highways, motels, food stalls and the oil slicks of motor boats.

The point is that man is undoing the work of organic evolution. By creating vast urban agglomerations of concrete, metal and glass, by overriding and undermining the complex, subtly organized ecosystems that constitute local differences in the natural world—in short, by replacing a highly complex, organic environment with a simplified, inorganic one— man is disassembling the biotic pyramid that supported humanity for countless millennia. In the course of replacing the complex ecological relationships, on which all advanced living things depend, for more elementary relationships, man is steadily restoring the biosphere to a stage which will be able to support only simpler forms of life. If this great reversal of the evolutionary process continues, it is by no means fanciful to suppose that the preconditions for higher forms of life will be irreparably destroyed and the earth will become incapable of supporting man himself.

Ecology derives its critical edge not only from the fact that it alone, among all the sciences, presents this awesome message to humanity, but also because it presents this message in a new social dimension. From an ecological viewpoint, the reversal of organic evolution is the result of appalling contradictions between town and country, state and community, industry and husbandry, mass manufacture and craftsmanship, centralism and regionalism, the bureaucratic scale and the human scale.

The Reconstructive Nature of Ecology

Until recently, attempts to resolve the contradictions created by urbanization, centralization, bureaucratic growth and statification were viewed as a vain counterdrift to "progress"—a counterdrift that could be dismissed as chimerical and reactionary. The anarchist was regarded as a forlorn visionary, a social outcast, filled with nostalgia for the peasant village or the medieval commune. His yearning for a decentralized society and for a humanistic community at one with nature and the needs of the individual —the spontaneous individual, unfettered by authority—were viewed as the reactions of a romantic, of a declassed craftsman or an intellectual "misfit." His protest against centralization and statification seemed all the less persuasive because it was supported primarily by ethical considerations—by utopian, ostensibly "unrealistic," notions of what man could be, not by what he was. In response to this protest, opponents of anarchist thought— liberals, rightists and authoritarian "leftists"—argued that they were the voices of historic reality, that their statist and centralist notions were rooted in the objective, practical world.

Time is not very kind to the conflict of ideas. Whatever may have been the validity of libertarian and non-libertarian views a few years ago, historical development has rendered virtually all objections to anarchist thought meaningless today. The modern city and state, the massive coal-steel technology of the Industrial Revolution, the later, more rationalized, systems of mass production and assembly-line systems of labor organization, the centralized nation, the state and its bureaucratic apparatus—all have reached their limits. Whatever progressive or liberatory role they may have possessed, they have now become entirely regressive and oppressive. They are regressive not only because they erode the human spirit and drain the community of all its cohesiveness, solidarity and ethico-cultural standards; they are regressive from an objective standpoint, from an ecological standpoint. For they undermine not only the human spirit and the human community but also the viability of the planet and all living things on it.

It cannot be emphasized too strongly that the anarchist concepts of a balanced community, a face-to-face democracy, a humanistic technology and a decentralized society—these rich libertarian concepts—are not only desirable, they are also necessary. They belong not only to the great visions of man's future, they now constitute the preconditions for human survival. The process of social development has carried them out of the ethical, subjective dimension into a practical, objective dimension. What was once regarded as impractical and visionary has become eminently practical. And what was once regarded as practical and objective has become eminently impractical and irrelevant in terms of man's development towards a fuller, unfettered existence. If we conceive of demands for community, face-to-face democracy, a humanistic liberatory technology and decentralization merely as reactions to the prevailing state of affairs—a vigorous "nay" to the "yea" of what exists today—a compelling, objective case can now be made for the practicality of an anarchist society.

A rejection of the prevailing state of affairs accounts, I think, for the explosive growth of intuitive anarchism among young people today. Their love of nature is a reaction against the highly synthetic qualities of our urban environment and its shabby products. Their informality of dress and manners is a reaction against the formalized, standardized nature of modern institutionalized living. Their predisposition for direct action is a reaction against the bureaucratization and centralization of society. Their tendency to drop out, to avoid toil and the rat race, reflects a growing anger towards the mindless industrial routine bred by modern mass manufacture in the factory, the office or the university. Their intense individualism is, in its own elemental way, a *de facto* decentralization of social life—a personal withdrawal from mass society.

What is most significant about ecology is its ability to convert this often nihilistic rejection of the status quo into an emphatic affirmation of life—indeed, into a reconstructive credo for a humanistic society. The essence of ecology's reconstructive message can be summed up in the word "diversity." From an ecological viewpoint, balance and harmony in nature, in society and, by inference, in behavior, are achieved not by mechanical standardization but by its opposite, organic differentiation. This message can be understood clearly only by examining its practical meaning.

Let us consider the ecological principle of diversity—what Charles Elton calls the "conservation of variety"—as it applies to biology, specifically to agriculture. A number of studies—Lotka's and Volterra's mathematical models, Bause's experiments with protozoa and mites in controlled environments, and extensive field research—clearly demonstrate that fluctuations in animal and plant populations, ranging from mild to pestlike proportions, depend heavily upon the number of species in an ecosystem and on the degree of variety in the environment. The greater the variety of prey and predators, the more stable the population; the more diversified the environment in terms of flora and fauna, the less likely there is to be ecological instability. Stability is a function of variety and diversity: if the environment is simplified and the variety of animal and plant species is reduced, fluctuations in population become marked and tend to get out of control. They tend to reach pest proportions.

In the case of pest control, many ecologists now conclude that we can avoid the repetitive use of toxic chemicals such as insecticides and herbicides by allowing for a greater interplay between living things. We must leave more room for natural spontaneity, for the diverse biological forces that make up an ecological situation. "European entomologists now speak of managing the entire plant-insect community," observes Robert L. Rudd. "It is called manipulation of the biocenose.[3] The biocenetic environment is varied, complex and dynamic. Although numbers of individuals will constantly change, no one species will normally reach pest proportions. The special conditions which allow high populations of a single species in a complex ecosystem are rare events. Management of the biocenose or ecosystem should become our goal, challenging as it is."[4]

The "manipulation" of the biocenose in a meaningful way, however, presupposes a far-reaching decentralization of agriculture. Wherever feasible, industrial agriculture must give way to soil and agricultural husbandry; the factory floor must yield to gardening and horticulture. I do not wish to imply that we must surrender the gains acquired by large-scale agriculture and mechanization. What I *do* contend, however, is that the land must be cultivated as though it were a garden; its flora must be diversified and carefully tended, balanced by fauna and tree shelter appropriate to the region. Decentralization is important, moreover, for the development of the agriculturist as well as for the development of agriculture. Food cultivation, practiced in a truly ecological sense, presupposes that the agriculturist is familiar with all the features and subtleties of the terrain on which the crops are grown. He must have a thorough knowledge of the physiography of the land, its variegated soils—crop land, forest land, pasture land —its mineral and organic content and its micro-climate, and he must be engaged in a continuing study of the effects produced by new flora and fauna. He must develop his sensitivity to the land's possibilities and needs while he becomes an organic part of the agricultural situation. We can hardly hope to achieve this high degree of sensitivity and integration in the food cultivator without reducing agriculture to a human scale, without bringing agriculture within the scope of the individual. To meet the de-

[3] Rudd's use of the word "manipulation" is likely to create the erroneous impression that an ecological situation can be described by simple mechanical terms. Lest this impression arise, I would like to emphasize that our knowledge of an ecological situation and the practical use of this knowledge are matters of insight rather than power. Charles Elton states the case for the management of an ecological situation when he writes: "The world's future has to be managed, but this management would not be like a game of chess . . . [but] more like steering a boat."

[4] Robert L. Rudd, "Pesticides: The *Real* Peril," *The Nation*, vol. 189 (1959), p. 401.

mands of an ecological approach to food cultivation, agriculture must be rescaled from huge industrial farms to moderate-sized units.

The same reasoning applies to a rational development of energy resources. The Industrial Revolution increased the *quantity* of energy used by man. Although it is certainly true that preindustrial societies relied primarily on animal power and human muscles, complex energy patterns developed in many regions of Europe, involving a subtle integration of resources such as wind and water power, and a variety of fuels (wood, peat, coal, vegetable starches and animal fats).

The Industrial Revolution overwhelmed and largely destroyed these regional energy patterns, replacing them first by a single energy system (coal) and later by a dual system (coal and petroleum). Regions disappeared as models of integrated energy patterns—indeed, the very concept of *integration through diversity* was obliterated. As I indicated earlier, many regions became predominantly mining areas, devoted to the extraction of a single resource, while others were turned into immense industrial areas, often devoted to the production of a few commodities. We need not review the role this breakdown in true regionalism has played in producing air and water pollution, the damage it has inflicted on large areas of the countryside, and the prospect we face in the depletion of our precious hydrocarbon fuels.

We can, of course, turn to nuclear fuels, but it is chilling to think of the lethal radioactive wastes that would require disposal if power reactors were our sole energy source. Eventually, an energy system based on radioactive materials would lead to the widespread contamination of the environment—at first in a subtle form, but later on a masssive and palpably destructive scale. Or we could apply ecological principles to the solution of our energy problems. We could try to re-establish earlier regional energy patterns, using a combined system of energy provided by wind, water and solar power. We would be aided by devices more sophisticated than any known in the past.

Solar devices, wind turbines and hydro-electric resources, taken singly, do not provide a solution for our energy problems and the ecological disruption created by conventional fuels. Pieced together as a mosaic, as an organic energy pattern developed from the potentialities of a region, they could amply meet the needs of a decentralized society. In sunny latitudes, we could rely more heavily on solar energy than on combustible fuels. In areas marked by atmospheric turbulence, we could rely more heavily on wind devices; and in suitable coastal areas or inland regions with a good network of rivers, the greater part of our energy would come from hydro-electric installations. In all cases, we would use a *mosaic* of non-combustible, combustible, and nuclear fuels. The point I wish to make is that by diversifying our use of energy resources, by organizing them into an ecologically balanced pattern, we could combine wind, solar and water power in a given region to meet the industrial and domestic needs of a given community with only a minimum use of harmful fuels. And, eventually, we might sophisticate our non-combustion energy devices to a point where all harmful sources of energy could be eliminated.

As in the case of agriculture, however, the application of ecological principles to energy resources presupposes a far-reaching decentralization of society and a truly regional concept of social organization. To maintain a large city requires immense quantities of coal and petroleum. By contrast, solar, wind and tidal energy reach us mainly in small packets; except for spectacular tidal dams, the new devices seldom provide more than a few thousand kilowatt-hours of electricity. It is difficult to believe that we will ever be able to design solar collectors that can furnish us with the immense blocks of electric power produced by a giant steam plant; it is equally difficult to conceive of a battery of wind turbines that will provide us with enough electricity to illuminate Manhattan Island. If homes and factories are heavily concentrated, devices for using clean sources of energy will probably remain mere playthings; but if urban communities are reduced in size and widely dispersed over the land, there is no reason why these devices cannot be combined to provide us with all the amenities of an industrialized civilization. To use solar, wind and tidal power effectively, the megalopolis must be decentralized. A new type of community, carefully tailored to the characteristics and resources of a region, must replace the sprawling urban belts that are emerging today.

To be sure, an objective case for decentralization does not end with a discussion of agriculture and the problems created by combustible energy resources. The validity of the decentralist case can be demonstrated for nearly all the "logistical" problems of our time. Let me cite an example from the problematical area of transportation. A great deal has been written about the harmful effects of gasoline-driven motor vehicles—their wastefulness, their role in urban air pollution, the noise they contribute to the city environment, the enormous death toll they claim annually in the large cities of the world and on highways. In a highly urbanized civilization it would be useless to replace these noxious vehicles by clean, efficient, virtually noiseless, and certainly safer, battery-powered vehicles. The best of our electric cars must be recharged about every hundred miles—a feature which limits their usefulness for transportation in large cities. In a small, decentralized community, however, it would be feasible to use these electric vehicles for urban or regional transportation and establish monorail networks for long-distance transportation.

It is fairly well known that gasoline-powered vehicles contribute enormously to urban air pollution, and there is a strong sentiment to "engineer" the more noxious features of the automobile into oblivion. Our age characteristically tries to solve all its irrationalities with a gimmick—afterburners for toxic gasoline fumes, antibiotics for ill health, tranquilizers for psychic disturbances. But the problem of urban air pollution is too intractable for gimmicks; perhaps it is more intractable than we care to believe.

Basically, air pollution is caused by high population densities—by an excessive concentration of people in a small area. Millions of people, densely concentrated in a large city, necessarily produce serious *local* air pollution merely by their day-to-day activities. They must burn fuels for domestic and industrial reasons; they must construct or tear down buildings (the aerial debris produced by these activities is a major source of urban air pollution); they must dispose of immense quantities of rubbish; they must travel on roads with rubber tires (the particles produced by the erosion of tires and roadway materials add significantly to air pollution). Whatever pollution-control devices we add to automobiles and power plants, the improvements these devices will produce in the quality of urban air will be more than canceled out by future megalopolitan growth.

There is more to anarchism than decentralized communities. If I have examined this possibility in some detail, it has been to demonstrate that an anarchist society, far from being a remote ideal, has become a precondition for the practice of ecological principles. To sum up the critical message of ecology: if we diminish variety in the natural world, we debase its unity and wholeness; we destroy the forces making for natural harmony and for a lasting equilibrium; and, what is even more significant, we introduce an absolute retrogression in the development of the natural world which may eventually render the environment unfit for advanced forms of life. To sum up the reconstructive message of ecology: if we wish to advance the unity and stability of the natural world, if we wish to harmonize it, we must conserve and promote variety. To be sure, mere variety for its own sake is a vacuous goal. In nature, variety emerges spontaneously. The capacities of a new species are tested by the rigors of climate, by its ability to deal with predators and by its capacity to establish and enlarge its niche. *Yet the species that succeeds in enlarging its niche in the environment also enlarges the ecological situation as a whole.* To borrow E. A. Gutkind's phrase, it "expands the environment,"[5] both for itself and for the species with which it enters into a balanced relationship.

How do these concepts apply to social theory? To many readers, I suppose, it should suffice to say that, inasmuch as man is part of nature, an expanding natural environment enlarges the basis for social development. But the answer to the question goes much deeper than many ecologists and libertarians suspect. Again, allow me to return to the ecological principle of wholeness and balance as a product of diversity. Keeping this principle in mind, the first step towards an answer is provided by a passage in Herbert Read's "The Philosophy of Anarchism." In presenting his "measure of progress," Read observes: "Progress is measured by the degree of differentiation within a society. If the individual is a unit in a corporate mass, his life will be limited, dull, and mechanical. If the individual is a

---

[5] E. A. Gutkind, *The Twilight of the Cities* (Free Press of Glencoe, Inc.: New York, 1962), pp. 55–144.

unit on his own, with space and potentiality for separate action, then he may be more subject to accident or chance, but at least he can expand and express himself. He can develop—develop in the only real meaning of the word—develop in consciousness of strength, vitality, and joy."

Read's thought, unfortunately, is not fully developed, but it provides an interesting point of departure. What first strikes us is that both the ecologist and the anarchist place a strong emphasis on spontaneity. The ecologist, insofar as he is more than a technician, tends to reject the notion of "power over nature." He speaks, instead, of "steering" his way through an ecological situation, of *managing* rather than *recreating* an ecosystem. The anarchist, in turn, speaks in terms of social spontaneity, of releasing the potentialities of society and humanity, of giving free and unfettered rein to the creativity of people. Both, in their own way, regard authority as inhibitory, as a weight limiting the creative potential of a natural and social situation. Their object is not to *rule* a domain, but to *release* it. They regard insight, reason and knowledge as means for fulfilling the potentialities of a situation, as facilitating the working out of the logic of a situation, not as replacing its potentialities with preconceived notions or distorting their development with dogmas.

Turning to Read's words, what strikes us is that both the ecologist and the anarchist view differentiation as a measure of progress. The ecologist uses the term "biotic pyramid" in speaking of biological advances; the anarchist, the word "individuation" to denote social advances. If we go beyond Read we will observe that, to both the ecologist and the anarchist, an ever-increasing unity is achieved by growing differentiation. *An expanding whole is created by the diversification and enrichment of its parts.*

Just as the ecologist seeks to expand the range of an ecosystem and promote a free interplay between species, so the anarchist seeks to expand the range of social experience and remove all fetters to its development. Anarchism is not only a stateless society but also a harmonized society which exposes man to the stimuli provided by both agrarian and urban life, to physical activity and mental activity, to unrepressed sensuality and self-directed spirituality, to command solidarity and individual development, to regional uniqueness and worldwide brotherhood, to spontaneity and self-discipline, to the elimination of toil and the promotion of craftsmanship. In our schizoid society, these goals are regarded as mutually exclusive, indeed as sharply opposed. They appear as dualities because of the very logistics of present-day society—the separation of town and country, the specialization of labor, the atomization of man—and it would be preposterous to believe that these dualities could be resolved without a general idea of the *physical* structure of an anarchist society. We can gain some idea of what such a society would be like by reading William Morris's *News From Nowhere* and the writings of Peter Kropotkin. But these works provide us with mere glimpses. They do not take into account the post–World War II developments of technology and the contributions made by the development of ecology. This is not the place to embark on "utopian writing," but certain guidelines can be presented even in a general discussion. And in presenting these guidelines, I am eager to emphasize not only the more obvious ecological premises that support them, but also the humanistic ones.

An anarchist society should be a decentralized society, not only to establish a lasting basis for the harmonization of man and nature, *but also to add new dimensions to the harmonization of man and man.* The Greeks, we are often reminded, would have been horrified by a city whose size and population precluded a face-to-face, often familiar, relationship between citizens. There is plainly a need to reduce the dimensions of the human community—partly to solve our pollution and transportation problems, partly also to create *real* communities. In a sense, we must *humanize* humanity. Electronic devices such as telephones, telegraphs, radios and television receivers should be used as little as possible to mediate the relations between people. In making collective decisions—the ancient Athenian ecclesia was, in some ways, a model for making social decisions—all members of the community should have an opportunity to acquire in full the measure of anyone who addresses the assembly. They should be in a position to absorb his attitudes, study his expressions, and weigh his motives as well as his ideas in a direct personal encounter and through face-to-face discussion.

Our small communities should be economically balanced and well rounded, partly so that they can make full use of local raw materials and energy resources, partly also to enlarge the agricultural and industrial stimuli to which individuals are exposed. The member of a community who has a predilection for engineering, for instance, should be encouraged to steep his hands in humus; the man of ideas should be encouraged to employ his musculature; the "inborn" farmer should gain a familiarity with the workings of a rolling mill. To separate the engineer from the soil, the thinker from the spade, and the farmer from the industrial plant promotes a degree of vocational overspecialization that leads to a dangerous measure of social control by specialists. What is equally important, professional and vocational specialization prevents society from achieving a vital goal: the humanization of nature by the technician and the naturalization of society by the biologist.

I submit that an anarchist community would approximate a clearly definable ecosystem; it would be diversified, balanced and harmonious. It is arguable whether such an ecosystem would acquire the configuration of an urban entity with a distinct center, such as we find in the Greek *polis* or the medieval commune, or whether, as Gutkind proposes, society would consist of widely dispersed communities without a distinct center. In any case, the ecological scale for any of these communities would be determined by the smallest ecosystem capable of supporting a population of moderate size.

A relatively self-sufficient community, visibly dependent on its environment for the means of life, would gain a new respect for the organic inter-relationships that sustain it. In the long run, the attempt to approximate self-sufficiency would, I think, prove more efficient than the exaggerated national division of labor that prevails today. Although there would doubt-less be many duplications of small industrial facilities from community to community, the familiarity of each group with its local environment and its ecological roots would make for a more intelligent and more loving use of its environment. I submit that, far from producing provincialism, relative self-sufficiency would create a new matrix for individual and communal development—a oneness with the surroundings that would vitalize the community.

The rotation of civic, vocational and professional responsibilities would stimulate the senses in the being of the individual, creating and rounding out new dimensions in self-development. In a complete society we could hope to create complete men; in a rounded society, rounded men. In the Western world, the Athenians, for all their shortcomings and limitations, were the first to give us a notion of this completeness. "The *polis* was made for the amateur," H. D. F. Kitto tells us. "Its ideal was that every citizen (more or less, according as the *polis* was democratic or oligarchic) should play his part in all of its many activities—an ideal that is recognizably descended from the generous Homeric conception of *arete* as an all-round excellence and an all-round activity. It implies a respect for the wholeness or the oneness of life, and a consequent dislike of specialization. It implies a contempt for efficiency—or rather a much higher ideal of efficiency; and efficiency which exists not in one department of life, but in life itself."[6] An anarchist society, although it would surely aspire to more, could hardly hope to achieve less than this state of mind.

If the ecological community is ever achieved in practice, social life will yield a sensitive development of human and natural diversity, falling to-gether into a well balanced, harmonious whole. Ranging from community through region to entire continents, we will see a colorful differentiation of human groups and ecosystems, each developing its unique potentialities and exposing members of the community to a wide spectrum of economic, cultural and behavioral stimuli. Falling within our purview will be an exciting, often dramatic, variety of communal forms—here marked by architectural and industrial adaptations to semi-arid ecosystems, there to grasslands, elsewhere by adaptation to forested areas. We will witness a creative interplay between individual and group, community and environment, humanity and nature. The cast of mind that today organizes differ-ences among humans and other life-forms along hierarchical lines, defining the external in terms of its "superiority" or "inferiority," will give way to an outlook that deals with diversity in an ecological manner. Differences

[6] H. D. F. Kitto, *The Greeks* (Aldine: Chicago, 1951), p. 16.

among people will be respected, indeed fostered, as elements that enrich the unity of experience and phenomena. The traditional relationship which pits subject against object will be altered qualitatively; the "external," the "different," the "other" will be conceived of as individual parts of a whole all the richer because of its complexity. This new sense of unity will reflect the harmonization of interests between individuals and between society and nature. Freed from an oppressive routine, from paralyzing repressions and insecurities, from the burdens of toil and false needs, from the trammels of authority and irrational compulsion, individuals will finally, for the first time in history, be in a position to realize their potentialities as members of the human community and the natural world.

SECTION 6

OBEDIENCE, CRIME, AND THE LAW

THE CHIEF PURPOSE of law and law enforcement is to uphold the interests of the ruling groups in a society. The function of police on the domestic level, and the army on the international level, is to protect existing privileges. In capitalist nations like the United States the laws stress protection of private property, because that is the chief concern of the ruling groups. In state socialist countries like Russia, though the laws may be different, their purpose is the same: to uphold the existing system of power and privilege.

There is an irremediable conflict between blacks and the police, because police are the guardians of the existing order and the blacks are its chief victims, Cleaver says.[1] However, policemen do their jobs because they are paid to do them. Cleaver warns that the real enemies of the blacks and others oppressed by the police are those who give the orders: the rich, the corporation executives, the government officials.

There are laws to protect property, government, and persons. But none of these laws promote justice in any way, according to Kropotkin, nor do they prevent crime. The best way to eliminate crime is to reconstruct

[1] This is true even where some blacks are co-opted into the police force.

174

society, not to pass laws. Eliminate private property[2] and economic in-quality, and you won't need laws protecting property. Abolish the state and you won't need legislation about crimes against the state. Crimes against the person, such as murder, rape, and assault, are not deterred by the existence of laws. There will probably always be some "crimes of passion," but their incidence will be much reduced in a properly reconstructed society.

If we really wanted to eliminate murder we would abolish the state, because states maintain themselves by preparing for and waging wars. As Bourne put it, war is the health of the state.[3] The state commits more crimes than individuals do, but individuals are punished and states are not.[4] The punishment of soldiers for perpetrating "war crimes" only masks the criminality of their governments. The trial of American officers for ordering the massacre of Vietnamese civilians at My Lai diverted public attention from the much greater culpability of the government that sent them there in the first place.

The experiment Milgram describes was designed to investigate the conditions under which subjects would obey or refuse orders to hurt other people. The experimenter instructed naive subjects to administer electric shocks to a third party. The subjects were made to believe that they were taking part in a study of the effect of punishment on learning. (The victims simulated pain, but did not actually receive any shocks.)

The subjects were college students and citizens from the surrounding community. They were paid in advance and told they could quit any time. The surprising finding was that a large proportion of subjects obediently administered "electric shocks" to the victim in spite of his protests and cries. When the victim was in another room, two-thirds of the subjects cooperated with the experimenter all the way. And even when the subjects were in close proximity to the victim and were ordered by the experimenter to force his hand onto the "shockplate" one quarter of them continued to obey to the end. Milgram concludes that average Americans will obey orders to mistreat their fellow human beings so long as they perceive the orders as coming from legitimate authority.

Cooperation with and obedience to authority that is seen as legitimate is what makes repressive government possible. Well-intentioned people

[2] The so-called right of private property, Kropotkin says, is actually the right to appropriate the product of other people's labor. Industrialists do not build their factories with their own hands, but exploit the labor of others and reap the profits. Similarly, the wealthy live in houses that others have built, and which derive much of their value from the labor that others have put into making roads, building other houses, and planting parks.

[3] Randolph S. Bourne, *War and the Intellectuals* (New York: Harper & Row, 1964).

[4] See Alex Comfort, *Authority and Delinquency in the Modern State* (London: Routledge and Kegan Paul, 1950).

who do not question their government go about their everyday jobs and pay their taxes because they don't see how their actions contribute to do harm to others far away. (Because most people obey voluntarily, force can be used effectively against the few who refuse.) Evils like the Vietnam War are facilitated by a complex system for the most part comprised of millions of individuals who never see the actual violence. This system includes the engineers and machinists who make the weapons, the revenue agents who collect taxes so the army can buy them, the truck drivers who transport them, and soldiers who finally use them. For every soldier sent to the front there are dozens of persons who carry out research, procure supplies, transmit messages, and so on. Once the entire war machine is set in motion, it takes relatively few individuals to do the actual dirty work of dropping bombs, burning villages, guarding concentration camps, and torturing or killing prisoners.

Law and Authority

Peter Kropotkin

In existing States a fresh law is looked upon as a remedy for evil. Instead of themselves altering what is bad, people begin by demanding a *law* to alter it. If the road between two villages is impassable, the peasant says:—"There should be a law about parish roads." If a park-keeper takes advantage of the want of spirit in those who follow him with servile observance and insults one of them, the insulted man says, "There should be a law to enjoin more politeness upon park-keepers." If there is stagnation in agriculture or commerce, the husbandman, cattle-breeder, or corn speculator argues, "It is protective legislation that we require." Down to the old clothes man there is not one who does not demand a law to protect his own little trade. If the employer lowers wages or increases the hours of labor, the politician in embryo exclaims, "We must have a law to put all that to rights." In short, a law everywhere and for everything! A law about fashions, a law about mad dogs, a law about virtue, a law to put a stop to all the vices and all the evils which result from human indolence and cowardice.

We are so perverted by an education which from infancy seeks to kill in us the spirit of revolt, and to develop that of submission to authority; we

FROM *Kropotkin's Revolutionary Pamphlets*, edited by Roger N. Baldwin. (New York: Vanguard Press, 1927), pp. 196–206; 212–218.

are so perverted by this existence under the ferrule of a law which regulates every event in life—our birth, our education, our development, our love, our friendship—that, if this state of things continues, we shall lose all initiative, all habit of thinking for ourselves. Our society seems no longer able to understand that it is possible to exist otherwise than under the reign of law, elaborated by a representative government and administered by a handful of rulers. And even when it has gone so far as to emancipate itself from the thralldom, its first care has been to reconstitute it immediately. "The Year I of Liberty" has never lasted more than a day, for after proclaiming it men put themselves the very next morning under the yoke of law and authority.

Indeed, for some thousands of years, those who govern us have done nothing but ring the changes upon "Respect for law, obedience to authority." This is the moral atmosphere in which parents bring up their children, and school only serves to confirm the impression. Cleverly assorted scraps of spurious science are inculcated upon the children to prove necessity of law; obedience to the law is made a religion; moral goodness and the law of the masters are fused into one and the same divinity. The historical hero of the schoolroom is the man who obeys the law, and defends it against rebels.

Later when we enter upon public life, society and literature, impressing us day by day and hour by hour as the water-drop hollows the stone, continue to inculcate the same prejudice. Books of history, of political science, of social economy, are stuffed with this respect for law. Even the physical sciences have been pressed into the service by introducing artificial modes of expression, borrowed from theology and arbitrary power, into knowledge which is purely the result of observation. Thus our intelligence is successfully befogged, and always to maintain our respect for law. The same work is done by newspapers. They have not an article which does not preach respect for law, even where the third page proves every day the imbecility of that law, and shows how it is dragged through every variety of mud and filth by those charged with its administration. Servility before the law has become a virtue, and I doubt if there was ever even a revolutionist who did not begin in his youth as the defender of law against what are generally called "abuses," although these last are inevitable consequences of the law itself.

* * *

The critics analyze the sources of law, and find there either a god, product of the terrors of the savage, and stupid, paltry and malicious as the priests who vouch for its supernatural origin, or else, bloodshed, conquest by fire and sword. They study the characteristics of law, and instead of perpetual growth corresponding to that of the human race, they find its distinctive trait to be immobility, a tendency to crystallize what should be modified and developed day by day. They ask how law has been maintained, and in its service they see the atrocities of Byzantinism, the cruelties of the Inquisition, the tortures of the middle ages, living flesh torn by the lash of the executioner, chains, clubs, axes, the gloomy dungeons of prisons, agony, curses and tears. In our own days they see, as before, the axe, the cord, the rifle, the prison; on the one hand, the brutalized prisoner, reduced to the condition of a caged beast by the debasement of his whole moral being, and on the other, the judge, stripped of every feeling which does honor to human nature, living like a visionary in a world of legal fictions, revelling in the infliction of imprisonment and death, without even suspecting, in the cold malignity of his madness, the abyss of degradation into which he has himself fallen before the eyes of those whom he condemns.

They see a race of law-makers legislating without knowing what their laws are about; today voting a law on the sanitation of towns, without the faintest notion of hygiene, tomorrow making regulations for the armament of troops, without so much as understanding a gun; making laws about teaching and education without ever having given a lesson of any sort, or even an honest education to their own children; legislating at random in all directions, but never forgetting the penalties to be meted out to ragamuffins, the prison and the galleys, which are to be the portion of men a thousand times less immoral than these legislators themselves.

Finally, they see the jailer on the way to lose all human feelings, the detective trained as a blood-hound, the police spy despising himself; "informing," metamorphosed into a virtue; corruption, erected into a system; all the vices, all the evil qualities of mankind countenanced and cultivated to insure the triumph of law.

All this we see, and, therefore, instead of inanely repeating the old formula, "Respect the law," we say, "Despise law and all its attributes!" In place of the cowardly phrase, "Obey the law," our cry is "Revolt against all laws!"

Only compare the misdeeds accomplished in the name of each law with the good it has been able to effect, and weigh carefully both good and evil, and you will see if we are right.

Relatively speaking, law is a product of modern times. For ages and ages mankind lived without any written law, even that graved in symbols upon the entrance stones of a temple. During that period, human relations were simply regulated by customs, habits and usages, made sacred by constant repetition, and acquired by each person in childhood, exactly as he learned how to obtain his food by hunting, cattle-rearing, or agriculture.

All human societies have passed through this primitive phase, and to this day a large proportion of mankind have no written law. Every tribe has its own manners and customs; customary law, as the jurists say. It has social habits, and that suffices to maintain cordial relations between the inhabitants of the village, the members of the tribe or community. Even amongst ourselves—the "civilized" nations—when we leave large towns, and go into the country, we see that there the mutual relations of the inhabitants are still regulated according to ancient and generally accepted customs, and not according to the written law of the legislators. The peasants of Russia, Italy, and Spain, and even of a large part of France and England, have no conception of written law. It only meddles with their lives to regulate their relations with the State. As to relations between themselves, though these are sometimes very complex, they are simply regulated according to ancient custom. Formerly, this was the case with mankind in general.

*   *   *

But as society became more and more divided into two hostile classes, one seeking to establish its domination, the other struggling to escape, the strife began. Now the conqueror was in a hurry to secure the results of his actions in a permanent form, he tried to place them beyond question, to make them holy and venerable by every means in his power. Law made its appearance under the sanction of the priest, and the warrior's club was placed at its service. Its office was to render immutable such customs as were to the advantage of the dominant minority. Military authority undertook to ensure obedience. This new function was a fresh guarantee to the power of the warrior; now he had not only mere brute force at his service; he was the defender of law.

If law, however, presented nothing but a collection of prescriptions serviceable to rulers, it would find some difficulty in insuring acceptance and obedience. Well, the legislators confounded in one code the two currents of custom of which we have just been speaking, the maxims which represent principles of morality and social union wrought out as a result of life in common, and the mandates which are meant to ensure external existence to inequality. Customs, absolutely essential to the very being of society, are, in the code, cleverly intermingled with usages imposed by the ruling caste, and both claim equal respect from the crowd. "Do not kill," says the code, and hastens to add, "And pay tithes to the priest." "Do not steal," says the code, and immediately after, "He who refuses to pay taxes, shall have his hand struck off."

Such was law; and it has maintained its two-fold character to this day. Its origin is the desire of the ruling class to give permanence to customs imposed by themselves for their own advantage. Its character is the skillful commingling of customs useful to society, customs which have no need of law to insure respect, with other customs useful only to rulers, injurious to the mass of the people, and maintained only by the fear of punishment.

Like individual capital, which was born of fraud and violence, and developed under the auspices of authority, law has no title to the respect of men. Born of violence and superstition, and established in the interests of consumer, priest and rich exploiter, it must be utterly destroyed on the day when the people desire to break their chains.

*   *   *

The millions of laws which exist for the regulation of humanity appear upon investigation to be divided into three principal categories: protection of property, protection of persons, protection of government. And by analyzing each of these three categories, we arrive at the same logical and necessary conclusion: *the uselessness and hurtfulness of law.*

Socialists know what is meant by protection of property. Laws on property are not made to guarantee either to the individual or to society the enjoyment of the produce of their own labor. On the contrary, they are made to rob the producer of a part of what he has created, and to secure to certain other people that portion of the produce which they have stolen either from the producer or from society as a whole. When, for example, the law establishes Mr. So-and-So's right to a house, it is not establishing his right to a cottage he has built for himself, or to a house he has erected with the help of some of his friends. In that case no one would have disputed his right. On the contrary, the law is establishing his right to a house which is *not* the product of his labor; first of all because he has it built for him by others to whom he has not paid the full value of their work, and next because that house represents a social value which he could not have produced for himself. The law is establishing his right to what belongs to everybody in general and to nobody in particular. The same house built in the midst of Siberia would not have the value it possesses in a large town, and, as we know, that value arises from the labor of something like fifty generations of men who have built the town, beautified it, supplied it with water and gas, fine promenades, colleges, theatres, shops, railways and roads leading in all directions. Thus, by recognizing the right of Mr. So-and-So to a particular house in Paris, London or Rouen, the law is unjustly appropriating to him a certain portion of the produce of the labor of mankind in general. And it is precisely because this appropriation and all other forms of property bearing the same character are a crying injustice, that a whole arsenal of laws and a whole army of soldiers, policemen and judges are needed to maintain it against the good sense and just feeling inherent in humanity.

Half our laws—the civil code in each country—serves no other purpose than to maintain this appropriation, this monopoly for the benefit of certain individuals against the whole of mankind. Three-fourths of the causes decided by the tribunals are nothing but quarrels between monopolists— two robbers disputing over their booty. And a great many of our criminal laws have the same object in view, their end being to keep the workman in a subordinate position towards his employer, and thus afford security for exploitation.

As for guaranteeing the product of his labor to the producer, there are no laws which even attempt such a thing. It is so simple and natural, so much a part of the manners and customs of mankind, that law has not given it so much as a thought. Open brigandage, sword in hand, is no feature of our age. Neither does one workman ever come and dispute the produce of his labor with another. If they have a misunderstanding they settle it by calling in a third person, without having recourse to law. The only person who exacts from another what the other has produced, is the proprietor, who comes in and deducts the lion's share. As for humanity in general, it everywhere respects the right of each to what he has created, without the interposition of any special laws.

As all the laws about property which make up thick volumes of codes and are the delight of our lawyers have no other object than to protect the unjust appropriation of human labor by certain monopolists, there is no reason for their existence, and, on the day of the revolution, social revolutionists are thoroughly determined to put an end to them. Indeed, a bonfire might be made with perfect justice of all laws bearing upon the so-called "rights of property," all title-deeds, all registers, in a word, of all that is in any way connected with an institution which will soon be looked upon as a blot in the history of humanity, as humiliating as the slavery and serfdom of past ages.

The remarks just made upon laws concerning property are quite as applicable to the second category of laws; those for the maintenance of government, i.e., constitutional law.

It again is a complete arsenal of laws, decrees, ordinances, orders in council, and what not, all serving to protect the diverse forms of representative government, delegated or usurped, beneath which humanity is writhing. We know very well—anarchists have often enough pointed out in their perpetual criticism of the various forms of government—that the mission of all governments, monarchical, constitutional, or republican, is to protect and maintain by force the privileges of the classes in possession, the aristocracy, clergy and traders. A good third of our laws—and each country possesses some tens of thousands of them—the fundamental laws on taxes, excise duties, the organization of ministerial departments and their offices, of the army, the police, the church, etc., have no other end than to maintain, patch up, and develop the administrative machine. And this machine in its turn serves almost entirely to protect the privileges of the possessing classes. Analyze all these laws, observe them in action day by day, and you will discover that not one is worth preserving.

About such laws there can be no two opinions. Not only anarchists, but more or less revolutionary radicals also, are agreed that the only use to be made of laws concerning the organization of government is to fling them into the fire.

The third category of law still remains to be considered; that relating to the protection of the person and the detection and prevention of "crime." This is the most important because most prejudices attach to it; because, if law enjoys a certain amount of consideration, it is in consequence of the belief that this species of law is absolutely indispensable to the maintenance of security in our societies. These are laws developed from the nucleus of customs useful to human communities, which have been turned to account by rulers to sanctify their own domination. The authority of the chiefs of tribes, of rich families in towns, and of the king, depended upon their judicial functions, and even down to the present day, whenever the necessity of government is spoken of, its function as supreme judge is the thing implied. "Without a government men would tear one another to pieces," argues the village orator. "The ultimate end of all government is to secure twelve honest jurymen to every accused person," said Burke.

Well, in spite of all the prejudices existing on this subject, it is quite time that anarchists should boldly declare this category of laws as useless and injurious as the preceding ones.

First of all, as to so-called "crimes"—assaults upon persons—it is well known that two-thirds, and often as many as three-fourths, of such "crimes" are instigated by the desire to obtain possession of someone's wealth. This immense class of so-called "crimes and misdemeanors" will disappear on the day on which private property ceases to exist. "But," it will be said, "there will always be brutes who will attempt the lives of their fellow citizens, who will lay their hands to a knife in every quarrel, and revenge the slightest offense by murder, if there are no laws to restrain and punishments to withhold them." This refrain is repeated every time the right of society to *punish* is called in question.

Yet there is one fact concerning this head which at the present time is thoroughly established; the severity of punishment does not diminish the amount of crime. . . .

* * *

We are continually being told of the benefits conferred by law, and the beneficial effect of penalties, but have the speakers ever attempted to strike a balance between the benefits attributed to laws and penalties, and the degrading effect of these penalties upon humanity? Only calculate all the evil passions awakened in mankind by the atrocious punishments formerly inflicted in our streets! Man is the cruelest animal upon earth. And who has pampered and developed the cruel instincts unknown, even among monkeys, if it is not the king, the judge, and the priests, armed with law, who caused flesh to be torn off in strips, boiling pitch to be poured into wounds, limbs to be dislocated, bones to be crushed, men to be sawn asunder to maintain their authority? Only estimate the torrent of depravity let loose in human society by the "informing" which is countenanced by judges, and paid in hard cash by governments, under pretext of assisting in the discovery of "crime." Only go into the jails and study what man becomes when he is deprived of freedom and shut up with other depraved beings, steeped in the vice and corruption which oozes from the very walls

of our existing prisons. Only remember that the more these prisons are reformed, the more detestable they become. Our model modern peniten-
tiaries are a hundred-fold more abominable than the dungeons of the
middle ages. Finally, consider what corruption, what depravity of mind is
kept up among men by the idea of obedience, the very essence of law; of
chastisement; of authority having the right to punish, to judge irrespective
of our conscience and the esteem of our friends; of the necessity for execu-
tioners, jailers, and informers—in a word, by all the attributes of law and
authority. Consider all this, and you will assuredly agree with us in saying
that a law inflicting penalties is an abomination which should cease to exist.

Peoples without political organization, and therefore less depraved than
ourselves, have perfectly understood that the man who is called "criminal"
is simply unfortunate; that the remedy is not to flog him, to chain him up,
or to kill him on the scaffold or in prison, but to help him by the most
brotherly care, by treatment based on equality, by the usages of life among
honest men. In the next revolution we hope that this cry will go forth:

"Burn the guillotines; demolish the prisons; drive away the judges,
policemen and informers—the impurest race upon the face of the earth;
treat as a brother the man who has been led by passion to do ill to his
fellow; above all, take from the ignoble products of middle-class idleness
the possibility of displaying their vices in attractive colors; and be sure that
but few crimes will mar our society."

The main supports of crime are idleness, law and authority; laws about
property, laws about government, laws about penalties and misdemeanors;
and authority, which takes upon itself to manufacture these laws and to
apply them.

No more laws! No more judges! Liberty, equality, and practical human
sympathy are the only effectual barriers we can oppose to the anti-social
instincts of certain among us.

Obedience and Disobedience to Authority

Stanley Milgram

The situation in which one agent commands another to hurt a third
turns up time and again as a significant theme in human relations. It is
powerfully expressed in the story of Abraham, who is commanded by God
to kill his son. It is no accident that Kierkegaard, seeking to orient his
thought to the central themes of human experience, chose Abraham's
conflict as the springboard to his philisophy.

FROM *Human Relations* Vol. 18, No. 1 (1965), pp. 57–75. Abridged with permission.

War too moves forward on the triad of an authority which commands a person to destroy the enemy, and perhaps all organized hostility may be viewed as a theme and variation on the three elements of authority, executant, and victim. We describe an experimental program, recently concluded at Yale University, in which a particular expression of this conflict is studied by experimental means.

In its most general form the problem may be defined thus: if X tells Y to hurt Z, under what conditions will Y carry out the command of X and under what conditions will he refuse. In the more limited form possible in laboratory research, the question becomes: if an experimenter tells a subject to hurt another person, under what conditions will the subject go along with this instruction, and under what conditions will he refuse to obey. The laboratory problem is not so much a dilution of the general statement as one concrete expression of the many particular forms this question may assume.

One aim of the research was to study behavior in a strong situation of deep consequence to the participants, for the psychological forces operative in powerful and lifelike forms of the conflict may not be brought into play under diluted conditions.

This approach meant, first, that we had a special obligation to protect the welfare and dignity of the persons who took part in the study; subjects were, of necessity, placed in a difficult predicament, and steps had to be taken to ensure their wellbeing before they were discharged from the laboratory. Toward this end, a careful, post-experimental treatment was devised and has been carried through for subjects in all conditions.[1]

Terminology

If Y follows the command of X we shall say that he has obeyed X; if he fails to carry out the command of X, we shall say that he has disobeyed X. The terms to *obey* and to *disobey*, as used here, refer to the subject's

---

[1] It consisted of an extended discussion with the experimenter and, of equal importance, a friendly reconciliation with the victim. It is made clear that the victim did not receive painful electric shocks. After the completion of the experimental series, subjects were sent a detailed report of the results and full purposes of the experimental program. A formal assessment of this procedure points to its overall effectiveness. Of the subjects, 83.7 per cent indicated that they were glad to have taken part in the study; 15.1 per cent reported neutral feelings; and 1.3 per cent stated that they were sorry to have participated. A large number of subjects spontaneously requested that they be used in further experimentation. Four-fifths of the subjects felt that more experiments of this sort should be carried out, and 74 per cent indicated that they had learned something of personal importance as a result of being in the study. Furthermore, a university psychiatrist, experienced in outpatient treatment, interviewed a sample of experimental subjects with the aim of uncovering possible injurious effects resulting from participation. No such effects were in evidence. Indeed, subjects typically felt that their participation was instructive and enriching. A more detailed discussion of this question can be found in Milgram (1964). [See references at end of article.—Ed.]

overt action only, and carry no implication for the motive or experiential states accompanying the action.

To be sure, the everyday use of the word *obedience* is not entirely free from complexities. It refers to action within widely varying situations, and connotes diverse motives within those situations: a child's obedience differs from a soldier's obedience, or the love, honor, and *obey* of the marriage vow. However, a consistent behavioral relationship is indicated in most uses of the term: in the act of obeying, a person does what another person tells him to do. Y obeys X if he carries out the prescription for action which X has addressed to him; the term suggests, moreover, that some form of dominance-subordination, or hierarchical element, is part of the situation in which the transaction between X and Y occurs.

A subject who complies with the entire series of experimental commands will be termed an *obedient* subject; one who at any point in the command series defies the experimenter will be called a *disobedient* or *defiant* subject. As used in this report, the terms refer only to the subject's performance in the experiment, and do not necessarily imply a general personality disposition to submit to or reject authority.

Subject Population

The subjects used in all experimental conditions were male adults, residing in the greater New Haven and Bridgeport areas, aged 20 to 50 years, and engaged in a wide variety of occupations. Each experimental condition described in this report employed 40 fresh subjects and was carefully balanced for age and occupational types. The occupational composition for each experiment was: workers, skilled and unskilled: 40 percent; white collar, sales, business: 40 percent; professionals: 20 percent. The occupations were intersected with three age categories (subjects in 20s, 30s, and 40s, assigned to each condition in the proportions of 20, 40, and 40 percent respectively).

The General Laboratory Procedure

The focus of the study concerns the amount of electric shock a subject is willing to administer to another person when ordered by an experimenter to give the "victim" increasingly more severe punishment. The act of administering shock is set in the context of a learning experiment, ostensibly designed to study the effect of punishment on memory. Aside from the experimenter, one naïve subject and one accomplice perform in each session. On arrival each subject is paid $4.50. After a general talk by the experimenter, telling how little scientists know about the effect of punishment on memory, subjects are informed that one member of the pair will serve as teacher and one as learner. A rigged drawing is held so that the naïve subject is always the teacher, and the accomplice becomes the learner. The learner is taken to an adjacent room and strapped into an "electric chair."

The naïve subject is told that it is his task to teach the learner a list of paired associates, to test him on the list, and to administer punishment whenever the learner errs in the test. Punishment takes the form of electric shock, delivered to the learner by means of a shock generator controlled by the naïve subject. The teacher is instructed to increase the intensity of electric shock one step on the generator on each error. The learner, according to plan, provides many wrong answers, so that before long the naïve subject must give him the strongest shock on the generator. Increases in shock level are met by increasingly insistent demands from the learner that the experiment be stopped because of the growing discomfort to him. However, in clear terms the experimenter orders the teacher to continue with the procedure in disregard of the learner's protests. *Thus, the naïve subject must resolve a conflict between two mutually incompatible demands from the social field. He may continue to follow the orders of the experimenter and shock the learner with increasing severity, or he may refuse to follow the orders of the experimenter and heed the learner's pleas. The experimenter's authority operates not in a free field, but against ever-mounting countervailing pressures from the person being punished.*

A few technical points need to be considered before the findings of the study are described. For the purpose of delivering shock, a simulated shock generator is used, with 30 clearly marked voltage levels that range from 15 to 450 volts (and each activated by one of 30 individual lever switches set in a horizontal line). The naïve subject is given a sample shock of 45 volts to convince him of the authenticity of the instrument. The generator bears verbal designations that range from "Slight Shock" to "Danger: Severe Shock."

The responses of the victim are standardized on tape, and each protest is coordinated to a particular voltage level on the shock generator. Starting with 75 volts the learner begins to grunt and moan. At 150 volts he demands to be let out of the experiment. At 180 volts he cries out that he can no longer stand the pain. At 300 volts he refuses to provide any more answers to the memory test, insisting that he is no longer a participant in the experiment and must be freed. In response to this last tactic, the experimenter instructs the naïve subject to treat the absence of an answer as equivalent to a wrong answer, and to follow the usual shock procedure. The experimenter reinforces his demand with the statement: "You have no other choice, you must go on!" (This imperative is used whenever the naïve subject tries to break off the experiment.) If the subject refuses to give the next higher level of shock, the experiment is considered at an end. . . .

*   *   *

Immediacy of the Victim

This series consisted of four experimental conditions. In each condition the victim was brought "psychologically" closer to the subject giving him shocks.

In the first condition (Remote Feedback) the victim was placed in another room and could not be heard or seen by the subject, except that, at 300 volts, he pounded on the wall in protest. After 315 volts he no longer answered or was heard from.

The second condition (Voice Feedback) was identical to the first except that voice protests were introduced. As in the first condition the victim was placed in an adjacent room, but his complaints could be heard clearly through a door left slightly ajar, and through the walls of the laboratory.

The third experimental condition (Proximity) was similar to the second, except that the victim was now placed in the same room as the subject, and 1½ feet from him. Thus he was visible as well as audible, and voice cues were provided. The fourth, and final, condition of this series (Touch-Proximity) was identical to the third, with this exception: the victim received a shock only when his hand rested on a shockplate. At the 150-volt level the victim again demanded to be let free and, in this condition, refused to place his hand on the shockplate. The experimenter order the naïve subject to force the victim's hand onto the plate. Thus obedience in this condition required that the subject have physical contact with the victim in order to give him punishment beyond the 150-volt level.

Forty adult subjects were studied in each condition. The data revealed that obedience was significantly reduced as the victim was rendered more immediate to the subject....

Expressed in terms of the proportion of obedient to defiant subjects, the findings are that 34 percent of the subjects defied the experimenter in the Remote condition, 37.5 percent in Voice Feedback, 60 percent in Proximity, and 70 percent in Touch-Proximity.

How are we to account for this effect? A first conjecture might be that as the victim was brought closer the subject became more aware of the intensity of his suffering and regulated his behavior accordingly. This makes sense, but our evidence does not support the interpretation. There are no consistent differences in the attributed level of pain across the four conditions (i.e., the amount of pain experienced by the victim as estimated by the subject and expressed on a 14-point scale). But it is easy to speculate about alternative mechanisms:

Empathic Cues. In the Remote and to a lesser extent the Voice Feedback condition, the victim's suffering possesses an abstract, remote quality for the subject. He is aware, but only in a conceptual sense, that his actions cause pain to another person; the fact is apprehended, but not felt. The phenomenon is common enough. The bombardier can reasonably suppose that his weapons will inflict suffering and death, yet this knowledge is divested of affect, and does not move him to a felt, emotional response to the suffering resulting from his actions. Similar observations have been made in wartime. It is possible that the visual clues associated with the victim's suffering trigger empathic responses in the subject and provide him with a more complete grasp of the victim's experience. Or it is possible that the empathic responses are themselves unpleasant, possessing drive properties which cause the subject to terminate the arousal situation. Diminishing obedience, then, would be explained by the enrichment of empathic cues in the successive experimental conditions.

Denial and narrowing of the cognitive field. The Remote condition allows a narrowing of the cognitive fields so that the victim is put out of mind. The subject no longer considers the act of depressing a lever relevant to moral judgment, for it is no longer associated with the victim's suffering. When the victim is close it is more difficult to exclude him phenomenologically. He necessarily intrudes on the subject's awareness since he is continuously visible. In the Remote conditions his existence and reactions are made known only after the shock has been administered. The auditory feedback is sporadic and discontinuous. In the Proximity conditions his inclusion in the immediate visual field renders him a continuously salient element for the subject. The mechanism of denial can no longer be brought into play. One subject in the Remote condition said: "It's funny how you really begin to forget that there's a guy out there, even though you can hear him. For a long time I just concentrated on pressing the switches and reading the words."

Reciprocal fields. If in the Proximity condition the subject is in an improved position to observe the victim, the reverse is also true. The actions of the subject now come under proximal scrutiny by the victim. Possibly, it is easier to harm a person when he is unable to observe our actions than when he can see what we are doing. His surveillance of the action directed against him may give rise to shame, or guilt, which may then serve to curtail the action. Many expressions of language refer to the discomfort or inhibitions that arise in face-to-face confrontation. It is often said that it is easier to criticize a man "behind his back" than to "attack him to his face." If we are in the process of lying to a person it is reputedly difficult to "stare him in the eye." We "turn away from others in shame" or in "embarrassment" and this action serves to reduce our discomfort. The manifest function of allowing the victim of a firing squad to be blindfolded is to make the occasion less stressful for him, but it may also serve a latent function of reducing the stress of the executioner. In short, in the Proximity conditions, the subject may sense that he has become more salient in the victim's field of awareness. Possibly he becomes more self-conscious, embarrassed, and inhibited in his punishment of the victim.

Phenomenal unity of act. In the Remote conditions it is more difficult for the subject to gain a sense of *relatedness* between his own actions and the consequences of these actions for the victim. There is a physical and spatial separation of the act and its consequences. The subject depresses a lever in one room, and protests and cries are heard from another. The two events are in correlation, yet they lack a compelling phenomenological unity. The structure of a meaningful act—*I am hurting a man*—breaks down because of the spatial arrangements, in a manner somewhat analogous to the disappearance of phi phenomena when the blinking lights are spaced too far apart. The unity is more fully achieved in the Proximity conditions as the victim is brought closer to the action that causes him pain. It is rendered complete in Touch-Proximity.

Incipient group formation. Placing the victim in another room not only takes him further from the subject, but the subject and the experimenter are drawn relatively closer. There is incipient group formation between the experimenter and the subject, from which the victim is excluded. The wall between the victim and the others deprives him of an intimacy which the experimenter and subject feel. In the Remote condition, the victim is truly an outsider, who stands alone, physically and psychologically.

When the victim is placed close to the subject, it becomes easier to form an alliance with him against the experimenter. Subjects no longer have to face the experimenter alone. They have an ally who is close at hand and eager to collaborate in a revolt against the experimenter. Thus, the changing set of spatial conditions leads to a potentially shifting set of alliances over the several experimental conditions.

Acquired behavior dispositions. . . . We may learn not to harm others simply by not harming them in everyday life. Yet this learning occurs in a context of proximal relations with others, and may not be generalized to that situation in which the person is physically removed from us. Or possibly, in the past, aggressive actions against others who were physically close resulted in retaliatory punishment which extinguished the original form of response. In contrast, aggression against others at a distance may have only sporadically led to retaliation. Thus the organism learns that it is safer to be aggressive toward others at a distance, and precarious to be so when the parties are within arm's reach. Through a pattern of rewards and punishments, he acquires a disposition to avoid aggression at close quarters, a disposition which does not extend to harming others at a distance. And this may account for experimental findings in the remote and proximal experiments.

Proximity as a variable in psychological research has received far less attention than it deserves. If men were sessile it would be easy to understand this neglect. But we move about; our spatial relations shift from one situation to the next, and the fact that we are near or remote may have a powerful effect on the psychological processes that mediate our behavior toward others. In the present situation, as the victim is brought closer to the man ordered to give him shocks, increasing numbers of subjects break off the experiment, refusing to obey. The concrete, visible, and proximal presence of the victim acts in an important way to counteract the experimenter's power and to generate disobedience.

Closeness of Authority

If the spatial relationship of the subject and victim is relevant to the degree of obedience, would not the relationship of subject to experimenter also play a part?

There are reasons to feel that, on arrival, the subject is oriented primarily to the experimenter rather than to the victim. He has come to the laboratory to fit into the structure that the experimenter—not the victim—would provide. He has come less to understand his behavior than to *reveal* that behavior to a competent scientist, and he is willing to display himself as the scientist's purposes require. Most subjects seem quite concerned about the appearance they are making before the experimenter, and one could argue that this preoccupation in a relatively new and strange setting makes the subject somewhat insensitive to the triadic nature of the social situation. In other words, the subject is so concerned about the show he is putting on for the experimenter that influences from other parts of the social field do not receive as much weight as they ordinarily would. This overdetermined orientation to the experimenter would account for the relative insensitivity of the subject to the victim, and would also lead us to believe that alterations in the relationship between subject and experimenter would have important consequences for obedience.

In a series of experiments we varied the physical closeness and degree of surveillance of the experimenter. In one condition the experimenter sat just a few feet away from the subject. In a second condition, after giving initial instructions, the experimenter left the laboratory and gave his orders by telephone; in still a third condition the experimenter was never seen, providing instructions by means of a tape recording activated when the subjects entered the laboratory.

Obedience dropped sharply as the experimenter was physically removed from the laboratory. The number of obedient subjects in the first condition (Experimenter Present) was almost three times as great as in the second, where the experimenter gave his orders by telephone. Twenty-six subjects were fully obedient in the first condition, and only 9 in the second (Chi square obedient vs. defiant in the two conditions, 1 d.f.=14.7 ; $p < .001$). Subjects seemed able to take a far stronger stand against the experimenter when they did not have to encounter him face to face, and the experimenter's power over the subject was severely curtailed.

Moreover, when the experimenter was absent, subjects displayed an interesting form of behavior that had not occurred under his surveillance. Though continuing with the experiment, several subjects administered lower shocks than were required and never informed the experimenter of their deviation from the correct procedure. (Unknown to the subjects, shock levels were automatically recorded by an Esterline-Angus event recorder wired directly into the shock generator; the instrument provided us with an objective record of the subjects' performance.) Indeed, in telephone conversations some subjects specifically assured the experimenter that they were raising the shock level according to instruction, whereas in fact they were repeatedly using the lowest shock on the board. This form of behavior is particularly interesting: although these subjects acted in a way that clearly undermined the avowed purposes of the experiment, they found it easier to handle the conflict in this manner than to precipitate an open break with authority.

Other conditions were completed in which the experimenter was absent during the first segment of the experiment, but reappeared at the point that the subject definitely refused to give higher shocks when commanded by telephone. Although he had exhausted his power via telephone, the experimenter could frequently force further obedience when he reappeared in the laboratory.

Experiments in this series show that the physical *presence* of an authority is an important force contributing to the subject's obedience or defiance. Taken together with the first experimental series on the proximity of the victim, it would appear that something akin to fields of force, diminishing in effectiveness with increasing psychological distance from their source, have a controlling effect on the subject's performance. As the victim is brought closer, the subject finds it harder to administer shocks to him. When the victim's position is held constant relative to the subject, and the authority is made more remote, the subject finds it easier to break off the experiment. This effect is substantial in both cases, but manipulation of the experimenter's position yielded the more powerful results. Obedience to destructive commands is highly dependent on the proximal relations between authority and subject.

Tensions

The description of final scores does not fully convey the character of the subjects' performance, and it would be useful to interrupt our reporting of quantitative relationships to remark on the subjects' general reaction to the situation.

One might suppose that a subject would simply break off or continue as his conscience and temperament dictated. Yet this is very far from what happened. There were powerful reactions of tension and emotional strain in a substantial proportion of the participants. Persons were observed to sweat, tremble, stutter, bite their lips, and groan as they found themselves increasingly implicated in the experimental conflict. Some sense of the subjects' mood can be gotten from a transcript of their remarks at break-off point. Here are the remarks of two defiant subjects:

Is he banging? . . . Is he hurt out there? Well, I don't want to be responsible for anything that happens to him. No, I can't go on with it. I don't know whether he's all right or not. I mean he may have a heart condition or something; I wouldn't feel right doing it. He's banging for help. He's evidently in trouble or he wouldn't bang . . . I don't see any sense to this—to knocking him out or something. I just can't see it.
(*Subject refuses to administer shocks*)   [*Subject 0108*]

The man is banging. He wants to get out . . . I'm sorry. If the man wants to get out I'd just as soon stop . . . I don't want to administer any more [extremely excited] . . . I will gladly refund the check, but I will not harm this man . . . I'm sorry, I will not give him any more if he obviously wants to get out. There is no money in the world that will make me hurt another individual.
[*Subject 010X*]

And here is a transcript from an obedient subject. He began the experiment calmly, but became increasingly tense as the experiment proceeded. After administering the 150-volt shock, he began to address the experimenter in agitated tones:

150 volts delivered. You want me to keep going?

165 volts delivered. That guy is hollering in there. There's a lot of them here. He's liable to have heart condition. You want me to go?

180 volts delivered. He can't stand it! I'm not going to kill that man in there! You hear him hollering? He's hollering. He can't stand it. What if something happens to him? . . . I'm not going to get that man sick in there. He's hollering in there. You know what I mean? I mean I refuse to take responsibility. He's getting hurt in there. He's in there hollering. Too many left here. Geez, if he gets them wrong. There's too many of them left. I mean who is going to take responsibility if anything happens to that gentleman? [*The experimenter accepts responsibility.*] All right.

195 volts delivered. You see he's hollering. Hear that. Gee, I don't know. [*The experimenter says: "The experiment requires that you go on."*]—I know it does, sir, but I mean—hugh—he don't know what he's in for. He's up to 195 volts.

210 volts delivered

225 volts delivered

240 volts delivered. Aw, no. You mean I've got to keep going up with the scale? No sir. I'm not going to kill that man! I'm not going to give him 450 volts!

[*The experimenter says: "The experiment requires that you go on."*]—I know it does, but that man is hollering in there, sir . . .

Despite his numerous, agitated objections, which were constant accompaniments to his actions, the subject unfailingly obeyed the experimenter, proceeding to the highest shock level on the generator. He displayed a curious dissociation between word and action. Although at the verbal level he had resolved not to go on, his actions were fully in accord with the experimenter's commands. This subject did not want to shock the victim, and he found it an extremely disagreeable task, but he was unable to invent a response that would free him from E's authority. Many subjects cannot find the specific verbal formula that would enable them to reject the role assigned to them by the experimenter. Perhaps our culture does not provide adequate models for disobedience.

One puzzling sign of tension was the regular occurrence of nervous laughing fits. In the first four conditions 71 of the 160 subjects showed definite signs of nervous laughter and smiling. The laughter seemed entirely out of place, even bizarre. Full-blown, uncontrollable seizures were observed for 15 of these subjects. On one occasion we observed a seizure so violently convulsive that it was necessary to call a halt to the experiment. In the post-experimental interviews subjects took pains to point out that they were not sadistic types and that the laughter did not mean they enjoyed shocking the victim.

In the interview following the experiment subjects were asked to indicate on a 14-point scale just how nervous or tense they felt at the point of maximum tension. The scale ranged from "Not at all tense and nervous" to "Extremely tense and nervous." Self-reports of this sort are of limited precision, and at best provide only a rough indication of the subject's emotional response. Still, taking the reports for what they are worth, it can be seen that the distribution of responses spans the entire range of the scale, with the majority of subjects concentrated at the center and upper extreme. A further breakdown showed that obedient subjects reported themselves as having been slightly more tense and nervous than the defiant subjects at the point of maximum tension.

How is the occurrence of tension to be interpreted? First, it points to the presence of conflict. If a tendency to comply with authority were the only psychological force operating in the situation, all subjects would have continued to the end and there would have been no tension. Tension, it is assumed, results from the simultaneous presence of two or more incompatible response tendencies (Miller, 1944). If sympathetic concern for the victim were the exclusive force, all subjects would have calmly defied the experimenter. Instead, there were both obedient and defiant outcomes, frequently accompanied by extreme tension. A conflict develops between the deeply ingrained disposition not to harm others and the equally compelling tendency to obey others who are in authority. The subject is quickly drawn into a dilemma of a deeply dynamic character, and the presence of high tension points to the considerable strength of each of the antagonistic vectors.

Moreover, tension defines the strength of the aversive state from which the subject is unable to escape through disobedience. When a person is uncomfortable, tense, or stressed, he tries to take some action that will allow him to terminate this unpleasant state. Thus tension may serve as a drive that leads to escape behavior. But in the present situation, even where tension is extreme, many subjects are unable to perform the response that will bring about relief. Therefore there must be a competing drive, tendency, or inhibition that precludes activation of the disobedient response. The strength of this inhibiting factor must be of greater magnitude than the stress experienced, else the terminating act would occur. Every evidence of extreme tension is at the same time an indication of the strength of the forces that keep the subject in the situation.

Finally, tension may be taken as evidence of the reality of the situations for the subjects. Normal subjects do not tremble and sweat unless they are implicated in a deep and genuinely felt predicament.

Background Authority

In psychophysics, animal learning, and other branches of psychology, the fact that measures are obtained at one institution rather than another is irrelevant to the interpretation of the findings, so long as the technical facilities for measurement are adequate and the operations are carried out with competence.

But it cannot be assumed that this holds true for the present study. The effectiveness of the experimenter's commands may depend in an important way on the larger institutional context in which they are issued. The experiments described thus far were conducted at Yale University, an organization which most subjects regarded with respect and sometimes awe. In post-experimental interviews several participants remarked that the locale and sponsorship of the study gave them confidence in the integrity, competence, and benign purposes of the personnel; many indicated that they would not have shocked the learner if the experiments had been done elsewhere.

This issue of background authority seemed to us important for an interpretation of the results that had been obtained thus far; moreover, it is highly relevant to any comprehensive theory of human obedience. Consider, for example, how closely our compliance with the imperatives of others is tied to particular institutions and locales in our day-to-day activities. On request, we expose our throats to a man with a razor blade in the barber shop, but would not do so in a shoe store; in the latter setting we willingly follow the clerk's request to stand in our stockinged feet, but resist the command in a bank. In the laboratory of a great university, subjects may comply with a set of commands that would be resisted if given elsewhere. *One must always question the relationship of obedience to a person's sense of the context in which he is operating.*

To explore the problem we moved our apparatus to an office building in industrial Bridgeport and replicated experimental conditions, without any visible tie to the university.

Bridgeport subjects were invited to the experiment through a mail circular similar to the one used in the Yale study, with appropriate changes in letterhead, etc. As in the earlier study, subjects were paid $4.50 for coming to the laboratory. The same age and occupational distributions used at Yale, and the identical personnel, were employed.

The purpose in relocating in Bridgeport was to assume a complete dissociation from Yale, and in this regard we were fully successful. On the surface, the study appeared to be conducted by RESEARCH ASSOCIATES OF BRIDGEPORT, an organization of unknown character (the title had been concocted exclusively for use in this study).

The experiments were conducted in a three-room office suite in a somewhat run-down commercial building located in the downtown shopping area. The laboratory was sparsely furnished, though clean, and marginally respectable in appearance. When subjects inquired about professional affiliations, they were informed only that we were a private firm conducting research for industry.

Some subjects displayed skepticism concerning the motives of the Bridgeport experimenter. One gentleman gave us a written account of the thoughts he experienced at the control board:

> . . . Should I quit this damn test? Maybe he passed out? What dopes we were not to check up on this deal. How do we know that these guys are legit? No furniture, bare walls, no telephone. We could of called the Police up or

the Better Business Bureau. I learned a lesson tonight. How do I know that Mr. Williams [the experimenter] is telling the truth . . . I wish I knew how many volts a person could take before lapsing into unconsciousness . . .

[*Subject 2414*]

Another subject stated:

I questioned on my arrival my own judgment [about coming]. I had doubts as to the legitimacy of the operation and the consequences of participation. I felt it was a heartless way to conduct memory or learning processes on human beings and certainly dangerous without the presence of a medical doctor.

[*Subject 2440 V*]

There was no noticeable reduction in tension for the Bridgeport subjects. And the subjects' estimation of the amount of pain felt by the victim was slightly, though not significantly, higher than in the Yale study.

A failure to obtain complete obedience in Bridgeport would indicate that the extreme compliance found in New Haven subjects was tied closely to the background authority of Yale University; if a large proportion of the subjects remained fully obedient, very different conclusions would be called for.

As it turned out, the level of obedience in Bridgeport, although somewhat reduced, was not significantly lower than that obtained at Yale. A large proportion of the Bridgeport subjects were fully obedient to the experimenter's commands (48 per cent of the Bridgeport subjects delivered the maximum shock *vs.* 65 per cent in the corresponding condition at Yale).

How are these findings to be interpreted? It is possible that if commands of a potentially harmful or destructive sort are to be perceived as legitimate they must occur within some sort of institutional structure. But it is clear from the study that it need not be a particularly reputable or distinguished institution. The Bridgeport experiments were conducted by an unimpressive firm lacking any credentials; the laboratory was set up in a respectable office building with title listed in the building directory. Beyond that, there was no evidence of benevolence or competence. It is possible that the *category* of institution, judged according to its professed function, rather than its qualitative position within that category, wins our compliance. Persons deposit money in elegant, but also in seedy-looking banks, without giving much thought to the differences in security they offer. Similarly, our subjects may consider one laboratory to be as competent as another, so long as it *is* a scientific laboratory.

It would be valuable to study the subjects' performance in other contexts which go even further than the Bridgeport study in denying institutional support to the experimenter. It is possible that, beyond a certain point, obedience disappears completely. But that point had not been reached in the Bridgeport office: almost half the subjects obeyed the experimenter fully.

*   *   *

Levels of Obedience and Defiance

One general finding that merits attention is the high level of obedience manifested in the experimental situation. Subjects often expressed deep disapproval of shocking a man in the face of his objections, and others denounced it as senseless and stupid. Yet many subjects complied even while they protested. The proportion of obedient subjects greatly exceeded the expectations of the experimenter and his colleagues. At the outset, we had conjectured that subjects would not, in general, go above the level of "Strong Shock." In practice, many subjects were willing to administer the most extreme shocks available when commanded by the experimenter. For some subjects the experiment provides an occasion for aggressive release. And for others it demonstrates the extent to which obedient dispositions are deeply ingrained, and are engaged irrespective of their consequences for others. Yet this is not the whole story. Somehow, the subject becomes implicated in a situation from which he cannot disengage himself.

* * *

Many people, not knowing much about the experiment, claim that subjects who go to the end of the board are sadistic. Nothing could be more foolish as an overall characterization of these persons. It is like saying that a person thrown into a swift-flowing stream is necessarily a fast swimmer, or that he has great stamina because he moves so rapidly relative to the bank. The context of action must always be considered. The individual, upon entering the laboratory, becomes integrated into a situation that carries its own momentum. The subject's problem then is how to become disengaged from a situation which is moving in an altogether ugly direction.

The fact that disengagement is so difficult testifies to the potency of the forces that keep the subject at the control board. Are these forces to be conceptualized as individual motives and expressed in the language of personality dynamics, or are they to be seen as the effects of social structure and pressures arising from the situational field?

A full understanding of the subject's action will, I feel, require that both perspectives be adopted. The person brings to the laboratory enduring dispositions toward authority and aggression, and at the same time he becomes enmeshed in a social structure that is no less an objective fact of the case. From the standpoint of personality theory one may ask: What mechanisms of personality enable a person to transfer responsibility to authority? What are the motives underlying obedient and disobedient performance? Does orientation to authority lead to a short-circuiting of the shame-guilt system? What cognitive and emotional defenses are brought into play in the case of obedient and defiant subjects?

* * *

Postscript

Almost a thousand adults were individually studied in the obedience research, and there were many specific conclusions regarding the variables that control obedience and disobedience to authority. Some of these have been discussed briefly in the preceding sections, and more detailed reports will be released subsequently.

There are now some other generalizations I should like to make, which do not derive in any strictly logical fashion from the experiments as carried out, but which, I feel, ought to be made. They are formulations of an intuitive sort that have been forced on me by observation of many subjects responding to the pressure of authority. The assertions represent a painful alteration in my own thinking; and since they were acquired only under the repeated impact of direct observation, I have no illusion that they will be generally accepted by persons who have not had the same experience.

With numbing regularity good people were seen to knuckle under to the demands of authority and perform actions that were callous and severe. Men who are in everyday life responsible and decent were seduced by the trappings of authority, by the control of their perceptions, and by the uncritical acceptance of the experimenter's definition of the situation, into performing harsh acts.

What is the limit of such obedience? At many points we attempted to establish a boundary. Cries from the victim were inserted; not good enough. The victim claimed heart trouble; subjects still shocked him on command. The victim pleaded that he be let free, and his answers no longer registered on the signal box; subjects continued to shock him. At the outset we had not conceived that such drastic procedures would be needed to generate disobedience, and each step was added only as the ineffectiveness of the earlier techniques became clear. The final effort to establish a limit was the Touch-Proximity condition. But the very first subject in this condition subdued the victim on command, and proceeded to the highest shock level. A quarter of the subjects in this condition performed similarly.

The results, as seen and felt in the laboratory, are to this author disturbing. They raise the possibility that human nature, or—more specifically— the kind of character produced in American democratic society, cannot be counted on to insulate its citizens from brutality and inhumane treatment at the direction of malevolent authority. A substantial proportion of people do what they are told to do, irrespective of the content of the act and without limitations of conscience, so long as they perceive that the command comes from a legitimate authority. If in this study an anonymous experimenter could successfully command adults to subdue a fifty-year-old man, and force on him painful electric shocks against his protests, one can only wonder what government, with its vastly greater authority and prestige, can command of its subjects. There is, of course, the extremely important question of whether malevolent political institutions could or would arise in American society. The present research contributes nothing to this issue.

In an article titled "The Dangers of Obedience," Harold J. Laski wrote:

> . . . civilization means, above all, an unwillingness to inflict unnecessary pain. Within the ambit of that definition, those of us who heedlessly accept the commands of authority cannot yet claim to be civilized men.
>
> . . . Our business, if we desire to live a life, not utterly devoid of meaning and significance, is to accept nothing which contradicts our basic experience merely because it comes to us from tradition or convention or authority. It may well be that we shall be wrong; but our self-expression is thwarted at the root unless the certainties we are asked to accept coincide with the certainties we experience. That is why the condition of freedom in any state is always a widespread and consistent skepticism of the canons upon which power insists.

References

BUSS, ARNOLD H. (1961). *The psychology of aggression.* New York and London: John Wiley.

KIERKEGAARD, S. (1843). *Fear and trembling.* English edition, Princeton: Princeton University Press, 1941.

LASKI, HAROLD J. (1929). The dangers of obedience. *Harper's Monthly Magazine* 159, June, 1–10.

MILGRAM, S. (1961). Dynamics of obedience: experiments in social psychology. Mimeographed report, *National Science Foundation*, January 25.

MILGRAM, S. (1963). Behavioral study of obedience. *J. Abnorm. Soc. Psychol.* 67, 371–8.

MILGRAM, S. (1964). Issues in the study of obedience: a reply to Baumrind. *Amer. Psychol.* 19, 848–52.

MILLER, N. E. (1944). Experimental studies of conflict. In J. McV. Hunt (Ed.), *Personality and the behavior disorders.* New York: Ronald Press.

Domestic Law
and International Order

Eldridge Cleaver

The police department and the armed forces are the two arms of the power structure, the muscles of control and enforcement. They have deadly weapons with which to inflict pain on the human body. They know how to bring about horrible deaths. They have clubs with which to beat the body and the head. They have bullets and guns with which to tear holes in the flesh, to smash bones, to disable and kill. They use force, to make you do what the deciders have decided you must do.

Every country on earth has these agencies of force. The people everywhere fear this terror and force. To them it is like a snarling wild beast which can put an end to one's dreams. They punish. They have cells and prisons to lock you up in. They pass out sentences. They won't let you go when you want to. You have to stay put until they give the word. If your mother is dying, you can't go to her bedside to say goodbye or to her graveside to see her lowered into the earth, to see her, for the last time, swallowed up by that black hole.

The techniques of the enforcers are many: firing squads, gas chambers, electric chairs, torture chambers, the garrote, the guillotine, the tightening rope around your throat. It has been found that the death penalty is necessary to back up the law, to make it easier to enforce, to deter transgressions against the penal code. That everybody doesn't believe in the same laws is beside the point.

Which laws get enforced depends on who is in power. If the capitalists are in power, they enforce laws designed to protect their system, their way of life. They have a particular abhorrence for crimes against property, but are prepared to be liberal and show a modicum of compassion for crimes against the person—unless, of course, an instance of the latter is combined with an instance of the former. In such cases, nothing can stop them from throwing the whole book at the offender. For instance, armed robbery with violence, to a capitalist, is the very epitome of evil. Ask any banker what he thinks of it.

If Communists are in power, they enforce laws designed to protect their system, their way of life. To them, the horror of horrors is the speculator, that man of magic who has mastered the art of getting something with nothing and who in America would be a member in good standing of his local Chamber of Commerce.

"The people," however, are nowhere consulted, although everywhere everything is done always in their name and ostensibly for their betterment, while their real-life problems go unsolved. "The people" are a rubber stamp for the crafty and sly. And no problem can be solved without taking the police department and the armed forces into account. Both kings and bookies understand this, as do first ladies and common prostitutes.

The police do on the domestic level what the armed forces do on the international level: protect the way of life of those in power. The police patrol the city, cordon off communities, blockade neighborhoods, invade homes, search for that which is hidden. The armed forces patrol the world, invade countries and continents, cordon off nations, blockade islands and whole peoples; they will also overrun villages, neighborhoods, enter homes, huts, caves, searching for that which is hidden. The policeman and the soldier will violate your person, smoke you out with various gases. Each will shoot you, beat your head and body with sticks and clubs, with rifle butts, run you through with bayonets, shoot holes in your flesh, kill you. They each have unlimited firepower. They will use all that is necessary to bring you to your knees. They won't take no for an answer. If you resist their sticks, they draw their guns. If you resist their guns, they call for reinforcements with bigger guns. Eventually they will come in tanks, in jets, in ships. They will not rest until you surrender or are killed. The policeman and the soldier will have the last word.

Both police and the armed forces follow orders. Orders. Orders flow from the top down. Up there, behind closed doors, in antechambers, in conference rooms, gavels bang on the tables, the tinkling of silver decanters can be heard as icewater is poured by well-fed, conservatively dressed men in hornrimmed glasses, fashionably dressed American widows with rejuvenated faces and tinted hair, the air permeated with the square humor of Bob Hope jokes. Here all the talking is done, all the thinking, all the deciding. Gray rabbits of men scurry forth from the conference room to spread the decisions throughout the city, as News. Carrying out orders is a job, a way of meeting the payments on the house, a way of providing for one's kiddies. In the armed forces it is also a duty, patriotism. Not to do so is treason.

Every city has its police department. No city would be complete without one. It would be sheer madness to try operating an American city without the heat, the fuzz, the man. Americans are too far gone, or else they haven't arrived yet; the center does not exist, only the extremes. Take away the cops and Americans would have a coast-to-coast free-for-all. There are, of course, a few citizens who carry their own private cops around with them, built into their souls. But there is robbery in the land, and larceny, murder, rape, burglary, theft, swindles, all brands of crime, profit, rent, interest—and these blasé descendants of Pilgrims are at each other's throats. To complicate matters, there are also rich people and poor people in America. There are Negroes and whites, Indians, Puerto Ricans, Mexicans, Jews, Chinese, Arabs, Japanese—all with equal rights but unequal possessions. Some are haves and some are have-nots. All have been taught to worship at the shrine of General Motors. The whites are on top in America and they want to stay there, up there. They are also on top in the world, on the international level, and they want to stay up there, too. Everywhere there are those who want to smash this precious toy clock of of a system, they want ever so much to change it, to rearrange things, to pull the whites down off their high horse and make them equal. Everywhere the whites are fighting to prolong their status, to retard the erosion of their position. In America, when everything else fails, they call out the police. On the international level, when everything else fails, they call out the armed forces.

A strange thing happened in Watts, in 1965, August. The blacks, who in this land of private property have all private and no property, got excited into an uproar because they noticed a cop before he had a chance to wash the blood off his hands. Usually the police department can handle such flare-ups. But this time it was different. Things got out of hand. The blacks were running amok, burning, shooting, breaking. The police department was powerless to control them; the chief called for reinforcements. Out came the National Guard, that ambiguous hybrid from the twilight zone where the domestic army merges with the international; that hypocritical force poised within America and capable of action on either level, capable of backing up either the police or the armed forces. Unleashing their formidable firepower, they crushed the blacks. But things will never be the same again. Too many people saw that those who turned the other cheek in Watts got their whole head blown off. At the same time, heads were being blown off in Vietnam. America was embarrassed, not by the quality of her deeds but by the surplus of publicity focused upon her negative selling points, and a little frightened because of what all those dead bodies, on two fronts, implied. Those corpses spoke eloquently of potential allies and alliances. A community of interest began to emerge, dripping with blood, out of the ashes of Watts. The blacks in Watts and all over America could now see the Viet Cong's point: both were on the receiving end of what the armed forces were dishing out.

So now the blacks, stung by the new knowledge they have unearthed, cry out: "POLICE BRUTALITY!" From one end of the country to the other, the new war cry is raised. The youth, those nodes of compulsive energy who are all fuel and muscle, race their motors, itch to do something. The Uncle Toms, no longer willing to get down on their knees to lick boots, do so from a squatting position. The black bourgeoisie call for Citizens' Review Boards, to assert civilian control over the activity of the police. In back rooms, in dark stinking corners of the ghettos, self-conscious black men curse their own cowardice and stare at their rifles and pistols and shotguns laid out on tables before them, trembling as they wish for a manly impulse to course through their bodies and send them screaming mad into the streets shooting from the hip. Black women look at their men as if they are bugs, curious growths of flesh playing an inscrutable waiting game. Violence becomes a homing pigeon floating through the ghettos seeking a black brain in which to roost for a season.

In their rage against the police, against police brutality, the blacks lose sight of the fundamental reality: that the police are only an instrument for the implementation of the policies of those who make the decisions. Police brutality is only one facet of the crystal of terror and oppression. Behind police brutality there is social brutality, economic brutality, and political brutality. From the perspective of the ghetto, this is not easy to discern: the TV newscaster and the radio announcer and the editorialists of the newspapers are wizards of the smoke screen and the snow job.

What is true on the international level is true also at home; except that the ace up the sleeve is easier to detect in the international arena. Who would maintain that American soldiers are in Vietnam on their own motion? They were conscripted into the armed forces and taught the wisdom of obeying orders. They were sent to Vietnam by orders of the generals in the Pentagon, who receive them from the Secretary of Defense, who receives them from the President, who is shrouded in mystery. The soldier in the field in Vietnam, the man who lies in the grass and squeezes the trigger when a little half-starved, trembling Vietnamese peasant crosses his sights, is only following orders, carrying out a policy and a plan. He hardly knows what it is all about. They have him wired up tight with the slogans of TV and the World Series. All he knows is that he has been assigned to carry out a certain ritual of duties. He is well trained and does the best he can. He does a good job. He may want to please those above him with the quality of his performance. He may want to make sergeant, or better. This man is from some hicky farm in Shit Creek, Georgia. He only knew whom to kill after passing through boot camp. He could just as well come out ready to kill Swedes. He will kill a Swede dead, if he is ordered to do so.

Same for the policeman in Watts. He is not there on his own. They have all been assigned. They have been told what to do and what not to do. They have also been told what they better not do. So when they continually do something, in every filthy ghetto in this shitty land, it means only that they are following orders.

It's no secret that in America the blacks are in total rebellion against the System. They want to get their nuts out of the sand. They don't like the way America is run, from top to bottom. In America, everything is owned. Everything is held as private property. Someone has a brand on everything. There is nothing left over. Until recently, the blacks themselves were counted as part of somebody's private property, along with the chickens and goats. The blacks have not forgotten this, principally because they are still treated as if they are part of someone's inventory of assets— or perhaps, in this day of rage against the costs of welfare, blacks are listed among the nation's liabilities. On any account, however, blacks are in no position to respect or help maintain the institution of private property. What they want is to figure out a way to get some of that property for themselves, to divert it to their own needs. This is what it is all about, and this is the real brutality involved. This is the source of all brutality.

The police are the armed guardians of the social order. The blacks are the chief domestic victims of the American social order. A conflict of interest exists, therefore, between the blacks and the police. It is not solely a matter of trigger-happy cops, of brutal cops who love to crack black heads. Mostly it's a job to them. It pays good. And there are numerous fringe benefits. The real problem is a trigger-happy social order.

The Utopians speak of a day when there will be no police. There will be nothing for them to do. Every man will do his duty, will respect the rights of his neighbor, will not disturb the peace. The needs of all will be taken care of. Everyone will have sympathy for his fellow man. There will be no such thing as crime. There will be, of course, no prisons. No electric chair, no gas chambers. The hangman's rope will be the thing of the past. The entire earth will be a land of plenty. There will be no crimes against property, no speculation.

It is easy to see that we are not on the verge of entering Utopia: there are cops everywhere. North and South, the Negroes are the have-nots. They see property all around them, property that is owned by whites. In this regard, the black bourgeoisie has become nothing but a ridiculous nuisance. Having waged a battle for entrance into the American main-stream continually for fifty years, all of the black bourgeoisie's defenses are directed outward, against the whites. They have no defenses against the blacks and no time to erect any. The black masses can handle them any time they choose, with one mighty blow. But the white bourgeoisie presents a bigger problem, those whites who own everything. With many shackled by unemployment, hatred in black hearts for this system of private property increases daily. The sanctity surrounding property is being called into question. The mystique of the deed of ownership is melting away. In other parts of the world, peasants rise up and expropriate the land from the former owners. Blacks in America see that the deed is not external, that it is not signed by God, and that new deeds, making blacks the owners, can be drawn up.

The Black Muslims raised the cry, *"WE MUST HAVE SOME LAND!" "SOME LAND OF OUR OWN OR ELSE!"* Blacks in America shrink from the colossus of General Motors. They can't see how to wade through that thicket of common stocks, preferred stocks, bonds and deben-tures. They only know that General Motors is huge, that it has billions of dollars under its control, that it owns land, that its subsidiaries are legion, that it is a repository of vast powers. The blacks want to crack the nut of General Motors. They are meditating on it. Meanwhile, they must learn that the police take orders from General Motors. And that the Bank of America has something to do with them even though they don't have a righteous penny in the bank. They have no bank accounts, only bills to pay. The only way they know of making withdrawals from the bank is at the point of a gun. The shiny fronts of skyscrapers intimidate them. They do not own them. They feel alienated from the very sidewalks on which they walk. This white man's country, this white man's world. Overflowing with men of color. An economy consecrated to the succor of the whites. Blacks are incidental. The war on poverty, that monstrous insult to the rippling muscles in a black man's arms, is an index of how men actually sit down and plot each other's deaths, actually sit down with slide rules and calculate how to hide bread from the hungry. And the black bourgeoisie greedily sopping up what crumbs are tossed into their dark corner.

There are 20,000,000 of these blacks in America, probably more. Today they repeat, in awe, this magic number to themselves: there are 20,000,000 of us! They shout this to each other in humiliated astonishment. No one need tell them that there is vast power latent in their mass. They know that 20,000,000 of anything is enough to get some recognition and consideration. They know also that they must harness their number and hone it into a sword with a sharp cutting edge. White General Motors also knows that the unity of these 20,000,000 ragamuffins will spell the death of the system of its being. At all costs, then, they will seek to keep these blacks from uniting, from becoming bold and revolutionary. These white property owners know that they must keep the blacks cowardly and intimidated. By a complex communications system of hints and signals, certain orders are given to the chief of police and the sheriff, who pass them on to their men, the footsoldiers in the trenches of the ghetto.

We experience this system of control as madness. So that Leonard Deadwyler, one of these 20,000,000 blacks, is rushing his pregnant wife to the hospital and is shot dead by a policeman. An accident. That the sun rises in the east and sets in the west is also an accident, by design. The blacks are up in arms. From one end of America to the other, blacks are outraged at this accident, this latest evidence of what an accident-prone people they are, of the cruelty and pain of their lives, these blacks at the mercy of trigger-happy Yankees and Rebs in coalition against their skin. They want the policeman's blood as a sign that the Viet Cong is not the only answer. A sign to save them from the deaths they must die, and inflict. The power structure, without so much as blinking an eye, wouldn't mind tossing Bova to the mob, to restore law and order, but it knows in the vaults of its strength that at all cost the blacks must be kept at bay, that it must uphold the police department, its Guardian. Nothing must be allowed to threaten the set-up. Justice is secondary. Security is the byword.

Meanwhile, blacks are looking on and asking tactical questions. They are asked to die for the System in Vietnam. In Watts they are killed by it. Now—NOW!—they are asking each other, in dead earnest: Why not die right here in Babylon fighting for a better life, like the Viet Cong? If those little cats can do it, what's wrong with big studs like us?

A mood sets in, spreads across America, across the face of Babylon, jells in black hearts everywhere.

WORK AND LEISURE

IN THE ADVANCED industrial societies it is technologically possible to eliminate poverty and unemployment and to free all citizens from toil. The authors of the selections included below explain that this can be done by abandoning wasteful standards of production and consumption and by making the tremendous productive capacity of modern technology serve not just a few but everyone.

The "triple revolution" refers to changes in technology, weaponry and civil rights taking place in the United States.

1. The application of computers and automation to production has resulted in almost unlimited productive capacity.

2 We now have weapons of mass destruction that cannot win wars but can obliterate all life on earth.

3. There is now an increasing militancy among blacks and other minority groups who have long been denied equal rights in America.

The manifesto of the Ad Hoc Committee concerns primarily the consequences of the technological changes.

The Ad Hoc Committee points to the paradox that in a country where there is more than enough for everyone some citizens lack even the necessities. There are not enough jobs to go around, and automation is causing existing jobs to disappear. The demands of minorities for full employment cannot be fulfilled within the system as presently organized. The thing that keeps millions of Americans poor is the link between jobs and income. The authors suggest this link be broken by providing everyone with a guaranteed minimum annual income, no strings attached.

This proposal is radical in that it promises freedom from toil, but it is also conservative in that it would stabilize the existing economic system by protecting it from the upheavals that accompany massive unemployment. Under the guaranteed income, those who wanted more than the minimum would continue to work for wages in the capitalist system. The corporations would continue to reap large profits from their operations in this country and abroad.

Our economic system dehumanizes man, says Theobald. It values people as consumers instead of as human beings, replaces men by machines when it becomes profitable to do so, accepts technological innovation regardless of its social consequences. (If it is technically possible to build hydrogen bombs, we build them; if it is possible to send rockets to the moon, we send them.)

Theobald also proposes a guaranteed income, which he terms Basic Economic Security. In addition, he suggests income maintenance for those previously used to well-paying jobs, which he calls Committed Spending. This program, he explains, will eliminate poverty and abolish welfare, and will free people to engage in work of their own choosing or to do no work at all.

In the portions of Communitas excerpted in this book, the Goodmans suggest two alternative models for an economy not dependent on alienated labor. In the first, production is decentralized and based on workers' understanding and control of the whole process. Though such a system might be less efficient than the present one, it would be more satisfying.

The second paradigm divides the economy into two sectors, necessity and luxury. Production of necessities is publicly controlled and accomplished by a relatively small amount of labor. Under the Goodmans' plan this labor is conscripted. Each person contributes only a few years out of his life to working on this side of the economy. In return he receives certificates that he can exchange for necessities. Luxuries can be produced by private entrepreneurs and craftsmen in a system that might be termed "capitalism by choice."

In modern industrial society, specialization and rationalization alienate man from his work. Work is channeled into patterns predetermined by the managers; roles and functions of personnel are defined without considering their human needs and desires. In my own article, I suggest two ways to reconstruct the economy to end alienation:

1. workers' control over policies, production, and profits, and
2. free distribution of necessities to all.

Workers' control can make work more meaningful and pleasant, but by itself it will not necessarily end alienation, for even in a democratic organization individuals may feel their talents and skills are not being expressed. Free distribution of necessities can liberate men to do the things they like best and are most suited for without having to worry about money. I simplify the Goodmans' plan for a dual economy by suggesting absolutely free distribution—no stamps, coupons, or money —and by substituting voluntary for conscripted labor in the subsistence economy.

The Triple Revolution[1]

Ad Hoc Committee

This statement is written in the recognition that mankind is at a historic conjuncture which demands a fundamental reexamination of existing values and institutions. At this time three separate and mutually reinforcing revolutions are taking place:

The Cybernation Revolution: A new era of production has begun. Its principles of organization are as different from those of the industrial era as those of the industrial era were different from the agricultural. The cybernation revolution has been brought about by the combination of the computer and the automated self-regulating machine. This results in a system of almost unlimited productive capacity which requires progressively less human labor. Cybernation is already reorganizing the economic and social system to meet its own needs.

The Weaponry Revolution: New forms of weaponry have been developed which cannot win wars but which can obliterate civilization. We are recognizing only now that the great weapons have eliminated war as a method for resolving international conflicts. The ever-present threat of total destruction is tempered by the knowledge of the final futility

FROM *Liberation* (April 1964). Reprinted by permission.
[1] Signed by *Donald G. Agger, Dr. Donald B. Armstrong, James Boggs, Louis Fein, W. H. Ferry, Maxwell Geismar, Todd Gitlin, Philip Green, Roger Hagan, Michael Harrington, Tom Hayden, Robert L. Heilbroner, Ralph L. Helstein, Frances W. Herring, Hugh B. Hester, Alice Mary Hilton, Irving Howe, Everett C. Hughes, H. Stuart Hughes, Gerald W. Johnson, Irving F. Laucks, Stewart Meacham, A. J. Muste, Gunnar Myrdal (with reservations), Linus Pauling, Gerard Piel, Michael D. Reagan, Bayard Rustin, Ben B. Seligman, Robert Theobald, John William Ward, William Worthy.*

of war. The need of a "warless world" is generally recognized, though achieving it will be a long and frustrating process.

The Human Rights Revolution: A universal demand for full human rights is now clearly evident. It continues to be demonstrated in the civil rights movement within the United States. But this is only the local manifestation of a world-wide movement toward the establishment of social and political régimes in which every individual will feel valued and none will feel rejected on account of his race.

We are particularly concerned in this statement with the first of these revolutionary phenomena. This is not because we underestimate the significance of the other two. On the contrary, we affirm that it is the simultaneous occurrence and interaction of all three developments which make evident the necessity for radical alterations in attitude and policy. The adoption of just policies for coping with cybernation and for extending rights to all Americans is indispensable for the creation of an atmosphere in the United States in which the supreme issue, peace, can be reasonably debated and resolved.

Interaction of Three Revolutions

The Negro claims, as a matter of simple justice, his full share in America's economic and social life. He sees adequate employment opportunities as a chief means of attaining this goal: the March on Washington demanded freedom *and* jobs. The Negro's claim to a job is not being met. Negroes are the hardest hit of the many groups being exiled from the economy by cybernation. Negro unemployment rates cannot be expected to drop substantially. Promises of jobs are a cruel and dangerous hoax on hundreds of thousands of Negroes and whites alike who are especially vulnerable to cybernation because of age or inadequate education.

The demand of the civil rights movement cannot be fulfilled within the present context of society. The Negro is trying to enter a social community and a tradition of work-and-income which are in the process of vanishing even for the hitherto privileged white worker. Jobs are disappearing under the impact of highly efficient, progressively less costly machines.

The United States operates on the thesis, set out in the Employment Act of 1946, that every person will be able to obtain a job if he wishes to do so and that this job will provide him with resources adequate to live and maintain a family decently. Thus job-holding is the general mechanism through which economic resources are distributed. Those without work have access only to a minimal income, hardly sufficient to provide the necessities of life, and enabling those receiving it to function as only "minimum consumers." As a result, the goods and services which are needed by these crippled consumers, and which they would buy if they could, are not produced. This in turn deprives other workers of jobs, thus reducing their incomes and consumption.

Present excessive levels of unemployment would be multiplied several times if military and space expenditures did not continue to absorb ten per cent of the gross national product (i.e., the total goods and services produced). Some six to eight million people are employed as a direct result of purchases for space and military activities. At least an equal number hold their jobs as an indirect result of military and space expenditures. In recent years, the military and space budgets have absorbed a rising proportion of national production and formed a strong support for the economy.

*   *   *

The Nature of the Cybernation Revolution

Cybernation is manifesting the characteristics of a revolution in production. These include the development of radically different techniques and the subsequent appearance of novel principles of the organization of production; a basic reordering of man's relationship to his environment; and a dramatic increase in total available and potential energy.

The major difference between the agricultural, industrial and cybernation revolutions is the speed at which they developed. The agricultural revolution began several thousand years ago in the Middle East. Centuries passed in the shift from a subsistence base of hunting and food gathering to settled agriculture.

In contrast, it has been less than two hundred years since the emergence of the Industrial Revolution, and direct and accurate knowledge of the new productive techniques has reached most of mankind. The swift dissemination of information is generally held to be the main factor leading to widespread industrialization.

While the major aspects of the cybernation revolution are for the moment restricted to the United States, its effects are observable almost at once throughout the industrial world and large parts of the non-industrial world. Observation is rapidly followed by analysis and criticism. The problems posed by the cybernation revolution are part of a new era in the history of all mankind but they are first being faced by the people of the United States. The way Americans cope with cybernation will influence the course of this phenomenon everywhere. This country is the stage on which the Machine-and-Man drama will first be played for the world to witness.

The fundamental problem posed by the cybernation revolution in the United States is that it invalidates the general mechanism so far employed to undergird people's rights as consumers. Up to this time economic resources have been distributed on the basis of contributions to production, with machines and men competing for employment on somewhat equal terms. In the developing cybernated system, potentially unlimited output can be achieved by systems of machines which will require little cooperation from human beings. As machines take over production from men, they absorb an increasing proportion of resources, while the men who are displaced become dependent on minimal and unrelated government measures —unemployment insurance, social security, welfare payments. These measures are less and less able to disguise a historic paradox: that a growing proportion of the population is subsisting on minimal incomes, often below the poverty line, at a time when sufficient productive potential is available to supply the needs of everyone in the United States.

The existence of this paradox is denied or ignored by conventional economic analysis. The general economic approach argues that potential demand, which if filled would raise the number of jobs and provide income to those holding them, is underestimated. Most contemporary economic analysis states that all of the available labor force and industrial capacity is required to meet the needs of consumers and industry and to provide adequate public services: schools, parks, roads, homes, decent cities, and clean water and air. It is further argued that demand could be increased, by a variety of standard techniques, to any desired extent by providing money and machines to improve the conditions of the billions of impoverished people elsewhere in the world, who need food and shelter, clothes and machinery and everything else the industrial nations take for granted.

There is no question that cybernation does increase the potential for the provision of funds to neglected public sectors. Nor is there any question that cybernation would make possible the abolition of poverty at home and abroad. But the industrial system does not possess any adequate mechanisms to permit these potentials to become realities. The industrial system was designed to produce an ever-increasing quantity of goods as efficiently as possible, and it was assumed that the distribution of the power to purchase these goods would occur almost automatically. The continuance of the income-through-jobs link as the only major mechanism for distributing effective demand—for granting the right to consume—now acts as the main brake on the almost unlimited capacity of a cybernated productive system.

Recent administrations have proposed measures aimed at achieving a better distribution of resources, and at reducing unemployment and underemployment. A few of these proposals have been enacted. More often they have failed to secure Congressional support. In every case, many members of Congress have criticized the proposed measures as departing from traditional principles for the allocation of resources and the encouragement of production. Abetted by budget-balancing economists and interest groups, they have argued for the maintenance of an economic machine based on ideas of scarcity to deal with the facts of abundance produced by cybernation. This time-consuming criticism has slowed the working of Congress and has thrown out of focus for that body the inter-related effects of the triple revolution.

An adequate distribution of the potential abundance of goods and services will be achieved only when it is understood that the major economic problem is not how to increase production but how to distribute the abundance that is the great potential of cybernation. There is an urgent need for a fundamental change in the mechanisms employed to insure consumer rights.

Facts and Figures

No responsible observer would attempt to describe the exact pace or the full sweep of a phenomenon that is developing with the speed of cybernation. Some aspects of this revolution, however, are already clear:

The rate of productivity increase has risen with the onset of cybernation.

An industrial economic system postulated on scarcity has been unable to distribute the abundant goods and services produced by a cybernated system or potential in it.

Surplus capacity and unemployment have thus co-existed at excessive levels over the last six years.

The underlying cause of excessive unemployment is the fact that the capability of machines is rising more rapidly than the capacity of many human beings to keep pace.

A permanent impoverished and jobless class is established in the midst of potential abundance.

Evidence for these statements follows:

1. The increased efficiency of machine systems is shown in the more rapid increase in productivity per man-hour since 1960, a year that marks the first visible upsurge of the cybernation revolution. In 1961, 1962, and 1963, productivity per man-hour rose at an average pace above three and a half per cent—a rate well above the historical average and the post-war rate.

Companies are finding cybernation more and more attractive. Even at the present early stage of cybernation, costs have already been lowered to a point where the price of a durable machine may be as little as one-third of the current annual wage-cost of the worker it replaces. A more rapid rise in the rate of productivity increase per man-hour can be expected from now on.

2. In recent years it has proved impossible to increase demand fast enough to bring about the full use of either men or plant capacities. The

task of developing sufficient additional demand promises to become more difficult each year. A thirty-billion-dollar annual increase in gross national product is now required to prevent unemployment rates from rising. An additional forty-to-sixty-billion-dollar increase would be required to bring unemployment rates down to an acceptable level.

3. The official rate of unemployment has remained at or above five and a half per cent during the Sixties. The unemployment rate for teenagers has been rising steadily and now stands at around fifteen per cent. The unemployment rate for Negro teenagers stands about thirty per cent. The unemployment rate for teenagers in minority ghettoes sometimes exceeds fifty per cent. Unemployment rates for Negroes are regularly more than twice those for whites, whatever their occupation, educational level, age or sex. The unemployment position for other racial minorities is similarly unfavorable. Unemployment rates in depressed areas often exceed fifty per cent.

These official figures seriously underestimate the true extent of unemployment. The statistics take no note of underemployment or featherbedding. Besides the five and a half per cent of the labor force who are officially designated as unemployed, nearly four per cent of the labor force sought full-time work in 1962 but could find only part-time jobs. In addition, methods of calculating unemployment rates—a person is counted as unemployed only if he has actively sought a job recently—ignore the fact that many men and women who would like to find jobs have not looked for them because they know there are no employment opportunities. Underestimates for this reason are pervasive among groups whose unemployment rates are high—the young, the old, and racial minorities. Many people in the depressed agricultural, mining and industrial areas, who by official definition hold jobs but who are actually grossly underemployed, would move if there were prospects of finding work elsewhere. It is reasonable to estimate that over eight million people are not working who would like to have jobs today as compared with the four million shown in the official statistics.

Even more serious is the fact that the number of people who have voluntarily removed themselves from the labor force is not constant but increases continuously. These people have decided to stop looking for employment and seem to have accepted the fact that they will never hold jobs again. This decision is largely irreversible, in economic and also in social and psychological terms. The older worker calls himself "retired"; he cannot accept work without affecting his social-security status. The worker in his prime years is forced onto relief: in most states the requirements for becoming a relief recipient bring about such fundamental alterations in an individual's situation that a reversal of the process is always difficult and often totally infeasible. Teenagers, especially "drop-outs" and Negroes, are coming to realize that there is no place for them in the labor force, but at the same time they are given no realistic alternative. These people and their dependents make up a large part of the "poverty" sector of the American population.

Statistical evidence of these trends appears in the decline in the proportion of people claiming to be in the labor force—the so-called labor-force-participation rate. The recent apparent stabilization of the unemployment rate at around five and a half per cent is therefore misleading: it is a reflection of the discouragement and defeat of people who cannot find employment and have withdrawn from the market, rather than a measure of the economy's success in creating jobs for those who want to work.

4. An efficiently functioning industrial system is assumed to provide the great majority of new jobs through the expansion of the private-enterprise sector. But well over half of the new jobs created during the period 1957–1962 were in the public sector—predominantly in teaching. Job creation in the private sector has now almost entirely ceased except in services; of the four million three hundred thousand jobs created in this period, only about two hundred thousand were provided by industry through its own efforts. Many authorities anticipate that the application of cybernation to certain service industries, which is only beginning, will be particularly effective. If this is the case, no significant job creation will take place in the private sector in coming years.

5. Cybernation raises the level of the skills of the machine. Secretary of Labor Willard Wirtz has recently stated that the machines being produced today, have, on the average, skills equivalent to a high-school diploma. If a human being is to compete with such machines, therefore, he must at least possess a high school diploma. The Department of Labor estimates, however, that on the basis of present trends as many as thirty per cent of all students will be high school dropouts in this decade.

6. A permanently depressed class is developing in the United States. Some thirty-eight million Americans, almost one-fifth of the nation, still live in poverty. The percentage of total income received by the poorest twenty per cent of the population was 4.9 per cent in 1944 and 4.7 per cent in 1963.

Secretary Wirtz recently summarized these trends: "The confluence of surging population and driving technology is splitting the American labor force into tens of millions of 'have's' and millions of 'have-nots.' In our economy of sixty-nine million jobs, those with wanted skills enjoy opportunity and earning power. But the others face a new and stark problem—exclusion on a permanent basis, both as producers and consumers, from economic life. This division of people threatens to create a human slag heap. We cannot tolerate the development of a separate nation of the poor, the unskilled, the jobless, living within another nation of the well-off, the trained, and the employed."

Need for a New Consensus

The stubbornness and novelty of the situation that is conveyed by these statistics is now generally accepted. Ironically, it continues to be assumed that it is possible to devise measures which will reduce unemployment to a minimum and thus preserve the overall viability of the present productive system. Some authorities have gone so far as to suggest that the pace of technological change should be slowed down "so as to allow the industrial productive system time to adapt."

We believe, on the contrary, that the industrial productive system is no longer viable. We assert that the only way to turn technological change to the benefit of the individual and the service of the general welfare is to accept the process and to utilize it rationally and humanely. The new science of political economy will be built on the encouragement and planned expansion of cybernation. The issues raised by cybernation are particularly amenable to intelligent policy-making: cybernation itself provides the resources and tools that are needed to ensure minimum hardship during the transition process.

But major changes must be made in our attitudes and institutions in the forseeable future. Today Americans are being swept along by three simultaneous revolutions while assuming they have them under control. In the absence of real understanding of any of these phenomena, especially of technology, we may be allowing an efficient and dehumanized community to emerge by default. Gaining control of our fortune requires the conscious formation of the society we wish to have. Cybernation at last forces us to answer historic questions: What is man's role when he is not dependent upon his own activities for the material basis of his life? What should be the basis for distributing individual access to national resources? Are there other proper claims on goods and services besides a job?

Because of cybernation, society no longer needs to impose repetitive and meaningless (because unnecessary) toil upon the individual. Society can now set the citizen free to make his own choice of occupation and vocation from a wide range of activities not now fostered by our value system and our accepted modes of "work." But in the absence of such a consensus about cybernation, the nation cannot begin to take advantage of all that it promises for human betterment.

Proposal for Action

As a first step to a new consensus it is essential to recognize that the traditional link between jobs and incomes is being broken. The economy of abundance can sustain all citizens in comfort and economic security whether or not they engage in what is commonly reckoned as work. Wealth produced by machines rather than by men is still wealth. We urge, therefore, that society, through its appropriate legal and governmental institutions, undertake an unqualified commitment to provide every individual and every family with an adequate income as a matter of right. This undertaking we consider to be essential to the emerging economic, social and political order in this country. We regard it as the only policy by which the quarter of the nation now dispossessed and soon-to-be dispossessed by lack of employment can be brought within the abundant society. The unqualified right to an income would take the place of the patchwork of welfare measures—from unemployment insurance to relief —designed to ensure that no citizen or resident of the United States actually starves.

We do not pretend to visualize all of the consequences of this change in our values. It is clear, however, that the distribution of abundance in a cybernated society must be based on criteria strikingly different from those of an economic system based on scarcity. In retrospect, the establishment of the right to an income will prove to have been only the first step in the reconstruction of the value system of our society brought on by the triple revolution.

The present system encourages activities which can lead to private profit and neglects those activities which can enhance the wealth and the quality of life of our society. Consequently national policy has hitherto been aimed far more at the welfare of the productive process than at the welfare of people. The era of cybernation can reverse this emphasis. With public policy and research concentrated on people rather than processes we believe that many creative activities and interests commonly thought of as non-economic will absorb the time and the commitment of many of those no longer needed to produce goods and services. Society as a whole must encourage new modes of constructive, rewarding and ennobling activity. Principal among these are activities, such as teaching and learning, that relate people to people rather than people to things. Education has never been primarily conducted for profit in our society; it represents the first and most obvious activity inviting the expansion of the public sector to meet the needs of this period of transition.

We are not able to predict the long-run patterns of human activity and commitment in a nation when fewer and fewer people are involved in production of goods and services, nor are we able to forecast the overall patterns of income distribution that will replace those of the past full employment system. However, these are not speculative and fanciful matters to be contemplated at leisure for a society that may come into existence in three or four generations. The outlines of the future press sharply into the present. The problems of joblessness, inadequate incomes, and frustrated lives confront us now; the American Negro, in his rebellion, asserts the demands—and the rights—of all the disadvantaged. The Negro's is the most insistent voice today, but behind him stand the millions of impoverished who are beginning to understand that cybernation, properly understood and used, is the road out of want and toward a decent life.

The Transition

We recognize that the drastic alterations in circumstances and in our way of life ushered in by cybernation and the economy of abundance will not be completed overnight. Left to the ordinary forces of the market, such change, however, will involve physical and psychological misery and perhaps political chaos. Such misery is already clearly evident among the unemployed, among relief clients into the third generation and more and more among the young and the old for whom society appears to hold no promise of dignified or even stable lives. We must develop programs for this transition designed to give hope to the dispossessed and those cast out by the economic system, and to provide a basis for the rallying of people to bring about those changes in political and social institutions which are essential to the age of technology.

*   *   *

. . . In our opinion, this is a time of crisis, the crisis of a triple revolution. Public philosophy for the transition must rest on the conviction that our economic, social and political institutions exist for the use of man and that man does not exist to maintain a particular economic system. This philosophy centers on an understanding that governments are instituted among men for the purpose of making possible life, liberty, and the pursuit of happiness and that government should be a creative and positive instrument toward these ends.

Change Must Be Managed

The historic discovery of the post-World War II years is that the economic destiny of the nation can be managed. Since the debate over the Employment Act of 1946, it has been increasingly understood that the Federal Government bears primary responsibility for the economic and social well-being of the country. The essence of management is planning. The democratic requirement is planning by public bodies for the general welfare. Planning by private bodies, such as corporations, for their own welfare does not automatically result in additions to the general welfare, as the impact of cybernation on jobs has already made clear.

The hardships imposed by sudden changes in technology have been acknowledged by Congress in proposals for dealing with the long and short-run "dislocations," in legislation for depressed and "impacted" areas, retraining of workers replaced by machines, and the like. The measures so far proposed have not been "transitional" in conception. Perhaps for this reason they have had little effect on the situations they were designed to alleviate. But the primary weakness of this legislation is not ineffectiveness but incoherence. In no way can these disconnected measures be seen as a plan for remedying deep ailments but only, so to speak, as the superficial treatment of surface wounds.

Planning agencies should constitute the network through which pass the stated needs of the people at every level of society, gradually building into a national inventory of human requirements, arrived at by democratic debate of elected representatives.

The primary tasks of the appropriate planning institutions should be:
—to collect the data necessary to appraise the effects, social and economic, of cybernation at different rates of innovation;
—to recommend ways, by public and private initiative, of encouraging and stimulating cybernation;
—to work toward optional allocations of human and natural resources in meeting the requirements of society;
—to develop ways to smooth the transition from a society in which the norm is full employment within an economic system based on scarcity, to one in which the norm will be either non-employment, in the traditional sense of productive work, or employment on the great variety of socially valuable but "non-productive" tasks made possible by an economy of abundance; to bring about the conditions in which men and women no longer needed to produce goods and services may find their way to a variety of self-fulfilling and socially useful occupations;
—to work out alternatives to defense and related spending that will commend themselves to citizens, entrepreneurs and workers as a more reasonable use of common resources;
—to integrate domestic and international planning. The technological revolution has related virtually every major domestic problem to a world problem. The vast inequities between the industrialized and the underdeveloped countries cannot long be sustained.

The aim throughout will be the conscious and rational direction of economic life by planning institutions and democratic control.

In this changed framework the new planning institutions will operate at every level of government—local, regional and federal—and will be organized to elicit democratic participation in all their proceedings. These bodies will be the means for giving direction and content to the growing demand for improvement in all departments of public life. The planning institutions will show the way to turn the growing protest against ugly cities, polluted air and water, an inadequate educational system, disappearing recreational and material resources, low levels of medical care, and haphazard economic development into an integrated effort to raise the level of general welfare.

We are encouraged by the record of the planning institutions both of the Common Market and of several European nations and believe that this country can benefit from studying their weaknesses and strengths. A principal result of planning will be to step up investment in the public sector. Greater investment in this area is advocated because it is overdue, because the needs in this sector comprise a substantial part of the content of the general welfare, and because they can be readily afforded by an abundant society. Given the knowledge that we are now in a period of transition it would be deceptive, in our opinion, to present such activities as likely to produce full employment. The efficiencies of cybernation should be as much sought in the public as in the private sector, and a chief focus of planning would be one means of bringing this about. A central assumption of planning institutions would be the central assumption of this statement, that the nation is moving into a society in which production of goods and services is not the only or perhaps the chief means of distributing income.

The Democratization of Change

The revolution in weaponry gives some dim promise that mankind may finally eliminate institutionalized force as the method of settling international conflict and find for it political and moral equivalents leading to a better world. The Negro revolution signals the ultimate admission of this group to the American community on equal social, political and economic terms. The cybernation revolution proffers an existence qualitatively richer in democratic as well as material values. A social order in which men make the decisions that shape their lives becomes more possible now than ever before; the unshackling of men from the bonds of unfulfilling labor frees them to become citizens, to make themselves and to make their own history.

But these enhanced promises by no means constitute a guarantee. Illuminating and making more possible the "democratic vistas" is one thing; reaching them is quite another, for a vision of democratic life is made real not by technological change but by men consciously moving toward that ideal and creating institutions that will realize and nourish the vision in living form.

Democracy, as we use the term, means a community of men and women who are able to understand, express and determine their lives as dignified human beings. Democracy can only be rooted in a political and economic order in which wealth is distributed by and for people, and used for the widest social benefit. With the emergence of the era of abundance we have the economic base for a true democracy of participation, in which men no longer need to feel themselves prisoners of social forces and decisions beyond their control or comprehension.

All Necessities Freely Available

Robert Theobald

. . . I believe the fundamental level of our problem is that we have a socio-economic system which *forces* the dehumanization of man. We will continue to dehumanize man until this socio-economic system is changed. This thesis, of course, was originally set out by Jacques Ellul in his book, *The Technological Society.* Everyone should read this book to get the flavor of the present debate. The issue can be stated, however, much more clearly and much more concisely. I believe man is trapped for four reasons.

First, we have a system which says that each country must be able to defend itself against all potential attacks. So long as we maintain this system, we must adopt any weapons-system that exists or is developed, because it *is* just possible that the next one will tip the balance of power. We never know which one will do it. Therefore, we cannot stop, because the overkill is qualitative as well as quantitative; in other words, we *can* shift the balance. The end result, as Herbert York and Jerome Weisner put it in speaking of the present arms-race, is "a steady downward spiral into oblivion." We do not have it in our power to stop this spiral without a change in something much deeper than the priorities system.

Second, we have to be able to find enough jobs for people. This means that we must find consumers for all of the possible production. This also means that we must value people as consumers and not as human beings. If you doubt me, I suggest that you look at the children's programming for a short while—remembering that television is the prime "parent" for children from age one through five. Television inculcates the values of frenetic consumership and permanent debt. I said this on television not long ago and someone replied, "Well, that is quite all right, because kids are really very sophisticated—by the age of ten they have learned not to take television seriously." I responded, "What I understand you now to be saying is that we have achieved the good society because we have managed to teach children in the first ten years of their lives never to believe anything that anybody tells them." I would say that this is a rather dubious accomplishment.

If you think we have seen anything in consumer seduction yet, by the way, I suggest you look around for what is going to come, and recognize that certain firms are now employing science-fiction writers to design environments in which their new products will be used. In other words, it is

FROM the *Journal* (Vol. 5, No. 5, February 1967), published by the Division of Higher Education, United Church Board for Homeland Ministries. Reprinted with permission.

their job to produce an environment in which man will be forced to buy things which they produce.

Third, as I think we all agree, it is necessary for firms to install specific equipment as soon as it becomes cheaper than human labor. We have an argument which is not going to be resolved very quickly concerning how rapidly machines are going to replace people in structured tasks. I believe this is going to be very rapid; some other people believe it is not. But in so far as machinery becomes cheaper than people, machinery will be used. Firms have no choice! Any talk about how we care for our human beings is icing on the cake which does not last very long when the chips are down. It can't—*firms have to make a profit*. In addition, of course, the fact that the West is monopolizing technology ensures that the position of the Western countries gets better and better, and that of the poor countries gets worse and worse. As RCA board chairman Sarnoff put it recently, "It is remarkable how knowledge stops at the water's edge." He was arguing for an international system of patents which would ensure that at least some of the patent information gets overseas. I go further. I claim that cybernation requires the end of all patents, and indeed all copyrights, except possibly on such things as poetry, music, and art.

Finally, we have a situation in which we must accept all technological developments. This is a strange situation, and it is cultural as much as anything else. We are so enamoured of technology that the institution with the latest technology is dominant. The supersonic aircraft is a good example of this phenomenon. You might think we were introducing the supersonic aircraft because it would lead to faster travel. But if you look at the ads you will find this is very seldom the reason given. We have instead three other reasons: First, we must produce jobs; second, we must protect our export markets or minimize our imports; and third, we must do it simply *because we can do it*. And I should add a fourth, which ties in with Professor Melman's theme*: It may be the best way to get a new military aircraft. This argument is just beginning to turn up at the edges of the debate on the supersonic aircraft.

What I am saying, and let me make this as clear as possible, is that so long as this socio-economic system exists, all of our efforts—however honest, however disinterested, however intelligent—will be destroyed. How long is it going to take us to realize that top-down programs cannot succeed? After all, we have had the urban renewal program and we all know its results. It failed not because of its bad direction but because we assumed that *buildings* rather than *people* make communities. The primary reason for the increasingly obvious failure of the poverty program is not a lack of planning or bad planning or even bad implementation; it is failing

* The reference is to Seymour Melman, "A Portrait of Depletion," which appears in the same issue of the United Church of Christ–Council for Higher Education *Journal* as Theobald's article.—Editor.

because we assume that the middle class can solve the problems of the poor. This is cultural imperialism at its very worst.

*   *   *

I believe that our first task, therefore, is to begin the restructuring of the socio-economic system to create a human order. I am convinced that we can move in this direction only through fundamental changes in our method of distributing resources. The first two changes must be through providing a guaranteed right to a minimum share of societal resources and through the development of a system of income maintenance for those who have held well-paying jobs over a period of time.

It is my intention to suggest not only some of the short-run implications of new patterns of income distribution but also to discuss some of the medium-run and long-run issues. In order to do this, I must move rapidly over the points which I have raised and discussed in *Free Men and Free Markets* and *The Guaranteed Income*. Briefly stated, however, this is the fundamental argument. First, man is entitled to at least a minimum share of resources, because without these resources no man can be free. Such a right, usually called the guaranteed income (my term is Basic Economic Security), was prefigured by Jefferson when he argued that it was only when man owned land that he could be free. Today, a right to a share in the production of machine-systems must take the place of land. Second, men who have received a certain level of resources over an extended period of time should be provided with a vested right to receive, up to a ceiling, a substantial portion of previous income. My term for this right is Committed Spending.

Basic Economic Security promises substantial immediate advantages. First, it would eliminate extreme poverty. I have a very unconventional view about poverty. I believe that being poor consists of a lack of money. As you know, this really is not the accepted view; poverty is a lack of cultural opportunity, or a lack of education, or a lack of something, but not a lack of money. This view arises from the security that most people directing the poverty program gain from having a very substantial income. Further, until we recognize that poverty produces apathy and degradation, we are not going to get very far. The immorality of talking about the fact that people really do not need money—that what they need is jobs, or that they need the qualities to hold jobs—ignores the fact that in order to motivate someone to learn when he is in an apathetic, degraded state, you must give him a base from which to start. It ignores even more the fact that a vast proportion of these people will never hold a job again. They are old, or sick, or they have great disadvantages. Yet we continue to say that somehow these people should have earned enough to support themselves. This is a remarkable piece of thinking!

Second, with the guaranteed income we could eliminate the means test and the other policing measures which are currently employed. In my opinion, there is far too little knowledge of the legally permissible but morally indefensible policing measures which result in the destruction of dignity and personal drive for the welfare recipient. In welfare we write somebody out of the functioning society. We write them into limbo, and then we complain bitterly when they act accordingly. It is not very reasonable. In other words, we say to them: Don't make a fuss, don't make a nuisance of yourself. If you do, we will take you off welfare. Then we come right back at them and say: But you didn't *try*. There is the same problem, incidentally, with the people who complain about the number of illegitimate children in the ghetto and at the same time fight viciously any attempt to produce decent birth-control programs.

Third, if we had the guaranteed income, instead of having social workers spending some 75 per cent of their time trying to determine how to get enough money for the family if they are good, or just filling in forms if they are bad, we would actually set them free to do something significant. They could actually *work* with the client, but in a non-power relationship. In other words, if the welfare client did not like his social worker, he could tell him or her to get out of his house. I can think of nothing more salutory for both sides!

This is the question: Do we want to maintain a power society? A power society is very comfortable for middle-class people so long as we have the money with which to employ other people. This is a very efficient sanction —people come in and smile very nicely and say: "Good morning, sir; Goodby, sir; Thank you very much, sir." If we did not have this and we wanted to employ somebody, he would have to want to come. I remember a reporter taking me to task for my naivete. He said, "Well, what would happen when Mr. Theobald's maid decided that she didn't like to work for him anymore because she wasn't getting her income from him?" My answer to this is that if she decided that she didn't want to work for me anymore, that is my problem. It shows that I am a very bad employer. If people don't want to come to you simply because they enjoy working for you, you have no reason for being an employer.

Fourth, there is the whole business of the economic base of the ghetto. We spend a great deal of time thinking about how we are going to bring business into the ghetto, how we are going to produce Negro businesses. Let me suggest that, on any level of significance, this is nonsense. If you want to bring money into the ghetto, let's get it from where it can be obtained—a guaranteed income. When you have a guaranteed income, firms with reasonable standards will be very pleased to move into the ghetto. The competition thus created would drive down the excessive consumer prices too often paid in the ghetto and would largely eliminate the door-to-door salesmen and fly-by-night mail-order houses which exploit the poor with shoddy merchandise and excessive credit charges.

Finally, Basic Economic Security establishes the most fundamental human right of all: the right to life regardless of whether the individual can find a job or not. As such, it is an extension of the civil rights—or, more accurately, human rights—movement of recent years. If we are to provide dignity to man, his right to an income must be absolute and not postulated on the administrative rules of any organization or the generosity of any individual. My belief is that a man has a right to live—*period!*

The reality of many of these advantages is accepted by many, including opponents of the proposal. But the proposal is opposed by arguing that the poor *should* hold jobs: That the individual's sense of dignity is indissolubly linked with the job which he holds, and that it is therefore inappropriate to pass a measure which would require him to accept his income as a right and be given the responsibility for developing himself and his society.

Such a position deserves serious consideration, for it is quite clear that many of those who would benefit immediately from Basic Economic Security would be those who perceive their inherent sense of dignity in terms of holding a job. It has been argued, therefore, that we should restrain the development of technology in order to prevent the too-rapid elimination of jobs. Quite apart from considerations of appropriateness or desirability, I believe that this Neo-Luddite approach must be rejected because of its infeasibility. Gross imbalances have developed because of our past use of technology. These can only be controlled for man's benefits through the introduction of further technological innovations.

It must be recognized, however, that the potential Neo-Luddite reaction will almost necessarily grow in scope if present patterns of income distribution persist. We are presently asking men to yield their jobs to the machine without a fuss. It seems improbable that workers will be willing to do this. It seems even less likely that middle-level managers, bankers, lawyers, accountants, etc., would give up their power without a struggle. The availability of Committed Spending as well as Basic Economic Security—that is, a generous income maintenance plan—seems essential if the degree of Neo-Luddism is to be kept at a tolerable level.

The fact that there will be insufficient jobs does not mean, of course, that we can afford to ignore the problem posed by the fact that life without a job appears totally lacking in meaning to many of those raised in the Protestant Ethic. There are many people who still wish to be "employed" but do not have the capacity to develop their own lives within the freedom provided by Basic Economic Security. It is extraordinarily unfortunate that many of those ultimately unemployable within the existing, job-structured, productive system seem likely to be those most in need of structured activity. This is true for the poor, for blue-collar workers, and for many in middle-management and similar groups with high levels of professional training.

The upbringing and education of those most immediately threatened by cybernation limited their horizons so severely that they cannot benefit fully from the potential abundance which their own work has created. Society crippled these people in order to get them to produce efficiently. As their productive efforts are no longer required, society must not only provide them with rights to adequate incomes but must *also* provide new types of activities which will give them a sense of satisfaction from their lives.

Recognition of the fact that our problem is a shortage of structured jobs, rather than a shortage of work or workers, moves the rather general fears about the unfavorable effects of Basic Economic Security on incentive into a more appropriate context. We need to encourage people to work with other human beings and to cease to work for machines and within bureaucratic structures.

This will require the development of what Arthur Pearl and Frank Riesman have called "New Careers for the Poor": the achievement of situations in which individuals, without extensive professional training but with empathy for the problems of those who need help, can act to aid others. This can only be done through new types of organization. The introduction of Basic Economic Security will greatly simplify the provision of new work roles for individuals who will not have to be paid wages. We can anticipate the organization of what I have called "Consentives": productive groups formed by individuals who will come together on a voluntary basis simply because they wish to do so. The goods produced by these consentives will not compete with mass-produced products available from cybernated, productive organizations. The consentive will normally produce the "custom-designed" goods and services which have been vanishing within the present economy.

This type of productive unit will continue far into the future, for the use of a man's hands is one of the most satisfying ways of spending time. The proportion of the population spending most of their time in this kind of production will decline, nevertheless, as other activities seem more challenging and education, in its fullest sense, takes an ever more central position.

It is essential that we recognize, however, that we face an acute transitional problem. We can reasonably hope to change the educational process so that those still within it come to perceive that structured toil is unnecessary and to accept the freedom made possible by cybernation. On the other hand, it will be far more difficult to help those brought up within the Protestant ethic to realize its irrelevance.

What do we do with people who were brought up to believe that life is 40 hours a week in a factory in a time when, if I am right, there is not going to be 40 hours a week in enough factories? Will people do anything if they are not given the lash or the carrot? This is the real issue: Are men fundamentally idle, irresponsible bums? I fear that a very strong proportion of people believe they are. It is deeply disturbing to count the number of *Christians* who have the lowest opinion of the human race. This is a problem which I do not understand, but I recognize it because I have faced enough church or church-related audiences. Somehow the doctrine of original sin has turned into a doctrine that if only people are left alone they will get into all sorts of mischief. "The devil makes mischief for idle hands" appears to be the dominant theme of Christianity today in many instances.

Let me quote from Erich Fromm:

Aside from the fact that there is already no work for an ever increasing sector of our population, and hence that the question of incentive for these people is irrelevant, the question of whether guaranteed income would not reduce the incentive for work is, nevertheless, a serious one. I believe, however, that it can be demonstrated that material incentive is by no means the only incentive for work and effort.

First of all, there are other incentives: pride, social recognition, pleasure in work itself. . . . Second, it is a fact that man, by nature, is not lazy but, on the contrary, suffers from the results of inactivity. People might prefer not to work for one or two months, but the vast majority would beg to work even if they were not paid for it. . . .

Economic abundance, liberation from fear of starvation would mark the transition from a prehuman to a truly human society.

I would suggest that we can make that a stronger and shorter statement: *Americans have a pathological desire to toil!* In other words, it is very difficult to find many people who would really sit down and do nothing for very long, and those who really would are scattered *throughout* our entire society. I remember a banker's statement to me one day. He said, "It is a very strange thing—we have bums in all classes of society, but we only get worried when they are among the poor."

What do I want then? I want a society of full unemployment. I want a society where man is set free to do what he wants to do. I want a society where rights to income are absolute, and man has a responsibility to develop himself and his society. I want a society where sanctions are internal, not external. I want a society of sane, intelligent, self-motivating individuals. Perhaps you will argue that all this is impossible; I am quite willing to admit the evidence suggests that it is. I believe, in fact, that the central issue lies here. I have spent many months trying to imagine a society in which man can continue to be dishonest, irresponsible, proud, and hateful —and still survive with the power that he has himself created. I have tried to imagine any sort of socio-economic system—however corrupt, however evil—which would allow us to cope with the destructive power about which Professor Melman speaks, and not blow ourselves off the face of the earth. I have failed. I know of no one who has really succeeded!

It seems to me that corruption and unlimited power do not mix, because the corruption will *use* the unlimited power at some point. This is what Teilhard de Chardin is saying, at least as I understand him. I believe he is saying that man must become man. Man must grow up. I think it is very startling how many scientists have said essentially the same thing—

that we have reached the point at which unless man becomes adult, he will not exist. Let me reiterate that I do not really expect him to. If I were an intelligent Martian and had visited earth, I would report back in this manner: I am convinced that there is a 99 per cent chance that the human society will wipe itself out within a reasonable period of time!

But I do not have to accept my own conclusions because I am a human being, not a rational Martian. I am also aware of the fact that we are the people who determine the odds. And *if* we decided to do what we have it in our power to do, and *if* we decided to move our programs into areas where they would be truly significant, and *if* we decided to kill the vast majority of our programs which actually impede forward movement, we would be able to change the percentage of probability. The reason I still have my 99 per cent is that, up to the present time, I have seen no evidence among any substantial groups of people that they are about to get rid of their past priorities and do something significant. It is not that we can't, it is that we won't!

This is not a conspiracy argument, it is not an argument about the evil of man. It is an argument about the extraordinary resilence of institutions and socio-economic systems which are intermeshed and interlocked in such a way that change is terribly difficult to achieve—where A is tied into B which is tied into C which is tied into D which is tied into A; and it is terribly difficult to get leverage.

I have developed an analogy about a train running on tracks headed over a cliff. Many of us are fighting to get at the controls. But the control board is not significant, however, because it does not slow the train down. The only significant act, therefore, is to jump off that train, get together, build a helicopter, get far enough ahead of the train to lay a new set of tracks which leads away from the cliff over which we are bound to go. The analogy, I think, is a useful one. It says several things. It says, first of all, that we are very unlikely to succeed. It also says that so long as one is on the train one cannot be truly significant—that we can fight any number of battles on that train, but they are not going to make much difference to the end result; and that it is only in designing and laying a new course—or in my analogy, a new set of tracks—that man can survive.

This requires the very difficult process of disengagement from immediate crisis, and examination of long-run patterns. What are we going to do? What is man going to do with his life? In the future if we move toward our full humanity, the first thing man would do would be to develop his mind and his body to the full. Within a very few years a flabby body among young people is going to be totally unacceptable. I think this is the lesson of modern dancing, which is a statement that the body is not a machine. It is something over which I have control, and I move it the way I *want* to move it.

Second, we would be engaged in the human care of human beings. But let me point out to you that, at the moment, we are moving *away* from the human care of human beings toward using human beings as machines to care for human beings. One of the quickest ways to get into trouble in a nursing school today is to spend a long time with any particular patient because she happens to need you at that particular point in time. This is liable to get you thrown out if you persist. According to the experts, this is not your job. What is wrong with that person, we are told, is his body. His machine is not functioning properly. Don't think about him as a human being—you might get involved, and that would be fatal!

Similarly, teachers now act as computers—but highly inefficient computers. What these teacher-computers do is teach structural knowledge, usually in the same way for several consecutive years. Computers can do that just as well, probably better, because they can be programmed by someone more intelligent than the individual teacher. If we are going to continue to teach in this manner, we will not need very many teachers because obviously they can be replaced. I do not mean that they *should* be, but they *can* be if we teach this way.

The third area of action would be human relationships. It is true that it takes a lifetime to get to know someone. But, do we really *want* to get to know anyone? I think the evidence at the moment is that we do not. At least, this is the way American society has been tending for a long time. We desire purely superficial relationships because they do not upset us.

I remember talking with men in a management-consulting firm. As I was leaving they asked: Have you read a book called *The Joy Seekers?* I said I had not. The consultant informed me that the book is about two sets of beings, one of which are human beings and the other, robots. The problem is you cannot tell one from the other. The man continued, "Our worry is that we are quite sure, in our business, we work exactly as an efficient robot would; but our concern is that we suspect that when we get home at night, we still act just like an efficient robot."

I will support it with the story of a Frenchman who went to Russia when the Russians were still taking dogma seriously. He asked the question: What happens in your ideal communist society when a beautiful young girl is run over by a trolley car? This broke up the meeting, literally, and the man waited until the next morning to receive the following reply: In the ideal communist societies, beautiful young girls are *not* run over by trolley cars!

This says, in effect, that in logical and rational and intelligent societies, tragic things don't happen. But in *human* societies, tragic things are always going to happen. The question is: Are we willing to accept tragedy? The current evidence is that we do not *want* tragedy, and that we avoid it by refusing to *feel* it. But there is a high cost. If one is insensitive to tragedy, he cannot have joy. We cannot cut off the bottom of the curve without also cutting off the top. We can live at a dull, nonexciting level and feel nothing—one way to do this is to go to a dark, padded room and stay there —or we can accept both tragedy and joy.

The fourth point is that we will be engaged in politics, which is the creation of the good community. There are any number of things for people to do. There are always more things to do for and with other people than one can ever get around to doing. But they cannot be done as *jobs*; because the nature of a job is that a man can be told what to do by someone else. This, of course, is profoundly destructive of any of these areas: *self-develop-ment*—you cannot have someone else telling you how to develop yourself; *human care of human beings*—only you can judge how long you should spend with another person; *human relationships*—by definition, this cannot be job-structured. If you look at these things, you will find that none of these are jobs today; or if they are, they should not be.

Why do we have teachers with tenure? Because we claim that the educational process cannot be job-structured. What is happening to us is the end of authority, the end of jobs; and this is where the "death of God" debate is relevant, because it, too, is a debate about the end of authority. It is a statement that, for the first time, man must make his own decisions, because nobody else can make them for him.

This is why I think Basic Economic Security and Committed Spending start us off on the right track. They begin the process of challenging man to behave responsibly: a process which must create a world in which all citizens are able to choose the right for themselves. It is perhaps worthwhile to set out one obvious and one of the less obvious consequences of this development. The obvious consequence is the end of all bureaucracies and administrative hierarchies. The less obvious consequence is that when man receives his income as a right, it will no longer be possible to buy an individual. Thus, it will no longer be possible to force a great talent to teach mediocrities by bribing him with money. This means that the great talents will teach those with great talents, and this will have incalculable results for the development of man.

It will, of course, be impossible to fully achieve this result until all necessary goods and mechanical services are free. It is, however, already clear that the end result of the guaranteed income and the recognition of the need for a more human system will be the creation of a society in which all necessities will be freely available.

Community Paradigms

Paul and Percival Goodman

The Elimination of the Difference
Between Production and Consumption

Men like to make things, to handle the materials and see them take shape and come out as desired, and they are proud of the products. And men like to work and be useful, for work has a rhythm and springs from spontaneous feelings just like play, and to be useful makes people feel right. Productive work is a kind of creation, it is an extension of human personality into nature. But it is also true that the private or state capitalist relations of production, and machine industry as it now exists under whatever system, have so far destroyed the instinctive pleasures of work that economic work is what all ordinary men dislike. (Yet unemployment is dreaded, and people who don't like their work don't know what to do with their leisure.) In capitalist or state-socialist economies, efficiency is measured by profits and expansion rather than by handling the means. Mass production, analyzing the acts of labor into small steps and distributing the products far from home, destroys the sense of creating anything. Rhythm, neatness, style belong to the machine rather than to the man.

The division of economy into production and consumption as two opposite poles means that we are far from the conditions in which work could be a way of life. A way of life requires merging the means in the end, and work would have to be thought of as a continuous process of satisfying activity, satisfying in itself and satisfying in its useful end. Such considerations have led many moralist-economists to want to turn back the clock to conditions of handicraft in a limited society, where the relations of guilds and small markets allow the master craftsmen a say and a hand in every phase of production, distribution, and consumption. Can we achieve the same values with modern technology, a national economy, and a democratic society? With this aim, let us reanalyze efficiency and machine production.

Characteristic of American offices and factories is the severe discipline with regard to punctuality. (In some states the law requires time clocks, to protect labor and calculate the insurance.) Now no doubt in many cases where workers cooperate in teams, where business is timed by the mails, where machines use a temporary source of power, being on time and on the same time as everybody else is essential to efficiency. But by and large it would make little difference at what hour each man's work began and ended, so long as the job itself was done. Often the work could be done at home or on the premises indifferently, or part here part there. Yet this laxity is never allowed, except in the typical instances of hack-writing or commercial art—typical because these workers have an uneasy relation to the economy in any case. (There is a lovely story of how William Faulkner asked M-G-M if he could work at home, and when they said, "Of course," he went back to Oxford, Mississippi.)

Punctuality is demanded not primarily for efficiency but for the discipline itself. Discipline is necessary because the work is onerous; perhaps it makes the idea of working even more onerous, but it makes the work itself much more tolerable, for it is a structure, a decision. Discipline establishes the work in an impersonal secondary environment where, once one has gotten out of bed early in the morning, the rest easily follows. Regulation of time, separation from the personal environment: these are signs that work is not a way of life; they are the methods by which, for better or worse, work that cannot be energized directly by personal concern can get done, unconfused by personal concern.

In the Garden City plans, they "quarantined the technology" from the homes; more generally, we quarantine the work from the homes. But it is even truer to say that we quarantine the homes from the work. For instance, it is calamitous for a man's wife or children to visit him at work; this privilege is reserved for the highest bosses.

Reanalyzing Production

In planning a region of satisfying industrial work, we therefore take account of four main principles:

1. A closer relation of the personal and productive environments, making punctuality reasonable instead of disciplinary, and introducing phases of home and small-shop production; and vice versa, finding appropriate technical uses for personal relations that have come to be considered unproductive.

2. A role for all workers in all stages of the production of the product; for experienced workers a voice and hand in the design of the product and the design and operation of the machines; and for all a political voice on the basis of what they know best, their specific industry, in the national economy.

3. A schedule of work designed on psychological and moral as well as technical grounds, to give the most well-rounded employment to each person, in a diversified environment. Even in technology and economics, the men are ends as well as means.

4. Relatively small units with relative self-sufficiency, so that each com-

munity can enter into a larger whole with solidarity and independence of viewpoint.

These principles are mutually interdependent.

1. To undo the present separation of work and home environments, we can proceed both ways: (a) Return certain parts of production to home-shops or near home; and (b) Introduce domestic work and certain productive family-relations, which are now not considered part of the economy at all, into the style and relations of the larger economy.

   (a) Think of the present proliferation of machine-tools. It could once be said that the sewing machine was the only widely distributed productive machine; but now, especially because of the last war, the idea of thousands of small machine shops, powered by electricity, has become familiar; and small power-tools are a best-selling commodity. In general, the change from coal and steam to electricity and oil has relaxed one of the greatest causes for concentration of machinery around a single driving-shaft.

   (b) Borsodi, going back to the economics of Aristotle, has proved, often with hilarious realism, that home production, such as cooking, cleaning, mending, and entertaining has a formidable economic, though not cash, value. The problem is to lighten and enrich home production by the technical means and some of the expert attitudes of public production, but without destroying its individuality.

   But the chief part of finding a satisfactory productive life in homes and families consists in the analysis of personal relations and conditions: e.g., the productive cooperation of man and wife as it exists on farms, or the productive capabilities of children and old folk, now economically excluded. This involves sentimental and moral problems of extreme depth and delicacy that could only be solved by the experiments of integrated communities.

2. A chief cause of the absurdity of industrial work is that each machine worker is acquainted with only a few processes, not the whole order of production. And the thousands of products are distributed he knows not how or where. Efficiency is organized from above by expert managers who first analyze production into its simple processes, then synthesize these into combinations built into the machines, then arrange the logistics of supplies, etc., and then assign the jobs.

   As against this efficiency organized from above, we must try to give this function to the workers. This is feasible only if the workers have a total grasp of all the operations. There must be a school of industry, academic and not immediately productive, connected with the factory. Now let us distinguish apprentices and graduates. To the apprentices, along with their schooling, is assigned the more monotonous work; to the graduates, the executive and coordinating work, the fine work, the finishing touches. The masterpiece that graduates an apprentice is a new invention, method, or other practical contribution advancing the industry. The masters are teachers, and as part of their job hold free discussions looking to basic changes.

Such a setup detracts greatly from the schedule of continuous production; but it is a question whether it would not prove more efficient in the long run to have the men working for themselves and having a say in the distribution. By this we do not mean merely economic democracy or socialist ownership. These are necessary checks but are not the political meaning of industrialism as such. What is needed is the organization of economic democracy on the basis of the productive units, where each unit, relying on its own expertness and the bargaining power of what it has to offer, cooperates with the whole of society. This is syndicalism, simply an industrial town meeting. To guarantee the independent power of each productive unit, it must have a relative regional self-sufficiency; this is the union of farm and factory.

3. Machine work in its present form is often stultifying, not a "way of life." The remedy is to assign work on psychological and moral as well as technical and economic grounds. The object is to provide a well-rounded employment. Work can be divided as team work and individual work, or physical work and intellectual work. And industries can be combined in a neighborhood to give the right variety. For instance, cast glass, blown glass, and optical instruments; or more generally, industry and agriculture, and factory and domestic work. Probably most important, but difficult to conjure with, is the division in terms of faculties and powers, routine and initiation, obeying and commanding.

The problem is to envisage a well-rounded schedule of jobs for each man, and to arrange the buildings and the farms so that the schedule is feasible.

4. The integration of factory and farm brings us to the idea of regionalism and regional relative autonomy. These are the following main parts:
   (a) Diversified farming as the basis of self-subsistence and, therefore, small urban centers (200,000).
   (b) A number of mutually dependent industrial centers, so that an important part of the national economy is firmly controlled. (The thought is always to have freedom secured by real power.)
   (c) These industries developed around regional resources of field, mine, and power.

Diversified farmers can be independent, and small farms have therefore always been a basis of social stability, though not necessarily of peasant conservatism. On the other hand, for the machines now desirable, the farmer needs cash and links himself with the larger economy of the town.

The political problem of the industrial worker is the reverse, since every industry is completely dependent on the national economy, for both materials and distribution. But by regional interdependence of industries and the close integration of factory and farm work—factory workers taking over in the fields at peak seasons, farmers doing factory work in the winter; town people, especially children, living in the country; farmers domestically making small parts for the factories—the industrial region as a whole can secure for itself independent bargaining power in the national whole.

* * *

Planned Security with Minimum Regulation

Our economy is gigantic by the quantity and number of kinds of goods and services, but as such it is not out of human scale, for to the immense civilized population the immense quantity of goods is appropriate. The increase of useless wealth of individuals, in the form of gadgets sold by advertising, may not add to human virtue, but then it adds to folly which is equally human. The inequitable distribution of wealth, especially considered internationally, is a subject of resentment, and this is an intensely human proposition.

But we have grown out of human scale in the following way: Starting from the human goods of subsistence and luxury, the increment of profit was reinvested in capital goods in order to earn more profits, to win for the enterprisers more luxury and power; this is still human motivation. But in recent decades the result has been that the center of economic concern has gradually shifted from either providing goods for the consumer or gaining wealth for the enterpriser, to keeping the capital machines at work and running at full capacity; for the social arrangements have become so complicated that, unless the machines are running at nearly full capacity, all wealth and subsistence are jeopardized, investment is withdrawn, men are unemployed. That is, when the system depends on all the machines running, unless *every* kind of goods is produced and sold, it is also impossible to produce bread. Then an economy is out of human scale.

Social Insurance vs. the Direct Method

But elementary subsistence and security cannot be neglected by any social order; they are political needs, prior to economic needs. So the governments of the most highly capitalized states intervene to assure elementary security which is no longer the first business of the economy. And the tack they take is the following: to guarantee social security by subsidizing the full productivity of the economy.

Security is provided by insurance paid in the money that comes from the operation of the whole economy. The amazing indirectness of this procedure is brilliantly exposed by the discovery of a new human "right"— as if the rights of man could be so easily amended. This is the "right to employment," failing which one gets the insurance. Full employment is the device by which we flourish; and so the old curse of Adam, that he must work in order to live, now becomes a goal to be struggled for, just because we have the means to produce a surplus, cause of all our woes. This is certainly out of human scale, yet the statesmen of America and England talk this way with absolute conviction; and anyone who spoke otherwise would be voted out of office.

The immediate result of such a solution, of insurance, social credit, or any other kind of give-away money, is to tighten even closer the economic trap. Whatever freedom used to come from free enterprise and free market —and they are freedoms which were indeed fought for with blood—is now trapped in regulation and taxes. The union of government and economy becomes more and more total; we are in the full tide toward statism. This is not a question of anybody's bad intentions, but follows from the connection of the basic political need of subsistence with the totality of an industrial economy.

So much for the indirect solution.

The direct solution, of course, would be to divide the economy and provide the subsistence directly, letting the rest complicate and fluctuate as it will. Let whatever is essential for life and security be considered by itself, and since this is a political need in an elementary sense, let political means be used to guarantee it. But the rest of the economy, providing wealth, power, luxury, emulation, convenience, interest and variety, has to do with varying human wishes and satisfactions, and there is no reason for government to intervene in it in any way. The divided economy has, therefore, the twofold advantage that it directly provides the essential thing that is in jeopardy, without having to underwrite something else; and it restricts the intervention of government to this limited sphere.

Up to, say, sixty years ago, more than half of the productive capacity of our economy was devoted to subsistence; subsistence could be regarded as the chief end of the economy; and whatever their own motives, most enterprisers served the subsistence market. Now, however, in the United States less than a tenth of the economy is concerned with subsistence goods. (Probably nearer a fifteenth; the exact figure would depend on what one considers an adequate minimum.) Except for the biological and political factors involved, the economic machinery could roll almost as usual though everybody were dead of starvation, exposure, and disease. When the situation is viewed in this way, one of the causes is at once clear why prosperity and surplus lead precisely to insecurity: namely, that too few people are busy about subsistence, and as we know from recent farming history, those who are busy about it try to get out of it; there's no real money in meat and potatoes.

But once the economy would be divided as we are suggesting, the very techniques of industry that, when applied incidentally to subsistence, lead to insecurity, would, applied directly to subsistence, produce it with an even smaller fraction of the social labor than at present.

Probably there are various political means by which this small fraction of production could be effectuated, and we will soon develop an obvious one, direct state production of subsistence by universally conscripted labor, run as a state monopoly like the post office or the army, but paying not money but its own scrip, exchangeable only for subsistence goods made by this same enterprise.

(This is a vast undertaking. It would be apparently simpler to effect approximately the same end by using private semi-monopolistic concession-aires in the state nonprofit subsistence-business. But if indeed the produc-tion cost is absolutely minimum and the types absolutely standard and non-competitive, how could a private firm profit? Further, it is intolerable, and unconstitutional, to *have* to work for a private concessionaire. There-fore we prefer the state production—taking over relevant private plant and building its own plant—because of its purity of method. It takes subsistence *out of the economy*. Subsistence is not something to profit by, to invest in, to buy or sell. On the part of the consumer, it is not something to choose or reject or contract for or exchange his labor for, but simply to work for.)

On whatever method—and there are no doubt possibilities we have not thought of—there is one principle: to assure subsistence by specific produc-tion of subsistence goods and services rather than by insurance taxed from the general economy. This involves a system of double money: the "money" of the subsistence production and consumption and the money of the general market. The subsistence-certificates are not money at all, for by definition a man's subsistence leaves nothing to exchange; this "money" is like wartime ration stamps, which are likewise not legally negotiable. A man's right to life is not subject to trade.

A major moral advantage of this proposal is that every person can know that the work he does for a living is unquestionably useful and necessary, and unexploited. It is life itself for himself and everybody else. In our times of so much frivolous production and synthetic demand, and the accompanying cynicism of the producers, the importance of such a moral cannot be overestimated.

Another consequence: To everyone, but especially to the small wage earner, the separation of his subsistence, employing a small fraction of his labor time, from the demands and values of the general economy employ-ing most of his labor time, would give a new security, a breath of freedom, and the possibility of choice. He is independent. He has worked directly for what he absolutely needs; he does not feel the pressure of being a drain on society; he does not fear that his insurance payments will cease. By the same token, people in general, including the small enterpriser, would be more fearless, for their risks are less fatal. But indeed, these things imply a change of social attitude so profound that we must think deeply about both the dangers and the opportunities.

The retrenchment of government from economic interference in the general part, again, might go very far, relaxing kinds of regulation that are now indispensable—protection of women and children, protection of

unions, and so forth. For where the prospective wage earner has a subsistence independently earned, the conditions under which he agrees to
work can be allowed to depend on his own education rather than on the
government's coercion of the employer.

Let us sum up by contrasting the actual plans offered by present-day
governments with the plan here suggested. They propose:

Security of subsistence.
A tax on the general economy.
Necessity to maintain the economy at full production to pay the tax: therefore, governmental planning, pump-priming, subsidies, and made work;
a still further tax, and possibly a falling rate of profit.
Insistence on the unemployed worker's accepting the third or fourth job
available, in order to prevent a continuing drain on the insurance fund.
Protection of the workers thus coerced by regulating the conditions of
industry and investment.

Against this we propose:

Security of subsistence.
Loss to the industrial and merchant of the subsistence market and a small
fraction of the social labor.
Coercion of a small fraction of the social labor to produce the subsistence
goods and services.
Economic freedom in all other respects.

Now financially, the choice between these two plans would depend on
the comparison between the insurance and subsidies tax and the loss of
labor time and market. (Unfortunately, for reasons explained below, this
comparison is hard to make accurately—at least by us.) Socially and
morally, however, there seems to be no comparison at all: our way is direct,
simple, liberating, and allows people a quiet interim to make up their
minds about things.

*   *   *

The Standard of Minimum Subsistence

What is the minimum standard on which a person will feel himself
secure and free, not struggling to get more in the private economy, unless
he chooses? The problem is subtle and difficult, for although as a medical
problem it has a definite solution, as a psychological and moral problem it
depends on emulation, and who is emulated, and these things themselves
are subject to alteration good or bad. What is minimum for even a poor
Southern sharecropper might be spendthrifty to an indio of Yucatan (who,
however, has other satisfactions).

We are speaking always of a going surplus technology. This technology which can provide all manner of things for everybody can also, in a different way, produce a few things of a very few kinds accompanied by a minimum regulation of time, living arrangements, and habits of life. How seriously are people willing to dispense with many things in order to have the freedom which they also think they want?

When combined with freedom, a minimum standard would be far less than what is estimated minimum in our present society. Let us give a single example. In estimating minimum standards of decency and safety, Stuart Chase finds it indispensable for every home to have a radio, because in an integrated society—especially during a total war—a person must have instant communications (and how desirable to have it one way!). But if the very point of our minimum standard is to free people from "integration," a radio is a convenience which a person might think twice about.

Other examples of reducing the "necessary" minimum could be found by considering how much of decency of appearance and how many contacts are required solely by the fact that we live in a society competitive through and through.

On the other hand, when combined with freedom, our minimum is far higher than exists in a scarcity economy, for instance China, where a person subsists in time-bound service to field or commune (and that standard too, since inevitable, is socially acceptable). But if the very point of our minimum is to free people for a selective choice of how they will regulate their time, mobility and independence of location are indispensable.

The minimum is based on a physiological standard, heightened by the addition of whatever is necessary to give a person a true possible freedom of social choice, and not violating our usual mores.

If freedom is the aim, everything beyond the minimum must be rigorously excluded, even if it should be extremely cheap to provide; for it is more important to limit political intervention than to raise the standard of living.

Then, the minimum economy must produce and distribute:

1. Food sufficient in quantity and kind for health, palatable but without variety.
2. Uniform clothing adequate for all seasons.
3. Shelter on an individual, family, and group basis, with adequate conveniences for different environments.
4. Medical service.
5. Transportation.

but *not* primary education, which is a public good taxed from the general economy.

Of these, food, clothing, and shelter are produced by absolute mass production in enormous quantities, without variation of style. Medicine and transportation are better provided by some arrangement between the subsistence and general economies.

The Cost of Subsistence

The extent and cost of the proposed subsistence system, measured in current money, is very hard to determine—and therefore it is hard to name, except by guesswork, the number of years of labor service that are bartered away for economic freedom.

In the first place, although the number of laborers is fixed—for even those who would buy off must furnish a laborer as a substitute—the amount of goods to be produced is fluctuating. For, obviously, though all are entitled to the minimal goods, many, and perhaps most, of the people who are used to better and can afford better, will not take them. There is no advantage in taking and wasting, for the less that needs to be produced, the less the exaction of universal service. Different kinds of goods will differ in demand: fewer will use the minimal housing and clothing; most perhaps can use some of the minimum food; very many will use the transportation and medical service. After a sufficient reserve is built up, production is geared to the prospective use of the next year. But further, this demand will fluctuate with the fluctuation of the general economy, though less sharply: in times of general economic crisis, the demand for subsistence goods increases; in times of prosperity, it diminishes. (The fluctuation is less sharp because of the ratio of minimum goods to substitutes of a higher standard, because of the ratio of the number of unemployed to the universal labor service, and because the reserve functions as an ever-normal granary.)

But secondly and most importantly, the price of goods under such a system of absolute mass production is impossible to estimate. It would be unbelievably cheap. . . .

Work, Automation, and Alienation*

Frank Lindenfeld

What constitutes the alienation of labor? First, that the work is external to the worker, that he does not fulfill himself in his work but denies himself, has a feeling of misery rather than well being, does not develop freely his mental and physical energies but is physically exhausted and mentally debased. The worker therefore feels himself at home only during his leisure time, whereas at work he feels homeless. His work is not voluntary but imposed, forced labor. It is not the satisfaction of a need, but only a means for statisfying other needs. Its alien character is clearly shown by the fact that as soon as there is no physical or other compulsion it is avoided like the plague.

KARL MARX
Economical and Philosophical Manuscripts

Up to the present, man has been constrained by economic conditions to a life of toil and alienated labor. In the advanced industrial societies, it is now possible to change the economic system to eliminate alienation in work. This can be done by establishing a dual economy, where the basic means of subsistence are produced so cheaply and in such quantities by automated machinery that they can be given away freely to all. This would free men from the necessity of working for a living. It would free them to do the kind of work they wanted to do. Improvements in technology have provided the *means* to eliminate both poverty and alienating labor. It remains for us to find the political *will*.

This essay is about conditions in the highly industrialized countries. The questions raised are more relevant to "affluent" economies like the United States than to underdeveloped economies. Where the level of technology is rudimentary, it is difficult to raise the social issue of alienating working conditions because the anterior problem of subsistence has not even been adequately dealt with.

I will make several points here:

1. The alienation of men from their work results from the job specialization and bureaucratization characteristic of modern industry. The alienating organization of the work process occurs under state "socialist" as well as capitalist forms of industrialism.
2. Alienation may not necessarily be consciously experienced. If it is, employees may tolerate it because they get high pay, pleasant working conditions and fringe benefits.
3. Work can be more satisfying if large factories are decentralized into smaller units and if the employees replace control from the top by democratic self-management.
4. The development of cybernation makes possible an economics (and a psychology) of abundance instead of scarcity. Automated, decentralized production and free distribution of the basic necessities of life to all can liberate men from the need to work for income. When work is voluntary, people can engage in freely chosen activities which allow them to express their creative capacities and talents to the fullest.

Work and Industrialism

Contemporary industrial societies drift increasingly toward specialization, rationalization, and managerial control of work. In the offices and factories, major policies are determined by a few at the top; decisions made by those lower in the hierarchies concern only the means to achieve predetermined ends, and often even the means are rigidly prescribed. Employees

* I wish to thank Robert Blauner, Annabelle Motz, John R. Seeley, Peter Reinhard, and Paul Thaxter for comments on earlier drafts of this essay.

are confined to a strictly limited sphere of competence, where they merely carry out orders to make some part of a larger product they may never see in completed form. Men accept these alienating working conditions because of economic compulsion—they need jobs in order to live.

These trends are associated with industrialism per se and do not necessarily disappear with the substitution of socialism for capitalism. Powerlessness, economic compulsion, and subordination are just as likely to be the lot of the average employee under socialism as under capitalism.[1] Indeed, these conditions may be even more pronounced in state socialist economies. In a socialist society, the feeling of alienation might be mitigated by the feeling that one is working for the good of all, rather than somebody's private profit. But I doubt whether the knowledge that industry is owned by the nation has given workers in the Soviet Union a sense of meaning and joy in their work. That feeling can come about only when work is freely chosen, and when workers have a direct say in the organization.

The modern division of labor is aptly described by Daniel Bell:

> The logic of hierarchy . . . is thus not merely the sociological fact of increased supervision which every complex enterprise demands, but a peculiarly technological imperative. In a simple division of labor, for example, the worker had a large measure of control over his own working conditions, that is, the set-up and make-ready, the cleaning and repairing of machines, obtaining his own materials, and so on. Under a complex division of labor these tasks pass out of his control, and he must rely on management to see that they are properly done. This dependence extends along the entire process of production. As a result, modern industry has had to devise an entirely new managerial superstructure which organizes and directs production. This superstructure draws all possible brain-work away from the shop; everything is centered in the planning and schedule and design departments. And in this new hierarchy there stands a figure known neither to the handicrafts nor to the industry in its infancy—the technical employee. With him, the separation of functions becomes complete. The worker at the bottom, attending only to a detail, is divorced from any decision or modification about the product he is working on.[2]

The logic of the division of labor is that of efficiency. The cooperation of many, each engaged in producing a small part, is thought to provide a greater output than the same number separately producing the whole item. The skilled worker who assembles a whole radio is replaced by semiskilled operatives who put together various subassemblies, and eventually these are replaced by automatic machines that make human labor superfluous. The

[1] As Bertrand Russell put it, "When an industry is transferred to the state by nationalization it may happen that there is still just as much inequality of power as there was in the days of private capitalism, the only change being that the holders of power are now officials, not owners." Bertrand Russell, *Authority and the Individual* (Boston: Beacon Press, 1963). For a solution to this problem, Russell comes close to advocating the establishment of local "soviets": "What is needed is local small-scale democracy in all internal affairs; foremen and managers should be elected by those over whom they are to have authority." Ibid., p. 50.

[2] Daniel Bell, "Work and Its Discontents," *The End of Ideology* (New York: Collier, 1962), pp. 234–235.

skilled carpenter who makes and fits doors, windows, and floors is replaced by a crew with less complex skills: those who specialize in laying prefabricated sections of floor, for example. In medicine, the general practitioner gives way to specialists in particular diseases or parts of the body. In academia, the broad ranging intellect is replaced by more narrowly trained experts who explore subsections of arbitrarily defined areas of ·knowledge.

The technically most efficient methods are not always the most satisfying to those engaged in the work. Often one has to choose between technical efficiency (concentration on *production*) and employee happiness (concentration on the *producers*). It would be a lovely world if efficiency and happiness could always be reconciled, but this is not the case. When efficiency and happiness conflict, we have to choose one over the other. Until modern times, the choices have generally been in the direction of efficiency.[3]

What makes the age of automation unique is the possibility of consistently resolving conflicts between efficiency and happiness in favor of the latter. There is no need to dream of the efficiency of a full and rational "utilization" of human and technological resources when muscle power becomes superfluous and machines are readily available. We may consciously opt for *inefficiency*, for less "production" than is theoretically attainable, because we place other values first.[4] Actually, decentralized organizations are often more efficient and less costly than centralized ones. But the important thing is that decentralization is a more desirable form of human association.[5]

Alienation

The thread of interest in alienation extends from such classical authors as Marx, Weber, and Mannheim to such contemporaries as Nisbet, Fromm, and Mills. In recent discussions, both Seeman and Blauner identify five separate dimensions of alienation.[6] The most important of these are powerlessness, meaninglessness, and self-estrangement.

[3] Thus the Israeli *kibbutzim*, committed to a communist ideology of nonspecialization in work, have nevertheless found that economic pressures make the attainment of this ideal difficult in practice. Nonspecialization was found to be less efficient from the strict, short-run, technical point of view. When production values are given highest priority, as they are in contemporary Israel, being able to change jobs is likely to remain an unrealized ideal. See Ivan Vallier, "Structural Differentiation, Production Imperatives, and Communal Norms: The Kibbutz in Crisis," *Social Forces* (1962), pp. 233–41.

[4] See Daniel Bell, op. cit.

[5] See some of the stimulating suggestions made by Paul Goodman in *People or Personnel* (New York: Random House, 1965).

[6] For some of the literature which has appeared on the subject of alienation in recent years, see Robert Blauner, *Alienation and Freedom* (Chicago: University of Chicago Press, 1964); Marvin B. Scott, "The Social Sources of Alienation," in *The*

Powerlessness refers to the employee's feeling that his voice doesn't count for much, that he is pushed around, that he cannot say what should be produced, or how, at what pace, and for whom. The growth of labor unions in the United States has provided many employees with the power to resist being pushed around and treated in a way that violates their dignity. Through collective bargaining, unions have resisted management pressures for speed-ups in production and arbitrary firing of employees. (In a number of nonunionized fields and in the smaller and marginal enterprises, however, many employees are still vulnerable to being pushed around.) But although unions can coerce employers into treating workers with more dignity, employees still accept the prerogative of management to decide what gets produced and what doesn't, what prices are set, and so on.

Meaninglessness refers to the fact that the employee in a bureaucratic organization is engaged in one small, standardized task, and rarely gets to see or understand the whole process or product. Only a few at the top know how all the highly subdivided jobs are interrelated. Self-estrangement occurs when work is undertaken for its extrinsic rather than its intrinsic value, when work is not done for its own sake, or for the sake of what the work itself accomplishes, but primarily for the money. Self-estrangement means that men do not express themselves fully or utilize their talents in their work.

The opposite of alienated labor is work pursued for its intrinsic worth and meaning. This, according to Mills, is the Renaissance view of work as craftsmanship:

> There is no ulterior motive in work other than the product being made and the processes of its creation. The details of daily work are meaningful because they are not detached in the worker's mind from the product of the work. The worker is free to control his own working action. The craftsman is thus able to learn from his work; and to use and develop his capacities and skills in its prosecution. There is no split of work and play, or work and culture. The craftsman's way of livelihood determines and infuses his entire mode of living.[7]

It is helpful at this point to distinguish between objective social conditions and the subjective perceptions and feelings that arise in response to them. Alienation can refer either to the relationship of the employee to his work, or to his awareness of that relationship.[8] The condition of alienation

---

New Sociology, Irving L. Horowitz, ed. (New York: Oxford University Press, 1964); Eric and Mary Josephson, eds., Man Alone (New York: Dell, 1962); Melvin Seeman, "The Meaning of Alienation," American Sociological Review (1959) pp. 783–91; Robert Nisbet, Community and Power (New York: Oxford University Press, 1962); C. Wright Mills, White Collar (New York: Oxford University Press, 1951); Erich Fromm, Marx's Concept of Man (New York: Ungar, 1961).

[7] C. Wright Mills, op. cit., p. 220.

[8] Blauner speaks of estrangement as the subjective aspect of alienation. See Robert Blauner, "Work Satisfaction and Industrial Trends in Modern Society," in Reinhard Bendix and Seymour Lipset, eds., Class Status and Power (New York: Free Press, 1966), p. 473.

may not necessarily be perceived or understood as such by the alienated.[9] Thus, I doubt whether any great number of American employees *feel* alienated from their work. They accept doing something they may not entirely like in return for their paycheck. As Blauner points out, the progress of automation may help to diminish certain aspects of alienation from work. For example, those employed in continuous process industries may be much freer in their movement and may have more leeway in varying their schedules than those who tend machines or work on the assembly line. This freedom makes work in automated plants more satisfying. Blauner dismisses the question of workers' control by saying (albeit correctly) that most employees are generally not interested in taking on managerial responsibilities: they are being used, but as they are well paid it's a good bargain, and at least on the surface they don't seem to mind.[10]

I will focus here on three dimensions of objective conditions of work: high vs. low pay, pleasant vs. unpleasant atmosphere, and using vs. nonusing relationships.

Pay is self-explanatory. Pleasantness includes friendly relations with co-workers and supervisors, fewer hours and longer coffee breaks, background music and air conditioning, looseness of supervision, and so forth. (The pleasantness of working conditions is, of course, relative; what would have been pleasant for most people two hundred years ago would not be acceptable today.)

By "using" I mean simply conditions under which the ends of work are not determined by the worker but by others to whom he is subordinate.[11] This is the typical condition of *employees*. Modern industrialism *uses* employees as means to the ends of those in control of industrial or

---

[9] There may be a connection between the repressed, unconscious frustration of modern employees and their being a willing part of a destructive system. Some employees, of course, do not take their work seriously and they good-humoredly trade their labor for pay. In many others, however, a basic aggressiveness may lurk just below their level of awareness. This aggressiveness, stemming from frustration at being powerless to control the course of their work or their lives, may lead to a secret glory in the possibility of the big bang of destruction. The alienated may indeed derive vicarious pleasure from their government's military aggression against the Vietnamese, the Chinese, or whoever the current "enemy" may be.

Benefiting as we do from life in the affluent society, we are less likely to worry about the conditions of people in other countries. As Marcuse puts it, "Loss of conscience due to the satisfactory liberties granted by an unfree society makes for a *happy consciousness* which facilitates acceptance of the misdeeds of this society." Herbert Marcuse, *One Dimensional Man* (Boston: Beacon Press, 1964), p. 76.

[10] See Robert Blauner, op. cit.

[11] I was tempted to use the term "exploitative" instead of "using." But exploitative is perhaps too strong. The larger American business firms do not generally have a policy of conscious exploitation of the domestic labor force. On the contrary, many managers of modern industrial bureaucracies pride themselves on their sense of public responsibility and believe in looking after the welfare of employees as "good business." Nor do most American employees feel exploited. Exploitation is a more appropriate term for those with the lowest-paying jobs, such as auto-wash attendants or farm laborers in this country or for employees of American corporations in Latin America.

governmental hierarchies.[12] The employer-employee relationship is *essentially* one of servitude for the employee. A certain amount of "using the other" is inherent in almost all social relationships, including work situations, but the question is not whether employees also "use" employers as a source of money, status, and so on. It is rather a question of which party has the decided advantage in the exchange.

WORKING CONDITIONS

		Using		Nonusing
	Unpleasant	*Pleasant*		
Low pay	1. Sweatshop operative; *bracero*	3. "girl friday"		Self-employed artist, craftsman or professional;
High pay	2. assembly-line worker	4. repairman in automated plant		independent farmer

In the above typology, the occupational categories on the right are less alienating, those on the left more alienating. The subjective awareness of alienation, however, may differ within the four categories on the left. Some of those who are being used may be aware of the fact and resent it; in which case we say they feel alienated. But many who are used are not particularly aware of this; or if they are they are not resentful, because they receive high pay or have pleasant working conditions. We would expect that consciousness of alienation would be highest among the sweatshop operatives, and lowest among repairmen in automated plants; it would be intermediate among assembly-line workers and secretaries. (The categories have been ranked from 1 (high) to 4 (low) to indicate expected degree of awareness of alienation.)

Herein lies the paradox of the relative contentment of American employees. If the work is dull, or even stupid and meaningless, at least the pay is high, the hours are short, and there are fringe benefits such as longer vacations, medical insurance, and pension systems. For meaning in their lives, people do not look so much to production as to consumption (of clothes, cars, television, homes) and they turn increasingly to do-it-yourself projects, gardening, travel, and so on.

American trade unions have not helped to develop the workers' consciousness of alienation. The role of the unions in the United States has been to raise wages and improve working conditions and fringe benefits through collective bargaining. The unions have never offered any serious challenge to management's prerogative of setting basic goals and policies. With the exception of groups such as the Industrial Workers of the

---

[12] The hierarchical principle need not be intrinsically bad. Voluntary deference to a co-worker on the basis of his greater knowledge and skill is quite different from deference based on the authoritative *position* of the co-worker.

World, unions have tended to accept the worker's powerlessness over broad policies in return for sharing with the managers a little bigger slice of the bread.

Unions have acquired a vested interest in the smooth running of business enterprises and often perform the very important function for management of "stabilizing" the labor situation. Moreover, the unions themselves have become large, bureaucratic structures over which the average worker has as little power as he has over management.

Progressive employers have attempted to cope with the negative attitudes of employees towards their work through such schemes as stock distribution, profit sharing, and "job enlargement." The first two are only a form of higher compensation. In enlarged jobs, workers participate in different phases of making a complex product, instead of engaging in only one repetitive task. This situation does make work more pleasant and less alienating; furthermore, the employees often turn out better-quality products.[13] However, integrated work patterns do not alter the powerless and subordinate position of the employee.

Workers' Control

One of my assumptions, implicit in the term "using," is that people should participate in deciding what they shall produce and how, and that the average man is a morally responsible and autonomous agent. But it is not certain that the results of democratic participation would necessarily be superior to those of the present hierarchical system. For the average man has become conditioned to consider various alien needs as his own.[14] Factory workers might upon due reflection decide that three-quarters of all their production should go into 1,000-horsepower automobiles, color television, or guided missiles. I would simply argue for the ethical superiority of making it *possible* for people to feel more responsible for their work, correct their own mistakes, and be the rulers of their own activity. Beyond this, perhaps we can find some way of turning the fiction that "the consumer is boss" into the reality of democratic control of the means of production and distribution by producers and consumers alike.

Alienated labor can be diminished when the workers themselves determine what products or services they will supply, how they will organize the

[13] See Abraham Maslow, *Eupsychian Management* (Homewood, Ill.: Dorsey Press, 1965).

[14] See Herbert Marcuse, op. cit., p. 6: "The question of what are true and false needs must be answered by the individuals themselves, but only in the last analysis; that is, if and when they are free to give their own answer. As long as they are kept incapable of being autonomous, as long as they are indoctrinated and manipulated (down to their very instinct) their answer to this question cannot be taken as their own. . . . How can the people who have been the object of effective and productive domination by themselves create the conditions of freedom?"

work and what they will do with the profits. Under workers' control, all those who work in an organization vote on production goals, wages, prices, and investments. All major decisions are shared: in small organizations problems are resolved by the group meeting as a whole. In large organizations, the group may elect a rotating executive committee.

Workers' control must be distinguished from mere participation in management, which is not the same thing at all. The difference is a question of power. Co-management means that workers are consulted, but that the final decision still rests with the boss. *Control* means that the final decision rests with the workers.

There have been attempts to implement workers' control, during the Spanish revolution of 1936–1937 and more recently in Yugoslavia and Algeria.[15] In Spain agricultural workers organized their own collective farms, and industrial workers took over and ran factories with the aid of sympathetic technicians. In all three countries, however, workers' management was hampered by government monopoly of banking and credit and by central government directives which set general policies within which local industries had to operate.

Workers' control has its difficulties. One is that in larger enterprises, elected management committees can become undemocratic and self-perpetuating. This might be avoided by rotating managers and by having periodic meetings of all who participate in the organization, but wherever possible the best method is to keep the organization small enough that problems can be resolved in general meetings.

A second difficulty is the parochialism encouraged by local autonomy, where rich enterprises keep their "profits" and do not share with poorer ones. The remedy for this would be some kind of coordination; but instead of achieving this by government intervention, it should be done through federation. Producers' organizations could elect representatives that would meet to determine how to share equipment, money, and resources and how they can cooperate in other ways. This method may not always be as efficient as central government control, but in the long run it will be more effective in encouraging free initiative and responsibility.

Still another difficulty is apparent when we try to extend workers' control to automated factories capable of producing large quantities of goods with only a handful of workers. It does not seem fair that the few persons needed to tend a continuous-process factory should determine its goals. The wealth embodied in the capital—the machinery—is a social product that belongs to the community. One solution would be for the

[15] For a general account of workers' control and attempts to apply it in various countries, see Daniel Guerin, *Anarchism* (New York: Monthly Review Press, 1970). Portions of Guerin's discussion on Spain are reprinted in Section 13 of this anthology.

On the Yugoslav experience, see David Riddell, "Social Self-Government: The Background of Theory and Practice in Yugoslav Socialism," *British Journal of Sociology*, XIX (March 1968), 47–75; Albert Meister, *Socialisme et Autogestion, L'Experience Jougoslave* (Paris: Editions du Seuil, 1964).

community to elect a factory board of directors on which the workers would have representation. The entire community, or the board, would decide what was to be produced. Those who wanted to would commit themselves to carrying out this decision. These would be engineers to draw up designs, machinists and technicians to make the production machinery, and operator-repairmen to operate and maintain the machines. The workers would decide *how* the work was to be accomplished and at what pace. Together with the board of directors they would decide what to do with any surplus, and how expansion should take place.

Workers' control is good because the people become active participants instead of passive servants. Workers' control will doubtless be accompanied by many mistakes and a certain inefficiency resulting from inadequate coordination of different enterprises, but it is a desirable system because it enables people to take initiative, to be directly responsible for their work, to correct their own mistakes, and to govern their own activity.

Automation and Freedom

Technology up to now has increased the alienation of man from his work. But this very technology applied in a different way can provide everyone with adequate food, shelter, clothing, and basic tools and services, so that all can be free to do the kind of work they want to, or not do any at all if they so desire. Production of necessities would require so few people that it could be done only by volunteers.

One way to translate automation into freedom from work is to introduce a dual economy with mass production of necessities on the one hand and a luxury market system on the other. (Another way is through the guaranteed income.[16]) What makes the dual economy possible is that food, clothing, shelter, and basic tools can be produced cheaply, well, and in such quantity as to be given away freely. Mass-produced items do not have to be of inferior quality; if designed for human use instead of profit they can be functional and beautiful. In fact, automation can supply more variation in the end products than older assembly-line techniques, and at no extra cost. The free distribution of necessities would allow more people to be artists or craftsmen, because they would not have to depend on selling their works. On the luxury side of the economy, those who did not want

[16] On the guaranteed annual income, see Robert Theobald, *Free Men and Free Markets* (New York: Doubleday, 1965); also, Ad Hoc Committee, "The Triple Revolution," *Liberation* (April 1964) [portions of which are reprinted on pp. 206–218 of this book]. On the dual economy, see the revised edition, Paul and Percival Goodman, *Communitas* (New York: Vintage, 1960) [portions of which appear on pp. 229–238]. The dual economy idea is also found in the writing of earlier generations. See Bertrand Russell, *Roads to Freedom* (London: Unwin, 1966, originally published in 1918). This concept goes back as far as William Godwin's *Inquiry Concerning the Principles of Political Justice*, published in 1793.

standardized goods could join with others to produce their own variants, or they could exchange their own products for those of others.[17]

The luxury economy would operate just as our economy now does except that nobody would be forced to work, since all would receive necessities free. Those who participated in the luxury side of the economy would be paid.

A mere fraction of the present labor force would suffice to produce all the necessities within a dual economy. Only a few million persons in the United States are engaged in producing subsistence goods. Many of the rest are employed in packaging, selling, advertising, insuring, inspecting, and transporting the commodities produced by these few. Others work for the government, the army, or in war plants, or are unemployed.[18]

A dual economy would not obviate the need to make certain political decisions. In fact it would clarify the political nature of economic decisions. When practically anything can be produced in large quantities and provided free it becomes a political question as to whether a particular item—automobiles, for instance—should be made for general distribution.

I assume that the subsistence portions of a dual economy would be decentralized, even where it would be technically possible to concentrate all production in one large plant. I assume further that the subsistence economy would have a system of workers' control, which would operate in conjunction with community-elected boards of directors. Decisions about general production goals would be discussed and debated by the entire community. Workers' control would probably also gradually overtake the luxury side of the economy, because economic security provided by the subsistence sector would allow people to leave immediately any organizations where they felt they did not have enough say.[19]

---

[17] Another paradigm, described in *Communitas*, consists of a decentralized system of independent communities, each relatively self-sufficient, where most persons are engaged in some form of craft or subsistence production. Isolated communities of this kind are beginning to form, but they are not likely to exist on a large scale in the foreseeable future.

[18] Documentation of this point is difficult because of the dispute about which occupations are necessary and which are superfluous. In 1961, Piel estimated there were close to 12 million persons either unemployed or working in the armed forces, the Defense Department, or industries supplying defense contracts. This means that all goods and services for the domestic civilian and export market were produced by 80 per cent of the labor force. See Gerald Piel, *Consumers of Abundance* (Santa Barbara: Center for the Study of Democratic Institutions, 1961).

Recent census and Labor Department data shows that the number of workers in certain essential occupations has been decreasing over the last two decades, while the number in nonproductive and nonessential occupations has increased enormously. The number of farm workers has decreased from more than 6 million to barely 2.5 million. During the same period, the number of those engaged in sales and clerical work jumped from 11.5 to 18.5 million (now more than one fourth of the total labor force!) The single fastest growing sector seems to be government. Government employment more than doubled in the last twenty years.

[19] I would favor minimum government control over the luxury half of the economy. *Cooperatively* structured organizations in the luxury economy might be allowed to grow naturally to include hundreds, possibly thousands of persons. It might be socially de-

In an economy where people didn't have to work for a living, it would be necessary for some to volunteer for people-oriented services like medicine, and for others to volunteer to build, maintain, and operate such mass-production machinery as might be needed. If a community found itself short of volunteers for essential occupations, it might resort to a sales or production tax on the luxury economy to provide wages for workers in scarce supply in the subsistence sector. This would probably be a rare occurrence. People would work voluntarily for much the same reasons that many have joined the Peace Corps. They would do the work because they wanted to help their fellow men, because the work was interesting to them, and because they felt they expressed and fulfilled themselves thereby.[20]

What would the average person do if the free availability of all basic necessities made working for pay unnecessary? Many would take jobs in the luxury economy to get money to buy fancy consumer goods as they do now. Some would spend much time looking for entertainment, or traveling from one community to another. Some would volunteer for jobs in the subsistence economy because they felt willing and able to do what was needed and because they knew that working in those jobs directly contributed to the welfare of the community. If economic compulsion were removed, many persons might redirect their energies into artistic work or handicraft production.

Given the opportunity to choose, many would leave large-scale organizations and form smaller voluntary associations of workers, while some would work alone. Large bureaucratic organizations such as General Motors could exist only if enough persons were persuaded to band together of their own free will. It is possible that the lure of money or power would interest some people in devoting their lives to such "old-fashioned" organizations. Nevertheless, I do not believe that their appeal would be great if the basic necessities of life were freely available and nobody had to work for money. There would be many candidates for corporation president, but few would want to be junior executives or secretaries.

An economy where necessities are freely available, where work is voluntary and where workers have control of the productive process is more than a utopian dream. The technological capacity of the America of the 1970's makes it a practical possibility which can be brought about when enough of us want it and join with others to bring it about.

---

sirable, however, to limit the size of hierarchical "private enterprise" organizations in the luxury sector. Here we could follow the example of Yugoslavia. In that country, there is both a public and a private sector, but private enterprises cannot employ more than six workers without being so heavily taxed that they lose money.

[20] Men work for more than just money, even in contemporary "materialist" America. This is indicated in a national sample survey of attitudes of persons in different occupations. Some four-fifths of the employed men interviewed said they would continue to work even if they didn't have to, although many would change the type of work they were doing if they could. See Nancy G. Morse and Robert S. Weiss, "The Function and Meaning of Work and the Job," *American Sociological Review*, XX, 2 (April 1955), pp. 191–98.

SECTION 8

POVERTY AND RACIAL INEQUALITY

BY CONTEMPORARY standards a substantial minority of the American population receives less than enough income to keep it adequately fed, clothed, and sheltered. As standards differ, so do the figures on the extent of poverty. Harrington, writing in 1969, claims the poor number between 40 and 50 million. A reasonable estimate is that at least one-fifth of the population lives below the poverty line.[1] Although the richest tenth has received more than one quarter of the national income, the poorest fifth has consistently received less than a twentieth.[2]

[1] See Robert Lampman, "The Low Income Population and Economic Growth," *Study Paper no. 12* (Washington, D.C.: U.S. Congress Joint Economy Committee, 1959).

[2] Poverty here is considered only in the context of the United States, in relation to its own general standard of living. This poverty, however, is relative to conditions of poverty in other countries. In Asia, Africa, and Latin America, the poor have nowhere near the material comforts of the poor in the United States, and poverty is a condition not merely of the few but of the majority. In both the Third World and the United States the distance between poverty and wealth is astronomical, and in both the rich keep down the poor; the difference is that in a country with an affluent majority it is possible for the poor to make it in one way or another, whereas in a country where most people are poor poverty means toil from childhood, slow starvation, and an early death.

On income differences within the United States, see Gabriel Kolko, *Wealth and Power in America* (New York: Praeger Pubs., Inc., 1962), Chaps. 1 and 2.

There are two nations, Harrington says: the well-to-do and the "other" America—the poor. The latter include a disproportionate number of the old, the sick, people in rural areas, and nonwhites. Many are unemployed. Some families move up, while others, hit by sickness or unemployment, become poor; but from year to year the total proportion of poor people remains inordinately large.

Most Americans do not consider poverty a problem because the poor have become invisible, Harrington says. Blacks are segregated in central city ghettos hardly ever seen by the white middle class. Old persons are hidden away in their rooms. In rural areas, poverty lies off the beaten track. When the poor appear in public they are not conspicuous, because in America they usually wear decent clothes and look not too different from everyone else.

For the poor, Harrington says, progress is misery. Urban renewal deprives them of housing. Automation takes their jobs away. The poor who participate in job training programs often find once they have finished their training that no jobs are available; those who attend night school for high school diplomas find that many jobs now require college degrees. Welfare benefits are higher than ever, but the poorest do not even know about the benefits available. Further, social security and unemployment insurance are calculated according to previous income, so that workers who have made the least receive the lowest benefits.

What is to be done? One answer is socialism. Another is the guaranteed annual income, or the free distribution of basic necessities.[3] Harrington implies that the most realistic solution is to apply more vigorously the principles of the welfare state. The only agency capable of ameliorating poverty, he says, is the federal government. He suggests that it embark on a massive welfare program.[4]

During the 1960s the federal government indeed launched a "war on poverty." But the program did not diminish poverty. Instead it provided jobs for middle-class social workers and professionals hired to "fight poverty." Also, it perpetuated the dependence of the poor, because like all government programs it was initiated at the top.

The feeling of hopelessness among the poor is not likely to be ameliorated until the poor themselves get together to define their own needs and take control of their own destiny. The poor do need money. But more important they need to run their own lives. Negroes have begun to do this, working through civil rights groups like SNCC (Student Nonviolent Coordinating Committee) and black nationalist groups such as the Black Panthers and the Black Muslims.

American Negroes have two problems, according to Carmichael: they are poor and they are black. To deal with these problems SNCC organized

[3] On socialism see Section 12 of this book. On the guaranteed annual income see Section 7.
[4] The Other America, p. 170.

to obtain political power in Southern communities. The "black power" they sought was power to participate in making the decisions affecting their lives. Black power means community control over police departments, school boards, and local welfare programs.

At present, if blacks want a better education they have to attend schools in white areas, and if they want better medical care they must be admitted to white hospitals. What the blacks want, Carmichael says, is schools and hospitals in their own communities as good or better than those serving whites. He urges radical whites to work to end racism in their own communities instead of trying to organize blacks.

Lincoln talks about the different ways that Negroes have dealt with racism. Some have avoided identification as Negroes and kept from threatening contact with whites by voluntarily remaining in the ghettos. Some have accepted "Uncle Tom" status, but only in outward appearance, and when they had no other choice. Increasing numbers, especially among the young have asserted their rights in militant actions such as sit-ins, while others have merely redirected toward each other the aggression meant for whites.

Black nationalism, Lincoln explains, is an attempt to cope with racism. It is a rebellion against white values and way of life, it asserts pride in a black culture and looks to the establishment of a black state. Black nationalism appeals most strongly to lower-class Negroes. Upper-class Negroes identify themselves with white society; middle-class Negroes see themselves as Negro Americans and seek equal privileges within the existing structure. Only the lower class is ready to repudiate both white culture and the "Negro" identity derived from that culture.

Black nationalism is revolutionary insofar as it provides a positive self-image that enables blacks to change their conditions. It is only through black power that the black community can be liberated. However, black power does not automatically lead to black liberation. Black mayors, police chiefs, and school superintendents can be just as bad as their white counterparts unless the people can exercise continuing democratic control over them. Also, full participation in national electoral politics will contribute little to black liberation, because national politics is only a part of a repressive system in which the most important decisions are monopolized by an elite not answerable to the public. Given the nature of electoral politics, the wider participation of Negroes may have little effect other than to push upward their status as an ethnic group, just as the Irish, Italians, and others have done in previous generations.

Black nationalism has its conservative side. Some nationalist groups hold to a doctrine of black supremacy, which by definition is as racist as white supremacy. Also some groups, instead of demanding an end to capitalism, merely seek to employ it themselves.

Groups such as SNCC, on the other hand, seek to break free from the confining assumptions of both the white and the black middle class. They reject white values and white culture, but also seek an entirely new way of life where there won't be room even for black capitalism. SNCC opposed the draft, the Vietnam war, and other interventions against foreign revolutions. It called for a drastic change in the economic system. As Carmichael put it, "The society we seek to build among black people . . . is not a capitalist one. It is a society in which the spirit of community and humanistic love prevail."

The Other America

Michael Harrington

The millions who are poor in the United States tend to become increasingly invisible. Here is a great mass of people, yet it takes an effort of the intellect and will even to see them.

I discovered this personally in a curious way. After I wrote my first article on poverty in America, I had all the statistics down on paper. I had proved to my satisfaction that there were around 50,000,000 poor in this country. Yet, I realized I did not believe my own figures. The poor existed in the Government reports; they were percentages and numbers in long, close columns, but they were not part of my experience. I could prove that the other America existed, but I had never been there.

My response was not accidental. It was typical of what is happening to an entire society, and it reflects profound social changes in this nation. The other America, the America of poverty, is hidden today in a way that it never was before. Its millions are socially invisible to the rest of us. No wonder that so many misinterpreted Galbraith's title and assumed that "the affluent society" meant that everyone had a decent standard of life. The misinterpretation was true as far as the actual day-to-day lives of two-thirds of the nation were concerned. Thus, one must begin a description of the other America by understanding why we do not see it.

There are perennial reasons that make the other America an invisible land.

Poverty is often off the beaten track. It always has been. The ordinary tourist never left the main highway, and today he rides interstate turnpikes. He does not go into the valleys of Pennsylvania where the towns look like movie sets of Wales in the thirties. He does not see the company houses in rows, the rutted roads (the poor always have bad roads whether they live in the city, in towns, or on farms), and everything is black and dirty. And even if he were to pass through such a place by accident, the tourist would not meet the unemployed men in the bar or the women coming home from a runaway sweatshop.

Then, too, beauty and myths are perennial masks of poverty. The traveler comes to the Appalachians in the lovely season. He sees the hills, the streams, the foliage—but not the poor. Or perhaps he looks at a run-down mountain house and, remembering Rousseau rather than seeing with his eyes, decides that "those people" are truly fortunate to be living the way they are and that they are lucky to be exempt from the strains and tensions of the middle class. The only problem is that "those people," the quaint inhabitants of those hills, are undereducated, underprivileged, lack medical care, and are in the process of being forced from the land into a life in the cities, where they are misfits.

These are normal and obvious causes of the invisibility of the poor. They operated a generation ago; they will be functioning a generation hence. It is more important to understand that the very development of American society is creating a new kind of blindness about poverty. The poor are increasingly slipping out of the very experience and consciousness of the nation.

If the middle class never did like ugliness and poverty, it was at least aware of them. "Across the tracks" was not a very long way to go. There were forays into the slums at Christmas time; there were charitable organizations that brought contact with the poor. Occasionally, almost everyone passed through the Negro ghetto or the blocks of tenements, if only to get downtown to work or to entertainment.

Now the American city has been transformed. The poor still inhabit the miserable housing in the central area, but they are increasingly isolated from contact with, or sight of, anybody else. Middle-class women coming in from Suburbia on a rare trip may catch the merest glimpse of the other America on the way to an evening at the theater, but their children are segregated in suburban schools. The business or professional man may drive along the fringes of slums in a car or bus, but it is not an important experience to him. The failures, the unskilled, the disabled, the aged, and the minorities are right there, across the tracks, where they have always been. But hardly anyone else is.

In short, the very development of the American city has removed poverty from the living, emotional experience of millions upon millions of middle-class Americans. Living out in the suburbs, it is easy to assume that ours is, indeed, an affluent society.

This new segregation of poverty is compounded by a well-meaning ignorance. A good many concerned and sympathetic Americans are aware that there is much discussion of urban renewal. Suddenly, driving through the city, they notice that a familiar slum has been torn down and that there are towering, modern buildings where once there had been tenements or hovels. There is a warm feeling of satisfaction, of pride in the way things are working out: the poor, it is obvious, are being taken care of.

The irony in this is that the truth is nearly the exact opposite to the impression. The total impact of the various housing programs in postwar America has been to squeeze more and more people into existing slums. More often than not, the modern apartment in a towering building rents at $40 a room or more. For, during the past decade and a half, there has been more subsidization of middle-and upper-income housing than there has been of housing for the poor.

Clothes make the poor invisible too: America has the best-dressed poverty the world has ever known. For a variety of reasons, the benefits of mass production have been spread much more evenly in this area than in many others. It is much easier in the United States to be decently dressed than it is to be decently housed, fed, or doctored. Even people with terribly depressed incomes can look prosperous.

This is an extremely important factor in defining our emotional and existential ignorance of poverty. In Detroit the existence of social classes became much more difficult to discern the day the companies put lockers in the plants. From that moment on, one did not see men in work clothes on the way to the factory, but citizens in slacks and white shirts. This process has been magnified with the poor throughout the country. There are tens of thousands of Americans in the big cities who are wearing shoes, perhaps even a stylishly cut suit or dress, and yet are hungry. It is not a matter of planning, though it almost seems as if the affluent society had given out costumes to the poor so that they would not offend the rest of society with the sight of rags.

Then, many of the poor are the wrong age to be seen. A good number of them (over 8,000,000) are sixty-five years of age or better; an even larger number are under eighteen. The aged members of the other America are often sick, and they cannot move. Another group of them live out their lives in loneliness and frustration: they sit in rented rooms, or else they stay close to a house in a neighborhood that has completely changed from the old days. Indeed, one of the worst aspects of poverty among the aged is that these people are out of sight and out of mind, and alone.

The young are somewhat more visible, yet they too stay close to their neighborhoods. Sometimes they advertise their poverty through a lurid tabloid story about a gang killing. But generally they do not disturb the quiet streets of the middle class.

And finally, the poor are politically invisible. It is one of the cruelest ironies of social life in advanced countries that the dispossessed at the bottom of society are unable to speak for themselves. The people of the other America do not, by far and large, belong to unions, to fraternal organizations, or to political parties. They are without lobbies of their own; they put forward no legislative program. As a group, they are atomized. They have no face; they have no voice.

*   *   *

Forty to 50,000,000 people are becoming increasingly invisible. That is a shocking fact. But there is a second basic irony of poverty that is equally important: if one is to make the mistake of being born poor, he should choose a time when the majority of the people are miserable too.

J. K. Galbraith develops this idea in *The Affluent Society*, and in doing so defines the "newness" of the kind of poverty in contemporary America. The old poverty, Galbraith notes, was general. It was the condition of life of an entire society, or at least of that huge majority who were without special skills or the luck of birth. When the entire economy advanced, a good many of these people gained higher standards of living. Unlike the poor today, the majority poor of a generation ago were an immediate (if cynical) concern of political leaders. The old slums of the immigrants had the votes; they provided the basis for labor organizations; their very numbers could be a powerful force in political conflict. At the same time the new technology required higher skills, more education, and stimulated an upward movement for millions.

Perhaps the most dramatic case of the power of the majority poor took place in the 1930's. The Congress of Industrial Organizations literally organized millions in a matter of years. A labor movement that had been declining and confined to a thin stratum of the highly skilled suddenly embraced masses of men and women in basic industry. At the same time this acted as a pressure upon the Government, and the New Deal codified some of the social gains in laws like the Wagner Act. The result was not a basic transformation of the American system, but it did transform the lives of an entire section of the population.

In the thirties one of the reasons for these advances was that misery was general. There was no need then to write books about unemployment and poverty. That was the decisive social experience of the entire society, and the apple sellers even invaded Wall Street. There was political sympathy from middle-class reformers; there were an élan and spirit that grew out of a deep crisis.

Some of those who advanced in the thirties did so because they had unique and individual personal talents. But for the great mass, it was a question of being at the right point in the economy at the right time in history, and utilizing that position for common struggle. Some of those who failed did so because they did not have the will to take advantage of new opportunities. But for the most part the poor who were left behind had been at the wrong place in the economy at the wrong moment in history.

These were the people in the unorganizable jobs, in the South, in the minority groups, in the fly-by-night factories that were low on capital and high on labor. When some of them did break into the economic mainstream—when, for instance, the CIO opened up the way for some Negroes to find good industrial jobs—they proved to be as resourceful as anyone else. As a group, the other Americans who stayed behind were not originally composed primarily of individual failures. Rather, they were victims of an impersonal process that selected some for progress and discriminated against others.

Out of the thirties came the welfare state. Its creation had been stimulated by mass impoverishment and misery, yet it helped the poor least of all. Laws like unemployment compensation, the Wagner Act, the various farm programs, all these were designed for the middle third in the cities, for the organized workers, and for the upper third in the country, for the big market farmers. If a man works in an extremely low-paying job, he may not even be covered by social security or other welfare programs. If he receives unemployment compensation, the payment is scaled down according to his low earnings.

One of the major laws that was designed to cover everyone, rich and poor, was social security. But even here the other Americans suffered discrimination. Over the years social security payments have not even provided a subsistence level of life. The middle third have been able to supplement the Federal pension through private plans negotiated by unions, through joining medical insurance schemes like Blue Cross, and so on. The poor have not been able to do so. They lead a bitter life, and then have to pay for that fact in old age.

Indeed, the paradox that the welfare state benefits those least who need help most is but a single instance of a persistent irony in the other America. Even when the money finally trickles down, even when a school is built in a poor neighborhood, for instance, the poor are still deprived. Their entire environment, their life, their values, do not prepare them to take advantage of the new opportunity. The parents are anxious for the children to go to work; the pupils are pent up, waiting for the moment when their education has complied with the law.

Today's poor, in short, missed the political and social gains of the thirties. They are, as Galbraith rightly points out, the first minority in history, the first poor not to be seen, the first poor whom the politicians could leave alone.

The first step toward the new poverty was taken when millions of people proved immune to progress. When that happened, the failure was not individual and personal, but a social product. But once the historic accident takes place, it begins to become a personal fate.

The new poor of the other America saw the rest of society move ahead. They went on living in depressed areas, and often they tended to become depressed human beings. In some of the West Virginia towns, for instance, an entire community will become shabby and defeated. The young and the adventurous go to the city, leaving behind those who cannot move and those who lack the will to do so. The entire area becomes permeated with failure, and that is one more reason the big corporations shy away.

Indeed, one of the most important things about the new poverty is that it cannot be defined in simple, statistical terms. Throughout this book a crucial term is used: aspiration. If a group has internal vitality, a will—if it has aspiration—it may live in dilapidated housing, it may eat an inadequate diet, and it may suffer poverty, but it is not impoverished. So it was in those ethnic slums of the immigrants that played such a dramatic role in the unfolding of the American dream. The people found themselves in slums, but they were not slum dwellers.

But the new poverty is constructed so as to destroy aspiration; it is a system designed to be impervious to hope. The other America does not contain the adventurous seeking a new life and land. It is populated by the failures, by those driven from the land and bewildered by the city, by old people suddenly confronted with the torments of loneliness and poverty, and by minorities facing a wall of prejudice.

In the past, when poverty was general in the unskilled and semi-skilled work force, the poor were all mixed together. The bright and the dull, those who were going to escape into the great society and those who were to stay behind, all of them lived on the same street. When the middle third rose, this community was destroyed. And the entire invisible land of the other Americans became a ghetto, a modern poor farm for the rejects of society and of the economy.

It is a blow to reform and the political hopes of the poor that the middle class no longer understands that poverty exists. But, perhaps more important, the poor are losing their links with the great world. If statistics and sociology can measure a feeling as delicate as loneliness . . . , the other America is becoming increasingly populated by those who do not belong to anybody or anything. They are no longer participants in an ethnic culture from the old country; they are less and less religious; they do not belong to unions or clubs. They are not seen, and because of that they themselves cannot see. Their horizon has become more and more restricted; they see one another, and that means they see little reason to hope.

Galbraith was one of the first writers to begin to describe the newness of contemporary poverty, and that is to his credit. Yet because even he underestimates the problem, it is important to put his definition into perspective.

For Galbraith, there are two main components of the new poverty: case poverty and insular poverty. Case poverty is the plight of those who suffer from some physical or mental disability that is personal and individual and excludes them from the general advance. Insular poverty exists in areas like the Appalachians or the West Virginia coal fields, where an entire section of the country becomes economically obsolete.

Physical and mental disabilities are, to be sure, an important part of poverty in America. The poor are sick in body and in spirit. But this is not an isolated fact about them, an individual "case," a stroke of bad luck. Disease, alcoholism, low IQ's, these express a whole way of life. They are, in the main, the effects of an environment, not the biographies of unlucky individuals. Because of this, the new poverty is something that cannot be dealt with by first aid. If there is to be a lasting assault on the shame of the other America, it must seek to root out of this society an entire environment, and not just the relief of individuals.

But perhaps the idea of "insular" poverty is even more dangerous. To speak of "islands" of the poor (or, in the more popular term, of "pockets of poverty") is to imply that one is confronted by a serious, but relatively minor, problem. This is hardly a description of a misery that extends to 40,000,000 or 50,000,000 people in the United States. They have remained impoverished in spite of increasing productivity and the creation of a welfare state. That fact alone should suggest the dimensions of a serious and basic situation.

And yet, even given these disagreements with Galbraith, his achievement is considerable. He was one of the first to understand that there are enough poor people in the United States to constitute a subculture of misery, but not enough of them to challenge the conscience and the imagination of the nation.

Finally, one might summarize the newness of contemporary poverty by saying: These are the people who are immune to progress. But then the facts are even more cruel. The other Americans are the victims of the very inventions and machines that have provided a higher living standard for the rest of the society. They are upside-down in the economy, and for them greater productivity often means worse jobs; agricultural advance becomes hunger.

In the optimistic theory, technology is an undisguised blessing. A general increase in productivity, the argument goes, generates a higher standard of living for the whole people. And indeed, this has been true for the middle and upper thirds of American society, the people who made such striking gains in the last two decades. It tends to overstate the automatic character of the process, to omit the role of human struggle. (The CIO was organized by men in conflict, not by economic trends.) Yet it states a certain truth—for those who are lucky enough to participate in it.

But the poor, if they were given to theory, might argue the exact opposite. They might say: Progress is misery.

As the society became more technological, more skilled, those who learn to work the machines, who get the expanding education, move up. Those who miss out at the very start find themselves at a new disadvantage. A generation ago in American life, the majority of the working people did not have high-school educations. But at that time industry was organized on a lower level of skill and competence. And there was a sort of continuum in the shop: the youth who left school at sixteen could begin as a laborer, and gradually pick up skill as he went along.

Today the situation is quite different. The good jobs require much more academic preparation, much more skill from the very outset. Those who lack a high-school education tend to be condemned to the economic underworld—to low-paying service industries, to backward factories, to sweeping and janitorial duties. If the fathers and mothers of the contemporary poor were penalized a generation ago for their lack of schooling, their children will suffer all the more. The very rise in productivity that created more money and better working conditions for the rest of the society can be a menace to the poor.

But then this technological revolution might have an even more disastrous consequence: it could increase the ranks of the poor as well as intensify the disabilities of poverty. At this point it is too early to make any final judgment, yet there are obvious danger signals. There are millions of Americans who live just the other side of poverty. When a recession comes, they are pushed onto the relief rolls. (Welfare payments in New York respond almost immediately to any economic decline.) If automation continues to inflict more and more penalties on the unskilled and the semi-skilled, it could have the impact of permanently increasing the population of the other America.

Even more explosive is the possibility that people who participated in the gains of the thirties and the forties will be pulled back down into poverty. Today the mass-production industries where unionization made such a difference are contracting. Jobs are being destroyed. In the process, workers who had achieved a certain level of wages, who had won working conditions in the shop, are suddenly confronted with impoverishment. This is particularly true for anyone over forty years of age and for members of minority groups. Once their job is abolished, their chances of ever getting similar work are very slim.

*   *   *

Throughout, I work on an assumption that cannot be proved by Government figures or even documented by impressions of the other America. It is an ethical proposition, and it can be simply stated: in a nation with a technology that could provide every citizen with a decent life, it is an outrage and a scandal that there should be such social misery. Only if one begins with this assumption is it possible to pierce through the invisibility of 40 to 50 million human beings and to see the other America. We must perceive passionately, if this blindness is to be lifted from us. A fact can be rationalized and explained away: an indignity cannot.

What shall we tell the American poor, once we have seen them? Shall we say to them that they are better off than the Indian poor, the Italian poor, the Russian poor? That is one answer, but it is heartless. I should put it another way. I want to tell every well-fed and optimistic American that it is intolerable that so many millions should be maimed in body and in spirit when it is not necessary that they should be. My standard of comparison is not how much worse things used to be. It is how much better they could be if only we were stirred.

Black Nationalism

C. Eric Lincoln

For any minority group, faced with a constant environment of prejudice and discrimination, three basic types of response are possible. These responses are *avoidance, acceptance* and *aggression*.

Avoidance

Group consciousness is a form of consolation derived from a shared sense of discrimination; it is often expressed in ambivalence and self-hatred. Such an acrid consolation is not for every taste. Many individuals would rather not be identified with a minority, they would prefer not to have a personal awareness of its existence or its claim on them as members. Such persons may seek to avoid entirely their identification with their group.

Avoidance may also be motivated by a haunting concern for personal security, physical or psychological. In this case, while acknowledging themselves as members of a group, individuals may seek to avoid the *meaning* of that identity in a wider context. Many Negroes, for example, avoid contact with whites by doing business with Negro businesses wherever possible; if they find it necessary to deal with white businesses, they order goods and pay their bills by mail. In this way, they minimize the likelihood of being insulted or otherwise humiliated by whites. Such avoidance also reduces the possibility of an inadvertent breach of the highly complex "etiquette" of race relations. In many parts of the South, a Negro who violates the etiquette requirements imposed by the whites may readily incur physical harm or even death.

For those individuals who wish to avoid their identification with a minority group, the most complete form of avoidance is to withdraw entirely by "passing" into the dominant group. But such passing is often hindered by distinctive names, accents or other cultural habits associated with the minority group. Racial minorities such as Negroes encounter a far more immediate obstacle: their distinctive color or "visibility," which is an unrelenting barrier to total acceptability. Thousands of fair-skinned Negroes do pass as white, however, and some dark-skinned Negroes pass as Filipinos, Spaniards, Italians or Mexicans.

In some Southern cities, light-skinned Negroes often pass in order to shop at certain stores or to use such facilities as libraries, toilets, theaters and hotels. In Memphis, one family of light-skinned Negroes regularly attends white churches. "This way," they explain, "we get to hear speakers not otherwise available to us, and the children have a chance to hear the great music and see the pageants performed on festival occasions." In Boston, at least two Negro businessmen passing as white operate businesses in white neighborhoods and because of their locations, cater almost exclusively to whites. In Birmingham, a fair-skinned Negro lunches occasionally at the best downtown hotels "just to look at the other side from time to time." In New Jersey, a Negro passing as white and married to a white woman holds a major executive position in a nationally-known drug firm. Such examples could be multiplied a thousandfold.

A second kind of avoidance is often exhibited by upper-class members of the Negro minority, especially those in the business or professional groups who are not dependent upon the white majority for a livelihood. These individuals often seek to insulate themselves from contact with lower-class Negroes as well as from the whites, and they do not identify themselves with the common problems of their group. They become a society unto themselves, "asking the white man for nothing" and sharing nothing with the Negroes from whom they derive their status and wealth. They form themselves into tight little cliques, which play at being part of the white society from which they are excluded.

For those individuals who wish to avoid the social *meaning* of their minority-group status, avoidance may take the form of developing towns or communities composed principally of members of their own group. Even when such residential segregation is initiated and enforced by the dominant group, minority-group members may actually *prefer* to live in the ghettos, rather than contend with the constant harassment incident to living in the larger community. But no ghetto, forced or voluntary, can really ward off the consequences of prejudice and discrimination; and the mere fact of its existence is a constant reminder of the lack of a more healthful and harmonious relationship.

Finally, avoidance may take the form of escape from feelings of inferiority and futility while maintaining contact with the dominant group. Those who choose this path attempt to obliterate the meaning of their minority-group status by emphasizing and enhancing their status as individuals. The result may be clearly beneficial—a determined self-improvement in order to meet the approved values of the dominant group in such areas as education and professional skill.

The other extreme, however, is an escape into a world of make-believe, where fantasies of wealth, power or position in "society" shut out the realities of a humiliating and frustrating day-to-day existence. Negroes of wealth and education, whose only barrier to unrestricted participation in the complete life of the community is that fact that they *are* Negroes, probably constitute the largest single class of social neurotics. Often their relationship to their white social counterparts is tenuous and marginal, but they can no longer find a place acceptable to their heightened sense of personal worth among the Negro classes out of which they rose. In their frustration, the creative talent which pushed them to the top and set them off from the masses is too often crudely dissipated.

Acceptance

Some minority-group members feel that it is sensible to accept what cannot be changed or avoided: "You don't like it, but what can you do?" This attitude of conscious resignation or futility is the most common form of acceptance, but it is not the whole story. At the other extreme is the whole-hearted acceptance of disparate social conditions characteristic of a caste society such as pre-Gandhian India. In such a society every group— high or low, favored or scorned—is felt to have a divinely ordained place in the sun. Social discrimination is no more than obedience to the divine order of the universe, and resentment against it would be as unthinkable as resentment of God. This attitude comes naturally, of course, to many white men in America; but there is some evidence that it was also widely held among American Negroes several decades ago, and vestiges of this kind of adjustment behavior are probably retained among the present "folk Negroes" of isolated rural areas and among certain family servants who identify closely with their employers.

Few Negroes today exhibit this wholehearted acceptance of discrimination and special privilege, but many will consciously defer in specific situations in which inferiority is implied. Many Negroes ride Jim-Crow buses, for example, when no other means of transportation is available; and a Negro servant may accept the epithet "boy" or "girl" because to reject it would mean the loss of employment and the possibility of livelihood. But, in both instances, the individuals involved may categorically reject the whole status pattern and its implications. They reason simply, "We've got to live if we're going to fight!"

These outward accommodations to specific situations of discrimination or prejudice are often misinterpreted as a whole-hearted acceptance of inferior role or status. Such an assumption is, of course, illogical, and it can only be made by a mind which brings to the situation a serious misconception of Negro intelligence. No healthy mind assumes that another healthy mind will welcome an inferior status or its degrading concomitants.

Prejudice has been called "the refuge of a sick mind" and "a method of transferring our sickness to others." Certainly the Negro who *welcomes* the kind of social subordination imposed upon him in our country may be considered to be quite ill. No more can be said for those who practice it.

Aggression

Aggression is an act or a pattern of behavior which aims to discomfort, injure or destroy a person or his values. As an individual response among American Negroes, it may express itself in very different forms. To be a "race man"—that is, a professional champion of the in-group, speaking or writing in its defense, or agitating for its rights—is a common expression of direct aggression, especially among the upper classes but increasingly among all classes. Boycott; inefficiency and sloppy work done for white employers; ostentation, such as expensive automobiles or homes; refusal to observe the customary forms of etiquette—all these are direct means of expressing personal hostility. Some physical attacks also take place. Negroes seldom initiate physical attacks against whites, but there is less hesitation now to return violence for violence, whatever the cost.

Literature, art and humor are readily available vehicles of direct aggression, and they are widely used as such. The Negro press is well known for its explicit posture against prejudice and discrimination, but countless individual Negro poets and novelists have also used their talents to express their resentment of and hostility toward the white man.

Not all aggression, however, is overt and outspoken. Silence or absolute immobility may also be aggressive, as, for example, when a Negro fails to respond to what he considers a degrading epithet or refuses to yield his seat on a public bus or trolley to a white person.

Even certain postures of meekness and deference may be expressions of aggression, as with the apparent humility and self-effacement often displayed in situations of great dependence or where intimidation is present. The suffering then experienced is accepted as a means to ultimate victory, for from the suffering, power is derived. Again, meekness is a Christian virtue, and through its expression the humble Negro asserts his moral superiority to the arrogant white. Aggressive meekness is also a common device for ridiculing the white man; while he egoistically accepts the meek behavior at face value, the Negro may be laughing at him secretly for his gullibility.

So sensitive are white men to any challenge to their position that even a *possibility* that aggression *might* be expressed is considered dangerous. In 1957 a Negro in North Carolina was arrested and charged with "assault" because he *looked* at a white woman; and in Georgia, a year later, a parade featuring a high school band and the usual corps of majorettes was stopped and disbanded because Negroes joined other citizens in standing along the street to watch. In the southern part of the United States and in South Africa, even a suspicion that a Negro might want to strike back can cost the Negro his freedom or his life.

But aggression can also be misdirected. Hurt and angry, yet too frightened to act against his powerful tormentor, the Negro sometimes thrashes about, seeking a target for his hostility. Often unconsciously, he displaces his aggression onto other minority groups—Jews, for example—which cannot retaliate so effectively. All too often, the aggression is simply inverted: Negroes turn their rage against other Negroes or against themselves. The result is sporadic intra-group violence and a general splintering of group solidarity, a disastrous development in a world unsympathetic to the dignity of powerless individuals or groups.

Even responsible and controlled aggression, as a response to offenses against one's human dignity, is a dangerous undertaking, and it is shrouded in moral and ethical ambivalence. Many individuals prefer the paths of avoidance and acceptance. In every minority, however, there will always be men who are willing to confront directly the source of their oppression and who will seek to remove, moderate, deflect or destroy it.

Stereotype and Identity

Aggression as an actual and continuing expression of Negro protest has long been underestimated in America. An image of the Negro as casual, passive and content with his lot was fabricated during the days of slavery. Manifestly absurd, it was accepted as fact and has persisted into modern times. Such a picture has done little to prepare Americans to live together in peace and mutual respect.

Historians have contributed to the confusion by stereotyping the Negro slave as a docile, devoted, contented servant, or else by ignoring him altogether. The Negro's active protests to the condition of slavery imposed upon him by a comparatively infinite power do not commonly appear in America's textbooks. Knowledge of the numerous slave revolts and insurrections, for example, is available only to the scholar who has the facilities for laborious research.

The problem is intensified by the racial segregation which prevents knowledgeable contact between whites and educated Negroes. Incredible as it seems, many Americans are surprised to learn that Negroes love and hate, accept and reject, with all the intensity of feeling common to human nature. Or perhaps it is not so incredible: he who would systematically degrade his fellow man must defend himself against reprisals. Since this cannot be done empirically, one way to gain a comforting sense of invulnerability is to pretend that the problem does not exist. If the Negro does not feel *anything*, his docility can be taken for granted.

Aggressive leaders will arise, however. Since they threaten the protective fantasy, the most militant of them must be discounted and isolated from the Negro masses. By dismissing them as "Communists" or "radicals" (or whatever is beyond the pale at any given moment), we can keep our fantasy of the contented Negro pure. But the Negro is not contented, and he will be heard. If his moderate leaders are dismissed as radical, then movements which are *in fact* radical will become more and more extreme, if only to get on ground where the white man will acknowledge their existence.

We are mired in complacency. The majority of unsuspecting whites are still shocked with disbelief and chagrin by the Negro's occasional public repudiation of the stereotype of good-natured, uncomplaining docility, which they have always accepted as true. When the Negro they thought they "knew" so well steps out of the role in which he has been cast, it seems to many like an act of treason. For example, when Marcus Garvey announced in 1920 that "the white man need expect no more Negro blood shed on his behalf" and that "the dying to be done by the black man in the future . . . will be done to make himself free," the speech was sufficiently alarming to be cited as sedition.[1] And when, forty years later, Negroes insisted upon being served at the lunch counters of stores which readily accepted their money in every other department, no less a person than ex-President Harry Truman—a man who had done much during his administration to remove racial barriers—cried out in outrage.

It is incredible that such expressions "against the system" should be viewed with surprise. It would be logically more surprising if resentment and hostility were *not* felt by a people who conceive themselves as oppressed and who can identify their oppressors. But this is precisely the tragedy of America, that she is oblivious of the smoldering resentments of millions for whom the American Creed is often a mockery. This "ignorance about the Negro is not, it must be stressed, just lack of interest and knowledge. It is a tense and high-strung restriction and distortion of knowledge, and it indicates much deeper dislocations within the mind of Southern whites"[2]—and, to a lesser extent, of the entire white community.

This "convenient ignorance"[3] on the part of whites compounds the frustrations of the Negro minority, which now more than ever before is determined to be heard—or at least seen. The conspicuous consumption; the overemphasis on titles; the preoccupation with such values as academic degrees, foreign travel and unique professional appointments; and the in-

---

[1] Edmund D. Cronon, *Black Moses* (Madison: The University of Wisconsin Press, 1955), p. 66.
[2] Arnold Rose, *The Negro in America* (Boston: Beacon Press, 1948), pp. 17–18.
[3] *Ibid.*, p. 16.

creasing activity of organized protest—all these add up to an open rejection of racial anonymity and the traditional stereotype. Many of these activities are also, of course, valuable in themselves. They are like the "double duty dollar"—the money a Negro spends with a business which employs Negroes, thus (1) buying goods for himself and (2) helping to provide jobs for others of his race.

Every important aspect of the Negro's behavior is likely to have a race angle, though he himself is not always conscious of that fact.

To the Negro himself, the Negro problem is all-important. A Negro probably seldom talks to a white man . . . without consciousness of this problem. Even in a mixed white and Negro group of closest friends in Northern intellectual circles, and probably even in an all-Negro group, the Negro problem constantly looms in the background. It steers the jokes and allusions if it is not one of the dominant topics of conversation.

The Negro leader, the Negro social scientist, the Negro man of arts and letters is likely to view all social, economic, political, indeed, even aesthetic and philosophical issues from the Negro angle. What is more, he is expected to do so. He would seem entirely out of place if he spoke simply as a member of a community, a citizen of America. . . . In the existing American civilization he can attain some degree of distinction, but always as a representative of "his people," not as an ordinary American. . . . The Negro genius is imprisoned in the Negro problem.[4]

Black Nationalism

Under the circumstances confronting him, the Negro is required to be "Negro" before—and sometimes to the exclusion of—anything else. At some point, therefore, he will inevitably be tempted to glorify that from which he cannot escape. He may repudiate the white man's stereotype, turn his eyes from the painful reality and substitute for them an idealized self-image. Drawing on the political parallel, in which each state considers itself distinct from and superior to its neighbors, this attitude has come to be known as *black nationalism*.

It would be absurd to say, of course, that all Negro race pride is only a rationalized form of acceptance. It is often a simple and spontaneous awareness of one's human dignity. Such, for example, was the pride of Denmark Vesey, an ex-slave who engineered an elaborate insurrection in Charleston in 1822:

Even whilst walking through the streets in company with another, he was not idle; for if his companion bowed to a white person he would rebuke him, and observe that all men were born equal, and that he was surprised that any one would degrade himself by such conduct; that he would never cringe to the whites, nor ought any one who had the feelings of a man. When answered,

4 *Ibid.*, pp. 11–12.

"We are slaves," he would sarcastically and indignantly reply, "You deserve to remain slaves."[5]

Vesey was hanged, along with thirty-four confederates, for leading the insurrection; but he died as he had lived, with courage and conviction, acknowledging no man his inherent superior.

Black nationalism is more than courage and rebellion; it is a way of life. It is an implicit rejection of the "alien" white culture and an explicit rejection of the symbols of that culture, balanced by an exaggerated and undiluted pride in "black" culture. It involves a drastic reappraisal not only of present realities but also of the past and future. The black nationalist revises history (or corrects it, as he would say) to establish that today's black men are descended from glorious ancestors, from powerful and enlightened rulers and conquerors. This reconstruction of history may reach ridiculous extremes; and it can never be accepted by white men, who, to bolster their own security, must perceive history as a record of *white* men's achievements. But a proud history is essential to the black nationalist's self-respect. Essential, too, is the certainty of a brilliant future, in which the inherent superiority of his race will triumph and he will again rule the world.

In any technical sense, of course, it is inaccurate for American Negroes to adopt a black nationalist position. The term implies that they are— politically, culturally, ethnically or racially—a distinct group. But this is emphatically not true. Politically they are Americans, as American as one can be (with the sole exception of the American Indian). Culturally they are merged into the American mainstream; as Lloyd Warner observes, they are "culturally more like the white 'old American' than [are] any other sub-groups in America."[6] Nor are they ethnically separated from other Americans, holding allegiance to an earlier shared culture. On the contrary:

> The conspicuous feature of the Negro in America is *that his aboriginal culture was smashed*. . . . The importance of this basic fact for the Negro in America cannot be overestimated. It means in effect that the old types of social organization and all their derivations could not continue, but a new type of emergent adjustment derived from the new conditions would have to be established.[7]

---

[5] E. Franklin Frazier, *The Negro in the United States* (New York: The Macmillan Co., 1949), p. 88. Quoting Lionel Kennedy and Thomas Parker, *An Official Report of the Trials of Sundry Negroes Charged with an Attempt to Raise an Insurrection in the State of South Carolina*.

[6] W. Lloyd Warner and Leo Srole, *The Social Systems of American Ethnic Groups* (New Haven: Yale University Press, 1945), p. 295.

[7] Abram Kardiner and Lionel Ovesey, *The Mark of Oppression* (New York: W. W. Norton & Co., 1951), p. 39. But see a somewhat broader concept of ethnocentrism in Brewton Berry, *Race and Ethnic Relations* (Houghton, 1951), p. 77. Says Berry, "The ethnic group is a human group bound together by ties of cultural homogeneity. . . . Above all, there is a consciousness of kind, a we-feeling. The ethnic group may even regard itself as a race, but the fact of such common descent is of much less importance than the *assumption* that there is a blood relationship, and the myths of the group develop to substantiate such an assumption."

Nor, finally, are they racially distinct. "Race" is at best a nebulous term.[8] There are no pure races, and it would be especially inappropriate to apply the term to the American Negro, who is at once African and Anglo-Saxon, Indian and French, Portuguese, Spanish, German and Italian—a composite of every major "racial stock"[9] and every nationality of Western Europe.[10]

W. E. B. DuBois observes that a common suffering, rather than a common biology or ethnic identity, has been the important factor uniting the Negro in what is usually referred to as "nationalism."

The so-called American Negro group . . . while it is in no sense absolutely set off physically from its fellow Americans, has nevertheless a strong, hereditary cultural unity born of slavery, of common suffering, prolonged proscription, and curtailment of political and civil rights. . . . Prolonged policies of segregation and discrimination have involuntarily welded the mass into a nation within a nation. . . .[11]

The "nationalism" of the American Negro is not voluntary, prompted by a desire to set himself apart in order to preserve some cultural values. It is, rather, a defensive response to external forces—hostile forces which threaten his creative existence. It is a unity born of the wish not to conserve but to *escape* a set of conditions.

Black nationalism seizes the conditions of disprivilege and turns them to advantage as a tool for eliminating the disprivilege. It challenges the supercilious attitude of the majority group by glorifying the unique symbols of the blacks—symbols which the whites consider repugnant. Some sociologists have labeled this behavior "negritude":

[8] For discussion on race, see the following: Ethel Alpenfels, *Sense and Nonsense About Race* (New York: Friendship Press, 1957); Ruth Benedict, *Race: Science and Politics* (New York: Viking Press, 1950); Franz Boas, *Anthropology and Modern Life* (New York: W. W. Norton & Co., 1928); J. Deniker, *The Races of Man* (London: Walter Scott Publishers, 1913); Oscar Handlin, *Race and Nationality in American Life* (New York: Doubleday & Co., 1957); F. H. Hankins, *The Racial Basis of Civilization* (New York: Alfred Knopf, 1926); Ben J. Marais, *Colour, the Unsolved Problem of the West* (Capetown: Howard B. Timmins, 1952); Simpson, George E., and Yinger, J. Milton, *Racial and Cultural Minorities in the United States*, 1st ed. rev. (New York: Harper and Brothers, 1958); W. Ashley Montague, *Man's Most Dangerous Myth* (New York: Columbia University Press, 1942); Gordon Allport, *The Nature of Prejudice* (New York: Doubleday, 1958).

[9] "A 'stock' may be defined as the descendants of a large group of people who once lived in the same geographical area and shared certain physical traits that are inherited. These traits set them apart from other groups who have other combinations of physical characteristics." Alpenfels, *Sense and Nonsense About Race*, p. 19.

[10] See Gunnar Myrdal, "Race and Ancestry," *An American Dilemma* (New York: Harper & Bros., 1944), pp. 113–136. See also John Hope Franklin, *From Slavery to Freedom* (New York: Alfred A. Knopf, 1956); E. Franklin Frazier, *Negro in the U.S.*, note 5.

[11] W. E. B. DuBois, "Three Centuries of Discrimination," *The Crisis*, LIV (December 1947), 362–363. Cf. Melville J. Herskovits: "The word 'Negro,' as employed in the United States has no biological meaning. . . . a social definition takes precedence over the biological reality." *Man and His Work* (New York: Alfred A. Knopf, 1950), p. 144.

. . . an exaltation of African-Negro specificity, a "kind of highly elaborated counterracism." . . . It involves a "particularly intense racial awareness," not uncoupled to political activity and demands. It is a term descriptive, also, of an appreciation of a new black unity experienced by its adherents, a consciousness of sharing in a past and in the making of the future. . . .[12]

Nationalism is ordinarily political; it refers to common values arising out of the existence of a state. Black nationalism addresses itself not to an existent state but to a state of mind.[13] But if there is no past or present black nation, what is to prevent the projection of a Black Nation of the future?

To the extent that it is couched in political terms—and this varies from movement to movement—black nationalism envisions and works toward the creation of such a state. In the creed of some movements, this political goal is relatively insignificant, a potentiality which the black man may or may not choose to realize. For the Black Muslims, however, the goal of a Black Nation is of consuming importance. The Muslims do not rest content with any concept of black nationalism that is not expressed in concrete economic and political terms.

Black Nationalism and Social Class

In the American Negro groups of highest and lowest status, hardly anyone wants to be a Negro. Upper-class Negroes seek to identify themselves with the white society; lower-class Negroes prefer to identify themselves with any group *except* the whites in order to escape the danger and humiliation that all Negroes incur. Only middle-class Negroes are generally willing to acknowledge themselves as Negroes and, at the same time, to seek an accommodation with the white society. Black nationalism, therefore, with its repudiation of both Negro identity and white culture, sinks its roots deepest in the lower class.

Upper-class Negroes are rarely "Negro" by choice. Those who have obvious strains of white ancestry are often at great pains to dissociate themselves from those who do not, and they are remarkably oblivious of the implications of their whiteness. Darker Negroes of the upper class must content themselves with pointed references to their "Indian ancestry" lest they be mistaken for full-blooded Negroes—an intolerable possibility.

The Negro of the upper class is largely committed to the idea that America's racial dilemma will be resolved when the Negro loses his distinctiveness, social and biological. He would prefer to become so thoroughly assimilated into the American mainstream as to be *biologically*

[12] Melvin Conant, *Race Issues on the World Scene* (Honolulu: University of Hawaii Press, 1955), p. 119.
[13] See Michael Clark's comprehensive article on the "Rise in Racial Extremism," *The New York Times*, January 25, 1960, p. 1.

indistinct, for his new status could not then be revoked or qualified in a future crisis. In short, the ultimate security in living among a white majority is to be white. But this security is almost impossible to achieve in view of the general disdain for miscegenation. The barrier is circular: unqualified social acceptance is the only gateway to racial anonymity, which in turn is the only gateway to unqualified social acceptance.

For the time being, therefore, the upper-class Negro is settling for that degree of assimilation which will make him *socially* indistinct from those whites who are his counterpart in terms of education, affluence and refinement. He tends to venerate everything that is "white" and "Western." In spite of the inconvenience of his color, he sees himself as part of this tradition; and he resents as irrational and unjust the social custom which emphasizes his black skin while overlooking the fact that his ancestry is partly European and his culture totally Western.

The members of the growing Negro middle class are least concerned about disestablishing themselves as Negroes. They ridicule the upper class as "neurotic sub-marginals" who make themselves ridiculous in trying to attract the white man's attention. Nor can they see the importance of having white ancestry, since almost all American Negroes share this qualification to some degree. Besides, white ancestry is not a criterion of the white man's judgment when he erects barriers to set himself apart from all others. Segregation is directed at a *class*, not at members within it; and all Negroes, whatever their names, ancestry or skin color, belong by definition to the segregated class.

The Negro middle class is somewhat ambivalent about black nationalism. The black nationalists' emphasis on a united struggle against subordination has a certain appeal, but the rejection of Negro identity and the search for cultural roots in Afro-Asian traditions has little or no appeal. The middle-class Negro feels no need to be either "Asiatic" or "European." He accepts the designation "American Negro" with no particular sense of opprobrium, and often with a certain pride, for he thus identifies himself with America's most important minority—a minority which has distinguished itself, in a brief span of history, by an achievement of progress unequaled by *either* "Europeans" or "Asiatics."

The self-image of the Negro middle class is one of ability and militancy, uncontaminated by either sycophancy or hatred for the white man. The middle-class Negro is not obsessed with status pretensions, as is the upper class, nor does he suffer the abject despair of the Negro masses. As a result, he seldom displays the kind of insecurity that needs to search for ancestral pegs upon which to hang a claim for present status and acceptance.

The main appeal of all black nationalist movements, then, is to the Negro lower class. Here the Negro's resentment is crystallized and open. He has long despaired of the white man's justice and of the trustworthiness of the "acceptable" Negro leaders who court the white man's favor. Moreover, he is already at the bottom of the ladder, so his economic and social position is not vulnerable. An indiscreet word, an admission of hostility or an identification with "radical" or "extremist" groups can cost him nothing. What has he to lose if the demagogues of black nationalism fan his resentment into hatred, openly expressed in defiance of all white men and their compliant Negro "friends"?

The lower-class Negro lives in a no man's land between two alien worlds, both of which he spurns. Unlike his upper-class brother, he has no conscious desire to be white or even "like the whites," whom he identifies with most of his misfortunes. But neither will he accept the implications of being "Negro"—a white man's word, which he sees as an epithet of contempt. The black race has a rich cultural heritage, extending thousands of years into the past; but the black men who were torn from their homes and shipped to the New World in chains were carefully isolated from that heritage. The history of the "Negro" begins in the torments and degradation of slavery in America. Unlike his better-educated brothers, the lower-class Negro is not generally aware that his ancestors served their new nation with distinction and that the term can be accepted with confidence —indeed, with pride. He is agonizingly aware of what "Negro" implies to most Americans, its humiliating connotations of white supremacy.

The lower-class Negro is ripe for the lure of black nationalism. He is proud to rediscover himself as a Black Man, linked to the great and venerable civilizations of the "single black continent" of Afro-Asia. He is grateful for a mystique, especially one dignified as a religion, that rationalizes his resentment and hatred as spiritual virtues in a cosmic war of good against evil. And he is jubilant at his new vision of the future—a future not of racial equality, for which he believes the white man has shown himself unfit, but of black supremacy. For "black," to the black nationalist, is a quality and symbol of all that is glorious, triumphant and divine.

Many counterpressures exist, of course, to restrain the lower-class Negro from active participation in black nationalist movements. The Christian church is still powerful, though its magic has been seriously eroded. Personal friendships with white men, where they exist, make the absolute generalizations of black nationalism difficult to accept. Some Negroes, like some white men, find a certain comfort and security in being considered inferior; they cling to the status in which all their personal failures are overlooked, since nothing much is expected of them. Others have experienced so rarely the feeling of superiority that they can scarcely imagine it as a way of life.

Above all, the lower-class Negro is a decent and responsible human being, loath to give his life over to hatred and vengeance. He will not do so unless forced to the wall by a smug and callous white society. The future of black nationalism, therefore, will ultimately be decided not by the demagogues but by ourselves.

Power and Racism

Stokely Carmichael

One of the tragedies of the struggle against racism is that up to now there has been no national organization which could speak to the growing militancy of young black people in the urban ghetto. There has been only a civil rights movement, whose tone of voice was adapted to an audience of liberal whites. It served as a sort of buffer zone between them and angry young blacks. None of its so-called leaders could go into a rioting community and be listened to. In a sense, I blame ourselves—together with the mass media—for what has happened in Watts, Harlem, Chicago, Cleveland, Omaha. Each time the people in those cities saw Martin Luther King get slapped, they became angry; when they saw four little black girls bombed to death, they were angrier; and when nothing happened, they were steaming. We had nothing to offer that they could see, except to go out and be beaten again. We helped to build their frustration.

For too many years, black Americans marched and had their heads broken and got shot. They were saying to the country, "Look, you guys are supposed to be nice guys and we are only going to do what we are supposed to do—why do you beat us up, why don't you give us what we ask, why don't you straighten yourselves out?" After years of this, we are at almost the same point—because we demonstrated from a position of weakness. We cannot be expected any longer to march and have our heads broken in order to say to whites: come on, you're nice guys. For you are not nice guys. We have found you out.

An organization which claims to speak for the needs of a community— as does the Student Nonviolent Coordinating Committee—must speak in the tone of that community, not as somebody else's buffer zone. This is the significance of black power as a slogan. For once, black people are going to use the words they want to use—not just the words whites want to hear. And they will do this no matter how often the press tries to stop the use of the slogan by equating it with racism or separatism.

An organization which claims to be working for the needs of a community—as SNCC does—must work to provide that community with a position of strength from which to make its voice heard. This is the significance of black power beyond the slogan.

FROM *The New York Review of Books* (September 22, 1966), pp. 5–8. Copyright © 1966 by the Student Nonviolent Coordinating Committee. Reprinted by permission.

Black power can be clearly defined for those who do not attach the fears of white America to their questions about it. We should begin with the basic fact that black Americans have two problems: they are poor and they are black. All other problems arise from this two-sided reality: lack of education, the so-called apathy of black men. Any program to end racism must address itself to that double reality.

Almost from its beginning, SNCC sought to address itself to both conditions with a program aimed at winning political power for impoverished Southern blacks. We had to begin with politics because black Americans are a propertyless people in a country where property is valued above all. We had to work for power, because this country does not function by morality, love, and nonviolence, but by power. Thus we determined to win political power, with the idea of moving on from there into activity that would have economic effects. With power, the masses could *make or participate in making* the decisions which govern their destinies, and thus create basic change in their day-to-day lives.

But if political power seemed to be the key to self-determination, it was also obvious that the key had been thrown down a deep well many years earlier. Disenfranchisement, maintained by racist terror, made it impossible to talk about organizing for political power in 1960. The right to vote had to be won, and SNCC workers devoted their energies to this from 1961 to 1965. They set up voter registration drives in the Deep South. They created pressure for the vote by holding mock elections in Mississippi in 1963 and by helping to establish the Mississippi Freedom Democratic Party (MFDP) in 1964. That struggle was eased, though not won, with the passage of the 1965 Voting Rights Act. SNCC workers could then address themselves to the question: "Who can we vote for, to have our needs met—how do we make our vote meaningful?"

SNCC had already gone to Atlantic City for recognition of the Mississippi Freedom Democratic Party by the Democratic convention and been rejected; it had gone with the MFDP to Washington for recognition by Congress and been rejected. In Arkansas, SNCC helped thirty Negroes to run for School Board elections; all but one were defeated, and there was evidence of fraud and intimidation sufficient to cause their defeat. In Atlanta, Julian Bond ran for the state legislature and was elected—twice—and unseated—twice. In several states, black farmers ran in elections for agricultural committees which make crucial decisions concerning land use, loans, etc. Although they won places on a number of committees, they never gained the majorities needed to control them.

All of the efforts were attempts to win black power. Then, in Alabama, the opportunity came to see how blacks could be organized on an independent party basis. An unusual Alabama law provides that any group of citizens can nominate candidates for county office and, if they win 20 per cent of the vote, may be recognized as a county political party. The same then applies on a state level. SNCC went to organize in several counties such as Lowndes, where black people—who form 80 per cent of the population and have an average annual income of $943—felt they could accomplish nothing within the framework of the Alabama Democratic Party because of its racism and because the qualifying fee for this year's elections was raised from $50 to $500 in order to prevent most Negroes from becoming candidates. On May 3, five new county "freedom organizations" convened and nominated candidates for the offices of sheriff, tax assessor, members of the school boards. These men and women are up for election in November—if they live until then. Their ballot symbol is the black panther: a bold, beautiful animal, representing the strength and dignity of black demands today. A man needs a black panther on his side when he and his family must endure—as hundreds of Alabamians have endured—loss of job, eviction, starvation, and sometimes death, for political activity. He may also need a gun and SNCC reaffirms the right of black men everywhere to defend themselves when threatened or attacked. As for initiating the use of violence, we hope that such programs as ours will make that unnecessary; but it is not for us to tell black communities whether they can or cannot use any particular form of action to resolve their problems. Responsibility for the use of violence by black men, whether in self-defense or initiated by them, lies with the white community.

This is the specific historical experience from which SNCC's call for "black power" emerged on the Mississippi march last July. But the concept of "black power" is not a recent or isolated phenomenon: it has grown out of the ferment of agitation and activity by different people and organizations in many black communities over the years. Our last year of work in Alabama added a new concrete possibility. In Lowndes county, for example, black power will mean that if a Negro is elected sheriff, he can end police brutality. If a black man is elected tax assessor, he can collect and channel funds for the building of better roads and schools serving black people—thus advancing the move from political power into the economic arena. In such areas as Lowndes, where black men have a majority, they will attempt to use it to exercise control. This is what they seek: control. Where Negroes lack a majority, black power means proper representation and sharing of control. It means the creation of power bases from which black people can work to change statewide or nationwide patterns of oppression through pressure from strength—instead of weakness. Politically, black power means what it has always meant to SNCC: the coming-together of black people to elect representatives and *to force those representatives to speak to their needs*. It does not mean merely putting black faces into office. A man or woman who is black and from the slums cannot be automatically expected to speak to the needs of black people. Most of the black politicians we see around the country today are not what SNCC means by black power. The power must be that of a community, and emanate from there.

SNCC today* is working in both North and South on programs of voter registration and independent political organizing. In some places, such as Alabama, Los Angeles, New York, Philadelphia, and New Jersey, independent organizing under the black panther symbol is in progress. The creation of a national "black panther party" must come about; it will take time to build, and it is much too early to predict its success. We have no infallible master plan and we make no claim to exclusive knowledge of how to end racism; different groups will work in their own different ways. SNCC cannot spell out the full logistics of self-determination but it can address itself to the problem by helping black communities define their needs, realize their strength, and go into action along a variety of lines which they must choose for themselves. Without knowing all the answers, it can address itself to the basic problem of poverty; to the fact that in Lowndes County, 86 white families own 90 per cent of the land. What are black people in that county going to do for jobs, where are they going to get money? There must be reallocation of land, of money.

Ultimately, the economic foundations of this country must be shaken if black people are to control their lives. The colonies of the United States—and this includes the black ghettoes within its borders, north and south—must be liberated. For a century, this nation has been like an octopus of exploitation, its tentacles stretching from Mississippi and Harlem to South America, the Middle East, southern Africa, and Vietnam; the form of exploitation varies from area to area but the essential result has been the same—a powerful few have been maintained and enriched at the expense of the poor and voiceless colored masses. This pattern must be broken. As its grip loosens here and there around the world, the hopes of black Americans become more realistic. For racism to die, a totally different America must be born.

This is what the society does not wish to face, this is why that society prefers to talk about integration. But integration speaks not at all to the problem of poverty, only to the problem of blackness. Integration today means the man who "makes it," leaving his black brothers behind in the ghetto as fast as his new sports car will take him. It has no relevance to the Harlem wino or to the cotton-picker making three dollars a day. As a lady I know in Alabama once said, "the food that Ralph Bunche eats doesn't fill my stomach."

Integration, moreover, speaks to the problem of blackness in a despicable way. As a goal, it has been based on complete acceptance of the fact that *in order to have* a decent house or education, blacks must move into a white neighborhood or send their children to a white school. This reinforces, among both black and white, the idea that "white" is automatically better and "black" is by definition inferior. This is why integration is a subterfuge for the maintenance of white supremacy. It allows

* In 1966.—Ed.

the nation to focus on a handful of Southern children who get into white schools, at great price, and to ignore the 94 per cent who are left behind in unimproved all-black schools. Such situations will not change until black people have power—to control their own school boards, in this case. Then Negroes become equal in a way that means something, and integration ceases to be a one-way street. Then integration doesn't mean draining skills and energies from the ghetto into white neighborhoods; then it can mean white people moving from Beverly Hills into Watts, white people joining the Lowndes County Freedom Organization. Then integration becomes relevant.

Last April, before the furor over black power, Christopher Jencks wrote in a *New Republic* article on white Mississippi's manipulation of the antipoverty program:

The war on poverty has been predicated on the notion that there is such a thing as *a community* which can be defined geographically and mobilized for a collective effort to help the poor. This theory has no relationship to reality in the Deep South. In every Mississippi county there are *two* communities. Despite all the pious platitudes of the moderates on both sides, these two communities habitually see their interests in terms of conflict rather than cooperation. Only when the Negro community can muster enough political, economic and professional strength to compete on somewhat equal terms, will Negroes believe in the possibility of true cooperation and whites accept its necessity. En route to integration, the Negro community needs to develop greater independence—a chance to run its own affairs and not cave in whenever "the man" barks . . . Or so it seems to me, and to most of the knowledgeable people with whom I talked in Mississippi. To oEO, this judgment may sound like black nationalism. . . .

Mr. Jencks, a white reporter, perceived the reason why America's antipoverty program has been a sick farce in both North and South. In the South, it is clearly racism which prevents the poor from running their own programs; in the North, it more often seems to be politicking and bureaucracy. But the results are not so different: In the North, nonwhites make up 42 per cent of all families in metropolitan "poverty areas" and only 6 per cent of families in areas classified as not poor. Sncc has been working with local residents in Arkansas, Alabama, and Mississippi to achieve control by the poor of the program and its funds; it has also been working with groups in the North, and the struggle is no less difficult. Behind it all is a federal government which cares far more about winning the war on the Vietnamese than the war on poverty; which has put the poverty program in the hands of self-serving politicians and bureaucrats rather than the poor themselves; which is unwilling to curb the misuse of white power but quick to condemn black power.

To most whites, black power seems to mean that the Mau Mau are coming to the suburbs at night. The Mau Mau are coming, and whites must stop them. Articles appear about plots to "get Whitey," creating an atmosphere in which "law and order must be maintained." Once again, responsibility is shifted from the oppressor to the oppressed. Other whites chide, "Don't forget—you're only 10 per cent of the population; if you get too smart, we'll wipe you out." If they are liberals, they complain, "What about me?—don't you want my help any more?" These are people supposedly concerned about black Americans, but today they think first of themselves, of their feelings of rejection. Or they admonish, "you can't get anywhere without coalitions," without considering the problems of coalition with whom?; on what terms?; when? Or they accuse us of "polarizing the races" by our calls for black unity, when the true responsibility for polarizing lies with whites who will not accept their responsibility as the majority power for making the democratic process work.

White America will not face the problem of color, the reality of it. The well-intended say: "We're all human, everybody is really decent, we must forget color." But color cannot be "forgotten" until its weight is recognized and dealt with. White America will not acknowledge that the ways in which this country sees itself are contradicted by being black—and always have been. Whereas most of the people who settled this country came here for freedom or for economic opportunity, blacks were brought here to be slaves. When the Lowndes County Freedom Organization chose the black panther as its symbol, it was christened by the press "the Black Panther Party"—but the Alabama Democratic Party, whose symbol is a rooster, has never been called the White Cock Party. No one ever talked about "white power" because power in this country *is* white. All this adds up to more than merely identifying a group phenomenon by some catchy name or adjective. The furor over that black panther reveals the problems that white America has with color and sex; the furor over "black power" reveals how deep racism runs and the great fear which is attached to it.

Whites will not see that I, for example, as a person oppressed because of my blackness, have common cause with other blacks who are oppressed because of blackness. This is not to say that there are no white people who see things as I do, but that it is black people I must speak to first. It must be the oppressed to whom SNCC addresses itself primarily, not to friends from the oppressing group.

From birth, black people are told a set of lies about themselves. We are told that we are lazy—yet I drive through the Delta area of Mississippi and watch black people picking cotton in the hot sun for fourteen hours. We are told, "If you work hard, you'll succeed"—but if that were true, black people would own this country. We are oppressed because we are black— not because we are ignorant, not because we are lazy, not because we're stupid (and got good rhythm), but because we're black.

I remember that when I was a boy, I used to go to see Tarzan movies on Saturday. White Tarzan used to beat up the black natives. I would sit there yelling, "Kill the beasts, kill the savages, kill 'em!" I was saying: *Kill me*. It was as if a Jewish boy watched Nazis taking Jews off to concentration camps and cheered them on. Today, I want the chief to beat hell out of Tarzan and send him back to Europe. But it takes time to become free of the lies and their shaming effect on black minds. It takes time to reject the most important lie: that black people inherently can't do the same things white people can do, unless white people help them.

The need for psychological equality is the reason why SNCC today believes that blacks must organize in the black community. Only black people can convey the revolutionary idea that black people are able to do things themselves. Only they can create in the community an aroused and continuing black consciousness that will provide the basis for political strength. In the past, white allies have furthered white supremacy without the whites involved realizing it—or wanting it, I think. Black people must do things for themselves; they must get poverty money they will control and spend themselves, they must conduct tutorial programs themselves so that black children can identify with black people. This is one reason Africa has such importance: The reality of black men ruling their own nation gives blacks elsewhere a sense of possibility, of power, which they do not now have.

This does not mean we don't welcome help, or friends. But we want the right to decide whether anyone is, in fact, our friend. In the past, black Americans have been almost the only people whom everybody and his momma could jump up and call their friends. We have been tokens, symbols, objects—as I was in high school to many young whites, who liked having "a Negro friend." We want to decide who is our friend, and we will not accept someone who comes to us and says: "If you do X, Y, and Z, then I'll help you." We will not be told whom we should choose as allies. We will not be isolated from any group or nation except by our own choice. We cannot have the oppressors telling the oppressed how to rid themselves of the oppressor.

I have said that most liberal whites react to "black power" with the question, What about me?, rather than saying: Tell me what you want me to do and I'll see if I can do it. There are answers to the right question. One of the most disturbing things about almost all white supporters of the movement has been that they are afraid to go into their own communities —which is where the racism exists—and work to get rid of it. They want to run from Berkeley to tell us what to do in Mississippi; let them look instead at Berkeley. They admonish blacks to be nonviolent; let them preach nonviolence in the white community. They come to teach me Negro history; let them go to the suburbs and open up freedom schools for whites. Let them work to stop America's racist foreign policy; let them press this government to cease supporting the economy of South Africa.

There is a vital job to be done among poor whites. We hope to see, eventually, a coalition between poor blacks and poor whites. That is the only coalition which seems acceptable to us, and we see such a coalition as the major internal instrument of change in American society. SNCC *has* tried several times to organize poor whites; we are trying again now, with an initial training program in Tennessee. It is purely academic today to talk about bringing poor blacks and whites together, but the job of creating a poor-white power bloc must be attempted: The main responsibility for it falls upon whites. Black and white can work together in the white community where possible; it is not possible, however, to go into a poor Southern town and talk about integration. Poor whites everywhere are becoming more hostile—not less—partly because they see the nation's attention focused on black poverty and nobody coming to them. Too many young middle-class Americans, like some sort of Pepsi generation, have wanted to come alive through the black community; they've wanted to be where the action is—and the action has been in the black community.

Black people do not want to "take over" this country. They don't want to "get whitey"; they just want to get him off their backs, as the saying goes. It was for example the exploitation by Jewish landlords and merchants which first created black resentment toward Jews—not Judaism. The white man is irrelevant to blacks, except as an oppressive force. Blacks want to be in his place, yes, but not in order to terrorize and lynch and starve him. They want to be in his place because that is where a decent life can be had.

But our vision is not merely of a society in which all black men have enough to buy the good things of life. When we urge that black money go into black pockets, we mean the communal pocket. We want to see money go back into the community and used to benefit it. We want to see the co-operative concept applied in business and banking. We want to see black ghetto residents demand that an exploiting landlord or store keeper sell them, at minimal cost, a building or a shop that they will own and improve cooperatively; they can back their demand with a rent strike, or a boycott, and a community so unified behind them that no one else will move into the building or buy at the store. The society we seek to build among black people, then, is not a capitalist one. It is a society in which the spirit of community and humanistic love prevail. The word love is suspect; black expectations of what it might produce have been betrayed too often. But those were expectations of a response from the white community, which failed us. The love we seek to encourage is within the black community, the only American community where men call each other "brother" when they meet. We can build a community of love only where we have the ability and power to do so: among blacks.

As for white America, perhaps it can stop crying out against "black supremacy," "black nationalism," "racism in reverse," and begin facing reality. The reality is that this nation, from top to bottom, is racist; that racism is not primarily a problem of "human relations" but of an exploitation maintained—either actively or through silence—by the society as a whole. Camus and Sartre have asked, can a man condemn himself? Can whites, particularly liberal whites, condemn themselves? Can they stop blaming us, and blame their own system? Are they capable of the shame which might become a revolutionary emotion?

We have found that they usually cannot condemn themselves, and so we have done it. But the rebuilding of this society, if at all possible, is basically the responsibility of whites—not blacks. We won't fight to save the present society, in Vietnam or anywhere else. We are just going to work, in the way *we* see fit, and on goals *we* define, not for civil rights but for all our human rights.

POWER, ECONOMY, AND THE
WARFARE STATE

TWO RIVAL THEORIES on who holds the power in contemporary
   American society are the elitist theory and the pluralist theory. A basic
   question is whether the United States is ruled by a unified power elite,
   as Mills maintains, or by a plurality of countervailing groups. Both
   elitists and pluralists agree that there are a number of centers of power
   in America. These include the executive branch of the federal government, the semi-autonomous government agencies (the most important
   and powerful being the CIA), the military establishment, and the
   major corporations. The question is whether these institutions balance
   and veto each other or whether they act in concert. A second issue is
   the degree of power exercised at the "middle" and "lower" levels of
   society by state and local governments, Congress, the universities, and
   the labor unions.
The power elite thesis of Mills is that incumbents of key positions in the
   major corporations, the military, and the executive branch of the federal
   government form a cohesive interlocking directorate that makes the
   fundamental decisions governing the course of American society. Members of the power elite are not always in agreement, but the assump-

tions and interests they share far outweigh their differences. Simply because they are at the top they view the world in a similar fashion. According to the power elite theorists, the more basic issues of national and international consequence are not, as the pluralists maintain, decided at the middle and lower levels.[1]

Hacker lists a dozen of the most powerful organizations in American society. These institutions are not directly accountable to the public, yet they have a great impact on the country. For example, the managements of the larger corporations bring prosperity or economic decline to particular areas by determining where new plants will be built or old ones abandoned. The CIA strongly influences our foreign relations by sifting intelligence information sent to the Chief Executive.

The policies of these agencies do not stem from the personalities of their managers, whose tenure is often brief. Mills too greatly emphasized the impact of individual men on the powerful institutions they command, Hacker says. Executives do initiate decisions, but even those decisions are largely determined by institutional momentum. Corporate institutions seem to have an organizational inertia. Previous investments in plants and equipment are often so heavy that sudden and drastic changes in policy would be uneconomical.

The United States today is a garrison society, according to Dibble, where the military, the corporations, and the government form one interdependent and interlocking system. In this system it makes no sense to talk about the distinction between civilian and military spheres, because there is no boundary between them. Key personnel move back and forth between business, government agencies, and the higher echelons of the armed forces. Industries such as aerospace and electronics depend on military contracts. The military penetrates into the university by financing research; through conscription it touches every young man in one way or another and influences his choices of occupation and schooling, regardless of whether or not he is actually drafted.

In their analysis of imperialism, Baran and Sweezy further discuss the relationship between corporations, the military, and the government. Corporations depend on the military to protect their investments abroad. Foreign operations of the major American corporations are becoming much more profitable than domestic operations and have been growing rapidly. Although only one third of the assets of the Standard

---

[1] For a good exposition of the pluralist view, see Arnold M. Rose, *The Power Structure* (New York: Oxford University Press, 1967). For the power elite view, see C. Wright Mills, *The Power Elite* (New York: Oxford University Press, 1956); G. William Domhoff, *Who Rules America?* (New York: Prentice Hall, 1967); Domhoff, "Some Friendly Answers to Radical Critics," *The Insurgent Sociologist*, 2,2 (Spring 1972); Marc Pilisuk and Thomas Hayden, "Is there a Military-Industrial Complex That Prevents Peace?" *Journal of Social Issues*, 21 (1965), pp. 67–117. Portions of Pilisuk and Hayden are reprinted in Frank Lindenfeld, ed., *Readings in Political Sociology* (New York: Funk & Wagnalls, 1968).

Oil Company of New Jersey are located in Latin America and in the Eastern hemisphere, fully two thirds of its profits come from those areas. The real purpose of foreign aid, according to Baran and Sweezy, is to make sure that foreign governments are friendly to American investments and profit-taking. When revolutions threaten to expropriate these investments, the government intervenes with military force. After the Cuban revolution when the new government took over American investments in Cuba such as refineries belonging to Jersey Standard, the United States attempted to overthrow the Castro regime —not merely to recover these losses, but to keep the Cuban example from spreading to other countries in Latin America.

I find the elite theory more convincing than the pluralist theory. The pluralists argue there is no concentration of power because there are disagreements among those at the top, and because many issues are debated and decided on by the legislature. But the pluralists exaggerate the influence of legislators, for the most important issues are decided at the top, and disagreement there concerns tactics rather than goals. Criticism of the Vietnam War has come from inside the Cabinet and from business executives, but such criticism has been based on pragmatic considerations and has rarely touched on the legitimacy of American intervention abroad.

At the apex of power in American society there is a basic agreement on the most vital issues—that "Communism" should be contained, that American intervention against revolutions for national liberation may be necessary, that capitalism must be preserved.

The Structure of Power in American Society

C. Wright Mills

I

Power has to do with whatever decisions men make about the arrangements under which they live, and about the events which make up the history of their times. Events that are beyond human decision do happen; social arrangements do change without benefit of explicit decision. But in so far as such decisions are made, the problem of who is involved in making

FROM Power, Politics and People: The Collected Papers of C. Wright Mills, edited by Irving Louis Horowitz (New York and London: Oxford University Press, 1963), pp. 23–38. Reprinted by permission of Irving Louis Horowitz.

them is the basic problem of power. In so far as they could be made but are not, the problem becomes who fails to make them?

We cannot today merely assume that in the last resort men must always be governed by their own consent. For among the means of power which now prevail is the power to manage and to manipulate the consent of men. That we do not know the limits of such power, and that we hope it does have limits, does not remove the fact that much power today is successfully employed without the sanction of the reason or the conscience of the obedient.

Surely nowadays we need not argue that, in the last resort, coercion is the "final" form of power. But then, we are by no means constantly at the last resort. Authority (power that is justified by the beliefs of the voluntarily obedient) and manipulation (power that is wielded unbeknown to the powerless)—must also be considered, along with coercion. In fact, the three types must be sorted out whenever we think about power.

In the modern world, we must bear in mind, power is often not so authoritative as it seemed to be in the medieval epoch: ideas which justify rulers no longer seem so necessary to their exercise of power. At least for many of the great decisions of our time—especially those of an international sort—mass "persuasion" has not been "necessary"; the fact is simply accomplished. Furthermore, such ideas as are available to the powerful are often neither taken up nor used by them. Such ideologies usually arise as a response to an effective debunking of power; in the United States such opposition has not been effective enough recently to create the felt need for new ideologies of rule.

There has, in fact, come about a situation in which many who have lost faith in prevailing loyalties have not acquired new ones, and so pay no attention to politics of any kind. They are not radical, not liberal, not conservative, not reactionary. They are inactionary. They are out of it. If we accept the Greek's definition of the idiot as an altogether private man, then we must conclude that many American citizens are now idiots. And I should not be surprised, although I do not know, if there were not some such idiots even in Germany. This—and I use the word with care—this spiritual condition seems to me the key to many modern troubles of political intellectuals, as well as the key to much political bewilderment in modern society. Intellectual "conviction" and moral "belief" are not necessary, in either the rulers or the ruled, for a ruling power to persist and even to flourish. So far as the role of ideologies is concerned, their frequent absences and the prevalence of mass indifference are surely two of the major political facts about the western societies today.

How large a role any explicit decisions do play in the making of history is itself an historical problem. For how large that role may be depends very much upon the means of power that are available at any given time in any given society. In some societies, the innumerable actions of innumerable men modify their milieux, and so gradually modify the structure itself. These modifications—the course of history—go on behind the backs of men. History is drift, although in total "men make it." Thus, innumerable entrepreneurs and innumerable consumers by ten thousand decisions per minute may shape and re-shape the free-market economy. Perhaps this was the chief kind of limitation Marx had in mind when he wrote, in *The 18th Brumaire*: that "Men make their own history, but they do not make it just as they please; they do not make it under circumstances chosen by them-selves. . . ."

But in other societies—certainly in the United States and in the Soviet Union today—a few men may be so placed within the structure that by their decisions they modify the milieux of many other men, and in fact nowadays the structural conditions under which most men live. Such elites of power also make history under circumstances not chosen altogeher by themselves, yet compared with other men, and compared with other periods of world history, these circumstances do indeed seem less limiting.

I should contend that "men are free to make history," but that some men are indeed much freer than others. For such freedom requires access to the means of decision and of power by which history can now be made. It has not always been so made; but in the later phases of the modern epoch it is. It is with reference to this epoch that I am contending that if men do not make history, they tend increasingly to become the utensils of history-makers as well as the mere objects of history.

The history of modern society may readily be understood as the story of the enlargement and the centralization of the means of power—in eco-nomic, in political, and in military institutions. The rise of industrial society has involved these developments in the means of economic production. The rise of the nation-state has involved similar developments in the means of violence and in those of political administration.

In the western societies, such transformations have generally occurred gradually, and many cultural traditions have restrained and shaped them. In most of the Soviet societies, they are happening very rapidly indeed and without the great discourse of western civilization, without the Renaissance and without the Reformation, which so greatly strengthened and gave political focus to the idea of freedom. In those societies, the enlargement and the co-ordination of all the means of power has occurred more brutally, and from the beginning under tightly centralized authority. But in both types, the means of power have now become international in scope and similar in form. To be sure, each of them has its own ups and downs; neither is as yet absolute; how they are run differs quite sharply.

Yet so great is the reach of the means of violence, and so great the economy required to produce and support them, that we have in the immediate past witnessed the consolidation of these two world centers, either of which dwarfs the power of Ancient Rome. As we pay attention to the awesome means of power now available to quite small groups of men we come to realize that Caesar could do less with Rome than Napoleon with France; Napoleon less with France than Lenin with Russia. But what was Caesar's power at its height compared with the power of the changing inner circles of Soviet Russia and the temporary administrations of the United States? We come to realize—indeed they continually remind us—how a few men have access to the means by which in a few days continents can be turned into thermonuclear wastelands. That the facilities of power are so enormously enlarged and so decisively centralized surely means that the powers of quite small groups of men, which we may call elites, are now of literally inhuman consequence.

My concern here is not with the international scene but with the United States in the middle of the twentieth century. I must emphasize "in the middle of the twentieth century" because in our attempt to understand any society we come upon images which have been drawn from its past and which often confuse our attempt to confront its present reality. That is one minor reason why history is the shank of any social science: we must study it if only to rid ourselves of it. In the United States, there are indeed many such images and usually they have to do with the first half of the nineteenth century. At that time the economic facilities of the United States were very widely dispersed and subject to little or to no central authority.

The state watched in the night but was without decisive voice in the day.

One man meant one rifle and the militia were without centralized orders.

Any American as old-fashioned as I can only agree with R. H. Tawney that "Whatever the future may contain, the past has shown no more excellent social order than that in which the mass of the people were the masters of the holdings which they ploughed and the tools with which they worked, and could boast . . . 'It is a quietness to a man's mind to live upon his own and to know his heir certain.' "

But then we must immediately add: all that is of the past and of little relevance to our understanding of the United States today. Within this society three broad levels of power may now be distinguished. I shall begin at the top and move downward.

II

The power to make decisions of national and international consequence is now so clearly seated in political, military, and economic institutions that other areas of society seem off to the side and, on occasion, readily subordinated to these. The scattered institutions of religion, education and family are increasingly shaped by the big three, in which history-making decisions now regularly occur. Behind this fact there is all the push and drive of a fabulous technology; for these three institutional orders have incorporated this technology and now guide it, even as it shapes and paces their development.

As each has assumed its modern shape, its effects upon the other two have become greater, and the traffic between the three has increased. There is no longer, on the one hand, an economy, and, on the other, a political order, containing a military establishment unimportant to politics and to money-making. There is a political economy numerously linked with military order and decision. This triangle of power is now a structural fact, and it is the key to any understanding of the higher circles in America today. For as each of these domains has coincided with the others, as decisions in each have become broader, the leading men of each—the high military, the corporation executives, the political directorate—have tended to come together to form the power elite of America.

The political order, once composed of several dozen states with a weak federal-center, has become an executive apparatus which has taken up into itself many powers previously scattered, legislative as well as administrative, and which now reaches into all parts of the social structure. The long-time tendency of business and government to become more closely connected has since World War II reached a new point of explicitness. Neither can now be seen clearly as a distinct world. The growth of executive government does not mean merely the "enlargement of government" as some kind of autonomous bureaucracy: under American conditions, it has meant the ascendency of the corporation man into political eminence. Already during the New Deal, such men had joined the political directorate; as of World War II they came to dominate it. Long involved with government, now they have moved into quite full direction of the economy of the war effort and of the post-war era.

The economy, once a great scatter of small productive units in somewhat automatic balance, has become internally dominated by a few hundred corporations, administratively and politically interrelated, which together hold the keys to economic decision. This economy is at once a permanent-war economy and a private-corporation economy. The most important relations of the corporation to the state now rest on the coincidence between military and corporate interests, as defined by the military and the corporate rich, and accepted by politicians and public. Within the elite as a whole, this coincidence of military domain and corporate realm strengthens both of them and further subordinates the merely political man. Not the party politician, but the corporation executive, is now more likely to sit with the military to answer the question: what is to be done?

The military order, once a slim establishment in a context of civilian distrust, has become the largest and most expensive feature of government; behind smiling public relations, it has all the grim and clumsy efficiency of a great and sprawling bureaucracy. The high military have gained decisive political and economic relevance. The seemingly permanent military threat places a premium upon them and virtually all political and economic actions are now judged in terms of military definitions of reality: the higher military have ascended to a firm position within the power of elite of our time.

In part at least this is a result of an historical fact, pivotal for the years since 1939: the attention of the elite has shifted from domestic problems—centered in the 'thirties around slump—to international problems—centered in the 'forties and 'fifties around war. By long historical usage, the government of the United States has been shaped by domestic clash and balance; it does not have suitable agencies and traditions for the democratic handling of international affairs. In considerable part, it is in this vacuum that the power elite has grown.

(i) To understand the unity of this power elite, we must pay attention to the psychology of its several members in their respective milieux. In so far as the power elite is composed of men of similar origin and education, of similar career and style of life, their unity may be said to rest upon the fact that they are of similar social type, and to lead to the fact of their easy intermingling. This kind of unity reaches its frothier apex in the sharing of that prestige which is to be had in the world of the celebrity. It achieves a more solid culmination in the fact of the interchangeability of positions between the three dominant institutional orders. It is revealed by considerable traffic of personnel within and between these three, as well as by the rise of specialized go-betweens as in the new style high-level lobbying.

(ii) Behind such psychological and social unity are the structure and the mechanics of those institutional hierarchies over which the political directorate, the corporate rich, and the high military now preside. How each of these hierarchies is shaped and what relations it has with the others determine in large part the relations of their rulers. Were these hierarchies scattered and disjointed, then their respective elites might tend to be scattered and disjointed; but if they have many interconnections and points of coinciding interest, then their elites tend to form a coherent kind of grouping. The unity of the elite is not a simple reflection of the unity of institutions, but men and institutions are always related; that is why we must understand the elite today in connection with such institutional trends as the development of a permanent-war establishment, alongside a privately incorporated economy, inside a virtual political vacuum. For the men at the top have been selected and formed by such institutional trends.

(iii) Their unity, however, does not rest solely upon psychological similarity and social intermingling, nor entirely upon the structural blending of commanding positions and common interests. At times it is the unity of a more explicit co-ordination.

To say that these higher circles are increasingly co-ordinated, that this is *one* basis of their unity, and that at times—as during open war—such co-ordination is quite wilful, is not to say that the co-ordination is total or continuous, or even that it is very surefooted. Much less is it to say that the power elite has emerged as the realization of a plot. Its rise cannot be adequately explained in any psychological terms.

Yet we must remember that institutional trends may be defined as opportunities by those who occupy the command posts. Once such opportunities are recognized, men may avail themselves of them. Certain types of men from each of these three areas, more far-sighted than others, have actively promoted the liaison even before it took its truly modern shape. Now more have come to see that their several interests can more easily be realized if they work together, in informal as well as in formal ways, and accordingly they have done so.

The idea of the power elite is of course an interpretation. It rests upon and it enables us to make sense of major institutional trends, the social similarities and psychological affinities of the men at the top. But the idea is also based upon what has been happening on the middle and lower levels of power, to which I now turn.

III

There are of course other interpretations of the American system of power. The most usual is that it is a moving balance of many competing interests. The image of balance, at least in America, is derived from the idea of the economic market: in the nineteenth century, the balance was thought to occur between a great scatter of individuals and enterprises; in the twentieth century, it is thought to occur between great interest blocs. In both views, the politician is the key man of power because he is the broker of many conflicting powers.

I believe that the balance and the compromise in American society— the "countervailing powers" and the "veto groups," of parties and associations, of strata and unions—must now be seen as having mainly to do with the middle levels of power. It is these middle levels that the political journalist and the scholar of politics are most likely to understand and to write about—if only because, being mainly middle class themselves, they are closer to them. Moreover these levels provide the noisy content of most "political" news and gossip; the images of these levels are more or less in accord with the folklore of how democracy works; and, if the master-image of balance is accepted, many intellectuals, especially in their current patrioteering, are readily able to satisfy such political optimism as they wish to feel. Accordingly, liberal interpretations of what is happening in the United States are now virtually the only interpretations that are widely distributed.

But to believe that the power system reflects a balancing society is, I think, to confuse the present era with earlier times, and to confuse its top and bottom with its middle levels.

By the top levels, as distinguished from the middle, I intend to refer, first of all, to the scope of the decisions that are made. At the top today, these decisions have to do with all the issues of war and peace. They have also to do with slump and poverty which are now so very much problems of international scope. I intend also to refer to whether or not the groups that struggle politically have a chance to gain the positions from which such top decisions are made, and indeed whether their members do usually hope for such top national command. Most of the competing interests which make up the clang and clash of American politics are strictly concerned with their slice of the existing pie. Labor unions, for example, certainly have no policies of an international sort other than those which given unions adopt for the strict economic protection of their members. Neither do farm organizations. The actions of such middle-level powers may indeed have consequence for top-level policy; certainly at times they hamper these policies. But they are not truly concerned with them, which means of course that their influence tends to be quite irresponsible.

The facts of the middle levels may in part be understood in terms of the rise of the power elite. The expanded and centralized and interlocked hierarchies over which the power elite preside have encroached upon the old balance and relegated it to the middle level. But there are also independent developments of the middle levels. These, it seems to me, are better understood as an affair of entrenched and provincial demands than as a center of national decision. As such, the middle level often seems much more of a stalemate than a moving balance.

(i) The middle level of politics is not a forum in which there are debated the big decisions of national and international life. Such debate is not carried on by nationally responsible parties representing and clarifying alternative policies. There are no such parties in the United States. More and more, fundamental issues never come to any point or decision before the Congress, much less before the electorate in party campaigns. In the case of Formosa, in the spring of 1955, the Congress abdicated all debate concerning events and decisions which surely bordered on war. The same is largely true of the 1957 crisis in the Middle East. Such decisions now regularly by-pass the Congress, and are never clearly focused issues for public decision.

The American political campaign distracts attention from national and international issues, but that is not to say that there are no issues in these campaigns. In each district and state, issues are set up and watched by organized interests of sovereign local importance. The professional politician is of course a party politician, and the two parties are semi-feudal organizations: they trade patronage and other favors for votes and for protection. The differences between them, so far as national issues are concerned, are very narrow and very mixed up. Often each seems to be forty-eight parties, one to each state; and accordingly, the politician as campaigner and as Congressman is not concerned with national party lines, if any are discernible. Often he is not subject to any effective national party discipline. He speaks for the interests of his own constituency, and he is concerned with national issues only in so far as they affect the interests effectively organized there, and hence his chances of re-election. That is why, when he does speak of national matters, the result is so often such an empty rhetoric. Seated in his sovereign locality, the politician is not at the national summit. He is on and of the middle levels of power.

(ii) Politics is not an arena in which free and independent organizations truly connect the lower and middle levels of society with the top levels of decision. Such organizations are not an effective and major part of American life today. As more people are drawn into the political arena, their associations become mass in scale, and the power of the individual becomes dependent upon them; to the extent that they are effective, they have become larger, and to that extent they have become less accessible to the influence of the individual. This is a central fact about associations in any mass society: it is of most consequence for political parties and for trade unions.

In the 'thirties, it often seemed that labor would become an insurgent power independent of corporation and state. Organized labor was then emerging for the first time on an American scale, and the only political sense of direction it needed was the slogan, "organize the unorganized." Now without the mandate of the slump, labor remains without political direction. Instead of economic and political struggles it has become deeply entangled in administrative routines with both corporation and state. One of its major functions, as a vested interest of the new society, is the regulation of such irregular tendencies as may occur among the rank and file.

There is nothing, it seems to me, in the make-up of the current labor leadership to allow us to expect that it can or that it will lead, rather than merely react. In so far as it fights at all it fights over a share of the goods of a single way of life and not over that way of life itself. The typical labor leader in the U.S.A. today is better understood as an adaptive creature of the main business drift than as an independent actor in a truly national context.

(iii) The idea that this society is a balance of powers requires us to assume that the units in balance are of more or less equal power and that they are truly independent of one another. These assumptions have rested, it seems clear, upon the historical importance of a large and independent middle class. In the latter nineteenth century and during the Progressive Era, such a class of farmers and small businessmen fought politically—and lost—their last struggle for a paramount role in national decision. Even then, their aspirations seemed bound to their own imagined past.

This old, independent middle class has of course declined. On the most generous count, it is now 40 per cent of the total middle class (at most 20 per cent of the total labor force). Moreover, it has become politically as well as economically dependent upon the state, most notably in the case of the subsidized farmer.

The *new* middle class of white-collar employees is certainly not the political pivot of any balancing society. It is in no way politically unified. Its unions, such as they are, often serve merely to incorporate it as hanger-on of the labor interest. For a considerable period, the old middle class *was* an independent base of power; the new middle class cannot be. Political freedom and economic security *were* anchored in small and independent properties; they are not anchored in the worlds of the white-collar job. Scattered property holders were economically united by more or less free markets; the jobs of the new middle class are integrated by corporate authority. Economically, the white-collar classes are in the same condition as wage workers; politically, they are in a worse condition, for they are not organized. They are no vanguard of historic change; they are at best a rearguard of the welfare state.

The agrarian revolt of the 'nineties, the small-business revolt that has been more or less continuous since the 'eighties, the labor revolt of the 'thirties—each of these has failed as an independent movement which could countervail against the powers that be; they have failed as politically autonomous third parties. But they have succeeded, in varying degree, as interests vested in the expanded corporation and state; they have succeeded as parochial interests seated in particular districts, in local divisions of the two parties, and in the Congress. What they would become, in short, are well-established features of the *middle* levels of balancing power, on which we may now observe all those strata and interests which in the course of American history have been defeated in their bids for top power or which have never made such bids.

Fifty years ago many observers thought of the American state as a mask behind which an invisible government operated. But nowadays, much of what was called the old lobby, visible or invisible, is part of the quite visible government. The "governmentalization of the lobby" has proceeded in both the legislative and the executive domain, as well as between them. The executive bureaucracy becomes not only the center of decision but also the arena within which major conflicts of power are resolved or denied resolution. "Administration" replaces electoral politics; the maneuvering of cliques (which include leading Senators as well as civil servants) replaces the open clash of parties.

The shift of corporation men into the political directorate has accelerated the decline of the politicians in the Congress to the middle levels of power; the formation of the power elite rests in part upon this relegation. It rests also upon the semi-organized stalemate of the interests of sovereign localities, into which the legislative function has so largely fallen; upon the virtually complete absence of a civil service that is a politically neutral but politically relevant, depository of brain-power and executive skill; and it rests upon the increased official secrecy behind which great decisions are made without benefit of public or even of Congressional debate.

IV

There is one last belief upon which liberal observers everywhere base their interpretations and rest their hopes. That is the idea of the public and the associated idea of public opinion. Conservative thinkers, since the French Revolution, have of course Viewed With Alarm the rise of the public, which they have usually called the masses, or something to that effect. "The populace is sovereign," wrote Gustave Le Bon, "and the tide of barbarism mounts." But surely those who have supposed the masses to be well on their way to triumph are mistaken. In our time, the influence of publics or of masses within political life is in fact decreasing, and such influence as on occasion they do have tends, to an unknown but increasing degree, to be guided by the means of mass communication.

In a society of publics, discussion is the ascendant means of communication, and the mass media, if they exist, simply enlarge and animate this discussion, linking one face-to-face public with the discussions of another. In a mass society, the dominant type of communication is the formal media, and publics become mere markets for these media: the "public" of a radio program consists of all those exposed to it. When we try to look upon the United States today as a society of publics, we realize that it has moved a considerable distance along the road to the mass society.

In official circles, the very term, "the public," has come to have a phantom meaning, which dramatically reveals its eclipse. The deciding elite can identify some of those who clamor publicly as "Labor," others as "Business," still others as "Farmers." But these are not the public. "The public" consists of the unidentified and the non-partisan in a world of defined and partisan interests. In this faint echo of the classic notion, the public is composed of these remnants of the old and new middle classes whose interests are not explicitly defined, organized, or clamorous. In a curious adaptation, "the public" often becomes, in administrative fact, "the disengaged expert," who, although ever so well informed, has never taken a clear-cut and public stand on controversial issues. He is the "public" member of the board, the commission, the committee. What "the public" stands for, accordingly, is often a vagueness of policy (called "open-mindedness"), a lack of involvement in public affairs (known as "reasonableness"), and a professional disinterest (known as "tolerance").

All this is indeed far removed from the eighteenth-century idea of the public of public opinion. That idea parallels the economic idea of the magical market. Here is the market composed of freely competing entrepreneurs; there is the public composed of circles of people in discussion. As price is the result of anonymous, equally weighted, bargaining individuals, so public opinion is the result of each man's having thought things out for himself and then contributing his voice to the great chorus. To be sure, some may have more influence on the state of opinion than others, but no one group monopolizes the discussion, or by itself determines the opinions that prevail.

In this classic image, the people are presented with problems. They discuss them. They formulate viewpoints. These viewpoints are organized, and they compete. One viewpoint "wins out." Then the people act on this view, or their representatives are instructed to act it out, and this they promptly do.

Such are the images of democracy which are still used as working justifications of power in America. We must now recognize this description as more a fairy tale than a useful approximation. The issues that now shape man's fate are neither raised nor decided by any public at large. The idea of a society that is at bottom composed of publics is not a matter of fact; it is the proclamation of an ideal, and as well the assertion of a legitimation masquerading as fact.

I cannot here describe the several great forces within American society as well as elsewhere which have been at work in the debilitation of the public. I want only to remind you that publics, like free associations, can be deliberately and suddenly smashed, or they can more slowly wither away. But whether smashed in a week or withered in a generation, the demise of the public must be seen in connection with the rise of centralized organizations, with all their new means of power, including those of the mass media of distraction. These, we now know, often seem to expropriate the rationality and the will of the terrorized or—as the case may be—the voluntarily indifferent society of masses. In the more democratic process of indifference the remnants of such publics as remain may only occasionally be intimidated by fanatics in search of "disloyalty." But regardless of that, they lose their will for decision because they do not possess the instruments for decision; they lose their sense of political belonging because they do not belong; they lose their political will because they see no way to realize it.

The political structure of a modern democratic state requires that such a public as is projected by democratic theorists not only exist but that it be the very forum within which a politics of real issues is enacted.

It requires a civil service that is firmly linked with the world of knowledge and sensibility, and which is composed of skilled men who, in their careers and in their aspirations, are truly independent of any private, which is to say, corporation, interests.

It requires nationally responsible parties which debate openly and clearly the issues which the nation, and indeed the world, now so rigidly confronts.

It requires an intelligentsia, inside as well as outside the universities, who carry on the big discourse of the western world, and whose work is relevant to and influential among parties and movements and publics.

And it certainly requires, as a fact of power, that there be free associations standing between families and smaller communities and publics, on the one hand, and the state, the military, the corporation, on the other. For unless these do exist, there are no vehicles for reasoned opinion, no instruments for the rational exertion of public will.

Such democratic formations are not now ascendant in the power structure of the United States, and accordingly the men of decision are not men selected and formed by careers within such associations and by their performance before such publics. The top of modern American society is increasingly unified, and often seems willfully co-ordinated: at the top there has emerged an elite whose power probably exceeds that of any small group of men in world history. The middle levels are often a drifting set of stalemated forces: the middle does not link the bottom with the top. The bottom of this society is politically fragmented, and even as a passive fact, increasingly powerless: at the bottom there is emerging a mass society.

These developments, I believe, can be correctly understood neither in terms of the liberal nor the marxian interpretation of politics and history. Both these ways of thought arose as guidelines to reflection about a type of society which does not now exist in the United States. We confront there a new kind of social structure, which embodies elements and tendencies of all modern society, but in which they have assumed a more naked and flamboyant prominence.

That does not mean that we must give up the ideals of these classic political expectations. I believe that both have been concerned with the problem of rationality and of freedom: liberalism, with freedom and rationality as supreme facts about the individual; marxism, as supreme facts about man's role in the political making of history. What I have said here, I suppose, may be taken as an attempt to make evident why the ideas of freedom and of rationality now so often seem so ambiguous in the new society of the United States of America.

Power to Do What?

Andrew Hacker

To return to the original problem: Mills' failure to show "what kinds of decisions the decision-makers make," to "specify what the big decisions are." A reading of *The Power Elite* makes clear that the men who run America's large corporations stand at the center of the topmost circle. They, more than their military and governmental counterparts, have power that is both autonomous and unchecked. The military are still heavily controlled by the politicians, and the politicians must be responsive to the public.

The conventional view, of course, is that the businessman is far from a free agent. Any executive will wax eloquent on how he is hemmed in on all sides. He will point to a plethora of government agencies, all of which regulate his conduct. There is the Federal Trade Commission, the National Labor Relations Board, the Anti-trust Division of the Justice Department, and of course the Internal Revenue Service. And then there are labor unions, further limiting his freedom of action. He has customers and suppliers, telling him what they want and what he can get; and he has stockholders clamoring for dividends, capital gains, and efficient management. And of course there is the ubiquitous public that must be satisfied at all stages, lest bankruptcy be the consequence. The question, however, is not whether businessmen feel hamstrung, for they have protested their powerlessness since they were first told to buy safety-devices for their dangerous machines. The point is whether or not these limiting factors take on much significance when weighed against the areas of unrestricted action open to the corporate elite.

It should be noted at the outset that large corporations do not go bankrupt. They can be inefficient, as the steel companies have demonstrated, and still be profitable. Their relative share of the market can rise or fall, and their rank in the industry may change slightly over the years. But mergers and reorganizations keep the assets and production facilities intact. To be sure, the corporate elite must make its decisions with an eye on profitability. But in the highest circles the concern is with the expansion of the enterprise over a period of several decades, and profits are but a means to this end. The real issue is how autonomous these enterprises are and what are the consequences of their decisions for society as a whole.

FROM *The New Sociology*, edited by Irving L. Horowitz, pp. 136–45. Copyright © 1964 by Oxford University Press, Inc. Reprinted by permission.

What, in short, can the corporate elite do with the power it is alleged to have?

First, in prices. Despite an occasional outburst from the White House, the corporate managers can administer prices as they see fit.[1] They are not required to submit proposed increases to any government agency for approval, and they may ask what the market will bear. Generally speaking, the market will pay what is asked.

On profits, stockholders expect only a certain modest dividend, and this is usually passed on to them without discussion.[2] Top management maintains a minimum level of earnings by its ability to fix prices. In addition it decides what proportion of the earnings will go to the stockholders and what proportion is to be retained by the company.

Wages are of course subject to collective bargaining. But this process simply maintains the status quo. For wage increases just about keep pace with the cost of living, and the share of a corporation's income going to wages remains about the same over the years. Management has even more freedom in setting salaries. Here it can determine who is to become wealthy and how great this wealth is to be. Decisions on executive compensation, in particular, go far toward determining aspirations for an entire society. The purchasing power bestowed on the men at and near the top makes for a style of life that becomes a goal for those lower in the pyramid.[3]

Enough has been said and written about organization men emphasizing that employee behavior is both scrutinized and shaped by those in the executive suites.[4] If it is asked why so many succumb to the pressure to conform, the answer is that most Americans want to succeed in their careers and are willing to pay the price of success. That such a high price is exacted by the corporate elite is itself instructive, for it has not been demonstrated that the bland and well-rounded personality results in more sales or higher production. Rather, this outlook is what management finds congenial to its own sensibilities. More significant, the habits inculcated in work-life inevitably spill over into private life—if such it can be called. The kinds of attitudes necessary for career-success are imparted to children and pervade marriage and other social relations.

The corporate elite decides what kinds of jobs are to be made available and how many of them there are to be. This is not simply management's traditional power to hire and fire. It is also the power to decide what kind

---

[1] The steel industry is, of course, the outstanding example. See Gardiner C. Means, *Pricing Policy and the Public Interest* (New York, 1962).

[2] The actual role of the presumed "owners" of American industry is laid bare in Joseph Livingston's *The American Stockholder* (Philadelphia, 1958).

[3] In a *New Yorker* advertisement aimed at recruiting advertisers for its own columns, a newspaper widely circulated in executive circles proclaimed: "What the *Wall Street Journal* reader learns to favor, others everywhere will yearn to possess."

[4] The better-known are: William H. Whyte, Jr., *The Organization Man* (New York, 1956); Vance Packard, *The Pyramid Climbers* (New York, 1962); and Martin Gross, *The Brain Watchers* (New York, 1962).

of work individuals will do for a living. The decision to automate, for example, lessened the need for blue-collar workers and created permanent underemployment for many groups in society. The earlier decision to expand the number of white-collar jobs opened new opportunities to millions of Americans, thus elevating them to new stations in life and creating not only new benefits but also new anxieties. People fill jobs; jobs are not made for people. Corporate decisions to create certain types of employment cause people to alter their lives in such ways as to qualify for those positions. Those who cannot make the changes are consigned to the human discard-heap.

Corporate managements are free to decide where they will locate their plants and offices. The decision of many companies to have their headquarters in New York, for example, has changed the face of that city. This power has also contributed, probably more than anything else, to the suburban explosion, for the burgeoning white-collar class must find a place to live. A handful of executives decide which parts of the country are to prosper and which are to stagnate. If over half the counties in the United States lost population in the 1950–60 decade, this is largely because the corporate elite was unwilling to locate facilities in areas it considered unsuitable. On the other hand, those regions it does favor experience a radical transformation. New citizens move in and old values must adjust themselves to new influences. Cities and towns, while welcoming branch plants as sources of jobs and revenue, find that what were once local decisions are now made from the outside and by outsiders.[5] Moreover, as corporations expand across the nation they turn many of their white-collar employees into transients, a rootless middle-class prepared to pick up stakes as management beckons it to new job opportunities. The nomadic life has consequences for family and personality that are not without their disturbing qualities.

Quite obviously even the most respected corporation, with the most persuasive advertising agency, cannot induce the American public to buy a white elephant. But the example of the Edsel—like President Kennedy's 1962 ultimatum on steel prices—is an exception proving the rule. For if management is sensitive to the kinds of products that consumers will be willing to purchase, it also has the power to persuade the public that it ought to own such goods. Even more autonomy surrounds decisions on methods and materials of production. What should be noted is that the number and character of possessions have a signal impact on the personality

[5] The question of changing power relations in local communities is just beginning to be studied. For a brief analysis, see Roland J. Pellegrin and Charles H. Coates, "Absentee-Owned Corporations and Community Power Structure," *American Journal of Sociology*, 61, March 1956, pp. 413–19. Mills himself did an important study in this area during World War II: "Small Business and Civic Welfare," Report of the Smaller War Plants Corporation to the Special Committee to Study Problems of American Small Business, Senate Document No. 135, 79th Congress, Second Session (Washington, 1946).

of the owner.[6] Materialism is not uniquely American, nor is the high valuation placed on material possessions entirely the result of management decisions. But the perpetuation of this system of values, with its stress on tangible possession and labor-saving devices, is due to the corporate elite's judgment about what sales are needed if rates and turnover of production are to be kept at the optimum level.

Investment is the most important area of corporate decision-making, and it governs most of the decisions mentioned up to this point. Management alone decides when to invest—in new capital equipment, in new locations, in new processes, products, and personnel. It need not receive the approval of any governmental agency, and no such agency can compel a corporation to go ahead with an investment program if it feels like retrenching. While top executives will be attuned to the public's buying expectations, it can just as well shape those expectations by announcing a buoyant expansion program. The good will of investors need not be courted, since large corporations can use their retained earnings for investment purposes. And there is increasing reliance on the huge investing institutions—insurance companies, pension funds, banks, brokerage houses—for funds.[7] Representatives of these institutions sit on or are close to the boards of the large corporations and are really part of the corporate elite. Together they decide how and in what amounts capital will be invested over the decades to come. The power to make investment decisions is concentrated in a few hands, and it is the power to decide what kind of a nation America will be. Instead of government planning there is planning by an elite that is accountable to no outside agency. Its decisions set the order of priorities on national growth, technological innovation, and ultimately the values and behavior of human lives. Investment decisions are sweeping in their ramifications, and no one is unaffected by their consequences. Yet, this is an area where neither the public nor its government is able to participate. If the contours of the economy and society are being shaped in a hundred or so boardrooms, so far as the average citizen is concerned these decisions are in the lap of the gods.

Finally, it should be noted that the corporate elite is free to decide when the power at its disposal will not be used. It has already been noted that corporations have concluded that civil rights is not a concern of theirs, that they have made no voluntary effort to establish equal employment opportunities for all Americans. Ministers and professors may work for desegregation but executives, by far a more influential group, simply are not interested. While companies might, on their own initiative, endeavor to locate, train, and promote Negroes for positions of responsibility, such a suggestion would be looked upon as outlandish in any executive suite.

---

[6] The best work on new consumption patterns and what they mean has been done by David Riesman. See his essays in *Individualism Reconsidered* (Glencoe, 1954).

[7] See A. A. Berle's two books, *The Twentieth Century Capitalist Revolution* (New York, 1954) and *Power Without Property* (New York, 1959).

Corporate management, by the same token, has decided that it bears no responsibility for upholding civil liberties, nor does it feel any obligation to stand behind employees who are attacked by self-appointed patriots. It might be proposed that corporations not only refuse to discharge employees who are unwilling to co-operate with legislative committees, but that they also make public their support for such dissenters. Needless to say, such a course of action does not occur to the corporate mind, even though such an exercise of influence would go far in the direction of defending freedoms of expression. Notwithstanding all the talk of a corporate conscience or a new dawn of corporate statesmanship, such rhetoric usually produces little more than a company contribution to the Boy Scouts or the Red Cross. On larger issues having political and moral overtones, the corporate elite remains quiescent, electing neither to lead the public when leadership is possible nor to defy the majority when that course is the only alternative.

These, then, are some of the decisions made by one segment of Mills' elite. These decisions add up to a substantial power, a power that is concentrated in a small circle of Americans who need not account for their behavior. The decisions of the corporate elite do not determine whether the nation is to have peace or war; but they do decide what will be the shape of the nation in the decades ahead. It should be clear by this time that the power of the corporate elite is not simply economic. On the contrary, its influence reaches far into society and has a deep impact on the character and personality of individual Americans. While additional forces are at work, the corporation is becoming our most characteristic institution and other agencies are taking secondary positions. As the corporation moves, so moves the nation. While predictions are difficult, it is possible to suggest that corporate tendencies will become accelerated in the years to come, with power growing more concentrated and individual citizens more dependent on large institutions for sustenance and direction. Yet, even as this development takes place, the power of the corporate elite will be invisible to the unaided eye and the forms of political democracy will perpetuate the view that the public is master of its own destiny.

Mills never suggested that the corporate elite was a "conspiracy." The top managers of the largest companies do not foregather at periodic intervals to make their key decisions in concert. At the same time it is clear that they know what is on one another's minds. Whether they come together casually at their clubs or hunting lodges, or slightly more formally at the Business Advisory Council or the Committee for Economic Development or the Foreign Policy Association, they are definitely not isolated from each other. Informal conversation elicits plans, hopes, and expectations. There is a community of interest and sentiment among the elite, and this renders any thought of a "conspiracy" both invalid and irrelevant. Moreover the critical investment decisions bring together many members of the elite—executives, bankers, brokers—and the agreement to expand or retrench is clearly based on consultation and consensus. Such decisions, in addition, are made with the knowledge of what others are doing or plan to do. The lines of communication are built into the system.

Nor is there any notion that the corporate elite is a "class," any more than the corporate world is "capitalist" in the traditional sense. The members of the elite come from a variety of backgrounds, or at least from every stratum of the middle class.[8] Birth and breeding are of negligible importance, and promotion to the highest corporate circles is based on talent more than manners or connections. The conception of a "ruling class" does not apply. Those in the elite group are simply the men who sit in particular chairs at any particular time. The chairs, moreover, have the power rather than their occupants. And it is this point that deserves some elaboration.

The greater part of *The Power Elite* was a discussion of the personal characteristics, backgrounds, and morals of the men at the top. This emphasis on persons rather than positions grew stronger as the book proceeded. Mills' closing paragraph deals exclusively with the "men," the "they" who travel in the upper circles of power:

> The men of the higher circles are not representative men; their high position is not a result of moral virtue; their fabulous success is not firmly connected with meritorious ability. Those who sit in the seats of the high and the mighty are selected and formed by the means of power, the sources of wealth, the mechanics of celebrity, which prevail in their society. They are not men selected and formed by a civil service that is linked with the world of knowledge and sensibility. They are not men shaped by nationally responsible parties that debate openly and clearly the issues this nation now so unintelligently confronts. They are not men held in responsible check by a plurality of voluntary associations which connect debating publics with the pinnacles of decision. Commanders of power unequaled in human history, they have succeeded within the American system of organized irresponsibility.[9]

This, unfortunately, is a misplaced emphasis. It caused the book to be regarded as an attack on the *individuals* who preside over the corporate, military and governmental bureaucracies. Mills, in so many words, accused these men of being not only pompous, vain, and ignorant, but also mediocre and immoral. This indictment has a great deal of truth in it. The men at the top are, as men, by no means an impressive group. Their character, however, is not at issue. For if the analysis is of power in contemporary American society, then the focus must be on the institutions rather than the individuals who staff them.

Mills gave some indication that this would be his line of approach in the opening pages of *The Power Elite*. There he pointed out that the elite are those with "access to the command of major institutions." Hope was held out that the institutions themselves would be analyzed in terms of their ability to make key decisions:

[8] For a study of the backgrounds of the presidents of America's 100 largest corporations, see Andrew Hacker, "The Elected and the Anointed," *American Political Science Review*, 55, Sept. 1961, pp. 539–49.

[9] C. Wright Mills, *The Power Elite* (New York, 1956), p. 361.

The elite are simply those who have the most of what there is to have, which is generally held to include money, power, and prestige—as well as all the ways of life to which these lead. But the elite are not simply those who have the most, for they could not "have the most" were it not for their positions in the great institutions. For such institutions are the necessary bases of power, of wealth, and of prestige. . . . No one, accordingly, can be truly powerful unless he has access to the command of major institutions, for it is over these institutional means of power that the truly powerful are, in the first instance, powerful.[10]

There is little point in discussing who has the power unless one explores the sources of that power. This needs to be stressed because there is strong reason to believe that the institutional structure determines the behavior of the men who hold positions in it. Put another way, it does not really matter who the officeholders are as individuals; for anyone placed in such an office would have much the same outlook and display much the same behavior.

To be sure, it is a lot easier to talk of people than positions, of individuals rather than institutions. For one thing, only the most technically-oriented reader can follow a discussion that omits personalities. Yet the really great social analysts—Marx, Weber, Veblen, Pareto—refused to be tempted in this direction. What is required, then, is an analysis of the great corporate institutions rather than the men who sit astride them.

Here are the names of a dozen of the institutions that direct the course of American society:

General Motors Corporation.
Standard Oil Company of New Jersey.
American Telephone and Telegraph Company.
Atomic Energy Commission.
Central Intelligence Agency.
Ford Foundation.
National Education Association.
Chase Manhattan Bank.
Metropolitan Life Insurance Company.
Columbia Broadcasting System.
The New York Times.
Merrill Lynch, Pierce, Fenner & Smith.

It is doubtful if even the well-informed citizen can name the president or chairman of half of these institutions. Nor should he feel any embarrassment about his ignorance. The man in one of the top chairs may have just arrived at his position last week, while the man in another may be just about to retire. Tenure is surprisingly short, and all incumbents are quite similar to those who have preceded and who will succeed them.

What is being said is that these institutions have lives and purposes of

[10] *Ibid.*, p. 9.

their own. No single person, not even the president or chairman, can be said to have made a critical corporate decision. If the man at the top sits at the controls, the car rides on rails he cannot move. The reason, of course, is that our corporate institutions are too large for a single individual to impress with his personality. Moreover the typical chief executive, sitting at the top for only a few years, spends much time in carrying out policies he did not himself inaugurate. His job is to organize his subordinates so that decisions will be carried out. He must, however, share the task of making those decisions, and it is hard to affix responsibility even at the top. The time has come when the institution in fact directs the man who in theory presides over it.[11]

The future holds in store a corporate America. The power that Mills attributed to the elite is a real power. The decisions the corporate elite is free to make are real decisions. Unfortunately the men at the top cannot in any meaningful way be held responsible for the actions the institutions take. Other men, in the same chairs, would behave no differently. At the same time we persist in thinking of great institutions as if they were small enterprises or voluntary associations. We assume either that they have no power or that their power is effectively nullified by countervailing forces. Corporate institutions are free to plan their future course of development, but they plan for their own purposes. The consequences are not simply profits but, more important, expansion of the corporate world into more and larger sectors of our national life. In defining their own roles and jurisdictions these institutions are oblivious to whether certain individuals are injured or neglected by the corporate thrust. At the same time they are above public control and take no responsibility for the social and psychological impact of their decisions. The situation, looked at from one vantage point, is highly rational and organized: corporate behavior is predictable and the corporate life is secure.

Viewed from a different direction a corporate America will hang on the edge of anarchy. Despite their sophisticated rhetoric and civilized demeanor, the great institutions of the nation have the power to carry the public along a road it has not consented to travel and for which there are no discernible alternatives.

---

[11] John K. Galbraith has written: "Organization replaces individual authority; no individual is powerful enough to do much damage. Were it otherwise, the stock market would pay close attention to retirements, deaths, and replacements in the executive ranks of large corporations. In fact it ignores such details in tacit recognition that the organization is independent of any individual." *The Affluent Society* (Boston, 1958), p. 102. A former president of Du Pont, Crawford Greenewalt, says much the same thing: "The more effective an executive, the more his own identity and personality blend into the background of his organization." *The Uncommon Man* (New York, 1959), p. 72.

The Garrison Society

Vernon K. Dibble

The brazen disregard of law in the Korean enterprise and in the setting up of an international army in Europe is further evidence that our State Department has long since repudiated any serious respect for law and justice. . . . My own feeling is that this policy in the field of foreign affairs, unless restrained, can only lead to arbitrary and totalitarian government at home, as foreign affairs come more and more to dominate our domestic activities, and to war in the world.

—SENATOR ROBERT A. TAFT, 1951

The United States today is a garrison society. A garrison society is one in which it makes no sense to ask whether or not civilians control the military. It is a society in which the institutions and the men who hold military, economic, and political power have become so dependent upon one another; in which their goals and interests are so complementary; and in which the traditional boundaries between military and civilian spheres have broken down to such an extent, that the very conception of civilian versus military control has no meaning.[1]

In militia societies, too, it makes no sense to talk of civilian control of the military. For in militia societies—England before the English Civil War, for example—there are few or no full-time soldiers, and no independent military establishment, for civilians to control.[2]

In a civilian society—the United States before the second World War—there are full-time soldiers and an independent military establishment. Professional soldiers live, in large measure, within their own, somewhat isolated world. Many of their values—obedience to hierarchical superiors, discipline, physical courage, military honor—are at odds with, or are at

FROM *New University Thought* (Spring 1967), pp. 106–15. Reprinted by permission.

[1] The term "garrison society" is, of course, a variation of Harold Lasswell's term, "garrison state." But the two terms do not refer to the same phenomena. In Lasswell's words, "The simplest version of the garrison-state hypothesis is that the arena of world politics is moving toward the domination of specialists in violence." . . . See Lasswell, "The Garrison State Hypothesis Today," in Samuel P. Huntington, ed., *Changing Patterns of Military Politics*, The Free Press of Glencoe: New York, 1952, 51–70.

[2] For more details about this example, see the section entitled "Lords Lieutenant And Their Deputies" in Vernon K. Dibble, "The Organization of Traditional Authority: English County Government, 1558–1640," in James G. March, ed., *Handbook of Organizations*, Rand McNally: Chicago, 1965, 879–909. See also the relevant chapters in Thomas G. Barnes, *Somerset, 1625–1640: A County's Government During the Personal Rule*, Harvard University Press: Cambridge, 1961.

least different from, the values of the rest of the society.[3] But they remain subordinate to civil authority.

In an old-fashioned militarist society—Bismarck's Germany, in some respects—the military establishment was not subordinate to civil authority. For example, military budgets in Imperial Germany did not require the approval of the *Reichstag*. Distinctly military values and styles, of which the duels in German fraternities are the best known example, spill over into civilian society.

But these old-fashioned distinctions between civilian or militarist societies, or between civilian versus military control, have no meaning in the United States today. For example, when hundreds of civilian institutions are closely involved with the military, civilian censorship of the public utterances of officers does not prevent them from having their say in public debate, or in public indoctrination. In August, 1914, President Wilson wrote to the Secretary of War as follows:[4]

> My dear Secretary, I write to suggest that you request and advise all officers of the service, whether active or retired, to refrain from public comment of any kind upon the military and political situation on the other side of the water . . . It seems to me highly unwise and improper that officers of the Army and Navy of the United States should make any public utterances to which any color of political or military criticism can be given where other nations are involved.

That policy still holds. The White House or civilian secretaries censor the speeches of officers, or forbid their presentation altogether. But in a garrison society the silencing of men in uniform is irrelevant. For hand-maidens of the military, out of uniform, abound in politics, in scholarship, in the mass media, and in business.

It makes little difference whether the men who make speeches are generals; or retired generals working for armaments firms; or professors whose research is paid for by the Pentagon, or by the CIA; or journalists whose bread and butter depend upon good relations with Pentagon sources; or Congressmen whose re-election may be jeopardized if the bases in their districts are shut down; or researchers in institutes and think shops that survive on military contracts; or corporate executives whose firms manufacture missiles or napalm.

Whoever makes the speeches, and whatever their disagreements with

---

[3] Samuel P. Huntington, in *The Soldier and the State*, notes a number of ways in which "the military ethic" is in conflict with the liberal ideology that has been dominant in American political history. For example, "The heart of liberalism is individualism. It emphasizes the reason and moral dignity of the individual, and opposes political, economic, and social restraints upon individual liberty. In contrast, the military ethic holds that man is evil, weak, and irrational and that he must be subordinated to the group. The military man claims that the natural relation among men is conflict." Quoted in Allen Guttman, "Political Ideals And The Military Ethic," *The American Scholar*, 34:2, Spring, 1965, p. 22.

[4] Quoted in Jack Raymond, *Power At The Pentagon*, Harper and Row: New York, 1964, p. 178.

one another—missiles or manned bombers, bomb Hanoi or hole up in enclaves, get tough with Russia or try peaceful coexistence—we will hear no challenge to the basic assumptions of American foreign and domestic policy. We will hear no challenge to the false view that freedom versus communism is what our cold wars and our hot wars are all about.

The point, then, is not simply the size and power of the American military establishment. To be sure, its size and power are basic features of the garrison society. The Pentagon is the headquarters of the largest corporation in the world. As Bert Cochran describes it:[5]

> The sprawling bureaucracy housed in this enormous fortress . . . controls an empire that elicits the respectful attention of any of the heads of our leading corporations. The Cordiner Report of several years ago set a valuation of $160 billion on the property owned by the Defense Department, "by any yardstick of measurement, the world's largest organization." This wealth includes weapons arsenals, air bases, naval stations, army reservations, in all, more than thirty-two million acres of land in the United States, and another two and a half million acres abroad. The total is larger than the combined area of Rhode Island, Connecticut, Massachusetts, Maryland, Vermont, and New Hampshire.
> . . . The assets of the military are three times the combined assets of United States Steel, American Telephone and Telegraph, Metropolitan Life Insurance, General Motors, and Standard Oil Company of New Jersey. Its paid personnel is three times as large as that of these corporations. Of a grand total of five million federal employees, more than three and one half million are working for the Defense Department: two and a half million in the armed forces, one million civilian workers. The civilian payroll alone is $11 billion a year, equal to one and a half times the combined payrolls of the iron and steel industry and of all other basic metal producers, and equal to twice the payroll of the automobile industry. The annual military budget is larger than the annual net income of all the corporations in the country.

But these figures alone do not define the garrison society. The garrison society consists, rather, of (1) a large and powerful military that penetrates deeply into civilian life; of (2) the great importance of civilians in military affairs, the increasing resemblance between military officers and civilian executives in politics and business, and the greater contact and cooperation between officers and civilians in politics, in science, and in business; such that (3) the traditional boundaries between civilian and military society break down; and (4) the military are blended into an alliance with government and with large corporations, whose goals include (a) counter revolution and American hegemony abroad and (b) a large dose of centralized, executive control of the economy and of politics at home.

Penetration into Civilian Life:—You cannot administer a military outfit as big as the Pentagon's without penetrating deeply into civilian society. And even if you could, the largest corporation in the world, like all large corporations, seeks to expand, and to reach out for monopoly control over its environment. It sets up or takes over subsidiary corporations like the

[5] Bert Cochran, *The War System*, Macmillan: New York, 1965, pp. 138–139.

nonprofit think shops. It diversifies its products. These products now include not only weapons, strategic theories, and military skills. They also include ideological indoctrination, social research, and, in Secretary McNamara's proposal to "salvage" the rejects of the draft, social work, pedagogical theory, an implicit denunciation of the failures of the welfare state, an attack upon the teaching profession, a veiled attack upon the humanities,[6] and "advanced educational and medical techniques." If our schools have failed, the Department of Defense will rescue us.[7]

". . . the imperatives of national security in our technological age make the Defense Department the world's largest educator of highly skilled men. Those same imperatives require that it also be the world's most efficient educator."

The present emergency found American trade-unions prepared to unite with other groups on a common program of national mobilization. They were keyed to an all-out extended battle against Communist totalitarianism, for they knew its dangers and the threat it represented to the people's well-being.

The military penetrates into education, into research and scholarship, into labor unions, into the political decisions of Senators and Congressmen, and, most crucially, into business and the economy. In education, the use of class standing as a basis for student deferments requires every college instructor in the country to confront his students as an agent of the state. He helps to decide which of his students shall live and which shall die. The selective service system has intruded into the internal government of colleges and universities, has appropriated the ordinary relations between students and teachers for its own administrative convenience, and has transformed these relations into instruments of the garrison society.[8]

The military's penetration into research and scholarship is even more direct. "There was a period after the war," writes Louis J. Halle, "when various departments of the Government tried to marry themselves to the universities." That marriage did not work well in the case of the State Department. But it "worked in the case of the Pentagon and the faculties of science and technology, a wartime precedent having already been established at Oak Ridge and Los Alamos."[9]

Since that time, the military has continued to purchase some of the best

[6] I take it that the Secretary's statement that "One of the department's key concepts is that traditional classroom training is often largely irrelevant to actual on-the-job performance requirements" and his reference to "pruning from existing courses all nonessential information" are veiled attacks on the humanities.

[7] The quotation which follows, the quotation in the previous sentence, and the quotation in Note 3 are from the excerpts from Secretary McNamara's address to the Veterans of Foreign Wars, New York Times, August 24, 1966, p. 18.

[8] The administration of a number of colleges (including Wayne State, Haverford, Cornell, and a few others) have indicated that their colleges will either submit no class standings to draft boards or will otherwise refuse to go along (for example, by refusing to compute class standings separately for male and female students). The faculties of a few other colleges, including Columbia College, have voted in favor of this position.

[9] Louis J. Halle, "On Teaching International Relations," *Virginia Quarterly Review*, 40:1, Winter, 1964, p. 13.

minds in the country. Professor Melman has described some of the consequences of that fact for civilian Research and Development, for the internal structure of American universities, and for the financially neglected fields outside the natural sciences.[10] The military provides large percentages of the annual budget of many major universities.[11] And it, along with the CIA, have transformed scholars and researchers into intelligence analysts, military technicians, and apologists. Michigan State University's fronting for the CIA in Vietnam, and the University of Pennsylvania's secret research for the Pentagon are extreme, but not unique instances. For example, at last count thirty-eight universities and institutes affiliated with universities were conducting research on chemical and biological warfare for the Department of Defense.[12]

Government money for research has consequences, in turn, for education. A professor who has research money from outside his university acquires an economic base that tends to free him from collegial and departmental control. Whether he operates alone with his assistants or in a research institute with colleagues, he is under less pressure to be concerned with all the varied tasks of a university, including the task of teaching students. He is more free, if so inclined, to regard his university as a home base for his operations elsewhere. One result, even among some teachers in undergraduate colleges, is professorial disdain for teaching and for education, as opposed to the specialized training of selected students. From the students' point of view, some of the best of them are suspicious of all scholars and of all scholarship, because they see the confusion of scholarship with military intelligence or apologetics.

In many labor unions, members and dues depend upon war plants. I doubt (as Isaac Deutscher recently expressed it) that most American workers are happy about working for death instead of for life. But a man needs a job. And a union needs members. Hence, unions help munitions firms to secure or retain military contracts, or lobby to prevent the closing down of shipyards and airplane plants. And some labor leaders are among the most chauvinistic heralds of the American counter-revolution abroad.

The no-strike pledge during the Second World War is to the unions' relations with the government as Oak Ridge and Los Alamos are to the post-war marriage between the Pentagon and departments or institutes of science and technology. That is, the organizational mobilization of American society that the Second World War brought about has continued

[10] Seymour Melman, *Our Depleted Society*, Dell Publishing Co.: New York, 1965, Chapter 4, entitled "Cold War Science and Technology."

[11] *Ibid.*, Appendix C, "Index of 500 Largest Military Prime Contractors for Experimental Development, Test and Research Work." See also Raymond, *op. cit.*, Chapter VIII, "Research and the Federal Government" and Cochran, *op. cit.*, pp. 155–161.

[12] This figure is from Carol Brightman, "The 'Weed Killers'—A Final Word," *Viet Report*, 2:7, 1966, 3–5. Miss Brightman relies on "a Pentagon spokesman" as reported in the *Washington Post*.

ever since. For the managers of unions, business firms, research institutes, and governmental agencies find advantages—less militant unions, access to power, money for research, or whatever—in continuing cooperation with one another. These advantages are quite independent of their original military significance. Hence, the organizational coordination of the Second World War goes on, but, of course, with a new definition of the enemy.

Thus, during the Korean War the Research Director of the Textile Workers Union wrote:[13]

The present emergency found American trade-unions prepared to unite with other groups on a common program of national mobilization. They were keyed to an all-out extended battle against Communist totalitarianism, for they knew its dangers and the threat it represented to the people's well-being.

One decade later the Executive Council of the AFL-CIO declared, "The nation's defense requirements obviously have top priority."[14] And in 1963, Secretary McNamara awarded the AFL-CIO a well-deserved citation for, among other things, military propaganda. The Secretary praised the union for "utilizing extensive communications media to promote greater understanding among its millions of members and the public of the vital objectives of defense programs."[15]

In Congress, we read, many silent Senators are "concerned" about Vietnam. But only three voted against the latest Vietnam appropriation. Dozens of Congressmen signed a statement of "concern" about escalation, and proceeded to vote in favor of the appropriation. In contrast, the draft was reinstated in 1948 by a vote of 70 to 10 in the Senate and 259 to 136 in the House.[16] For (except when they want to appropriate more money than the Pentagon requests) a mere Senator or Congressman does not tangle with the largest corporation in the world, whether his state or district wants to keep the bases and war plants it already has, or feels neglected and wants to acquire some. Its economic importance stifles debate. And with most labor unions, or their leaders, committed to the garrison system, one potential source of pressure on Congressmen to behave differently is eliminated.

The acquiescence of Congress and of the labor movement has repercussions, in turn, on education. Many of the most intelligent and most serious college students today spend more time on political activity than on their studies. For as they see it, and they see it correctly, America faces desperate problems that almost no one in public life is willing to face. If a dozen silent Senators who are "concerned" about Vietnam would only

[13] Solomon Barkin, "American Trade-Unions in the Present Emergency," *Monthly Labor Review*, the Bureau of Labor Statistics. 73.4. October, 1951, 409.

[14] *Proceedings of the AFL-CIO Fourth Constitutional Convention*, 1961, Vol. II, p. 70.

[15] *Proceedings of the AFL-CIO Fifth Constitutional Convention*, 1963, Vol. I, p. 355.

[16] *New York Times*, June 11, 1948 and June 23, 1948.

speak up, political activists on college campuses would feel free to spend more time on chemistry formulae and the Greek dative.

In the economy, some ten to twenty percent—depending on what you include and how you measure it—of the national product depends on the military. And some ten to twenty percent of the labor force work at jobs that also depend upon the military. About 25,000 private industrial plants operate under systems of military security, over four million employees were required to obtain security clearance during a period of ten years, and, to be on the safe side, some firms have extended military security to all of their operations, including those which have nothing to do with military work.[17]

To be sure, many, perhaps most, American firms do not benefit directly from the garrison society. If twenty percent depend upon it, eighty percent pay taxes to make it possible. Nor would all munitions firms, even, be hurt seriously by sudden disarmament. And some firms, in banking and in men's clothing for example, have been hurt by the war in Vietnam. But we cannot look to businessmen who are left out of the profits of the garrison society, or to firms that are hurt by the war, to lead the way toward "dismantling the cold war institutional machine."[18] For to do so would be a basic challenge to their aerospace colleagues; to the existing system of political power; in some cases to the unions that operate in their plants; and to the entire ideology of anti-communism from which they, too, derive strength and comfort in these trying times. Terminating the war in Vietnam tomorrow would be in the economic interest of many American firms. But adherence to the reigning ideology, and class solidarity with other businessmen more directly involved in the garrison society, seem thus far to be stronger than immediate economic interests. In short, as concerns the military and the American economy, a little penetration goes a long, long way.

The Boundaries Break Down:—But, as noted in the second element in our definition of the garrison society, the penetration of the military into civilian society is only part of the story. While civilian life has become increasingly militarized, civilians have become more important in military

[17] The information on military security in business is from Raymond, *op. cit.*, pp. 154–156. On the extent to which the economy depends upon military spending, Harry Magdoff, using the estimates of the U.S. Arms Control And Disarmament Agency in its volume, *Economic Impacts of Disarmament* (Washington, D.C., 1962), writes as follows: "The more than $55 billion spent annually on what the government agencies classify as 'national defense' has a chain-reaction effect on the rest of the economy, just as other forms of investment and spending have a 'multiplier' effect. It is estimated that for every $1 spent on 'national defense' another $1 to $1.40 of economic product is stimulated. A crude, but conservative, calculation shows that in addition to the approximately 7.4 million people engaged in some phase of 'national defense,' another 6 to 9 million are employed due to the economic stimulus of defense spending." Harry Magdoff, "Problems of United States Capitalism," in R. Miliband and J. Savile, eds., *The Socialist Register: 1965*, Monthly Review Press: New York, 1965, p. 63. See also Cochran, *op. cit.*, pp. 140–41.

[18] This phrase is the title of Chapter 12 of Melman, *op. cit.*

affairs, military men have more contact with civilians, and military men come to resemble civilians more than ever before. The office of the Secretary of Defense is no longer that of a coordinator. The Secretary and his civilian aides are makers of military policy. The number and the influence of civilian military theorists, in and out of the Department of Defense, moved General Thomas D. White, former Air Force Chief of Staff, to remark, "in common with other military men I am profoundly apprehensive of the pipe-smoking, trees-full-of-owls type of so-called defense intellectuals who have been brought into this nation's capitol."[19] And no longer do armaments firms simply manufacture what the military orders. They have their own staffs to devise their own weapons systems, which they try to sell to Congress and to the Pentagon.

But the military, too, is developing its own generation of military intellectuals and technological specialists. Advanced technology and a complex sprawling organization (no longer limited to a simple command structure plus some staff positions) make brains and managerial talent more important than old-fashioned heroism in the upper reaches of military hierarchies. And, of course, constant dealings with corporate executives, plus the prospect of a career in business after retirement from the service, reinforce tendencies within the services themselves toward making the work of military leaders increasingly similar to the work of corporate executives.[20] More generally, as Allen Guttman suggests, the end of *laissez faire* liberalism in this country—the transformation, in Guttman's words, "from an imperfect liberal democracy to an imperfect social democracy"— means that "the American soldier can for the first time in our history square the dictates of his professional ethic with the accepted values and institutions of our society."[21]

In short, the traditional social and cultural boundaries between civilian and military society have broken down. The military, civilian government, and large corporations do not form a single, monolithic ruling group. There are conflicts within, and between, each party to the alliance. But on all essentials—American world power, the Cold War and anti-communism, and the shape of our domestic economy and social structure—they are as one.

The historical origins of the garrison society are reflected in this coalescence of military and civilian executives, and in this fading away of traditional boundaries. The garrison society did not come about because a military clique imposed itself on the rest of America. It was built—base by base, contract by contract, and professor by professor—through the cooperation of military leaders, politicians, and corporate executives that

[19] Quoted in Raymond, *op. cit.*, p. 289. More generally, see Raymond's Chapter 16, "The 'McNamara Monarchy'."

[20] See Morris Janowitz, *The Professional Soldier: A Social and Political Portrait*, The Free Press: Glencoe, Illinois, 1960. Especially Section II, "Organizational Realities: Heroic And Managerial" and Chapter 20, "The Future of the Military Profession."

[21] Guttman, *op. cit.*, p. 237. See note #3, above for further explanation of this point.

began during the Second World War. Universities, labor leaders, intellectuals, and the mass media followed along.

One of the earliest prophets of the garrison society was Charles E. Wilson, former president of General Electric. In January, 1944, in an address before the Army Ordnance Association, Wilson proposed an alliance of the military, the executive branch of the Federal government, and large corporations in "a permanent war economy." He proposed that every large corporation have on its roster a colonel in the reserves for liaison with the military, and he spelled out the role of the Federal executive, of Congress, and of business as follows:[22]

First of all a [preparedness] program must be the responsibility of the Federal government. It must be initiated and administered by the executive branch—by the President as Commander-in-Chief and by the War and Navy Departments. Of equal importance is the fact that this must be, once and for all, a continuing program and not the creature of an emergency. In fact one of its objects will be to eliminate emergencies so far as possible. The role of Congress will be limited to voting the needed funds . . .

Industry's role in this program is to respond and cooperate . . . in the execution of the part allotted to it; industry must not be hampered by political witch hunts, or thrown to the fanatical isolationist figure tagged with a 'merchants of death' label.

The cooperation that Wilson proposed, and that in fact came about, does not create a monolithic ruling group. But it does create a system in which each party has a great stake in the other party's interests and success. That is one of the system's strong points. If one party to the alliance were imposing itself on the other two, the whole system would be weaker than it is. The economy is dependent in an important degree on the military. But it is equally true that the military are dependent on big business. If armaments firms acted like old-fashioned entrepreneurs, keeping their capital mobile and seeking out the most profitable markets, they might go in for pea canning plants in Sicily instead of missiles. The military and the government depend upon their continued preference for government-sponsored, low-risk capitalism.

Another source of the alliance's strength is the fact that most participants—politicians, generals, corporate executives, and professors—really believe in what they are doing. They are, by their lights, patriotic servants of the public weal. And the combination of power, profits, and sincerity is more powerful than power and profits alone.

International Power and Domestic Controls:—This powerful combination, of motives and of institutions, has profound consequences for American society. The world-wide goals of the garrison society—preventing social

[22] Quoted in Fred J. Cook, *The Warfare State*, Macmillan: New York, 1962, pp. 76–77. Mr. Cook, in turn, quotes from an article by John M. Swomley in *The Progressive*, January 1959. I was unfortunately not able to locate the full text of Mr. Wilson's speech in any of the usual sources such as *Vital Speeches* or *The New York Times*. Note that this man is Wilson of G.E., not Wilson of General Motors.

revolution and preserving both capitalism and American world power abroad—have repercussions on domestic politics and on the domestic political economy. The preservation of the American imperial system requires economic stability and steady, manageable, predictable economic growth at home. Management and predictability are crucial.

Suppose the United States had a free market economy, subject to uncontrolled fluctuations. Think of the international consequences. A big depression, a great and sudden decline in profits and in employment, would mean a great decline in Federal revenues. There would also be increased political pressure to use these declining revenues for more domestic relief of one kind or another. Foreign aid programs might be threatened. American purchases abroad, public and private, would be curtailed. American multi-national corporations might import more of their undistributed profits from abroad and engage in less foreign investment, especially if low prices in capital goods made the depression a good time to invest here. And imports of the products of other nations, including unstable and potentially revolutionary nations, would go down. Previously friendly governments and businessmen in foreign countries would have to look elsewhere for friends. And, what is more crucial, what would happen to our counter-revolution in Colombia if we could not buy Colombian coffee?

On the other hand, a boom that is too big or too sudden is no good either. For one thing, booms tend to produce their opposite. But apart from that fact, too great an increase in dividends and in corporate investment creates inflationary pressure and invites social conflict in the form of wage demands and perhaps crippling strikes. Inflation means that foreign nations have less purchasing power in the United States and would take their business elsewhere, while production at high capacity forces American business to purchase more from abroad than they otherwise would. Both developments place further strain on the balance of payments, which might require, at some later point, either great cuts in foreign purchases, or a great cut in the foreign military bases of the United States.

In short, some of the international repercussions of a big boom are identical to those of a big depression. Both must be avoided if the American imperial system is to remain intact.

Avoiding both the big boom and the big depression requires an increasingly guided economy—guidelines, dumping surplus commodities on the market to prevent an increase in price, the confrontation between President Kennedy and the steel industry, using the White House instead of old-fashioned bargaining sessions to settle strikes, and using tax policy to make investment and consumption go up or down as the moment requires. These policies, in turn, have further consequences for the society.

For example, labor leaders come under pressure to suppress any signs of an active internal life, and of mass rank-and-file involvement in labor unions. Such things are unmanageable. They have unpredictable consequences. To cite a second example, we cannot permanently abolish unemployment—the classic test of the success of the welfare state—because we must worry about attendant inflationary pressure. That fact, in turn, makes any genuine integration of the mass of Negroes into American society most unlikely, so long as the garrison system lasts.

There are, to be sure, strains in the system. The airline machinists did not go along. The guidelines are breaking down. And there is probably an inherent contradiction between the requirements of the system and the interests of each single firm or industry. Guidelines are most advantageous to you if your firm or your union is the only one that does not go along with them.

But suppose, for the moment, that the economic management that is inherent in the garrison society works well enough for the foreseeable future. What, then, are the lessons of Vietnam? The obvious lesson is that future garrison governments, in time of peace, must always manage to keep unemployment relatively high and production well below capacity. For reasons that Professor Terence McCarthy has expounded that extra slack is needed in order to fight our next colonial war without overheating the economy. That is how you incorporate Keynesian economics and the historic achievements of the New Deal and of American liberalism into the garrison society.

Militarism and Imperialism

Paul A. Baran and Paul M. Sweezy

The international relationships and interests of the typical giant corporation today are likely to be diverse and extremely complex, much more so than mere exporting or importing. There is perhaps no better way to make this clear than by summarizing the world-wide scope and character of what is unquestionably the leading United States "multinational corporation"—Standard Oil of New Jersey. The facts and figures which follow are taken from official publications of the company.[1]

In terms of dollar assets, Jersey Standard is the largest industrial corporation in the United States, the total at the end of 1962 amounting to

FROM *Monopoly Capital* by Paul A. Baran and Paul M. Sweezy (New York: Monthly Review Press, 1966), pp. 193–207. Copyright © 1966 by Paul M. Sweezy; reprinted by permission of Monthly Review Press.

[1] *Notice of Special Stockholders' Meeting* (October 7, 1959); *Form 10-K for the Fiscal Year Ended December 31, 1962* (filed with the Securities and Exchange Commission pursuant to Section 13 of the Securities Act of 1934); and 1962 *Annual Report.*

$11,488 million. Aggregate revenues for the same year were $10,567 million and net income (profit) $841 million. It is only when these figures are broken down geographically, however, that the crucial importance of foreign operations becomes clear. As of the end of 1958, the percentage distribution of assets and profits by regions was as follows:

	Assets	Profits
United States and Canada	67	34
Latin America	20	39
Eastern Hemisphere	13	27
Total	100	100

While two thirds of Jersey's assets were located in North America, only one third of its profits came from that region. Or to put the point differently, Jersey's foreign investments were half as large as its domestic investments but its foreign profits were twice as large as its domestic profits. The indicated profit rate abroad is thus four times the domestic rate.

That Jersey's operations are truly world-wide can be gathered from the facts that in 1962 the company sold its products in more than a hundred countries and owned 50 percent or more of the stock in 275 subsidiaries in 52 countries. By regions, we find that Jersey had 114 subsidiaries in the United States and Canada, 77 in Europe, 43 in Latin America, 14 in Asia, 9 in Africa, and 18 elsewhere.

The tremendous variety and scope of Jersey's foreign operations might lead one to suppose that over the years the company has been a large and consistent exporter of capital. Nothing could be further from the truth. Apart from a small initial export of capital many years ago, the expansion of Jersey's foreign assets has been financed from the profits of its foreign operations. Moreover, so great have been these foreign profits that after all foreign expansion needs have been taken care of, there have still been huge sums left over for remittance to the parent company in the United States. Separate figures on the amount of these remittances from foreign profits are not published, but an idea of the orders of magnitude is conveyed by the following figures for 1962. In that year, as already noted, total profits were $841 million. Of this sum, $538 million were paid out as dividends to stockholders, the vast majority of whom are residents of the United States. The remaining $303 million were added to the company's investments, at home and abroad. Elsewhere in the same Annual Report that records these figures we learn that profits from operations in the United States in 1962 were $309 million. This figure, it will be seen, is $229 million less than the amount of dividends paid. In other words, approximately 40 percent of dividends paid to stockholders plus whatever net investment was made in the United States during the year were financed from the profits of foreign operations. In a word: Standard Oil of New Jersey is a very large and consistent *importer* of capital.

At this point, however, we must pause and ask whether Standard Oil of New Jersey is really an ideal type which helps us to distill the essence of capitalist reality, or whether on the contrary it may not be an exceptional case which we should ignore rather than focus attention on.

Up to the Second World War, it would have been correct to treat Standard Oil as a sort of exception—a very important one, to be sure, exercising tremendous, and at times even decisive, influence on United States world policy. Nevertheless in the multinational scope and magnitude of its operations not only was it far ahead of all the others; there were only a handful which could be said to be developing along the same lines. Many United States corporations of course had large interests in import and export trade, and quite a few had foreign branches or subsidiaries. In neither respect, however, was the situation much different in 1946 from what it had been in 1929. Indeed, direct foreign investments of United States corporations actually declined from $7.5 billion to $7.2 billion, or by 4 percent, between these two dates.[2] Most of the giant corporations which dominated the American economy in those years were, in the words of *Business Week*, "domestically oriented enterprises with international operations" and not, like Standard Oil, "truly world oriented corporations."[3]

A big change took place during the next decade and a half. To quote *Business Week* again, "In industry after industry, U. S. companies found that their overseas earnings were soaring, and that their return on investment abroad was frequently much higher than in the U.S. As earnings abroad began to rise, profit margins from domestic operations started to shrink. . . . This is the combination that forced development of the multinational company."[4] As a result, of course, foreign direct investments of American corporations shot up—from $7.2 billion in 1946 to $40.6 billion in 1963, a more than fivefold increase in the years since the Second World War.[5] Parallel to this growth in foreign investments has gone an increase in the sales and profits of foreign branches and subsidiaries. In manufacturing (excluding petroleum and mining), sales of such affiliates amounted to $18.3 billion in 1957 (the first year for which figures are available) and to $28.1 billion in 1962, an increase of 54 percent in six years.[6]

Some idea of the growing relative importance of these foreign opera-

[2] United States Department of Commerce, Office of Business Economics, *U.S. Business Investments in Foreign Countries: A Supplement to the Survey of Current Business*, Washington, 1960, p. 1.

[3] "Multinational Companies," *Business Week*, April 20, 1963. It is interesting to note that in the United States the business press is often far ahead of the economic profession in recognizing, and even trying to analyze, the latest developments in the capitalist economy.

[4] *Ibid.*

[5] *Survey of Current Business*, August 1964, p. 10.

[6] Fred Cutler and Samuel Pizer, "Foreign Operations of U. S. Industry: Capital Spending, Sales, and Financing," *Survey of Current Business*, October 1963, p. 19.

TABLE 1:   Growth of Foreign and Domestic
Manufacturing Sales and Merchandise Exports, 1957–1962
(Billions of dollars)

	Sales of Foreign Manufacturing Affiliates	Total Domestic Manufacturing Sales	Merchandise Exports (Excluding foodstuffs)
1957	18.3	341	16.8
1958	n.a.	314	13.8
1959	21.1	356	13.7
1960	23.6	365	16.6
1961	25.6	368	16.9
1962	28.1	400	17.3

n.a. = not available
SOURCES: Foreign sales, Fred Cutler and Samuel Pizer, "Foreign Operations of U.S. Industry," *Survey of Current Business*, October 1963; domestic sales and exports, *Economic Indicators*, current issues.

tions of American corporations may be gathered from Table 1, which presents data on the sales of foreign manufacturing affiliates, total domestic manufacturing sales, and non-agricultural merchandise exports.

It would of course be preferable to compare the foreign and domestic sales and exports of those corporations which have foreign branches or subsidiaries; and it would be still better if we could include the profits of these corporations from foreign and domestic operations respectively. If such data were available, we could form a very clear picture of the degree of involvement of the United States giant corporations in foreign activities. But even the figures presented in Table 1 bear eloquent testimony to the rapid growth of that involvement. In the six years beginning with 1957, the sales of foreign affiliates grew by 54 percent, while total domestic manufacturing sales expanded only 17 percent and non-agricultural exports hardly changed at all.

So much for the record of recent years. If we look ahead, we find that American corporate business, far from regarding its expansion abroad as having come to an end, is relying heavily for its future prosperity on the continued penetration of other countries' economies. "America as the 'land of opportunity' is beginning to lose that title in the eyes of many U.S. businessmen," says a Special Report in *U. S. News & World Report*.[7] And the Report goes on to tell why:

[7] "For New Opportunities: Now, the Word Is 'Go Abroad,' " *U. S. News & World Report*, June 1, 1964. In order to gather material for this report, "members of the International Staff of *U. S. News & World Report* talked with scores of U. S. firms abroad. Added material was gathered from corporations in the U. S. heavily engaged in the foreign field."

These businessmen increasingly are deciding that markets abroad—not those in this country—offer the biggest potential for future growth. The feeling grows that the U. S. market, while huge, is relatively "saturated."

It is overseas that businessmen see the big, untapped market with hundreds of millions of customers wanting—and increasingly able to buy—all kinds of products and services.

To go after this market, U. S. firms are building and expanding factories all around the world. Since 1958, more than 2,100 American companies have started new operations in Western Europe alone. . . .

All types of business—from autos to baby food—predict a glowing future for markets outside the U. S.

Says L. E. Spencer, president of Goodyear Tire & Rubber Company of Canada: "Foreign markets will expand several times as fast as North American markets over the next 10 years."

From C. C. Smith, vice president of International Business Machines' World Trade Corporation: "The rate of increase in our foreign business is greater than in the U.S. in every major product category. In time, we expect volume to overtake that in the U. S."

Listen to the comment by an official of Colgate-Palmolive Company: "You're in a saturated market here in the U. S., where new products are the only answer to growth. Abroad there are millions of people each year who reach the stage in their cultural, social and economic development where they buy soap, toothpaste, other things we sell."

This flat prediction is made by Fred J. Borch, president of General Electric Corporation: "Regardless of economic or political ups and downs, the most rapidly expanding markets will be abroad in the next 25 years."

Against that background, the survey of U. S. firms abroad turned up these major findings—

1. Foreign sales of U. S. companies are growing much faster than sales of the same companies in this country. Often, the percentage gains are three or four times as great.

2. Profit rates abroad generally are higher than those in similar activities in the U. S. Many firms report a percentage return "twice as high abroad as in America." Most cite lower wage costs overseas—and less competition.

3. Foreign markets usually can best be tapped by an on-the-scene operation, rather than by exporting from the U.S. A plant abroad can avoid tariff and other trade barriers erected against exports from this country. . . .

It thus appears both from the record of the past and from the plans and hopes for the future that American corporate business has irrevocably embarked on the road long since pioneered by Standard Oil. Standard is still the model of a multinational corporation, but it is no longer an exception. It simply shows us in the most developed form what the other giants either already are or are in the process of becoming.

As it happens, the recent history of Standard Oil of New Jersey also supplies us with a textbook example of why multinational corporations are profoundly hostile to the spread of socialism. Before the Cuban Revolution, Jersey was heavily involved in Cuba in several ways. It owned refining facilities on the island and operated an extensive distribution system, involving altogether properties valued at $62,269,000.[8] In addition, Jersey's

---

[8] Standard and Poor, *Standard Corporate Descriptions*, July 24, 1961.

Cuban subsidiary bought its crude from Creole Petroleum, Jersey's Venezuelan subsidiary, at the high prices maintained by the international oil cartel. The company therefore reaped profits in two countries and on three separate operations—sale of crude, refining of crude, and sale of finished products. As a result of the Revolution, the company's properties in Cuba were nationalized without compensation, and Creole lost its Cuban market. More than $60 million in assets and all three sources of current profit were lost in one blow—and without in any way involving exports from or imports to the United States.

It might be argued that if Jersey and the United States government had pursued different policies toward Cuba, the revolutionary regime would have been glad to continue buying oil from Venezuela, which after all is the nearest and most rational source of supply. This is no doubt true—but with a big proviso. The revolutionary regime would have been glad to continue buying oil from Venezuela, but it would not have been glad to continue paying prices and meeting terms of payment dictated by Standard Oil. And since it could turn to the Soviet Union as an alternative source of supply, it was no longer obliged to go on submitting to the cartel's terms. Hence to remain in the Cuban market, Jersey would at the least have to cut its prices and offer better credit terms. This not only would have meant less profits on sales to Cuba but would have threatened the whole structure of cartel prices. Jersey and Washington decided instead to make war on the Cuban Revolution.

That what is at stake in the conflict between the United States and Cuba is not trade between the two countries is confirmed by Cuba's relations with other capitalist countries. Long after the socialization of the Cuban economy, the Havana government was vigorously promoting its trade with Britain, France, Spain, Canada, Japan—in short, with any country willing and able to do business with Cuba. It is true, of course, that Cuba's capacity to export and import has been seriously curtailed by the disorganization and other difficulties of the early years of the change-over to socialism, but there seems to be no reason to doubt the Cubans' own contention that in a few years the island will be a much better trading partner than it was under the old neo-colonial regime. Nor is there any reason to doubt that the United States could capture a major share of the Cuban trade if the blockade were called off and normal relations re-established between the two countries.

But this is not what really interests the giant multinational corporations which dominate American policy. What they want is *monopolistic control* over foreign sources of supply and foreign markets, enabling them to buy and sell on specially privileged terms, to shift orders from one subsidiary to another, to favor this country or that depending on which has the most advantageous tax, labor, and other policies—in a word, they want to do business on their own terms and wherever they choose. And for this what they need is not trading partners but "allies" and clients willing to adjust their laws and policies to the requirements of American Big Business.

Against this background, one can see that Cuba's crime was to assert, in deeds as well as in words, her sovereign right to dispose over her own resources in the interests of her own people. This involved curtailing and, in the struggle which ensued, eventually abrogating the rights and privileges which the giant multinational corporations had previously enjoyed in Cuba. It was because of this and not because of a loss of trade, still less because of any irrational fears or prejudices, that the corporations and their government in Washington reacted so violently to the Cuban Revolution.

It might perhaps be thought that since Cuba is a small country, the violence of the reaction was out of all proportion to the damage suffered. But this would be to miss the main point. What makes Cuba so important is precisely that she is so small, plus the fact that she is located so close to the United States. If Cuba can defect from the "free world" and join the socialist camp with impunity, then any country can do so. And if Cuba prospers under the new setup, all the other underdeveloped and exploited countries of the world will be tempted to follow her example. The stake in Cuba is thus not simply the exploitability of one small country but the very existence of the "free world" itself, that is to say, of the whole system of exploitation.

It is this fact that has dictated the Cuban policy of the United States. The strategy has been to damage and cripple the Cuban economy in every possible way, with a threefold objective. First, it is hoped that the Cuban people will sooner or later become disillusioned with their revolutionary leadership, thus setting the stage for a successful counter-revolution. Second, the peoples of the underdeveloped countries are to be taught that revolution does not pay. And third, the burden of supporting the Cuban economy thrown on the rest of the socialist camp, and especially on the Soviet Union as its economically most developed member, is to be maximized so that these other socialist countries may be induced to use their influence to restrain any new revolutions which might place further burdens on their already overstrained economies.

Military "Aid"

This is of course not the only way the "free world" is being defended. The United States failed to understand the nature of the revolution which overthrew the Batista regime in Cuba until it was too late to keep the revolutionaries from consolidating their power. Every precaution is being taken to see that the same mistake is not made again. All revolutionaries are automatically suspect; no regime is too reactionary to merit all-out United States backing.

Partly, this backing takes the form of so-called economic aid—in reality handouts to corrupt oligarchies designed to insure their loyalty to Washington rather than to the interests of their own countries.[9] And partly it takes the form of military aid, which is predominantly of two types.

First, there is direct participation by United States armed forces on the territory of the client state: stationing of troops in bases controlled by the United States (as we saw above, there are some 275 major base complexes and 1,400 bases either occupied by or prepared for American forces); "emergency" deployment of troops anywhere on the host country's national territory that the two governments may decide (Lebanon in the summer of 1958, Thailand in the spring of 1962, the Dominican Republic in the spring of 1965); and various kinds of advisory and training missions accredited to the armed forces of the clients (in 1957, a total of forty Army, Navy, and Air Force missions were in Latin America alone, in every country except Mexico). As South Vietnam shows, training missions can be quickly and almost imperceptibly transformed into counter-revolutionary combat forces.[10]

The second form of military aid is the provision of material and financial support for the armed forces of the client states. While the dozens of military assistance pacts which the United States has signed with underdeveloped countries around the world are ostensibly designed to meet the "threat" of aggression from the Soviet Union or China, no serious military planner imagines that this is the real purpose. Such a threat, if it really existed, could be countered only by the United States itself, and an attempt to coordinate military strategy with a large number of feeble allies would be a source of weakness rather than strength. The real purpose of this military aid is clearly spelled out by Lieuwen in his pioneer study of the role of the military in Latin America:

> Those [military] policies . . . are not designed to meet the military threat of communism, but rather to gain Latin America's friendship, to win its cooperation and support in the United Nations and the Organization of American States. The Rio military alliance, the M[utual] D[efense] A[ssistance] Pacts, the arms grants, the reimbursable aid, the work of the I[nter] A[merican] D[efense]

[9] A lot of the criticism of foreign aid," according to D. A. Fitzgerald, a high official in the succession of United States government agencies in charge of foreign aid from 1948 to 1961, "is because the critic thought the objective was to get economic growth, and this wasn't the objective at all. . . . It depends on what the major purpose is, and half the time the major purpose is to meet a short-term political crisis—and economic development, if any, is only an incidental result." Interview in *U. S. News & World Report*, February 25, 1963, pp. 49, 50.

[10] South Vietnam also shows that in the underdeveloped countries today reactionary regimes, no matter how lavishly equipped and "advised" by the United States, cannot win wars against dedicated and experienced revolutionary guerrillas. This is not the place to attempt to assess the implications of this momentous fact. We only record our conviction that its significance will loom larger and larger as the years go by and that in retrospect the struggle in South Vietnam will be recognized as one of the turning points of the history of the second half of the twentieth century.

B[oard] and the military missions—all of these have no great military significance. They are designed, above all, to draw the Latin American officer corps, which exercise great influence over the political scene in most of the republics, closer to the United States, in the hope that they will exclude Soviet influence, give the United States their support, maintain political stability, ensure continued access to strategic raw materials, and provide rights to the use of bases.[11]

To put the matter more bluntly, the purpose of United States military aid to underdeveloped countries is to keep them in the American empire if they are already there and to bring them in if they are not—and in any case to insure that there are no further defections from the "free world." The consequences for the recipient countries are tragic. "What we are doing," said the Colombian statesman Eduardo Santos, "is building up armies which weigh nothing in the international scale but which are juggernauts for the internal life of each country. Each country is being occupied by its own army."[12] And the same point is made and heavily underlined in a remarkable study of relations between the United States and Pakistan published by a group of Pakistani students in London:

In the long run, the worst aspect of military aid lies in the complete change it produces in the balance of social and political forces in favor of conservatism and established vested interests. The dragon seeds sown by military aid have produced a fearful crop of military officers, with their social roots in the most conservative sections of our society, who have learnt to sit in judgment on our people. It is an overwhelming force without any countervailing force to hold it in check.[13]

This world-wide spawning of little military machines loyal to Washington does not in any way reduce the need for a big military machine in the United States itself. As the tide of revolutionary protest rises in the exploited countries of the "free world," it is only by increasingly direct and massive intervention by American armed forces that the old order can be held together a while longer. As the shift to nuclear weapons and intercontinental missiles proceeds, even the pretense that the global system of bases is for protection against Russian aggression is given up. "Little by little," writes Cyrus L. Sulzberger, foreign affairs columnist of *The New York Times*, "the requirement for bases on the periphery of the NATO area is dwindling. Medium-range and long-range plus seaborne missiles are changing the emphasis of our counter-strike force. But the time has not yet come when one can envision the disappearance of all need for U. S. overseas bases; on the contrary." There follows a revealing analogy with British policy after the Napoleonic Wars, though the naked term "empire" is used only in referring to that bygone era:

Today Washington stresses preparations to fight limited wars if necessary. These need mobility, the ability to transfer men and supplies from one quarter

[12] Quoted by Lieuwen, *ibid.*, pp. 237–238.
[11] Edwin C. Lieuwen, *Arms and Politics in Latin America*, New York, 1960, p. 226.
[13] "The Burden of U. S. Aid," *Pakistan Today*. New Series, No. 1. Autumn 1961.

to the other, using staging points abroad. They also necessitate what is called "forward stockpiling" at strategically important havens.

A study of this particular problem is now under way in the Pentagon. After the Napoleonic Wars, the British Navy made such a study to ascertain London's requisites in defending its vast overseas empire. Later the U.S. Navy made a similar analysis of how to operate globally.

The focus of present Washington research is more on aspects of limited war than total war. . . .

Likewise, the administration sees the possibility we might be engaged in limited wars on other fronts, conflicts similar to that in South Vietnam where we are not belligerents but are increasingly committed. For example, were Iran to be subjected to Russian pressure, initial efforts to aid it might be "limited" rather than "total." To be ready for such actions, the United States must maintain sufficient bases overseas to permit accumulation of stocks for swift reaction by other means than holocaust.[14]

Is not Sulzberger really saying that the United States, like Great Britain in the nineteenth century, needs a global military machine to police a global empire? But, as we know, the United States needs a global military machine also for carrying on its unremitting struggle against the advance of socialism. And the truth is that policing the empire and fighting socialism are rapidly becoming, if they are not already, one and the same. For the threat to the empire comes from revolutionary movements which, like the American Revolution two hundred years ago, are sparked by a deep-seated yearning for national independence and are fueled by an increasingly urgent need for economic development, which experience is proving cannot be achieved by underdeveloped countries today except on the basis of public enterprise and comprehensive planning—in short, only if their nationalist revolutions are also socialist revolutions.

As these two great socio-political transformations merge into a single process, so likewise does the struggle against them. For the United States to defend its empire today means to fight socialism, not only in the empire but wherever it exists; for socialism is by its very nature an international movement which gains strength everywhere from a success anywhere. Hence all revolutions must be opposed, every source which gives them material or moral aid must be weakened and if possible destroyed. It is this two-sided, world-wide commitment to the political and social status quo which defines and determines the military needs of the United States oligarchy.

[14] *New York Times*, April 23, 1962.

THE MASS SOCIETY

DEMOCRACY in the classical sense, Mills says, can exist only in a community of publics where issues are debated by the people and where their subsequent decisions are translated into effective political action. A community of publics may never have existed in its ideal form, but modern industrial society is moving closer to the opposite, the mass society. The mass society consists of an elite at the top and a mass of individuals at the bottom who lack intermediate associations through which they can exercize effective power.[1] In a mass society the people are consumers of the mass media. Communication is one-way, and the individual listener cannot answer back. Having little access to the mass media, dissenting voices have difficulty making themselves heard.

In the United States, Mills says, political parties and interest organizations have become so large that they are not responsive to their individual members. (Most people, feeling powerless, do not exercise even the limited influence they might have within these organizations.) Voluntary associations small enough to be democratic in the classic sense are

[1] See William Kornhauser, *The Politics of Mass Society* (New York: The Free Press, 1959).

too small to be effective in a mass society. For their information on the world, men have become increasingly dependent on the mass media, whose selective and simplistic presentation of events keeps people from transcending their own milieux and understanding the political world.

Marcuse would undoubtedly agree that there is a power elite at the top and an incipient mass society at the bottom. But he would emphasize that both managers and managed are motivated by false needs required by the system's imperative of expansion and profitable production. The system is authoritarian in that issues are not solved by political discussion in public but by administrative fiat. The system is not merely dominated by a minority, it is carried along by legions of administrators who make the routine decisions called for by their office. The "comfortable, smooth, reasonable, democratic unfreedom" operates primarily through cultural indoctrination and positive reinforcement of desired behavior with high material and status rewards. Only as a last resort does the system make use of imprisonment and physical coercion.

The system is repressive in that it implants false standards and needs that bind human beings to unnecessary and degrading labor. Liberation is precluded by an increasing "non-terroristic economic-technical coordination which operates through the manipulation of needs by vested interests." The modern technology whose unlimited production capacity could be employed to liberate man from unnecessary and degrading labor is used instead to serve capitalism with an ever larger cycle of wasteful production and consumption and to provide the state with more sophisticated tools for manipulation and repression. In view of all this, the outlook for change appears hopeless. Nevertheless, says Marcuse, we must try. The first step toward freedom, he says, consists in a great refusal—a refusal to consume, to work under alienating conditions, to participate in sham electoral politics.[2]

The fight against veiled oppression will be more difficult than that against open domination. In a dictatorship we know who the enemy is. Liberation from the system of administrative repression is likely to be a confusing process because the enemy is not only the ruling class. It may also be the friendly administrator who is trying to make the organization run smoothly; our coworkers who urge us not to "make waves"; our parents and others who say they love us and are only concerned for our best interests. To the extent that we have introjected alien needs binding us to the system, it may also be ourselves.

[2] See Marcuse, *One Dimensional Man*, Chap. 10.

Mass Society

C. Wright Mills

The transformation of public into mass is of particular concern to us, for it provides an important clue to the meaning of the power elite. If that elite is truly responsible to, or even exists in connection with, a community of publics, it carries a very different meaning than if such a public is being transformed into a society of masses.

The United States today is not altogether a mass society, and it has never been altogether a community of publics. These phrases are names for extreme types; they point to certain features of reality, but they are themselves constructions; social reality is always some sort of mixture of the two. Yet we cannot readily understand just how much of which is mixed into our situation if we do not first understand, in terms of explicit dimensions, the clearcut and extreme types:

At least four dimensions must be attended to if we are to grasp the differences between public and mass.

I. There is first, the ratio of the givers of opinion to the receivers, which is the simplest way to state the social meaning of the formal media of mass communication. More than anything else, it is the shift in this ratio which is central to the problems of the public and of public opinion in latter-day phases of democracy. At one extreme on the scale of communication, two people talk personally with each other; at the opposite extreme, one spokesman talks impersonally through a network of communications to millions of listeners and viewers. In between these extremes there are assemblages and political rallies, parliamentary sessions, law-court debates, small discussion circles dominated by one man, open discussion circles with talk moving freely back and forth among fifty people, and so on.

II. The second dimension to which we must pay attention is the possibility of answering back an opinion without internal or external reprisals being taken. Technical conditions of the means of communication, in imposing a lower ratio of speakers to listeners, may obviate the possibility of freely answering back. Informal rules, resting upon conventional sanction and upon the informal structure of opinion leadership, may govern who can speak, when, and for how long. Such rules may or may not be in congruence with formal rules and with

FROM *The Power Elite* by C. Wright Mills, pp. 302–309; 320–24. Copyright © 1956 by Oxford University Press, Inc. Reprinted by permission.

institutional sanctions which govern the process of communication. In the extreme case, we may conceive of an absolute monopoly of communication to pacified media groups whose members cannot answer back even "in private." At the opposite extreme, the conditions may allow and the rules may uphold the wide and symmetrical formation of opinion.

III. We must also consider the relation of the formation of opinion to its realization in social action, the ease with which opinion is effective in the shaping of decisions of powerful consequence. This opportunity for people to act out their opinions collectively is of course limited by their position in the structure of power. This structure may be such as to limit decisively this capacity, or it may allow or even invite such action. It may confine social action to local areas or it may enlarge the area of opportunity; it may make action intermittent or more or less continuous.

IV. There is, finally, the degree to which institutional authority, with its sanctions and controls, penetrates the public. Here the problem is the degree to which the public has genuine autonomy from instituted authority. At one extreme, no agent of formal authority moves among the autonomous public. At the opposite extreme, the public is terrorized into uniformity by the infiltration of informers and the universalization of suspicion. One thinks of the late Nazi street-and-block-system, the eighteenth-century Japanese kumi, the Soviet cell structure. In the extreme, the formal structure of power coincides, as it were, with the informal ebb and flow of influence by discussion, which is thus killed off.

By combining these several points, we can construct little models or diagrams of several types of societies. Since "the problem of public opinion" as we know it is set by the eclipse of the classic bourgeois public, we are here concerned with only two types: public and mass.

In a *public*, as we may understand the term, (1) virtually as many people express opinions as receive them. (2) Public communications are so organized that there is a chance immediately and effectively to answer back any opinion expressed in public. Opinion formed by such discussion (3) readily finds an outlet in effective action, even against—if necessary— the prevailing system of authority. And (4) authoritative institutions do not penetrate the public, which is thus more or less autonomous in its operations. When these conditions prevail, we have the working model of a community of publics, and this model fits closely the several assumptions of classic democratic theory.

At the opposite extreme, in a *mass*, (1) far fewer people express opinions than receive them; for the community of publics becomes an abstract collection of individuals who receive impressions from the mass media. (2) The communications that prevail are so organized that it is difficult or impossible for the individual to answer back immediately or with any effect. (3) The realization of opinion in action is controlled by authorities who organize and control the channels of such action. (4) The mass has no autonomy from institutions; on the contrary, agents of authorized institutions penetrate this mass, reducing any autonomy it may have in the formation of opinion by discussion.

The public and the mass may be most readily distinguished by their dominant modes of communication: in a community of publics, discussion is the ascendant means of communication, and the mass media, if they exist, simply enlarge and animate discussion, linking one *primary public* with the discussions of another. In a mass society, the dominant type of communication is the formal media, and the publics become mere *media markets*: all those exposed to the contents of given mass media.

From Public to Mass

From almost any angle of vision that we might assume, when we look upon the public, we realize that we have moved a considerable distance along the road to the mass society. At the end of that road there is totalitarianism, as in Nazi Germany or in Communist Russia. We are not yet at that end. In the United States today, media markets are not entirely ascendant over primary publics. But surely we can see that many aspects of the public life of our times are more the features of a mass society than of a community of publics.

What is happening might again be stated in terms of the historical parallel between the economic market and the public of public opinion. In brief, there is a movement from widely scattered little powers to concentrated powers and the attempt at monopoly control from powerful centers, which, being partially hidden, are centers of manipulation as well as of authority. The small shop serving the neighborhood is replaced by the anonymity of the national corporation: mass advertisement replaces the personal influence of opinion between merchant and customer. The political leader hooks up his speech to a national network and speaks, with appropriate personal touches, to a million people he never saw and never will see. Entire brackets of professions and industries are in the "opinion business," impersonally manipulating the public for hire.

In the primary public the competition of opinions goes on between people holding views in the service of their interests and their reasoning. But in the mass society of media markets, competition, if any, goes on between the manipulators with their mass media on the one hand, and the people receiving their propaganda on the other.

Under such conditions, it is not surprising that there should arise a conception of public opinion as a mere reaction—we cannot say "response" —to the content of the mass media. In this view, the public is merely the collectivity of individuals, each rather passively exposed to the mass media and rather helplessly opened up to the suggestions and manipulations that flow from these media. The fact of manipulation from centralized points of control constitutes, as it were, an expropriation of the old multitude of little opinion producers and consumers operating in a free and balanced market.

In official circles, the very term itself, "the public"—as Walter Lippmann noted thirty years ago—has come to have a phantom meaning, which dramatically reveals its eclipse. From the standpoint of the deciding elite, some of those who clamor publicly can be identified as "Labor," others as "Business," still others as "Farmer." Those who can *not* readily be so identified make up "The Public." In this usage, the public is composed of the unidentified and the non-partisan in a world of defined and partisan interests. It is socially composed of well-educated salaried professionals, especially college professors; of non-unionized employees, especially white-collar people, along with self-employed professionals and small businessmen.

In this faint echo of the classic notion, the public consists of those remnants of the middle class, old and new, whose interests are not explicitly defined, organized, or clamorous. In a curious adaptation, "the public" often becomes, in fact, "the unattached expert," who, although well informed, has never taken a clear-cut, public stand on controversial issues which are brought to a focus by organized interests. These are the "public" members of the board, the commission, the committee. What the public stands for, accordingly, is often a vagueness of policy (called open-mindedness), a lack of involvement in public affairs (known as reasonableness), and a professional disinterest (known as tolerance).

Some such official members of the public, as in the field of labor-management mediation, start out very young and make a career out of being careful to be informed but never taking a strong position; and there are many others, quite unofficial, who take such professionals as a sort of model. The only trouble is that they are acting as if they were disinterested judges but they do not have the power of judges; hence their reasonableness, their tolerance, and their open-mindedness do not often count for much in the shaping of human affairs.

The Organized Society

All those trends that make for the decline of the politician and of his balancing society bear decisively upon the transformation of public into mass. One of the most important of the structural transformations involved is the decline of the voluntary association as a genuine instrument of the public. As we have already seen, the executive ascendancy in economic, military, and political institutions has lowered the effective use of all those voluntary associations which operate between the state and the economy on the one hand, and the family and the individual in the primary group on the other. It is not only that institutions of power have become large-scale and inaccessibly centralized; they have at the same time become less political and more administrative, and it is within this great change of framework that the organized public has waned.

In terms of *scale*, the transformation of public into mass has been underpinned by the shift from a political public decisively restricted in size (by property and education, as well as by sex and age) to a greatly enlarged mass having only the qualifications of citizenship and age.

In terms of *organization*, the transformation has been underpinned by the shift from the individual and his primary community to the voluntary association and the mass party as the major units of organized power.

Voluntary associations have become larger to the extent that they have become effective; and to just that extent they have become inaccessible to the individual who would shape by discussion the policies of the organization to which he belongs. Accordingly, along with older institutions, these voluntary associations have lost their grip on the individual. As more people are drawn into the political arena, these associations become mass in scale; and as the power of the individual becomes more dependent upon such mass associations, they are less accessible to the individual's influence.[1]

Mass democracy means the struggle of powerful and large-scale interest groups and associations, which stand between the big decisions that are made by state, corporation, army, and the will of the individual citizen as a member of the public. Since these middle-level associations are the citizen's major link with decision, his relation to them is of decisive importance. For it is only through them that he exercises such power as he may have.

The gap between the members and the leaders of the mass association is becoming increasingly wider. As soon as a man gets to be a leader of an association large enough to count he readily becomes lost as an instrument of that association. He does so (1) in the interests of maintaining his leading position in, or rather over, his mass association, and he does so (2) because he comes to see himself not as a mere delegate, instructed or not, of the mass association he represents, but as a member of "an elite" composed of such men as himself. These facts, in turn, lead to (3) the big gap between the terms in which issues are debated and resolved among members of this elite, and the terms in which they are presented to the members of the various mass associations. For the decisions that are made must *take into account* those who are important—other elites—but they must be *sold* to the mass memberships.

The gap between speaker and listener, between power and public, leads

---

[1] At the same time—and also because of the metropolitan segregation and distraction, which I shall discuss in a moment—the individual becomes more dependent upon the means of mass communication for his view of the structure as a whole.

less to any iron law of oligarchy than to the law of spokesmanship: as the pressure group expands, its leaders come to organize the opinions they "represent." So elections, as we have seen, become contests between two giant and unwieldy parties, neither of which the individual can truly feel that he influences, and neither of which is capable of winning psychologically impressive or politically decisive majorities. And, in all this, the parties are of the same general form as other mass associations.[2]

When we say that man in the mass is without any sense of political belonging, we have in mind a political fact rather than merely a style of feeling. We have in mind (I) a certain way of belonging (II) to a certain kind of organization.

I. The way of belonging here implied rests upon a belief in the purposes and in the leaders of an organization, and thus enables men and women freely to be at home within it. To belong in this way is to make the human association a psychological center of one's self, to take into our conscience, deliberately and freely, its rules of conduct and its purposes, which we thus shape and which in turn shape us. We do not have this kind of belonging to any political organization.

II. The kind of organization we have in mind is a voluntary association which has three decisive characteristics: first, it is a context in which reasonable opinions may be formulated; second, it is an agency by which reasonable activities may be undertaken; and third, it is a powerful enough unit, in comparison with other organizations of power, to make a difference.

It is because they do not find available associations at once psychologically meaningful and historically effective that men often feel uneasy in their political and economic loyalties. The effective units of power are now the huge corporation, the inaccessible government, the grim military establishment. Between these, on the one hand, and the family and the small community on the other, we find no intermediate associations in which men feel secure and with which they feel powerful. There is little live political struggle. Instead, there is administration from above, and the political vacuum below. The primary publics are now either so small as to be swamped, and hence give up; or so large as to be merely another feature of the generally distant structure of power, and hence inaccessible.

Public opinion exists when people who are not in the government of a

2 On elections in modern formal democracies, E. H. Carr has concluded: "To speak today of the defence of democracy as if we were defending something which we knew and had possessed for many decades or many centuries is self-deception and sham —mass democracy is a new phenomenon—a creation of the last half-century—which it is inappropriate and misleading to consider in terms of the philosophy of Locke or of the liberal democracy of the nineteenth century. We should be nearer the mark, and should have a far more convincing slogan, if we spoke of the need, not to defend democracy, but to create it." (ibid. pp. 75–6).

country claim the right to express political opinions freely and publicly, and the right that these opinions should influence or determine the policies, personnel, and actions of their government.[3] In this formal sense there has been and there is a definite public opinion in the United States. And yet, with modern developments this formal right—when it does still exist as a right—does not mean what it once did. The older world of voluntary organization was as different from the world of the mass organization as was Tom Paine's world of pamphleteering from the world of the mass media.

*   *   *

Structural Trends

The structural trends of modern society and the manipulative character of its communication technique come to a point of coincidence in the mass society, which is largely a metropolitan society. The growth of the metropolis, segregating men and women into narrowed routines and environments, causes them to lose any firm sense of their integrity as a public. The members of publics in smaller communities know each other more or less fully, because they meet in the several aspects of the total life routine. The members of masses in a metropolitan society know one another only as fractions in specialized milieux: the man who fixes the car, the girl who serves your lunch, the saleslady, the women who take care of your child at school during the day. Prejudgment and stereotype flourish when people meet in such ways. The human reality of others does not, cannot, come through.

People, we know, tend to select those formal media which confirm what they already believe and enjoy. In a parallel way, they tend in the metropolitan segregation to come into live touch with those whose opinions are similar to theirs. Others they tend to treat unseriously. In the metropolitan society they develop, in their defense, a blasé manner that reaches deeper than a manner. They do not, accordingly, experience genuine clashes of viewpoint, genuine issues. And when they do, they tend to consider it mere rudeness.

Sunk in their routines, they do not transcend, even by discussion, much less by action, their more or less narrow lives. They do not gain a view of the structure of their society and of their role as a public within it. The city is a structure composed of such little environments, and the people in them tend to be detached from one another. The "stimulating variety" of the city does not stimulate the men and women of "the bedroom belt," the

---

[3] Cf. Hans Speier, *Social Order and The Risks of War* (New York: George Stewart, 1952), pp. 323–39.

one-class suburbs, who can go through life knowing only their own kind. If they do reach for one another, they do so only through stereotypes and prejudiced images of the creatures of other milieux. Each is trapped by his confining circle; each is cut off from easily identifiable groups. It is for people in such narrow milieux that the mass media can create a pseudo-world beyond, and a pseudo-world within themselves as well.

Publics live in milieux but they can transcend them—individually by intellectual effort; socially by public action. By reflection and debate and by organized action, a community of publics comes to feel itself and comes in fact to be active at points of structural relevance.

But members of a mass exist in milieux and cannot get out of them, either by mind or by activity, except—in the extreme case—under "the organized spontaneity" of the bureaucrat on a motorcycle. We have not yet reached the extreme case, but observing metropolitan man in the American mass we can surely see the psychological preparations for it.

We may think of it in this way: When a handful of men do not have jobs, and do not seek work, we look for the causes in their immediate situation and character. But when twelve million men are unemployed, then we cannot believe that all of them suddenly "got lazy" and turned out to be "no good." Economists call this "structural unemployment"—meaning, for one thing, that the men involved cannot themselves control their job chances. Structural unemployment does not originate in one factory or in one town, nor is it due to anything that one factory or one town does or fails to do. Moreover, there is little or nothing that one ordinary man in one factory in one town can do about it when it sweeps over his personal milieu.

Now, this distinction, between social structure and personal milieu, is one of the most important available in the sociological studies. It offers us a ready understanding of the position of "the public" in America today. In every major area of life, the loss of a sense of structure and the submergence into powerless milieux is the cardinal fact. In the military it is most obvious, for here the roles men play are strictly confining; only the command posts at the top afford a view of the structure of the whole, and moreover, this view is a closely guarded official secret. In the division of labor too, the jobs men enact in the economic hierarchies are also more or less narrow milieux and the positions from which a view of the production process as a whole can be had are centralized, as men are alienated not only from the product and the tools of their labor, but from any under-standing of the structure and the processes of production. In the political order, in the fragmentation of the lower and in the distracting proliferation of the middle-level organization, men cannot see the whole, cannot see the top, and cannot state the issues that will in fact determine the whole struc-ture in which they live and their place within it.

This loss of any structural view or position is the decisive meaning of the lament over the loss of community. In the great city, the division of milieux and of segregating routines reaches the point of closest contact with the individual and the family, for, although the city is not the unit of prime decision, even the city cannot be seen as a total structure by most of its citizens.

On the one hand, there is the increased scale and centralization of the structure of decision; and, on the other, the increasingly narrow sorting out of men into milieux. From both sides, there is the increased dependence upon the formal media of communication, including those of education itself. But the man in the mass does not gain a transcending view from these media; instead he gets his experience stereotyped, and then he gets sunk further by that experience. He cannot detach himself in order to observe, much less to evaluate, what he is experiencing, much less what he is not experiencing. Rather than that internal discussion we call reflection, he is accompanied through his life-experience with a sort of unconscious, echoing monologue. He has no projects of his own: he fulfills the routines that exist. He does not transcend whatever he is at any moment, because he does not, he cannot, transcend his daily milieux. He is not truly aware of his own daily experience and of its actual standards: he drifts, he fulfills habits, his behavior a result of a planless mixture of the confused standards and the uncriticized expectations that he has taken over from others whom he no longer really knows or trusts, if indeed he ever really did.

He takes things for granted, he makes the best of them, he tries to look ahead—a year or two perhaps, or even longer if he has children or a mortgage—but he does not seriously ask, What do I want? How can I get it? A vague optimism suffuses and sustains him, broken occasionally by little miseries and disappointments that are soon buried. He is smug, from the standpoint of those who think something might be the matter with the mass style of life in the metropolitan frenzy where self-making is an externally busy branch of industry. By what standards does he judge himself and his efforts? What is really important to him? Where are the models of excellence for this man?

He loses his independence, and more importantly, he loses the desire to be independent: in fact, he does not have hold of the idea of being an independent individual with his own mind and his own worked-out way of life. It is not that he likes or does not like this life; it is that the question does not come up sharp and clear so he is not bitter and he is not sweet about conditions and events. He thinks he wants merely to get his share of what is around with as little trouble as he can and with as much fun as possible.

Such order and movement as his life possesses is in conformity with external routines; otherwise his day-to-day experience is a vague chaos—although he often does not know it because, strictly speaking, he does not truly possess or observe his own experience. He does not formulate his desires; they are insinuated into him. And, in the mass, he loses the self-confidence of the human being—if indeed he has ever had it. For life in a society of masses implants insecurity and furthers impotence; it makes men uneasy and vaguely anxious; it isolates the individual from the solid group; it destroys firm group standards. Acting without goals, the man in the mass just feels pointless.

The idea of a mass society suggests the idea of an elite of power. The idea of the public, in contrast, suggests the liberal tradition of a society without any power elite, or at any rate with shifting elites of no sovereign consequence. For, if a genuine public is sovereign, it needs no master; but the masses, in their full development, are sovereign only in some plebiscitarian moment of adulation to an elite as authoritative celebrity. The political structure of a democratic state requires the public; and, the democratic man, in his rhetoric, must assert that this public is the very seat of sovereignty.

But now, given all those forces that have enlarged and centralized the political order and made modern societies less political and more administrative; given the transformation of the old middle classes into something which perhaps should not even be called middle class; given all the mass communications that do not truly communicate; given all the metropolitan segregation that is not community; given the absence of voluntary associations that really connect the public at large with the centers of power— what is happening is the decline of a set of publics that is sovereign only in the most formal and rhetorical sense. Moreover, in many countries the remnants of such publics as remain are now being frightened out of existence. They lose their will for rationally considered decision and action because they do not possess the instruments for such decision and action; they lose their sense of political belonging because they do not belong; they lose their political will because they see no way to realize it.

The top of modern American society is increasingly unified, and often seems willfully co-ordinated: at the top there has emerged an elite of power. The middle levels are a drifting set of stalemated, balancing forces: the middle does not link the bottom with the top. The bottom of this society is politically fragmented, and even as a passive fact, increasingly powerless: at the bottom there is emerging a mass society.

New Forms of Control

Herbert Marcuse

A comfortable, smooth, reasonable, democratic unfreedom prevails in advanced industrial civilization, a token of technical progress. Indeed, what could be more rational than the suppression of individuality in the mechanization of socially necessary but painful performances; the concentration of individual enterprises in more effective, more productive corporations; the regulation of free competition among unequally equipped economic subjects; the curtailment of prerogatives and national sovereignties which impede the international organization of resources. That this technological order also involves a political and intellectual coordination may be a regrettable and yet promising development.

The rights and liberties which were such vital factors in the origins and earlier stages of industrial society yield to a higher stage of this society: they are losing their traditional rationale and content. Freedom of thought, speech, and conscience were—just as free enterprise, which they served to promote and protect—essentially *critical* ideas, designed to replace an obsolescent material and intellectual culture by a more productive and rational one. Once institutionalized, these rights and liberties shared the fate of the society of which they had become an integral part. The achievement cancels the premises.

To the degree to which freedom from want, the concrete substance of all freedom, is becoming a real possibility, the liberties which pertain to a state of lower productivity are losing their former content. Independence of thought, autonomy, and the right to political opposition are being deprived of their basic critical function in a society which seems increasingly capable of satisfying the needs of the individuals through the way in which it is organized. Such a society may justly demand acceptance of its principles and institutions, and reduce the opposition to the discussion and promotion of alternative policies *within* the status quo. In this respect, it seems to make little difference whether the increasing satisfaction of needs is accomplished by an authoritarian or a non-authoritarian system. Under the conditions of a rising standard of living, non-conformity with the system itself appears to be socially useless, and the more so when it entails tangible economic and political disadvantages and threatens the smooth operation of the whole. Indeed, at least in so far as the necessities of life are involved, there seems to be no reason why the production and distribu-

FROM *One Dimensional Man*, by Herbert Marcuse, pp. 1–12. Copyright © 1964. Reprinted by permission of Beacon Press, and of Routledge & Kegan Paul Ltd.

tion of goods and services should proceed through the competitive concurrence of individual liberties.

Freedom of enterprise was from the beginning not altogether a blessing. As the liberty to work or to starve, it spelled toil, insecurity, and fear for the vast majority of the population. If the individual were no longer compelled to prove himself on the market, as a free economic subject, the disappearance of this kind of freedom would be one of the greatest achievements of civilization. The technological processes of mechanization and standardization might release individual energy into a yet uncharted realm of freedom beyond necessity. The very structure of human existence would be altered; the individual would be liberated from the work world's imposing upon him alien needs and alien possibilities. The individual would be free to exert autonomy over a life that would be his own. If the productive apparatus could be organized and directed toward the satisfaction of the vital needs, its control might well be centralized; such control would not prevent individual autonomy, but render it possible.

This is a goal within the capabilities of advanced industrial civilization, the "end" of technological rationality. In actual fact, however, the contrary trend operates: the apparatus imposes its economic and political requirements for defense and expansion on labor time and free time, on the material and intellectual culture. By virtue of the way it has organized its technological base, contemporary industrial society tends to be totalitarian. For "totalitarian" is not only a terroristic political coordination of society, but also a nonterroristic economic-technical coordination which operates through the manipulation of needs by vested interests. It thus precludes the emergence of an effective opposition against the whole. Not only a specific form of government or party rule makes for totalitarianism, but also a specific system of production and distribution which may well be compatible with a "pluralism" of parties, newspapers, "countervailing powers," etc.

Today political power asserts itself through its power over the machine process and over the technical organization of the apparatus. The government of advanced and advancing industrial societies can maintain and secure itself only when it succeeds in mobilizing, organizing, and exploiting the technical, scientific, and mechanical productivity available to industrial civilization. And this productivity mobilizes society as a whole, above and beyond any particular individual or group interests. The brute fact that the machines's physical (only physical?) power surpasses that of the individual, and of any particular group of individuals, makes the machine the most effective political instrument in any society whose basic organization is that of the machine process. But the political trend may be reversed; essentially the power of the machine is only the stored-up and projected power of man. To the extent to which the work world is conceived of as a machine and mechanized accordingly, it becomes the *potential* basis of a new freedom for man.

Contemporary industrial civilization demonstrates that it has reached the stage at which "the free society" can no longer be adequately defined in the traditional terms of economic, political, and intellectual liberties, not because these liberties have become insignificant, but because they are too significant to be confined within the traditional forms. New modes of realization are needed, corresponding to the new capabilities of society.

Such new modes can be indicated only in negative terms because they would amount to the negation of the prevailing modes. Thus economic freedom would mean freedom *from* the economy—from being controlled by economic forces and relationships; freedom from the daily struggle for existence, from earning a living. Political freedom would mean liberation of the individuals *from* politics over which they have no effective control. Similarly, intellectual freedom would mean the restoration of individual thought now absorbed by mass communication and indoctrination, abolition of "public opinion" together with its makers. The unrealistic sound of these propositions is indicative, not of their utopian character, but of the strength of the forces which prevent their realization. The most effective and enduring form of warfare against liberation is the implanting of material and intellectual needs that perpetuate obsolete forms of the struggle for existence.

The intensity, the satisfaction and even the character of human needs, beyond the biological level, have always been preconditioned. Whether or not the possibility of doing or leaving, enjoying or destroying, possessing or rejecting something is seized as a *need* depends on whether or not it can be seen as desirable and necessary for the prevailing societal institutions and interests. In this sense, human needs are historical needs and, to the extent to which the society demands the repressive development of the individual, his needs themselves and their claim for satisfaction are subject to overriding critical standards.

We may distinguish both true and false needs. "False" are those which are superimposed upon the individual by particular social interests in his repression: the needs which perpetuate toil, aggressiveness, misery, and injustice. Their satisfaction might be most gratifying to the individual, but this happiness is not a condition which has to be maintained and protected if it serves to arrest the development of the ability (his own and others) to recognize the disease of the whole and grasp the chances of curing the disease. The result then is euphoria in unhappiness. Most of the prevailing needs to relax, to have fun, to behave and consume in accordance with the advertisements, to love and hate what others love and hate, belong to this category of false needs.

Such needs have a societal content and function which are determined by external powers over which the individual has no control; the development and satisfaction of these needs is heteronomous. No matter how much such needs may have become the individual's own, reproduced and fortified by the conditions of his existence; no matter how much he identifies himself with them and finds himself in their satisfaction, they continue to be what they were from the beginning—products of a society whose dominant interest demands repression.

The prevalence of repressive needs is an accomplished fact, accepted in ignorance and defeat, but a fact that must be undone in the interest of the happy individual as well as all those whose misery is the price of his satisfaction. The only needs that have an unqualified claim for satisfaction are the vital ones—nourishment, clothing, lodging at the attainable level of culture. The satisfaction of these needs is the prerequisite for the realization of *all* needs, of the unsublimated as well as the sublimated ones.

For any consciousness and conscience, for any experience which does not accept the prevailing societal interest as the supreme law of thought and behavior, the established universe of needs and satisfactions is a fact to be questioned—questioned in terms of truth and falsehood. These terms are historical throughout, and their objectivity is historical. The judgment of needs and their satisfaction, under the given conditions, involves standards of *priority*—standards which refer to the optimal development of the individual, of all individuals, under the optimal utilization of the material and intellectual resources available to man. The resources are calculable. "Truth" and "falsehood" of needs designate objective conditions to the extent to which the universal satisfaction of vital needs and, beyond it, the progressive alleviation of toil and poverty, are universally valid standards. But as historical standards, they do not only vary according to area and stage of development, they also can be defined only in (greater or lesser) *contradiction* to the prevailing ones. What tribunal can possibly claim the authority of decision?

In the last analysis, the question of what are true and false needs must be answered by the individuals themselves, but only in the last analysis; that is, if and when they are free to give their own answer. As long as they are kept incapable of being autonomous, as long as they are indoctrinated and manipulated (down to their very instincts), their answer to this question cannot be taken as their own. By the same token, however, no tribunal can justly arrogate to itself the right to decide which needs should be developed and satisfied. Any such tribunal is reprehensible, although our revulsion does not do away with the question: how can the people who have been the object of effective and productive domination by themselves create the conditions of freedom?

The more rational, productive, technical, and total the repressive administration of society becomes, the more unimaginable the means and ways by which the administered individuals might break their servitude and seize their own liberation. To be sure, to impose Reason upon an entire society is a paradoxical and scandalous idea—although one might dispute the righteousness of a society which ridicules this idea while making its own population into objects of total administration. All liberation depends on the consciousness of servitude, and the emergence of this consciousness is always hampered by the predominance of needs and satisfactions which, to a great extent, have become the individual's own. The process always replaces one system of preconditioning by another; the optimal goal is the replacement of false needs by true ones, the abandonment of repressive satisfaction.

The distinguishing feature of advanced industrial society is its effective suffocation of those needs which demand liberation—liberation also from that which is tolerable and rewarding and comfortable—while it sustains and absolves the destructive power and repressive function of the affluent society. Here, the social controls exact the overwhelming need for the production and consumption of waste; the need for stupefying work where it is no longer a real necessity; the need for modes of relaxation which soothe and prolong this stupefication; the need for maintaining such deceptive liberties as free competition at administered prices, a free press which censors itself, free choice between brands and gadgets.

Under the rule of a repressive whole, liberty can be made into a powerful instrument of domination. The range of choice open to the individual is not the decisive factor in determining the degree of human freedom, but *what* can be chosen and what *is* chosen by the individual. The criterion for free choice can never be an absolute one, but neither is it entirely relative. Free election of masters does not abolish the masters or the slaves. Free choice among a wide variety of goods and services does not signify freedom if these goods and services sustain social controls over a life of toil and fear —that is, if they sustain alienation. And the spontaneous reproduction of superimposed needs by the individual does not establish autonomy; it only testifies to the efficacy of the controls.

Our insistence on the depth and efficacy of these controls is open to the objection that we overrate greatly the indoctrinating power of the "media," and that by themselves the people would feel and satisfy the needs which are now imposed upon them. The objection misses the point. The preconditioning does not start with the mass production of radio and television and with the centralization of their control. The people enter this stage as preconditioned receptacles of long standing; the decisive difference is in the flattening out of the contrast (or conflict) beween the given and the possible, between the satisfied and the unsatisfied needs. Here, the so-called equalization of class distinctions reveals its ideological function. If the worker and his boss enjoy the same television program and visit the same resort places, if the typist is as attractively made up as the daughter of her employer, if the Negro owns a Cadillac, if they all read the same newspaper, then this assimilation indicates not the disappearance of classes, but the extent to which the needs and satisfactions that serve the preservation of the Establishment are shared by the underlying population.

Indeed, in the most highly developed areas of contemporary society, the transplantation of social into individual needs is so effective that the difference between them seems to be purely theoretical. Can one really distinguish between the mass media as instruments of information and entertainment, and as agents of manipulation and indoctrination? Between the automobile as nuisance and as convenience? Between the horrors and the comforts of functional architecture? Between the work for national defense and the work for corporate gain? Between the private pleasure and the commercial and political utility involved in increasing the birth rate?

We are again confronted with one of the most vexing aspects of advanced industrial civilization: the rational character of its irrationality. Its productivity and efficiency, its capacity to increase and spread comforts, to turn waste into need, and destruction into construction, the extent to which this civilization transforms the object world into an extension of man's mind and body makes the very notion of alienation questionable. The people recognize themselves in their commodities; they find their soul in their automobile, hi-fi set, split-level home, kitchen equipment. The very mechanism which ties the individual to his society has changed, and social control is anchored in the new needs which it has produced.

The prevailing forms of social control are technological in a new sense. To be sure, the technical structure and efficacy of the productive and destructive apparatus has been a major instrumentality for subjecting the population to the established social division of labor throughout the modern period. Moreover, such integration has always been accompanied by more obvious forms of compulsion: loss of livelihood, the administration of justice, the police, the armed forces. It still is. But in the contemporary period, the technological controls appear to be the very embodiment of Reason for the benefit of all social groups and interests—to such an extent that all contradiction seems irrational and all counteraction impossible.

No wonder then that, in the most advanced areas of this civilization, the social controls have been introjected to the point where even individual protest is affected at its roots. The intellectual and emotional refusal "to go along" appears neurotic and impotent. This is the socio-psychological aspect of the political event that marks the contemporary period: the passing of the historical forces which, at the preceding stage of industrial society, seemed to represent the possibility of new forms of existence.

But the term "introjection" perhaps no longer describes the way in which the individual by himself reproduces and perpetuates the external controls exercised by his society. Introjection suggests a variety of relatively spontaneous processes by which a Self (Ego) transposes the "outer" into the "inner." Thus introjection implies the existence of an inner dimension distinguished from and even antagonistic to the external exigencies—an individual consciousness and an individual unconscious *apart from* public opinion and behavior.[1] The idea of "inner freedom" here has its reality: it

---

[1] The change in the function of the family here plays a decisive role: its "socializing" functions are increasingly taken over by outside groups and media. See my *Eros and Civilization* (Boston: Beacon Press, 1955), p. 96 ff.

designates the private space in which man may become and remain "himself."

Today this private space has been invaded and whittled down by technological reality. Mass production and mass distribution claim the *entire* individual, and industrial psychology has long since ceased to be confined to the factory. The manifold processes of introjection seem to be ossified in almost mechanical reactions. The result is, not adjustment but *mimesis*: an immediate identification of the individual with *his* society and, through it, with the society as a whole.

This immediate, automatic identification (which may have been characteristic of primitive forms of association) reappears in high industrial civilization; its new "immediacy," however, is the product of a sophisticated, scientific management and organization. In this process, the "inner" dimension of the mind in which opposition to the status quo can take root is whittled down. The loss of this dimension, in which the power of negative thinking—the critical power of Reason—is at home, is the ideological counterpart to the very material process in which advanced industrial society silences and reconciles the opposition. The impact of progress turns Reason into submission to the facts of life, and to the dynamic capability of producing more and bigger facts of the same sort of life. The efficiency of the system blunts the individuals' recognition that it contains no facts which do not communicate the repressive power of the whole. If the individuals find themselves in the things which shape their life, they do so, not by giving, but by accepting the law of things—not the law of physics but the law of their society.

I have just suggested that the concept of alienation seems to become questionable when the individuals identify themselves with the existence which is imposed upon them and have in it their own development and satisfaction. This identification is not illusion but reality. However, the reality constitutes a more progressive stage of alienation. The latter has become entirely objective; the subject which is alienated is swallowed up by its alienated existence. There is only one dimension, and it is everywhere and in all forms. The achievements of progress defy ideological indictment as well as justification; before their tribunal, the "false consciousness" of their rationality becomes the true consciousness.

This absorption of ideology into reality does not, however, signify the "end of ideology." On the contrary, in a specific sense advanced industrial culture is *more* ideological than its predecessor, inasmuch as today the ideology is in the process of production itself.[2] In a provocative form, this proposition reveals the political aspects of the prevailing technological rationality. The productive apparatus and the goods and services which it produces "sell" or impose the social system as a whole. The means of mass

---

[2] Theodor W. Adorno, *Prismen. Kulturkritik und Gessellschaft.* (Frankfurt: Suhrkamp, 1955), p. 24 f.

transportation and communication, the commodities of lodging, food, and clothing, the irresistible output of the entertainment and information industry carry with them prescribed attitudes and habits, certain intellectual and emotional reactions which bind the consumers more or less pleasantly to the producers and, through the latter, to the whole. The products indoctrinate and manipulate; they promote a false consciousness which is immune against its falsehood. And as these beneficial products become available to more individuals in more social classes, the indoctrination they carry ceases to be publicity; it becomes a way of life. It is a good way of life—much better than before—and as a good way of life, it militates against qualitative change. Thus emerges a pattern of *one-dimensional thought and behavior* in which ideas, aspirations, and objectives that, by their content, transcend the established universe of discourse and action are either repelled or reduced to terms of this universe. They are redefined by the rationality of the given system and of its quantitative extension.

PART THREE

Ideologies and Agencies of Change

POLITICS AND SOCIAL CHANGE:
THE NEW LEFT

THE NEW LEFT is an international movement to replace the system of corporate liberalism with a decentralized society based on brotherhood, love, and freedom. Strictly speaking there is no single movement, but a congeries of parties, organizations, communes, groups, and individuals who reject for similar reasons the prevailing system. The different tendencies and factions in the movement within and between countries cooperate loosely at times, but they are not centrally organized and often disagree with each other. Many drop-outs, anarchists, and participants in counter-institutions do not consider themselves "members" of any movement, and yet this disavowal most clearly exemplifies the new left determination to decentralize.

In the United States part of the movement grew out of the civil rights struggles of the early 1960s. The new left has been embodied in such groups as SNCC (Student Nonviolent Coordinating Committee) and SDS (Students for a Democratic Society), and in explosions like the Berkeley Free Speech Movement. It is above all a certain mood, which finds its expression now is one organization and now in another. Much of its support has come from young people outraged by the continuing

Vietnam War and the system of military conscription that helps make it possible.

Adherents of the new left share a number of characteristics:

1. They tend to be eclectic in their world view. Some identify themselves as socialists, anarchists, or liberals, but most lack any coherent theory of society or social change. Some favor reforms; others, while supporting efforts to ameliorate immediate social conditions, struggle for the complete change of the entire system. The minimum program that different segments of the movement might agree on is an end to economic exploitation and military intervention abroad, abolition of capitalism at home, and democratic control of all social organizations. The main disagreements in the new left are about how much government will be needed in the future, and about the tactics necessary to achieve social change.

2. They emphasize participatory democracy within their groups and organizations and as a goal for the society. They de-emphasize leadership, and believe that all the people should share in the decisions that affect their lives. They oppose the bureaucratic paternalism of the schools, corporations, and government agencies. They try to bring about students' control of schools, community control of police, and workers' control of the factories.

3. They call for direct action, including civil disobedience, to bring about immediate social change, because they believe that working through legal channels and parliamentary elections is inappropriate and ineffective. To desegregate lunch counters, activists have "sat in" and demanded to be served; in schools and universities they exercise free speech by distributing literature in defiance of administrative regulations, and they assert their sexuality by sleeping together in open violation of dormitory rules. Activists impede or obstruct oppressive institutions by direct confrontations. Some burn draft board files, others physically interfere with campus recruiting by corporations with war contracts, try to stop troop trains and ships carrying war materiel, and so on.

4. Many are drop-outs who participate in a growing counterculture. They have created anti-institutions such as free schools and underground newspapers. A growing number reject the conventional family pattern and live together in urban and rural communes. Some engage in handicrafts, others in subsistence farming. Many drop-outs, however, still depend on the system for occasional jobs and for welfare and other benefits.

The drop-outs will not greatly threaten the social order unless and until there are enough of them—because they are basically apolitical. They even draw people away from organized radical political groups. They are not out to capture political power, although they are revolutionary by implication. For example, if most young men dropped out by not registering for the draft, then that part of the system based on conscription would fall apart. If millions refused to consume, work in the system, or pay taxes, the entire economy might begin to collapse.

Like all political groups, the new left has had to face the ethical dilemmas of means and ends discussed by Weber:

> In numerous instances the attainment of "good" ends is bound to the fact that one must be willing to pay the price of using morally dubious means or at least dangerous ones—and facing the possibility or even the probability of evil ramifications. From no ethics in the world can it be concluded when and to what extent the ethically good purpose "justifies" the dangerous means and ramifications.[1]

The current movement has been unable to resolve these moral dilemmas any more effectively than previous ones. There is sharp disagreement over what conditions can justify violent action. Many in the movement believe in revolutionary nonviolence,[2] although they agree with Gandhi that it is better to resist evil violently than not to resist it at all. Others distinguish between the oppressive violence of the state and self-defense against that violence.

One of the key questions for any theory of social change is which social groups are to be the historical agency of that change. The answer of the Marxists has been that change will be effected by the industrial working class. Today's blue collar workers, however, tend to be conservative. The new left sees change coming about primarily through the efforts of students,[3] drop-outs, and members of the "new working class" of technicians, teachers, and other professionals.

Alternative institutions such as free universities, free radio, and so on are necessary but not sufficient conditions for the construction of a new society, says Teodori. To succeed in its goals, he points out, the new left must not only build counter-institutions but it must also wage a continuing battle against the concentrated power of the corporations and the government. This struggle takes the form of demonstrations, strikes, propaganda, and community organization.

The growth of the movement is partly a response to contradictions in the existing system, according to Berke (such as the need of capitalism to expand in an ever-increasing cycle of consumption and production). The contradictions lead to continual conflict, and, eventually, to a crisis of the system in which the movement successfully challenges its power.

The new society will be decentralized and nonauthoritarian, and will provide essential goods and services free. It will not be a static utopia, but

[1] See Hans Gerth and C. Wright Mills, *From Max Weber* (New York: Oxford University Press, 1958), p. 121.

[2] See David Dellinger, *Revolutionary Nonviolence* (Indianapolis, Bobbs Merrill, 1970).

[3] See Irving Louis Horowitz and William H. Friedland, *The Knowledge Factory* (Carbondale, Ill.: Southern Illinois University Press, 1972), especially the chapter on "Students as a Social Class."

will itself evolve through continuing conflict. Berke sees three phases in the struggle to reach this new society. In the first stage, thousands of youth drop out and begin to organize counter-institutions. In the second, which Berke says is just beginning, people move out of bourgeois society into the newly emerging counter society. The third phase begins with a confrontation precipitated by police violence which ignites a previously explosive situation. This clash leads to a general strike, the occupation of key institutions by the people, and the collapse of the bourgeois state.

The events in France of May, 1968, described by the Cohn-Bendits, marked just such a crisis. The action initiated by students at the University of Nanterre escalated into an insurrection that threatened to topple the entire regime and to replace it with a second French Commune. It nearly succeeded.

Following a sit-in at Nanterre, a wave of student demonstrations and strikes swept the country. In spite of the initial opposition of the French Communist Party, the student action encouraged the unions to call a general strike, which lasted for weeks. During this time workers began to occupy large factories.

Further demonstrations organized by the students drew the support of thousands of Parisians. The marchers took over and burned the stock exchange and were ready to occupy the government ministries, radio and television stations, and public buildings. Because of lack of unity and the treachery of Communist leaders, the movement failed to capture these objectives, but it came close to its goal: "to smash the entire state apparatus, to show the people how well they could get on without it, and how the whole of society had to be reconstructed afresh on the basis of workers' control."

After a decade of growth, the American new left is divided and disorganized. Few people in the movement are sure exactly where it is going. Radical organizations have been killed by in-fighting between Maoists, Trotskyists, and other factions. There is distrust between black and white radicals, between drop-outs and political activists. The questions facing the movement are hard to answer: What to do in the next election—support a political candidate or abstain? What if abstention means the American government becomes even more repressive and imperialist? Do you subvert the system by taking jobs within it and acting on your own values, or do you create new alternatives outside it? If you devote your time to counter-institutions, how do you reach the many people who are still caught up in the educational "establishment" or still working at alienating jobs in the corporations and civil service? As there are no clear-cut answers to these questions, the new left will probably continue to follow divergent and sometimes contradictory policies.

The direction taken by the organizations, groups, and individuals that comprise the movement will be partly determined by what the estabtablishment does. If local authorities do not harass the new counter-institutions, and if the federal government ceases its most blatant military intervention abroad and expands the benefits of the welfare state at home, the movement may become coopted and acceptable. If the authorities launch a new war, or vigorously persecute and repress alternative life styles and dissenting politics, however, they may succeed in welding the new left together into a cohesive, self-conscious opposition movement.

Beyond Politics—Social Revolution?

Mässímo Teodorí

Something Is Happening

Although the various movements of the past three years must be considered individually, they are all expressions of a common context: the formation of a new culture and politics opposed to the existing order in the United States. If we wish to go beyond the mere succession of events and the phenomenology of the antiwar, antidraft, Black Power, and student power movements, we must ask a number of questions about how and why dissent, protest, resistance, and a new "life-style" are developing.

What actually is this Movement of which an entire segment of America's younger generation feels itself a part? Is it an abstract and metaphysical phenomenon for those in search of an identity, or can it also be considered the expression of new historical forces capable of bringing about profound changes in the society and its institutions? How widespread is the Movement, and how many people are involved in it? What kinds of individuals, which groups and classes participate in this new dimension of culture and politics? What is the importance of the Movement as a whole; what repercussions does it have on the political structures and social and economical order of American life? What do the new radicals want? What is the New Left? Is a revolution in the process of developing? Although our approach is essentially political, we should, in order to answer these questions, consider three different levels of analysis and evaluation:

1. *Psychological:* concerning transformation occurring in the realms of "life-style," morality, and culture within a few groups in the society,

FROM *The New Left: A Documentary History*, copyright © 1969, Mässímo Teodorí, reprinted by permission of the publisher, The Bobbs-Merrill Company, Inc.

and the consequent repercussions on the manner of looking at the social order in general.

2. *Social:* concerning the formation of new social institutions in opposition or as alternatives to those of the existing order.

3. *Political:* regarding the development of analyses and strategies about the entire societal order and the organization of forces capable of bringing about changes in the structures of power.

The phenomena of each of these three levels are not really separate and distinct. In the Movement they exist side by side, interact, and sometimes come into conflict with one another. The reasons for the development of certain actions are sometimes psychological, at other times social or political, but most often all three levels are involved, because protest and the search for alternative values spring from a "one dimensional" society in which not only have all the organized left-wing forces been rendered impotent in the past, but also where attempts have been made to make values, instincts, and behavior conform to accepted patterns, as we have already pointed out. The process of individual liberation from the oppression of uniformity and conformity often leads to the formation of new social structures in which different relationships between individuals are made possible, and to organized political action for the purpose of transforming power structures. The very dynamics of the Movement and the development of the New Left indicate the simultaneous presence and evolution of all three elements—psychological, social, and political—during the period from the beginning of the 1960s until today. Political action during this period moved through a cycle: originally it was principally by moral considerations and a sense of individual commitment (civil rights, peace, and free speech); then it became collective and community-oriented (participatory democracy), and finally it took on a more specifically political character in the classical sense, with the establishment of a struggle for power at different levels. Nevertheless, the three levels of transformation still remain tightly connected and often complement one another. The Movement must be seen precisely as this open process which affects public and private, psychological and political life. The New Left, with its strong leaning toward experiment, attempts to express all of this in a political praxis which is meant to give direction to the ongoing process of change.

We must look briefly at the composition of the Movement if we are to understand its social roots.

The first group of insurgents is made up of college and university students, who no longer represent an élite coming from restricted groups, but constitute in themselves an entire segment of the social structure. Before the war, there were no more than a million and a half college and university students in the United States; by the mid-1950s, the number had grown to about 2.7 million, and in 1968 there were over seven million, i.e., nearly three percent of the whole population. Campus life makes them a mass of individuals virtually separate from the rest of the population, with their own cultural needs which relate both to their situation as young people and to the nature and level of the education they receive. Their concentration within certain limited areas creates a completely special situation in which they develop interpersonal relationships particularly intense in degree of change and growth, and collective activities that express ideas, values, and general interests which the very process of "studying" and "learning" makes them respond to more deeply than would occur elsewhere.

The second group of protestors is that of the "dropouts." We use this term here to indicate the wide spectrum of all those who, out of either desire or necessity, are outside of those educational, productive, or social processes considered "normal." It includes those young people—about one-third of the total number—who leave school before they are eighteen years old, one-quarter of nonwhite and one-sixth of white youths who, at the beginning of the normal working age (eighteen and nineteen years), are unemployed and in danger of remaining chronically out of work; the one-third or more of students who drop out of colleges or universities because they feel their education is irrelevant and finally all those who deliberately choose not to become involved in permanent productive activity and get along in one way or another, through temporary or part-time marginal jobs.

This wide and heterogeneous category also includes the hippies. The period when they attracted the greatest publicity, the summer of 1967 (when several hundred thousand dropouts converged on the psychedelic meccas of Haight-Ashbury in San Francisco and New York's East Village) is now past, and the "flower children" are dispersing into small groups scattered over different areas of the country. But in spite of the numerical smallness of this nonmovement, the phenomenon has a strong emblematic importance. The New Bohemia, above and beyond its leaders, is the visible reflection of a state of mind which exists on a more or less conscious level in groups larger than that of the hippies and signifies a psychological break with "one-dimensional" society.

Finally, the third social source of the Movement is the group of adults inside the middle-class melting pot, who are engaged in more or less skilled and well-paying productive activities but do not actively participate in decision-making processes because of their subordinate positions and the centralized structure of the institutions in which they work. Among these we can include teachers, scientific workers at the intermediate level, technicians, and small professionals. The members of this social group, unlike the dropouts, feel the need to have a place in the productive process and to put their intellectual and technical abilities to creative use; they constitute that "new working class" which is numerically expanding in modern society and is finding increasing moral dissatisfaction and decreasing power to control its own activity.

Although their sociological conditions, relationships to the economic structure, and ideal objectives are very different, the protestors who come from these different categories—students, dropouts, and the "new working class"—have nevertheless a common characteristic which draws them to protest against and reject the existing order. This characteristic is the rejection, on an individual level, of the American way of life in general and of all the by-products generated by the "system": affluence (enjoyed at the expense of a poor minority) carried to preposterous lengths by the vicious cycle of consumption; education, with its effects of mass stultification and its efforts to make individuals conform to stereotyped models; the undifferentiated use of erotic messages, accompanied by sexual repression and double moral standards; the cult of ownership and the accompanying loss of strong emotional ties with people.

This unity of negation which characterizes the new protest does not go against the democratic values proclaimed by American rhetoric, but against what Paul Goodman calls the "Empty Society," i.e., the incapability of a society at the height of its collective wealth and technological development to bring about conditions of greater material and spiritual freedom.

The unity on positive issues is more vague, although certain major goals are shared widely throughout the Movement. One of these is the rediscovery of the "worldly" value of life, which some have referred to as a "new hedonism," but which can be summed up more accurately as realization "here and now" of all possible conditions of happiness and freedom in a world liberated from the former slavery of labor and struggle against nature. There is also the need for total participation in the life of a community where education, work, and intelligence can be utilized for other than purely materialistic ends. There is the search for new relationships of individuals to one another and of individuals to institutions, relationships not dictated by purely functional needs but by more truly human values.

On the other hand, there are many basic disagreements. If it is possible to proceed to a generalization in a field where there is a great variety of positions and goals, we can use two conceptual categories as means of interpretation. On one hand, there are those who believe that the revolution needed today is a psychological one, and that the movement it is necessary to build must have an exclusively spiritual character. On the other hand, there are those involved in organizing political forces and changing the power relationships in the society, and their goal is the transformation of institutions.

Those who make up the first group, best exemplified by the psychedelic movement, although they represent an attitude that is also widespread elsewhere, reject politics, which is "used to gain power," and seek a "deeper vision of themselves and society." Although it is not accepted by all of them, their general philosophy may be summed up in the slogan "Turn On, Tune In, Drop Out," a process which is to be followed up by the building of a new society through nonpolitical means. "What we need to realize is that there can be, shall we say, a movement . . . a stirring among people . . . which can be *organically* designed instead of *politically* designed. It has no boss. Yet all the parts recognize each other in the same way as the cells of the body all cooperate together."[1]

The members of the second group, the "political" people, are those who developed all the organized movements we have discussed in the preceding chapters.

If we leave aside the various phenomena which become fashionable for a brief period only and those aspects of the Movement which are quickly incorporated into the advertising arsenal of consumer industry and the "swinging" style of public relations of Madison Avenue, a "life-style" can be seen to emerge from a significant portion of the new generation which, on the individual level, expresses itself in the search for a new morality and, on the collective level, in the form of a youth subculture or even a real counterculture.

In all the different components of the Movement, it seems that barriers between private and public life are being broken down, i.e., that the continuity between the psychological and social (or political) moments of existence is being affirmed. It is no accident that for many new radicals the choice of political involvement has coincided with the abandonment of fixed professional careers and "traditional" family groups and with the acceptance of prospectives which, not rarely, lead to prison sentences. Double standards, which in so many respects are an accepted condition of "normal" life, are rejected on every level. In this sense, the experimentation in the realms of sex and drugs, and particularly the open affirmation of their morality, are part of the necessary psychological break from prevalent modes of behavior, even though new values have not yet completely replaced the old ones. A tradition consistently based on the rejection of sex and pleasure, which were seen as negative things, is being replaced by the notion of the body itself as an integral element of the human patrimony. The widespread practice of cohabitation among young people seems to recall—on the level of custom rather than of ideological awareness—the old practice of the anarchists and socialists of the last century, who proved by their own way of living that they assumed individual responsibilities outside and beyond the institutions of the bourgeoisie. Experience with drugs, in itself, is really nothing but a means of accelerating the process of breaking with the past and searching for a genuine "inwardness" which social pressure constantly rejects in favor of a series of models for behavior. Marijuana has been the sign of rebellion, first of all, against the ethic of work and success which require control, outside discipline, and double standards.

---

[1] Alan Watts, "Changes," *San Francisco Oracle*, February 1967. The conversation among Allen Ginsberg, Timothy Leary, Gary Snyder, and Alan Watts, published in the *Oracle*, is the most important document on the coexistence of completely different goals and tendencies within the psychedelic movement itself.

"Anything that can be done chemically can be done in other ways. You don't need drugs to get high, but drugs do serve as a useful shortcut at certain stages of the training."[2] And this is precisely what the new generations are doing: looking for a shortcut to the transformation of personality structure and the building of a "new man."

Part of this new morality also consists of a wide search for specific qualities and values typical of different human conditions—sex, age, race—and for a reevaluation of them in the kind of society where there can be no dominant groups and modes of behavior. It is within this framework that one must consider the demands of young people and women for a role in society not defined in relation to the prevalent adult and male culture. Young people are making demands in the realms of economic opportunities, political rights, and social participation. The Women's Liberation Movement is, in turn, organized around all those aspects of life in which women in today's society are exploited, treated like consumer items and thrown back on activities considered "proper." Here also, as in other aspects of the Movement, psychology and politics are fused and the struggle for individual liberation coincides with a more general singling-out of the oppressive structures of the productive system.

The youth subculture or counterculture expresses all these attempts and experiments at the collective level. This culture has not yet taken a precise form, and for this reason passing fads and lasting values exist side by side: pop music, with its existential rhythms and its participatory potential, together with forms of dress and appearance which call attention to regained individuality; the tendency toward mysticism and Oriental cults which place their emphasis not on good and evil but on the discovery of a deeper self, together with rejection of material consumption and opposition to all technological development. These are all signs of a search taking place at the cultural level, a symptom more than a statement of opposition to the system of ethics some have identified with the "Western Judeo-Christian tradition," including Marxism, which has led to moral bankruptcy.

More generally, we may say that what is taking place is a process of redefinition of behavior, instincts, values, attitudes and mores, i.e., a collective process of building a new identity.

Toward a Parallel Society

A strong tendency to work outside of and in opposition to existing institutions pervades the Movement. This tendency manifests itself in diverse actions which have varying purposes; sometimes these begin before politics itself has been formed, creating the premises for its development. At other

2 William Burroughs, "Academy 23: A Deconditioning," *Village Voice*, July 6, 1967.

times, the actions are undertaken to complement political actions of a general nature, in an attempt to transform institutions and create new ones which can embody "here and now" that ideal of new values and new life-style which we have discussed before. At other times, finally, creating *ex novo* communities or institutions is the very means of rejecting not only the existing society but also any attempt to become involved in changing it.

We have already noted that, from the time of the first appearances of the new movements, "freedom schools" were begun in the South; in the North there were attempts at community organizing, and after the Berkeley revolt a free university was organized which soon became the model for other projects of the same type. These examples, in addition to being specifically alternative in content, were also concrete applications of the "participatory democracy" which at the time provided the methodological reference for the new radicals.

With the development of the new movements and the formation of more specific social groups than those the early "populist" phase of the New Left had concerned itself with, the idea of parallel or alternative structures also evolved.

In their own way, even the hippies are creating their own counter-communities: groups gathered in small rural or urban communes. They are attempting to overcome the usual "bourgeois" style of living in organized family groups and emphasize such psychological elements as communion of feelings, experiences, and the joy of living among similar closely knit groups. Their objectives lie within the group rather than with institutional demands on the society at large.

At the other extreme are plans for the creation of alternative institutions which function not as symbolic elements but on the complex levels within society. The attempt is to relate technical instrumentalities to the political movement in a mutual enrichment of radical ideological experiences. The plan for the Movement for a Democratic Society to organize professional people and technicians to challenge existing organizations and/or to create counterinstitutions exemplifies the way some radical groups are trying to provide a theoretical framework and a political outlet for a tendency already manifesting itself spontaneously.[3]

In both of these cases, as in the whole range of attempts to build the foundations of a new structure with which to oppose and substitute for the old one, the phenomenon no longer touches only isolated exceptions, but a significant minority of people in the new generations.

The mirror of the growth of this parallel society is the "underground" press—itself an alternative structure, the most highly developed and suc-

---

[3] Bob Gottlieb and Marge Piercy, "Movement for a Democratic Society—Beginning to Begin to Begin," *Radicals in the Professions Newsletter*, March 1968.

cessful one so far. It began in 1965 with the birth of the first two newspapers of this new type, the *Los Angeles Free Press* and the *Berkeley Barb*. The underground, or free press, as it is sometimes called, burst forth during the years 1967 and 1968, when hundreds of new papers appeared not only in the large metropolitan areas where there is an avant-garde audience, but also in small communities, sometimes associated with colleges and universities. It is impossible to calculate the number of new publications or their circulation, because the underground press is a continually changing, decentralized and diversified phenomenon. The Liberation News Service (LNS) in September 1968, for example, listed about 400 papers, of which 111 were called "underground" and 44, "movement." Whatever the exact number of publications and the general breadth of circulation (330,000, according to *The Wall Street Journal* of April 1968; 4.6 million, according to Marshall Bloom of LNS; and 5 million, according to the *Underground Press Directory* published in autumn 1968), this journalistic network certainly represents an alternative structure on a nationwide scale.

In the underground press, as in the Movement as a whole, important distinctions in a political evaluation are necessary. There is the part of the press which performs a service for all the groups in the subculture of protestors and dropouts in a certain geographical area (a typical example is the *Berkeley Barb*); there is the kind which is clearly psychedelically oriented (the *San Francisco Oracle* and the *East Village Other* of New York); and finally there is the political type (*San Francisco Express Times; Rat* of New York) which are involved in formulating and informing radically oriented public opinion. Still, there are certain characteristics common to many of these publications. For the first time in the United States, a press which expresses a culture of opposition (with its undeniable political-radical character and its by-products of conformism "anti") is reaching a mass audience, certainly a few million individuals, who have never before been exposed to left-wing publications. It represents an independent economic structure which cannot be subjugated by pressures from the usual economic or financial channels or forced to alter the manner in which its production, distribution, and publicity are organized. Finally, this means of regulating a mass-communications medium is also significant from the aspect of internal democracy: very often the editors of an underground paper are also its owners and participate in determining the line the paper is to take without there being any separation or subordination between managers and managed.

The underground press is the example of how new alternative structures can begin to vie with existing ones, replacing them not only in the technical sense but also in the quality of their direction. The tendency toward decentralized programs run by the resources and creativeness of particular groups is itself an indication of the kind of strictly anticentralized and libertarian work carried on by the Movement and the New Left: there is no Watchword handed down from Washington or New York, no Correct Analysis, but a common policy which develops from below on the basis of original, independent experiences.

The press is not the only existing parallel structure working along these lines, although it is the most successful one so far. There are press services operating on a national basis, such as Liberation News Service (LNS) and the Underground Press Syndicate (UPS), which, with their information services and mutual exchange of material, fulfill and increase the possibilities for independent journalism. Other means of expression and mass communication are flourishing as well; there is cinema (Newsreel), theater (Guerrilla Theatre), radio and television (Radio Free People), etc.; attempts are even being made to apply computer technology in a radical context (Meta Information Applications).

The development of autonomous structures is a sign that the transformations taking place in American society do not concern only life-style and the psychological needs of a certain number of individuals or an attempt by a small group of radical activists to "gain power." It is rather an indication of the vitality of the Movement, to the extent that its membership and bases are numerous, varied, and active, each component maintaining its own autonomy and independence. The ongoing tendency is, in a certain sense, utopian, because the intention is to build a new society in the lap of the old. At the moment, there are only a few threads with which to create this new fabric; some are rapidly expanding, such as the communications media; others, like those based on the alternative uses of technical, scientific and professional personnel, are just beginning. On the whole, there is no doubt that a basic movement does exist, and the new fabric is getting larger.

In all cases where two societies—old and new—coexist, the tendency of the established and consolidated institutions is either to incorporate the new ones by assimilation or to crush them by force. Today, in the United States, both tendencies are present. When mutual incompatibility intensifies the conflict, both the method of control and that of repression will probably be perfected and brought fully to bear. Therefore, the contest is open: the creation of structures from below is a guarantee of the strength of the new forces, in the numbers of people involved, the energies which have been mobilized, the value of the patterns and examples provided by the new experiments. However, these are not enough. Dual powers, counterinstitutions, parallel structures are the necessary but not sufficient conditions for the construction of a new society, particularly where power, such as military and industrial power, is concentrated. It is also necessary to build a movement which will work toward the transformation of the central powers of the state and be able to offer tentative solutions to the immense organizational problems which a complex, supertechnological society presents. The response to systematic rationalization and concentration of power can only be anti-authoritarian and decentralized, as is the response being developed by New Lefts everywhere. The response to the failure of the "systems" which have proposed the Final Solution can only be anti-systematic and antitotalist, as is the response which emerges in some of the alternative structures of the New Left in the United States. But it is also necessary to resolve the problem of the general strategy the new forces are to follow. It is not a minor problem, and the American New Left has not yet solved it.

*   *   *

If we can, in a single phrase, define the New Left as the continuing struggle for freedom, which concentrates on those crucial points where antifreedom is most clearly visible in America today, it is obvious that such a struggle cannot be guided by a definitive vision of future society, i.e., a program for that hypothetical future time when it will take power. The objection to the New Left's lack of a concrete alternative program, held by those who support the system but at the same time would like to change some aspects of it, is actually quite naïve. A movement must be judged according to the way it carries on its political struggles, in other words, by what it is able to accomplish historically, and not by what it professes. In this sense, the New Left is full of suggestive possibilities, even though, as we have already pointed out, these exist more as potential than as consciously held goals.

The New Left has supplanted the Marxist models of dictatorship of the proletariat and supremacy of a single class in governing the state by the widely shared goal of decentralization of administration and economic bodies and social institutions. The concept of ownership of the means of production is giving way to an emphasis on participation in decision-making processes which affect the lives of individuals in the various institutions of society, and therefore on the realization, not so much of a "socialist state," as of a society which all citizens can take part in running. The importance of economic structures in the struggle for freedom is taking on a new dimension. The emphasis is on making available effective instruments with which people can control their own lives; in other words, a psychological rather than a purely political or economic dimension. The society dominated by the work ethic is being replaced by one in which creativity and imagination can play an important role in the realization of human potentialities. Faced with the fetishes of economic and technological development as absolute goods, people are seeking new productive arrangements which will permit the creation of a postscarcity economy in which "human activity can be defined by man's own consciously determined needs, and not by needs determined from the outside," and connected with the myth of expansion. In rejecting the concept of rationality that has grown out of the gradual identification of *homo humanus* with *homo economicus*, whose basic law is material incentive and competition, this Movement with its imprecise boundaries is striving toward a society in which behavior and instinct will be inspired by love, brotherhood, and freedom. So the New Left, like every left-wing movement worthy of the name, is introducing a necessary utopian dimension into the society of today.

The Creation of an Alternative Society

Joseph Berke

America is the end product of two thousand years of EUROPEAN-CHRISTIAN culture, now synonymous with what is called THE WEST. For our very survival AMERICA must be destroyed.

The destruction/DE-STRUCTURING of America has begun. At this moment many cracks in the monolith are evident. Their presence has been announced by the spontaneous development of MICRO-REVOLUTIONARY groups throughout the West—"COUNTER" INSTITUTIONS whose existence subverts the social-economic-political roles prescribed by advance bourgeois society for itself. These will lead to the creation of an ALTERNATIVE and COUNTER CULTURE.

What is necessary is to recognize the importance of these groups in the unfolding of a new basis for revolutionary social change. What must follow is the destruction/DE-STRUCTURING of our entire civilization and the movement toward a fundamentally different, necessarily utopian basis for our collective experience.

First, look at this WEST, and examine what happens to those who live in it, as well as to those external to it who are trapped in its wake. In doing so, I will refer, in particular, to the situation in the United States which is prototypical for the West as a whole. Citizens of the United States may have achieved the HIGHEST standards of material living, or not,[1] but they have achieved the LOWEST QUALITY OF HUMAN LIFE.

It is the quality of life which expresses such questions as how much does a person enjoy his existence, how well do people get on with each other, and how do they treat other nonhuman objects.

For us the answer to these questions is simple. The relations of

---

FROM *Counter Culture*, edited by Joseph Berke, published by Peter Owen Ltd, London, 1969, pp. 14–18; 28–34. Reprinted by permission.

[1] Mass poverty is a pervasive feature of life in the United States. Over 80,000,000 people (that is, 40% of the entire population) live at a poverty or sub-poverty level. Of these, over 10,000,000 are actually starving, wasting away from chronic hunger and malnutrition. For further discussion of this, refer to Michael Harrington's *The Other America* and the *Report of the Citizens' Board of Inquiry into Hunger and Malnutrition in the United States*, 1968. [For excerpts from Harrington, see section 8 of this book—Ed.]

people(s) toward one another are characterized by the uninterrupted and highly organized application of violence and destruction. The country is split into irreconcilable subunits who no longer communicate with each other except to threaten mutual annihilation. Rape and pollution of natural resources are indiscriminate and occur on a massive scale. Every single person is affected by this. No one escapes—whether rich, middle class or poor, young or old, man or woman. What differs is how you experience it, and this depends on how much money you have.

The prime function of wealth is its use as an anaesthetic against the circumstances of living. As a group, but certainly not in terms of any given individual, those with the most wealth think they are the best off. Those with the least wealth know they are not, and in the absence of this anaesthetic, are most directly exposed to the systematic violence, both personal and social, which is generated by the structure of American society. The net effect is a massive self-destruction—explosive, barely controlled, internalized in our bodies, which, in desperation, is projected around the rest of the world. It was not an accident that the United States was the first to develop the atomic bomb. It was typical.

Internally, the principal social correlates are the very high rates of suicide, murder, alcoholism, use of tranquillizers and sedatives,[2] automobile accidents (*themselves the major form of suicide or murder*), crime, divorce, and disease. Most directly, the violence is perpetrated by people against people,[3] and by institutions against people.[4] Externally, the whole world lies prostrate under the yoke of the American war machine, necessi-

[2] Tranquillizers and sedatives are used by one out of four people in the United States (50,000,000+). In 1967, $510 million were spent on prescriptions for them. Eight hundred thousand pounds of barbiturates were sold (2,109 pounds a day). Ten billion amphetamine tablets ("pep pills," "happy pills," "speed") were produced, many used to offset the effects of them. Report in the *International Herald Tribune*, 28th November, 1968.

[3] In 1967, there were over 19,000 reported deaths by gunshot, and at least half of those killed were murdered by a member of his or her immediate family. Report in the *International Herald Tribune* at the time of the assassination of Martin Luther King. At present in the United States about 1,000 people are killed and 70,000 seriously injured on the highways *each week*. Report in the *International Herald Tribune*, 12th April, 1969.

[4] Illustrative is institutionalized racialism or the organized murder of old people. In the United States a comparison of black/white mortality rates at childbirth shows that two to three times as many black babies die at childbirth than their white neighbours. Similarly, the life expectancy of a coloured person is five to ten years less than his white neighbour (depending on the region of the country). Local and state mental hospitals are now the favoured means for getting rid of old people, who are the waste products of the American way of life. Unwanted, uncared for and unnecessary, the only problem is how to dispense with them as quickly and unobtrusively as possible. Easy, send them to the bughouse. For example, in certain states, the LD 50 for old people sent to mental .hospital is six months. This means that for every 1,000 old folk sent to a state hospital in a given week, within six months, 50% of them, that is 500, will be dead. (The average life expectancy of these people before commitment is between five to twenty years.) For further discussion refer to Jules Henry's *Culture Against Man*. (New York: Random House, 1963).

tated (?) by the expansion of trade, the blood-sucking of the Third World, and the violence endemic to American society. (If you can't kill 'em here, do it there.) For the United States this century has been one vast WAR. It continues to be one vast WAR. Americans have not seen peace for more than fifty years.

Periods of cold war, that is when actual fighting is not taking place, are merely interludes between battles—major battles such as World War I and World War II and minor battles or skirmishes such as our interventions in China, the Congo, Cuba, Dominican Republic, Greece, Guatemala, Iran, Korea, Lebanon, the Philippines, Russia, VIETNAM, etc. etc. These interludes allow for the regroupment and resupplying of forces, while hostilities and military expansion continue at fever pace.

The United States has become the mainstay of death and destruction throughout the world, whenever it occurs, as in VIETNAM, or has occurred, as in Korea, Cuba, the Dominican Republic; or will occur, the next country after VIETNAM.

The United States exists solely to create, develop, feed, encourage and participate in wars, anywhere in the world, all over the world.[5]

What we must realize is that VIOLENCE, WAR, POVERTY and RACISM are integral parts of the social-economic-political system which is the United States. What we must realize is that this VIOLENCE, WAR, POVERTY, RACISM and DESTRUCTION exist independently of any stated policy of the American government. They exist independently of any given person in political power. It does not matter whether a Republican, Democrat or Independent is elected to any given post. It does not matter whether said person is a radical, liberal, conservative or reactionary. The VIOLENCE,[6] the WAR, the POVERTY, the RACISM, the DESTRUCTION will CONTINUE. These are the components of the American way of life. These are aspects of the very organization and structure of American society. These happen regardless of whether ANYONE wants them to happen. They cannot be prevented within the terms by which American society operates.

What is true for the United States is also true for all of Europe and all other Western countries. The United States is the child of Western Europe. Any single aspect of life in the United States may be magnified or

---

[5] For documentation of this—how, why, where, and when, facts and figures—refer to: (1) *Pentagonism: A Substitute for Imperialism* (New York: Grove Press, 1969), by Juan Bosch; (2) *Report from Iron Mountain on the Possibility and Desirability of Peace* (Penquin); (3) *Monopoly Capital* (Monthly Review Press), by Paul A. Baran and Paul M. Sweezy. [See excerpts from *Monopoly Capital* in section 9 of this book—Ed.]

[6] The average American between his second and sixty-fourth year spends 3,000 entire days (nearly nine years of his life) watching television. These TV programmes contain (on the average) a violent incident every fourteen minutes and a killing every three-quarters of an hour. (This is equivalent to being present at/participating in more than 300,000 violent incidents and 100,000 killings.) Evidence presented to the United States Congress, National Commission on the Causes and Prevention of Violence, quoted in *The Observer* (5th January, 1969).

minimized in any other Western country, but, as a whole the picture is the same. NO single person or change of policy in any Western country or countries can affect this.

By America I now indicate not only the United States, but all of the Western world—that which is interrelated and interlocked by a web, a network of shared social, economic and political practices.[7]

We can only conclude that the WEST—its structure—has to be dismantled piece by piece, not only in the United States, but wherever Western hegemony exists.

IT IS OUR SOLE TASK TO ACCOMPLISH THIS AND TO PROVIDE FOR OURSELVES AND OUR FUTURE IN SO DOING.

This work has already begun, generated out of the conflicts and contradictions of Western society. It is rooted in innumerable projects of social erosion and practical self-survival which are decentralized, heterogeneous, self-supporting, and non-participatory in the parent system. It is exemplified by the tens of thousands who have "dropped out" and begun to engage in spontaneous social experiment: the commune and community, collective living and working; the anti-university, free university, critical university; the anti-hospital; the "underground" communication and publishing networks—all seeds of a counter culture. And it is exemplified by the rapidly emerging political consciousness of the black people in the United States, as expressed in the Black Power movement. Its roots are the young—of the white middle class and the black ghetto dwellers, with a similar orientation but different emphasis, dependent on class and colour.

THIS is the first expression of a historic development of cultural-political guerrilla warfare, whose purpose is to utilize the contradictions within the West as a system of social organization and operation to destroy it AND AT THE SAME TIME CREATE A NEW WAY OF LIFE FOR OURSELVES.

The principle is simple. Contradictions within the system create conflict, whether intra- or inter-personal. People respond and in so doing confront the discrepancy between themselves and the repressive demands of the state. The basic rule is to avoid any head-on clash with the state and/or state institutions, but to deal with the overwhelming power of the state by forcing it to respond to you on your own terms. Actions are decentralized and unpredictable, multifocal, and heterogeneous. The result: PERSONAL— "dropping out"; SOCIAL—*counter society, Black Power, Student Power;* POLITICAL—*organization.* Each generates counter-repressive measures on the part of the state, which are confronted, in turn. The issues are immediate, direct and flow from the personal experience of the participants.

At all times, but especially at the early stages of the struggle, a major function of these actions is to penetrate, demystify the confusion of social reality, that black veil perpetrated by the institutional infrastructure of

[7] This web is exemplified by the ever-increasing number of international corporations whose operations extend far beyond a given country, or even group of countries.

the country. We can only comprehend the existing economic, social, cultural and political forces and their relation to one another and their relation to ourselves by engaging them and forcing them to reveal themselves. Each confrontation lifts the veil that much more and points to further areas of contradiction, conflict and confrontation.

What we do is to penetrate, de-structure and destroy the system and at the same time re-structure, create it anew in our own terms, and vice versa. THESE ARE INSEPARABLE. One does not wait for the other. In the beginning, each act of confrontation, of resistance, or rebellion—either of one person, two, or many—exists as a break in the infrastructure.

The system is honeycombed as a Swiss cheese, eroded from within, until it is no longer able to sustain itself. The crisis comes. The system collapses and is quickly replaced by the new social units which have been organized and now function collectively—that is, at this point the revolution *manifests* itself.

Of great importance is that even when the larger parameters of power are taken over, the process-movement of criticism, conflict and confrontation must continue. You destroy the structure in order to create the structure in order to destroy the structure in order to create the structure. . . . [Ellipsis in original, not indicating elision there. F. L.]

THE STRUCTURE IS OURSELVES. THE REVOLUTION IS OURSELVES. THE REVOLUTION IS THE REVOLUTION.

THIS REVOLUTION NEVER OCCURS, BUT ALWAYS IS IN THE PROCESS OF OC-CURRING. THIS REVOLUTION IS CHANGE. THIS REVOLUTION IS THE MOVEMENT BY WHICH ANY INDIVIDUAL OR SOCIETY CONFRONTS, CREATES AND RECREATES ITSELF.

*   *   *

. . . At this moment, the framework of current cultural/political events can be seen to encompass four phases of development and expansion.

Phase 1:
The Invisible Insurrection—Cultural Conflict
The Reawakening of Black Power
Multifocal Confrontation

In the United States this began in the early 1950s. The single most important feature of this period is the large number of young people who "dropped out" of school and work in order to wander around the country, often turning on to various psychoactive drugs such as pot and LSD, (itself facilitating the process of "dropping out" and living as-catch-can). In doing so, they escape the social strait-jacket of middle-class life and initiated an Invisible Insurrection of the young.

It was invisible because the political effect of their action was masked by the form of their dissent. They were the vanguards of the tens of thousands who now respond to the American way of life by running away, dropping out, opting out, and making a go of their lives in their own terms.

And in order to survive (easy on a marginal basis because of the wealth of the country), they have entered into a wide variety of social experiments in communal organization, sex, education, even medical care—THE COUNTER CULTURE —which demonstrates the ways and means of breaking down the structure of middle-class life—both externally and internally. (Of necessity, the communes are an ongoing experiment in social therapy whereby the commune members have to exorcise past social wounds—inter-personal games and gamesmanship—in order to coexist with other people.)

Furthermore, these varied elements of the COUNTER CULTURE have generated a tremendous amount of conflict with local, state, and general authorities which has served to educate the participants as to the exercise of power (and violence) in American society and to point to ways of undermining it.[23] The confrontations with the power structure, accelerated by the war in Vietnam and the domestic consequences of it, has led an unwilling middle class to criticize directly American society and the way things are run. It has forced them to politicize their dissent.[24]

At the same time that white kids were fleeing home and school, black kids from the Northern ghettoes and Southern towns began to confront the oppressive position that was theirs within the terms of American society. For them it was not drop out but drop in—to themselves. They soon saw that the point was not to integrate into a corrosive white bourgeois world—just putting them into a new but equally vicious bag—but to rediscover their own history. This reverberated with another major feature of America, which cannot be explained away by poverty or caste. It is the fact of their own cultural castration, as has been perpetrated on every single non-Aryan people with whom the West has come in contact.

Black Power is the historic awakening of their sense of peoplehood, and self-respect. Concomitantly, the black people have become a major revolutionary force in the United States both in terms of their own struggle and their linking up with the revolutionary struggle in the Third World, particularly Cuba and Vietnam.

[23] That thousands of people should be harassed and sent to jail for the use of harmless mind stimulants such as marijuana exposes the underlying political struggle. It is not the drug itself, but the effect of the drug which is a threat to THEM. Pot makes it easier to see what they cannot tolerate.

[24] An example is the Boston, Mass., hippie paper *Avatar*. Initially, it featured articles on drugs, sex, mysticism, psychedelics. But almost at the same time as its first issue came out, it began to be harassed by the Boston police, till no copies were allowed to be sold in the stores and the kids who peddled them on the streets were being arrested and sent to jail. Concomitant with this the tone of the paper began to change. It published many articles questioning the tactics of the authorities and gradually expanded its criticism to include all aspects of the city administration and government as well as the Vietnam war, national policy, etc. In the space of a couple of months it was politicized, and now most of the paper is concerned with draft resistance, confrontation with the authorities, etc. It has recently expanded its coverage to include a New York edition. [Date referred to is 1969.—Ed.]

Thus, the *Phase* 1 consists of a multilevel opting out from our parent culture and the creation of a counter society. (The term is similar for both white and black, the content differs.) It looks toward a spiralling series of conflicts and confrontations whose logical purpose can only be a struggle to revolutionize—that is, recreate society.

Phase 2:
Expansion
Organization
Planned Confrontation

We have just begun to enter this phase of events, which is characterized by the large-scale movement of people out of bourgeois society and into a counter society which they develop for themselves, encompassing far more vigorous experiment and social invention. All manner of communes and communities spring up, especially in the cities. They become self-supporting. They associate themselves with each other for self-protection (from the authorities) and to provide mutual services. There is a continued emphasis on figuring out ways of living in small groups in a non-authoritarian, non-ego hang-up manner, and always with an intense inter-action to break down hard programmed life patterns.

A second generation appears who are not sent to "schools" but make their way in "anti-schools" created among the communes to take care of the young. All work is shared and services provided free.[25] Communal shops are set up to provide goods. Free Universities, Anti-Universities counter, bypass existing educational channels. The "underground" communications network is extended. It includes newspapers, magazines, books, radio, TV and theatre.

The total non-involvement in the system is part of the guerrilla war waged against the system and is emphasized by the non-payment of taxes, as well as the refusal to consume non-subsistence, that is, unnecessary products or engage in "work." *The technocracy is vacated.*

Concomitantly the black people become increasingly militant. There occurs a massive draft refusal and organized occupation of the ghettoes. They set up their own schools, stores and communal facilities—the elements of a COUNTER CULTURE.

During this period, an increasing number of planned provocations are directed against state institutions. These take the form of a quick, direct and dispersed jab, such as temporary occupation of a television station to mobile demonstrations in the streets, jamming traffic.

There develops increasing contact between white and black militants, as well as like-minded groups throughout the West and Third World, to provide for mutual aid and defence, this being necessitated by the escala-

---

[25] Facilitated by utilizing existing "welfare" services as well as the "guaranteed annual income" seen to be forthcoming in the States.

tion of violent clashes with the authorities and their hired hoodlums—the police.[26]

Phase 2 realizes itself with a broadly expanding and militant Counter Society in the United States, and the beginning of such in all parts of the West. The large numbers of people involved pose a serious threat to all governments because of their disruptive effect on the economy and pressures on existing institutions.[27] The West reacts with ever-increasing violent and repressive measures.

Phase 3:
Crisis

Collapse of the Bourgeois State

The movement of people into a counter society and the erosion of social control will create a highly unstable and explosive situation. This will culminate in the taking of political power from THEM which may take the form of either: (1) a pre-planned confrontation, i.e. general strike accompanied by the occupation of all state institutions; or (2) a spontaneous crisis precipitated by police violence in attempting to enforce some bureaucratic regulation, i.e. closing down a commune for infringement or breaking up a demonstration.[28]

In theory, a combination of both is likely, especially as the government will try to maintain itself in power through military means, this to be dealt with by organized and armed resistance of the people.

In practice, one cannot say how it will happen, only that it will hap-

[26] As indicated by black and white militants running together as candidates on the Peace and Freedom and Freedom and Peace Parties during the 1968 United States presidential campaign. More important is the growing alliance between the Black Panthers and Yippies. (Panthers have begun to protect Yippies from attack in Haight-Ashbury. White students have joined the Panthers in attacking the racist administration of San Francisco State College.)

[27] Mass refusal to consume unnecessary goods undermines the basis of the consumer economy—ever-expanding demand. The warehouses are clogged and the factories grind to a halt. Mass refusal to work or contribute to existing institutions leaves them powerless, an empty façade, unable to exert their prime function of social control and manipulation. We can therefore anticipate laws requiring people to buy X amount of goods per year, or patronize Y institution, Z number of hours per month or face fine or imprisonment.

[28] The *Mechanism* of spontaneous crisis is illustrated by events in Czechoslovakia and France in 1968. In Czechoslovakia, without prior indication, communications personnel decided to liberate television, radio and the newspapers for free discussion and criticism of the government. This precipitated the downfall of a tyrannical regime and the liberalization of political life. In France, the demands of students seeking reform of the universities occasioned a chain of events leading to explosion. The first links in the chain were simple requests for change, forcibly rebuffed by the authorities. Logical escalation of the situation led to the students occupying what had previously been the seat of their own oppression—that is, the concrete structure of the university; whereupon the police were called to dislodge them, whereupon violent and massive demonstrations broke out involving the whole of the country. Similar situations are likely to develop in France again in 1969 and in Spain and Mexico.

pen. The form is solely dependent on social conditions existent at that time. The result is a historical necessity.

Phase 4:
  The Counter Society
  The Revolution Continues

The withering away of the state is the withering away of its institutional infrastructure. This is concretized as the developing social experiments—anti-institutions—of the Counter Culture become the only effective media of social exchange and function. It is confirmed by the inability of the state forcibly to maintain an operational façade. What the new "society" will be like, i.e. its content, cannot be predicted in advance because it is based on a multiplicity of personal and inter-personal transactions which have yet to occur. However, its form—that is, its relational structure—will clearly follow from what is currently happening. As such, it will be heterogeneous, decentralized, non-authoritarian and freely providing of all essential goods and services to all its members.

The withering away of the STATE does not mark the success of the revolution, but, most tangibly, ITS BEGINNING. Only at this point will people no longer need to be concerned with THEIR power and structure (organization) but be free to focus on the central issue—that is, their own power and their own structure. Conflict will continue to occur between divers groups reflecting their particular circumstances and/or their degree of understanding and commitment to the revolution. Criticism of all existing social practices and institutions (anti-institutions) will increase.

The fundamental difference between previous attempts at changing society[29] and the current scene is that revolution is no longer imprisoned in itself as a single static event. Revolution realizes itself as continuous conflict. It asserts itself in the tearing down of old and reified structures both in the external world and as internalized in the individual.

The organization of the West is not a static structure, but rather a system of relationships which is reflected in the internal make-up of every person in the society. Concomitantly the internal make-up—that is, structure, relational system—of every individual is the foundation stone of society. In other words, individual structure recapitulates the structure of society and societal structure recapitulates the structure of the individual. This is why the CULTURAL MEDIA—family, school, work, religion, etc.— are so important in the maintenance of social stasis, that is, the *status quo*. The similar (and inter-digitating) relational systems embodied in each of these institutions[30] are internalized by each of us in the process of growing

---

[29] There has never been a successful revolution in the West. Either they failed to achieve their political objectives as in Germany or France, or they degenerated into subtle parodies of the previous regime as in the Soviet Union.

[30] This structure is even expressed in the way we walk, talk, hold ourselves erect, or not. It is embodied as a pattern of muscle tension, most concretely known as individual

up, and are the means by which the state perpetuates itself. After all, how can you attack, or even question, society—i.e. what happens out there— if, at the same time, you are attacking yourself—Mummy, Daddy, Teacher, God and the relations between them and you, as well as all else carried inside.[31]

It is at this level that the revolution really takes place, for if people cannot find some way collectively to destroy—de-structure this system of operations inside themselves—then the overthrow of the state degenerates into a simple power struggle between X and Y with the nature of society remaining the same.[32] And it is at this level that what is now happening is qualitatively different from previous attempts at revolution.

The destruction-destructuring of the system in people is fundamentally a political event.

It is the means by which any given person exorcizes, and gets rid of, THE WEST, which he carries inside himself by virtue of his having been born into it and it into him. The way this takes place, and the basis for a re-structuring of oneself—that is, one's internal and external relationships —is the cultural/political struggle now taking place, a transactional spiral-ling of criticism, conflict and confrontation. It is epitomized by the opting out from society and the social experiments of the Counter Culture.

These are the first steps in our liberation. These are the means by which we can deal with our lives—right now, concretely, here.

---

character. Relationship between character and society is discussed by Wilhelm Reich in *Character Analysis*, as well as in many other of his works.

[31] The family ("The Family is the Bulwark of Society") refers to the organization of a relationship between parent and child. This is repeated in the school where the teacher acts as a parent surrogate, or the Church (God As Big Daddy) or even in the mental hospital whose structure mimics what takes place at home. (See *Asylums* by Erving Goffman). The points raised here have developed out of discussion with Dr. R. D. Laing, Dr. David Cooper and their colleagues over the past three years. See R. D. Laing "Family and Individual Structure" in *The Predicament of the Family*, ed. Peter Lomas, and Dr. Laing's opening address to the Dialectics of Liberation Congress, en-titled "The Obvious," in the proceedings of the Congress. [David Cooper (ed.) *To Free a Generation* (New York: Collier Books, 1969)—Ed.]

[32] As mentioned, the best example of this is the Soviet Union. Those who over-threw the Czarist government, while motivated by high ideals, were not able to deal with their own internal make-up (patterned by growing up in Czarist Russia). What resulted is a society whose political structure closely mimics the Czarist state—highly centralized, bureaucratic and authoritarian.

The Revolutionary Movement in France

Gabriel and Daniel Cohn-Bendit

... In Nanterre, the first term of the "historic" year of 1967/68 saw a student strike which went far beyond the traditional political and union framework. Some 10,000 to 12,000 of us boycotted all lectures in order to force the authorities to improve our working conditions. This "model strike" as *Le Figaro* called it, was not, in effect, anything but a protest against overcrowding. . . .

*   *   *

The second term brought a series of incidents, most of them the spontaneous expression of widespread student dissatisfaction. The "Missoffe affair" during the opening of the swimming pool at the end of January 1968 will long be remembered, because this banal incident had wide repercussions. An exceedingly stupid minor police official (whom we salute in passing) started extradition proceedings against D. Cohn-Bendit, who had accused Missoffe, the Minister for Youth, of talking like a Hitler Youth. By way of retaliation, the students stuck up photographs of plainclothes policemen mingling with members of the faculty, and also denounced the administration and the Dean as so many "tools of the prefecture." A convincing demonstration of solidarity and of protest against the proposed expulsion of Cohn-Bendit ended in scuffles with the riot police whom the Dean had called in. A short battle, in which students bombarded the police with anything handy, ended in victory: the police beat a hasty retreat. But the students had felt the iron fist under the liberal glove of the university.

In fact, M. Grappin, the Dean, was not the "Nazi" people made him out to be but a "good" man of the Left. Our struggle was not one against Fascism as such but against *bourgeois* authoritarianism. The mediocrity of university teaching is no accident, but reflects the life style of a civilization in which culture itself has become a marketable commodity and in which the absence of all critical faculties is the safest guarantee of "profitable specialization of university studies." The only way to oppose this type of stupidity is to attack all those academic restrictions whose only justification is that they exist: curricula; tests; set lectures and competitive entrance examinations.

Why Sociologists?

It was against this background that the events of 22 March 1968 must be viewed. Towards the middle of March, students in the department of social psychology, finding their courses too academic, decided to boycott the examinations and they sealed their decision by singing the Internationale. At the same time, a leaflet was distributed on the campus. It was called: "Why do we need sociologists?"

*   *   *

The 22 March Movement

On Friday, 22 March, following the arrest of six militants of the National Vietnam Committee, a crowd of students assembled quite spontaneously for a protest at Nanterre. At the end of the meeting, it was decided to occupy the administrative building. That evening, more than 150 students, of whom at least 50 per cent were politically uncommitted, met in the Staff Common Room and carried on a heated debate until two in the morning. (The Union of Communist Students naturally washed its hands of the whole affair.) The results of the discussion were summarized in a statement, 5,000 copies of which were distributed the next day.

Action and Reaction

Following a demonstration organized by the National Vietnam Committee, several demonstrators have been arrested in the street or in their homes, and charged with organizing attacks on American buildings in Paris. Once again we have come face to face with the usual police repression. After the invasion of Nanterre and Nantes by plain-clothes cops—
THE BLACK LISTS;
After the arrest and imprisonment of thirty workers and students in Caen;
After continuous raids, searches and arrests of students inside the university, a further step—
the arrest of militants no longer stops with the end of demonstration, but is continued by house arrests.
For us this is no mere coincidence. The authorities have been driven into a corner; capitalism is badly in need of repair. To achieve this end, the ruling class has seen fit to tighten up the reins. It now:
—challenges the workers' right of association
—nibbles away at social security
—tries to run society like an army
—introduces psychosociological techniques into industry in a desperate attempt to play down class conflicts (some of us are being trained for this very task).

Capitalism Can No Longer Conceal Its Hand

We must stop challenging capitalism by means of *outdated* techniques.

The Socialist Wilson has clamped down on England and now de Gaulle is clamping down on us. It is too late for the kind of peaceful procession organized by the SNESUP (University Teachers' Union) for next Thursday.

We have to thrash out the problems inside the university and act right where we work.

We call on you to transform the 29th into a vast debate on
—*Capitalism in 1968 and the workers' struggles*
—*University and Anti-University*
—*The Anti-Imperialist Struggle*
—*The Workers' and Students' Struggle in the East and the West.*

We shall accordingly occupy Block C and divide for discussions in the various lecture halls.

As the authorities are becoming more and more brazenly brutal we are forced to become increasingly militant ourselves. We shall demonstrate our determination not to be cowed by holding a demonstration outside the Prefecture of *Hauts-de-Seine.*

Resolution passed by 142 students, occupying the Administrative Block of Nanterre with 2 against and 3 abstentions.

On reading this proclamation, the university authorities took fright and their fright turned into panic when, by way of preparing for the 29th, we plastered the walls with tracts, placards and slogans, some of which caused a real sensation.

"Professors, you are past it and so is your culture!"

"When examined, answer with questions!"

"Please leave the Communist Party as clean on leaving as you would like to find it on entering."

The challenge of these slogans was one which forced people to take a stand. The authorities, no less than the Stalinists, were furious and tried to incite the staff of the faculty against the "terrorist minority." The library was closed in order to stop alleged thefts; there was a stay-in strike by the maintenance staff.

Under pressure from above, from neo-Fascist groups who had sworn to exterminate the revolutionary "rabble," and from reactionary lecturers, the Dean, on Thursday, 28 March, one week after the closure of the University of Warsaw, ordered the suspension of lectures and of laboratory work until the following Monday. Three hundred students assembled immediately after this announcement and decided not to leave but to spend the next day drafting a political manifesto to be published on 2 April. Having made up our minds to introduce politics into the campus, we were not going to retreat like a flock of frightened sheep at a bark from the sheepdog.

The weather helped us—the 29 March was a glorious and sunny day. A large police guard ringed the campus, while five hundred students divided into discussion groups on the lawn in front of the closed faculty doors. The gentlemen of the press were completely at a loss to understand what was going on; they had been led to expect a small band of anarchist bomb-throwers with long hair, and what they found instead was more than five hundred students seriously discussing the fundamental problems of our age.

On Monday, 1 April, second year sociology students decided, after a vote, to boycott their current examinations. Then they passed a resolution condemning sociology as a capitalist fraud. Meanwhile the professors themselves were at loggerheads, for while some (particularly in the Faculty of Letters and Social Science) were in favour of opening one of the lecture halls for political discussions, others (Faculty of History) wanted the "ringleaders" arrested.

Tuesday, 2 April, was a great day for the students. We turned down the small room put at our disposal by the Dean and faced the administration with a *fait accompli:* we took over the large lecture theatre for our inaugural meeting, which was attended by more than 1,200 students including Karl-Dietrich Wolff representing the German SDS.

* * *

On 2 April, we decided to set aside 2 and 3 May for the study of imperialism, with special film shows, discussions in committee and in general assembly, etc. But it did not work out like that. Threatened by an attack from such semi-Fascist groups as *Occident*, we had instead to see to our defences, and arm ourselves with stones and other improvised weapons.

Panic-stricken, misinformed and above all under pressure from some of the professors, the Dean ordered Nanterre to be closed once again. Moreover, seven of the most militant students of the 22 March Movement, together with a prominent member of the Trotskyist Federation of Revolutionary Students were ordered to appear on the following Monday, 6 May, before a disciplinary board at the Sorbonne. We decided to go along Monday at 9 o'clock to march on the Sorbonne.

By their disciplinary action the university administration had hoped to strike our movement a fatal blow. They had calculated that student agitation must surely subside in the third term, what with the crucial examinations only four weeks away. As the Rector himself put it on 9 May:

"The systematic disturbances brought about by a small gang of students who have been trying, on their own admission, for some time to paralyse our lectures, and now threaten to stop the examinations, have forced us to take strong measures. We intend to preserve the freedom of all to sit for their examinations in order that the vast majority of students can derive legitimate recognition for their work."

Now, at the time, the politically conscious students were, in fact, still a minority, and they knew it. Hence they never set themselves up as champions of the "common interest of all students," but simply demanded the right to express political opinions within the campus and without police interference. They realized full well that the main body of students were far more interested in furthering their careers than in social justice.

It was because of this that the Communist Party has accused us of despising the students. In fact, we only despise the sons of the bourgeoisie, who, not only content with belonging to a privileged class, clamour for its privileges and are ready to defend them. Students differ in their political opinions as in everything else. Moreover, they are not a class, and they have no objective interests to defend. In a truly democratic society, higher education will be open to all, and students will cease to be a group apart. We do not, therefore, despise students as such but only those who applaud the men with the whip, who move in against every revolution.

But let us return to the events themselves. It was the action of the authorities that opened the eyes of many previously uncommitted students. Our "provocation" daily brought the latent authoritarianism of the bureaucracy into the open. As soon as any real problems were brought up, dialogue gave place to the policeman's baton: in Berkeley and Berlin no less than in Paris. The pathetic excuses put forward by the university dignitaries, who thought every pussy cat was a tiger, have left many a liberal observer perplexed.

"Was it really necessary, on account of a handful of troublemakers, to suspend all lectures in two faculties? It seems that the authorities lacked sang-froid. It is certainly true that small groups of the extreme Left, or at least several among them, have turned provocation into a weapon of war. Loving absolute truths and even more the fear they arouse in the 'bourgeoisie,' they claim that examinations help to perpetuate an archaic and meaningless system of education. But do we really have to take them so seriously?" (B. Girod de l'Ain in Le Monde, 6 May, 1968.)

If we ignore the paternalistic tone of this and similar articles in the liberal press, we must admit that there is a great deal of truth in them. In reality, everything hangs on the use of provocation in the crystallization of thought and latent emotion. Provocation is not a "weapon of war" except in special circumstances. It can only be used to arouse feelings that are already present, albeit submerged. In our case we exploited student insecurity and disgust with life in an alienated world where human relationships are so much merchandise to be used, bought and sold in the market place. All we did therefore was to "provoke" students to express their passive discontent, first by demonstrations for their own sake, and then by political actions directly challenging modern society. The justification for this type of provocation is its ability to arouse people who have been crushed under the weight of repression. Now, to speak of "repression" in the case of an institution such as a university which has no physical means of repression may seem ridiculous. But repression lies in the very function of that institution, in its blinding of the student to the fact that he is daily being spoon-fed with poisonous rubbish. Most students, as we saw, are willing to swallow it all, for the sake of a privileged position in the future, and because they believe that a rigid hierarchy is necessary for the efficient functioning of society. As a result, they lose all real desire, every ounce of creative spirit, all expression of life. The use of provocation is to drive this point home to them and to show how empty their lives have become.

We show them first of all that the petty hostel* regulations are an impertinent infringement of their personal liberty, that learning is no substitute for the warmth of human companionship. In learning to question these regulations, the student is forced to explore repression in general and the forms it takes in the modern world. Open physical repression with the point of a bayonet, as it was seen in the nineteenth century, is now reserved strictly for the suppression of the Third World. A complex and sophisticated industrial bureaucracy cannot function efficiently with a resentful proletariat. What it needs is apathy—just this apathy against which we are agitating. If we in the universities can show factory workers how authoritarianism and the official hierarchy can be overthrown in our own institutions, they will not be slow in applying similar methods to theirs. Hence the panic of the authorities—they do not mind criticism, however radical, but they cannot afford to let us express our disgust in action. Our threat is that we offer students real liberty by overthrowing, not only in theory, but in practice, the class-based university system. We do this by our boycott of lectures dispensing "pure" and "objective" knowledge and, worst of all, by our determination to carry the debate from the lecture hall into the streets and the factories. Our first task is to make the students themselves more politically conscious. In practice, this means developing new ways of communication: improvising meetings in the various faculty common rooms, occupying lecture halls, interrupting lectures with denunciations of their ideological basis, boycotting the examinations, sticking up posters and slogans, taking over the public address system—in short, taking any action that openly challenges the authorities.

The university bureaucracy cannot really cope with student power. True, it made an attempt to let the movement run its course for a while, but soon afterwards Rector Roche or, rather, the government felt impelled to take a strong line.

Following our distribution of a pamphlet calling for the boycott of examinations, the Dean put out the following notice: "The Dean and Professors of the Faculty of Letters of Paris would like to remind students that the examinations (May and October) will take place on the usual days, and state categorically that no supplementary arrangements can be made under any circumstances."

The Dean, moreover, proscribed the distribution of our pamphlet which said, among other things:

"In the present circumstances . . . any attempt to test the qualifica-

* Dormitory.—Ed.

tions of students by competitive exams is little more than a sham. All candidates ought therefore to be considered as having passed the examinations."

Monday, 6 May, was the official day for the competitive examinations. It is at this point that the Rector's "lack of sang-froid" seems to have degenerated into complete panic. Instead of proceeding with his "sacrosanct examinations," he decided to close the Sorbonne and to put it under the protection of the police.

Part of the explanation for his actions was that, whereas the most militant students were at the Sorbonne, the vast majority of "good" students were at home feverishly preparing for their examinations, so that this seemed a golden opportunity for crushing the enemy's "shock troops." How badly he miscalculated was shown by subsequent events.

*   *   *

The unwelcome presence of the police on the campus gained the students the support of the University Teachers' Association (SNESUP), and also of four professors in Nanterre: Messrs. Lefèvre, Michaud, Touraine and Ricœur, who declared themselves willing to undertake the defence of those students who had been summoned to appear before the Disciplinary Committee in the Sorbonne on the following Monday. Their moral support took the press completely by surprise and did much to gain the students fresh sympathizers.

On Saturday, 4 May, the police swooped again, and on Sunday, 5 May, an emergency court sent six student demonstrators to gaol. Proclamations in the press and over the radio then made it known that the demonstrations in support of the condemned students which had been called for Monday at 9 o'clock were officially banned.

"On Monday, Paris saw its most impressive and threatening demonstration for many years. Even during the Algerian war there has never been a movement of such breadth and above all of such staying power." *Le Monde*, 8 May 1968.

"We cannot allow those who are openly opposed to the university to seize that institution. We cannot tolerate violence in the streets, for violence is no way of starting any kind of dialogue." Charles de Gaulle, 7 May 1968.

Many people have asked themselves how it was possible that so vast a movement should have erupted from what was apparently so unimportant an event as the closure of a university and the intervention of the police in student affairs. It is therefore important to explain how a relatively small number of students succeeded in broadening the struggle against police repression to such an extent that it culminated in the occupation of the universities and the total rejection of its function in capitalist society. Learning through action plays a basic part in the genesis and growth of all revolutionary movements. From analysing what is closest at hand, we can come to understand society at large.

The complexity of modern life and the frustration it brings in its wake are such that we are forced most of the time to submerge our deepest aspirations. Students, who have to swallow humiliation every day, are particularly subject to these frustrations, and so react all the more violently once they are aroused. Lull them with sweet promises about the future and they may be prepared to put up with petty restrictions, false values, hypocritical doctrines and the lot, but bring out the police against them and you will find that you have stirred up a hornets' nest. The students started demonstrating at 9 A.M. and by the time they dispersed fourteen hours later, a mere trickle had swelled into a torrent, and "barricades" had sprung up in the streets. The students' determination, and above all their willingness to take on the police, were truly astonishing. They asserted their right to enter their own university, and to run it themselves for the benefit of all. The almost continuous confrontation with the police merely hardened their determination not to go back on their first claims: the release of all the imprisoned demonstrators, withdrawal of the police and re-opening of the faculties. I must add in parentheses that during the "Long March" of 7 May, and during the demonstrations at the university annex at the Halle aux vins, the various factions of the Left tried desperately to insinuate their own marshals in the vain hope of taking control. There were some 35,000 demonstrators present in the Champs Elysées alone and—*mirabile dictu*—they managed without any leaders at all. Unfortunately, the bureaucratic officials of UNEF, that moribund Student Union, who had been frustrated in their earlier attempts to take over the movement, now called in the help of the trade union bureaucrats who, at the Halle aux vins and in the demonstrations that followed, were able to divert the movement away from its original aim: the recapture of the Sorbonne. I do not want to pass an opinion on the strategic and tactical possibilities of capturing the Sorbonne at this point, but merely to show that all hierarchical and bureaucratic organizations must necessarily pervert all activities in which they participate to their own ends. Thus Alain Geismar explained to the General Assembly of the 22 March Movement on 8 May, how trade union officials had used every trick in the book to force the student movement to opt for a programme that would divert the struggle into purely reformist channels. In this they were greatly helped by Communist students and lecturers, who played a particularly treacherous part on 8 May at the Place du Luxembourg, when they called upon the students to disperse. This might well have spelled the end of the movement, long before it had a chance to express its real demands: the overthrow of repressive society. Luckily the revolutionary students were not taken in; they realized that they themselves had the power to beat repression, even in the face of Communist Party and other bureaucratic obstruction. Indeed, UNEF, by launching appeals to "reason" and issuing communiqués through the press, merely mobilized an ever larger number of demonstrators. And so when Roche announced he would re-open the Sorbonne under police protection, the students replied with an improvised "teach-out," assembled in their thousands and completely stopped the traffic in the Boulevard St. Michel. This teach-out was the first attempt to turn the Latin Quarter into a "public forum." Those responsible for the dispersal of the students in the Place du Luxembourg during the previous night were severely taken to task and asked to explain their actions. Direct democracy was being put into effect—under the very noses of the police. All the political and strategic problems of the past few days were brought up for discussion and thrashed out, not least among them the role of the university of the future.

*   *   *

. . . The people were clearly sympathetic, the National Assembly was divided, and we saw our chance to prove that the power of General de Gaulle would collapse like a house of cards if we went about it the right way. And here the police force itself came to our aid: by barring the route we had planned to take, they forced us into the Latin Quarter. Once there, we were determined not to disperse until all our demands had been met. And so we found ourselves drawn up in front of the CRS, facing their clubs, 30,000 of us standing united and ready for action, but with no definite plan. No one seriously envisaged attacking the Sorbonne, no one wanted a massacre. All we knew was that we had to defend ourselves where we stood; we split up into small groups, so that the police services were unable to launch a single, directed attack. Every barricade became a centre of action and of discussion, every group of demonstrators a squad acting on its own initiative. Barricades sprang up everywhere; no one felt the lack of a general in charge of overall strategy; messengers kept everyone informed of what was happening on the other barricades and passed on collective decisions for discussion. In our new-found solidarity our spirits began to soar. For the first time in living memory, young workers, young students, apprentices and high school pupils were acting in unison. We could not guess what turn the events were going to take, but that did not bother us—all that mattered was that, at long last, we were all united in action. The Gaullist régime proved completely helpless in the face of this youthful demonstration of strength, and this was only a beginning! None of the lies that have been told since, nor yet the final sell-out by the CGT,* can detract from this achievement. In a society which seeks to crush the individual, forcing him to swallow the same lies, a deep feeling of collective strength had surged up and people refused to be browbeaten. We were no longer thousands of little atoms squashed together but a solid

* The Communist-led French trade union federation.—Ed.

mass of determined individuals. We who had known the nagging ache of frustration were not afraid of physical hurt. This "rashness of youth" did not spring from despair, the cynicism of impotence, but on the contrary from the discovery of our collective strength. It was this feeling of strength and unity which reigned on the barricades. In such moments of collective enthusiasm, when everything seems possible, nothing could be more natural and simple than a warm relationship between all demonstrators and quite particularly between the boys and the girls. Everything was easy and uncomplicated. The barricades were no longer simply a means of self-defence, they became a symbol of individual liberty. This is why the night of 10 May can never be forgotten by those who were "there." For bourgeois historians the barricades will doubtless become symbols of senseless violence, but for the students themselves they represented a turning point that should have its place among the great moments of history. The memory of the raids, the gas grenades, the wounds and the injuries will surely remain, but we will also remember that night for the exemplary bravery of the "communards" or "sans-culottes" of the rue Gay-Lussac, of young men and women who opened a new and cleaner page in the history of France.

So great was their impact, in fact, that the trade unions and parties of the Left were forced, willy nilly, to call a general strike for 13 May 1968, in an attempt to take the political sting out of the student movement. But, having demonstrated their solidarity with the working class throughout the day, the students did not meekly disperse—that very night they took the Sorbonne. Students were suddenly freed from their intellectual imprisonment, and communication, discussion, explanation were, all at once, easy and meaningful. The Sorbonne became a spectacular focus of intellectual liberation, and one that, unlike the Liberation of 1945, refused to be gagged by the authorities.

*　　*　　*

... Not a train was running on the main lines or underground, not a letter, not a telegram could be sent, not a car or a ton of coal was being produced, workers in every industry, from every branch of the state, had joined the students. Even the football clubs were taken over by their players! Just as the strike itself came about spontaneously, without specific grievances, in the wake of the student revolt, so, now, new forms of organization of society were being discussed everywhere. Passionate and entirely novel ideas were being mooted throughout France.

It was at Charlety Stadium on Monday, 27 May, that Barjonet, recently resigned from the CGT, openly confessed that a revolution was possible after all. Barjonet only expressed what hundreds of other trade union militants had suddenly come to realize.

Perhaps the most concrete expression of this new sense of purpose was the occupation of the Sud-Aviation works in Nantes. The workers, by "imitating the students," were rediscovering a form of action that they had far too long discarded while playing the parliamentary game of the reformists and Stalinists. The applied psychoanalysis of the revolutionary students was clearly bringing on a general cure; on 20 May, even the most apathetic joined in, the Citröen works were occupied and a host of others followed suit soon afterwards.

Recourse to direct action changed the whole tenor of the struggle, for the workers' self-confidence is enormously increased once they act without delegating any of their power to political parties or trade unions. "The factory is ours so do we need to start working for the bosses again?" This idea arose quite spontaneously, not by command, or under the aegis of the so-called vanguard of the proletariat, but simply as a *natural response to a concrete situation.*

Discussions took place everywhere—there was hardly a factory where the question of "workers' control" was not raised and debated, so much so that, on Tuesday, 21 May, Séguy, speaking officially for the CGT, felt impelled to inform a press conference that "self-management is a hollow formula; what the workers really want is immediate satisfaction of their claims."

The revolution burst the old dams, its force took the entire world by surprise, and, of course, no one more so than the French authorities and bureaucracy of the CGT. The CGT realized that it was no longer sufficient to fight Leftism with invective in *L'Humanité* and a bit of character assassination in the factories. It had somehow to intervene on the shop floor if it was to stop the rot. And in this field the CGT was a past master —it had played the same part in 1936 and 1945 and, in a smaller way, in daily practice.

On 22 May, the government, in a desperate attempt to quieten things down, voted a general amnesty. But if they hoped to stop the movement in that way, they were badly mistaken. The movement was no longer restricted to the students, it had assumed wider proportions.

During this period everything was still possible, authority no longer existed except as a threat, and even part of the professional army was known to be sympathetic to the strikers. Moreover, the government no longer enjoyed the confidence of the public and finally it could not count on enough genuine, sick Fascists to carry out a counter-revolutionary coup.

The various police forces were dispersed in the streets, in the factories and even in the fields, since even the peasants had begun talking socialism and revolution. As a result, the police stations were unmanned and the administration left to its own, diminishing, devices. At this moment, I repeat, everything was still possible.

It was against this background that de Gaulle delivered his speech on 24 May. After blackmailing us with the threat of civil war (by whom against whom?) the Head of State graciously gave us permission to vote for a new set of laws and to give him a new mandate.

This generous offer fell spectacularly flat. Moreover, two hundred thousand peasants downed tools in various parts of France, blocking the roads and organizing mass meetings.

Then came the night of the 24th, which could have spelled the end of de Gaulle, but merely revealed a lack of political awareness among the masses and the narrowness of outlook of the different left-wing splinter groups who, instead of making common cause, tried to bend the situation to their own petty ends.

That day the CGT organized two marches in support of the strikers in different parts of Paris. These marches were restrained and highly organized—they were meant to pass off "in calm and dignity" and not to provoke the police. The whole idea was out of touch with the spirit of the more militant workers, and also with the advanced stage we had reached in our struggle: we were on the brink of overthrowing the government, and felt no need for appeasement.

And so we decided to let the processions take their peaceful course, while we ourselves would spill out of the Latin Quarter and plant the banner of revolution over the rest of Paris. Unfortunately, the way we of the 22 March Movement saw things was not the way the other student groups saw them. UNEF and PSU (United Socialist Party) were opposed to the whole idea, while the Trotskyists felt that no final push could be made before a revolutionary party was ready to step into the shoes of the bourgeoisie. As far as they were concerned we were simply a "band of irresponsible adventurists."

Nevertheless, they joined our appeal for a massed assembly at the Gare de Lyons. With the help of scores of action committees, in which high-school pupils played an important part, we organized five assembly points from which we would converge at 5 P.M. on the Gare de Lyons.

During the day, we got the Action Committees to distribute the following pamphlet:

Toilers, it is time we looked after ourselves! To ten million strikers! To all workers!

—No to all parliamentary solutions! De Gaulle may go but the bosses will stay!

—No to negotiations which only prop up capitalism!

—Enough referendums, no more circuses!

No one can speak for us. We ourselves must remain masters of our factories! The struggle must go on! The factories must support all those who are now engaged in battle.

This is the time to plan our rule of tomorrow—

Direct supplies of food, organization of public services, transport, information, housing, etcetera.

In the street, in the committees, wherever you may be! Workers! Peasants! Students! Teachers! Schoolboys! Let us organize and coordinate our struggle: For the abolition of Bosses! All power to the Workers!

The campaign had been launched. The CGT demonstration in the afternoon collected more than 200,000 workers, that of the 22 March

Movement and the Action Committees started with far less but very quickly grew in number, for as we marched through the various quarters, the people fell in behind us. At the Place de la Bastille and elsewhere, many from the CGT demonstration who had refused to disperse, joined us as well. In the end, more than 100,000 people assembled at the Gare de Lyons, while several thousand others were demonstrating in other parts of Paris. The atmosphere was electric. We then marched on the Stock Exchange as we had planned (the Hotel de ville*, another objective, was too well defended by the CRS and the army), captured it with remarkable ease and set it on fire. Paris was in the hands of the demonstrators, the Revolution had started in earnest! The police could not possibly guard all the public buildings and all the strategic points: the Elysée, the Hôtel de ville, the bridges, the ORTF (the French Broadcasting Service). Everyone felt it and wanted to go on. But then the political boys stepped in. It was a leader of the far-left JCR (Revolutionary Communist Youth) who, in the Place de l'Opéra, took charge and turned us back towards the Latin Quarter—when most of us thought we had done with the fatal attraction of the Sorbonne. It was officers of UNEF and PSU who stopped us taking the Ministry of Finance and the Ministry of Justice. These "revolutionaries" were quite incapable of grasping the potential of a movement that had left them far behind and was still gaining momentum. As for us, we failed to realize how easy it would have been to sweep all these nobodies away. We should never have allowed them to divert us, should have occupied the Ministries and public buildings, not to put in a new lot of "revolutionary" bureaucrats, but to smash the entire state apparatus, to show the people how well they could get on without it, and how the whole of society had to be reconstructed afresh on the basis of workers' control.

* City hall.—Ed.

TOWARD A RADICAL IDEOLOGY

TWO OF THE MOST important ideologies of social change are Marxist
socialism (or communism) and anarchism. The two theories are alike
insofar as both insist on the abolition of private property and look
forward to a society where people contribute and produce what they
are able and receive what they need. Anarchists, however, insist on the
abolition of government, whereas the Communists leave room for a
"temporary" dictatorship after the revolution. Anarchists point out that
this state will not just "wither away" and that the history of Russia
has proved them correct.

Marxist theory holds that there is an inherent contradiction in the capitalist system, an imbalance between its ever-increasing production
and the consumption that lags behind it. As Sweezy explains, the boss
pays the worker only part of the value the worker creates and keeps
the surplus. The surplus accumulates and is invested in further production. Output expands, but the purchasing power of the workers is not
enough to buy more than a portion of it. This process is accelerated
by the introduction of labor-saving machines that create more goods
with fewer workers. The imbalance between production and consump-

tion and other contradictions inherent in the economic system will force it to break down and enable the workers to take over the means of production. The industrial working class, according to Marx, was to be the main lever of social change. Both Sweezy and Macdonald point out that the proletarian revolution Marx believed would take place in the advanced industrial nations has not occurred. The communist revolutions that did sweep Russia, China, and Cuba were led by intellectuals and supported mainly by the peasants.

Anarchists in the past shared the Marxist belief that factory workers were to be the main agency of social change in the highly industrialized countries. Many contemporary anarchists have shifted their hopes to other groups: students, ethnic minorities, intellectuals, and the "new working class" of teachers, technicians, and other middle-level white-collar workers.

I would add that whether Marx's predictions were correct is less important than how they have been used. National leaders in underdeveloped countries have been able to use Marxism to organize the people to destroy the system that had kept them hungry and exploited. On the other hand, revolutionary leaders have used Marxist doctrine to justify repressive policies of their own once they have obtained power.

Macdonald proposes an ideology in which "the root is man." He agrees with the ethical goals originally stated by Marx: the withering away of the state, production for use instead of profit, distribution on the basis of need instead of work, abolition of toil. He criticizes Marxism for its illusion that the victory of one side or the other in a modern war may advance the cause of socialism, and for its belief that progress is inevitable. He also criticizes the belief shared by some Marxists, liberals, and progressives that the development of science and technology will necessarily lead to a better world.

Macdonald feels it is important to refrain from the political game of choosing between the lesser of two evils, as represented by the major parties. He suggests that dissenters go beyond electoral politics and engage in direct action such as draft refusal and sabotage.[1] He suggests trying to communicate with small audiences, face to face, instead of trying all at once to "convert the masses." Because centralized organizations are vulnerable to attack by the state, he suggests decentralized, loosely coordinated organization for radical political groups. Finally, he emphasizes the revolutionary importance of individuals living their lives the way they feel is right.

Malatesta was an Italian anarchist active from the turn of the century until his death in 1932. The manifesto he drafted in 1920 shows the kind

---

[1] At the time he wrote the article (1946) Macdonald was against all war. He subsequently retreated from this pacifist outlook; some of his latter comments are contained in the footnotes.

of social changes that anarchists want. The most important of these are:
1. abolition of private ownership of land and means of production;
2. abolition of government, laws, police, armies, frontiers; 3. voluntary
organization of social life by free association and federations of producers
and consumers; and 4. reconstruction of the family, to be based on love
and voluntary association instead of economic or legal compulsion.

The first stage in bringing about a revolution, Malatesta says, is persuasion
and propaganda. When enough people have recognized the need for
change and when circumstances are right, the people will take over
the means of production by force, destroy the government, and prevent
the establishment of a new one. While preparing for the future insurrection, he counsels continual participation in the day-to-day struggles against the system.

Anarchism, it seems to me, is more relevant today than ever and is more
convincing than either liberalism or Marxism. Like Marxism, anarchism
sees the need to destroy the power of the existing state, its military
machine, and the giant corporations. Unlike Marxism, however, it does
not see this change as coming about through the leadership of a centralized party, but through the decentralized, loosely coordinated efforts
of many small groups. Anarchists see government as necessarily repressive, and thus cannot share the Marxist idea that the revolution must
set up a temporary dictatorship. They call for immediate decentralization—direct control of production by the people at the local level.
Anarchists believe not only in working for the future revolution, but
in living as free people here and now.

Marxian Socialism

Paul M. Sweezy

Marxism is a body of ideas about the nature of the universe, of man, of
society, and of history. It bears the name of Karl Marx, a German who was
born in 1818 and died in 1883, and who lived the latter half of his life in
London. Marx was a man of prodigious learning and enormously powerful
intellect, one of the greatest thinkers not only of the nineteenth century
but of all recorded history.

Marx combined in his system of ideas the realistic philosophy of the
English and French Enlightenment, the comprehensive and dynamic

FROM *Monthly Review* Pamphlet Series (Number 13), pp. 6–13. Reprinted by permission of the *Monthly Review*.

point of view of the German idealists and particularly of Hegel, and the hardheaded analysis of the capitalist economy which we owe to the great British classical economists. The result was a brilliant new synthesis which is both highly original and at the same time stands squarely in the mainstream of modern intellectual development from the Renaissance onward. Here, in desperate brevity, are what I understand to be the central elements of the Marxian view of society and history:

The universe is real and existed for eons before there was human life, or for that matter life of any kind, on our planet. Life here on the earth is a natural by-product of the earth's cooling, and humanity is the result of a long process of evolution. In the earliest stages of society, human labor was still so unproductive that it yielded no surplus over and above the requirements of life and reproduction. As long as this was true, men lived in a state of primitive communism—cooperating, sharing, fighting, but not yet exploiting each other.

Later, techniques improved so much that a man could produce a surplus over and above what he needed for himself, and from this dates the beginning of economic exploitation and social classes. When one tribe fought and defeated another, it was now worthwhile to take captive the vanquished and force them to work for the victors. Some men became rulers living off the surplus produced by others; while the actual producers lost their independence and spent their lives toiling for their masters. It was in this way that exploitation of man by man and the division of society into classes originated.

But the form of exploitation has not remained unchanged—indeed, nothing remains unchanged, everything is in a constant state of flux. The exploiters seek to expand the surplus at their disposal, and with this end in view they invent and introduce new and better techniques of production; the exploited seek to improve their condition and therefore carry on a never-ending struggle to enlarge their share of the product. As a result the forms of exploitation change, and with them the whole structure of society. At first it was slavery, in which the laborer is the property of his master. Next came serfdom, in which the laborer has attained a certain degree of freedom but is still tied to the soil. And finally there is wage labor, in which the laborer is legally entirely free but must work for the profit of others because he lacks means of production of his own.

A society based on private ownership of the means of production and wage labor is called capitalism. It came into the world first in England and certain parts of Western Europe, not all at once but gradually and painfully between the sixteenth and nineteenth centuries. It brought with it social and political upheavals, new ways of thinking, and a deep awareness of the vast creative potentials of human labor and industry. Historically speaking, capitalism was a long leap forward. In the words of the *Communist Manifesto*: "It has been the first to show what man's activity can bring about. It has accomplished wonders far surpassing Egyptian pyramids, Roman aqueducts, and Gothic cathedrals; it has conducted expeditions that put in the shade all former migrations and crusades."

But capitalism contains within itself what Marx called contradictions which prevent it from fully realizing the potentials which it was the first to uncover. The capitalist class, comprising those who own the instruments of production and set them in motion, is and must be concerned with making profits, not with the general welfare. Capitalists subordinate other aims to the maximization of profit. In pursuit of this objective, they pay workers as little as they can get away with and steadily introduce labor-saving machinery. The consequence, of course, is to hold down the consuming power of the working class. At the same time, the capitalists restrict their own consumption in the interests of accumulating more and more capital. But accumulating more and more capital means adding to society's productive capacity. We, therefore, have the paradox that capitalism steps on the brake as far as consumption is concerned and on the accelerator as far as production is concerned. This is its basic contradiction, and it cannot be eliminated except through changing the system from one of production for profit to one of production for use.

On the basis of this analysis, Marx believed that it was to the interest of the workers to organize themselves politically in order eventually to gain power and replace capitalism by a system based upon common ownership of the means of production and economic planning, a system to which he and his followers came in time to give the name of socialism. Moreover, Marx had no doubt that the workers would in fact follow this course, and that their growing numbers, importance, and discipline under capitalism would sooner or later ensure their victory. As to *how* the transition would be effected, Marx at first thought that it would have to be everywhere by means of a violent revolution. But as political democracy spread, especially in the English-speaking countries, he modified this view and in the last decades of his life believed that a peaceful and legal transition was quite possible in some countries and under some conditions. "We know," he said in a speech at Amsterdam in 1872, "that special regard must be paid to the institutions, customs, and traditions of various lands; and we do not deny that there are certain countries, such as the United States and England, in which the workers may hope to achieve their ends by peaceful means."

What Is Socialism?

So much then for Marxism. Naturally, my account is oversimplified and very incomplete, but I hope it may serve to give you some idea of the scope and quality of Marx's thought—so different from the impressions which demagogic opponents have always sought to convey. Let us now ask: What is socialism?

Socialism, according to Marx, is the form of society which will succeed capitalism, just as capitalism is the form of society which succeeded feudalism.

The fundamental change would consist in the abolition of private ownership of the means of production. Please note that neither Marx nor (so far as I know) any other modern socialist of importance ever advocated or expected that private ownership of consumer goods would or should be abolished. On the contrary, he favored the multiplication of consumer goods in the hands of the lower-income groups, hence a great extension of private ownership in this sphere.

As to the form of ownership of the means of production which would characterize socialism, Marxists have never been dogmatic. Ownership must be by public bodies, but that does not necessarily mean only the central government: local governments, special public authorities of one sort or another, and cooperatives can also own means of production under socialism. And there can even be a certain amount of private ownership, provided it is confined to industries in which production takes place on a small scale.

A corollary of public ownership of the means of production is economic planning. The capitalist economy is governed by the market, that is to say, by private producers responding to price movements with a view to maximizing their own profits. It is through this mechanism that supply and demand are adjusted to each other and productive resources are allocated to various industries and branches of production. But public bodies have no compelling reason to maximize their profits (though, admittedly, under certain circumstances they may be *directed* to make as much profit as they can). In general, therefore, they must have some other principle to guide their economic conduct, and this can only be the following of a plan which coordinates the activities of all the public bodies.

Now socialists claim that it is precisely the freedom from the necessity to make profits and the coordination of all economic activities by a general plan which allows socialism to overcome the contradictions of capitalism and to develop its resources and technology for the greatest good of the people as a whole. Under such a system, crises and unemployment could only result from bad planning; and while bad planning is certainly not impossible, especially in the early stages of socialist society, there is no reason why planners should not learn to correct their mistakes and to reduce the resulting maladjustments and disproportions to smaller and smaller dimensions.

What about the non-economic aspects of socialism? Here Marx had a well-developed theory. He expected socialism to come first in the more advanced industrialized countries and to build on the political foundations which they had already achieved. Since in such countries the workers were in a majority, he believed that the taking of political power by the working class would mean full democracy and liberty for most of the people, though he also expected that there would be a period of greater or lesser duration when the rights and freedoms of the former exploiters would be subject to certain restrictions. As to the longer-run future, he reasoned that the full development of society's economic potential under socialism would gradually raise the well-being and education of everyone so that eventually all classes and class distinctions would be done away with. When that happened—but not before—the state as a repressive apparatus for dealing with class and other forms of social conflict would "wither away." The final goal of Marx and his followers can therefore be said to be the same as that of the philosophical anarchists. It would be a state of society in which, to quote Marx's words, "the free development of each is the condition for the free development of all" and in which distribution takes place according to the principle "from each according to his ability, to each according to his need."

Others before Marx had had a similar vision of a good society to come —a society of abundance and brotherhood in place of the society of scarcity and alienation which the human race had always been condemned to live in. What particularly distinguished Marx from his predecessors is that he purported to prove that this society of the future, which he called socialism, is not only a dream and a hope but is in fact the next stage of historical evolution. It would not come automatically, to be sure—not as the result of the blind decrees of fate. It would come rather as the result of the conscious, organized activity of working people, the vast majority of mankind. Given this perspective, the task of the humanitarian could only be to devote his energies to educating and organizing the working class to fulfill its historic mission. That, in a word, is what Marxists have been trying to do for nearly a hundred years now.

Was Marx Right?

Marx's prophetic forecast of the end of capitalism and the opening of a new era in human history was given to the world in the *Communist Manifesto* in 1848. More than a century has passed since. Do the facts of this intervening period permit us to say whether Marx was right or wrong?

In the broadest sense, I do not see how it can be denied that Marx has been brilliantly vindicated. A mighty socialist movement based on the working class grew up during his lifetime. The crises of capitalism, far from abating, grew in intensity and violence, culminating in the holocausts of two world wars. Beginning with the Russian Revolution of 1917, more and more of the earth's population has withdrawn from the orbit of capitalism and has undertaken to reconstruct its economy and society on the basis of public ownership and planning. Today, something like a third of the human race has definitely abandoned private enterprise and, under Communist leadership, is building up a network of planned economies.

But it is not only in Communist-led countries that this is happening, though elsewhere the pace is slower. Since World War II, Great Britain has moved a considerable distance along the road to a socialized economy, and one of the two big political parties is a socialist party. Even more recently, India, next to Communist China the most populous country in the world, has adopted a Five Year Plan which the sober London *Times* calls "India's Socialist Plan."

The fact is that over most of the world's surface the trend is now visibly away from private enterprise and toward public ownership of the means of production, away from market-dominated economies and toward economic planning. Only in the United States and a few countries closely allied to the United States does the trend seem to be in the other direction. Here, it is true, the socialist movement is at a low ebb, and private enterprise is very much in the saddle.

Should we perhaps conclude that Marx was right for the rest of the world but wrong for the United States? Are we the great exception? Or are we merely lagging somewhat behind in a movement which eventually will be as universal as Marx predicted it would?

These are crucial questions, especially for us Americans. In what time remains to me, I shall attempt to indicate some possible answers.

There is one respect, and it is an important one, in which Marx was certainly wrong. As I noted earlier, he expected socialism to come first in the most advanced industrial countries. It did not. For reasons having to do with the late 19th- and early 20th-century development of relations between the advanced countries and the colonial and semi-colonial backward countries, the revolutionary movement grew more rapidly and had more opportunities in the backward than in the advanced regions. When the capitalist system was wracked by the destruction and disasters of the two world wars, it broke at its weakest points not at its strongest. Socialism came first to the Tsarist Empire, and spread from there to Eastern Europe and China.

This has, of course, meant that the early stages of the development of socialism have been very different from what Marx foresaw.

The new order could not build directly on the achievements of the old. It had no developed industrial base, no educated and trained labor force, no political democracy. It had to start from scratch and work under conditions of utmost difficulty.

Many people, including Marxists, expected socialism to proceed at once, or at any rate within a short time, to achieve its great goals: an economy of abundance, increasing democracy and freedom for the workers, a richer life for all. It could have happened that way if Britain, Germany, and the United States had been the first socialist countries. But it could not possibly happen that way in backward Russia standing alone for a whole generation. The industrial base had to be built, and that meant belt-tightening. The Russians had no traditions of democracy and civil liberty, and under the difficult conditions of the '20s and '30s it was natural that a new police state should arise on the foundations of the old Tsarist police state. Moreover, like all police states this one committed excesses and horrors which had little if anything to do with the central tasks of construction the regime had set itself.

Under these circumstances, socialism in practice had little attraction for the people of the advanced countries. The standard of living of those living under it remained abysmally low, and political conduct, both among leaders and between leaders and people, often seemed closer to oriental despotism than to enlightened socialism. It was widely assumed in the West either that the Soviet Union was not socialist at all, or that socialism had been tried and failed.

In the underdeveloped countries, however, the USSR made a very different impression. They saw rapid economic advance, a vast process of popular education, some improvement in living standards—and never having experienced democracy themselves, they hardly noticed its absence in Russia. Communism was imposed on Eastern Europe by the Red Army chasing Hitler back to Berlin, but in China it was the product of a great popular revolution. And it is now expanding its influence throughout the underdeveloped regions of the world.

The Competition of the Systems

The two systems of capitalism and socialism exist side by side in the world today. They are competing for the support and emulation of the backward and uncommitted countries. They are also competing in terms of absolute performance. How will this contest turn out? Will those now in the capitalist camp remain there? Or will they tend to join the socialist camp as time goes on? And finally, what about the United States, the leader of the capitalist camp?

These are questions which every serious person in the world is asking today. I predict that they will be increasingly the center of attention in the years and decades ahead.

The answers, I think, will depend very largely on the relative success of the two systems in the following fields: production and income, education, and liberty.* I believe that socialism will win out in this great world-shaking contest, and I am going to conclude . . . by trying to give you some of the reasons why I hold this view. I should add perhaps that I don't expect you to agree with me at this stage of the game. The decisive forces and trends are still operating for the most part below the surface, and it will be some time yet before they can be seen and evaluated by all. But I hope that I may succeed in making you *think* seriously about these matters.

* The concluding section of Sweezy's pamphlet is omitted here. In it, he compares the performance of the United States and the Soviet Union in these areas.—Ed.

It is, I believe, important that Americans should be put on notice that things are happening in the world, and will increasingly happen, which contradict their established thought patterns and expectations. You may not believe me yet, but at any rate if you pay serious attention to what I say you should not be surprised when things turn out differently from the way you have been taught to expect.

The Root Is Man

Dwight Macdonald

We Need a New Political Vocabulary

The first great victory of Bureaucratic Collectivism came in 1928, when Stalin finally drove Trotsky into exile and prepared, the following year, to initiate the First Five Year Plan. Between the French Revolution (1789) and 1928, political tendencies could fairly accurately be divided into "Right" and "Left." But the terms of the struggle for human liberation shifted in 1928—the shift had been in process long before then, of course, but 1928 may be taken as a convenient watershed. It was Trotsky's failure to realize this that gave an increasingly unreal character to his handling of "the Russian question," just as it is the continued blindness of liberals and socialists to this change that makes academic, if not worse, their present-day political behavior.

Let me try to define the 1789–1928 "Left" and "Right."

The Left comprised those who favored a change in social institutions which would make the distribution of income more equal (or completely equal) and would reduce class privileges (or do away with classes altogether). The central intellectual concept was the validity of scientific method; the central moral concept was the dignity of Man and the individual's right to liberty and a full personal development. Society was therefore conceived of as a means to an end: the happiness of the individual. There were important differences in method (as, reform v. revolution, liberalism v. class struggle) but on the above principles the Left was pretty much agreed.

The Right was made up of those who were either satisfied with the status quo (conservatives) or wanted it to become even more inegalitarian

FROM *The Root Is Man*, by Dwight Macdonald (Alhambra, Calif.: The Cunningham Press), pp. 17–54. Copyright 1953 by Dwight Macdonald. Reprinted by permission of the author.

(reactionaries). In the name of Authority, the Right resisted change, and in the name of Tradition, it also, logically enough, opposed what had become the cultural motor of change: that willingness, common alike to Bentham and Marx, Jefferson and Kropotkin, to follow scientific inquiry wherever it led and to reshape institutions accordingly. Those of the Right thought in terms of an "organic" society, in which society is the end and the citizen the means. They justified inequalities of income and privilege by alleging an intrinsic inequality of individuals, both as to abilities and human worth.

This great dividing line has become increasingly nebulous with the rise of Nazism and Stalinism, both of which combine Left and Right elements in a bewildering way. Or, put differently, both the old Right and the old Left have almost ceased to exist as historical realities, and their elements have been recombined in the dominant modern tendency: an inegalitarian and organic society in which the citizen is a means, not an end, and whose rulers are antitraditional and scientifically minded. Change is accepted in principle—indeed, the unpleasant aspects of the present are justified precisely as the price that must be paid to insure a desirable future, whether it be Hitler's domination of lesser races by the Nordics, or Stalin's emancipation of the world workingclass, or our own liberals' peaceful future world to be achieved through war. The whole idea of historical process, which a century ago was the badge of the Left, has become the most persuasive appeal of the apologists for the status quo.

In this Left-Right hybrid, the notion of Progress is central. A more accurate terminology might therefore be to reserve the term "Right" for such old-fashioned conservatives as Herbert Hoover and Winston Churchill and to drop the term "Left" entirely, replacing it with two words: "Progressive" and "Radical."

By "Progressive" would be understood those who see the Present as an episode on the road to a better Future; those who think more in terms of historical process than of moral values; those who believe that the main trouble with the world is partly lack of scientific knowledge and partly the failure to apply to human affairs such knowledge as we do have; those who, above all, regard the increase of man's mastery over nature as good in itself and see its use for bad ends, as atomic bombs, as a perversion. This definition, I think, covers fairly well the great bulk of what is still called the Left, from the Communists ("Stalinists") through reformist groups like our own New Dealers, the British Laborites, and the European Socialists to small revolutionary groups like the Trotskyists.[1]

---

[1] It is not intended to suggest there are not important differences between these tendencies. The Stalinists, in particular, should be most definitely set off from the rest. Their Progressivism is a complete abandonment to the historical process, so that absolutely anything goes, so long as it is in the interests of Russia, a "higher" form of society. The other groups, although they put more emphasis on the historical process than is compatible with the values they profess, do stand by certain general principles and do recognize certain ethical boundaries.

"Radical" would apply to the as yet few individuals—mostly anarchists, conscientious objectors, and renegade Marxists like myself—who reject the concept of Progress, who judge things by their present meaning and effect, who think the ability of science to guide us in human affairs has been overrated and who therefore redress the balance by emphasizing the ethical aspect of politics. They, or rather we, think it is an open question whether the increase of man's mastery over nature is good or bad in its actual effects on human life to date, and favor adjusting technology to man, even if it means—as may be the case—a technological regression, rather than adjusting man to technology. We do not, of course, "reject" scientific method, as is often charged, but rather think the scope within which it can yield fruitful results is narrower than is generally assumed today. And we feel that the firmest ground from which to struggle for that human liberation which was the goal of the old Left is the ground not of History but of those non-historical values (truth, justice, love, etc.) which Marx has made unfashionable among socialists.

The Progressive makes History the center of his ideology. The Radical puts Man there. The Progressive's attitude is optimistic both about human nature (which he thinks is basically good, hence all that is needed is to change institutions so as to give this goodness a chance to work) and about the possibility of understanding history through scientific method. The Radical is, if not exactly pessimistic, at least more sensitive to the dual nature of man; he sees evil as well as good at the base of human nature; he is sceptical about the ability of science to explain things beyond a certain point; he is aware of the tragic element in man's fate not only today but in any conceivable kind of society. The Progressive thinks in collective terms (the interests of Society or the Workingclass); the Radical stresses the individual conscience and sensibility. The Progressive starts off from what actually is happening; the Radical starts off from what he wants to happen. The former must have the feeling that History is "on his side." The latter goes along the road pointed out by his own individual conscience; if History is going his way, too, he is pleased; but he is quite stubborn about following "what ought to be" rather than "what is."

Because its tragic, ethical and non-scientific emphasis corresponds partly with the old Right attitude, leading to criticisms of Progressive doctrine that often sound very much like those that used to be made from the Right, the Radical viewpoint causes a good deal of confusion today. It is sometimes called "objectively reactionary." It would not be hard, however, to show the peculiar bedfellows, notably the Stalinists, the Progressives have today. For the fact is that *both* the Progressive and the Radical attitudes, as here defined, cut across the old Left-Right dividing line, and in this sense both are confusing and even "objectively reactionary" if one continues to think in the old terms.

*   *   *

The World We Live In

The social systems of the victorious powers are developing a common tendency towards a planned, State-controlled economy which considers the citizen a cell in the social organism and thus at once the ward of the State, entitled to a job and to average living standards in exchange for his usefulness in production or the armed forces, and also the State's docile instrument who could no more rebel than a cell could develop independently of the total organism. If this latter *does* happen, modern political theory agrees with biology in calling the result cancer, which must be cut out lest the organism die. The Organic State is directed towards one great end: to assert effectively against competing States its own nationalistic interests, which means preparation for World War III. All this is a matter of common knowledge in upperclass circles in the USA, the USSR and other big powers, although, for obvious reasons, it is not discussed in public.

Now, with such a society developing, what kind of demands do the tribunes of the people put forth today? Do they proclaim a new Rights of Man? Do they turn pacifist, denounce war as the greatest of evils, insist on immediate disarmament, beginning with their own country, expose the fraudulent character of World War II? Do they agitate for greater freedom of the press and opinion? Do they push toward decentralization of industry until its scale becomes human, regardless of the effects on munitions production? Do they take up arms against the growing power of the State? Do they fight against the growth of nationalism?

These are, of course, rhetorical questions. The reformist movements like the British Labor Party and our own labor unions are apathetic on such issues. The Communists are not apathetic; they are intensely hostile. What kinds of aims do both liblabs and Communists actually have? They want Full Production, Nationalization, Planning, and above all Security, of both the Social and the National varieties. There is nothing in these demands incompatible with the interest of the ruling class in organizing a strong nation to compete militarily with other nations. There are antagonisms, it is true, sharp and sometimes bloody battles. But these clashes are on secondary issues; they do not affect the trend towards war and social regimentation. For the struggle is not over a kind of society, but over who is to dominate the existing society, the Old Guard or the Tribunes of the People. It is becoming increasingly difficult to distinguish the "Right" from the "Left" wing.

The reason for this confusion is basically simple: the historical process to which the Left has traditionally looked for progress in a desirable direction has been going on but the result is often not progress but the reverse. The liberals put their faith in social and economic reforms; these are being made, but often go hand in hand with moral barbarism. The Marxists looked to the expropriation of the bourgeoisie; this is taking place, but new and in many ways even more oppressive rulers are replacing the old ones. We are all in the position of a man going upstairs who thinks there is another step and finds there is not. We are off balance.

*　　*　　*

The Question of Marxism

The Ambiguity of Marxism

Marxism is not simply, or even primarily, an interpretation of history. It is a guide to political action. The worst fate that can befall a philosophy of action is for it to become ambiguous. This is what has happened to Marxism. Its ambiguity stems from the fact that Marx's ethical aims have not been realized—quite the contrary!—while the historical process by which he thought they would be realized has to a large extent worked out as he predicted it would. It is possible to reach opposite conclusions, on the basis of Marxism, about Soviet Russia, depending on whether one emphasizes Marx's ethical values or his idea of the historical process. Since Marx himself made the process significant rather than the values, the Stalinists would seem to have a somewhat better claim to be the "real" Marxists than their more ethically-minded opponents. But the point is not which is "really" the Marxist view; the point is that each view may be maintained, on the basis of Marx's thought, with a good deal of reason. There is an ambiguity here, fatal to a philosophy conceived as a basis for action, which was not apparent during Marx's lifetime, when history seemed to be going his way, but which is all too clear now that history is going contrary to socialist values.

What Marx Wanted

Marx's vision of a good society was essentially the same as that of the anarchists, the Utopian socialists, and the great 18th century liberals—also as that of those today whom I call "Radicals." The same theme runs through his writings from beginning to end. The *Communist Manifesto* (1848): "an association in which the free development of each is the condition for the free development of all." *Capital*, Vol. 1 (1867): "a society in which the full and free development of every individual becomes the ruling principle . . . production by freely associated men." The *Critique of the Gotha Program* (1875) gives us the most explicit and famous formulation:

"In a higher phase of communist society, after the enslaving subordination of individuals under division of labor, and therewith also the antithesis between mental and physical labor, has vanished; after labor, from a means of life, has itself become the prime necessity of life; after the productive forces have also increased with the all-round development of the individual, and all the springs of cooperative wealth flow more abundantly—only then can the narrow horizon of bourgeois right be fully left behind and society inscribe on its banners: from each according to his ability, to each according to his needs."

The political seal of this future society would be the elimination of all forms of coercion, i.e., the withering away of the State. Some critics of Marx, in particular certain anarchists whose sectarian intemperance matches that of certain Marxists, make him out an ideological apologist for the State. There is indeed a potential towards Statism in Marxism, but it lies not in Marx's values, but, as I shall show presently, in his "historical" method of thinking about those values. From the splendid polemic against Hegel's *Philosophy of Law* in 1844 to the Gotha Critique thirty years later, Marx consistently criticised Statism from the standpoint of human liberation. As a moralist, Marx viewed the individual as the End and society as the Means.

How He Thought It Would Come About

So much for Marx's ethical aims. I think it needs no demonstration that such a society is farther off today than it was in Marx's time. Now what about the way Marx conceived the historical process that would realize these aims? Two passages will give us the grand outlines:

"At a certain stage of their development, the material forms of production in society come into conflict with the existing relations of production or—what is but a legal expression for the same thing—with the property relations within which they had been at work before. From forms of development of the forces of production, these relations turn into their fetters. Then comes the period of social revolution. With the change of the economic foundation, the entire immense superstructure is more or less rapidly transformed. . . . In broad outline we can designate the Asiatic, the ancient, the feudal, and the modern bourgeois methods of production as so many epochs in the process of the economic formation of society. The bourgeois relations of production are the last antagonistic form of the social process of production—antagonistic not in the sense of individual antagonism, but of one arising from conditions surrounding the life of individuals in society. At the same time, the productive forces developing in the womb of bourgeois society create the material conditions for the solution of that antagonism. This social formation constitutes, therefore, the closing of the prehistoric stage of human society." (Marx's Preface to *A Contribution to the Critique of Political Economy*.)

"Along with the constantly diminishing number of magnates of capital . . . grows the mass of misery, oppression, slavery, degradation, exploitation; but with this too grows the revolt of the workingclass, a class always increasing in numbers, and disciplined, united, organized by the very mechanism of the process of capitalist production itself. The monopoly of capital becomes a fetter upon the mode of production. . . . Centralization of the means of production and socialization of labor at last reach a point where they become incompatible with their capitalist integument. This integument is burst asunder. The knell of capitalist private property sounds. The expropriators are expropriated. . . . The transformation of scattered private property, arising from individual labor, into capitalist private property is, naturally, a process incomparably more protracted, violent and difficult than the transformation of capitalistic private property, already practically resting on socialised production, into socialised property. In the former case, we had the expropriation of the mass of the people by a few usurpers; in the latter, we have the expropriation of a few usurpers by the mass of people." (*Capital*, Vol. I.)

How It Really Is Coming About

Two aspects of these passages concern us here: (1) the assumption that there is a progressive evolution in history from worse to better; (2) the description of how the overthrow of capitalism, the final step in this evolution, would come about.

(1) The belief in Progress is central to Marx's thought, although his more sophisticated followers today, for understandable reasons, say as little as possible about it. As I shall show later on, Marx's concept of historical Progress has not only proved to be empirically false, but it has also been used by the Communists as an ideology to justify the most atrocious policies. So long as we are bemused by the will-o-the-wisp of Progress, we can never become truly radical, we can never make man the root.

(2) Marx predicted that the contradiction between the increasing productivity of industry and the forms of private property would "burst asunder" the capitalist "integument" and lead to "socialised property." The agency that would accomplish this change would be the proletariat, lashed to the task by increasing misery and historically fitted for it by the fact that collectivism was to its interest as a class (and, so far as Marx ever states, to the interest of no other class). The result of the change would be a non-antagonistic form of social production in which, for the first time in history, the masses would expropriate "a few usurpers" instead of the other way around. As we have seen already in this article, private capitalism is indeed decaying and the bourgeoisie are being expropriated, but the agency is not the proletariat but rather a new *political* ruling-class which is substituting its rule for the old ruling class in the time-honored way. The process on which Marx banked so heavily is being brought about from the top, not the bottom, and is directed towards nationalism and war. The result is not the liberation of the masses but their even more complete enslavement, not the coming of the Kingdom of Freedom but the creation of an even more crushing Kingdom of Necessity. The external process is working out, but the inner spirit is the reverse of what Marx expected.

The weakness of Marxism seems to me to be precisely its most distinctive contribution to socialist thinking: the expectation that external, materialistic factors (such as changes in class and property relationships) will bring about certain desired results with "iron necessity." Ends, values, cannot safely be treated only as functions of materialistic factors but must be defined and communicated in their own terms. Even that concept of change, the essence of his dialectical method, which Marx thought was intrinsically progressive, has become ambiguous. One is attracted to his "critical and revolutionary" spirit which "lets nothing impose on it"—and yet one cannot but recall that the Nazis were revolutionaries in their own way, who considered nothing sacrosanct, who let nothing impose on them, and whose only principle was a willingness to change anything at any time. This problem of how one roots one's values, which will be treated more extensively later on, seems to me to be the heart of "the question of Marxism."

The Rock That Turned Out to Be Sand

When Marx concentrated his great intellectual powers on the economic process of capitalism, he thought he was building on a rock. In the preface to *Capital* he quotes approvingly from a Russian review: "The one thing which is of moment to Marx is to find the law of the phenomena with whose investigation he is concerned. . . . This law once discovered, he investigates in detail the effects in which it manifests itself in social life. Consequently, Marx only troubles himself about one thing: to show, by rigid scientific investigation, the necessity of successive determinate orders of social conditions. . . . Marx treats the social movement as a process of natural history, governed by laws not only independent of human will, consciousness and intelligence, but rather on the contrary, determining that will, consciousness and intelligence. . . . The scientific value of such an inquiry lies in the disclosing of the special laws that regulate the origin, existence, development and death of a given social organism and its replacement by another and higher one." The optimism of the 19th century, both about Progress and about the possibilities of scientific inquiry, is strikingly expressed here. Also the influence of Darwin's evolutionary theory on Marx, with its reinforcement of the idea of Progress that had arisen in the 18th century and its emphasis on external environmental factors over human consciousness. In the same preface, Marx grandiosely writes of "the natural laws of capitalist production . . . working with iron necessity towards inevitable results." The necessity has proved to be putty, the results quite evitable. The rock of Historical Process on which Marx built his house has turned out to be sand. . . .

In the following three sections, I try to show that (1) the workingclass has "come of age" without advancing us towards socialism; (2) a great shift away from capitalism is taking place without advancing us towards socialism; (3) modern war, far from offering "revolutionary opportunities" for socialism, is creating new conditions which make the struggle for socialism even more difficult. This failure of history to take the anticipated course might not be fatal to some systems of political thought but it is so to Marxism, because that system is built not on ethical principles but on the historical process itself.

The Mirage of the Proletarian Revolution

It was to the workingclass that Marx looked to bring in a better society. And it is in that direction that his followers today still look, as a glance at the minute coverage of labor news in almost any Marxist organ will show. I think it is time for us to recognize that, although the workingclass is certainly *an* element in any reconstitution of society along more tolerable lines, it is not now, and possibly never was, *the* element Marx thought it was. The evidence for this is familiar, and most Marxists will admit almost every item in detail. They shrink, however, and understandably enough, from drawing the logical but unpleasant conclusions that follow.

In my opinion, the weight that Marx attached to the proletariat was excessive *economically* in that the organization of the workers into unions has failed to develop into the broader kind of action Marx expected it to. And it was excessive *politically* in that neither the reformist nor the Bolshevik tactic has led to the hoped-for results. . . .

Economic: The Unions

Instead of broadening their objectives, as Marx expected them to, and aspiring finally to "the emancipation of the downtrodden millions," unions have usually followed precisely the opposite course.

. . . The early struggle to establish unions had an anti-capitalist character which more and more disappeared as time went on. The evolution has been at first into simple pressure groups fighting for labor's interests *against* the rest of society (which does not by any means consist only of bankers in silk hats) and with an attitude of devil take the hindmost so long as "we get ours"; Lewis' United Mine Workers and the old-line A.F. of L. unions are still in this stage. There is also a later stage, more typical of mature capitalism, which indeed involves the assumption of a broad social responsibility, but as an integral part of capitalism rather than as a force for labor's emancipation *from* capitalism. Industrialists often find it advantageous to have their work force controlled by a "responsible" union bureaucracy with whom they can deal on a "reasonable" basis—in England, for example, the employer himself often makes union membership a condition of employment. The State also finds unions of great value as agencies of control, especially in wartime. In short, the modern union is a bureaucratized mass-organization which simply extends the conventional patterns of society into the workingclass and has little significance as an expression of a specific workingclass consciousness. It may be a narrow-minded economic pressure-group, or, more typically, the kind of a prop to a disintegrating status quo the Social Democracy was in Weimar Germany and the T.U.C. is today in somewhat similar circumstances in England. In either case, what it has to do with either socialism or revolution is obscure.

Political: The Parties

The most obvious fact about the Proletarian Revolution is that it has never occurred.[2] Such revolutions as have taken place have not followed the workingclass pattern which Marxism anticipates. The Paris Commune had a very mixed class character and materialized more along the lines of Blanqui or Proudhon than of Marx. The other revolutionary upheavals have been in the least advanced, not the most advanced, countries, and have therefore had a mixed peasant-worker character (Russia, China, Spain). These revolutions in backward lands have either failed or have produced new tyrannies; the Marxist explanation is that the low level of economic development made socialism impossible. But when countries are highly developed, their workers don't make revolutions at all.

The proletarian revolution today is even less of a historical possibility than it was in 1900. The first world war was the turning point. The reformist-socialist movements of Europe, by supporting their capitalist governments in that war, permanently discredited the Second International.

* * *

Our Own Experience in America

For the last thirty years, socialism in America has been an "as if" movement; we middleclass intellectuals who have comprised its main body of adherents have generally behaved "as if" our movement were a historical reality. It has not been anything of the sort since 1918; that is, socialism of any variety has not in that period influenced the behavior of a historically significant number of Americans; even the Communists, despite the material and psychological help of their success in Russia, have never played the role in the trade union movement or in national politics which the pre-war radical groups played. After the first world war, American Radicalism lost its mass roots. This fact should always be kept in mind in evaluating the American leftist movement; it explains many things.

* * *

The first step towards the A.F. of L. was taken in 1875 when the Gompers group circulated a call to a conference of trade unions. This

---

[2] And probably never will occur.

letter begins: "Throughout the United States, there exist numerous organized bodies of workingmen who declare that the present degraded dependence of the workingman upon the capitalist for the means of livelihood is the cause of the greater part of the intellectual, moral and economic degradation that afflicts society, every political movement must be subordinate to the first great social end, viz., the economic emancipation of the workingclass." And the preamble to the constitution which the A.F. of L. adopted ten years later—and which is still its official program— begins with an echo of the thunder of the Communist Manifesto: "A struggle is going on in all the nations of the civilized world between the oppressors and the oppressed . . . the capitalist and the laborer."

Compare the preamble to the constitution of an exceptionally militant and progressive present-day union, the United Automobile Workers. This begins not with an echo of the Communist Manifesto but with a literal reproduction of . . . the Declaration of Independence—self-evident truths, life, liberty and the pursuit of happiness, and all the rest. But even the 1776 brand of radicalism is too strong for these modern proletarians: they include the statement about governments "deriving their just powers from the consent of the governed," but they omit the rest of the sentence, which declares that the people have a right to overthrow a government if they don't like it. The builders of the new Jefferson Memorial in Washington made precisely the same excision when they cut this quotation into the marble wall of that pompous edifice. But the auto workers go them one better: they actually substitute for Jefferson's subversive idea, the following: "Within the orderly process of such Government lies the hope of the worker." The rest of their preamble is in the same spirit. Far from unions being called on to change society, the growth of unionism itself is presented as evidence of such a change *already accomplished!* ("We believe the right of the workers to organize for mutual protection is . . . evidence . . . of an economic and social change in our civilization.") These proletarians roar gently as any sucking dove. They have nothing against capitalism or the wage system; all they want is "a mutually satisfactory and beneficial employer-employee relationship" and "a place at the conference table, together with management." And this is in many ways the most class-conscious union in the country!

"The grandiose economic crisis, acquiring the character of a social crisis," wrote Trotsky in 1931, "will inevitably become transformed into the crisis of the political consciousness of the American workingclass." Fifteen years later, some 150,000 American proletarians, each carrying a union card, labored for many months on an unknown product in the plants of the "Manhattan District" project. When the first atomic bombing revealed to them what they had been making, they reacted with patriotic cheers. There may have been other reactions, but I have seen no reports of them. Furthermore, the petty-bourgeois scientists who developed The Bomb have expressed the utmost concern over the effects of their creation—forming associations, issuing statements, proposing various policies, trying to arouse the public. But I have seen not a single protest, recommendation, or any other expression from the union locals that worked on The Bomb.[3]

* * *

Modern War and the Class Struggle

In the century after Waterloo (1815–1914), there was only one war in Europe between first-class powers: the Franco-Prussian War. In the first half of the 20th century, there have already occurred two world wars which involved not only all the great European powers but also the USA, Russia and Japan; and a third world war is generally anticipated. Furthermore, World War II was much more destructive of lives, property and culture than World War I, and the atomic bomb promises to make World War III devastating beyond any historical parallel.

These are commonplaces, but it is easy (and pleasant) to forget them. It is also easy to forget that the whole body of socialist theory, from the Utopians through Marx, Engels, Proudhon and Kropotkin to Luxemburg, Lenin and Trotsky (after whom it ceased to develop significantly) was built up during the "Hundred Years' Peace" after Waterloo.

From these facts, two conclusions emerge. (1) The preparation and waging of war is now the normal mode of existence of every great nation; the creation of military force is no longer one among other means of advancing the national interest but rather, it *is* now the national interest. (2) Since the chronic world warfare of our day was unknown to them, the theoreticians of socialism devoted their attention mainly to the internal class struggle and failed to work out an adequate theory of the political significance of war; this gap still remains to be filled; until it is, modern socialism will continue to have a somewhat academic flavor.[4]

---

[3] When, in the summer of 1946, some pacifist members of the Workers Defense League planned to picket the Oak Ridge atom bomb plant to protest atomic warfare, the League was pressured to prevent them by the local CIO leadership, which feared the picketing would do "irreparable harm to our current organizing drive among the Oak Ridge workers." The director of the CIO's Tennessee Regional Office wrote that if the pickets persisted, "We will be forced to take drastic measures to denounce your program, which we would not like to do." Confronted by this unexpected opposition, the would-be pickets, who were mostly socialists and so starry-eyed about labor unions, called off the demonstration. . . .

[4] For some nonacademic thinking on modern war & politics, see Simone Weil's "Reflections on War" (*Politics*, Feb. 1945) and "Words and War" (*Politics*, March 1946); also two remarkable and not-enough-noticed-at-the-time pieces by "European" in *Politics*: "Is a Revolutionary War a Contradiction in Terms?" (April 1946) and "Violence and Sociability" (Jan. 1947); also, of course, that little classic from the First World War, Randolph Bourne's *The State*, with its sombre refrain: "War is the health of the State."

The Inadequacy of the Marxian View of War

Marxism regards war as a means to an end, a method of advancing certain definite class interests; as a means, it is subordinated to its end, so that if the destruction it causes seems likely to exceed the gains to those groups using this means, they will presumably not use it; there is implied in this whole view a certain rationality, even moderation and limit, to warfare, so that one can say that a given war may offer a "revolutionary opportunity" or that the victory of one side may be more advantageous to the cause of socialism than the victory of the other.

There was some truth in these ideas in Marx's time, but they are now obsolete. War has become an end in itself; instead of advancing certain class or national interests at the expense of others, war tends more and more to make the situation of the "victors" indistinguishable from that of the "defeated," as in Europe today; the effects of the technical measures that must be taken to fight a modern war have become more important than any political effect of the war's outcome. In a word, war seems to have lost its rationality, so that one might say there will probably be a third world war because there has been a second world war; that is, the existence of powerful warmaking apparatuses, with economies and social institutions deformed to support them, and the quite justified fears of every nation of attack from every other nation—these factors are the key to the problem, rather than the expansive needs of capitalist imperialism (which the new State-capitalist economic techniques have largely obviated) or the "contradiction" between Soviet collectivism and American private capitalism (which exists but is not so automatic in its effects as Marxists think). The machine is out of control and is grinding away according to its own logic. Here is another example of "reification" ("thing-ification"): human creations developing their own dynamic and imposing their own laws on their creators. . . .

A related Marxian illusion is that the victory of one or the other side in a modern war may advance the cause of socialism. Marx and Engels took sides, on this basis, in the American Civil War and in the Franco-Prussian War. I think it may be questioned now whether the beneficial results they expected from these conflicts (abolition of slavery, unification of Germany) have turned out to be quite so important to "progress" as they expected. The hardboiled pragmatic attitude of Marxism shows up at its worst in this now crucial matter of taking a stand in a war. . . .

Not only has it become impossible to fit modern war into the Marxian framework, but a reverse action has also taken place: war has had a shattering effect on that framework.

Economic: "More Work, Better Pay"

Marx and Engels regarded the periodic economic crises which they predicted would occur under capitalism as the immediate causes of revolutions. "We can almost calculate the moment," wrote the latter in his preface to the first volume of *Capital*, "when the unemployed, losing patience, will take their own fate into their hands." And Marx, in *The Class Struggles in France*, noted that "a real revolution is only possible in the periods when these two factors, the modern productive forces and the bourgeois production forms, come into collision with each other. . . . A new revolution is only possible in consequence of a new crisis. It is, however, just as certain as this." How do these crises arise? Marx sums it up in *Capital* (V. 3, p. 568): "The last cause of all real crises always remains the poverty and restricted consumption of the masses as compared to the tendency of capitalist production to develop productive forces in such a way that only the absolute power of consumption of the entire society would be the limit."

In a fully-developed Bureaucratic Collectivist society like that of Russia, none of the above applies: crises may occur, but they have a political character and cannot be shown—or at least have not been shown—to arise from the kind of periodic and automatic economic imbalance described by Marx. The forms of production still conflict with the productive forces—but along new lines. In societies like our own and England, which are still capitalist but in which Bureaucratic Collectivism is spreading, techniques of State spending, economic control, and deficit financing have been developed which in practice *have* avoided crises and in theory *should* be able to do so. These new economic forms are closely related to preparation for warfare. As Stalin's recent election speech emphasized, the Five Year Plans were primarily armament-building programs. Hitler's rearming of Germany was made possible by the brilliant adaptation Dr. Schacht made of Keynes' theories, which he carried so far as to produce by 1936 (and quite without intending to do so) an economy that was more Bureaucratic Collectivist than it was capitalist. As for the military implications of New Deal economics, note that in 1933, after four years of Hoover's laisser-faire capitalism, there were 16 million unemployed, or one out of every three workers. The New Deal's Keynesian approach did reduce unemployment to manageable proportions—from 7 to 10 millions. But it was war that really solved the problem: by 1943, unemployment had practically vanished (1 million), nor has it to date—since the hot war has been followed by the cold—again risen to significant heights.

The modern warmaking State, even if it is still mainly capitalist, thus avoids Marx's "inevitable" economic crises. Through deficit spending, it enlarges the purchasing power of the masses. And it brings to bear "the power of consumption of the entire society" through vast orders for munitions (a form of buying which has the further advantage of removing the goods entirely outside the market sphere so that they don't compete for a share of the public spending power: the ultimate consumer of munitions —and the adjective is most fitting—is the Enemy soldier). There is also largely eliminated another one of the factors to which Marx looked for the self-disintegration of capitalism: the "industrial reserve-army of the unemployed." In wartime, this becomes a real army. In peacetime, it gets employment through the measures just noted. For, while Marx was able to demonstrate how essential "an industrial reserve army" was to the bourgeoisie to keep down the price of labor, such an army is of no advantage to the rulers of a warmaking society, which needs two things above all: "national unity" and full production. Unemployment, with its idle and discontented millions, from this standpoint has only disadvantages.

Finally, nothing improves the economic position of the working class and strengthens its trade unions more than a really good war. This phenomenon, which was uneasily noted by Marxists in World War I, has become positively absurd in World War II. In this country, there was a considerable increase in union membership during the war, and "maintenance-of-membership" clauses, which give the union a certain degree of stability, became standard procedure in War Labor Board awards. Manufacturing wages went up 71% (from $26 to $45 a week average) between 1940 and 1943. This is all common knowledge, but it puts an odd twist on the idea that the improvement of the class position of the workers is necessarily connected with progress. And it makes it very difficult to convince the workers *as workers* that war is a curse.

Jesús Espinosa, a Mexican gardener of the city of San Antonio, Texas, was asked last week to venture an opinion on an important subject. What did he think of the atomic bomb?
Jesús stared, then shrugged his shoulders eloquently.
Should the U.S. give it to other nations?
"Why not?" said Jesús.
But what if the other nations started a war with it?
Jesús brightened. "More work, better pay," he said.
Did he and his friends discuss the possibilities of atomic energy?
Jesús gave his interviewer a long, pitying look and went back to shoveling dirt. (*Time*, March 18, 1945.)

Political: The Dominance of Foreign Policy

It is true that Mussolini was demagogic when he transposed the class-struggle theme by speaking of "proletarian nations" like Italy whose hope lay in rebellion against "bourgeois nations" like England (stifling at the same time his own workingclass movement the better to fight what might be—demagogically—called "the international class struggle"). But the point is he was not *just* being demagogic. Nor was Hitler when he joined those hitherto warring concepts "national" and "socialism." Everywhere today we see the class struggle *inside* nations yielding to struggle *between* nations, so that the main conflict nowadays is between peoples and not between exploiters and exploited. If history has indeed *a* motor—which I doubt, just as I doubt the existence of History with a capital "H"—then the motor is war, not revolution. Everywhere "national unity" is weakening the class struggle: politically, it moderates class conflicts by emphasizing the common national enemy; economically, it makes concessions to the masses in return for their support in warmaking. In Russia, where Hitler's "national socialism" has been realized far more completely than it ever was in Germany, the political control of the rulers over the ruled is so complete that the economic concessions are the most trifling, the gap between the living standards of the masses and their exploiters is the widest.

Marxists will retort that revolutionary class struggle inside each nation is the way to weaken the present supernationalism that is leading us to a third world war. I would agree that it is certainly an important method, but this simply raises the question of WHY there is so little class struggle today. WHY the masses follow their leaders to war with such docility. It is one purpose of this article to suggest that the Marxist answers to this question of WHY are superficial and in large measure obsolete. And certainly, until we can answer the question WHY the condition exists, we cannot do much effectively about changing it.

The more war becomes dominant, the more the ruling classes can monopolize continually—not just in time of actual hostilities—the most powerful ideological weapon they have ever grasped: the appeal for "unity" of the whole nation against a threat from outside. This weapon is powerful psychologically, because it plays on very deep fears and in-group loyalties. It is also powerful in rational terms, because it is perfectly true that national defeat is catastrophic for *all* classes, not just for the ruling class. Thus the strongest appeal of the Nazis in the terrible final year of the war was their picture of what the consequences of defeat would be for the German people; and now we see—and doubtless the Germans see even better—that the Nazis were quite right in all their predictions.

One striking confirmation of the way war rather than class struggle has become the center of our world is the importance that foreign policy now assumes. The disagreements between "Left" and "Right" on domestic policy, unsubstantial enough precisely because of the needs of "national unity" in order to present a strong front to competing nations, vanish completely when the really vital question of foreign policy arises. . . .

Now that the national State has become the great menace, and war and foreign policy the great issues, the "realistic" attitude that has always distinguished Marx and his followers on these matters has become quite unrealistic (if one's aim is not effective warmaking or the furtherance of nationalistic ambitions). The Anarchists' uncompromising rejection of the State, the subject of Marxian sneers for its "absolutist" and "Utopian" character, makes much better sense in the present era than the Marxian relativist and historical approach.[5] The pacifists also seem to be more real-

[5] "Bakunin has a peculiar theory," Engels wrote to Cuno in 1872, "the chief point of which is that he does not regard capital, and therefore the class contradiction between capitalists and wage-earners . . . as the main evil to be abolished. Instead, he regards the State as the main evil. . . . Therefore, it is above all the State which must

istic than the Marxists both in their understanding of modern war and also in their attempts to do something about it. A very interesting essay could be written today about the unrealism of Realism and the metaphysical nature of Materialism.

*　　*　　*

Scientific Method and Value Judgment

The fact that "everybody" agrees that war, torture, and the massacre of helpless people are Evil is not reassuring to me. It seems to show that our ethical code is no longer *experienced*, but is simply *assumed*, so that it becomes a collection of "mere platitudes." One does not take any risks for a platitude. Ask a dozen passersby, picked at random, whether they believe it is right to kill helpless people; they will reply "of course not" (the "of course" is ominous) and will probably denounce the inquirer as a monster for even suggesting there could be two answers to the question. But they will all "go along" with their government in World War III and kill as many helpless enemy people as possible. (While the monstrous questioner may well become a conscientious objector.) Good and Evil can only have reality for us if we do not take them for granted, if they are not regarded as platitudes but as agonizing problems. Thus the easy, universal agreement that war is Evil is a matter for suspicion, not congratulation.[6]

*　　*　　*

The Idea of Progress

The Metaphysics of Progress

As D. S. Savage has pointed out ("Socialism in Extremis," *Politics*, January 1945), those who build their political philosophy on the idea of progress tend to justify the Means by the End, the Present by the Future, the Here by the There. The Progressive can swallow war as a Means to the End, peace; he can overlook the unsatisfactory Present by fixing his eyes on a distant and perfect Future, as in the case of the USSR; he can justify the loss of the individual's freedom Here as necessary to a workable organization of society There. He is able to perform these considerable feats of abstract thinking because he, who makes so free with the charge of

---

be done away with, and then capitalism will go to hell of itself. We, on the contrary, say: do away with capital, the appropriation of the whole means of production in the hands of the few, and the State will fall away of itself. The difference is an essential one." It is indeed.

[6] Since I'm no longer a pacifist, I could no longer write this eloquent paragraph.

"metaphysician" and "Utopian," is actually the arch-metaphysician of our time, quite prepared to sacrifice indefinitely and on the most grandiose scale the real, material, concrete interests of living human beings on the altar of a metaphysical concept of Progress which he assumes (again metaphysically) is the "real essence" of history.

And what an assumption this idea is based on: nothing less than the daring hypothesis—which the Progressive advances as if it were the most elementary common sense—that the "real" nature of scientific advance is to benefit humanity. There are, and it is admitted, certain regrettable by-products of this advance. The atomic bomb is one, and another is the new "germ spray" developed by our own scientists which promises to make The Bomb look positively benevolent. . . . :

"They have developed a weapon that can wipe out all forms of life in a large city. It is a germ proposition and is sprayed from airplanes . . . It is quick and certain death. You would not have to drop a germ on every person in a city. One operation would be sufficient, for the effects would spread rapidly." (N. Y. *Times*, May 25, 1946.)

According to the scientific metaphysician, this sort of thing is a regrettable by-product of Progress, a perversion, in fact. He will point out that this lethal germ spray has also been developed, in the form of DDT, to rid mankind of those insect pests which cause $5,678,945,001 worth of damage *in this country alone* every year (or fill in your own figures). And he will conclude that the problem is to use it for Good instead of Evil, or more specifically, to spray it on insects but not on people.

*   *   *

1. Personally, I am not particularly ascetic. It is, indeed, just because I do value human, this-worldly satisfactions that I am skeptical about Scientific Progress. The real materialists today are those who reject Historical Materialism. For man's mastery of nature has led to nature's mastering man. The ever more efficient organization of technology in the form of large, disciplined aggregations of producers implies the modern mass-society which implies authoritarian controls and the kind of irrational—sub-rational, rather—nationalist ideology we have seen developed to its highest pitch in Germany and Russia. The one great power today whose culture is most materialistic, whose leaders proclaim themselves Marxists, where the crudest optimism of progress is rampant is also the one where the alienation of man from his own products has gone the farthest, the one whose citizens lead the lives of bees or of ants but not of men, the one whose soldiers, fresh from the land of materialistic progress and Five Year Plans, are astounded at the ease, luxury and comfort of life in Bulgaria and will commit any crime to possess themselves of a bicycle. So we, too, may perish in the next war because atomic fission is the latest stage of scientific discovery, and Progress depends on the advancement of science. But a simple-minded person might see in such modern truisms as that you

must reach socialism through dictatorship ("Sure, the Soviet Union isn't democratic, but that's the only way a backward country can be raised to an industrial level that will support democratic institutions later on—just wait fifty years!") or that atomic fission holds ultimate promise of the Abundant Life—such a simple person might see in these propositions a similarity to that promise of a better life in Heaven on which the Catholic Church banks so heavily.

2. It may be that the fact that Western intellectuals are showing more and more signs of what Sidney Hook has called "the new failure of nerve" —*i.e.*, skepticism about scientific progress—is of some historical significance, for intellectuals often sense now what most people will believe later on. Is it fantastic to imagine that large masses of people may become, as life grows increasingly unbearable in our scientifically-planned jungle, what might be called Human materialists (as against the Historical and Progressive variety)? That they may conclude that they don't want electric iceboxes if the industrial system required to produce them also produces World War III, or that they would prefer fewer and worse or even no automobiles if the price for more and better is the regimentation of people on a scale which precludes their behaving humanly toward each other?

*   *   *

Wanted: A New Concept of Political Action

As socialists, our central problem today is what Georg Lukacs calls "reification" ("thing-ification"), that process which Marx prophetically described in his theory of "alienation": the estrangement of man from his own nature by the social forces he himself generates.

"This crystallization of social activity," write the young Marx and Engels in *The German Ideology*, "this consolidation of what we ourselves produce into an objective power above us, growing out of control, thwarting our expectations, bringing to naught our calculations, is one of the chief factors in historical development up to now. And out of this very contradiction between the interest of the individual and that of the community, the latter takes an independent form as THE STATE, divorced from the real interests of individual and community . . . The social power, *i.e.*, the multiplied productive forces . . . appears to these individuals, since their cooperation is not voluntary but coerced, not as their own united power but as an alien force existing outside them, of the origin and end of which they are ignorant, which they thus cannot control, which on the contrary passes through a peculiar series of phases and stages independent of the will and action of men—nay, even being the prime governor of these! . . .

"How does it come about that personal interests continually grow, despite the persons, into class-interests, into common interests which win an independent existence over against the individual persons . . . enter as such into opposition with the real individuals . . . ? How does it come about that, within this process of the self-assertion of personal interests as class-interests, the personal behavior of the individual must become hard and remote, *estranged* from itself . . . ?"[7]

It is not difficult to sketch out the kind of society we need to rescue modern man from his present alienation. It would be one whose only aim, justification and principle would be the full development of each individual, and the removal of all social bars to his complete and immediate satisfaction in his work, his leisure, his sex life, and all other aspects of his nature. (To remove all social bars does not, of course, mean to remove all bars; complete happiness and satisfaction is probably impossible in any society, and would be dull even if possible; regardless of the excellence of social institutions, there will always be, for example, persons who are in love with others who aren't in love with them.) This can only be done if each individual understands what he is doing and has the power, within the limitations of his own personality and of our common human imperfection, to act exactly as he thinks best for himself. This in turn depends on people entering into direct personal relationships with each other, which in turn means that the political and economic units of society (workshops, exchange of goods, political institutions) are small enough to allow the participants to understand them and to make their individual influence felt. If effective wars cannot be fought by groups the size of New England town meetings, and I take it they cannot, this is one more reason for giving up war (rather than the town meeting). If automobiles cannot be made efficiently by small factories, then let us make them inefficiently. If scientific research would be hampered in a small-unit society, then let us by all means hamper it. Said the young Marx: "For Hegel, the starting-point is the State. In a democracy, the starting-point is man . . . Man is not made for the law, but the law is made for man.

This is all clear enough. What is not so generally understood is that the traditional Progressive approach, taking History as the starting-point and thinking in terms of mass political parties, bases itself on this same alienation of man which it thinks it is combating. It puts the individual into

[7] English translation, International Publishers, 1939, pp. 22, 23, 24, and 203. I have put "coerced" instead of this edition's "natural," a change I think justified by its own Note 12, p. 202. These formulations are so wonderfully precise and imaginative as to make one regret all the more that Marx, instead of making his theory of alienation the cornerstone of his intellectual effort, chose to waste years on economic analysis which today has only historical interest. Nor was it just a matter of a lost opportunity. The remedy for this alienation of man by his own creations which Marx evolved, misled by his historical-materialist concepts—that is, the class struggle conducted by parties and trade unions directed towards replacing capitalism with collectivism—this has turned out to be simply the 20th century aspect of that alienation which the above passage so admirably describes.

the same powerless, alienated role vis-à-vis the party or the trade union as the manipulators of the modern State do, except that the slogans are different. The current failure of the European masses to get excited about socialist slogans and programs indicates that the masses are, as Rosa Luxemburg constantly and rightly insisted, much smarter and more "advanced" than their intellectual leaders. The brutal fact is that the man in the street everywhere is quite simply *bored* with socialism, as expounded by the Socialist, Stalinist, and Trotskyist epigones of Marx, that he suspects it is just a lot of stale platitudes which either have no particular meaning (Socialists, Trotskyists, British Labor Party), or else a sinister one (Stalinists). Above all, he feels that there is no interest in it for *him*, as an individual human being—that he is as powerless and manipulated vis-à-vis his socialist mass-organization as he is towards his capitalistic employers and their social and legal institutions.

Here is observable a curious and unexpected (to Progressives) link between the masses and those dissident intellectuals here and there who are beginning to show a distrust of the old Marxian-Deweyan-Progressive verities and to cast about for some firmer ground. Each party, in its own way, has come to find the old slogans and axioms either treacherous or boring—mostly the latter. Boring because they give no promise of leading to that which they proclaim and meanwhile still further alienate man from his true and spontaneous nature.

From all this one thing seems to follow: we must reduce political action to a modest, unpretentious, personal level—one that is real in the sense that it satisfies, here and now, the psychological needs, and the ethical values of the particular persons taking part in it. We must begin way at the bottom again, with small groups of individuals in various countries, grouped around certain principles and feelings they have in common. These should probably not be physically isolated as was the case in the 19th century since this shuts one off from the common experience of one's fellow men. They should probably consist of individuals—*families*, rather —who live and make their living in the everyday world but who come together often enough and intimately enough to form a *psychological* (as against a geographical) community. The purpose of such groups would be twofold. Within itself, the group would exist so that its members could come to know each other as fully as possible as human beings (the difficulty of such knowledge of others in modern society is a chief source of evil), to exchange ideas and discuss as fully as possible what is "on their minds" (not only the atomic bomb but also the perils of child-rearing), and in general to learn the difficult art of living with other people. The group's purpose toward the outside world would be to take certain actions together (as, against Jim Crow in this country, or to further pacifism), to support individuals whether members of the group or not who stand up for the common ideals, and to preach those ideals—or, if you prefer, make propaganda—by word and by deed, in the varied everyday contacts of the group members with their fellow-men. . . .

The ideas which these groups would advance, by word and deed, would probably run along something like the following lines:

1. The dominance of war and the development of weapons atrocious beyond all past imagination make pacifism, in my opinion, a sine-qua-non of any Radical movement. The first great principle would, therefore, be that killing and hurting others is wrong, always and absolutely, and that no member of the group will use such methods or let himself be drafted to do so.[8]

2. Coercion of the individual, whether by the State or by a revolutionary party, is also wrong in principle, and will be opposed with sabotage, ridicule, evasion, argument, or simple refusal to submit to authority— as circumstances may require. Our model here would be the old I.W.W. rather than the Marxist Internationals.[9]

3. All ideologies which require the sacrifice of the present in favor of the future will be looked on with suspicion. People should be happy and should satisfy their spontaneous needs here and now.[10] If people don't

[8] Again, I am now more moderate in my absolutism. Under certain extreme circumstances, I would use force, personally and even as a soldier.

[9] Though I still hold to the *tendency* expressed here, the actual formulation now seems to me absurdly overstated. Even the Wobblies, after all, since they lived in a world of cops and judges, must have submitted to authority far more often than they rebelled against it or evaded it—or else, they would have spent *all* their time in jail (where, again, if they consistently flouted authority, they would have spent *all* their time in solitary confinement if not worse). Also certain kinds of social authority—as, traffic laws, sanitary regulations—are from even the purest anarchist viewpoint not objectionable and indeed useful. Proudhon drew the line sensibly: he was willing to submit to the State in matters which did not seem to him to importantly affect his interests adversely.

[10] "To make such a statement," a friend wrote me, "amounts to saying in so many words that one doesn't give a damn about moral ideals. Morality, in fact, is nothing at all if it is not giving up something in the present in favor of something not only of the future but even of the purely 'ideal.' And it isn't even a question of morality: no intelligent activity of any kind would be possible if your statement, and your demand for immediate satisfaction, had to be taken seriously." Even though I qualify this statement as "a leaning rather than a principle," I still must admit it is onesided as put here, and that acting out an ethical ideal may often involve some sacrifice of the present to the future and perhaps also of one's spontaneous, or at least immediate, needs. But the prevailing morality, Christian or Marxian, I think involves far too much of that kind of thing, going to the extremes of the Puritan and of the Communist fanatic. I think pleasure and virtue ought to be re-introduced to each other, and that if there's too much of the sacrificial and not enough of the enjoyable about one's political or ethical behavior, it's a bad sign. Those who have a real vocation for saintliness, like Gandhi, generally strike one as happy to the point of positive gaiety. But too many of us are self-alienated drudges of virtue or work, like Poseidon in Kafka's sketch: "Poseidon sat at his desk, doing figures. The administration of all the waters gave him endless work. . . . It cannot be said that he enjoyed his work; he did it only because it had been assigned to him; in fact, he had already filed frequent petitions for—as he put it—more cheerful work, but every time the offer of something different was made to him, it would turn out that nothing suited him quite so well as his present position. . . . Actually, a shift of

enjoy what they are doing, they shouldn't do it. (This includes the activities of the group.) This point is a leaning, a *prejudice* rather than a principle; that is, the extent to which it is acted on would be relative to other things.

4. Socialism is primarily an ethical matter. The number of people who want it at any given moment has nothing to do with its validity for the individual who makes it his value. What *he* does, furthermore, is considered to be just as "real" as what History does.

5. Members of the groups would get into the habit, discouraged by the Progressive frame of mind, of acting here and now, on however tiny a scale, for their beliefs. They would do as the handful of British and American scientists did who just refused, as individuals and without any general support, to make atomic bombs; not as Albert Einstein and other scientists are now doing—raising money for an educational campaign to show the public how horrible The Bomb is, while they continue to cooperate with General Groves in making more and bigger bombs.

6. They will think in human, not class terms. This means they will free themselves from the Marxian fetishism of the mass, preferring to be able to speak modest meaningful truths to a small audience rather than grandiose empty formulae to a big one. This also means, for the moment, turning to the intelligentsia as one's main supporters, collaborators and audience, on the assumption that what we are looking for represents so drastic a break with past traditions of thinking and behaving that at this early stage only a few crackpots and eccentrics (*i.e.,* intellectuals) will understand what we're talking about, or care about it at all. We may console ourselves that all new social movements, including Marxism, have begun this way: with a few intellectuals rather than at the mass level.

Five Characteristics of a Radical

While it is still too soon to be definite about what a Radical *does* (beyond the vague suggestions just indicated), it is possible to conclude

---

posts was unthinkable for Poseidon—he had been appointed God of the sea in the beginning and that he had to remain. What irritated him most—and it was this that was chiefly responsible for his dissatisfaction with his job—was to hear of the conceptions formed about him: how he was always riding about through the waves with his trident. When all the while he sat here in the depths of the world-ocean, doing figures uninterruptedly, with now and then a trip to Jupiter as the only break in the monotony —a trip, moreover, from which he usually returned in a rage. Thus he had hardly seen the sea. . . . and he had never actually travelled around it. He was in the habit of saying that what he was waiting for was the fall of the world. Then, probably, a quiet moment would be granted in which, just before the end and after having checked the last row of figures, he would be able to make a quick little tour."

with a more concrete idea of what he is. What are his attitudes toward politics? They may be summed up under five heads:

1. Negativism.
2. Unrealism.
3. Moderation.
4. Smallness.
5. Self-ishness.

The Positiveness of Negativism

The first two adjectives which occur to a Progressive when confronted with a Radical attitude are: "negativistic" and "unrealistic." In this section, let us consider the former.

During the late war, those of us who opposed it were told by Progressives who supported it that our position was absurd because we couldn't "do anything" about it; that is, we couldn't stop the war. They felt that they were at least *acting* in accordance with their convictions; that is, they were helping bring about an Allied victory. This criticism, however, reveals an incomprehension of the nature of modern social organization: there is no place in the orderly, bureaucratized workings of a first-class power today for individual emotion, will, choice, or action. As the late Dr. Goebbels well expressed it: "Moods and emotions, the so-called 'morale' of the population, matters little. What matters is that they should preserve their bearing (*Haltung*) . . . Expressions such as patriotism and enthusiasm are quite out of place. The German people simply do their duty, that's all." (*Das Reich*, April 9, 1943.) The Progressive is the victim of an illusion which he could puncture for himself in a moment if, instead of doing what his Draft Board told him to do, he had tried to volunteer for the work he thought he could do best. He would have been told by some harrassed bureaucrat: "For God's sake, go home and wait till we call you. Don't come around upsetting our Selective Service system, which is a delicate and complex affair geared to process so many of you patriots in such and such a time for such and such kinds of service." Thus the only difference between those who *submit* to the draft because they are afraid not to and those who *welcome* it because they want their country to win the war, is in the ethical value attached to an identical action. But the Progressive, as a good Deweyan or Marxian, does not believe in values apart from action. The Radical, however, does not submit to the draft; he refuses to do what the State wants him to do; by not acting, he is thus acting—and in the Deweyan sense that what he does (or rather doesn't) distinguishes him from those with different values. The only way to be positive vis-à-vis the modern State is to be negative, *i.e.*, refuse to do what it wants one to do. The situation might be compared to a group of people being driven in a high-powered automobile along a road that ends in a precipice. They see the Radicals sitting by the side of the road—just sitting. "Yaahh, negativists!" they cry. "Look at us! *We're* going somewhere, *we're* really *doing* something!" (There is no space here to develop the relevance of Lao-Tse's principle of "non-acting"—and perhaps it is not necessary.)

The Realism of Unrealism

The Progressive insists that one has a duty in every situation to choose between what he calls "real" alternatives, and that it is irresponsible to refuse to make such a choice. By "real" he means an alternative which has a reasonably good chance of success. Thus in World War II, he saw two real alternatives: to support the Allies or to support Hitler. He naturally chose the former. The trouble with his "real" alternatives is that each of them is part of the whole system of war and exploitation, to put an end to which is the very justification of his choice. The Radical believes—and I think logic is on his side—that only an alternative which is antithetical to the existing system can lead one to the abolition of that system. For him, it is unrealistic to hope to secure a peaceful world through war, to hope to defeat the brutality and oppression of Hitler by the brutality and oppression of the American and Russian political systems. Consider the Radical approach to the present situation of France, for example. Today that country lies between two mighty imperialisms: Russian and Anglo-American. The French Progressive wants to create a decent socialist society in France and to avoid the destruction of France in a future war between the two blocs. But in his terms of "real" alternatives, he can only think of aligning France with one or the other of the two powerblocks (with Russia if he is a Communist, with Anglo-America if he is a Socialist) and making France as strong a power as possible. It is not hard to show that a weak power which allies itself to a stronger one does not thereby avert war and does not even escape being sacrificed as a pawn in that coming war; and that, as the examples of Nazi Germany and Stalinist Russia show us, to build a strong army and munitions industry means to enslave and oppress the people, regardless of the literary charm of the slogans under which the dirty work is done. The Radical Frenchman would begin by himself, personally, refusing cooperation in the above policy, sabotaging it at every chance, and trying to persuade by argument and emotional appeal his fellow men and women to do likewise. The final perspective would be a pacifist-socialist revolution; this would have at least a chance of striking fire in the hearts of other peoples, spurring them to similar action against their oppressors. Success would be problematical, but at least (1) it would not be logically and historically inconceivable (as in the case with the Progressive's armament-and-alliance program), and (2) his end would be congruent with his means, so that he could view the situation with clear eyes and a whole heart, free from the befuddling and stultifying evasions and compromises which the Progressive must resort to in such a situation.[11]

The greatest living theorist of Progressivism, as defined in this article, is John Dewey. It seems not irrelevant to recall that Dewey gave active support to both World War I and II. The contrast between the Progressive and the Radical notions of "realistic" and "positive" action comes out in the contrasting behavior in World War I of Dewey and his brilliant young disciple, Randolph Bourne.

"In 1916," we read in Louis Filler's life of Bourne, "Bourne broke with John Dewey, and a rift opened that was to become wider as both men formulated their stands on the war. The differences between them were to culminate in a statement of principles by Bourne which was to stand as perhaps his supreme literary achievement. Dewey had slowly come around to the conviction that war represented a state of affairs which had to be faced and mastered by men who wished to be effective social agents . . . The justice of the Allied cause was the assumption behind the articles which Dewey contributed to *The New Republic* and *The Dial* in the interim between American isolation and America's entrance into the war. Dewey's role was to provide the theoretical base for armed preparedness.

"Dewey's conclusions followed logically from his philosophy because the essence of pragmatism was action. 'Our culture,' he wrote, 'must be consonant with realistic science and machine industry, instead of a refuge from them.' ('American Education and Culture,' *New Republic*, July 1, 1916.) If the task of the day was war, then our culture must be 'consonant' with war. Dewey, therefore, called for army training as a form of contemporary education. (*New Republic*, April 22, 1916.)

"The very thought of military regimentation aroused in Bourne the keenest agitation, and out of his desperate denial of the idea came one of his most brilliant essays: "A Moral Equivalent for Universal Military Service" (*New Republic*, July 1, 1916.) . . . It was persuasive but was it practical? It demonstrated how essentially the poet Bourne was, that the relative value of education and war, and not the question of how he or anyone else could most effectively influence American affairs for the better, seemed to him the immediate question demanding solution . . . Bourne was fighting for a doomed cause."

*   *   *

Against the Fetishism of the Masses

To Marx's "fetishism of commodities" I would counterpoise our modern fetishism—that of the masses. The more Progressive one's thinking, the more one assumes that the test of the goodness of a political program

---

[11] This paragraph now seems nonsensical to me.

is how wide a popular appeal it makes. I venture to assert, for the present
time at least, the contrary: that, as in art and letters, communicability
to a large audience is in inverse ratio to the excellence of a political approach. This is not a good thing: as in art, it is a deforming, crippling factor. Nor is it an eternal rule: in the past, the ideas of a tiny minority,
sometimes almost reduced to the vanishing-point of one individual, have
slowly come to take hold on more and more of their fellow-men; and we
may hope that our own ideas may do likewise. But such, it seems to me, is
our situation today, whether we like it or not. To attempt to propagate
political ideas on a mass scale today results in either corrupting them or
draining them of all emotional force and intellectual meaning. The very
media by which one must communicate with a large audience—the radio,
the popular press, the movies—are infected; the language and symbols of
mass comunication are infected; if one tries to use these media, one gets
something like the newspaper *PM*, and something like the political writings of Max Lerner. Albert Camus, for example, edited the underground
Resistance paper, *Combat*, during the German occupation of France. After
the liberation, *Combat* quickly won a large audience, and Camus became
one of the most widely read and influential political journalists in France.
Yet, as he told me, he found that writing about politics in terms of the
great parties and for a mass audience made it impossible for him to deal
with reality, or to tell the truth. And so he has withdrawn from *Combat*,
giving up what in traditional terms would seem to be a supremely fortunate
chance for a socially-minded intellectual to propagate his ideas among the
masses, in order to cast about for some better way of communicating. This
will be found, I suspect, in talking to fewer people more precisely about
"smaller" subjects.

As it is with communication, so is it with political organization. The
two traditional Marxian approaches to organization are those of the Second
and the Third International. The former puts its faith in mass parties, tied
in with the great trade unions; the latter, in a disciplined, centralized,
closely organized corps of "professional revolutionaries" which will lead
the masses in revolutionary situations. Superficially, it would seem that the
vast scale of modern society calls for mass parties to master it, while the
centralized power of the modern State can be countered only by an equally
centralized and closely organized revolutionary party. But the fact seems to
be just the contrary: the State can crush such groups, whether organized
as mass parties or as Bolshevik elite corps, the moment they show signs of
becoming serious threats, precisely because they fight the State on its own
grounds, they *compete* with the State. The totalization of State power
today means that only something on a different plane can cope with it,
something which fights the State from a vantage point which the State's
weapons can reach only with difficulty. Perhaps the most effective means
of countering violence, for example, is non-violence, which throws the
enemy off balance ("moral ju-jitsu" some one has called it) and confuses

his human agents, all the more so because it appeals to traitorous elements in their own hearts.[12]

All this means that individual actions, based on moral convictions, have *greater* force today than they had two generations ago. As an English correspondent wrote me recently: "The main reason for Conscientious Objection is undoubtedly that it does make a personal feeling have weight. In the present world, the slightest sign of individual revolt assumes a weight out of all proportion to its real value." Thus in drafting men into that totalitarian society, the U.S. Army, the examiners often rejected anyone who stated openly that he did not *want* to enter the Army and felt he would be unhappy there. We may assume this action was not due to sympathy, but rather to the fact that, as practical men, the examiners knew that such a one would "make trouble" and that the smooth running of the vast mechanism could be thrown out by the presence of such a gritty particle precisely because of the machine's delicately-geared hugeness.

Another conclusion is that group action against The Enemy is most effective when it is most spontaneous and loosest in organization. The opposition of the romantic clubs of German youth ("Edelweiss," "Black Pirates") was perhaps more damaging to the Nazis than that of the old parties and unions. So, too, World-over Press reports that a recently discovered secret list of British leaders to be liquidated by the Nazis after the invasion of England gave top priority not to trade unionists nor to leftwing political leaders but to well-known pacifists.

What seems necessary is thus to encourage attitudes of disrespect, scepticism, ridicule towards the State and all authority, rather than to build up a competing authority. It is the difference between a frontal attack all along the line and swift flanking jabs at points where The Enemy is weakest, between large-scale organized warfare and guerrilla operations. Marxists go in for the former: the Bolsheviks emphasize discipline and unity in order to match that of The Enemy; the reformists try to outweigh The Enemy's power by shepherding great masses of voters and trade unionists into the scales. But the status quo is too powerful to be overthrown by such tactics; and, even worse, they show a disturbing tendency to lead one over to the side of The Enemy.

Self-ishness, or the Root Is Man

Granted that individual actions can never overthrow the status quo, and also that even spontaneous mass rebellion will be fruitless unless it has some kind of conscious program and also unless certain elementary steps of coordination and organization are taken. But today we confront this situation: the masses just do not act towards what most of the readers of

---

[12] As of 1953, I admire the ingenuity of this argument almost as much as I deplore its insubstantiality. I fear that I overestimated the fermenting power of the yeast and underestimated the doughiness of the dough.

this magazine* would recognize as some fundamental betterment of society. The only way, at present, of so *acting* (as against just "making the record" for the muse of Marxian history by resolutions and manifestoes "against imperialist war," "for the international proletarian revolution," etc.) seems to be through symbolic individual actions, based on one person's insistence on his own values, and through the creation of small fraternal groups which will support such actions, keep alive a sense of our ultimate goals, and both act as a leavening in the dough of mass society and attract more and more of the alienated and frustrated members of that society. These individual stands have two advantages over the activities of those who pretend that mass action is now possible:

1. They make a dramatic appeal to people, the appeal of the individual who is bold enough and serious enough to stand alone, if necessary, against the enormous power of The State; this encourages others to resist a little more than they would otherwise in *their* everyday life, and also preserves the living seeds of protest and rebellion from which later on bigger things may grow.
2. They at least preserve the revolutionary vitality and principles of the few individuals who make such stands, while the mass-actionists become, if they stick by their principles, deadened and corrupted personally by their constant submission in their own personal behavior to the standards of The Enemy—and much more corrupted than the simple bourgeois who feels himself at one with those standards (any one who has been through the Trotskyist movement, for example, as I have, knows that in respect to decent personal behavior, truthfulness, and respect for dissident opinion, the "comrades" are generally much inferior to the average stockbroker). On the other hand, if they compromise with principles in order to establish contact with the masses, they simply become part of The Enemy's forces, as is the case with the British Labor Party and the French Socialists. Marxists always sneer at the idea of individual action and individual responsibility on the grounds that we are simply interested in "saving our own souls." But what is so terrible about that? Isn't it better to save one's soul than to lose it? (And NOT to "gain the whole world," either!)

The first step towards a new concept of political action (and political morality) is for each person to decide what he thinks is right, what satisfies *him*, what *he* wants. And then to examine with scientific method the environment to figure out how to get it—or, if he can't get it, to see how much he can get without compromising his personal values. Self-ishness must be restored to respectability in our scheme of political values. Not that the individual exists apart from his fellow men, in Max Stirner's sense. I agree with Marx and Proudhon that the individual must define himself

* Reference is to *Politics*, in which the article originally appeared.—Ed.

partly in his social relations. But the point is to make these real *human* relations and not abstract concepts of class or history. It has often been observed that nations—and, I might add, classes, even the proletariat—have a lower standard of ethical behavior than individuals do. Even if all legal constraints were removed, I take it we can assume that few people would devote themselves exclusively to murder or would constantly lie to their friends and families; yet the most respected leaders of present societies, the military men and the political chieftains, in their public capacities become specialists in lying and murder. Always, of course, with the largest aims, "for the good of humanity."[13]

A friend put it well in a letter I received several months ago: "So long as morality is all in public places—politics, Utopia, revolutions (nonviolent included), progress—our private mores continue to be a queasy mixture of chivalry and cynicism: all in terms of *angles*, either for or against. We're all against political sin, we all love humanity, but individuals are sort of tough to love, even tougher to hate. Goldenhaired dreams, humanitarian dreams—what's the difference so long as they smell good? Meanwhile, patronize any whore, fight in any war, but don't marry the girl and don't fight the boss—too dangerous . . . No. Damn, our only chance is to try to get as small, private, honest, selfish as we can. Don't you agree that one can't have a moral attitude toward Humanity? Too big."

Or to put it more generally. Technological progress, the organization from the top of human life (what Max Weber calls "rationalization"), the overconfidence of the past two centuries in scientific method—these have led us, literally, into a dead end. Their trend is now clear: atomic warfare, bureaucratic collectivism, "the crystallization of social activity into an objective power above us, growing out of our control, thwarting our expectations, bringing to naught our calculations . . ." To try to fight this trend, as the Progressives of all shades do, with the same forces that have brought it about appears absurd to me. We must emphasize the emotions, the imagination, the moral feelings, the primacy of the individual human being, must restore the balance that has been broken by the hypertrophy of science in the last two centuries. The root is man, here and not there, now and not then.

---

[13] "For God's sake, do not drag me into another war! I am worn down and worn out with crusading and defending Europe and protecting mankind; I *must* think a little of myself. I am sorry for the Spaniards—I am sorry for the Greeks—I deplore the fate of the Jews—the people of the Sandwich islands are groaning under the most detestable tyranny—Bagdad is oppressed—I do not like the present state of the Delta—Tibet is not comfortable. Am I to fight for all these people? The world is bursting with sin and sorrow. Am I to be champion of the Decalogue and to be eternally raising fleets and armies to make all men good and happy? We have just done saving Europe, and I am afraid the consequence will be that we shall cut each other's throats. No war, dear Lady Grey; no eloquence; but apathy, selfishness, common sense, arithmetic." So, Sydney Smith, shortly after the Napoleonic wars.

Il Programma Anarchico*

Errico Malatesta

Aims and Objectives

We believe that most of the ills that afflict mankind stem from a bad social organisation; and that Man could destroy them if he wished and knew how.

*   *   *

... Step by step through a most complicated series of struggles of every description, of invasions, wars, rebellions, repressions, concessions won by struggle, associations of the oppressed united for defence, and of the conquerors for attack, we have arrived at the present state of society, in which some have inherited the land and all social wealth, while the mass of the people, disinherited in all respects, is exploited and oppressed by a small possessing class.

From all this stems the misery in which most workers live today, and which in turn creates the evils such as ignorance, crime, prostitution, diseases due to malnutrition, mental depression and premature death. From all this arises a special class (government) which, provided with the necessary means of repression, exists to legalise and protect the owning class from the demands of the workers; and then it uses the powers at its disposal to create privileges for itself and to subject, if it can, the owning class itself as well. From this the creation of another privileged class (the clergy), which by a series of fables about the will of God, and about an after-life etc., seeks to persuade the oppressed to accept oppression meekly, and (just as the government does), as well as serving the interest of the owning class, serves its own. From this the creation of an official science which, in all those matters serving the interests of the ruling class, is the negation of true science. From this the patriotic spirit, race hatred, wars and armed peace, sometimes more disastrous than wars themselves. From this the transformation of love into torment or sordid commerce. From this hatred, more or less disguised, rivalry, suspicion among all men, insecurity and universal fear.

We want to change radically such a state of affairs. And since all these

FROM *Malatesta, His Life and Ideas*, by Vernon Richards. Copyright 1965. Pp. 182–188; 195–198. Reprinted by permission of the author.
* *Il Programma Anarchico* was drafted by Malatesta and adopted by the Unione Anarchica Italiana at its Congress in Bologna (1920).—Ed.

ills have their origin in the struggle between men, in the seeking after well-being through one's own efforts and for oneself and against everybody, we want to make amends, replacing hatred by love, competition by solidarity, the individual search for personal well-being by the fraternal cooperation for the well-being of all, oppression and imposition by liberty, the religious and pseudo-scientific lie by truth.
Therefore:

1. Abolition of private property in land, in raw materials and the instruments of labor, so that no one shall have the means of living by the exploitation of the labor of others, and that everybody, being assured of the means to produce and to live, shall be truly independent and in a position to unite freely among themselves for a common objective and according to their personal sympathies.
2. Abolition of government and of every power which makes the law and imposes it on others: therefore abolition of monarchies, republics, parliaments, armies, police forces, magistratures and any institution whatsoever endowed with coercive powers.
3. Organisation of social life by means of free association and federations of producers and consumers, created and modified according to the wishes of their members, guided by science and experience, and free from any kind of imposition which does not spring from natural needs, to which everyone, convinced by a feeling of overriding necessity, voluntarily submits.
4. The means of life, for development and well-being, will be guaranteed to children and all who are prevented from providing for themselves.
5. War on religions and all lies, even if they shelter under the cloak of science. Scientific instruction for all to advanced level.
6. War on rivalries and patriotic prejudices. Abolition of frontiers; brotherhood among all peoples.
7. Reconstruction of the family, as will emerge from the practice of love, freed from every legal tie, from every economic and physical oppression, from every religious prejudice.
This is our ideal.

Ways and Means

We have outlined under a number of headings our objectives and the ideal for which we struggle.

But it is not enough to desire something; if one really wants it adequate means must be used to secure it, and these means are not arbitrary, but instead cannot but be conditioned by the ends we aspire to and by the circumstances in which the struggle takes place, for if we ignore the choice of means we would achieve other ends, possibly diametrically opposed to those we aspire to, and this would be the obvious and inevitable consequence of our choice of means. Whoever sets out on the highroad and takes a wrong turning does not go where he intends to go but where the road leads him.

It is therefore necessary to state what are the means which in our opinion lead to our desired ends, and which we propose to adopt.

Our ideal is not one which depends for its success on the individual considered in isolation. The question is of changing the way of life of society as a whole; of establishing among men relationships based on love and solidarity; of achieving the full material, moral and intellectual development not for isolated individuals, or members of one class or of a particular political party, but for all mankind—and this is not something that can be imposed by force, but must emerge through the enlightened consciences of each one of us and be achieved with the free consent of all.

Our first task therefore must be to persuade people.

We must make people aware of the misfortunes they suffer and of their chances to destroy them. We must awaken sympathy in everybody for the misfortunes of others and a warm desire for the good of all people.

To those who are cold and hungry we will demonstrate how possible and easy it could be to assure to everybody their material needs. To those who are oppressed and despised we shall show how it is possible to live happily in a world of people who are free and equal; to those who are tormented by hatred and bitterness we will point to the road that leads to peace and human warmth that comes through learning to love one's fellow beings.

And when we will have succeeded in arousing the sentiment of rebellion in the minds of men against the avoidable and unjust evils from which we suffer in society today, and in getting them to understand how they are caused and how it depends on human will to rid ourselves of them; and when we will have created a lively and strong desire in men to transform society for the good of all, then those who are convinced, will by their own efforts as well as by the example of those already convinced, unite and want to as well as be able to act for their common ideals.

As we have already pointed out, it would be ridiculous and contrary to our objectives to seek to impose freedom, love among men and the radical development of human faculties, by means of force. One must therefore rely on the free will of others, and all we can do is to provoke the development and the expression of the will of the people. But it would be equally absurd and contrary to our aims to admit that those who do not share our views should prevent us from expressing our will, so long as it does not deny them the same freedom.

Freedom for all, therefore, to propagate and to experiment with their ideas, with no other limitation than that which arises naturally from the equal liberty of everybody.

But to this are opposed—and with brute force—those who benefit from existing privileges and who today dominate and control all social life.

In their hands they have all the means of production; and thus they suppress not only the possibility of free experimentation in new ways of communal living, and the right of workers to live freely by their own efforts, but also the right to life itself; and they oblige whoever is not a boss to have to allow himself to be exploited and oppressed if he does not wish to die of hunger.

They have police forces, a judiciary, and armies created for the express purpose of defending their privileges; and they persecute, imprison and massacre those who would want to abolish those privileges and who claim the means of life and liberty for everyone.

Jealous of their present and immediate interests, corrupted by the spirit of domination, fearful of the future, they, the privileged class, are, generally speaking incapable of a generous gesture; are equally incapable of a wider concept of their interests. And it would be foolish to hope that they should freely give up property and power and adapt themselves to living as equals and with those who today they keep in subjection.

Leaving aside the lessons of history (which demonstrates that never has a privileged class divested itself of all or some of its privileges, and never has a government abandoned its power unless obliged to do so by force or the fear of force), there is enough contemporary evidence to convince anyone that the bourgeoisie and governments intend to use armed force to defend themselves, not only against complete expropriation, but equally against the smallest popular demands, and are always ready to engage in the most atrocious persecutions and the bloodiest massacres.

For those people who want to emancipate themselves, only one course is open: that of opposing force with force.

It follows from what we have said that we have to work to awaken in the oppressed the conscious desire for a radical social transformation, and to persuade them that by uniting they have the strength to win; we must propagate our ideal and prepare the required material and moral forces to overcome those of the enemy, and to organise the new society; and when we will have the strength needed we must, by taking advantage of favourable circumstances as they arise, or which we can ourselves create, make the social revolution, using force to destroy the government and to expropriate the owners of wealth, and by putting in common the means of life and production, and by preventing the setting up of new governments which would impose their will and to hamper the reorganisation of society by the people themselves.

All this is, however, less simple than it might appear at first sight. We have to deal with people as they are in society today, in the most miserable moral and material condition; and we would be deluding ourselves in thinking that propaganda is enough to raise them to that level of intellectual development which is needed to put our ideas into effect.

Between man and his social environment there is a reciprocal action. Men make society what it is and society makes men what they are, and the result is therefore a kind of vicious circle. To transform society men must be changed, and to transform men, society must be changed.

*　　*　　*

The Political Struggle

While preaching against every kind of government, and demanding complete freedom, we must support all struggles for partial freedom, because we are convinced that one learns through struggle, and that once one begins to enjoy a little freedom one ends by wanting it all. We must always be with the people, and when we do not succeed in getting them to demand a lot we must still seek to get them to want something; and we must make every effort to get them to understand that however much or little they may demand should be obtained by their own efforts and that they should despise and detest whoever is part of, or aspires to, government.

Since government today has the power, through the legal system, to regulate daily life and to broaden or restrict the liberty of the citizen, and because we are still unable to tear this power from its grasp, we must seek to reduce its power and oblige governments to use it in the least harmful ways possible. But this we must do always remaining outside, and against, government, putting pressure on it through agitation in the streets, by threatening to take by force what we demand. Never must we accept any kind of legislative position, be it national or local, for in so doing we will neutralise the effectiveness of our activity as well as betraying the future of our cause.

The struggle against government in the last analysis is physical, material.

Governments make the law. They must therefore dispose of the material forces (police and army) to impose the law, for otherwise only those who wanted to would obey it, and it would no longer be the law, but a simple series of suggestions which all would be free to accept or reject. Governments have this power, however, and use it through the law, to strengthen their power, as well as to serve the interests of the ruling classes, by oppressing and exploiting the workers.

The only limit in the oppression of government is the power with which the people show themselves capable of opposing it. Conflict may be open or latent; but it always exists since the government does not pay attention to discontent and popular resistance except when it is faced with the danger of insurrection.

When the people meekly submit to the law, or their protests are feeble and confined to words, the government studies its own interests and ignores the needs of the people; when the protests are lively, insistent, threatening, the government, depending on whether it is more or less understanding, gives way or resorts to repression. But one always comes back to insurrection, for if the government does not give way, the people will end by rebelling; and if the government does give way, then the people gain confidence in themselves and make ever increasing demands, until such time as the incompatibility between freedom and authority becomes clear and the violent struggle is engaged.

It is therefore necessary to be prepared, morally and materially, so that when this does happen the people will emerge victorious.

A successful insurrection is the most potent factor in the emancipation of the people, for once the yoke has been shaken off, the people are free to provide themselves with those institutions which they think best, and the time lag between passing the law and the degree of civilisation which the mass of the population has attained is breached in one leap. The insurrection determines the revolution, that is, the speedy emergence of the latent forces built up during the "evolutionary" period.

Everything depends on what the people are capable of wanting.

In past insurrections unaware of the real reasons for their misfortunes, they have always wanted very little, and have obtained very little.

What will they want in the next insurrection?

The answer, in part, depends on our propaganda and what efforts we put into it.

We shall have to push the people to expropriate the bosses and put all goods in common and organise their daily lives themselves, through freely constituted associations, without waiting for orders from outside and refusing to nominate or recognise any government or constituted body in whatever guise (constituent, dictatorship, etc.) even in a provisional capacity, which ascribes to itself the right to lay down the law and impose with force its will on others.

And if the mass of the population will not respond to our appeal we must—in the name of the right we have to be free even if others wish to remain slaves and because of the force of example—put into effect as many of our ideas as we can, refuse to recognise the new government and keep alive resistance and seek that those localities where our ideas are received with sympathy should constitute themselves into anarchist communities, rejecting all governmental interference and establishing free agreements with other communities which want to live their own lives.

We shall have to, above all, oppose with every means the re-establishment of the police and the armed forces, and use any opportunity to incite workers in non anarchist localities to take advantage of the absence of repressive forces to implement the most far reaching demands that we can induce them to make.

And however things may go, to continue the struggle against the possessing class and the rulers without respite, having always in mind the complete economic, political and moral emancipation of all mankind.

Conclusion

What we want, therefore, is the complete destruction of the domination and exploitation of man by man; we want men united as brothers by a conscious and desired solidarity, all cooperating voluntarily for the well-being of all; we want society to be constituted for the purpose of supplying everybody with the means for achieving the maximum well-being, the maximum possible moral and spiritual development; we want bread, freedom, love, and science for everybody.

And in order to achieve these all-important ends, it is necessary in our opinion that the means of production should be at the disposal of everybody and that no man, or groups of men, should be in a position to oblige others to submit to their will or to exercise their influence other than through the power of reason and by example.

Therefore: expropriation of landowners and capitalists for the benefit of all; and abolition of government.

And while waiting for the day when this can be achieved: the propagation of our ideas; unceasing struggle, violent or non-violent depending on the circumstances, against government and against the boss class to conquer as much freedom and well-being as we can for the benefit of everybody.

SECTION 13

UTOPIAN PRACTICE

WHEN SOCIAL institutions are unsatisfactory, we can try to change them or to create alternatives. In this section, I include descriptions of some alternative institutions. Both the anti-hospital described by Cooper and the school that Neill writes about were isolated, small-scale units. The social experiments described in the last two articles were part of larger movements to transform society. All these examples of "utopian practice" are drawn from outside the United States.

Cooper describes the reorganization of a wing of a mental hospital in England that reversed some usual preconceptions. Whatever medication and psychotherapy they prescribe, most mental hospitals have a social organization that perpetuates mental illness. The authority structure and hospital rules continue the process of violence to the self that often began in the family situation and precipitated the "illness" in the first place. Participants in the experiment Cooper describes began to clarify and act upon the distinction between authority based on expertise and authority based merely on social position.

Paradoxically, the doctors in this mental hospital used the traditional authority of their position to initiate changes from the top, including the abolition of their own authority. This model may have only limited applicability because most administrators are not as enlightened as these. Subsequently, Cooper, with R. D. Laing and other associates, sponsored the formation of nonhospital communities where doctors and patients lived together divested of their artificial roles.[1]

Another utopian experiment is described by the English educator A. S. Neill. His school, Summerhill, is based on a philosophy that children are naturally curious, and that all one need do is provide the conditions under which this curiosity can ripen into learning. He does not force children to attend classes if they do not wish to. Above all, he realizes that students have to learn for themselves and that it is useless to feed them predigested knowledge. Needless to say, he doesn't employ extrinsic rewards such as grades.

Since Neill wrote his book, an entire free schools movement has blossomed.[2] By 1972 there were several hundred such schools in the United States. These schools have two main functions. First, they are alternatives to the public schools, where children can grow and develop in an atmosphere of love and freedom. Instead of trying to make the student fit the society, they try to make him feel strong enough to fit a part of the society to his needs. Second, they are vehicles of social change whose very existence is a positive political act. Free schools can exercise a liberalizing effect on public schools; they also offer teachers as well as students a way of life responsive to their needs.

The Israeli kibbutz described by Spiro was founded as a utopian venture by people who were ready to explore a new way of life, based on economic and social equality. The absence of inequality in the kibbutz has led to a new family form and a different way of raising children. Marriage is based on love and not on economic considerations. Neither husband nor wife is economically dependent on the work of the other. Parents don't individually hand down privileges to children. The kibbutz is an extended family where children are reared separately from their parents in a communal nurseries and children's houses.[3]

During the 1960's, the commune movement began to revive in the United States.[4] There are now many urban communes, especially in the university towns, and there is a small drift "back to the land." In contrast with the Israeli kibbutz, most American communes are not strongly involved in national politics.

[1] See the description of Kingsley Hall by Morton Schatzman in his article "Madness and Morals," *Salamagundi*, No. 16 (Spring 1971), 170–84.

[2] See for example Jonathan Kozol, *Free Schools* (Boston: Houghton Mifflin, 1972).

[3] In the course of a brief visit to several *kibbutzim* in the spring of 1971, I found that they overemphasized work and production. Instead of lingering over the meals they shared in the common dining room, people gulped them down in order to get back to work. It also seemed to me that the *kibbutz* was sexually puritan. Finally, individuals' decisions about going to school, traveling, or working on their art during the day had to be approved by the group; I felt this gave too much weight to the group and not enough to the individual. The liberation of the group may be a precondition

In his discussion of the Spanish revolution, which began with the electoral victory of a left-wing coalition in 1936, Guerin shows how the people spontaneously ran their own agricultural collectives and took over the management of factories in parts of Spain without waiting for the new government to legislate better conditions. In the factories the workers exercised control by electing managerial committees. The workers' management was not totally autonomous, however, because the government appointed controllers, exercised a veto over the nomination of managers of large factories, and monopolized finance and credit.[5]

The Spanish military chiefs, led by Franco, attempted a putsch against the Republican government, which led to a civil war. This was in fact the first stage of World War II, for Hitler sent soldiers to support Franco's side while Stalin sent military equipment to the Republicans. Thousands of volunteers went to Spain and formed what were known as the international brigades to fight on the side of the Republicans against the fascists. The Spanish revolution was eventually defeated by the power of Franco's army on the outside and conflict between anarchists and pro-Stalinists on the inside. The pro-Stalinists, who controlled the Republican government, were hostile to the anarchist social experiments and undermined them by lack of cooperation. Before it was crushed, however, the Spanish revolution demonstrated that when the people are given a chance they can efficiently run their own factories and farms and build a new life for themselves by cooperation without control from above.

The utopian experiments outlined below show what some people have done to alter their conditions. They are not meant as blueprints, but only as examples of new social arrangements. It is up to the reader to dream up his own utopian visions and to get together with others of a like mind to make those visions a reality. This can be readily accomplished on a small scale. The example of Spain, however, warns that broad-scale social revolution will encounter formidable opposition from the ruling circles within any particular country as well as from their counterparts in other countries, who will if necessary intervene with military force to protect the prevailing system.

---

for the effective liberation of the individual; but in the final analysis the latter is what utopian ventures are about.

[4] See Benjamin Zabloski, *The Joyful Community* (Baltimore: Penguin Books, 1971); and Rosabeth Kanter, *Commitment and Community: Communes and Utopias in Sociological Perspective* (Cambridge, Mass.: Harvard University Press, 1972.)

[5] For recent discussions of the social revolution and the civil war in Spain, see: Noam Chomsky, "Objectivity and Liberal Scholarship," in his *American Power and the New Mandarins* (New York: Pantheon, 1969); and the selections on Spain in volumes III and IV of Daniel Guerin's anthology of anarchism, *Ni Dieu ni Maitre* (Paris: Maspero, 1970). See also George Orwell, *Homage to Catalonia*, originally published in 1938 and Vernon Richard, *Lessons of the Spanish Revolution* (London: Freedom Press, 1953).

The Anti-Hospital: An Experiment in Psychiatry

David Cooper

Psychiatrists set out to cure people. Somehow or other a bad (ill, mad) state of affairs arises in someone and somehow or other this has to be transformed into a good (well, sane) state of affairs. The implicit model of psychiatric thinking has been predominantly one according to which a disease process, organic or psychological, afflicts a person and then, secondarily, affects other persons. The emphasis is on passivity and process. The model demands a patient, someone who undergoes the process of pathological change, who submits to treatment, who waits to be cured. It is only in the last few years that some workers have begun seriously to question whether this invalid is in fact invalid or invalidated.

Nowhere does this distinction become more crucially relevant and nowhere is it more smothered in ambiguity than in the field of schizophrenia. Schizophrenics occupy about two thirds of the beds in most mental hospitals and mental hospital beds are nearly half the total hospital beds in the country. In most European countries about 1 per cent of the population go to hospital at least once in their lifetime with the diagnosis schizophrenia and the Swiss psychiatrist E. Bleuler estimated that for every one schizophrenic in hospital there are about ten "at large" in the community. If one takes note of recent research into the familial origin of schizophrenia (see *Sanity, Madness and the Family* by R. D. Laing and A. Esterson, Tavistock Publications, 1964) and its conclusion, that schizophrenia is not a disease in one person but rather a crazy way in which whole families function, then one realises the massive social problem presented by this disease or perhaps pseudo-disease. For the emerging view is that acute schizophrenia is not a disease process with as yet undetermined somatic or psychological causes, but rather that it is a microsocial crisis situation in which one member of a group, usually a family group, is elected by a process which is often violent and arbitrary to become the patient.

The implication for the psychiatric ward is that we must understand very clearly the nature of this sort of violence. We must understand how the patient-to-be becomes mystified by others and then progressively invalidated as an autonomous person. The invalidation must not be continued in the ward and staff must begin to refuse to enter into the traditional covert collusion with the patient's family. In the past this collusion has

FROM *New Society* (March 11, 1965), pp. 11–16. Reprinted by permission.

often meant that staff become implicated in a progressive violence that is perpetrated, in the name of treatment, against the labelled patient.

Staff Selection

If the conventional psychiatric ward and hospital are in many ways opposite to those indicated by the nature of the schizophrenia problem, why not explore this contradiction by setting up in the heart of a mental hospital an experimental unit which ideologically would be in some sense an anti-hospital? It was agreed that we should do this at our hospital—a large mental hospital of 2,300 patients just northwest of London.

To carry this out in a wholly responsible way entailed taking certain precautions. One had to be quite sure that the patients in the anti-hospital stood to gain significantly more than they would in a conventional ward (although in practice this would not be likely to prove difficult). One would have to be on the look out for disintegrative effects on the rest of the hospital that might harm the other patients. Finally, one had fully to realise that extremely difficult problems would arise for the anti-hospital staff and that some might not stay the course: careful initial selection and adequate help subsequently were clearly necessary.

After a year during which staff were selected and emotionally prepared, we commenced the unit in January 1962 with 19 male patients in what, until that time, had been the insulin coma ward. About two thirds of the patients had been diagnosed as schizophrenic and they were adolescent or young adult men. In the second year the unit expanded into a 30 bed ward. Both wards were close to the geographical centre of the hospital. The original programme was highly structured. It began every morning with a community meeting of all the patients and staff, followed after a staff meeting by three sub-groups each meeting with a doctor therapist, and then, in the afternoon and evening, occupational therapy and recreational groups. In addition to the patient and staff group transactions there were family meetings consisting of the patient, his nuclear family and a therapist. No "physical treatments" were used, apart from occasionally tranquillisers. It took the staff about a year to become disenchanted with this way of functioning and to be prepared to tolerate a progressive destructuring of the programme in a way that was felt might be liberating and creative for the patients and which might also ultimately have similar results for the staff.

We had one central conviction, founded on repeated unhappy experiences in conventional psychiatric admission wards, that before we have any chance of understanding what goes on in the patients the staff have to have at least some elementary awareness about what goes on in themselves. We therefore aimed to explore in our day to day work the whole range of preconceptions, prejudices and fantasies that staff have about each other and about the patients.

This is undoubtedly a major task. The psychiatric institution throughout its history has found it necessary to defend itself against the madness which it is supposed to contain—disturbance, disintegration, violence, contamination. The staff defences, insofar as they are erected against illusory rather than real dangers, may be collectively termed *institutional irrationality*: What, then, is the reality of madness in the mental hospital and what is illusion? What are the defining limits of institutional irrationality?

It has long been recognised that a great deal of violent behaviour in mental patients is a direct reaction to physical restraint. If any member of the public were to be seized by several burly men and thrust into a straitjacket for reasons which were obscure to him, and if his attempts to find an explanation were without avail, his natural reaction would be to struggle. We are no longer in the era of straitjackets and padded rooms are on the way out, but it is not so long ago that the writer saw a patient, kicking and screaming in a straitjacket, carried by several policemen into the observation ward: one had only to dismiss the policemen and remove the straitjacket to end the patient's violent reactions.

Today psychiatrists resort to "chemical restraint"—sedatives and tranquillisers—and to electroshock and bedrest. The effect of these less drastic measures, however, is much the same if they are used, as they often are, without any reasonable explanation. The expectation set up when a patient is given a large dose of tranquilliser is that there is danger in him which must be controlled. Patients who are very sensitive to such expectations often oblige by providing the violence—at least until they are subdued by a larger dose of the same "treatment." This is not to say that disturbed patients should not be given tranquillisers but simply that there should be clarity in the mind of the doctor and of the patient about what is being done.

There rarely is. The meaning of this situation is only too often lost in the quasi-medical mystique of "illness" and "treatment." Why should one not, for instance, tell the patient: "I'm giving you this stuff called Largactil to quieten you down a bit so that we can get on with the rest of our job without feeling too anxious about what you are going to get up to next!"

Let us look at some of the ways in which we have tried to put our philosophy into action.

Rebelling in Bed

One of the commonest staff fantasies in mental hospitals is that if patients are not coerced verbally or physically into getting out of bed at a certain hour in the morning they will stay in bed until they rot away. Behind this is staff anxiety over non-conformism with the time regulation and general control in their own lives. The patient is that frightening aspect of themselves that sometimes does not want to get out of bed in the morning and come to work. It is obviously true that if they succumbed to this temptation they would lose their jobs. It is also true that young schizophrenic patients will eventually leave hospital and take jobs which they will have to attend punctually. But all this ignores the life historical significance of the "staying in bed problem." In the past the patient has probably depended entirely on his mother to get him up in the morning. Shortly prior to his admission he has often rebelled against this enforced dependence by what, for various reasons, is the only course available to him, namely staying in bed despite his mother's efforts to get him up. This "withdrawal" is often one of the "presenting symptoms" of schizophrenia.

In hospital one can repeat the family pattern, that is to say gratify the patient's dependent needs by getting him up; this is really getting up *for him*. Or one can take the "risk" of leaving the decision to him in the hope that he will one day *get up himself*. In fact, after many heated discussions of this issue in the unit and a great deal of policy difference between the nursing shifts it was found that if the usual vigorous rousing procedures were abandoned and patients left to get up themselves they invariably did rise, even if in some cases they would spend most of the day in bed for several weeks. No one rotted away after all and the gain in personal autonomy seemed worthwhile.

Staff at first and then patients would comment in the community meetings on the getting up problem in terms of dependent need but the point was also brought home in more active ways. At one time all the occupants of a six bed dormitory rebelled against the community meeting by staying in bed until after eleven o'clock. One of the charge nurses went upstairs to see what was going on. One of the patients left to go to the toilet and the nurse seized the opportunity to take off his white coat (worn not as uniform but as protective clothing for certain messy jobs like washing up) and climb into the vacant bed. The patient, on his return, appreciating the irony of the situation, had little option but to take the vacated "staff role," put on the white coat and get the others out of bed.

Another fantasy prevalent in the mental hospital concerns patient work. It is held implicitly, and sometimes stated, that if patients are not fully occupied in domestic ward jobs and the various occupational therapy projects, or helping in hospital maintenance departments, they will become "withdrawn," "institutionalised," "chronic patients." The bitter truth is that if they submissively carry out all these required tasks they become what is implied by these labels anyhow. If one wishes to encounter the ultimate in withdrawn chronic institutionalisation one has only to visit one of the more "active" and productive "factories in a hospital" or "industrial occupational therapy departments." There is, relatively speaking, something remarkably healthy about the chronic schizophrenic, preoccupied with his inner world, spending the day hunched over the central heating fitting in a decrepit back ward. If he does not have the solution to the riddle of life at least he has fewer illusions.

What Should Patients Do?

In the unit we had some desperate confrontations on this matter. Patients resisted conventional occupational therapy projects. We had begun to question the ancient myth that tells us that Satan makes work (destructiveness, masturbation, promiscuity) for idle hands, but were not certain about where we went from there. Work projects would at least form a group, make a happy ward family. But perhaps people had come to the hospital to get away from "happy families." Or rather they had been sent to hospital to keep the family happy. We worked through a number of virile destructive jobs, knocking down an air raid shelter, breaking up an aero engine: these jobs it was felt would provide a "safe outlet" for "dangerous aggressive impulses." The jobs were done without enthusiasm and the staff soon began to realise their irrelevance to the real problems of anger. People had real reasons to be angry with real other people at home and in hospital (this was not entirely reducible to projection). The aero engine was an innocent party.

Our anxieties led us to put forward, consider, and then reject a number of other typical hospital projects of a trivial nature, such as putting together the manufactured elements in (ironically) toy doctor's sets. Patients reacted contemptuously to these tasks and we came to share their feelings. Most of them were young men of at least average intelligence, well able to acknowledge the incongruity of the projects offered them.

It was only after the first year of the unit's life that the staff group, including the young female occupational therapist, were able to tolerate a situation in which no organised work project was presented to the community. Whatever project had been offered disintegrated after some weeks when patients "skived off" to private activities elsewhere within and outside the hospital. Sanctions in the form of reduction of pocket money (up to 22s 6d per week allowance for patients who work in the hospital) did not affect the issue at all. What were we getting so anxious about and what were we trying to do anyhow?

The occupational therapist who had already abandoned her green uniform found herself gravitating towards a role that seemed nearer to the nursing role. She even considered resigning and joining the staff as an assistant nurse. It was at this time that we became particularly aware of the fact of role diffusion, the breakdown of role boundaries which was a necessary stage on the way to staff and patients defining themselves and their relationships with each other not on the basis of an imposed abstract labelling system, based on a few technical or quasi-technical functions, but in terms of the personal reality of each member of the community.

There was a progressive blurring of role between nurses, doctors, occupational therapist and patients which brought into focus a number of disturbing and apparently paradoxical questions: for example, can patients "treat" other patients and can they even treat staff? Can staff realise quite frankly and acknowledge in the community their own areas of incapacity and "illness" and their need for "treatment"? If they did, what would happen next and who would control it?

It was at this point that the most radical departure from conventional psychiatric work was initiated. If the staff rejected prescribed ideas about their function and if they did not quite know what to do next, why do anything? Why not withdraw from the whole field of hospital staff and patient expectation in terms of organising patients into activity, supervising the ward domestic work and generally "treating patients." The staff group decided to limit their function to controlling the drug cupboard as was legally required (some of the more "overactive and impulsive" patients were on the tranquilliser Largactil) and to dealing with ward administrative issues involving other hospital departments over the telephone.

A necessary prelude to this major policy change was explanation to the nursing office and other hospital departments. The kitchen staff, for instance, were informed that if the aluminium food containers were returned unwashed they should leave them until they were cleaned. If people wanted to eat they would have to clean the containers. These decisions were made quite clear to everyone in the community meetings.

Despite these explanations and superficial acceptance of them, subsequent events were dramatic. In the first phase dirt accumulated higher and higher in the corridors. Dining room tables were covered with the previous day's unwashed plates. Signs of horror were evoked in visiting staff, in particular nursing officers on their twice daily rounds. Patients decided their own leave periods, getting out of bed, attendance at meetings. Staff were anxious throughout but particularly since no patients showed signs of organising themselves to attend to these matters.

External administrative pressure on the ward staff rapidly mounted. The patients were divided in their response. A few began to demand more nurse attention. Those less urgently dependent expressed some dissatisfaction but at the same time made it clear that they appreciated the more authentic elements in the policy change.

Breaking Down Authority

Subsequent events must be seen in relation to the problem of doctor centredness in mental hospital ward administration. In conventional wards all but the most trivial decisions have to be either made by or blessed by the doctor. The doctor is invested and sometimes invests himself with magical powers of understanding and curing. Whether the formal training of psychiatrists includes qualifications in magical omnipotence is perhaps uncertain, but the image is reinforced and perpetuated in many ways. The same person who is supposed to have a psychotherapeutic relationship with patients assumes a general practitioner role in relation to their bodily ailments. Not only that but psychiatrists attend the staff sick bay and medically care for nurses with whom they work. The resulting confusion of controlled frustration and wholesale gratification can well be imagined.

If the white coat and stethoscope is one means by which the psychiatrist defends himself from patients, that is to say from his own projected disturbance, the printed form is another. Doctors have accepted, only too readily in many cases, a mass of legal and administrative responsibilities which keep them from getting near their patients but which, to a far greater extent than is commonly admitted, could be left to efficient, suitably trained non-medical administrators. As things stand, however, the doctor visiting the ward includes a pile of official forms and certificates in his (often unwanted) armamentarium and these forms structure his relationships with staff and patients before anything else he does or they do can have any effect.

In addition to this medical, legal and administrative prestructuring of the psychiatrist's role there are occasionally more realistic factors which lead to his assumption of the central position in the ward, namely training and experience in psychotherapeutic skills and small group sociology, although these skills are by no means universal among psychiatrists.

In the staff groups the level of dependency on the doctor is not much different from that in the staff-patient groups. The problem for nurses is to change their position from one in which they mediate the doctor-for-the-patient and the patient-for-the-doctor to one in which they involve themselves in relationships without the mediating or mediated "third." This shift of position is fantastically difficult. After two years of work centred largely on this issue we have barely shifted at all in the unit—but we have shifted a little.

It was during the "experimental" phase of staff withdrawal that the staff group was able to make some advance. The author was away on holiday for a month. Official pressure on the unit to introduce conventional controls was at its peak. Anxiety among the staff was considerable and there was an added factor of conflict between the two shifts (7 A.M. to 2 P.M. and 2 P.M. to 9 P.M.) of nurses. Much of the latter conflict was based on the mistaken attribution of certain intentions to the doctor. The suggestion that staff should withdraw from their supervisory, directive role, informing the patients how this would happen, was in fact generated by one shift of nurses. This had been gently confirmed by the doctor (the author) and was accepted with only a few, unimportant reservations by the whole staff group. Because of earlier happenings in the unit which had led to the idea among hospital staff that the unit doctor had new, ultra-permissive ideas, the staff decision was regarded as the "doctor's policy"—it might be pretty crazy but if it originated in the mind of a senior doctor it had unquestionably to be carried out.

The advance made by the staff group was frankly to recognise their anxiety as intolerable and, in the doctor's absence, to arrive at a group decision to reimpose some staff controls on what went on in the ward. It was decided to supervise eating and cleaning arrangements and to insist on attendance at community meetings and adherence to the rule that week-end leave was only granted from Saturday morning (after the community meeting) to Sunday night. It was decided that persistent offenders against these rules would have to choose between conforming to them or discharge from the unit. On my return I lent my confirmation to these decisions and in fact two patients who had blatantly broken the rules were shortly discharged (and in both cases this confrontation with a group reality led to consequences which were favourable).

This leads us on to the central problem of the psychiatric hospital of distinguishing between authentic and inauthentic authority. The "official" practice of psychiatry in this country, whatever progressive mantle it may don, aims only too often at enforcing conformism to the rigid, stereotyped dictates and needs of authority persons who refract on to the patient massified and alienated social expectations and hidden injunctions as to who and what he may be. The authority of the authority person is granted him by arbitrary social definition rather than on the basis of any real expertise he may possess. If staff have the courage to shift themselves from this false position they may discover real sources of authority in themselves. They may also discover such sources of authority in "the others" who are defined as their patients.

This begins to get disturbing—particularly when the patients sometimes happen to be those who are clinically the most psychotic in the ward. One of the most memorable group meetings in the unit was dominated by an extremely fragmented patient who was just beginning a lengthy project of reintegration: all the staff and patients were lulled into a fascinated somnolence by his account of a "bizarre," imaginary world tour. We became a sort of collective infant at the breast of the mother-narrator. I made a formal comment in these terms but interpretation was not necessary. At a certain point indicated by the narrator everyone snapped themselves out of the fantasy awareness to find themselves on a more integrated level of group reality. And there was no doubt about who had led them there.

Murdering Personality

Perhaps the most central characteristic of authentic leadership is the relinquishing of the impulse to dominate others. Domination here means controlling the behaviour of the others where their behaviour represents for the leader projected aspects of his own experience. By domination of the other the leader produces for himself the illusion that his own internal organisation is more and more perfectly ordered.

The Nazi extermination camps were one product of this Dream of Perfection. The mental hospital, along with other institutions in our society, is another. In the camp bodily existences were systematically annihilated, each body containing, in terms of the illusion, the projected badness, sexual anomaly, meanness of the camp officials and the society they represented. This murder was always ritual murder aimed at the purification of the murderer and as it was essentially a manner of evading guilt, how can one suppose that the murderers should feel guilty *because* of it? In the mental hospital which functions traditionally bodies are assiduously cared for but individual personalities are murdered. The model system for the conventional mental nurse and psychiatrist is the delightfully landscaped cabbage patch. As cabbages exist comfortably enough, at least until they go into the soup, many patients choose to collude with the illusions of their keepers, and this interplay of illusion and collusion is the basic social fantasy system upon which the structure of the conventional mental hospital is erected. It is plainly a totally alienated structure.

Although staff in the unit have been able to discover in themselves some elements of authentic leadership the situation in which they function is replete with contradictions. Most of the nurses live in hospital accommodation (the nurses' home or separate houses), the student nurses and sometimes staff nurses have to leave to work in other wards, all nurses are dependent on the central nursing administration for promotion. Outside the unit they are subjected to very strong social and financial pressures to conform and this inevitably becomes a pressure to conform inside the unit. But conformism in this context means a reversion to the prevalent primitive, ritualised nursing attitudes that run counter to the culture that has developed in the unit. This means that nurses must choose between submission to external pressures on the one hand and adherence to the unit principles on the other. Until they do choose, their existence in the unit is inevitably painfully confused. The extent to which the staff group in the unit can help them is limited by the reality of the dilemma and the necessity for commitment one way or the other.

The Staff Feel Threatened

We should reflect a moment here on the magnitude of the anxieties involved. For the unit nurses these issues quite literally went "right home"— to their families involved in the social life and promotion struggle of the hospital as a whole. When they refused to quit their ideological ground they faced ridicule, sometimes amounting to attributions, half behind their backs, of madness. For senior nurses outside the unit, on the other hand, the demand to re-establish controls and "tidy up" things assumed the dimentions of a desperate struggle between life and death forces, sanity and madness. They felt intensely threatened by all the things in the unit that infringed the staff-patient dividing line, like patients calling staff by their first names, staff and patients having tea together, the suggestion that ex-patients be employed as nurses (since there was an acute shortage of nurses and since we felt that their personal qualities and experience of breakdown and recovery in the unit would make them particularly useful in the staff group).

These developments and many others challenged their conceptions of themselves as sane in relation to the mad patients. The gravity of these anxieties was sometimes masked by the ludicrously trivial nature of incidents that led to crises. On one occasion for instance a nursing officer on his rounds sent in a report criticising ward staff for lack of supervision when he observed a patient pouring milk into his tea from a bottle rather than use the thoughtfully provided milk jug in the cupboard. When one of the staff commented that he often did this himself at home the situation was not helped.

Nowhere were anxieties more evident than in the highly significant distortions of the hospital communication process. Reports are submitted to the nursing office by the nurse in charge of the unit at the end of each shift. Sometimes these reports travel via the night nursing superintendent to the day shift of nursing administrators. At each change of hands the reports are edited, "significant" happenings in each ward being selected for presentation in a final version to the daily meeting of doctors, social workers and nursing officers on the division. (The whole hospital of 2,300 patients is divided into three more or less self-contained divisions each led by a consultant psychiatrist.)

A typical incident processed by this communication system was as follows. A young man in the unit had a girl friend in a female ward; one night she became hysterically upset about an issue connected with her ward and treatment and he and a friend attempted to console her and help her back to her ward: she noisily resisted these attempts and a member of the portering staff who witnessed the incident called a nurse who took her back to her ward. The porter informed the night nursing superintendent who informed the unit and reported to the day nursing administration who reported finally to the divisional meeting.

The final version related was that two male patients from the unit had attacked a female patient and, it was implied, were attempting to carry her off for sexual purposes. The fantasy existing in the minds of many staff outside the unit is that rape, sexual orgies and murder are daily occurrences in the unit—and this is not entirely rhetorical exaggeration. In fact, during the last two years there has been no significant injury produced by patient violence in the unit, and no pregnancy in young female patients who frequently visited boy friends in the unit and went out with them.

Readmission Results

The dilemma one encounters when one attempts an assessment of "results" in a project of this nature is that either one puts forward a series of propositions that are impressive in their statistical workout but are either meaningless or misleading in terms of what has actually happened to the persons concerned, or one attempts a phenomenological description of the changes in the inner—and outer—world complexes of these persons. This latter course will inevitably fail to satisfy the obsessional needs of those who would attempt to reduce the reality of human transactions to massified pseudo-generalisations. In practical terms, however, there are some conventional criteria of improvement in this sort of sample that are less objectionable than others, and one such criterion is the tendency for schizophrenics to be readmitted within one year of their discharge from hospital.

Together with two other workers using family orientated therapy with hospitalised schizophrenics I have worked out results, shortly to be published, according to this criterion. It has proved very difficult to find comparable national figures but as compared with Medical Research Council figures (1964) of 43 per cent of discharged schizophrenics who were readmitted within one year, our figures are 17 per cent. This difference is statistically significant ($X^2 = 8.34$, p. 005).

About one third of patients at any time in the unit, however, have non-schizophrenic diagnoses, and other factors have been involved since the original series of patients (all admitted in 1962). For example we have more recently developed a policy of encouraging discharged patients to return voluntarily to the unit for a night or a few days if they were running into difficulties outside that might result in further invalidation by their families or others. This strategy became necessary in view of difficulties in finding reasonable living situations outside hospital in many cases. This is clearly a major deficiency in community care provision.

The situation I have somewhat schematically presented here has already indicated certain conclusions about a future "schizophrenic" unit. A traditional psychiatric social context severely inhibits the internal evolution of such a community, even in a progressive, permissive hospital with considerable goodwill toward experimental developments. If staff attempt to meet psychotic patients on all levels of their existential voyage and if they aspire, through increasing vision into their own "inner worlds," to become genuine guides to such patients, then they must be free of conventional institutional conformist pressures and their subtle violence.

The need for a fully autonomous unit in which these things may happen is clear and urgent.

Summerhill

A. S. Neill

Obviously, a school that makes active children sit at desks studying mostly useless subjects is a bad school. It is a good school only for those who believe in *such* a school, for those uncreative citizens who want docile, uncreative children who will fit into a civilization whose standard of success is money.

Summerhill began as an experimental school. It is no longer such; it is now a demonstration school, for it demonstrates that freedom works.

When my first wife and I began the school, we had one main idea: *to make the school fit the child*—instead of making the child fit the school.

I had taught in ordinary schools for many years. I knew the other way well. I knew it was all wrong. It was wrong because it was based on an adult conception of what a child should be and of how a child should learn. The other way dated from the days when psychology was still an unknown science.

Well, we set out to make a school in which we should allow children freedom to be themselves. In order to do this, we had to renounce all discipline, all direction, all suggestion, all moral training, all religious instruction. We have been called brave, but it did not require courage. All it required was what we had—a complete belief in the child as a good, not an evil, being. For almost forty years, this belief in the goodness of the child has never wavered; it rather has become a final faith.

My view is that a child is innately wise and realistic. If left to himself without adult suggestion of any kind, he will develop as far as he is capable of developing. Logically, Summerhill is a place in which people who have the innate ability and wish to be scholars will be scholars; while those who are only fit to sweep the streets will sweep the streets. But we have not produced a street cleaner so far. Nor do I write this snobbishly, for I would rather see a school produce a happy street cleaner than a neurotic scholar.

What is Summerhill like? Well, for one thing, lessons are optional. Children can go to them or stay away from them—for years if they want to. There *is* a timetable—but only for the teachers.

The children have classes usually according to their age, but sometimes according to their interests. We have no new methods of teaching, because we do not consider that teaching in itself matters very much.

FROM *Summerhill: A Radical Approach to Child Rearing*, by A. S. Neill, pp. 4–5; 25–26; 109–115; 153–69. Copyright, 1960, Hart Publishing Company, New York.

Whether a school has or has not a special method for teaching long division is of no significance, for long division is of no importance except to those who *want* to learn it. And the child who *wants* to learn long division *will* learn it no matter how it is taught.

* * *

How much of our education is real doing, real self-expression? Handwork is too often the making of a pin tray under the eye of an expert. Even the Montessori system, well known as a system of directed play, is an artificial way of making the child learn by doing. It has nothing creative about it.

In the home, the child is always being taught. In almost every home, there is always at least one ungrown-up grownup who rushes to show Tommy how his new engine works. There is always someone to lift the baby up on a chair when baby wants to examine something on the wall. Every time we show Tommy how his engine works we are stealing from that child the joy of life—the joy of discovery—the joy of overcoming an obstacle. Worse! We make that child come to believe that he is inferior, and must depend on help.

Parents are slow in realizing how unimportant the learning side of school is. Children, like adults, learn what they want to learn. All prize-giving and marks and exams sidetrack proper personality development. Only pedants claim that learning from books is education.

Books are the least important apparatus in a school. All that any child needs is the three R's; the rest should be tools and clay and sports and theater and paint and freedom.

Most of the school work that adolescents do is simply a waste of time, of energy, of patience. It robs youth of its right to play and play and play; it puts old heads on young shoulders.

When I lecture to students at teacher training colleges and universities, I am often shocked at the ungrownupness of these lads and lasses stuffed with useless knowledge. They know a lot; they shine in dialectics; they can quote the classics—but in their outlook on life many of them are infants. For they have been taught to *know*, but have not been allowed to *feel*. These students are friendly, pleasant, eager, but something is lacking —the emotional factor, the power to subordinate thinking to feeling. I talk to these of a world they have missed and go on missing. Their textbooks do not deal with human character, or with love, or with freedom, or with self-determination. And so the system goes on, aiming only at standards of book learning—goes on separating the head from the heart.

It is time that we were challenging the school's notion of work. It is taken for granted that every child should learn mathematics, history, geography, some science, a little art, and certainly literature. It is time we realized that the average young child is not much interested in any of these subjects.

I prove this with every new pupil. When told that the school is free, every new pupil cries, "Hurrah! You won't catch me doing dull arithmetic and things!"

I am not decrying learning. But learning should come after play. And learning should not be deliberately seasoned with play to make it palatable.

Learning is important—but not to everyone. Nijinsky could not pass his school exams in St. Petersburg, and he could not enter the State Ballet without passing those exams. He simply could not learn school subjects—his mind was elsewhere. They faked an exam for him, giving him the answers with the papers—so a biography says. What a loss to the world if Nijinsky had had to really pass those exams!

*   *   *

The usual argument against freedom for children is this: *Life is hard, and we must train the children so that they will fit into life later on. We must therefore discipline them. If we allow them to do what they like, how will they ever be able to serve under a boss? How will they compete with others who have known discipline? How will they ever be able to exercise self discipline?*

People who protest the granting of freedom to children and use this argument do not realize that they start with an unfounded, unproved assumption—the assumption that a child will not grow or develop unless forced to do so. Yet the entire thirty-nine years of experience of Summerhill disproves this assumption. Take, among one hundred others, the case of Mervyn. He attended Summerhill for ten years, between the ages of seven to seventeen. During those ten years, Mervyn never attended a single class. At age seventeen, he hardly knew how to read. Yet when Mervyn left school and decided to become an instrument maker, he quickly taught himself how to read and absorbed in a short time through self-study all the technical knowledge he needed. Through his own efforts, he made himself ready for his apprenticeship. Today, this same chap is thoroughly literate, commands a good salary, and is a leader in his community. As to self-discipline, Mervyn built a good part of his house with his own hands and he is bringing up a fine family of three boys from the fruits of his daily labors.

Similarly, each year boys and girls at Summerhill who up to then have rarely studied, decided to enter college; and of their own accord, they then begin the long and tiresome grind of preparing themselves for college entrance examinations. Why do they do it?

The common assumption that good habits that have not been forced into us during early childhood can never develop in us later on in life is an assumption we have been brought up on and which we unquestioningly accept merely because the idea has never been challenged. I deny this premise.

Freedom is necessary for the child because only under freedom can he grow in his natural way—the good way. I see the results of bondage in new pupils coming from prep schools and convents. They are bundles of insincerity, with an unreal politeness and phony manners.

Their reaction to freedom is rapid and tiresome. For the first week or two, they open doors for the teachers, call me "Sir," and wash carefully. They glance at me with "respect," which is easily recognized as fear. After a few weeks of freedom, they show what they really are. They become impudent, unmannerly, unwashed. They do all the things they have been forbidden to do in the past: they swear, they smoke, they break things. And all the time, they have a polite and insincere expression in their eyes and in their voices.

It takes at least six months for them to lose their insincerity. After that, they also lose their deference to what they regarded as authority. In just about six months, they are natural, healthy kids who say what they think without fluster or hate. When a child comes to freedom young enough, he does not have to go through this stage of insincerity and acting. The most striking thing about Summerhill is this absolute sincerity among the pupils.

This business of being sincere in life and to life is a vital one. It is really the most vital one in the world. If you have sincerity, all other things will be added to you. Everyone realizes the value of sincerity in, say, acting. We expect sincerity from our politicians (such is the optimism of mankind), from our judges and magistrates, teachers and doctors. Yet we educate our children in such a way that they dare not be sincere.

Possibly the greatest discovery we have made in Summerhill is that a child is born a sincere creature. We set out to let children alone so that we might discover what they were like. It is the only possible way of dealing with children. The pioneer school of the future must pursue this way if it is to contribute to child knowledge and, more important, to child happiness.

The aim of life is happiness. The evil of life is all that limits or destroys happiness. Happiness always means goodness; unhappiness at its extreme limits means Jew-baiting, minority torture, or war.

* * *

People are always saying to me, "But how will your free children ever adapt themselves to the drudgery of life?" I hope that these free children will be pioneers in *abolishing* the drudgery of life.

We must allow the child to be selfish—ungiving—free to follow his own childish interests through his childhood. When the child's individual interests and his social interests clash, the individual interests should be allowed precedence. The whole idea of Summerhill is release: allowing a child to live out his natural interests.

A school should make a child's life a game. I do not mean that the child should have a path of roses. Making it all easy for the child is fatal to the child's character. But life itself presents so many difficulties that the artificially made difficulties which we present to children are unnecessary.

I believe that to impose anything by authority is wrong. The child should not do anything until he comes to the opinion—his own opinion —that it should be done. The curse of humanity is the external compulsion, whether it comes from the Pope or the state or the teacher or the parent. It is fascism in toto.

Most people demand a god; how can it be otherwise when the home is ruled by tin gods of both sexes, gods who demand perfect truth and moral behavior? Freedom means doing what you like, so long as you don't interfere with the freedom of others. The result is self-discipline.

In our educational policy as a nation, we refuse to let live. We persuade through fear. But there is a great difference between compelling a child to cease throwing stones and compelling him to learn Latin. Throwing stones involves others; but learning Latin involves only the boy. The community has the right to restrain the antisocial boy because he is interfering with the rights of others; but the community has no right to compel a boy to learn Latin—for learning Latin is a matter for the individual. Forcing a child to learn is on a par with forcing a man to adopt a religion by act of Parliament. And it is equally foolish.

*   *   *

A child should not be asked to face responsibilities for which he is not ready, nor be saddled with decisions he is not yet old enough to make. The watchword must be common sense.

At Summerhill we do not ask our five-year-olds whether or not they want fireguards. We do not ask a six-year-old to decide whether or not he should go outdoors when he is running a temperature. Nor do we ask a rundown child whether or not he should go to bed when he is overtired. One does not seek a child's permission to give him prescribed remedies when he is sick.

But the imposition of authority—necessary authority—on a child does not in any way conflict with the idea that a child should be given just about as much responsibility as he can accept at his particular age. In determining the amount of responsibility that a parent should give his child, the parent must always consult his inner soul. He must first examine himself.

*   *   *

Discipline is a means to an end. The discipline of an army is aimed at making for efficiency in fighting. All such discipline subordinates the individual to the cause. In disciplined countries life is cheap.

There is, however, another discipline. In an orchestra, the first violinist obeys the conductor because he is as keen on a good performance as the conductor is. The private who jumps to attention does not, as a rule, care about the efficiency of the army. Every army is ruled mostly by fear, and the soldier knows that if he disobeys he will be punished. School discipline can be of the orchestra type when teachers are good. Too often it is of the army type. The same applies to the home. A happy home is like an orchestra and enjoys the same kind of team spirit. A miserable home is like a barracks that is ruled by hate and discipline.

* * *

The danger in rewarding a child is not as extreme as that of punishing him, but the undermining of the child's morale through the giving of rewards is more subtle. Rewards are superfluous and negative. To offer a prize for doing a deed is tantamount of declaring that the deed is not worth doing for its own sake.

No artist ever works for a monetary reward only. One of his rewards is the joy of creating. Moreover, rewards support the worst feature of the competitive system. To get the better of the other man is a damnable objective.

Giving rewards has a bad psychological effect on children because it arouses jealousies. A boy's dislike of a younger brother often dates from mother's remark, "Your little brother can do it better than you can." To the child, mother's remark is a reward given to brother for being better than he is.

When we consider a child's natural interest in things, we begin to realize the dangers of both rewards and punishment. Rewards and punishment tend to pressure a child into interest. But true interest is the life force of the whole personality, and such interest is completely spontaneous. It is possible to compel attention, for attention is an act of consciousness. It is possible to be attentive to an outline on the blackboard and at the same time to be interested in pirates. Though one can compel attention, one cannot compel interest. No man can force me to be interested in, say, collecting stamps; nor can I compel myself to be interested in stamps. Yet both rewards and punishment attempt to compel interest.

* * *

To repeat: hitting a child gives him fear *only when it is associated with a moral idea, with the idea of wrong.* If a street urchin knocked off my hat with a lump of clay and I caught him and gave him a swat on the ear, my reaction would be considered by the boy to be a natural one. No harm would have been done to the boy's soul. But if I went to the principal of his school and demanded punishment for the culprit, the fear introduced by the punishment would be a bad thing for the child. The affair would at once become an affair of morals and of punishment. The child would feel that he had committed a crime.

The ensuing scene can easily be imagined! I stand there with my muddy hat. The principal sits and fixes the boy with a baleful eye. The boy stands with lowered head. He is overawed by the dignity of his accusers. Running him down on the street, I had been his equal. I had no dignity after my hat had been knocked off. I was just another guy. The boy had learned a necessary lesson of life—the lesson that if you hit a guy he'll get angry and sock you back.

Punishment has nothing to do with hot temper. Punishment is cold and judicial. Punishment is highly moral. Punishment avows that it is wholly for the culprit's good. (In the case of capital punishment, it is for society's good.) Punishment is an act in which man identifies himself with God and sits in moral judgment.

Many parents live up to the idea that since God rewards and punishes, they too should reward and punish their children. These parents honestly try to be just, and they often convince themselves that they are punishing the child for his own good. *This hurts me more than it hurts you* is not so much a lie as it is a pious self-deception.

Children of the Kibbutz

Melford Spiro

The Nature of a Kibbutz

From the deserts of the Negev to the mountains of the upper Galilee, the Israeli landscape is dotted with over 300 *kibbutzim* (collective agricultural settlements). Divided into several federations on the basis of varying ideological and structural criteria, their similarities are fundamental enough to permit us—and them—to refer to them collectively as "the kibbutz movement." This movement, comprised of less than 5 per cent of the total Israeli population, is of much greater importance than its numerical strength would indicate. Its ideals were instrumental in bringing the young state into being; from its manpower the country obtained its most valiant fighters for defense against a foreign attack which threatened its very existence; its representatives occupy important positions of leadership in almost all phases of contemporary Israeli life. It is no coincidence that the present premier of Israel lists as his perma-

REPRINTED by permission of the publishers from Melford E. Spiro, *Children of the Kibbutz*, Cambridge, Mass.: Harvard University Press, Copyright, 1958, by the President and Fellows of Harvard College, pp. 3–10.

nent address a young kibbutz in the Negev, or that many of his ministers are members of kibbutzim.

Kiryat Yedidim [the kibbutz . . . described in this essay] was founded thirty years prior to this study by a small group of Eastern European Jews. Motivated by the desire to escape from the anti-Semitism to which European Jewry was heir, by the dream of reconstituting the Jewish people as a Nation in its ancient homeland, by the conviction that physical —and, particularly, agricultural—labor was the noblest means to self-expression, and by the zeal to establish a society based on freedom and equality, this band of intellectual youths migrated to Palestine and, after a few years, began their experiment in what was then a malarial swampland. At the time of this study, Kiryat Yedidim was a prosperous and attractive village of five hundred. Its original membership had been augmented, not only by natural increase, but by the inclusion of two later adult contingents. The members of the second, and younger, contingent married the adult children of the kibbutz.

As an agricultural village, Kiryat Yedidim is characterized by group living, communal ownership, and cooperative enterprise. All land is owned by the Jewish National Fund, an arm of the Jewish Agency, which rents it to the kibbutz on a long-term lease for a nominal fee; and all capital goods are owned by the kibbutz, although individuals possess a few personal effects. Though a most efficient instrument in the agricultural colonization of a barren and malaria-infested land, kibbutz collectivism is predicated on moral rather than on pragmatic grounds. Zealously devoted to the ideals of brotherhood, equality, and freedom, the kibbutz believes that these can best be implemented in a collectivistic community. Communal ownership, it is believed, prevents the development of economic classes and the inevitable social inequality that seems to characterize societies stratified by class. Similarly, cooperative enterprise is believed to promote brotherhood and freedom by muting the more vicious aspects of a competitive economy, by precluding the rise of entrenched power and of the exploitation which, it is believed, accompanies the conjunction of power and privilege. Hence, labor is performed in work crews under the leadership of a foreman who, perceived as a *primus interpares*, serves his tenure of office at the pleasure of his peers.

Kibbutz opposition to exploitation extends to non-kibbutz members as well. Thus, despite the shortage of manpower in Kiryat Yedidim, it will not hire workers from the outside since this would entail the reaping of profit from another's labor. This means, of course, that all who live in the kibbutz are members of it,[1] and as kibbutz members all are comrades (*chaverim*).

[1] There are some exceptions to this generalization. Elderly parents of kibbutz founders who have been brought there from their European homes are residents, but not members. Similarly, various youth groups—either refugees or children from urban, economically depressed homes—are taken into the kibbutz for both training and rehabilitation.

Having abolished money within the kibbutz both as a medium of exchange and a symbol of wealth, the kibbutz has also eliminated the profit motive as a stimulus for economic production. The distribution of goods is determined by the principle of "from each according to his ability, to each according to his needs," the latter being determined to a great extent by the entire group assembled in Town Meeting. This biweekly Meeting is the ultimate authority on all other matters which affect the kibbutz or any of its individual members. Authority is delegated by the Meeting to democratically elected officials who carry out policy determined by the Meeting, and who administer the various economic and social institutions of the kibbutz. Tenure of office is brief—never more than three years—which, it is believed, prevents the rise of a leadership caste or an entrenched bureaucracy.

Despite the absence of a highly developed formal system of authority, the kibbutz exhibits a remarkably high degree of congruence between its social norms and the behavior of its members. Group pressure, expressed in public opinion and in the ultimate threat of expulsion, is a sufficient deterrent to deviant behavior.

Unlike a few kibbutzim, Kiryat Yedidim has tenaciously opposed the introduction of industry into its economy, persisting in maintaining the generic kibbutz emphasis on the primacy of the land. Its agricultural economy is diversified, comprising eight distinct branches: dairy, field crops, vegetable gardens, fishery, fruit orchards, flocks, poultry, and fodder. Its agriculture is not only diversified, it is highly rationalized and mechanized. The resulting efficiency has produced a prosperous agricultural economy.

Although they have been highly successful farmers, the members of Kiryat Yedidim are not merely farmers. And, despite its peasant-like devotion to the land, Kiryat Yedidim is not a village of peasants either in fact or in its self-image. On both scores the members of the kibbutz comprise a landed intelligentsia. In the fields one hears discussions not only of crops and machinery, but of books and music, of politics and literature. At the end of the working day, the interest of a chaver may turn to a class in English, a lecture on genetics, a chamber-music concert, a discussion of politics, a dramatic performance. This is not to say that all chaverim turn their attention to such intellectual pursuits, nor that all who do, display equal zeal in them. It is to say, however, that these activities are available, that they are valued by many, and that the kibbutz self-image demands at least lip-service devotion to them. It is this same self-image, and not merely kibbutz prosperity, which accounts for the attractive kibbutz landscaping, the lovely private gardens, the tasteful interior decor that impress even the most casual visitor.

But Kiryat Yedidim is not content with merely a prosperous economy and the opportunity to enjoy the pleasures of the mind and heart. And this brings us to still another component of its self-image. As a kibbutz, Kiryat Yedidim is not only an agricultural village. As a kibbutz it perceives itself as the vanguard of man's quest for the ideal society, part of the shock troops in the future social revolution. The kibbutz, together with the urban proletariat with whom it identifies, will—it is hoped—bring socialism and, ultimately, the classless society to the entire country. These political convictions, stemming from an avowedly Marxist ideology,[2] have led Kiryat Yedidim to join with other kibbutzim of like mind in a large kibbutz federation. In turn, the Federation has joined with urban workers of similar political persuasion to form a political party.[3]

If the kibbutz has still to achieve its goal of external political revolution, it has already achieved a major internal revolution: it has revolutionized the structure of the family and the educational system. Love is not only the basis for the kibbutz marriage; it is the sufficient solemnizer of the relationship. Nevertheless, since marriage is also a social relationship, the kibbutz confers social sanction on the relationship by granting a common room to the couple. This room is their home. Since meals are cooked in the communal kitchen and eaten in the communal dining room, and since children live in the various children's houses, a combined bedroom-sitting room is sufficient for their needs.

Marriage entails few changes in the life of either spouse. The woman, whose membership in the kibbutz is legally distinct from that of her husband, changes neither her name nor her work when she marries. She is supported, not by her husband, but by the entire kibbutz to whose economic well-being she, in turn, contributes by her labor. Women, like men, work a nine-hour day, although relatively few women today work in the agricultural branches of the kibbutz economy. If the wife is economically independent of her husband, so is the husband independent of his wife for domestic services. These—meals, laundry, mending, and so forth—are provided in the various communal institutions of the kibbutz. Should either become ill, he is assured of complete and continuing economic support, not by dint of special initiative on the part of his spouse, but because the kibbutz continues to provide for his needs. Having a child poses no economic problems for the couple. The kibbutz assumes complete responsibility for its economic welfare. In brief, economic factors play no role in cementing the relationship between *husband* and *wife*. The marital bond is compounded of emotional, sexual, and social ties exclusively. The advent of children does not alter this generalization; the kibbutz family is not an economic unit.

[2] Though opposed to and opposed by the tiny Communist party in Israel, the Marxism of the federation has been Stalinist in conception and pro-Soviet in practice. Disquieting events in the Soviet Union subsequent to the death of Stalin—disquieting both to its socialist and its Zionist convictions—has led to much soul searching. The future Marxist orientation of the Federation, however, is not, at the time of this writing, entirely clear.

[3] The Party has been only mildly successful in the Israeli political arena, polling less than 10 percent of the votes in the last national elections. Though opposed to much of the platform of the leading party in the present coalition government, the Party has joined the Government after some years of steadfast refusal. It currently holds two portfolios in the cabinet.

Marriage in the kibbutz almost inevitably results in children. And it is in the care and training of children that the kibbutz has instituted one of its crucial social revolutions. It is this educational revolution which is the subject of this monograph.

Collective Education

The educational system of Kiryat Yedidim is known as *chinuch meshutaf*, or collective education. Its characteristic feature is the fact that the children live in communal nurseries with age peers, where they are reared by "nurses," nursery teachers, and teachers, rather than by their parents. Since parents of both sexes work in the kibbutz economy, the daily interaction between parent and child is in general restricted to the interval between the parents' return from work in the afternoon and the child's bedtime.

When a child is born in Kiryat Yedidim, he becomes an official member, not of the kibbutz, but of the Children's Society (*chevrat yeladim*); and in this Society he remains until, upon graduation from high school, he is elected to membership in the kibbutz. Kiryat Yedidim is similar to a religious sect in that membership is not a right conferred upon an individual at birth, but is, rather, a privilege that the group confers upon an adult who, at the age of consent, knowingly and willingly accepts its values and its way of life. Thus it is that, although the children live in and are raised by Kiryat Yedidim, they are not viewed as members of the kibbutz until their candidacy is announced and they are formally elected as chaverim.

The children do not live in one immense institution-like dwelling. They are organized into small peer groups—the number of children in a group varying and increasing with age—which occupy scattered dwellings or "cottages" within the kibbutz. All the houses are designed for the convenience of the particular age groups occupying them. Until they enter high school, the children's houses, as well as their communal kitchen, lie within the living area of the kibbutz, although they all lie to one side of this area. While in general these houses may be said to form a separate community from their parents' dwellings, they are in actuality not isolated from the rest of the kibbutz, for adult dwellings are scattered throughout the children's area, and, indeed, some of the nurseries are actually parts of adult dwellings that have been converted.

When the children enter the junior-senior high school (*mosad*), however, they do move to a separate community—for the land occupied by the high school lies across the road from the kibbutz living area. The high school has its own dwellings, classrooms, dining room and kitchen, and library.

An infant enters the kibbutz educational system when he returns with his mother from the hospital at the age of four or five days. The Nursery is designed to care for a maximum of sixteen babies, who are in the care of kibbutz women who qualify as infants' "nurses." Thus, the responsibility for the kibbutz child is assumed immediately by some one or more persons other than his parents. This is not to say that the kibbutz infant never sees his parents; he is visited at least once a day by his father and many times a day by his mother, who comes not only to play with him but to nurse him.

The first important change in the infant's life occurs at the age of six months, when he may be taken to his parents' room in the afternoon for approximately one hour. The second important change occurs at the age of about one year, when he is moved from the Nursery to the Toddlers' House (beth peutot). In the Toddlers' House, which consists of two nurses and eight children, the infant is gradually toilet trained; he is taught to feed himself; and he learns to interact with his age mates. At this age the infant may remain in his parents' room for approximately two hours in the evening, and he may be taken to their room not only on Saturdays, but on other days when they may be free.

In some instances the group of eight children in the Toddlers' House remain with the same nurse or nurses until they enter the Kindergarten (gan), at which time they not only change buildings, but nurses as well. In most instances, however, the group remains with its nurses until it reaches nursery age—between two and three—at which time a nursery teacher (ganenet) generally replaces one of the nurses.

Sometime between their fourth and fifth birthdays, the children encounter another important change. At this time the group passes into the Kindergarten. This not only involves a new building and sometimes a new nurse and Kindergarten teacher, but it also involves the enlargement of their original group to include sixteen members. This is accomplished by merging two nursery groups into one Kindergarten. This merger is an important event in the lives of the children, for this enlarged group, or kevutza, will remain together as a unit until its members reach high school age. The kevutza is in many ways the child's most important social group, not only because of its long duration, but also because of the frequency and intensity of interaction within it.

Between the ages of five and six the children in the Kindergarten pass into a new dwelling, where they receive their first formal intellectual instruction, including the study of reading and writing; when they have completed a year in this "Transitional Class" (kitat ma'avar), they are ready to enter the primary school and its dormitory. For the first time children live in a building that includes not only their own (approximate) age-peers, but other children whose ages span a wide range—from seven to twelve. Each kevutza, or group of sixteen children, remains distinct in that it has its own teacher, classroom, and bedrooms. But the entire student body eats together, plays together, and participates in the same extracurricular activities. Hence, the functional "children's society" for these children includes not only their kevutza, but the entire school population, known as their *chevra*.

The completion of the sixth grade, when the children are twelve, marks another turning point in their lives. They enter the high school, an event which is important not only for its intellectual implications, but for other reasons as well. They are physically separated from the rest of the kibbutz; their kevutza is split up; for the first time they encounter male educational figures (except for their fathers) in the person of the teacher; and they begin to work in the kibbutz economy.

Upon graduation from high school the students are expected to live outside the kibbutz for approximately one year, so that their decision to become kibbutz members may be based on the experience of non-kibbutz living. After election to membership, they become full-fledged *chaverim*.

Workers' Control in Spain

Daniel Guerin

An "Apolitical" Revolution

The Spanish Revolution was, thus, relatively well prepared, both in the minds of libertarian thinkers and in the consciousness of the people. It is therefore not surprising that the Spanish Right regarded the electoral victory of the Popular Front in February 1936 as the beginning of a revolution.

In fact, the masses soon broke out of the narrow framework of their success at the ballot box. They ignored the rules of the parliamentary game and did not even wait for a government to be formed to set the prisoners free. The farmers ceased to pay rent to the landlords, the agricultural day laborers occupied land and began to cultivate it, the villagers got rid of their municipal councils and hastened to administer themselves, the railwaymen went on strike to enforce a demand for the nationalization of the railways. The building workers of Madrid called for workers' control, the first step toward socialization.

The military chiefs, under the leadership of Colonel Franco, responded

FROM *Anarchism*, by Daniel Guerin (New York: Monthly Review Press, 1970), pp. 126–27; 129–43. Copyright © 1970 by Monthly Review Press; reprinted by permission of Monthly Review Press.

to the symptoms of revolution by a *putsch*. But they only succeeded in accelerating the progress of a revolution which had, in fact, already begun. In Madrid, in Barcelona, in Valencia particularly, in almost every big city but Seville, the people took the offensive, besieged barracks, set up barricades in the streets and occupied strategic positions. The workers rushed from all sides to answer the call of their trade unions. They assaulted the strongholds of the Franco forces, with no concern for their own lives, with naked hands and uncovered breasts. They succeeded in taking guns from the enemy and persuading soldiers to join their ranks.

Thanks to this popular fury the military *putsch* was checked within the first twenty-four hours; and then the social revolution began quite spontaneously. It went forward unevenly, of course, in different regions and cities, but with the greatest impetuosity in Catalonia and, especially, Barcelona. When the established authorities recovered from their astonishment, they found that they simply no longer existed. The State, the police, the army, the administration, all seemed to have lost their *raison d'être*. The Civil Guard had been driven off or liquidated and the victorious workers were maintaining order. The most urgent task was to organize food supplies: committees distributed foodstuffs from barricades transformed into canteens, and then opened communal restaurants. Local administration was organized by neighborhood committees, and war committees saw to the departure of the workers' militia to the front. The trade-union center had become the real town hall. This was no longer the "defense of the republic" against fascism, it was the Revolution—a Revolution which, unlike the Russian one, did not have to create all its organs of authority from scratch: the election of soviets was made unnecessary by the omnipresent anarcho-syndicalist organization with its various committees at the base. In Catalonia the CNT and its conscious minority, the FAI, were more powerful than the authorities, which had become mere phantoms.*

*   *   *

Anarchists in Government

This underestimation of government, however, was very rapidly reversed and the Spanish anarchists suddenly became governmentalists. Soon after the Revolution of July 19 in Barcelona, an interview took place between the anarchist activist García Oliver and the president of the Catalonian government, the bourgeois liberal Companys. He was ready to resign but was kept in office. The CNT and the FAI refused to

* The CNT was the National Federation of Labor; a number of its members were also members of the Iberian Anarchist Federation (FAI).—Ed.

exercise an anarchist "dictatorship," and declared their willingness to collaborate with other left groupings. By mid-September, the CNT was calling on the prime minister of the central government, Largo Caballero, to set up a fifteen-member "Defense Council" in which they would be satisfied with five places. This was as good as accepting the idea of participating in a cabinet under another name.

The anarchists ended up by accepting portfolios in two governments: first in Catalonia and subsequently in Madrid. The Italian anarchist, Camillo Berneri, was in Barcelona and, on April 14, 1937, wrote an open letter to his comrade, minister Federica Montseny, reproaching the anarchists with being in the government only as hostages and fronts "for politicians who flirt with the [class] enemy."[1] It is true that the State with which the Spanish anarchists had agreed to become integrated remained a bourgeois State whose officials and political personnel often had but little loyalty to the republic. What was the reason for this change of heart?

The Spanish Revolution had taken place as the consequence of a proletarian counterattack against a counter-revolutionary *coup d'état*. From the beginning the Revolution took on the character of self-defense, a military character, because of the necessity to oppose the cohorts of Colonel Franco with anti-fascist militia. Faced by a common danger, the anarchists thought that they had no choice but to join with all the other trade-union forces, and even political parties, which were ready to stand against the Franco rebellion. As the fascist powers increased their support from Franco, the anti-fascist struggle degenerated into a real war, a total war of the classical type. The libertarians could only take part in it by abandoning more and more of their principles, both political and military. They reasoned, falsely, that the victory of the Revolution could only be assured by first winning the war and, as Santillan was to admit, they "sacrificed everything" to the war. Berneri argued in vain against the priority of the war as such, and maintained that the defeat of Franco could only be insured by a *revolutionary* war. To put a brake on the Revolution was, in fact, to weaken the strongest arm of the Republic: the active participation of the masses. An even more serious aspect of the matter was that Republican Spain, blockaded by the Western democracies and in grave danger from the advancing fascist troops, needed Russian military aid in order to survive. The aid was given on a two-fold condition: 1) the Communist Party must profit from it as much as possible,

---

[1] The International Workers' Association to which the CNT was affiliated held a special congress in Paris, June 11–13, 1937, at which the anarcho-syndicalist trade-union center was reproached for participating in government and for the concessions it had made in consequence. With this backing, Sébastien Faure decided to publish a series of articles in the July 8, 15, and 22 issues of *Le Libertaire*, entitled "The Fatal Slope." These were severely critical of the decision of the Spanish anarchists to take part in government. The CNT was enraged and brought about the resignation of the secretary of the International Workers' Association, Pierre Besnard.

and the anarchists as little as possible; 2) Stalin wanted at any price to prevent the victory of a social revolution in Spain, not only because it would have been libertarian, but because it would have expropriated capital investments belonging to Britain which was presumed to be an ally of the U.S.S.R. in the "democratic alliance" against Hitler. The Spanish Communists went so far as to deny that a revolution had taken place: a legal government was simply trying to overcome a military mutiny. In May 1937, there was a bloody struggle in Barcelona and the workers were disarmed by the forces of order under Stalinist command. In the name of united action against the fascists the anarchists forbade the workers to retaliate. The sad persistence with which they threw themselves into the error of the Popular Front, until the final defeat of the Republic, cannot be dealt with in this short book.

Self-Management in Agriculture

Nevertheless, in the field to which they attached the greatest importance, the economic field, the Spanish anarchists showed themselves much more intransigent and compromised to a much lesser degree. Agricultural and industrial self-management was very largely self-propelled. But as the State grew stronger and the war more and more totalitarian, an increasingly sharp contradiction developed between a bourgeois republic at war and an experiment in communism or rather in libertarian collectivism. In the end, it was self-management which had to retreat, sacrificed on the altar of "antifascism." According to Peirats, a methodical study of this experiment in self-management has yet to be made; it will be a difficult task, since self-management presented so many variants in different places and at different times. This matter deserves all the more attention, because relatively little is known about it. Even within the Republican ranks it was either passed over or under-rated. The civil war submerged it and even today overshadows it in human memory. For example, there is no reference to it in the film *To Die in Madrid*, and yet it is probably the most creative legacy of Spanish anarchism.

The Revolution of July 19, 1936, was a lightning defensive action by the people to counter the *pronunciamento* of Franco. The industrialists and large landowners immediately abandoned their property and took refuge abroad. The workers and peasants took over this abandoned property, and the agricultural day laborers decided to continue cultivating the soil on their own. They associated together in "collectives" quite spontaneously. In Catalonia a regional congress of peasants was called together by the CNT on September 5 and agreed to the collectivization of land under trade-union management and control. Large estates and the property of fascists were to be socialized, while small landowners would have free choice between individual property and collective property. Legal sanction came later: on October 7, 1936, the Republican central government confiscated without indemnity the property of "persons compromised in the fascist rebellion." This measure was incomplete from a legal point of view, since it only sanctioned a very small part of the take-overs already carried out spontaneously by the people; the peasants had carried out expropriation without distinguishing between those who had taken part in the military *putsch* and those who had not.

In underdeveloped countries where the technical resources necessary for large-scale agriculture are absent, the poor peasant is more attracted by private property, which he has not yet enjoyed, than by socialized agriculture. In Spain, however, libertarian education and a collectivist tradition compensated for technical underdevelopment, countered the individualistic tendencies of the peasants, and turned them directly toward socialism. The latter was the choice of the poorer peasants, while those who were slightly better off, as in Catalonia, clung to individualism. A great majority (90 percent) of land workers chose to join collectives from the very beginning. This decision created a close alliance between the peasants and the city workers, the latter being supporters of the socialization of the means of production by the very nature of their function. It seems that social consciousness was even higher in the country than in the cities.

The agricultural collectives set themselves up with a twofold management, economic and geographical. The two functions were distinct, but in most cases it was the trade unions which assumed them or controlled them. A general assembly of working peasants in each village elected a management committee which was to be responsible for economic administration. Apart from the secretary, all the members continued their manual labor. Work was obligatory for all healthy men between eighteen and sixty. The peasants were divided into groups of ten or more, each led by a delegate, and each being allocated an area to cultivate, or an operation to perform, appropriate to the age of its members and the nature of the work concerned. The management committee received the delegates from the groups every evening. With regard to local administration, the commune frequently called the inhabitants together in general assembly to receive reports of activities undertaken. Everything was put into the common pool with the exception of clothing, furniture, personal savings, small domestic animals, garden plots, and poultry kept for family use. Artisans, hairdressers, shoemakers, etc., were grouped in collectives; the sheep belonging to the community were divided into flocks of several hundreds, put in the charge of shepherds, and methodically distributed in the mountain pastures.

With regard to the distribution of products, various systems were tried out, some based on collectivism and others on more or less total communism, and still others resulting from a combination of the two. Most commonly, payment was based on family needs. Each head of a family received a daily wage of specially marked pesetas which could only be exchanged for consumer goods in the communal shops, which were often set up in the church or its buildings. Any balance not consumed was placed in a peseta credit account for the benefit of the individual. It was possible to draw a limited amount of pocket money from this balance. Rents, electricity, medical care, pharmaceuticals, old-age assistance, etc., were all free. Education was also free and often given in schools set up in former convents; it was compulsory for all children under fourteen, who were forbidden to perform manual labor.

Membership in the collective continued to be voluntary, as was required by the basic concern of the anarchist for freedom. No pressure was brought to bear on the small farmers. Choosing to remain outside the community, they could not expect to receive its services and benefits since they claimed to be sufficient unto themselves. However, they could opt to participate as they wished in communal work and they could bring their produce to the communal shops. They were admitted to general assemblies and the enjoyment of some collective benefits. They were forbidden only to take over more land than they could cultivate, and subject to only one restriction: that their presence or their property should not disturb the socialist order. In some places socialized areas were reconstituted into larger units by voluntary exchange of plots with individual peasants. In most villages individualists, whether peasants or traders, decreased in number as time went on. They felt isolated and preferred to join the collectives.

It appears that the units which applied the collectivist principle of day wages were more solid than the comparatively few which tried to establish complete communism too quickly, taking no account of the egoism still deeply rooted in human nature, especially among the women. In some villages where currency had been suppressed and the population helped itself from the common pool, producing and consuming within the narrow limits of the collectives, the disadvantages of this paralyzing self-sufficiency made themselves felt, and individualism soon returned to the fore, causing the breakup of the community by the withdrawal of many former small farmers who had joined but did not have a really communist way of thinking.

The communes were united into cantonal federations, above which were regional federations. In theory all the lands belonging to a cantonal federation were treated as a single unit without intermediate boundaries[2] Solidarity between villages was pushed to the limit, and equalization funds made it possible to give assistance to the poorest collectives. Tools, raw materials, and surplus labor were all made available to communities in need.

The extent of rural socialization was different in different provinces.

2 "In theory," because there was some litigation between villages on this subject.

As already said, Catalonia was an area of small- and medium-sized farms, and the peasantry had a strong individualistic tradition, so that here there were no more than a few pilot collectives. In Aragon, on the other hand, more than three-quarters of the land was socialized. The creative initiative of the agricultural workers in this region had been stimulated by a libertarian militia unit, the Durruti Column, passing through on its way to the northern front to fight the Franco troops, and by the subsequent establishment of a revolutionary authority created at the base, which was unique of its kind in Republican Spain. About 450 collectives were set up, with some half a million members. In the Levant region (five provinces, capital Valencia), the richest in Spain, some 900 collectives were established, covering 43 percent of the geographical area, 50 percent of citrus production, and 70 percent of the citrus trade. In Castile, about 300 collectives were created, with around 100,000 members. Socialization also made headway in Estremadura and part of Andalusia, while a few early attempts were quickly repressed in the Asturias.

It should be remembered that grass-roots socialism was not the work of the anarcho-syndicalists alone, as many people have supposed. According to Gaston Leval, the supporters of self-management were often "libertarians without knowing it." In Estremadura and Andalusia, the social-democratic, Catholic, and in the Asturias even communist, peasants took the initiative in collectivization. However, in the southern areas not controlled by the anarchists, where municipalities took over large estates in an authoritarian manner, the day laborers unfortunately did not feel this to be a revolutionary transformation: their wages and conditions were not changed; there was no self-management.

Agricultural self-management was an indisputable success except where it was sabotaged by its opponents or interrupted by the war. It was not difficult to beat the record of large-scale private ownership, for it had been deplorable. Some 10,000 feudal landowners had been in possession of half the territory of the Spanish Peninsula. It had suited them to let a large part of their land lie fallow rather than to permit the development of a stratum of independent farmers, or to give their day laborers decent wages; to do either of these would have undermined their medieval feudal authority. Thus their existence had retarded the full development of the natural wealth of the Spanish land.

After the Revolution the land was brought together into rational units, cultivated on a large scale and according to the general plan and directives of agronomists. The studies of agricultural technicians brought about yields 30 to 50 percent higher than before. The cultivated areas increased, human, animal, and mechanical energy was used in a more rational way, and working methods perfected. Crops were diversified, irrigation extended, reforestation initiated, and tree nurseries started. Piggeries were constructed, rural technical schools built, and demonstration farms set up, selective cattle breeding was developed, and auxiliary agricultural industries put into operation. Socialized agriculture showed itself superior on the one hand to large-scale absentee ownership, which left part of the land fallow; and on the other to small farms cultivated by primitive techniques, with poor seed and no fertilizers.

A first attempt at agricultural planning was made, based on production and consumption statistics produced by the collectives, brought together by the respective cantonal committees and then by the regional committee which controlled the quantity and quality of production within its area. Trade outside the region was handled by a regional committee which collected the goods to be sold and in exchange for them bought the goods required by the region as a whole. Rural anarcho-syndicalism showed its organizational ability and capacity for coordination to best advantage in the Levant. The export of citrus required methodical modern commercial techniques; they were brilliantly put into play, in spite of a few lively disputes with rich producers.

Cultural development went hand in hand with material prosperity: a campaign was undertaken to bring literacy to adults; regional federations set up a program of lectures, films, and theatrical performances in all the villages. These successes were due not only to the strength of the trade-union organization but, to a considerable degree, also to the intelligence and initiative of the people. Although the majority of them were illiterate, the peasants showed a degree of socialist consciousness, practical good sense, and spirit of solidarity and sacrifice which drew the admiration of foreign observers. Fenner Brockway, then of the British Independent Labour Party, now Lord Brockway, visited the collective of Segorbe and reported: "The spirit of the peasants, their enthusiasm, and the way they contribute to the common effort and the pride which they take in it, are all admirable."

Self-Management in Industry

Self-management was also tried out in industry, especially in Catalonia, the most industrialized area in Spain. Workers whose employers had fled spontaneously undertook to keep the factories going. For more than four months, the factories of Barcelona, over which waved the red and black flag of the CNT, were managed by revolutionary workers' committees without help or interference from the State, sometimes even without experienced managerial help. The proletariat had one piece of good fortune in being aided by technicians. In Russia in 1917–1918, and in Italy in 1920, during those brief experiments in the occupation of the factories, the engineers had refused to help the new experiment of socialization; in Spain many of them collaborated closely with the workers from the very beginning.

A trade-union conference representing 600,000 workers was held in Barcelona in October 1936, with the object of developing the socialization of industry. The initiative of the workers was institutionalized by a decree of the Catalan government dated October 24, 1936. This ratified the *fait accompli*, but introduced an element of government control alongside self-management. Two sectors were created, one socialist, the other private. All factories with more than a hundred workers were to be socialized (and those with between fifty and a hundred could be, on the request of three-quarters of the workers), as were those whose proprietors either had been declared "subversive" by a people's court or had stopped production, and those whose importance justified taking them out of the private sector. (In fact many enterprises were socialized because they were heavily in debt.)

A factory under self-management was directed by a managerial committee of five to fifteen members representing the various trades and services. They were nominated by the workers in general assembly and served for two years, half being changed each year. The committee appointed a manager to whom it delegated all or part of its own powers. In very large factories the selection of a manager required the approval of the supervisory organization. Moreover, a government controller was appointed to each management committee. In effect it was not complete self-management but a sort of joint management in very close liaison with the Catalonian government.

The management committee could be recalled, either by the general meeting of the workers or by the general council of the particular branch of the industry (composed of four representatives of management committees, eight of the trade unions, and four technicians appointed by the supervisory organization). This general council planned the work and determined the division of the profits, and its decisions were mandatory. In those enterprises which remained in private hands an elected workers' committee was to control the production process and conditions of work "in close collaboration with the employer." The wage system was maintained intact in the socialized factories. Each worker continued to be paid a fixed wage. Profits were not divided on the factory level and wages rose very little after socialization, in fact even less than in the sector which remained private.

The decree of October 24, 1936, was a compromise between aspirations to self-management and the tendency to tutelage by the leftist government, as well as a compromise between capitalism and socialism. It was drafted by a libertarian minister, and ratified by the CNT, because anarchist leaders were in the government. How could they object to the intervention of government in self-management when they themselves had their hands on the levers of power? Once the wolf is allowed into the sheepfold he always ends up by acting as its master.

In spite of the considerable powers which had been given to the general council of branches of industry, it appeared in practice that workers' self-management tended to produce a sort of parochial egoism, a species of "bourgeois cooperativism," as Peirats called it, each production unit concerning itself only with its own interests. There were rich collectives and poor collectives. Some could pay relatively high wages while others could not even manage to maintain the wage level which had prevailed before the Revolution. Some had plenty of raw materials, others were very short, etc. This imbalance was fairly soon remedied by the creation of a central equalization fund, which made it possible to distribute resources fairly. In December 1936, a trade-union assembly was held in Valencia, where it was decided to coordinate the various sectors of production into a general organic plan, which would make it possible to avoid harmful competition and the dissipation of effort.

At this point the trade unions undertook the systematic reorganization of whole trades, closing down hundreds of small enterprises and concentrating production in those that had the best equipment. For instance: in Catalonia foundaries were reduced from over 70 to 24, tanneries from 71 to 40, glass works from about 100 to about 30. However, industrial centralization under trade-union control could not be developed as rapidly and completely as the anarcho-syndicalist planners would have wished. Why was this? Because the Stalinists and reformists opposed the appropriation of the property of the middle class and showed scrupulous respect for the private sector.

In the other industrial centers of Republican Spain the Catalonian socialization decree was not in force and collectivizations were not so frequent as in Catalonia; however, private enterprises were often endowed with workers' control committees, as was the case in the Asturias.

Industrial self-management was, on the whole, as successful as agricultural self-management had been. Observers at first hand were full of praise, especially with regard to the excellent working of urban public services under self-management. Some factories, if not all, were managed in a remarkable fashion. Socialized industry made a major contribution to the war against fascism. The few arms factories built in Spain before 1936 had been set up outside Catalonia: the employers, in fact, were afraid of the Catalonian proletariat. In the Barcelona region, therefore, it was necessary to convert factories in great haste so that they might serve the defense of the Republic. Workers and technicians competed with each other in enthusiasm and initiative, and very soon war materiel made mainly in Catalonia was arriving at the front. No less effort was put into the manufacture of chemical products essential for war purposes. Socialized industry went ahead equally fast in the field of civilian requirements; for the first time the conversion of textile fibers was undertaken in Spain, and hemp, esparto, rice straw, and cellulose were processed.

Self-Management Undermined

In the meanwhile, credit and foreign trade had remained in the hands of the private sector because the bourgeois Republican government wished it so. It is true that the State controlled the banks, but it took care not to place them under self-management. Many collectives were short of working capital and had to live on the available funds taken over at the time of the July 1936 Revolution. Consequently they had to meet their day-to-day needs by chance acquisitions such as the seizure of jewelry and precious objects belonging to churches, convents, or Franco supporters who had fled. The CNT had proposed the creation of a "confederal bank" to finance self-management. But it was utopian to try to compete with private finance capital which had not been socialized. The only solution would have been to put all finance capital into the hands of the organized proletariat; but the CNT was imprisoned in the Popular Front, and dared not go as far as that.

The major obstacle, however, was the increasingly open hostility to self-management manifested by the various political general staffs of Republican Spain. It was charged with breaking the "united front" between the working class and the small bourgeoisie, and hence "playing the game" of the fascist enemy. (Its detractors went so far as to refuse arms to the libertarian vanguard which, on the Aragon front, was reduced to facing the fascist machine guns with naked hands—and then being reproached for its "inactivity.")

It was the Stalinist minister of agriculture, Vincente Uribe, who had established the decree of October 7, 1936, which legalized part of the rural collectivizations. Appearances to the contrary, he was imbued with an anti-collectivist spirit and hoped to demoralize the peasants living in socialized groups. The validation of collectivizations was subjected to very rigid and complicated juridical regulations. The collectives were obliged to adhere to an extremely strict time limit, and those which had not been legalized on the due date were automatically placed outside the law and their land made liable to being restored to the previous owners.

Uribe discouraged the peasants from joining the collectives and fomented discontent against them. In December 1936 he made a speech directed to the individualist small proprietors, declaring that the guns of the Communist Party and the government were at their disposal. He gave them imported fertilizer which he was refusing to the collectives. Together with his Stalinist colleague, Juan Comorera, in charge of the economy of Catalonia, he brought the small- and medium-scale landowners together into a reactionary union, subsequently adding the traders and even some owners of large estates disguised as smallholders. They took the organization of food supplies for Barcelona away from the workers' unions and handed it over to private trade.

Finally, when the advance guard of the Revolution in Barcelona had been crushed in May 1937,[3] the coalition government went so far as to liquidate agricultural self-management by military means. On the pretext that it had remained "outside the current of centralization," the Aragon "regional defense council" was dissolved by a decree of August 10, 1937. Its founder, Joaquín Ascaso, was charged with "selling jewelry," which was actually an attempt to get funds for the collectives. Soon after this, the 11th Mobile Division of Commander Lister (a Stalinist), supported by tanks, went into action against the collectives. Aragon was invaded like an enemy country, those in charge of socialized enterprises were arrested, their premises occupied, then closed; management committees were dissolved, communal shops emptied, furniture broken up, and flocks disbanded. The Communist press denounced "the crimes of forced collectivization." Thirty percent of the Aragon collectives were completely destroyed.

Even by this brutality, however, Stalinism was not generally successful in forcing the peasants of Aragon to become private owners. Peasants had been forced at pistol point to sign deeds of ownership, but as soon as the Lister Division had gone, these were destroyed and the collectives rebuilt. As G. Munis, the Spanish Trotskyist, wrote: "This was one of the most inspiring episodes of the Spanish Revolution. The peasants reaffirmed their socialist beliefs in spite of governmental terror and the economic boycott to which they were subjected."

There was another, less heroic, reason for the restoration of the Aragon collectives: the Communist Party had realized, after the event, that it had injured the life force of the rural economy, endangered the crops from lack of manpower, demoralized the fighters on the Aragon front, and dangerously reinforced the middle class of landed proprietors. The Party, therefore, tried to repair the damage it had itself done, and to revive some of the collectives. The new collectives, however, never regained the extent or quality of land of their predecessors, nor the original manpower, since many militants had been imprisoned or had sought shelter from persecution in the anarchist divisions at the front.

Republicans carried out armed attacks of the same kind against agricultural self-management in the Levant, in Castile, and in the provinces of Huesca and Teruel. However, it survived, by hook or by crook, in many areas which had not yet fallen into the hands of the Franco troops, especially in the Levant.

The ambiguous attitude, to put it mildly, of the Valencia government to rural socialism contributed to the defeat of the Spanish Republic: the poor peasants were not always clearly aware that it was in their interests to fight for the Republic.

[3] This refers to the time when the POUM (Partido Obrero Unido Marxista) together with rank-and-file anarchists came into armed conflict with the police and were defeated and crushed. (Translator's note.)

In spite of its successes, industrial self-management was sabotaged by the administrative bureaucracy and the authoritarian socialists. The radio and press launched a formidable preparatory campaign of denigration and calumny, questioning the honesty of the factory management councils. The Republican central government refused to grant any credit to Catalonian self-management even when the libertarian minister of the Catalonian economy, Fabregas, offered the billion pesetas of savings bank deposits as security. In June 1937, the Stalinist Comorera took over the portfolio of the economy, and deprived the self-managed factories of raw materials which he lavished on the private sector. He also failed to deliver to the socialist enterprises supplies which had been ordered for them by the Catalan administration.

The central government had a stranglehold over the collectives; the nationalization of transport made it possible for it to supply some and cut off all deliveries to others. Moreover, it imported Republican army uniforms instead of turning to the Catalonian textile collectives. On August 22, 1937, it passed a decree suspending the application of the Catalonian October 1936 socialization decree to the metal and mining industries. This was done on the pretext of the necessities of national defense; and the Catalonian decree was said to be "contrary to the spirit of the Constitution." Foremen and managers who had been driven out by self-management, or rather, those who had been unwilling to accept technical posts in the self-managed enterprises, were brought back, full of a desire for revenge.

The end came with the decree of August 11, 1938, which militarized all war industries under the control of the Ministry of War Supplies. An overblown and ill-behaved bureaucracy invaded the factories—a swarm of inspectors and directors who owed their position solely to their political affiliations, in particular to their recent membership in the Stalinist Communist Party. The workers became demoralized as they saw themselves deprived of control over enterprises which they had created from scratch during the first critical months of the war, and production suffered in consequence.

In other branches, Catalan industrial self-management survived until the Spanish Republic was crushed. It was slowed down, however, for industry had lost its main outlets and there was a shortage of raw materials, the government having cut off the credit necessary to purchase them.

To sum up, the newborn Spanish collectives were immediately forced into the straitjacket of a war carried on by classic military methods, in the name of which the Republic clipped the wings of its own vanguard and compromised with reaction at home.

The lesson which the collectives have left behind them, however, is a stimulating one. In 1938 Emma Goldman was inspired to praise them thus: "The collectivization of land and industry shines out as the greatest achievement of any revolutionary period. Even if Franco were to win and the Spanish anarchists were to be exterminated, the idea they have launched will live on." On July 21, 1937, Federica Montseny made a speech in Barcelona in which she clearly posed the alternatives: "On the one hand, the supporters of authority and the totalitarian State, of a state-directed economy, of a form of social organization which militarizes all men and converts the State into one huge employer, one huge entrepreneur; on the other hand, the operation of mines, fields, factories and workshops, by the working class itself, organized in trade-union federations." This was the dilemma of the Spanish Revolution, but in the near future it may become that of socialism the world over.